Jahrbuch Junge Rechtsgeschichte 2
Yearbook of Young Legal History 2

Oliver Brupbacher, Nadine Grotkamp,
Jana Osterkamp, Tilmann Röder,
Stefan Ruppert, David Sörgel (ed.)

Erinnern und Vergessen

Remembering and Forgetting

Martin Meidenbauer »

Die Herausgeber waren und sind Doktoranden des Max-Planck-Instituts für europäische Rechtsgeschichte.

Die Deutsche Bibliothek verzeichnet diese Publikation in der Deutschen Nationalbibliografie; detaillierte bibliografische Daten sind im Internet über http://dnb.ddb.de abrufbar.

Gedruckt auf
chlorfrei gebleichtem, säurefreiem und alterungsbeständigem Papier (ISO 9706)

ISBN 978-3-89975-595-4

Verlagsverzeichnis schickt gern:
Martin Meidenbauer Verlagsbuchhandlung
Erhardtstr. 8
D-80469 München

www.m-verlag.net

Inhaltsverzeichnis

Vorwort

Das zweite „Jahrbuch Junge Rechtsgeschichte" umfasst die Beiträge des *Europäischen Forums Junger Rechtshistorikerinnen und Rechtshistoriker*, das vom 25. bis 28. Mai 2006 in Frankfurt am Main stattfand. Der Einladung waren nicht nur juristisch ausgebildete Rechtshistoriker gefolgt, sondern auch Philologen, Politologen und allgemeine Historiker. Von den 68 eingereichten Vortragsvorschlägen konnten 30 berücksichtigt werden, deren Sprachenvielfalt und deren unterschiedliche, häufig national geprägte Forschungsstile sich auch in diesem Band widerspiegeln. Gleichwohl eröffnete das gemeinsame Forumsthema unter dem Begriffspaar „Erinnern und Vergessen" die Sicht auf zahlreiche Bezüge zwischen den Präsentationen.

Während in der Geschichtswissenschaft schon seit Jahren über Aspekte des sozialen, kulturellen oder kollektiven Gedächtnisses diskutiert wird, haben diese Konzepte in der Rechtsgeschichte bisher nicht die gleiche Aufmerksamkeit gefunden. Dies verwundert, sind doch „Erinnern und Vergessen" nicht nur für den Rechtshistoriker, sondern für jeden Juristen relevant. Denn das Recht als sozialer Mechanismus zur Konfliktlösung muss, um seiner Befriedungsfunktion nachzukommen, Antworten auf und Lösungen für die beschränkte Gedächtnisleistung seiner Erfinder und Anwender finden. Es kennt spezielle Rechtsinstitute, die dem Erinnern und Vergessen feste Formen geben, wie etwa Mahnung, Verjährung oder Amnestie, es kennt Urkunden, welche die Erinnerung an ein bestimmtes Recht oder an bestimmte Sachverhalte sichern, und es kennt eigene Erinnerungsmechanismen zur Sammlung und Verbreitung von Gesetzen. In seinen Prozessen bestimmt es, was auszusondern und zu vergessen, was weiter zu tragen und zu erinnern ist.

Der Zugang über die allgemeinen Funktionen „Erinnern und Vergessen" erwies sich auf der Tagung als fruchtbar, da er Anknüpfungspunkte lieferte, um unterschiedliche Epochen und Forschungsansätze – von der Technik- und Mediengeschichte bis hin zu Geschichten der Identitätsbildung – miteinander zu verbinden. Das Tagungsprogramm als ganzes überblickend, lassen sich grob vier überlappende thematische Bereiche ausmachen. Zum ersten gilt es bei der Mnemonik ebenso wie bei historischen Forschungsarbeiten allgemein, praktische Fragen nach den konkreten Techniken zu stellen, wie etwas vor dem Vergessen bewahrt wurde. Schriftlichkeit in ihren unterschiedlichen Kontexten (Buis, Komáromi, Moniuszko, Schennach) wird ergänzt um physische Erinnerungshilfen (Dariescu) und um Beweisregeln (Desnos, Petrović).

Zum zweiten wurden aus dem vielbehandelten Bereich der Vergangenheitsbewältigung mithilfe des Rechts einige, vor allem weniger prominente Schauplätze ausgewählt, wie die aktuellen Debatten in Spanien, Mexiko und Russland (Aragoneses Aguado, Olaiz, Zezekalo) sowie die das Selbstverständnis der internationalen Beziehungen berührenden Fragen der Erinnerung an den Umgang mit eingeborenen Völkern in den Kolonialgebieten (Vega, Murtfeld[1]). Juristen diskutierten in Italien, wie als falsch erkannte Kategorien aus den Gesetzen zu beseitigen seien, ohne die Kategorienbildung zu wiederholen (Falconieri), Historiker konnten sich in den Kriegsverbrecherprozessen nach Nürnberg in einer neuen Rolle wiederfinden und zu Experten werden (Petrović). An den Universitäten stellte und stellt sich auch die Frage nach dem Umgang mit den Werken der Rechtsprofessoren der NS-Zeit und ihrem weiteren Wirken (Winkler).

Die Begnadigung der Kriegsverbrecher nach den französischen Oradourprozessen in den fünfziger Jahren verweist auf einen dritten Bereich, den der Steuerung von Erinnerung und Vergessen (Meyer). Recht steuert die Erinnerung nicht nur durch Archivrecht, das bestimmt, welche Akten zukünftigen Historikern zur Verfügung stehen werden (Rügge), sondern auch mit der Anordnung von Amnestien (wörtlich: Nichterinnern – Scheibelreiter, Stronati) und der Verdammung von Schriften, etwa durch die kirchliche Zensur (Beck

---

[1] Die Beiträge von Pablo Gutierrez Vega, „The Minutes of the Savages. Treaties between the Hispanic Monarchy and Indigenous Nations in Latin America (XVIII-XIX Centuries)" und Robert Murtfeld, „Memory and the History of International Law: The Case of the Ovaherero and Ovambanderu" werden zu einem späteren Zeitpunkt veröffentlicht.

Varela). Allerdings kann trotz eines radikalen „Vergessens“, das Alte durch praktische Anwendung fortwirken (Schulze, Fastenmayer).

Schließlich, viertens, ist das Recht selbst von der Erinnerung geprägt. Besonders deutlich wird dies in Verfassungen, die explizit gegen eine vorangehende Erfahrung gesetzt wurden (Delbecke, Müller, Engel). Aber auch die Privatrechtswissenschaft wurde von ihrem selektiven Gedächtnis auf verschiedene Weise geprägt (Aldous, Święcicka, Hofri-Winogradow, Thompson, Fastenmayer). In diesen Bereich fallen auch die – teilweise erst zu konstruierenden – Ideale früher Zeiten, die das Recht junger Nationen prägen und ihre Identität stärken, demonstriert am Rückgriff auf ein utopisches altirisches Recht im Irland des 19. Jahrhunderts (Mohr) oder am jüdischen Recht in Israel nach 1948 (Kedar).

Neben den allgemeinen theoretischen und historischen Erkenntnissen zeigte sich mithin, dass Recht als steuerndes und gesteuertes Instrument auf beiden Seiten des „Erinnerns und Vergessens“ steht.

Für den Eröffnungsvortrag danken wir herzlich dem Frankfurter Mediävisten Prof. Dr. Johannes Fried. Prof. Dr. Marie-Theres Fögen verabschiedete die Tagungsteilnehmer mit einem Grußwort des Max-Planck-Instituts für europäische Rechtsgeschichte, aus dem die Tradition des *Forums* entsprungen war. Auch ihr sei herzlich gedankt, ebenso wie dem Verwaltungsleiter des genannten Instituts, Herrn Gerhard H. Gräber, für seine kontinuierliche, verlässliche Unterstützung sowie den anderen Mitarbeitern der Verwaltung.

Das finanzielle Fundament für die Tagung und für diese Publikation schufen großzügige Spenden des Max-Planck-Instituts für europäische Rechtsgeschichte, der Generalverwaltung der Max-Planck-Gesellschaft, der Vereinigung von Freunden und Förderern der Johann Wolfgang Goethe-Universität Frankfurt am Main, der Dr. Bodo Sponholz-Stiftung für Wohlfahrt, Kunst und Wissenschaft und des Verlages Vittorio Klostermann. Ihnen gilt unser ganz besonderer Dank, sind doch Nachwuchstagungen mehr als andere wissenschaftliche Zusammenkünfte auf das Vertrauen von Sponsoren angewiesen.

Hervorzuheben bleibt schließlich die hervorragende Zusammenarbeit mit Herrn Dr. Jörg Meidenbauer vom Martin Meidenbauer Verlag, der sich geduldig auf den Wechsel vom Luzerner zum Frankfurter Organisationsteam des *Forums* eingelassen hat und hoffentlich noch viele weitere Bände dieser Reihe betreuen wird. Denn das *Forum* lebt weiter: Im Jahr 2007 sind die jungen Rechtshistoriker und Rechtshistorikerinnen nach Sevilla eingeladen. ¡Mucho exito y diversión!

Frankfurt, im März 2007

Die Organisatoren und Herausgeber:
Oliver Brupbacher
Nadine Grotkamp
Jana Osterkamp
Tilmann Röder
Stefan Ruppert
David Sörgel

The Selective Memorialization of Sir John Fortescue in Early Modern England: A Short Case Study in Legal Antiquarianism

Kenneth E. Aldous

It has been observed that English lawyers during the seventeenth century expended considerable effort "constructing and challenging the lineages of local and constitutional customs extending back beyond memory into 'immemorial' antiquity."[1] Immersed as they were in a "memorial culture"[2] captivated by a seemingly all-encompassing commitment to find meaning in history – or, in true antiquarian fashion, to find history in meaning – English lawyers during the early modern period played a pivotal role in the overall re-conceptualization of a particularly English past. In practice, this involved the continued recollection and interpretation of certain legal and constitutional ideas from England's rather checkered history, including contributions from Bracton, Glanvill, Littleton and the late-fifteenth-century jurist, Sir John Fortescue.

Interest in Fortescue, along with interest in Littleton before him, represented a true revival of legal scholarship "in the spirit of Bracton."[3] And yet, although Fortescue returned to the project begun by Bracton, where Bracton's works were essentially "legal," Fortescue's task was predominantly constitu-

---

[1] Ross, Richard J.: The Memorial Culture of Early Modern English Lawyers: Memory as Keyword, Shelter, and Identity, 1560-1640. In: 10 Yale Journal of Law and the Humanities 229 (1998), p. 230.

[2] Ross (as in note 1), p. 230.

[3] Hazeltine, Harold Dexter: The Age of Littleton and Fortescue: Its Significance in the History of English Law and Its Literature. In the General Preface to Stanley Bertram Chrimes (ed.): Sir John Fortescue, De Laudibus Legum Anglie. Cambridge 1942 (reprinted 1949), p. xix-xxii. For another discussion of Fortescue and Littleton, see Sir William S. Holdsworth's third lecture, aptly entitled "Littleton and Fortescue," in: Some Makers of English Law: The Tagore Lectures. Cambridge, 1937-38, pp. 46-68.

tional and comparative,[4] lauding the English form of government, where both the king and parliament assume critical roles – *dominium politicum et regale.*

Arguably, unlike his medieval predecessors, Fortescue overcame the austerity and distance characteristic of a great deal of medieval learning, with his numerous references to practical affairs and the existing state of things. In fact, his involvement with the affairs of his own day enabled Fortescue to engage in, and make significant contributions to, political theory.[5] In this way, Fortescue is among the first of the medieval writers to "bring political philosophy [down] from the clouds to earth by basing his theoretical analysis upon observation of existing conditions."[6]

This article traces the place of Fortescue, and his notion of the English constitution as *dominium politicum et regale*, within an admittedly thin slice of the socio-political disputes that revolutionized Tudor and Stuart society. The general purpose is to examine briefly some of the ways in which exponents, on both sides of those disputes, memorialized Fortescue in aid of their respective legal, jurisdictional and constitutional causes. After briefly previewing Fortescue's life and principal literary achievements, the article briefly discusses how – as part of a process of recollection rooted firmly in an antiquarian consciousness – Fortescue's authority grew as a preeminent source from England's jurisprudential past.

As recognition of Fortescue's accessibility and overall "timelessness" developed, his renown as a defender of the constitutional legitimacy and political force of the people also increased. With the cessation of the relative tranquility occasioned by the Tudor compromise, the strong monarchic rule of the early Stuarts cast into sharp relief the apparent paradox inherent in a *dominium* that is both *politicum* and *regale.* Thus, the largest part of the article examines the

---

[4] See Plummer, Charles (ed.): Sir John Fortescue: The Governance of England: Otherwise Called The Difference Between an Absolute and a Limited Monarchy. London 1885 (second impression, 1926), p. 82.

[5] See Holdsworth, William S.: Sources and Literature of English Law. Oxford, 1925 p. 135 (noting that Fortescue shared with Bentham the fame of being both a lawyer and a practical philosopher). See also, Hallam, Henry: View of the State of Europe During the Middle Ages. 6th ed., New York, 1837, pp. 426-428.

[6] Plummer (as in note 4), p. 82.

"debate touching impositions" (c.1602-1610), one well-recognized precursor to the legal, political and constitutional changes that occurred during the mid-to-late seventeenth century.

A. Fortescue's Life & Principal Literary Achievements

Fortesuce was born sometime during the last decade of the fourteenth century.[7] By the time the infant Henry VI succeeded to the thrones of England and France in 1422, Fortescue had been admitted to Lincoln's Inn. By 1442, he ascended to the lofty position of Chief Justice of the King's Bench, and he was an instrumental figure in a number of important cases. As a member of the Lancastrian Party, Fortescue was actively engaged in "extra-judicial" activities during the early years of the War of the Roses. He found himself in exile in Scotland with Queen Margaret and Prince Edward and, during those years, he became nominal chancellor to Henry and wrote a number of works in support of the House of Lancaster.[8]

In 1463, Fortescue fled to France and Flanders with Margaret and Edward, remaining with them in exile until 1471. During this time, he wrote what is perhaps his most important work, *De Laudibus Legum Angliae*.[9] In addition to the value of *De Laudibus* as one of the earliest expositions on English constitutional theory, its unique literary form set it apart. It was expressly written in Latin for the benefit of Edward so that he might learn how a prince is made

---

[7] For a review of Fortescue's life, see Chrimes (as in note 3), pp. lxix-lxxvii; Jacob, E.F.: The Fifteenth Century, 1399-1485. Oxford, 1961, pp. 309-16; Campbell, John Lord: Lives of the Lord Chancellors and Keepers of the Great Seal of England, From the Earliest Times Till the Reign of King George IV, 5th ed., vol. 1. London, 1868, chp. XXII.

[8] These works included: *De Titulo Edwardi Comitis Marchiae*, "On the title of the House of York;" *Defensio Juris Domus Lancastriae*, "A Defence of the title of the House of Lancaster, or a Replication to the claim of the Duke of York;" and *Opusculum de Natura Legis Naturae et eius Censura in Successione Regnorum Suprema.*

[9] Fortescue also wrote a number of other works while in exile, including: (i) a work for Louis XI entitled, "Memoranda on the political situation," (ii) "Articles from Prince Edward to the Earl of Warwick," and (iii) as is thought by some, a translation of the works of Alain Chartier. See Blayney, Margaret Statler: Sir John Fortescue and Alain Chartier's "Traité de L'Esperance". In: 48 Modern Language Review 385 (1953).

happy by the laws and how he might acquire a love of justice.[10] *De Laudibus* was written in the form of a conversation between young Edward and the Chancellor, an early form of didactic dialogue, that had a defensive and distancing effect.[11]

In *De Laudibus*, the Chancellor, addressing the young prince and drawing upon examples from the Bible, classical philosophy and Roman law, emphasized the centrality of the king's duty to do justice by means of the law.[12] Framed in this context, Fortescue centralized the notion of *dominium politicum et regale*.[13] A law is political because the people assent to it, but it is also royal because it is administered by the king.[14] According to Fortescue, this characteristic is preferable to the purely royal kingship of, for instance, France.[15]

---

[10] See Skeel, Caroline A.J.: The Influence of the Writings of Sir John Fortescue. In: 10 Transactions of the Royal Historical Society 77 (1916), p. 80-81.

[11] In this way, Fortescue was able to write about English government as it *ought* to be. As Shelley Lockwood explains: "Fortescue's concern was to establish a defense of political monarchy on the grounds of reason, law and justice and thereby to provide a theory to fit the practice of that monarchy *as it should be*. . . . He was creating a theory to which he felt English practice *should ideally* conform: England should conform to '*dominium politicum et regale*' because that was the best form of *dominium* for England." Fortescue, Sir John: On the Laws and Governance of England. Cambridge, 1997, pp. xiv-xxv.

[12] See *De Laudibus*, chps. I-VI.

[13] See generally, Blythe, James M.: Ideal Government and the Mixed Constitution in the Middle Ages. Princeton, NJ, 1992; Burns, J.H.: Fortescue and the Political Theory of Dominium. In: 28 The Historical Journal 777 (1985); Gilbert, Felix: Sir John Fortescue's "Dominium Regale et Politicum", 2 Medievalia et Humanistica 88 (1944).

[14] See *De Laudibus*, chp. XXXIV.

[15] According to Fortescue, not only does the political and royal kingship of England provide a more secure defense against the danger of tyranny, but it serves as a more effective guarantor of justice. What is more, he claims that English laws are uniquely suited to the realm of England. See *De Laudibus*, chps. IX, XII-XV, XXIX. Fortescue's prejudice, both as an Englishman and as a common lawyer, is noteworthy. As Caroline A.J. Skeel explained: "As a common lawyer he was convinced that the common law of England was better than the civil law; as an Englishman he was equally convinced that English institutions excelled the French. His attitude is hardly scientific; but the mere fact that he institutes the comparison is worth something." Skeel, C.A.J.: The Influence of the Writings of Sir John Fortescue. In: 10 Transactions of the Royal Historical Society 77 (1916), pp. 79-80.

Thus, with an apparent Anglo-centricity, Fortescue traced the origins of the English realm and its form of law.[16] He asserted that what distinguished English constitutional form, over and above the French form, was the unique relation of the king (as the head) to the people (as the body). This organic model demonstrated that the kingdom comes from the people (*ex populo errumpit*) and is best understood as a mystical body (*corpus extat mysticum*).[17]

After his return from exile, in May 1471, Fortescue was captured along with Margaret at the Battle of Tewksbury. Prince Edward was killed during that battle, and with his death, Fortescue's hopes of Lancastrian ascendance came to an end.[18] After writing "Declaration upon Certain Writings sent out of Scotland against the King's title to the realm of England," for which he received a pardon,[19] Fortescue presented the king with a copy of "The Governance of England, otherwise called, The Difference Between an Absolute and a Limited Monarchy" or *Monarchia*, perhaps his most technically sophisticated work. In *The Governance of England*, Fortescue appealed to certain "myths of the realm," explaining that fellowship among English subjects came with Brutus. At that time – as the theory went – the people of England assented to his rule as their "head and king." Thus, in an appeal of truly mythic proportions, Fortescue purported to bridge the gap between absolute and limited monar-

---

[16] See Plucknett, Theodore F.T.: A Concise History of the Common Law, 5th ed. Boston, 1956, p. 279. Plucknett states that Fortescue took this idealization – which resulted largely from his living abroad – to the point of preferring the French language of the English Year Books to the French language as then actually spoken in France. Id.

[17] See *De Laudibus*, chp. XIII. Theological in origin, this latter concept, to the extent that it allows for the perpetuation of the plurality of the realm, provides a more nuanced understanding of precisely how the body functions. See Kantorowicz, E.H.: The King's Two Bodies: A Study in Medieval Political Theology. Princeton, 1957, cited in Lockwood (as in note 11), p. xxvi.

[18] Although the details of Fortescue's later life remain somewhat sketchy, the date of his death is generally reckoned sometime around 1477.

[19] In 1475, Fortescue received a reversal of the attainder issued against him while in exile. One historian quoted Edward Coke as follows: "[Fortescue] wrote . . . a book in defence of the title of King Henry VI, his sovereign Lord and Master, to the crown of England; but after, out of truth and conscience retracted the same. . . . Wherein he deserved singular commendation in that he was not amongst the number of those 'qui suos amassent errores' but yielded to truth when he found it." Lord Clermont: Life and Works of Fortescue, vol. 1 (1869), p. 49.

chy within a constitutional framework whose foundation was both vividly consensual and descriptively antiquarian.[20]

B. Fortescue During the Early Modern Period

Although Fortescue occupied various important political offices, took active roles in critical events, and wrote extensively concerning matters of contemporary concern, there is little evidence that his works enjoyed much acclaim during his lifetime.[21] Nonetheless, during the centuries following his own, Fortescue's works were at least modestly influential.[22]

Fortescue's repute lies in his expositions concerning the nature of kingly rule as grounded in the law of nature and *dominium politicum et regale*.[23] Although some scholars have noted that these assertions lack for originality – as largely employing concepts and categories found in Aristotle, Augustine and Aquinas – many of the ambiguities and shifts in thought that appear in his works are arguably attributable to "Renaissance tendencies toward intellectual rational-

---

[20] See Lockwood (as in note 11), p. xxvi.

[21] For a discussion of the English contribution to the new political science of the fifteenth century, see Ullmann, Walter: Law and Politics in the Middle Ages: An Introduction to the Sources of Medieval Political Ideas. Ithaca, NY, 1975, pp. 299-306. See also Wilkinson, B.: Constitutional History of England in the Fifteenth Century (1399-1485), New York, 1964; Chrimes, Stanley Bertram: English Constitutional Ideas in the Fifteenth Century. Cambridge, 1936.

[22] See generally, Genet, J.P. : Droit et Histoire en Angleterre: La Préhistoire de la 'Révolution Historique. In: 87 Annales de Bretagne 319 (1980). Comparing Fortescue to his fifteenth-century companions Littleton, Pecock and Gascoigne, Plummer remarked: "In all the literature of the [fifteenth-century Lancastrion] period which I have read, I have found no single reference to any of his works. But in the seventeenth century he was constantly appealed to as an authority by the constitutional party; and his writings played a part not altogether inconsiderable in the preservation of English liberties." Plummer (as in note 4), p. 105. Skeel, likewise, explained how Fortescue's ideas, although largely ignored in the fifteenth century, contributed greatly to the Tudor monarchy and the seventeenth-century debates. See Skeel (as in note 10), p. 83. See also Holdsworth, Sir William S.: Makers of English Law (as in note 4), p. 137.

[23] See generally, Doe, Norman: Fundamental Authority in Late Medieval English Law. Cambridge, 1990).

ism and pluralism."[24] Perhaps it is at least partly due to these tendencies that Fortescue's stature as a legal and constitutional authority grew considerably during the generations following his own. What is more, it should be remembered that Fortescue's works – although somewhat rudimentary when compared with the more advanced political philosophy of succeeding centuries – first appeared at a time when discussion of constitutional matters was severely limited.[25]

As Caroline Skeel noted in her article surveying Fortescue's works across the centuries, the opulent Henry VII stands in stark contrast to the poverty-stricken Lancastrians of Fortescue's own day.[26] No doubt, Henry recognized, along with Fortescue in The Governance, both the "harm that comyth off a Kynges pouerte"[27] and the "perellis that may come to the Kyng by ouer myghtye subgettes."[28] In this way, one might speculate that Fortescue would have approved of the Act of 1487, granting the jurisdiction of the Council in the Court of the Star Chamber, as well as the resumption of the royal domain. And yet, it remains questionable whether Fortescue would have approved of the harshness and injustice that these institutions visited upon individual subjects.[29]

During the early years of Henry VIII's reign, as well as during the continued development of Tudor rule throughout the sixteenth century, Fortescue's no-

---

[24] Lockwood O'Donovan, Joan: Theology of Law and Authority in the English Reformation. Emory University Studies in Law and Religion, Atlanta, 1991, p. 45.

[25] As Skeel noted: "[W]hile Fortescue's notions may have been revolutionary during his own day, his assertions regarding the importance of strong monarchic rule (*dominium regale*) were not fully instituted until the Tudors came to the throne, particularly during their glorious ascendance in the sixteenth century. However, Henry VII, the first of the Tudor monarchs, resolved to remedy some of the problems that Fortescue pointed out would arise in the event of weak monarchy. This fact is illustrated by Henry's strict taxation policy which increased his wealth greatly, as well as his express policy directed at suppressing the power of the nobles." Skeel (as in note 10), pp. 84-88.

[26] Skeel (as in note 10), p. 85.

[27] The Governance of England, chp. 5. The full quote states: "But the grettest harme that comyth of a Kynges pouerte is, that he shal bi necessite be arted to fynde exquysite meanes of geytinge of good."

[28] The Governance of England, chp. 9.

[29] See Skeel (as in note 10), pp. 86-87.

tions of strong royal prerogative appear to have strengthened the English nation at a time when defendable sources for executive power were in considerable demand. This strengthening came in response to the Lancastrian downfall, which left governance wanting and national power, on a world-scale, diminished.[30] Yet, Fortescue's notions surrounding the monarchy were tempered by guarantees against arbitrary rule.[31]

These notions, coupled with the overall accessibility and timelessness of Fortescue's constitutional vision, elevated him as a force to be reckoned with during the decades following the War of the Roses. Paramount among the precepts accounting for this renown was the idea that the people – much in the spirit of *Magna Carta* – possessed not only true constitutional legitimacy, but also considerable political force. No longer could an English monarch simply look up to heaven and extol the luminary virtue of divine right. After Fortescue – though admittedly not solely because of Fortescue – those in power would need to look down to their subjects as well. Failure to do so could, and did, have dire consequences. Indeed, this tempered recognition came to characterize Tudor rule. As one historian has observed:

"[P]olemical writings such as those of Sir John Fortescue, directed towards and capable of influencing the 'people,' must be regarded as both a threat and

---

[30] As Chrimes stated: "The weakness of the Crown during the fifteenth century had been the source of great evils, the cause of that "lack of governance and politic rule" that had resulted in a widespread breakdown of the enforcement of law and order, and in a recrudescence of a bastard sort of feudalism, in sporadic civil war. The great Lancastrian chief justice, Sir John Fortescue, had unerringly perceived the reasons for the Crown's ineffectiveness, and had propounded a scheme for administrative reform. No one could have anticipated that the obscure, untried Earl of Richmond, Henry Tudor . . . was destined not only to carry into effect wise measures very similar to those foreshadowed by Fortescue, but also to found the greatest of the English dynasties." Chrimes, Stanley Bertram: English Constitutional History. London, 1947, pp. 123-24.

[31] As Chrimes elsewhere has stated: "[D]uring the sixteenth century some of Fortescue's ideas had considerable influence, though others were for the time unfruitful. The security of life, liberty and property which he had extolled as the birthright of Englishmen we too often impaired in days when *salus populi* was regarded as *suprema lex*. But his views on the advantages of limited monarchy played some considerable part in the opposition to arbitrary government, when the monarchy built up by the Tudors had in the hands of their successors lost national support." Chrimes (as in note 30), p. 88.

an offensive weapon, to be feared yet used. Henceforth a crowned head would ignore such writings at his own peril."[32]

It was perhaps when the Stuarts, choosing a path purposefully side-stepped by the Tudors, claimed an absolute legitimacy and sovereignty that the inevitability of revolution began to loom large.

C. An Example from the Early Seventeenth Century: The "Debate Touching Impositions" (c.1602-1610)

Although sown much earlier, the ideological seeds of the legal and jurisdictional debates of the seventeenth century blossomed with Elizabeth's death in 1603; an event which resulted in her distant and confidently non-Protestant relative, James, taking the throne. Although James ruled England for less than a quarter century, his policies set in motion legal and constitutional turmoil that would eventually lead up to, and transcend, the English Civil War.

The importance of Fortescue's influence during this period is apparent when one considers that the medieval constitution reached its peak under the Tudors.[33] Yet, Fortescue could not have so significantly influenced the shape of the English constitution if the Stuarts had not refashioned, repackaged and re-emphasized the Tudor prerogative.

Throughout the course of Elizabeth's reign, and particularly near its end, foreign trade was an important and lucrative enterprise. Impositions in the form of taxes on imports and exports greatly enriched royal coffers. During the early years of James's reign, the matter of the constitutionality of the king's power to impose taxes assumed dynamic proportions. The question essentially turned on whether the king's prerogative was absolute or whether impositions on his subjects required popular consent.

The evolution of the medieval constitution had resulted in not only the recognition that the king was limited by the rule of law, but increasingly, that the

---

[32] Gill, Paul E.: Politics and Propaganda in Fifteenth-Century England: The Polemical Writings of Sir John Fortescue, In: 46 Speculum 333 (1971), p. 347.
[33] See Chrimes (as in note 29), p. 118.

king should look to the Commons for rulemaking authority. In the wake of the assertions of private right embodied in *Magna Carta*, this evolution was occasioned and quickened by the practical necessities and political wranglings that have come to typify early modern England.[34]

Yet, events during the early part of the seventeenth century being what they were – or, more to the point, James being who he was – Forstescue's notion of *dominium politicum et regale* was put to the test in a practical fashion.

I. Bate's Case

In 1606, the merchant John Bate disobeyed a royal command pertaining to the garnishment of certain customs.[35] The debate over the king's prerogative that followed brought some of the most influential expositors of English constitutionalism to center stage – advocates who collected and refined their ideas with a palpable reverence for the past.

The facts of the case were fairly straightforward. Bate was a member of the Levant Company, an enterprise which had at one time operated under the auspices of a royal monopoly, trading extensively in the Mediterranean and Middle East. He had instructed his servant to depart from the waterside with a cartful of recently imported currants before customs agents had the opportunity to examine the cargo and levy a tax. Bate believed the imposition to be illegal. Because the government was eager to declare the legality of the tax in a friendly forum, Bate's "test case" was quickly brought before the Exchequer. At the same time, Bate, together with others implicated in the case, introduced the matter to the Commons, who included the issue in their Petition of Grievances, forcefully maintaining that, without parliament's consent, the king lacked the power to tax.[36]

When the case came before the Exchequer, the judges declared that Bate was required to pay the duty. The four barons deciding the case each declared

---

[34] See Chrimes (as in note 3), p. civ n.2.
[35] See generally, Gardiner: History of England, vol. II. London, 1904, pp. 4-6.
[36] Gardiner (as in note 35), pp. 4-6.

that the king was entitled to levy impositions, unequivocally and without reservation, as a function of his royal prerogative. When the decisions were delivered, many in the Commons feared they seriously jeopardized certain fundamental freedoms. In fact, it was largely for this reason that the Exchequer's highly politicized judgments failed to resolve the issue in a universally acceptable manner. Thereafter, and for the duration of his reign, James tirelessly championed his so-called prerogative. With the stage set, the matter of the king's power to impose would unearth a firestorm of legal, constitutional and political rhetoric.

II. The "Shadows of Kings"

On May 21, 1610, James delivered a speech to parliament at Whitehall.[37] Although many who heard it hoped James would be as "a loving father to dear children,"[38] many "went away exceeding sad and heavy."[39] During the speech, James asserted his royal prerogative in starkly absolutist terms:

"When I lay at Thetford, I sent a message to will and require you to forbear to meddle touching prerogative and the privilege of a king. . . . That . . . you mistake not my message nor think that I mistake your proceedings, I told you my meaning was [not] to forbid you to complain if there were inconvenience or heaviness, inequality, disproportion or disorder in matter of trade; from this I meant not to restrain you, for I acknowledge it becomes you in your duty not only in that particular but in all other in general in that place to complain where you find any just grievance that may be hurt to the people. But that under the pretense of complaining . . . to me you should go to the root and dispute my prerogative and call in question that power which I have in possession, confirmed by law, derived from my progenitors and which my judges have denounced, to search into these mysteries or to judge of my right in that kind, I thought did not belong unto you. Leave to the king that which is his in power, and do you take into your consideration the inconveniences."[40]

On the specific point of his power to impose, James continued:

"Three arguments there are tossing among you . . . why impositions should not be laid without parliament. [1] The first is precedents, that divers kings, having laid impositions without parliament, have in parliament recalled them. [2] The second is that there be acts of parliament to restrain them. [3] The

---

[37] See Gardiner, Samuel Rawson (ed.): Parliamentary Debates in 1610. London, 1862 (reprinted 1968), pp. 32-34.

[38] Read Foster, Elizabeth (ed.): Proceedings in Parliament, 1610, vol. 2. New Haven, 1966, pp. 100-07.

[39] Foster (ed., as in note 38), p. 108 (quoting Thomas Wentworth).

[40] Foster (ed., as in note 38), pp. 101-02. See also Gardiner, ed. (as in note 36), pp. 34-36.

third is out of the light of human reason, why should a king have it in his power to take what he will, he need not then have subsidies, if he might impose he might bring in all the money of the kingdom into his purse. [1] As to the first, it is an ill consequent I am sure yourselves know and false logic to say . . . that because kings have done so they have no power to do otherwise. . . . [2] To the second, men that study the laws may best speak in that, yet I that am a king ought to know them and this I dare affirm, no act of parliament deludes the king of power to impose. . . . [3] To the third, I am sure none of you, when you shall have advised wisely and considered, but will cross his mouth and deny that to be a reason, that because a king may do in excessive manner, therefore he shall not do it at all. Because he may pardon all offenders, which were inconvenient, therefore he shall pardon none. Because he may be good or may be ill, should we have power to set him limits? Pray beware of such arguments. You must not set such laws as make the *shadows of kings* and dukes of Venice. . . ."[41]

James's insistence that he functioned as the sole repository of his subjects' interests set the tone for the many parliamentary discussions that followed. In fact, when the Commons gathered to consider the matter of the king's prerogative, many were greatly disturbed. During the discussions that ensued, references to Fortescue appeared. He was cited the very next day by Thomas Wentworth, who argued:

"Fortescue, that brought up the Prince and might have favored prerogative, in that he tells him the difference between England and France is that by the law of England no imposition can be without assent of parliament as in France. . . ."[42]

The surviving transcript of the speech contains a footnote reporting the observations of Boderie, the French ambassador, who reported that Wentworth quoted Fortescue for the proposition that the English monarchy is

---

[41] Foster (ed., as in note 38), pp. 102-03 (emphasis & brackets added).
[42] Foster (ed., as in note 38), p. 108.

"politique," making it impossible for the English king to dispose of affairs without popular consent.[43]

As the Commons continued to debate, appeals to Fortescue mounted on both sides. On June 23, Nicholas Fuller appealed to Fortescue:

"Mr. Fortescue, a learned judge of this realm, which was after Chancellor to the Prince . . . upon great deliberation saith in his book printed that . . . the king of England cannot charge or make impositions upon the subjects' goods and merchandise without their consents . . . and according to [the] good precedent [of *Magna Carta*], I hope that it will be granted by this parliament that all new customs or impositions granted or any way encroached upon the subjects' goods or merchandise without parliament . . . shall be taken away . . ., notwithstanding Charta Mercatoria or any grant, ordinance, or judgment in the Exchequer or elsewhere had or made . . . [T]he same appear to be contrary to the laws of the realm and directly contrary to the great Charter, which laws having once a settled allowance cannot be altered, changed, or made void by act of prince or people, but by mutual consent in parliament . . . of prince and people as all learned men know."[44]

Fuller's reference to Fortescue would not go unchallenged. On June 29, Sir John Doderidge clarified what, to his mind, represented Fortescue's true intention. Responding to Fuller, Doderidge added a gloss recognizing a qualified right of the king to impose – an interpretation turning on Fortescue's use of the word "strange."

"You say Fortescue, a learned man and Chancellor, in his commendation of the laws of England, writeth that the king can lay impositions upon his people but by parliament. In this quotation under favor he dealt not clearly that delivered the words, for the words are lay strange impositions, strange being a word equivalent to unreasonable, and so this authority insisteth upon the same

[43] Foster (ed., as in note 38), p. 108.
[44] Foster (ed., as in note 38), p. 108.

ground that the records and statutes before alleged did, the error being in the quantity, not the right."[45]

Doderidge's position was expanded upon by one of James's faithful supporters, Francis Bacon. Bacon's position turned on precisely whose rights parliament should guard. As one observer noted:

"[Bacon] sayd that he had bene a parliamente man ever synce he was 17 years olde, within which tyme he did observe that the parliament had receaved divers inhibicions from the Queene to restrayne theyme from debating the matter then in question; whearin he tooke this difference, that, if the matter debated concerned the right or interest of any subject or the Commonwealth, if in that case an Inhibicion came, he, for his parte, would not advise the Howse to proceed. But, if the matter in question were an esssentiall thinge which concerned the prerogative and the power of the Crowne, then the Howse did allwayes desist from proceeding any further upon such inhibicions receaved."[46]

Yet, despite both Bacon's appealing bifurcation and Doderidge's nuanced interpretation, the weight of authority and reason appears to have resided with those who saw themselves as custodians of the common law, property rights and individual liberties.

James Whitelocke strikingly appealed to Fortescue in opposition to the royal prerogative. Whitelocke proclaimed:

"So we see that the power of imposing and power of making laws are *convertibilia et coincidentia*, and whatsoever can do the one can do the other. And this was the opinion of Sir John Fortescue, that reverend and honourable judge and very learned professor of the common law, and chief justice of the King's Bench in the time of Henry VI. . . . [H]e maketh these two powers of making law and imposing to be concomitant in the same hand and that one of

---

[45] Foster (ed., as in note 38), p. 220. See also: The case of mines, 8 Eliz. I, Mich.
[46] Gardiner (ed., as in note 36), p. 38.

them is not without the other. He giveth the same reason for this as we do now, but in other words; because (as he saith) in England it is *principatus mixtus et politicus*, the King hath his sovereign power in Parliament assisted and strengthened with the consent of the whole Kingdom, and therefore these powers are to be exercised by him only in Parliament."[47]

Sir Heneage Finch, illustrating his point with reference to Tudor absolute power, also appealed to Fortescue for the proposition that, absent the express consent of parliament, the king cannot lay impositions.

"For authorities in the point whether the king may by law impose or no, I find not any in our books, only in I Elizabeth it is made a question upon an impost laid upon cloth by Queen Mary, but the book says that the merchants of London found great grief and made exclamation and suit to the Queen to be unburthened of that impost because it was not granted by parliament but assessed by Queen Mary of her absolute power, by which it appears the complaint was not in regard of the excess but of the unlawfulness and that the imposition was against law is intimated by the book which says it was assessed by the absolute power without parliament. And Fortescue . . . who was Chief Justice of England and after Chancellor, writes expressly that the king of England cannot lay impositions upon his people without parliament (as hath been already often remembered). . ."[48]

In November 1610, Whitelocke led the charge to reform the king's impositions, so that the judges' decisions in *Bate's Case* could be reversed and a law passed to restrain the king's power to lay impositions.[49] And yet, the "debate touching impositions" did not end with these deliberations; for indeed, the

---

[47] Cobbett (ed.): State Trials and Proceedings Upon High Treason and Other Crimes and Misdemeanors, vol. II. London, 1731, p. 486. Quoted in: Skeel (as in note 10), pp. 94-95.
[48] Foster (ed., as in note 37), p. 245, citing I Mary, Mich. (Dyer, fol. 92).
[49] See Gardiner (ed., as in note 36), p. 142.

matter of impositions remained a fundamental focus of inquiry throughout a great deal of the seventeenth century.[50]

D. Conclusion

The various citations to Fortescue during the seventeenth century set the revival of his ideas squarely within a cognizable antiquarian movement. The questions which occupied the minds of seventeenth-century jurists largely concerned "legality" in a general sense; and notions of precedence and antiquity greatly aided and supported the search for this legality. As Samuel Gardiner, more than a century ago, observed:

"The legality which [such jurists] cherished was the legality of a nation which had hitherto preserved unbroken the traditions of self-government. . . . It was a new thing that a king should treat the policy and religion of the nation as if they concerned himself alone; but the men who opposed it because it was new, opposed it still more because it was degrading."[51]

No doubt, some of Fortescue's ideas were viewed as effective remedies against such degradation. At a minimum, they represented a link to the political traditions of the land – a link to which both the king and the self-regarded protectors of the common law would claim possession.

As the role of the lawyer in public affairs grew throughout the seventeenth century, the explication and memorialization of legal authority, gleaned from England's jurisprudential past, gained prominence. Perhaps fittingly, no legal authority – with the exceptions of Bracton and perhaps Glanvill – garnered more attention during the century than Fortescue.[52] Richard Ross has observed that to the English lawyers of the seventeenth century:

"[M]emory became an intellectual keyword, a shelter, and a badge of guild identity no less than a subject of lawyerly manipulation and a repository of in-

[50] For example, see Bidwell, William B. and Maija Jansson (eds.): Proceedings in Parliament, 1626, vol. II. New Haven, 1992, p. 74; vol. IV, p. 216.

formation. The centrality of memory to the thought and practices of this legal culture created forensic advantages and vulnerabilities for a profession at the center of political, jurisdictional, and dignitary conflicts."[53]

Viewed in the light of legal authority distinctly and firmly grounded in the precedent and tradition of the English nation, the construction of a past in which Fortescue played a central role emerges as a noticeable preoccupation of a legal culture that placed a premium on the past.

---

[51] Gardiner (as in note 34), vol. VIII, p. 271.

[52] "Fortescue's authority was quoted on both sides of the struggle (although more frequently, for rather obvious reasons) on the side of the common law. The most cursory survey of the constitutional disputes from 1603 onwards shows the leading part taken by lawyers and the importance they attached to legal authorities." Chrimes (as in note 29), p. 91. With respect to Bracton's place in the seventeenth-century debates, see Hearnshaw, F.J.C.: Legal Literature. In: The Cambridge History of English Literature, vol. III. Sira A.W. Ward and A.R. Waller (eds.), Cambridge, 1932, pp. 312-13.

[53] Ross (as in note 1), p. 230.

Entre el Dictador i jo: Gedächtnis und Recht der Diktatur im heutigen Spanien

Alfons Aragoneses Aguado

Ein Ausflug nach "El Valle de los Caídos”

50 Kilometer nördlich von Madrid, in der Sierra de Guadarrama, liegt das „Valle de los Caídos“; das Tal der Gefallene. Dort wurden zwischen 1940 und 1958 eine in Stein gegrabene Basilika und ein 150 Meter hohes Steinkreuz gebaut. Die Bauarbeiter waren politische Zwangsarbeiter, von denen viele dort starben. Ziel dieses pharaonischen Denkmals war, so ein „Decreto“ von 1940, die Erinnerung an die Gestorbenen des „Cruzada nacional“ zu bewahren[1]. Seit 1975 ist der Diktator Francisco Franco in der Basilika begraben.

Trotz dieser historischen Bedeutung ist das „Valle de los Caídos“ für die öffentliche Institution „Patrimonio Nacional“, die die königliche Denkmale pflegt, ein ganz normales Grabmal. Für viele Bürger ist es ein sehenswerter Ort wie der Palacio Real oder der Kloster in San Lorenzo de el Escorial. Nur jetzt, 30 Jahre nach dem Tod des Diktators, sprechen einige Stimmen über die politische Symbolik dieses Denkmals.

Das ist der Grund warum die junge Regisseurin Sandra Ruesga diese normalen Ausflüge ins Valle de los Caídos in einem kurzen Film thematisiert hat. Ihr Film ist einer der 6 Kurzfilme des Projektes „Entre el dictador i jo“, „Zwischen dem Diktator und mir“[2], die am 20. November 2005 auf über hundert

---

[1] Sieh. Decreto de 1 de Abril de 1940, disponiendo se alcen Basílica, Monasterio y Cuartel de Juventudes, en la finca situada en las vertientes de la Sierra de Guadarrama (El Escorial), conocida por Cuelgamuros, para perpetuar la memoria de los caídos de nuestra gloriosa Cruzada (BOE von 2.04.1940).

[2] Verschiedene Autoren, *Entre el Dictador i jo*, Barcelona (2005). Gefördert von der katalanischen Regierung und dem Programm del Memorial democràtic. (Sieh. www.entreeldictadorijo.com).

Plätzen in ganz Europa gezeigt wurden. Sechs junge Regisseure, alle nach 1975 geboren, wurden eingeladen, unter diesem Motto einen Kurzfilm zu drehen. Sie stellten sich selbst die Fragen: Was ist Franco für Dich? Wann hast Du zum ersten Mal von Franco gehört? Diese Filme gehören zu einem Projekt der katalanischen Regierung zur Rückkehr des so genannten historischen Gedächtnisses[3].

Die Regisseurin Sandra Ruesga zeigt in ihrem Film alte Bilder von ihrer Kindheit und lässt uns eine Diskussion mit ihren Eltern hören:

– Papa, ich bin jetzt dabei Videos von der Zeit als wir Kinder waren zu sehen und es gibt Dinge, an die ich versuche, mich wieder zu erinnern.

– Vielleicht kann ich deinem Gedächtnis helfen.

– Zum Beispiel denke ich an das Valle de los Caídos. Ich weiß nicht warum wir in das Valle de los Caídos gegangen sind?

– Wir sind nicht so oft hingegangen, obwohl es nah bei uns lag. Nur... es war ziemlich nah und deswegen haben wir Ausflüge dorthin gemacht.

– Ja aber hinzugehen finde ich schon komisch. Ich würde jetzt nicht hingehen, da Franco dort begraben ist. Hatte das für Euch...

– Gut also das ist auf jeden Fall Geschichte. Also was wir nicht machen können ist die Geschichte zu zerstören oder zu vergessen. Das ist Geschichte. Franco gehört der Geschichte und das ist alles.

(...)

– Aber hatte das für Dich keine politische Bedeutung?

– Nein, nein: Wir sind einfach zu dem Grab von Franco gegangen. Wenn es das Grab des Königs gewesen wäre, wäre es das gleiche gewesen.

Der Dialog zwischen Sandra Ruesga, der Regisseurin des kurzen Films, und ihrem Vater scheint mir sehr repräsentativ für die Erinnerung an Franco in der spanischen Gesellschaft zu sein. Franco ist politisch unbedeutende Geschichte, Vergangenheit, oder, wie einige Journalisten noch heute schreiben, „der vorherige Staatschef“. Dieser Film zeigt uns, dass die Funktion des Ge-

---

[3] Über das Programm del Memorial Democràtic der katalanischen Regierung sieh http://www10.gencat.net/drep/AppJava/cat/Memorial/index.jsp.

dächtnisses in der spanischen Gesellschaft und auch im spanischen Recht, wie ich zeigen werde, geringer ist als in anderen Gesellschaften, die auch eine Diktatur erlebt haben.

Erinnerung an den Bürgerkrieg. Vergessen der Diktatur.

Erinnerung und Gedächtnis sind nur Metaphern. Sie haben aber eine wichtige Funktion im sozialen und politischen System. Geschichte, so der Anthropologe Christian Giordano, ist nicht nur eine Disziplin, sondern auch ein „way to build reality here and now“[4]. Dann müssen wir uns wie der Anthropologe fragen und ich zitiere wiederum Giordano, „How do specific social actors use past events in the present? In what way is history reinterpreted, manipulated, and even reinvented?” Ich frage nun, wie das Gedächtnis im heutigen spanischem Recht operiert.

Die Diktatur ist heute ein Thema sowohl in der historiographischen, wie auch in der sozialen und politischen Agenda. Man kann heute über einen „Boom“ des Franquismus im Buchhandel, der Film- und Dokumentarindustrie und in der politischen Diskussionen sprechen[5]. Die Gründe dieses Booms liegen nicht nur darin, dass die Generation der Enkel des Bürgerkrieges jetzt ihre Stimme in der Gesellschaft gewonnen hat. Sie liegen auch darin, dass sich am 20. November 2005 der Todestag des Diktators zum 20. Mal jährte. Am 23. Februar dieses Jahres wurde des Putschversuches von Kolonel Tejero 1981 gedacht, was eine sehr wichtige Rolle in der Politik der Erinnerung meines Landes hat.

Diese Erinnerung an Franco vergisst aber oft wichtige Perioden oder Aspekte der Diktatur. Sie privilegiert den Bürgerkrieg und die „Transición“, den Übergang zur Demokratie und, wie die Eltern dieser Regisseurin, vergisst sie Repression und den Kampf gegen das Regime während der langen Diktatur.

---

[4] Christian Giordano, The past in the present: actualized history in the social construction of reality, in Focaal 26/27 (1996), 97-107, S. 106.

[5] Sieh. Alfons Aragoneses, “Atomisierte Geschichte. Der Franquismus-Boom in Spanien“, Rechtsgeschichte 5 (2004), 293-297.

Diese selektive Erinnerung an den Franquismus vermittelt natürlich ihre eigene Kultur und Ideologie. Diese haben meiner Meinung nach sehr wichtige Konsequenzen für das Recht, wie ich im Folgenden zeigen werde.

Der Rechtstaat von 1978 wurde nicht aus dem Nichts geschaffen, sondern er basiert auf einer staatlichen Struktur, die bereits zuvor existierte und die von einer eigene juristischen Kultur getragen wurde. Viele Faktoren dieser Struktur sind nach 1978 nicht verschwunden.

Der Übergang zur Demokratie und das Amnestie-Gesetz von 1977[6] brachten die Freiheit für viele politische Gefangene, aber auch die juristische Kontinuität von der Diktatur zur Demokratie. Die Urteile gegen antifranquistische Kämpfer unter den Kommunisten, Nationalisten oder Gewerkschaftern haben heute nach spanischem Recht immer noch Bestandskraft. Zwei wichtige Beispiele finden wir in den Urteilen gegen die Diktaturkämpfer Julián Grimau und Salvador Puig Antich, über die jetzt ein Film erschienen ist[7].

Aber die Kontinuität steht nicht nur in den Gesetzen oder Gerichtsurteilen, sondern auch in den Verhaltenmustern solcher juristischen Institutionen wie Richter oder Gerichte. Diese entwickeln sich langsamer als die Gesetzte. Juan José del Águila hat in seiner Arbeit über den Tribunal de Orden Público gezeigt, wie im Einklang mit der Verfassung die Richter dieses „Tribunals“ nicht verurteilt, sondern einfach in anderen Institutionen weiter beschäftigt wurden[8].

Ähnliches geschieht heute im Tribunal Supremo, dem obersten ordentlichen Gericht in Spanien. Der Franquismus führte das Tribunal Supremo als politisch wirkende Kraft ein[9]. Wie im 19. Jahrhundert war dieses Gericht unter der Diktatur die höchste Instanz. Und der Supremo entwickelte eine Doktrin, die eine Identifikation mit dem Staat und dem politischen Regime bewirkte. Das heißt, es gab keine Ausdifferenzierung zwischen den juristischen Normen und den politischen, moralischen und religiösen Werten des Franquismus, zwischen Recht und Unrecht. Die Unabhängigkeit des Richters verschwand,

---

[6] Ley 46/1977, de 15 de octubre, de amnistía (BOE von 17.10.1977).

[7] Manuel Huerga, *Salvador Puig Antich*, Barcelona (2006).

[8] Juan José del Águila, El TOP. La represión de la libertad, Barcelona 2001.

[9] Francisco J. Bastida, Jueces y Franquismo. El pensamiento político del Tribunal Supremo en la Dictadura, Barcelona, 1986.

und die Richter, so Tomás y Valiente, waren auf politische Neutralität – aber nicht auf ihre Autonomie bedacht[10].

Seit 1979 existiert in Spanien ein Verfassungsgericht, welches mit der höchsten Jurisdiktion über Menschenrechte betraut ist und dem deutschen Bundesverfassungsgericht in Karlsruhe vergleichbar ist. Der Supremo versucht aber trotzdem, eine politische Rolle zu spielen und auch über Menschenrechte das letzte Wort zu haben[11]. Dies zeigen die vielen Konflikte der letzten Jahre zwischen beiden Institutionen. Diese Konflikte wurden von den Juristen unterschätzt. Die Verfassungsrechtler Tomás y Valiente, Rubio y Llorente und andere Verfassungsrechtler und Richter des Verfassungsgerichts behaupteten, es seien „kleine Kompetenzkonflikte“[12]. Aber sie dauern bis heute noch an. Das Problem sitzt tiefer und ist in der juristischen Kultur des Tribunals Supremo begründet. Diese Institution übt noch heute eine Kultur der Rechte und des Rechts aus, die der Vergangenheit angehört, und sie ist nicht zufrieden mit ihrer neuen Rolle.

Erinnerung und Vergessens im spanischen Rechtssystem

Das Gedächtnis hat wichtige Konsequenzen auch im Bereich des Verfassungsrechts. Nach José-Ignacio Lacasta Zabalza konzentriert sich die Erinnerung auf die weit entfernten Gefilden der II. Republik, (oder) des Bürgerkrieges oder die nahe gelegenen „Transición” von 1973 bis 1978”[13]. Die lange Diktatur und die Kämpfe gegen den Franquismus bleiben vergessen. Das bedeutet, dass die spanische Verfassung keine antifranquistische Vergangenheit hat. Die II. Republik und die antifranquistischen Bewegungen in den fünfziger

---

[10] Francisco Tomás y Valiente, Poder judicial y Tribunal Constitucional. Escritos sobre y desde el Tribunal Constitucional, Madrid, 1993, S. 66.

[11] Rosario Serra Cristóbal, La guerra de las Cortes. La revisión de la jurisprudencia del Tribunal Supremo a través del recurso de amparo, Madrid, 1999.

[12] Sieh. Alfons Aragoneses, Verfassungsgerichtsbarkeit im Umgang mit ihrem Vorzimmer. Reminiszenzen nicht-rechtstaatlicher Kultur im spanischen Recht, Rainer Maria Kiesow, Dieter Simon (Hg.), Vorzimmer des Rechts, Frankfurt am Main, 2006, 1-12, S. 8.

[13] José Ignacio Laasta Zabalza, Tiempos difíciles para el patriotismo constitucional español, in Cuadernos Electrónicos de Filosofía del Derecho 2 (1999).

und sechziger Jahren gehören nicht zur Vergangenheit der spanischen Verfassung. Dann liegt die Vergangenheit der Verfassung, so Lacasta-Zabalza, in der Angst und der Katastrophe des Krieges. Das ist natürlich keine erfreuliche Perspektive, denn

> „Der Bürgerkrieg und die Angst davor, das Regime Franco und die Diktatur von Primo de Rivera dürfen auf keinen Fall als Gründungsmomente oder gültige Voraussetzungen des sozialen und demokratischen Rechtsstaates der 1978er Verfassung gelten“[14].

Man stellt die Transición als die natürliche Folge der Diktatur dar. Natürlich muss man auch den Übergang zur Demokratie der siebziger Jahre als Legitimationsquelle und Vergangenheit der Verfassung benennen. Aber gerade in dieser so genannten „Transición" hat die Angst vor dem Bürgerkrieg eine große Rolle gespielt, wie Paloma Fernández gezeigt hat[15].

Der Rechtsphilosoph Elías Díaz kritisiert auch die Logik der Argumentation, welche besagt, dass der Bürgerkrieg eine Konsequenz des zu fortschrittlichen Regimes der II. Republik war. Das würde zur Folge haben, dass der Bürgerkrieg eine natürliche Konsequenz der II. Republik und die Verfassung von 1978 eine natürliche Konsequenz von der Diktatur und der „Transición“ waren.

Um die Begriffe der historischen Anthropologie zu gebrauchen, könnte man sagen, dass die „Transición“ als Gründungsmythos der spanischen Demokratie immer noch präsent ist, was eine Überlegitimation dieser Verfassung bedeutet und die demokratischen Verfassungen von 1931 und 1870 und auch 1812 in Vergessenheit geraten lässt.

Das hat auch Konsequenzen für die Zukunft der Verfassung. Diese „Sakralisierung“ der „Transición“ führt in eine „Sakralisierung“ der Verfassung. Nun ist die Rede in Spanien von der Verfassungsreform. Oft ist die Verfassungsfeindlichkeit vieler Sektoren auf dieser mythischen Bedeutung der „Transición“ gegründet. Man appelliert an den Geist der „Transición“ oder an den

---

[14] Idem.

[15] Paloma Aguilar Fernández, Memoria y olvido de la Guerra civil, Madrid, 1996.

„Consenso de la transición", der unberührbar ist, um die Änderungen in der Verfassung, in den regionalen Verfassungen oder in den Beziehungen zwischen Kirche und Staat zu verhindern[16]. Dies natürlich erschwert viele Reformen, die besonders im Bereich der territorialen Struktur des Staates sehr notwendig sind.

Welche Zukunft für die vergangene Diktatur

Heutzutage diskutiert das katalanische Parlament ein Projekt über das demokratische Gedächtnis. In Madrid wird dieses Thema ebenfalls in naher Zukunft diskutiert. Ferner ist auch ein Gesetz zum Gedenken in Planung. Beide sind mehr als notwendig, um den Gründungsmythos der spanischen Demokratie zu aktualisieren. Für das Rechtssystem ist dies besonders wichtig, weil durch die Mystifizierung der „Transición" und der Verfassung von 1978 jeder Reformvorschlag erschwert wird.

Aber diese Reform wird leider niemals die Energie der alten juristischen Agenten stoppen können. Darunter gibt es wichtige juristisch-kulturelle Wurzeln, die nur eine große Reform des Wahlsystems von Richtern in Spanien ändern könnte. Wenn das nicht geschafft wird, werden wir noch lange Zeit über zwei juristische Kulturen in Spanien sprechen.

Einige Parteien haben vorgeschlagen, ein Denkmal der Repression und der Diktatur zu bauen. Aber im Moment pflegt noch Patrimonio Nacional das Valle de los Caídos, wo keine Denkmal an die unter Franco gestorbenen Zwangsarbeiter erinnert. Die Arbeiter dieser öffentlichen Institution stellen noch heute jeden Tag frische Blumen auf das Grab von Francisco Franco Bahamonde.

---

[16] Dieses Bild hat oft die Kirche gegen die Bildungssystemsreform benutzt:El presidente de los obispos apela al espíritu de la Transición para pedir un acuerdo educativo, in: El País vom 21.11.2005.

Verdammt zum Vergessen – oder zum Erinnern? Kirchliche Zensur und juristische Literatur im Spanien des 18. Jahrhunderts

Laura Beck Varela

Von den zahlreichen sozialen Erinnerungs- und Vergessensmechanismen der frühen Neuzeit sind wenige so eng mit der Umformung und Disziplinierung des kulturellen Gedächtnisses verbunden, wie die kirchliche Buchzensur und ihre Polizeimaßnahmen mit dem Ziel der „*damnatio memoriae*" (Verdammung des Gedächtnisses).[1]

Die *Indices librorum prohibitorum* waren das Instrument *par excellence* dieser besonderen Art von Wissenskontrolle, die in verschiedener Weise die Produktion, die Transfer- und Verbreitungsprozesse des Textes im Zeitalter des Frühdrucks bestimmt hat.[2] Die historische Forschung hat ihre Aufmerksamkeit

---

* Ich danke Viktor Winkler für die kritische Lektüre sowie für die zahlreichen Anregungen während unserer gemeinsamen Zeit in der I.M.P.R.S. Auch für die Anregungen Nadine Grotkamps bin ich dankbar.

Die hier vorliegenden Überlegungen bearbeite ich ausführlicher in einem Dissertationsvorhaben, das im Rahmen des von Bartolomé Clavero geleiteten wissenschaftlichen Projekts HICOES 2004-2007 („Historia Cultural e Institucional del Constitucionalismo en España. Cultura jurisdiccional y orden constitucional en España y América, siglos XVIII-XIX") entwickelt wird. Für die Unterstützung der rechtsgeschichtlichen Abteilung der Universität von Sevilla, des Kultusministeriums Brasiliens und des Internationalen Max-Planck Forschungskollegs für vergleichende Rechtsgeschichte möchte ich mich bedanken.

[1] „Estinguere le forme rivali e cancellarne le tracce è l'opera che ha assorbito gran parte delle energie del cristianesimo occidentale. Ai suoi caratteri storici di religione giuridicamente strutturata appartiene l'elaborazione di regole e strumenti per cancellare le memorie sconfite: è stato nell'ambito dell'Inquisizione ecclesiastica che la 'damnatio memoriae' ha raggiunto la sua formalizzazione più ricca" (Prosperi, Adriano: „Damnatio memoriae". Nomi e libri in una proposta della controriforma: In: Inquisizioni: percorsi di ricerca. Hrsg. von Giovanna Paolin. Trieste 2001, S. 11-34; hier S. 12).

[2] Zum komplexen Netzwerk der Buchproduktion im Zeitalter des Frühdrucks als einem „*communication circuit*", an dem verschiedene Akteure, wie Autoren, Drucker, Herausgeber, Buchhändler,

überwiegend auf die theologischen, literarischen, philosophischen und politischen Werke gerichtet. Wenig ist aber über die Auswirkung der Wissenskontrolle auf die juristische Literatur bekannt,[3] und das, obwohl ihre Produktion und Zirkulation unter denselben buchgeschichtlichen Bedingungen verstanden werden sollten.

Paradigmatisch im spanischen Kontext ist die besondere Verbreitung des holländischen Juristen Arnoldus Vinnius (1588-1657),[4] des ersten im Jahr 1723 in Spanien gedruckten protestantischen juristischen Autors,[5] dessen erfolgreiche Werke sich die inquisitorische Zensur systematisch vornahm. Er wurde einer der zahlreichen Zielscheiben der Politik der sogenannten *damnatio memo-*

Zensoren, Leser, teilnehmen, siehe: Darnton, Robert: What is the history of books? In: The Kiss of Lamourette. Reflections in Cultural History. London 1990, S. 107-135.

[3] Ausnahmen sind die Studien von Savelli, Rodolfo: Da Venezia a Napoli: Diffusione e censura delle opere di Du Moulin nel cinquecento italiano. In: Censura ecclesiastica e cultura politica in Italia tra cinquecento e seicento. Hrsg. von Cristina Stango. Firenze 2001, S. 101-154; Ders.: The censoring of law books. In: Church, Censorship and Culture in Early Modern Italy. Hrsg. von Gigliola Fragnito. Cambridge 2001, S. 223-253; Ders.: Allo scrittorio del censore. Fonti a stampa per la storia dell'espurgazione dei libri di diritto in Italia tra Cinque e Seicento. Società e storia (2003), XXVI, Nr.100-101, S. 293-330; Ders.: Giuristi francesi, biblioteche italiane. Prime note sul problema della circolazione della letteratura giuridica in età moderna. In: Manoscritti, editoria e biblioteche dal medioevo all' età contemporanea. Hrsg. von Mario Ascheri; Gaetano Colli. Studi offerti a Domenico Maffei per il suo ottantesimo compleanno. Roma 2006, S. 1239-1270; Alvarado, Javier: Juristas turbadores: la censura inquisitorial a la literatura jurídica y política (siglos XVI-XVII). In: Historia de la literatura jurídica en la España del Antiguo Régimen. Hrsg. von Dems. Band I. Madrid 2000, S. 331-385; Becker, Gisela: Deutsche Juristen und ihre Schriften auf den römischen Indices des 16. Jahrhunderts. Berlin 1970; Tomás y Valiente, Francisco: Expedientes de censura de libros jurídicos por la Inquisición a finales del siglo XVIII y principios del XIX. Anuario de Historia del Derecho Español (1964) 34, S. 417-462; Reusch, Franz Heinrich. Der Index der verbotenen Bücher. Ein Beitrag zur Kirchen- und Literaturgeschichte. Band 2, Abteilung 2. Aalen 1967 [Neudruck der Ausgabe Bonn 1885], S. 167-174. Douglas Osler stellt die Auswirkung auf die Sammlungen der heutigen juristischen Bibliotheken fest (Osler, Douglas: Teramo and the ius commune. In: Le Cinquecentine della Facoltà di Giurisprudenza. Fondi antichi e di pregio dell'Università degli Studi di Teramo. Hrsg. von Paolo Campanella; Rita Viola. Teramo 2004, S. XIV-XIX; Ders.: The Myth of European Legal History. Rechtshistorisches Journal (1997) Nr. 16, S. 393-410).

[4] Über die Zirkulation von Vinnius anhand der Zahl der Nachdrucke seines Werks: Feenstra, Robert; C. J. D. Waal: Seventeenth-century Leyden Law Professors and their influence in the development of the Civil Law. A study of Bronchorst, Vinnius and Voet. Amsterdam, Oxford 1975.

[5] Für diese Information danke ich Douglas Osler.

riae, die sich offensichtlich eher auf die Leser als auf die oft schon verstorbenen oder abwesenden Autoren ausgewirkt hat.

Die Leser stehen auch im Mittelpunkt der vorliegenden Betrachtung, insbesondere die verschiedenen Lesegewohnheiten,[6] die gesellschaftlichen Strategien und Mechanismen von Selbstdisziplinierung,[7] die eine Zensurdynamik von gleichzeitigem Verdrängen und Überzeugen darstellen. Dadurch wird eine differenzierte Annäherung an das Phänomen der Verbreitung Vinnius' ermöglicht, die sich von den Maßstäben der Rezeptionsforschung und der Ideengeschichte unterscheidet.[8] Unter dieser Voraussetzung kann man auf die unfruchtbare allgemeine Debatte um die Auswirkung der Inquisitionskontrolle auf das spanische intellektuelle Leben[9] verzichten, und den Blick auf die konkrete soziale Praxis und Reaktionen eines Fachpublikums werfen – der Juristen und Jurastudenten. Durch einige konkrete Beispiele bezüglich der Praxis der Zensur, der Zirkulation und des Besitzes der Werke Vinnius' können so auch einige Interpretationen über die Buchkontrolle im 18. Jahrhundert Spaniens in Frage gestellt werden.

---

[6] Price, Leah: Reading: The State of the Discipline. Book history (2004), Nr. 7, S. 303-320.

[7] Meine Untersuchung bezieht ihren theoretischen Orientierungsrahmen aus einigen Überlegungen zur Entstehung der „Disziplinargesellschaft" im Rahmen der geschichtswissenschaftlichen Diskussion über Diskurs- und Machttheorie, die im Gefolge der Werke von Michel Foucault und Gerhard Oestreich statt fand. Eine Skizzierung der Debatte findet sich bei: Breuer, Stefan: Sozialdisziplinierung. Problem und Problemverlagerungen eines Konzepts bei Max Weber, Gerhard Oestreich und Michel Foucault. In: Soziale Sicherheit und Soziale Disziplinierung. Hrsg. von C. Sachβe; F. Tennstedt. Frankfurt am Main 1986, S. 45-69.

[8] Foucault, Michel: La arqueología del saber. Aus dem Französisch übersetzt von Aurelio Garzón del Camino. México, 1970. Eine Aufsatzsammlung zu der Debatte der 70er/80er Jahre in: Teoria della ricezione. Hrsg. von Robert Holub. Torino 1989. Zur aktuellen buchgeschichtlichen Forschung siehe: Darnton, Robert: Discourse and Diffusion. Contributions (2005) Nr. 1, S. 21-28; Skinner, Quentin: On Intellectual History and the History of Books. Contributions (2005) Nr. 1, S. 29-36.

[9] Eine kritische Analyse der klassischen Debatte in der spanischen Geschichtsschreibung findet sich in: Goodman, David: Intellectual Life under the Spanish Inquisition: A Continuing Historical Controversy. History (2005), Bd. 90, Nr. 299, S. 375-386; López Vela, Roberto: Historiografía inquisitorial, catolicismo y España. Análisis de una trayectoria historiográfica. In: Historia de la Inquisición en España y América. Tomo III, Temas y problemas. Hrsg. von Joaquín Pérez Villanueva; Bartolomé Escandell Bonet. Madrid 2000, S. 83-168.

Seit seinem ersten Erscheinen auf dem spanischen Index im Jahr 1707, wurde Vinnius der ersten Kategorie (*prima classis*) zugeordnet. Dies bedeutete, dass sein gesamtes Werk verboten war, mit Ausnahme jener Werke, die explizit durch Bereinigung oder Expurgation (d. h., Auslösung oder Streichen bestimmter Textpassagen) erlaubt waren: *Prima Classis Auctorum Damnatae memoriae, quórum Opera edita, & adenda sunt prohibita: nisi expurgata, aut, quod videantur innoxia, nominatim permittantur.*[10]

In dem Fall Vinnius' lag die Ausnahme in seinem schon damals populären Institutionenkommentar,[11] insofern dieser bereinigt (*expurgatus*) war.[12]

Durch die Indizierung *sub* erste Kategorie wird ein Autor einem präventiven Verbot unterworfen.[13] Damit wollte die Inquisition eine „häresiefreie Lage"

---

[10] Eine andere Behandlung erhielten die Autoren der 2. Klasse: *secunda classis, in qua Libri certorum Auctorum expurgati, aut prohibiti, etc.* Bei der dritten handelte es sich um anonyme Werke: *Libri incertorum Auctorum expurgati, aut prohibiti etc.*

[11] Commentarius locupletissimus, academicus et forensis, in quatuor libros Institutionum imperialium (...). Lugduni Batavorum, ex officina Ioannis Maire 1642.

[12] Die zu expurgierenden Textpassagen betrafen sowohl umstrittene Fragen des Eherechts (z. B. die geistliche Verwandtschaft, die heimlichen Ehe, die Zustimmung der Eltern und andere von der 24. Session des Konzils von Trient behandelten Themen) als auch Asylrecht und kleinere Aussagen Vinnius' über die katholische Kirche. So der Index librorum prohibitorum et expurgandorum, pro Regis catholicis Hispaniarum Regnis Catholicis. Matriti: ex typographia Musicae, 1707. *Idem* in späteren Ausgaben des Index, etwa die vom 1747, die die expurgierten Absätze erweitert, und die vom 1790: „Vinius (Arnoldus), J. C. I. cl. Ejus In quatuor Lib. Institutionum Imperial, Lugd. 1666: corrijase como en el *Expurgat.* de 1747, pag. 25." (*Indice ultimo de los libros prohibidos y mandados expurgar: para todos los reynos y señoríos del catolico rey de las Españas, el señor Don Carlos IV, contiene en resumen todos los Libros puestos en el Indice Expurgatorio del año 1747, y en los Edictos posteriores, hasta fin de Diciembre de 1789. Formado y arreglado con toda claridad y diligencia, por mandato del Excmo. Sr. D. Agustin Rubin de Cevallos, Inquisidor General, y Señores del Supremo Consejo de la Santa General Inquisicion: impreso de su orden, con arreglo al Exemplar visto y aprobado por dicho Supremo Consejo.* Madrid, en la Imprenta de Don Antonio Sancha, 1790, S. 278).

[13] Das Prinzip wurde in der Erklärung des Bereinigungsverfahrens („*In Titulo apponatur nota Auctoris damnati, Opus vero cum expurgatione permissum*") und in den einleitenden Regeln des Index immer wieder aufgegriffen: „IV. Para los que ignoran estas materias del Expurgatorio, se advierte que todas las veces que hallaren en este Catálogo autor ó autores de primera clase, con el nombre desnudo, sin noticia de patria, profesion ó escritos, tengan entendido que por el mismo caso que se ponen de dicha primera clase, están prohibidas todas sus obras impresas y manuscritas, aunque no se haga mencion de ellas; porque para permirtirse es preciso que se señale tal y tal obra; y así, todo

sicherstellen, ohne den orthodoxen Inhalt der Bücher überprüfen zu müssen. Diese Strategie wurde ab dem Index von 1612 immer wieder intensiviert.[14] Weiterhin setzte sie andere polizeilichen Maßnahmen in Kraft, etwa die schon erwähnte Politik der Bereinigung oder Expurgation. Der gelehrte Leser wurde ständig zur Mitarbeit an der kollektiven Zensuraufgabe aufgerufen.[15] Exkommunikation und Geldstrafen waren für die Leser verbotener und unbereinigter Bücher vorgesehen, falls sie nicht innerhalb von 90 Tagen nach dem Erscheinen eines neuen Index oder Dekret die entsprechenden Bücher bei dem inquisitorischen Behörden vorgelegt hatten.[16] Dadurch unterschieden sich die Zen-

---

lo que se omite está prohibido" (Nachgedruckt in Indice de los Libros Prohibidos por el Santo Oficio de la Inquisición Española (...). Madrid 1873, S. 13).

[14] Der Index von 1612 schloß mehr als 1500 Schriftsteller der ersten Kategorie ein (Pardo Tomás, José: Censura inquisitorial y lectura de libros científicos. Una propuesta de replanteamiento. Tiempos modernos: Revista Electrónica de Historia Moderna (2003-2004), (4) 9, S. 9 (http://www.tiemposmodernos.org/viewarticle.php?id=35).

[15] Nach dem Vorwort (*Nota ad lectorem*) des Index von Sandoval von 1612 „Schriften von verdammten Autoren, die nicht über Religion handeln, sind sorgfältig expurgirt worden, um sie den Gläubigen gestatten zu können. Auch in Schriften von Orthodoxen sind einige Versehen oder missverständliche Ausdrücke gefunden worden, die zu einer Expurgation oder zur Beifügung einer Erklärung oder Warnung Anlass gegeben haben, während im übrigen die Frömmigkeit und Gelehrsamkeit dieser Schriftsteller und ihr Eifer für die katholische Religion das höchste Lob verdienen. Einige wenige andere sind, obschon sich in ihren Werken einiges findet, was mit der gesunden Lehre nicht übereinstimmt, mit Stillschweigen übergangen worden, weil einerseits ihr höheres Alter, ihre nicht zu verachtende Würde und Autorität und ihre großen Verdienste um die Kirche sie schützen, anderseits weil das, was zu der Zeit, in welcher sie schreiben, vielleicht noch nicht genügend klar gestellt worden war, später von gelehrten und frommen Männern in Disputationen, Vorlesungen und Schriften genügend widerlegt worden ist und darum zu unserer Zeit so gut wie gar keinen Anstoß und keine Gefahr mehr bringt... Es wird jetzt die Expurgation von mehr als 300 Schriften, und zwar den verbreitetsten, geboten. Weitere Expurgationen bleiben vorbehalten. Die Gelehrten mögen dabei die Inquisition unterstützen". Zitiert nach Reusch, Index (wie Fn. 3), S. 44.

[16] Erst ab 1790 durften die Leser ihre Bücher selbst expurgieren. Die Indices' Regeln sprachen von „excomunion mayor latae sententiae trina canonica monitioni premissa" für diejenigen „(...) que tuvieren ó leyeren libros prohibidos ó expurgados por otras causas, que no estuvieren expurgados, ademas del pecado mortal (que es cierto que por la inobediencia habrán cometido), incurran en pena de excomunion ferenda. Y á los unos y á los otros, condenados á perdimiento de los libros y de seiscientos ducados, aplicados por tercias partes á gastos del Santo Oficio, jueces y denunciador, y otras penas á nuestro arbitrio, y del Consejo y tribunales de la Santa y general Inquisicion...". Reglas, nachgedruckt in: Indice (wie Fn. 13), S. 26-27.

surstrategien Spaniens und Portugals, die voluminöse *Indices prohibitorum et expurgatorium* veröffentlichten, von der römischen. Die römische Inquisition hat nur *Indices prohibitorum* veröffentlicht, trotz einiger niedergeschlagener Entwürfe[17] und der ständigen Anforderung des professionellen Publikums und des Produktionskreises. Beispielhaft für dieses Spannungsfeld im 16. Jahrhundert ist der Fall Charles du Moulins. Obwohl die Juristen um eine offizielle Expurgation seiner Werke gebettelt hatten, lehnte die römische Inquisition dies immer wieder ab[18]. Unter der großen Anzahl von Rom indizierter Autoren hat aber nur eine Minderheit eine *donec corrigatur* Klausel verdient,[19] u. a. wieder Arnoldus Vinnius und sein Kommentar zu den Institutionen.[20]

Aber die offiziellen Vorschriften sind offensichtlich nur eine der zahlreichen Elemente innerhalb einer komplexeren Zensurpraxis.

Bei einer quantitativen Untersuchung der Exemplare des Institutionenkommentars fällt die große Zahl unbereinigter Exemplare auf. Nur ca. 35% wurden von einem offiziellen Zensor vollständig oder teilweise expurgiert und weitere 20% enthalten Spuren von selbst gemachten Zensuren, d. h. ca. 45% unzensierte Exemplare wurden ausgezählt.[21]

Auf den ersten Blick könnte man diese Angaben als Zeichen für ein massives Unterlaufen oder als Widerstand betrachten. Schenkten die spanischen

---

[17] Fragnito, Gigliola: Aspetti e problemi della censura espurgatoria. In: L'Inquisizione e gli storici: un cantiere aperto. Atti dei convegni lincei, 162. Roma 2000, S. 161-178.

[18] Savelli erwähnt die Bemühungen der Jurafakultät von Pisa: Savelli, Allo scrittoio (wie Fn. 3), S. 304.

[19] Nach Bujanda „La pratique de condamner des ouvrages avec la clause *donec corrigatur* devient de plus en plus rare avec le temps. Pendant la période de trois siècles et demi (1600-1966), on décompte quelque 260 ouvrages interdits, dont près des deux tiers au XVIIe siècle, et uniquement deux au XXe siècle" (Bujanda, Jesús Martínez de: Introduction. In: Index des livres interdits. Band XI: Index librorum prohibitorum, 1600-1966. Hrsg. von dems. Genève Montréal 2002, S.27-44, hier S. 33. Unter den von Benedikt XIV eingeführten Veränderungen im Zensursverfahren war die Förderung der Expurgationspolitik (Bulle *Sollicita ac provvida*, 1753). Über seine Funktion von Selbstzensur und Verstärkung der kirchlichen Mechanismen von Wissenskontrolle siehe: Delpiano, Patrizia. Per una storia della censura ecclesiastica nel Settecento. Aspetti e problemi. Società e Storia (2004), Nr. 105, S. 487-530.

[20] Nach dem Dekret der römischen Indexkongregation vom 4. Dezember 1725.

[21] Dieser Untersuchung liegen insgesamt 80 in verschiedenen spanischen Bibliotheken vorhandene Exemplare zugrunde.

Leser der Institution keinen Glauben mehr? Unter diesen scheinbar „heterodoxen" Lesern gab es aber sicher diejenigen, die eine spezielle persönliche oder institutionelle Leseerlaubnis genossen.[22] Auch die damaligen Schwierigkeiten angesichts des Zugangs zu der offiziellen Norm müssen im Panorama der Zensurpraxis berücksichtigt werden.[23] Auch nach der Bekanntmachung der Norm herrschte eine fortdauernde Unsicherheit bezüglich der genauen Maßstäbe für die Bereinigungen: Sowohl ein neues Dekret von 1741, das die zu expurgierenden Textpassagen erweiterte, als auch die Veränderungen der in Venedig und Lyon neugedruckten Versionen des Kommentars verursachten eine heterogene Expurgationspraxis. Die erste *secundum Indicem expurgata* gedruckte spanische Ausgabe von 1723/1724, die eine wichtige Rolle für die Verbreitung des Kommentars gespielt hatte, musste auch ab 1741 wieder handschriftlich bereinigt werden. Dem disziplinierten Leser war dieses fließende Wesen des gedruckten Textes durchaus bewusst.[24]

Eine weitere wichtige Angabe, die das Bild massiver Gleichgültigkeit gegenüber der Buchzensur relativiert, bezieht sich auf die 20% derjenigen Exemplare, die keine Spuren offizieller Zensur enthalten. Diese haben wahrscheinlich

---

[22] Defourneaux erwähnt eine große Zahl von Leseerlaubnissen, die am Ende des 18. Jahrhunderts sowohl Individuen als auch Gesellschaften (wie z. B. für die *Sociedades de Amigos del País*) das Lesen verbotener Bücher gestatteten (Defourneaux, Marcelin: Inquisición y censura de libros en la España del siglo XVIII. Aus dem Französisch übersetzt von Ignacio Tellechea Idigoras. Madrid 1973).

[23] Zahlreiche Beispiele dafür in: Defourneaux, Inquisición (wie Fn. 22) und Domergue, Lucienne: La censure des livres en Espagne à la fin de l'Ancien Régime. Madrid 1996.

[24] Als ein Beispiel unter vielen kann diese handschriftliche Bemerkung auf einem an der Universität von Sevilla vorhandenen Exemplar gelten: „*Esta impresión de Madrid del año 1723 no es la que se manda expurgar: por que exstá expurgada. La impresión de Leon del año 1666 por Lorenzo Anison es solamente la que debe expurgarse, como puede verse en el 1°. tomo del expurgatorio fol.22 verbo Arnoldus Vinnius J. C. etc. esta impresión está conforme a la de Valencia del año 1767. Dedicada al Exmo. Conde de Aranda*" (*Arnoldi Vinnii J.C., authoris damnati, opus vero cum expurgatione permissum, in quatuor libros Institutionum imperialium commentarius academicus et forensis. Editio novissima ... Correcta atque emendata secundum Indicem expurgatorium Sanctissimae Inquisitionis Hispaniae, publicatum anno 1707*. Tomus primus. Matriti, sumpt. Francisci Lasso et Iosephi Lasso filii, ex officina regia, apud Iosephum Rodriguez de Escobar, 1724. Signatur: A 150/16). Für die Debatte um die Bedeutung der „typographical fixity" siehe die Kritik von Adrian Johns um Eisensteins Werk: Johns, Adrian: The Nature of the Book: Print and Knowledge in the Making. Chicago 1998; Eisenstein, Elisabeth: The Printing Press as an Agent of Change, Band I. Cambridge 1979, S. 116.

dieselben Benutzer oder die Buchhändler hinterlassen. Bei diesen ca. 20%, die keine Zeichen von offiziellen Zensoren enthalten, ist ein gleichsam „mildes" Selbstzensurverfahren auffällig. Die verbotenen Absätze sind nämlich in einer so zurückhaltenden Weise gestrichen, daß die verbotenen Absätze ohne Schwierigkeiten zu lesen waren.[25] Die Leser, oder die Buchhändler, wussten, was nicht gelesen werden sollte; sie kannten die Index-Befehle, aber sie erfüllten sie nicht im Ganzen. Es ist auch zu vermuten, daß sie sich vor einem unwahrscheinlichen Besuch des Zensors schützen wollten.

Neben diesem Umgang gibt es andere Spuren disziplinierter Lesegewohnheiten. Ein weiteres, oft anzutreffendes Beispiel ist jenes von dem Leser, der andere Kleinigkeiten in dem Buch strich; Kleinigkeiten, die nicht durch den spanischen Index formell verboten wurden, aber die doch der Orthodoxie des Konzils von Trient widersprachen und dem Glaubenswächter unangenehm ins Auge fallen konnten. Manchmal kann man nicht mit Sicherheit entscheiden, ob sie von dem Leser oder von dem Zensor gemacht wurden.[26] Auf jeden Fall weisen diese besonderen Lesegewohnheiten auf eine Internalisierung der Maßstäbe, auf eine Sorte von „Überzensur" hin. Solche informelle Me-

---

[25] Wie z. B. bei einem Exemplar der Ausgabe von 1761, das an der Bibliothek der Universität von Barcelona vorhanden ist (In quatuor libros Institutionum imperialium commentarius academicus et forensis. Jo. Gottl. Heineccius Recensuit et praefationem notulasque adjecit. Praemittuntur in hac novissima editione ex Jacobo Gothofredo Historia et Bibliotheca juris civilis Romani. Tomus primus. Venetiis, ex typographia Balleoniana, 1761. Signatur XVIII-30).

[26] Dies ist es bei einem in der Bibliothek des Seminars der Diözese von Menorca vorhandenen Exemplar zu finden, wo die von Heineccius hinzugefügten Notizen zum Vinnius' Kommentar auch gestrichen wurden, obwohl sie nicht offiziell verboten worden waren. Es enthält keine Unterschrift oder andere Zeichen des Zensors, sondern nur ein *Exlibris* des damaligen Besitzers (In quatuor libros Institutionum imperialium commentarius academicus et forensis. Jo. Gottl. Heineccius JC. recensuit et praefationem notulasque adjecit. Tomus primus. Venetiis, ex typographia Balleoniana, 1736. Signatur 2633). In anderen Fällen, wo Zeichen des Zensors zu finden sind, wurden „erlaubte" Textpassagen gestrichen, etwa im Exemplar der Bibliothek des Vatikans, das einem spanischen Besitzer gehörte (Arnoldi Vinnii, auctoris damnati, cum expurgatione vero permissi, in quatuor libros Institutionum imperialium commentarius academicus et forensis, correctus secundum Indicem erxpurgatorium Sanctissimae Inquisitionis Hispaniae anno 1707 publicatum. Editio recentissima ac emendatissima, cui praeter auctoris notas commentario adjunctas accedunt ejusdem Quaestiones iuris selectae, duobus libris inclusae, cum indicibus locupletissimis. Coloniae Allobrogum et Lugduni, apud fratres de Tournes 1729. Signatur: Racc. Gen. Dir. Civ. IV 1639).

chanismen, die jenseits der offiziellen Ebene der Indexvorschriften derenselben Kriterien ergänzen und potenzieren konnten, müssen in einer Analyse des Phänomens der Wissenskontrolle auch Betrachtung finden.[27]

Neben dem Vinnius' expurgierten Institutionenkommentaren, waren seine übrigen Schriften generell verboten, so die Werke: Jurisprudentiae contractae sive partitionum juris civilis libri quatuor (...)[28] und Tractatus de iurisdictione et imperio academico-forensis und Tractatus de collationibus academico-forensis, die gewöhnlich zusammen in erweiterten Ausgaben zirkulierten.[29] Trotz des Verbotes gerieten diese Werke nicht in Vergessenheit: Sie wurden aus dem Ausland nach Spanien eingeführt und sind zahlreich in den heutigen

---

[27] Über die verschiedenen Strategien von *subjectivation* durch die *pouvoir pastorel*: Foucault, Michel: Deux essais sur le sujet et le pouvoir. In: Michel Foucault. Un parcours philosophique au delà de l'objectivité et de la subjectivité. Hrsg. von Hubert Dreyfus; Paul Rabinow. Aus dem Englisch übersetzt von Fabienne Durand-Bogaert. Paris 1984, S. 297-321. Nach der Kritik von Schilling vernachlässigte das geschichtswissenschaftliche Sozialdisziplinierungsmodell diese Arten von Sozialpraxis: „Nicht Disziplinierung von oben durch Institutionen wie Staat oder Kirchen habe die alteuropäische Welt bestimmt, sondern *Selbstregulierung* und soziales *Aushandeln* durch die Betroffenen selbst in Gemeinde, Korporation und Nachbarschaft" (Schilling, Heinz: Profil und Perspektiven einer interdisziplinären und komparatistischen Disziplinierungsforschung jenseits einer Dichotomie von Gesellschafts- und Kulturgeschichte. In: Institutionen, Instrumente und Akteure sozialer Kontrolle und Disziplinierung im frühneuzeitlichen Europa. Hrsg. von Heinz Schilling. Frankfurt am Main 1999, S.4-36, hier S. 14).

[28] Erste Ausgabe: Iurisprudentiae contractae sive partitionum iuris civilis libri IIII, variis observationibus notisque perpetuis illustrati. Pars prima, quae nunc prodit, omnem juris sui cuiusque cognitionem II voluminibus circumplexa est. Hagae-Comitis, apud viduam et haeredes Hillebrandi Jacobi à Wouw, 1624 (Feenstra, Robert; Margreet Ahsmann: Bibliografie van Hoogleraren in de Rechten aan de Leidse Universiteit 1811. Amsterdam 1984, Nr. 824).

[29] Tractatus IV academico-forenses, de jurisdictione, pactis, transactionibus, collationibus, quorum tertius nunc primum in lucem exit caeteri iterum sed ab auctore recogniti et ampla dote locupletati. Amstelredami, apud Abrahamum Commelinum, 1651. Ein anderes Werk, das Selectarum juris quaestionum libri duo (erste Ausgabe Lugduni Batavorum, apud Joh. et Danielem Elsevier, 1653 – Feenstra, Bibliografie [wie Fn. 28], Nr. 931) wurde von dem Dekret von 1741 expurgiert (Kapitel XIII des 2. Buches, *An quo jure licitum sit leviri aut gloris filiam neptemve uxorem ducere,* in dem es auch um die geistliche Verwandtschaft ging). Ab 1747 verbreiteten sich die *Selectarum Juris* als Anhang vieler Ausgaben des Kommentars (u. a. In quatuor libros Institutionum imperialium commentarius academicus et forensis. Jo. Gottl. Heineccius JC. recensuit et praefationem notulasque adjecit. Editio novissima, cui accedunt ejusdem Vinnii Quaestiones juris selectae (...) Lugduni, sumptibus Petri Bruyset et sociorum, 1747).

Bibliotheken vorhanden. Mehr als 50 Exemplare konnten ermittelt werden.[30] Vinnius schien also eine Ausnahme zur negativen Nebenauswirkung der Politik der *damnatio memoriae* zu sein, denn seine Indizierung verursachte kein allgemeines Misstrauen unter den spanischen Lesern.[31] Im Gegenteil weisen die Quellen auf eine verbreitete Verwendung der Werke hin. Wie ist dies zu erklären? Welches sind die Gründe für dieses scheinbar massive Unterlaufen der Inquisitionsbefehle?[32] Wie schon erwähnt beeinflusste die Unkenntnis und der schwierigen Zugang zu den kirchlichen Befehlen den Abstand zwischen offizieller Norm und gesellschaftlicher Praxis. Die Schwierigkeiten angesichts der Bekanntmachung der Normen war eine jener typischen Eigenschaften des Rechts im *Ancien Régime*, die sich bis ins 19. Jahrhundert auswirkten.[33] Das rechtliche Prinzip des *neminem excusat ignorantia legis* blieb der zeitgenössischen offiziellen Praxis und den Mentalitäten fremd. In diesem Zusammenhang sind die Aussagen derselben Zensoren beachtenswert, die eben diese Unkenntnis als legitimen Grund für die Nichterfüllung der Befehle akzeptierten.[34]

---

[30] In verschiedenen Bibliotheken von Sevilla, Cádiz, Madrid, Barcelona und Vitoria.

[31] Pardo Tomás, José: Ciencia y censura. La Inquisición española y los libros científicos en los siglos XVI y XVII. Madrid 1991, S. 345.

[32] Andererseits fehlen nicht die Quellen, die auf eine fieberhafte Tätigkeit der Inquisition zu dieser Zeit hinweisen: Dufour, Gérard: El libro y la Inquisición. In: Historia de la edición y de la lectura en España (1472-1914). Hrsg. von Victor Infantes (et alii). Madrid, Fundación Germán Sánchez Ruipérez, 2003, S. 285-290.

[33] Lorente, Marta: La Voz del Estado. La publicación de las normas (1810-1889). Madrid 2001.

[34] Wie z. B. das Vorwort des Index, Reglas, Mandatos y Advertencias Generales (wie Fn. 16): „Y como tan constante solicitud haya excitado nuestra gravisima obligacion á ocurrir por todos caminos á la malicia humana, particularmente en los presentes tiempos, en que muchas prensas de afuera se fatigan excesivamente por hacer prevalecer en el campo del Señor la cizaña, repetidamente arrancada, cortada y abrasada con los mas formidables anatemas; y aun dentro de los dominios de S. M. Católica se han reimpreso algunas obras de las contenidas en el Expurgatorio del año de 1747, excusando la transgresion con la ignorancia de que estuviesen comprendidas en él; haciendo creible la buena fé la suma escasez de ejemplares del expresado Indice expurgatorio y su crecido coste, por ser muy raros los que se hallan, y estos sin el aumento ó adicion de las obras prohibidas ó mandadas expurgar en el crecido número de edictos posteriores; cuya noticia no puede conservarse con la debida puntualidad en las oficinas de los impresores y libreros, ni aun en las bibliotecas públicas y de diferentes particulares, como es necesario para su observancia: dispusimos, con acuerdo y parecer de los señores del consejo, se formase é imprimiese un Resumen ó Compendio alfabético, en que se incluyesen no solo todas las obras contenidas en el expresado

Aber auch als die offiziellen Befehle bekannt waren, war immerhin in bestimmten sozialen Kreisen ein gewisser Spielraum bezüglich seiner Interpretation möglich.

Berühmte Rechtsgelehrte wie Gregorio Mayans y Siscar[35] empfahlen offensichtlich ihren Studenten das Lesen verbotener Vinnius-Werke.[36] Das *Jurisprudentiae contractae sive partitionum juris civilis libri IV*... gehörte auch zu seinem bekanntem Entwurf für die Reform des Jurastudiums.[37] Die Unkenntnis der Indexvorschriften ist in seinem Fall auszuschließen: Als Professor in Valencia und selbst Autor einiger Zensuren und Zensurentwürfe juristischer Werke kannte er sie gut. Er durfte solche Werke lesen, da er für eine begrenzte Zeit eine außerordentliche Erlaubnis für das Lesen verbotener Bücher genoss[38], die trotz seiner Bemühungen nicht weiter verlängert wurde.[39]

Indice de 1747 y su Suplemento, sino tambien cuantas obras se han prohibido ó mandado expurgar en los citados edictos, hasta el último publicado en 13 de Diciembre de 1789, y asimismo las prohibidas hasta su examen y censura (...)" (nachgedruckt in Indice general de los libros prohibidos, compuesto del Indice último de los libros prohibidos y mandados expurgar hasta fin de diciembre de 1789 por el señor Inquisidor General y señores del Supremo Consejo de la Santa General Inquisicion, de los suplementos del mismo, que alcanzan hasta 25 de agosto de 1805. Madrid, Imprenta de José Felix Palacios, editor, 1844, S. V).

[35] Über den Juristen aus Valencia, der einer der bekanntesten Juristen und eine paradigmatische Figur der spanischen Aufklärung war, gibt es zahlreiche Studien: U. a. von Mestre, Antonio: Mayans y la España de la Ilustración. Madrid, 1990; und Peset, Mariano; José Luis Peset. Gregorio Mayáns y la Reforma Universitaria. Idea del nuevo método que se puede practicar en la enseñanza de las universidades de España, 1 de abril de 1767. Valencia 1975.

[36] Briefe von Pedro Andrés Burriel an Mayáns, vom 22. Januar 1746. In: Gregorio Mayans y Siscar. Epistolario. Bd. II: Mayáns y Burriel. Hrsg. von Antonio Mestre. Valencia 1972, S. 224.

[37] Peset, Gregorio Mayáns y la Reforma (wie Fn. 35), S. 240-241. Das *Jurisprudentia contractae*... wurde nicht von der römischen Inquisition verboten, sondern explizit in einem Briefwechsel mit der lokalen Inquisition von Florenz erlaubt (Archivio della Congregazione per la Dottrina della Fede: ACDF, S. O. Tit. Lib., 1729-1745, fasc. 55), obwohl es ähnliche „heterodoxe" Passagen über das Eherecht wie der Institutionenkommentar enthielt.

[38] Über die Rolle der *licentiae legendi* zur Verstärkung und Legitimierung der kirchlichen Kontrolle siehe Frajese, Vittorio: Le licenze di lettura tra vescovi ed inquisitori. Aspetti della politica dell'indice dopo il 1596. Società e Storia (1999), Nr. 86, XXII, S. 767-818.

[39] Brief vom G. Mayans an F. J. de Charola vom 20. März 1751 zitiert nach Alemany Peiró, Amparo: Estudio introductorio: ¿Era posible una apertura en la Inquisición española a principios del XVIII? In: Gregorio Mayans y Siscar. Epistolario, Band XX. Los hermanos Mayans y los Inquisi-

Wie aber könnte er dieses verbotene Werk den Studenten, die in der Mehrzahl der Fälle nie solche Leseerlaubnisse hatten, systematisch empfehlen? Diese öffentlichen Empfehlungen verbotener Bücher sollten nicht für eine lebensgefährliche „Unbesonnenheit" gehalten werden. Sie werden in einem historischen Zusammenhang verständlich, in dem der Index nicht als Ausdruck einer absoluten Macht verstanden wurde,[40] sondern als eine noch offene und unvollständige Norm. Der Index vermittelte eher bestimmte Maßstäbe für die Lesenormierung der sozialen Akteure, die sich je nach der Position in dem sozialen Feld mit einer gewissen Unabhängigkeit bewegen konnten und die ständig zur Zusammenarbeit aufgerufen wurden. Die Inquisition hat die Mitarbeit Gelehrter wie Mayans, der über ein großes soziales Prestige verfügte und mit mächtigen Figuren des bourbonischen Reiches verkehrte,[41] in der Expurgationspolitik besonders gefördert, da sie wegen der ständigen Zunahme der gedruckten Produktion die Grenzen ihres Verfahrens erkannte.[42] Mayans, der sich der willkürlichen Art und Weise der Inquisitoren bewusst war,[43] engagier-

---

dores, 1. La „clientela" del Inquisidor Andrés Orbe. Hrsg. von Amparo Alemany Peiró. Valencia 2005, S.7-90; hier S. 72.

[40] „... mesurer l'efficacité des mécanismes de censure non pas du point de vue d'un contrôle absolu, irréalisable" (Bethancourt, Francisco: L'Inquisition à l'époque moderne: Espagne, Italie, Portugal, XVe- XIXe siècle. Paris 1995, S. 226).

[41] Bei den Schwierigkeiten, die Mayans mit der Zivilzensur hatte (d. h. mit dem *Juez de Imprentas*, dessen Funktionen ab 1752 erweitert und verstärkt wurden), wurde ihm von einem seiner einflussreichen Freunde wie dem *Consejero* Fernando José de Velasco geholfen (Mestre, Antonio; Pablo Pérez García: Estudio preliminar. La amistad de dos bibliófilos. In: Gregorio Mayans y Siscar. Epistolario. Band XVI: Mayans y los altos cuadros de la magistratura y administración borbónica, 3. Fernando José de Velasco Ceballos (1753-1781). Hrsg. von Antonio Mestre. Valencia, 1998, S. 23-28). Über die Zivilzensur im Spanien des 18. Jahrhunderts: García Martín, Javier: El juzgado de imprentas y la utilidad pública. Cuerpo y alma de una Monarquía vicarial. Bilbao, 2003 und die kürzlich veröffentlichte Dissertation von Esteban Conde Naranjo: El Argos de la Monarquía. La policía del libro en la España ilustrada (1750-1834). Madrid 2006.

[42] Siehe Fn. 15.

[43] In seiner Antwort an den Genfer Drucker Cramer über die Einführung der *Opera omnia* des Heineccius in Spanien schrieb Mayans: „Yo estoy muy bien informado de la utilidad de dichas obras, y puedo decir que soy el que las ha dado a conocer en España años ha; pero como, cuando vienen, paran en manos de teólogos revisores de libros, que no atienden sino a si ven algunas proposiciones contrarias a los dogmas católicos, nadie es capaz de impedir que se delaten a la inquisición y se expurguen, que es lo menos que puede suceder, o se prohiban absolutamente, por

te sich bei der Expurgationspolitik juristischer Werke. Dies zeigt seine Initiative hinsichtlich eines Zensurentwurfs des moralisch-philosophischen Lehrbuch Heineccius', den er vergebens bei der Inquisition vorgelegt hatte.[44] Außerdem schrieb er auch Zensuren und Vorworte im Auftrag des Königs.[45] Er genoß in verschiedenen Phasen die Gunsten der Inquisitoren[46] erlebte aber auch die Verfolgung seiner eigenen Werke.[47] Unterschiedliche Umstände gaben ihm mehr oder weniger Verhandlungsmacht.

„Verdammt" wurden bestimmte Schriftsteller nicht nur um vergessen, sondern auch um erinnert werden zu können. Neben der formellen Maßnahmen der Verdammung des Gedächtnisses und der Expurgationspolitik, die die Zirkulation der Werke unter sicheren Umständen für Drucker und Publikum ermöglichte, ebenso bedeutend für den Lauf des mannigfaltiges Netzwerk der Zensur[48] waren die verschiedenen Strategien des Unterlaufens und des Wider-

---

huir del trabajo de ir particularizando las proposiciones. Estas prohibiciones salen antes que se tenga noticia de las delaciones y son inevitables en España" (Carta de Gregorio Mayáns al impresor Cramer, 4-I-1749, Biblioteca-Archivo-Hispano-Mayansiana (BAHM), Valencia, 154 zitiert nach Mestre, Antonio: Los libreros ginebrinos y la Ilustración española. In: Livres et libraires en Espagne et au Portugal (XVI-XXè siècles). Paris 1989, S.61-79; hier S.64).

[44] S. Brief an Martínez Pingarrón vom 18. Oktober 1768 in: Gregorio Mayans y Siscar. Epistolario. Band IX: Mayans y Martínez Pingarrón, 3. Real Biblioteca y Política Cultural. Hrsg. von Antonio Mestre. Valencia, 1989, S. 165. Auch: Rus Rufino, Salvador: Existe una teoría española sobre el derecho natural en el siglo XVIII? In: La historia de la filosofía jurídica española. Hrsg. von Francisco Puy Muñoz; Salvador Rus Rufino. Santiago, 1998, S. 131-162; S. 138. Nur die *Praelectiones academicae in Hugonis Grotii De iure belli ac pacis libros III* von Heineccius wurden später von der spanischen Inquisition verboten.

[45] Veröffentlicht in Gregorio Mayans y Siscar. Obras completas. Band V: *Ensayos y varia.* Hrsg. von Antonio Mestre. Valencia 1986.

[46] Als der Inquisitor Marmanillo eine Kritik an dem Werk Orador cristiano von Mayans veröffentlichen wollte, bat Mayans um die Unterstützung seiner Bekannten bei der Inquisition, die die Veröffentlichung der Schrift verhindern konnten (u. a. der Brief vom 19. September 1733 von dem Inquisitor Andrés Orbe an Mayans. In: Epistolario, Bd. XX, S. 113).

[47] Die kritische Ausgabe von Mayans des Censura de Historias Fabulosas von Nicolas Antonio, wurde systematisch verfolgt (siehe u. a. der Brief von Mayans an dem Inquisidor general Orozco Manrique de Lara am 26. Januar 1743, in: Epistolario, Bd. XX, S. 98-100).

[48] „Disziplinierung ist nicht mehr ein einseitiges Verhältnis der Repression, sondern ein umfassendes Kontrollnetz, das sich in einer Vielzahl ganz unterschiedlicher Formen gesellschaftlichen Wissens und gesellschaftlicher Praktiken manifestiert. Und gerade indem sich Disziplinierung ver-

standes, die disziplinierten Lesegewohnheiten und die verschiedenen Formen aktiver Interaktion zwischen Zensoren, Drucker und Leser. Die Disziplinierung der Erinnerung und des Vergessens für die juristischen Leser in Spanien war kein geradliniger von oben nach unten durchgeführter Prozess. Weitere Beiträge wären aber noch wünschenswert, um ein tieferes Verständnis der Formation dieser besonderen Disziplin des Erinnerns und des Vergessens zu erreichen.

---

allgemeinert, tritt ihre offen repressive Seite zurück“ (Sachße, Christoph; Florian Tennstedt: Sicherheit und Disziplin: Eine Skizze zur Einführung. In: Soziale Sicherheit (wie Fn. 7), 1986, S.14).

From Inscriptions to the Dramatic Text: Literary Reminders of Lawmaking in Athenian Old Comedy

Emiliano J. Buis

A. Introduction

The enactment of legislation constituted for Athenians an exercise of active participation. Ancient testimonies confirm that legislative proposals could originate from different sources and could respond to quite different interests. Therefore, we should not be surprised to discover that references to law are frequent in a well-known literary genre such as Greek Old Comedy. In fact, legal expressions – identified as such and frequently remembered by those citizens attending the theatre – became useful as a source for laughter.

Our purpose here is to work on several passages of Aristophanes' plays in which comic characters and *choreutai* imitate legislative language and propose the approval of laws and decrees on stage. In the framework of this analysis, the contrast of epigraphic testimonies and comic discourse can shed light on a number of parodic strategies put forward within the dramatic text in order to achieve both artistic and political goals.

B. Lawmaking in Classical Athens: From Oral Arguments to Written Laws

Popular participation in Athens could be seen, at different levels, all along the steps of the legislative procedure, and the Assembly (ἐκκλησία), the Council (βουλή) and any citizen were granted an extended capacity of initiative. If an Athenian decided it was suitable to propose a new law within the established set of norms, he was obliged to persuade others that this was the right way to act. Its benefits to the community were publicly expressed, and in the meeting – soon after – their decision on the legal proposal, voted by show of hands, became definite.[1] In any case, once the decree was drafted, passed and voted on, it was finally inscribed in stone for publicity.[2]

It must be said that the aim of writing statutes (θεσμοί) for their preservation is significant. During the classical period, written law was regarded as conductive to fairness, justice and equality.[3] A stable medium offered stability, security and permanence.[4] Consequently, inscribing laws, as a way of constructing a sort of collective juridical memory in Athens and elsewhere in the Greek world, was considered to be an active measure to promote the widespread consultation of their content and, at the same time, to impress and symbolically intimidate the population with their authority.

In this sense, an interesting interaction between oral transmission and writing was achieved, since the Athenians regarded public argumentation as the appropriate way to discuss laws but considered written publicity to stand as the legitimate means to make laws officially known and valid.

---

[1] D. 20.89-99, 20.91, 24.20-3; cf. MacDowell, D. M: Law-Making at Athens in the Fourth Century B.C.. In: Journal of Hellenic Studies vol. 95, pp. 62-74, here on p. 73.

[2] Athenian democracy was based on the notion of informed citizens, and thus writing laws in inscriptions was obviously the way to let the populace know about their content (Meritt, B. D.: Epigraphica Attica [Martin Classical Lectures, Vol. 9]. Cambridge MA 1940, pp. 89-93). See further a survey of recent discussions in Hedrik, C. W.: Writing, Reading, and Democracy. In: Ritual, Finance, Politics: Athenian Democratic Accounts Presented to David Lewis. Ed. by R. Osborne/S. Hornblower. Oxford 1994, pp. 157-174.

[3] Thomas, R.: Writing, Law, and Written Law. In: M. Gagarin/D. Cohen (eds.): The Cambridge Companion to Ancient Greek Law. Cambridge 2005, pp. 41-60, here on p. 43. See also Hölkeskamp, K.-J.: Nomos, Thesmos und Verwandtes. Vergleichende Überlegungen zur Konzeptualisierung geschriebenen Rechts im klassischen Griechenland. In: D. Cohen/E. Müller-Luckner (eds.) Demokratie, Recht und soziale Kontrolle im klassischen Athen (Schriften des Historischen Kollegs. Kolloquien 49). München 2002, pp. 109-114.

[4] *"Written law can be – and often is – fundamental in checking arbitrary judgement: when justice was in the hands of a few elders and governed by unwritten law, it was clearly open to arbitrary judgement and inconsistency"*, Thomas, R.: Written in Stone? Liberty, Equality, Orality and the Codification of Law. In: L. Foxhall/A. D. E. Lewis, Greek Law in its Political Setting. Justifications not Justice. Oxford 1996, pp. 9-31, here on p. 30. On the same subject of legal writing and orality, see also Papakonstantinou, Z.: Written Law, Literacy and Social Conflict in Archaic and Classical Crete. In: Ancient History Bulletin (2002) 16 (3-4), pp. 135-150; Bertrand, J.-M.: De l'écriture à l'oralité. Lectures des "Lois" de Platon. Paris 1999, inter multa alia.

But in what sense did the audience of a comic play know, for instance, this praxis of law and was able to perceive the echoes of legal language?

C. Assembly, Courtrooms and Theatre: The (Common) Experience of Civic Performance

In democratic times, civic action was mainly exercised through the staging of public speeches in spaces open for participation. Theater, courtrooms and the Assembly, in this sense, constituted three fields which could be clearly connected within the broad field of political activity.[5] As formal instances in which every citizen could have his place, where the actors and the audience were clearly discernible in a prepared scenario of solemnity,[6] legislative procedures and theatrical representations were basically "performative" activities.[7]

---

[5] This relationship does not only occur in Antiquity. In fact, several points can be discovered if theater is put in contact with the practice of law: *"(...) drama itself is a vital part of the tissue of experience that develops our ideas and expectations of justice"*, Larner, D.: Justice and Drama: Historical Ties and 'Thick' Relationships. In: Legal Studies Forum (1998) 22 (1, 2 & 3), pp. 2-17, here on p. 17; cf. Laster, K.: The Drama of the Courtroom. Annandale 2000. Whereas tragedy is probably the dramatic experience that is most often attached to the exercise of justice, comedy cannot be left aside when drawing this parallel: *"The action of a civil society is what on stage is known as comedy – that form of drama which displays how individuals grow and learn, and how societies integrate youth and age, the conventional and the rebellious, the ordinary and the odd, into community"*, Larner, D.: Teaching Justice: The Idea of Justice in the Structure of Drama. In: Legal Studies Forum (1999) 23 (1 & 2), pp. 201-210, here on pp. 209-210; *"(...) we see how integral the development of cultural conceptions of justice are to the very fabric and essence of the drama, and how, for more than two thousand years, we have found the essential forms of those ideas in the tissues of our drama where its tragic and comic sensibilities collide, conflict, and connect."*, Larner, D.: Justice and Drama: Conflict and Advocacy. In: Legal Studies Forum (1999) 23 (4), pp. 417-429, here on p. 429.

[6] Cf. Duvignaud, J.: Sociologie du théatre: essai sur les ombres collectives. Paris 1965.

[7] On the recent importance granted to the notion of performance in order to explain several aspects of Greek culture, see the textual analyses suggested by Taplin, O.: The Stagecraft of Aeschylus. Oxford 1977, and: Greek Tragedy in Action. London/Berkeley 1978, and the more recent volume edited by Goldhill, S./Osborne, R. (eds.): Performance culture and Athenian democracy. Cambridge 1999. From this perspective, it is possible to read both legal activities and dramatic competitions as socially dynamic and public creations; drama, festivals, rites and spectacles can all be taken as cultural instances (MacAloon, J. (ed.): Rite, Drama, Festival, Spectacle: Rehearsals to-

As Garner points out, "(...) these legal and dramatic verbal contests shared various details of procedure and administration which suggested their equivalence to democratic audiences. Some of the resemblances were elaborately specific".[8] They were meant to be prepared in advance to be performed in front of others. In the core of the debate, litigants-actors-assemblymen were definitely playing the roles society attributed to them. In these agonistic games of characters, a public dimension was achieved: theater, courts and the ἐκκλησία were meant to represent both collective and symbolic events in a public sphere.[9] Broadly speaking, they consolidated social shows or political rituals.[10] Certain conventional elements shared by them[11] were capable of turning them into formal and deeply structured ceremonies.

A number of parallels remain obvious; from a global perspective, dramatic plays seem to derive part of their formal structure, to a certain extent, from legal proceedings. We regularly find two individuals pitted against each other, and each used to address a speech of approximately equal length. As Hall has very well demonstrated,[12] speeches in law courts were essentially *dramatic* because they were represented as a spectacle: actors and orators had to rehearse in advance, memorizing the speech and afterwards pretending to improvise. Like tragic or comic characters, the plaintiff and the defendant, standing on two platforms facing the audience, were engaged in a process of self-dramatization.[13]

---

ward a Theory of Cultural Performance. Philadelphia 1984) which are performed on their scenes in front of a democratic audience sharing a common ideology on the power of the *demos*.

[8] Garner, R.: Law and Society in Classical Athens. New York 1987, p. 97.

[9] Soulier, G.: Le théâtre et le procès. In: Droit et société. Revue internationale de théorie du droit et de sociologie juridique (1991) 17-18, pp. 9-24, here p. 17.

[10] On the importance of the 'community' and theatre as "a public event par excellence", see Longo, O.: The Theater of the *Polis*. In: J. J. Winkler/F. I. Zeitlin (eds.): Nothing to Do With Dionysos? Athenian Drama in Its Social Context. Princeton NJ 1990, pp. 12-19.

[11] On theatrical conventions, cf. Dedoussi, C.: Greek Drama and Its Spectators: Conventions and Relationships. In: A. Griffiths (ed.): Stage Directions. Essays in Ancient Drama in Honour of E. W. Handley (BICS Suppl. 66). London 1995, pp. 123-132.

[12] Cf. Hall, E.: Lawcourt Dramas: The Power of Performance in Greek Forensic Oratory. In: Bulletin of the Institute of Classical Studies (1995) 40, pp. 39-58.

[13] Wills, D.: Greek Theater Performance: An Introduction. Cambridge 2000, p. 57.

Several other interesting similarities between public hearings in the legal sphere and those that were staged before citizens in the theatre have often been acknowledged.[14] In their public dimension, trials, meetings at the Assembly and dramatic festivals were not only performed but also attended, seen and heard by a large number of participants[15] – jurors and public, respectively – which became involved with the action.[16] In both of them, agonistic performances were aimed at a majority decision by the jury about the winner.

It is possible to conclude therefore that the proximity of legal and dramatic experiences in Athens must be taken into consideration when dealing with their specific nature and potential interactions. Spectators attending the staging of comedies or tragedies were used to listening at the βουλή or the ἐκκλησία to legal proposals. It remains evident, in this sense, that dramatic texts were capable of exploiting this shared knowledge as a functional literary device.

D. (En)acting Legislation in Old Comedy: The Parody of Legal Documents in Aristophanes

Despite the considerable number of studies on Ancient Greek Law published in the last decades,[17] Old Comedy – mostly known to us through the

---

[14] Wills, Greek Theater (as in note 13), p. 131; Ober, J./Strauss, B.: Drama, Politicial Rhetoric and the Discourse of Athenian Democracy. In: Winkler/Zeitlin, Nothing to Do With Dionysos? (as in note 10), pp. 237-270, here on p. 237.

[15] Wallace, R. W.: Poet, Public, and 'Theatrocracy': Audience Performance in Classical Athens. In: L. Edmunds/R. W. Wallace (eds.): Poet, Public, and Performance in Ancient Greece. Baltimore-London 1997, pp. 97-111, speaks of a real "theatocracy" in Athens in the course of an interpretation of the cultural importance of the public in social performances such as the drama.

[16] In the theatre, the spectators became identified with the chorus, as they became involved with the dramatic fiction through the civic performance of the *choreutai* (Calame, C.: Performative aspects of the choral voice in Greek tragedy: civic identity in performance. In: Goldhill/R. Osborne, Performance culture (as in note 7), pp. 125-153, here on p. 149).

[17] Since 1980, and apart from the works quoted elsewhere in this paper, we may recall the publication of some interesting monographs on Greek Law: Biscardi, A.: Diritto Greco Antico. Bari 1982; Todd, S.C.: The Shape of Athenian Law. Oxford 1993; Hunter, V.: Policing Athens: Social Control in the Attic Lawsuits, 420-320 BC. Princeton 1994; Sealey, R.: The Justice of the Greeks. Ann Arbor 1994; Cohen, D.: Law, Violence and Community in Classical Athens. Cambridge

preservation of eleven complete plays written by Aristophanes, out of more than forty, between 427 and 388 BC – seems to be still ignored or left aside by legal historians. An incomplete vision of the genre, limited to the identification of political upside-down fictions, grotesque characters and utopian worlds in which carnivalesque celebrations dominated the stage, boycotted any interest of legal historians in its "serious" content.[18] It was not until recently that fresh perspectives on comedy have finally showed the inadequacy of the traditional partial point of view and have succeeded in presenting it as a complex phenomenon. A number of recent volumes have acknowledged the importance of technical languages in Ancient Comedy.[19] Even if they only grant a few pages to describing the specificity of a legal technical vocabulary in Aristophanes' works, they have at least opened the door to the further study of juridical references in comic testimonies. In order to show the ways in which comic plays become useful as a literary source for the reconstruction of Athenian law, it is our purpose here to deal with the texts themselves.

1995; Christ, M. R.: The Litigious Athenian. Baltimore 1998; Johnstone, S.: Disputes and Democracy. The Consequences of Litigation in Ancient Athens. Austin 1999; Martini, R.: Diritti greci. Siena 1999; Rubinstein, L.: Litigation and Cooperation. Supporting Speakers in the Courts of Classical Athens. Stuttgart 2000; Allen, D. S.: The World of Prometheus. The Politics of Punishment in Democratic Athens. Princeton 2002; Gagarin, M.: Antiphon the Athenian. Oratory, Law, and Justice in the Age of the Sophists. Austin 2002; Harris, E. M.: Democracy and the Rule of Law in Classical Athens: Essays on Law, Society, and Politics. Cambridge 2006; Lanni, A.: Law and Justice in the Courts of Classical Athens. Cambridge 2006, among many others.
In the same period of time, several collective books have also dealt with the legal aspects of classical Greek societies: Cartledge, P. Millett, P. Todd, S. (eds.): Nomos. Essays in Athenian law, politics and society. Cambridge 1990; Boegehold, A. L. Scafuro, A. C. (eds.): Athenian Identity and Civic Ideology. Baltimore-London 1993; Harris, E. M. Rubinstein, L. (eds.): Law and the Courts in Ancient Greece. Cambridge 2000; Hunter, V./Edmonson, J. (ed.): Law and Social Status in Classical Athens/Oxford 2001; Leão, D. F. Rossetti, L. do Céu Fialho, M. (eds.): Nomos. Direito e sociedade na antiguidade Clássica / Derecho y sociedad en la Antigüedad Clásica. Coimbra-Madrid 2004; Cairns, D. (ed.): Law, Rhetoric and Comedy in Classical Athens. London 2004.

[18] For a recent re-examination of these visions of comedy, see MacDowell, M.: Aristophanes and Athens. An Introduction to the Plays. Oxford 1995.

[19] For example, we can mention the works by Kloss, G.: Erscheinungsformen komischen Sprechens bei Aristophanes. Berlin 2001; Beta, S.: Il linguaggio nelle commedie di Aristofane. Parola positiva e parola negativa nella commedia antica. Roma 2004, and Willi, A.: The Languages of Aristophanes: Aspects of Linguistic Variation in Classical Attic Greek. Oxford 2003.

I. Indictments

A first clear example of the comic use of legal material in Aristophanic comedy is *Wasps*, put on stage in 422 BC at the festival of the Lenaia. Its plot is arranged around a harsh critique of the Athenian judicial system. The main character of the play, Philocleon, is an old man addicted to court proceedings, suffering thus from a dangerous dikastic illness which desperately makes him spend all his life acting as a juror. To help him with his inconvenient paranoia, his son Bdelycleon manages, at a certain point of the plot, to lock him up and to set up a court in his own home for his father to preside over. For the lack of anyone else to pass judgment on, the protagonist puts the family dog on trial. By apparently making a parodic reference to a recent event – known by the audience – in which the politician Cleon intended to accuse an Athenian general (Laches) for accepting bribes in Southern Italy, Philocleon is ready to sentence the dog for having entered the kitchen and having devoured a Sicilian cheese on his own. Bdelycleon himself reads the statement of the claim (*V.* 894-897):

> ἀκούετ᾽ ἤδη τῆς γραφῆς. "ἐγράψατο
> Κύων Κυδαθηναιεὺς Λάβητ᾽ Αἰξωνέα
> τὸν τυρὸν ἀδικεῖν ὅτι μόνος κατήσθιεν
> τὸν Σικελικόν. τίμημα κλῳὸς σύκινος."

Now all hear the charge: "Demadogue, the watchdog of Cydathenaeum, indicts Gabres of Aexone because he committed the offense of devouring a Sicilian cheese all by himself. Proposed penalty: a collar of impeach wood."[20]

---

[20] We have generally relied upon the Oxford editions for the quotation of Aristophanes' plays in Greek: Austin, C./Olson, S. D. (eds.): Aristophanes' Thesmophoriazusae. Oxford 2004; Dover, K. J. (ed.): Aristophanes: Clouds. Oxford 1968, and (ed.): Aristophanes' Frogs. Oxford 1993[1] (2002); Dunbar, N. (ed.): Aristophanes' Birds. Oxford 1995[1] (1997); MacDowell, D. M. (ed.): Aristophanes' Wasps. Oxford 1971; Olson, S. D. (ed.): Aristophanes' Acharnians. Oxford 2002; Ussher, R. G. (ed.): Aristophanes Ecclesiazusae. Oxford 1973. As for the translations, we have reproduced here the English versions of Henderson, J. (ed.): Aristophanes. Clouds, Wasps, Peace, vol. II (The Loeb Classical Library). Cambridge, Mass./London 1998, and idem (ed.): Aristo-

The syntactic structure of these verses, listened to by the audience, carefully responds to the judicial initiatives of the period. It is possible to recall – for comparison – the famous indictment against Socrates for the charge of impiety, according to the testimony of Diogenes Laertius 2.40.3-7, which reveals the typical terms of a public accusation:

> "τάδε ἐγράψατο καὶ ἀντωμόσατο Μέλητος Μελήτου Πιτθεὺς Σωκράτει Σωφρονίσκου ᾽Αλωπεκῆθεν· ἀδικεῖ Σωκράτης, οὓς μὲν ἡ πόλις νομίζει θεοὺς οὐ νομίζων, ἕτερα δὲ καινὰ δαιμόνια εἰσηγούμενος· ἀδικεῖ δὲ καὶ τοὺς νέους διαφθείρων. τίμημα θάνατος."
>
> *Meletos son of Meletos of Pithos indicts and takes an oath against Socrates son of Sophroniscos of Alopece. Socrates has committed the offence of not recognizing the gods whom the state recognizes and introducing other new divinities; he has also committed the offence of corrupting the youth. Proposed penalty: death.*

As it is clearly perceived, the basic linguistic structure in both cases remains the same: at the beginning, we find the name of the prosecutor and the defendant, accompanied by the patronymic and *deme* of residence in order to identify the litigants. The verb indicating the type of the indictment is also included: in both cases, we find the aorist ἐγράψατο, showing that it was a *graphe* or a public action.[21] The nature of the crime committed (shown by the

---

phanes. Birds, Lysistrata, Women at the Thesmophoria. Vol. III (The Loeb Classical Library). Cambridge, Mass./London 2000, as well as those offered by Sommerstein, A. H. (ed.): The Comedies of Aristophanes, vol. 1-12. Warminster 1980-2002.

[21] As opposed to private *dikai*, *graphai* were judicial actions that – under Athenian Law – could be initiated by any interested citizen. Cf. MacDowell, D. M.: The Law in Classical Athens. London 1978, pp. 57-58. According to Osborne, R.: Law in Action in Classical Athens. In: Journal of Hellenic Studies (1985) 105, pp. 40-58, here on p. 43, a citizen could have the possibility of choosing the most appropriate procedure to win his case: "*Since most offences for which the law specified procedure by* graphē *could be redefined to fall within the scope of a law specifying procedure by* dikē *it was frequently possible for an Athenian litigant to choose between processes. The man who acted by* dikē *had to act himself but ran no risk; the man who wanted action by* graphē *could prosecute himself or find another who was willing to do so, and*

verb ἀδικεῖν) is also mentioned, and at the end the denunciations point to the proposed sanction or τίμημα.

Despite the close similarities between both passages, the text of *Wasps* is openly ridiculous. In this domestic mock trial, it is precisely the nature of the offence – not the illegal consumption of the cheese, but the fact of not having shared it – and the characteristics of the litigants which constitute the hilarity of the scene. The final allusion to the figwood (σύκινος) as a punishment is also humorous, since it plays on the Greek term to designate the *sycophantai* – i.e. the professional Athenian blackmailers who used to take people to trial in order to receive the financial reward granted to successful litigants. As it is evident, the formalities of traditional indictments – such as the one that Diogenes would mention coming from the early 4th Century BC – are displaced by Aristophanes and set within the framework of a comic plot.

II. Laws

In its first verses, the comedy *Birds* (represented at the city of Dionysia in 414 BC) shows two old men – Peisetaerus and Euelpides – who, tired of Athenian litigiousness, decide to escape and travel in search of Tereus, the ancient king transformed into a Hoopoe. In their own initial words, they confess that they are looking for an ideal place, far from problems and trials (*Av.* 39-45):

Οἱ μὲν γὰρ οὖν τέττιγες ἕνα μῆν' ἢ δύο
ἐπὶ τῶν κραδῶν ᾄδουσ', Ἀθηναῖοι δ' ἀει
ἐπὶ τῶν δικῶν ᾄδουσι πάντα τὸν βίον.
Διὰ ταῦτα τόνδε τὸν βάδον βαδίζομεν,
κανοῦν δ' ἔχοντε καὶ χύτραν καὶ μυρρίνας

whoever undertook the prosecution faced the possibility of a heavy fine if completely unsuccessful. The variety of actions both constrains a man and frees him to fit his actions to his circumstances."

πλανώμεθα ζητοῦντε <u>τόπον ἀπράγμονα</u>,
ὅποι καθιδρυθέντε διαγενοίμεθ' ἄν.

No, it's that the cicadas chirp on their boughs for only a month or two, whereas <u>the Athenians harp on their lawsuits their whole lives long</u>. That's why we're trekking this trek, and wandering with basket, kettle, and myrtle boughs in search of a <u>peaceable place</u>, where we can settle down and pass our lives.

The objects they are carrying correspond to the ordinary elements used in foundation rituals. In this sense, their objective seems to take place as soon as they manage to convince Tereus of building a new city for the birds, Cloud-cuckooland, in the middle of the sky. At the beginning, the πόλις is intended to host a society only ruled by the laws (νόμοι) of nature and not by Attic legislation.[22] Consequently, the protagonist starts a dispute with an Athenian decree-seller (ψηφισματοπώλης)[23] who appears on stage to offer new possible νόμοι for the place. In the dialogue, a number of specific statutes are quoted by the visitor (*Av.* 1035-45):

---

[22] On *nómos* in Aristophanic comedy, see Lopez Férez, J. A.: *Nómos* chez Aristophane. In: P. Thiercy/M. Menu (eds.): Aristophane: la langue, la scène, la cité (Actes du colloque de Toulouse, 17-19 mars 1994). Bari 1997, pp. 379-396. The word in Greek refers both to written law and to customary rules, as Ostwald, M. (Nomos and the Beginnings of the Athenian Democracy. Oxford 1969, and: From Popular Sovereignity to the Sovereignity of Law. Law, Society and Politics in Fifth-Century Athens. Berkeley/Los Angeles/London 1986) has consistently explained. By the end of the century, a specific difference is established between νόμοι (identified as general laws) and ψηφίσματα (decrees in particular), as Wilson Nightingale, A.: Plato's Lawcode in Context: Rule by Written Law in Athens and Magnesia. In: Classical Quarterly (1999) 49, 1, pp. 100-122, clarifies on p. 105: "*(…) in the last decade of the fifth century, the Athenians attempted to codify all their laws, which seems to have involved revising the laws to eliminate inconsistencies, collecting them together, and inscribing on the Stoa Basileios. In addition, they introduced an important change into the legal system by distinguishing nomoi from psêphismata, and giving precedence to the former: nomoi were now 'laws' of a general nature with permanent standing, while psêphismata were mere 'decrees' which dealt with immediate and individual issues and did not establish legal precedent (…).*" On the same topic, see Quass, F.: Nomos und Psephisma. Untersuchungen griechischen Staatsrecht. München 1971, and Hansen, M. H.: Nomos and Psephisma in Fourth-Century Athens. In: Greek, Roman, and Byzantine Studies (1978) 19, pp. 315-330.

[23] On this character, see Jackson, C. N.: The Decree-Seller in the *Birds* and the Professional Politicians at Athens. In: Harvard Studies in Classical Philology (1919) 30, pp. 89-109.

{ΨΗ} "Ἐὰν δ' ὁ Νεφελοκοκκυγιεὺς τὸν Ἀθηναῖον ἀδικῇ–"
{ΠΙ.} Τουτὶ τί ἐστιν αὖ κακόν, τὸ βιβλίον;
{ΨΗ.} Ψηφισματοπώλης εἰμὶ καὶ νόμους νέους
ἥκω παρ' ὑμᾶς δεῦρο πωλήσων.
{ΠΙ.} Τὸ τί;
{ΨΗ.} Χρῆσθαι Νεφελοκοκκυγιᾶς τοῖς αὐτοῖς μέτροισι
καὶ σταθμοῖσι καὶ ψηφίσμασι καθάπερ Ὀλοφύξιοι
{ΠΙ.} Σὺ δέ γ' οἷσπερ Ὠτοτύξιοι χρήσει τάχα.
{ΨΗ.} Οὗτος, τί πάσχεις;
{ΠΙ.} Οὐκ ἀποίσεις τοὺς νόμους;
Πικροὺς ἐγώ σοι τήμερον δείξω νόμους.

Decree-Seller [reading]: And if a Cloudcuckoolander commits an offence against an Athenian – Peisetaerus: What sort of nuisance is this now, this little book? – Decree-Seller: I'm a decree-seller, and I'm here to sell you some new laws. – Peisetaerus: For instance? – Decree-Seller: The Cloudcuckoolanders must use the selfsame measures, weights and decrees as the Olophyxians. – Peisetaerus: And you'll soon be getting the same as the Black-and-Bluesians! [strikes him] – Decree-Seller: Hey, what's the matter with you? – Peisetaerus: Take your laws away from here! In a moment I'll be showing you some laws you won't like!

In the verse 1035, the decree-seller reads a legal text which resembles the sanction clauses included in several contemporary decrees. In fact, we know that conditional structures such as this one reproduce the linguistic formalities which are typical to legal provisions. In Athens, and according to the principle of imputation, a sanction is virtually always expressed as a third person conditional sentence; the offense is stated in the protasis and the penalty in the apodosis (e.g. "*If a man kills another, he is to be exiled.*").[24] In our case, we can

---

[24] The explanation and the example are based on Gagarin, M.: Drakon and Early Athenian Homicide Law. New Haven/London 1981, p. 82: "*In Greek Laws a sanction is virtually always expressed as a third person conditional sentence; the offense is stated in the protasis and the penalty in the apodosis (e.g. 'If a man kills another, he is exiled.'). Legal sanctions in this form are the regular means for expressing legislation in most societies, and it has been said that there is no true law without them*". On the legal syntax of statutes in

easily identify the eventual hypothesis (introduced by ἐὰν) with the verb in the subjunctive mood (ἀδικῇ) and the generalization through the inclusion of the possible offender (ὁ Νεφελοκοκκυγιεὺς).

Inscriptional testimonies dating from the same period of Athenian history can shed light on this passage and help to illustrate the comic mechanism employed by the playwright.[25] In the text published as *IG* I³ 19 (from 450 BC),[26] concerning the granting of *proxenia* to a certain Achelaion, we find a similar vocabulary as the one contained in the decree-seller's proposal. In fact, lines 2-7 of the text set the case of penalties which are imposed for acting unjustly against him (l. 2-7), by stating εὰν δέ ὑπό τινον [ἀδικε͂τ]αι Ἀχελαΐο[ν.

Other decrees also include clauses beginning with the conditional apodosis ἐὰν δέ τις ἀδικῇ, such as *IG* I³ 34, ll 31-32: εὰν δέ τις Ἀθ[εναῖος ἒ χσύμμαχος ἀδικεῖ περὶ τὸ]ν φόρον. Finally, the decree for the city of Chalcis (446-5 BC), transcribed in a marble stele in the south of the Athenian Acropolis (*IG* I³ 40, 30-31), includes the text of the oath that had to be taken by the Chalcian citizens. One of the clauses (ll. 29-31) provides that they would protect their allies and that they would defend them, if anyone commits a crime against the Athenian people (καὶ το͂ι δέμοι το͂ι Ἀθεναίον βοεθέσ-| ο καὶ ἀμυνο͂, ἐάν τις ἀδικε͂ι τὸν δε͂μον τὸν | Ἀθεναίον). [27] Both in structure and terminology, similar patterns are reproduced.

The law quoted in *Birds*, therefore, is similar to the formulae which are frequent in several Attic laws and which the dramatic audience must have been well able to recognize and understand.[28] However, the clause in the comedy

---

Athenian Law, see also Carey, Ch.: The Shape of Athenian Laws. In: Classical Quarterly (1998) 48 (i), pp. 93-109, here on p. 95. I have worked elsewhere with this formulation and its frequent use in Aristophanes' *Birds*: Buis, E. J. :Persuadir, legislar y juzgar en *Aves*. Aristófanes y los alcances jurídico-políticos del uso de hipótesis eventuales. In: Argos (2001) 24, pp. 7-22.

[25] Despite the scarce evidence for classical times, it remains true that epigraphy allows the only direct source for our reconstruction on Ancient Greek Law. On the subject, see Maffi, A.: Studi di epigrafia giuridica greca. Milano 1983.

[26] For the Athenian inscriptions, I have followed the texts edited by Kirchner, I. (ed.): Inscriptiones Graecae. Inscriptiones Atticae. Vol. I²-II². Editio Minor. Berlin 1913 [= *IG* I²-II²].

[27] Cf. also Xen. Hell. 1.7.20.

[28] Another interesting example of this kind of legal clauses within *Birds* is provided by lines

remains incomplete, and the whole legal text – even before the main legal consequence providing the sanction is mentioned – is qualified by Peisetaerus as a nuisance (κακόν).

The second law referred to by the ψηφισματοπώλης is interesting, too. When he imposes that *"The Cloudcuckoolanders are to use the selfsame measures, weights and decrees as the Olophyxians"*, there is a clear parallelism with the famous Athenian decree of about 423 BC,[29] which established the enforcement of uniform criteria for measuring and weighing around the Empire. In fact, the engraved legal document – now lost but copied already at Smyrna by A. Baumeister and edited in 1969 by Erxleben – contained a clause establishing that if a city used foreign coins and did not respect the coinage system, weights and measures of Athens, it would be condemned and punished in accordance with the previous decree proposed by Clearchos:

> ἐάν τις κόπτηι νόμισ[μα] ἀργυρίου ἐν τῆσι πό-||[λεσι καὶ μ]ὴ χρῆται νομ[ίσμασιν τοῖς 'Αθηνα]ίων ἢ σταθμοῖς ἢ μέτ-[ροις, ἀλλὰ ξενικοῖς | νομίσμασι]ν καὶ μ̣έτροις καὶ σταθμοῖς, [τὴν | τιμωρίαν εἶναι κατὰ τὸ πρότε]ρον ψήφισ-μα, ὃ | Κλέαρχ[ος εἶπεν.

Once again, the comic effect is obvious. Aristophanes not only uses a humorous *variatio* to replace one of the three elements of the enumeration (including decrees – ψηφίσματα – instead of coins – νομίσματα –); he manages to introduce an additional play on word as well.

1072-9, in which we identify the same conditional structure. In the passage, the chorus of birds parody a decree that allegedly offered a bounty of one talent of silver to the person that would kill Diagoras of Melos, who had unveiled the secrecy of the mysteries and was accused of impiety. We do not include the analysis of this passage in our discussion on legal parody here because – despite the discussions on the subject – the only available evidence that seems to talk about the existence of such a decree is the *scholium* to Aristophanes' verse 1073 and, therefore, it could be nothing but an inference from the comic text itself. At least, we have no means of knowing how independent this source of information is.

[29] Cf. Tod, M. N.: Greek Historical Inscriptions from the Sixth Century BC to the Death of Alexander the Great in 323 BC. Chicago 1946-8[1] (1985), pp. 163-166, n. 67.

The analogy with the situation of the Olophyxians (καθάπερ ᾿Ολοφύξιοι, l. 1040) allows for a new joke. It should first be recalled that the use of the comparative is a common feature in contemporary legal statutes, as we can see – to quote only the example of an inscription which we have already mentioned – in the expression τὰ μὲν ἄλλα καθάπερ ᾿Α-|ντικλε͂ς (*IG* I³ 40, ll. 70-1) or, short afterwards, in ἐν Χαλκίδι καθάπερ ᾿Αθ-|ένεσιν (ll.72-3).[30] But after this formal association with the Olophyxians – who were the inhabitants of a small city on the Attos peninsula –, Peisetaerus changes the noun into Ototyxians (῾Ωτοτύξιοι), a comic ethnic term phonetically related to the Greek interjection ὠτοτοι, frequently used in Greek to describe pain.

As the last verse in the passage indicates, the decree-seller is expelled from Cloudcuckoodland by the angry Peisetaerus. Nevertheless, he seems to reappear in order to introduce a last legal text (*Av.* 1050-1):

᾿Εὰν δέ τις ἐξελαύνῃ τοὺς ἄρχοντας καὶ μὴ δέχηται κατὰ τὴν στήλην–

And should anyone expel the officials and refuse them entry under the terms of the inscription –

There appears the same syntactic structure we have already discovered in the first law. In fact, just as in the previous case, the conditional sentence is also interrupted by Peisetaerus' insults. As it becomes clear from the Greek text, the verse 1051 does not mention the words ψήφισμα or νόμος, but στήλη, which specifically refers to the pillar into which the laws were inscribed. In order to understand the protagonist's attitude towards inscribed legislation, it is important to look at the last intervention by the decree-seller before his definitive disappearance from stage, in which he accuses him of having defecated on the pillar (v. 1054):

---

[30] Other examples of the use of καθάπερ in 5th Century Athenian inscriptions include IG I³ 46 (lines 38-40), and IG I³ 127 (lines 17-18).

Μέμνησ' ὅτε τῆς στήλης κατετίλας ἑσπέρας;

Do you recall those evenings when you used to crap on the inscription?

The disrespectful behaviour of Peisetaerus as far as the laws are concerned[31] seems, however, to be left aside and transformed into a pious reverence as soon as they are useful for his personal purposes of becoming the tyrant of the birds. Therefore, when a father beater appears on stage saying that he wants to get wings to be able to peck and throttle his father, Peisetaerus invents a law – by reproducing the linguistic framework of Attic rules – that does not allow this violence (*Av.* 1353-7):

{ΠΙ.} ᾿Αλλ᾿ ἔστιν ἡμῖν τοῖσιν ὄρνισιν νόμος
παλαιὸς ἐν ταῖς τῶν πελαργῶν κύρβεσιν·
"Επὴν ὁ πατὴρ ὁ πελαργὸς ἐκπετησίμους
πάντας ποήσῃ τοὺς πελαργιδέας τρέφων,
δεῖ τοὺς νεοττοὺς τὸν πατέρα πάλιν τρέφειν."

But we birds have a law, an ancient one on the Storks' Tablets: "When the father stork has provided for all his storklings and got them fully fledged, then the chicks must in their turn provide for their father."

The reference to the storks' κύρβεις points to the ancient wooden tablets in the Athenian Agora on which the traditional laws of Draco and Solon had been inscribed,[32] and gives an idea of the character's ability of using the Attic legal documents to impose his will. But it is not until the end of the play that the use of Athenian law reaches its highest level. In verses 1660-6, Peisetaerus

[31] Slater, N. W.: Literacy and Old Comedy. In: Worthington, I. (ed.): Voice into Text. Orality and Literacy in Ancient Greece. Leiden/New York/Köln 1996, pp. 99-112, on p. 103 deals with this passage and considers: "*Another very quick joke suggests that the stone versions of decrees were actually points of resistance or display of disrespect to the laws(…).*"

[32] On the notion of *kyrbeis*, see Stroud, R.S.: The axones and kyrbeis of Drakon and Solon. Berkeley/Los Angeles/London 1979.

quotes a complete Solonian νόμος on bastardy as a strategy to convince Heracles that he will not inherit Zeus' property because he is an illegitimate son:

Ἐρῶ δὲ δὴ καὶ τὸν Σόλωνός σοι νόμον·
"Νόθῳ δὲ μὴ εἶναι ἀγχιστείαν παίδων ὄντων γνησίων·
ἐὰν δὲ παῖδες μὴ ὦσι γνήσιοι, τοῖς ἐγγυτάτω γένους μετεῖναι τῶν χρημάτων."

I'll tell you what Solon's law dictates: "If there are lawful children, then a bastard has no rights as a close blood relative. If there are no lawful children, the goods go to the nearest next of kin."

III. Decrees

The so-called feminine comedies also allow us to discover this use of legal texts, through male actors disguised as women under the light of a utopian framework. The *Thesmophoriazusae* (represented in 411 BC, probably in the city of Dionysia) show women deciding to put Euripides to trial and accuse him of misogyny. In verses 372-9, one of them informs the audience about the decision they have taken during their official meeting:

Ἄκουε πᾶσ'. Ἔδοξε τῇ βουλῇ τάδε
τῇ τῶν γυναικῶν· Τιμόκλει' ἐπεστάτει,
Λύσιλλ' ἐγραμμάτευεν, εἶπε Σωστράτη·
ἐκκλησίαν ποεῖν ἕωθεν τῇ μέσῃ
τῶν Θεσμοφορίων, ᾗ μάλισθ' ἡμῖν σχολή,
καὶ χρηματίζειν πρῶτα περὶ Εὐριπίδου,
ὅ τι χρὴ παθεῖν ἐκεῖνον· ἀδικεῖν γὰρ δοκεῖ
ἡμῖν ἁπάσαις. Τίς ἀγορεύειν βούλεται;

Crytilla: Hear ye all! [reading] "The following was resolved by the Council of the women (chairwomen, Timocleia; secretary, Lysilla; proposer of motion, Sostrate): to hold an assembly at sunrise on the middle day of the Thesmophoria, being the day on which we have most free time, and to consider as first business the subject of Euripides, namely what penalty he shall suffer, since we are unanimously of opinion that he committed unjust acts." Who wishes to speak?

The formal aspects of the motion confront the spectators, once again, with well-known formulae. The expression ἔδοξε τῇ βουλῇ in v. 372 is found as the obligatory prescript in every decree issued by the Athenian βουλή, and it is used to include the content of the legal decision. An example like the one quoted by Rhodes & Lewis[33] is useful to clarify this traditional scheme (*IG* I³ 84, of 418-7):

> [ἔ]δοχσεν τε̂ι βόλει καὶ το̂ι δέμοι· Πανδιονὶς ἐπρυτάνευε Ἀριστό-[σ]ε νος ἐγραμμάτευε· Ἀντιοχίδες ἐπεστάτει· Ἀντιφο̂ν ἐ̂ρχε· Ἀδοσιο-[ς ε] ἶπε.

Resolved by the council and the people, <the tribe> Pandionis was in prytany; Aristoxenos was secretary; Antiochides was chairman; Antiphon was archon; Adosios proposed the motion.

In Aristophanes' passage, it is clear that the structure is reproduced with the inclusion of the names of the chairman, the secretary and the proposer of the final decision. However, the context is – once again – burlesque, since the members of the Council are women who were traditionally excluded from political activities.

Similarly, in the text of the *Ecclesiazusae* (put on stage in 393 or 391 BC) another written decree which was voted on by women after they assumed power in the πόλις is fully presented (vv. 1014-1020):

> λέγ' αὐτὸ τί ποτε κἄστι. καὶ δή σοι λέγω.
> ἔδοξε ταῖς γυναιξίν, ἢν ἀνὴρ νέος
> νέας ἐπιθυμῇ, μὴ σποδεῖν αὐτὴν πρὶν ἂν
> τὴν γραῦν προκρούσῃ πρῶτον. ἢν δὲ μὴ 'θέλῃ

[33] Rhodes, P. J./Lewis, D. M.: The Decrees of Greek States. Oxford 1997, p. 19.

πρότερον προκρούειν, ἀλλ' ἐπιθυμῆ τῆς νέας,
ταῖς πρεσβυτέραις γυναιξὶν ἔστω τὸν νέον
ἕλκειν ἀνατεὶ λαβομένας τοῦ παττάλου.

And I read it to you. "It was resolved by the women that if a young man desires a young girl, he can only lay her after having (...) satisfied an old woman; and if he refuses and goes to seek the maiden, let the old women be authorized to seize him by his (...) tail and drag him in with impunity."

The prescript ἔδοξε ταῖς γυναιξίν, the presence of conditional structures headed by ἤν and including a verb in the subjunctive mood (v. 1015) and a general indefinite noun to indicate the general scope of the measure (ἀνὴρ) are all aspects which reproduce the technical vocabulary of the decrees at the βουλή. The imperative form ἔστω (v.1019), typical of juridical language, contributes to reinforcing the formality of the whole passage.[34] But, as we have already seen, the situation in which this legal text is introduced deprives the document of an expected seriousness. The text is quoted here by a disgusting old women that reads it (καὶ δή σοι λέγω) with the purpose of convincing a young man, by legal means, to have sex with her. In this context, the comic device consists – as it is usually the case within Aristophanic plays – in the overlapping of an elevated discourse and a low-level language: regulating sexual matters, the legal provisions are vulgarized and merged with an obscene terminology (προκρούειν, τοῦ παττάλου).[35]

Summing up, we can say that in all the cases of laws and decrees quoted within the play, it is worth noting an emphasis on the written nature of the document. In this sense, the characters in charge of pronouncing the legal formulae carefully insist on the fact that these rules are not improvised but that their terms and clauses have been agreed on and laid down. Sometimes they address the other characters and the audience in order to prepare them

---

[34] In this sense, the expression ἕλκειν ἀνατεί, "drag off", can mean in judicial contexts "manhandle with impunity"; for this legal use, also used by Pl. Leg. 871d, see Ussher, Aristophanes Ecclesiazusae (as in note 20), p. 217.

[35] On this specific vocabulary in Aristophanes, see Henderson, J.: The Maculate Muse: Obscene Language in Attic Comedy. Oxford 1990.

and ask them to listen (ἀκούετ' , *V.* 894; ἄκουε, *Th.* 372) because a text is about to be read (ἐρῶ, *Av.* 1660; λέγω, *Ecc.* 1014). The fact that it is always written decisions which are referred to is also perceived by the use of the noun βιβλίον (*Av.* 1036) or by direct allusions to legal inscriptions (κύρβεις, *Av.* 1354; στήλη, *Av.* 1051 and 1054). As a whole, these references provide a framework for the literal quotations and a solid background to the decrees; they give them a formal validity which contradicts, in the end, their ridiculous provisions. The comic effect is ensured, then, by the drastic collision between the apparent authority of the written laws and their comic application.

Apart from these specific situations of intertextuality in the dramatic script, a few other examples in comedy do not reproduce the structure of juridical documents but focus instead on the oral aspects of the lawmaking process itself.

IV. Legislative Proposals

An active participation of the citizens at the Assembly is well attested for classical Athens. Since every legal draft would generally rely on a defense of a position, usually followed by the replies from opposite points of views on a measure to be taken onwards, it is clear that the legislative procedure in Athens – quite like real controversies before the tribunals – was sustained by the logic of rhetorical confrontation.[36] It is therefore clear why Aristotle, in his *Rhetoric* 1358.b.2-8, attributes to the assemblymen a deliberative speech addressed to the future time:

> ἀνάγκη δὲ τὸν ἀκροατὴν ἢ θεωρὸν εἶναι ἢ κριτήν, κριτὴν δὲ ἢ τῶν γεγενη-μένων ἢ τῶν μελλόντων. ἔστιν δ' ὁ μὲν περὶ τῶν μελλόντων κρίνων ὁ ἐκκλησιαστής, ὁ δὲ περὶ τῶν γεγενημένων [οἷον] ὁ δικαστής, ὁ δὲ περὶ τῆς δυνάμεως ὁ θεωρός, ὥστ' ἐξ

[36] "*L'action législative se déroule comme celle d'un procès. L'auteur de la proposition se présente comme l'accusateur des lois existantes*", Hansen, M. H.: La démocratie athénienne à l'époque de Demosthène. Structures, principes et idéologie. Paris 1993, p. 203.

ἀνάγκης ἂν εἴη τρία γένη τῶν λόγων τῶν ῥητορικῶν, συμβουλευτικόν, δικανικόν, ἐπιδεικτικόν.

Now the hearer must necessarily be either a mere spectator or a judge, and a judge either of things past or of things to come. For instance, a member of the general assembly is a judge of things to come; the dicast, of things past; the mere spectator, of the ability of the speaker. Therefore there are necessarily three kinds of rhetorical speeches, deliberative, forensic, and epideictic.

Three different types of speech are distinguished, according to the kind of addressee in charge of judging (κρίνειν) the arguments and time: the deliberative speech, based on future events (τῶν μελλόντων) and directed to the assemblyman (ὁ ἐκκλησιαστής), the judicial speech, centered on past events (τῶν γεγενεμένων) and presented to the juror (ὁ δικαστής) and, finally, the epideictic speech, constructed on the present activities of the speaker (τῆς δυνάλεως) and pointing to the spectator (ὁ θεωρός).

The interaction of a deliberative discourse and the present tense of the speaker is clear in some passages of Aristophanes in which the practice of politically persuasive speech is introduced on stage.[37] Several examples of parodic proposals and discussions of legislative texts may be identified in the corpus.

In *Acharnians* (represented at the Lenaia in 425 BC), the chorus of elderly charcoal-burning poor fellows from the *deme* of Acharnai develops in the *parabasis* a real complaint in the way trials were carried out at that time. They affirm that they are unfairly brought before the court by young prosecutors who take advantage of their weakness and their age, and they manage to make an interesting proposal in front of the audience. They suggest a way of avoiding the maltreatment of elders in court, with the main purpose of balancing the adverse positions of applicants and respondents in judicial claims (*Ach.* 713-8):

---

[37] On persuasion and argumentative skills in Aristophanes, cf. Murphy, C. T.: Aristophanes and the Art of Rhetoric. In: Harvard Studies in Classical Philology (1938) 49, pp. 69-113 and Heath, M.: Aristophanes and the Discourse of Politics. In: G. W. Dobrov (ed.): The City as Comedy. Society and Representation in Athenian Drama. Chapel Hill/London 1997, pp. 230-249.

᾽Αλλ᾽ ἐπειδὴ τοὺς γέροντας οὐκ ἐᾶθ᾽ ὕπνου τυχεῖν,
ψηφίσασθε χωρὶς εἶναι τὰς γραφάς, ὅπως ἂν ᾖ τῷ γέροντι μὲν γέρων
καὶ νωδὸς ὁ ξυνήγορος,
τοῖς νέοισι δ᾽ εὐρύπρωκτος καὶ λάλος χὠ Κλεινίου.
Κἀξελαύνειν χρὴ τὸ λοιπόν- κἂν φύγῃ τις ζημιοῦν-
τὸν γέροντα τῷ γέροντι, τὸν νέον δὲ τῷ νέῳ.

But since you won't allow the old a peaceful night of sleeping, at least you ought to pass a decree to make indictments separate, in order for an old man to have a prosecutor just as old and toothless, and for youngsters an Alcibiades, the glib-tongued little pansy. In the future – and if anyone refuses, he must be fined –, an oldster shall charge the oldster, and a youngster shall charge the youngster.

The subject clause in v. 713 is rounded out by an appeal to the audience embodied in an imperative which efficiently increases the feeling of presence of the viewers[38] and the text makes it explicit that we are facing a legislative proposal: ψηφίσασθε ("*pass a decree*").

After the inclusion of the general considerations justifying the need to modify the law (introduced, as it happens in decrees, by ἐπειδὴ), the last two verses embrace the final request of the chorus' intervention, restoring both situations: the imperative, the absence of a first or second person – now replaced by an impersonal χρὴ – and the suggestion of implementing a sanction in case the rule is not fully respected: κἂν φύγῃ τις ζημιοῦν. In this last parenthetic expression, we discern once again the linguistic formalities which correspond to a legal provision: the eventual hypothesis (κἂν), the verb in the subjunctive mood (φύγῃ) and the generalization through the indefinite pronoun τις.

[38] Perelman, C./Olbrechts-Tyteca, L.: Tratado de la argumentación. La nueva retórica. Madrid 1989[1] (1994), p. 255 (Original Edition: Traité de l'argumentation. La nouvelle rhétorique. Paris 1958[1]).

The future dimension, distinctive of the deliberative speech according to Aristotle, is also present in the passage with the expression τὸ λοιπόν,[39] which indicates the non-retroactivity of the measure which is proposed. In contemporary decrees, τὸ λοιπόν ("*henceforth*") is frequently found. The inscription *IG* I[3] 32 (from 448 BC) concerning the selection of overseers for the goddesses Demeter and Kore provides, for instance, in lines 18-20 that τὸ λοιπ|ὸν κατὰ ταὐτὰ ηαιρε͂σθαι κ[α]τ' ἐνιαυτὸν τ|ὸς ἄνδ[ρ]ας, "*in the future the men are to be elected in the same way every year*") and, some lines afterwards (28-30), that ἀναλίσκεν δὲ ὅ τι ἀν [μά]|λιστα δέει μετὰ το͂ν ηιερέον καὶ τε͂ς β[ολ]|ε͂ς βολευομένος τὸ λοιπόν ("*to spend in the future whatever is necessary in consultation with the Priests and the Council*").[40]

From a syntactic perspective, we are here, in fact, in front of a suggested statute which responds to all formal requisites and becomes rhetorically defended by the chorus of old Acharnians.

In *Clouds* (written in 423 BC for the city of Dionysia, but the text which has been preserved corresponds to a revision, possibly dating from 418 or 417 BC), the protagonist Strepsiades is worried because he is about to be taken to trial by creditors because of the unpaid debts of his son, Pheidippides. In order to make Pheidippides learn the appropriate legal arguments and help him to twist the decrees and evade lawsuits, he decides to send him to Socrates' Thinkery, a place in which he will easily acquire a sophistic knowledge of judicial chicanery. As soon as the young man leaves the Thinkery, he shows on stage some interesting juridical subterfuges. At a certain point, then, Pheidippides manages to propose a new law allowing children to beat their fathers (οἶμαι διδάξειν ὡς δίκαιον τὸν πατέρα κολάζειν, v. 1405). In fact, he explains that the law imposing respect for parents is conventional, since it was a man who managed to persuade others on the convenience of its content.

---

[39] This expression can be taken adverbially; we could translate it – following Olson, Aristophanes' Acharnians (n. 20), p. 256 – as "in the future"; cf. Nu. 677, V. 299.

[40] A more or less complete list of Athenian inscriptional evidence from the V Century B. C. including the expression τὸ λοιπόν can be found in Harris, E. M.: Pheidippides the Legislator. A Note on Aristophanes' Clouds. In: Zeitschrift für Papyrologie und Epigraphik (2002) 140, pp. 3-5.

Thus, statutes can be amended or modified whenever it is necessary (*Nu.* 1421-6):

> οὔκουν ἀνὴρ ὁ τὸν νόμον θεὶς τοῦτον ἦν τὸ πρῶτον,
> ὥσπερ σὺ κἀγώ, καὶ λέγων ἔπειθε τοὺς παλαιούς;
> ἧττόν τι δῆτ' ἔξεστι κἀμοὶ καινὸν αὖ τὸ λοιπὸν
> θεῖναι νόμον τοῖς υἱέσιν, τοὺς πατέρας ἀντιτύπτειν;
> ὅσας δὲ πληγὰς εἴχομεν πρὶν τὸν νόμον τεθῆναι,
> ἀφίεμεν, καὶ δίδομεν αὐτοῖς προῖκα συγκεκόφθαι.

Well, wasn't it a man who established that law in the first place, a man like you or me, and didn't he persuade the men of old by argument to accept it? Is it then any less open to me in my turn to establish a new law for sons in the future, that they should be their parents in return? All the blows we received before the law was established we wipe from the record, and we make it a concession to them that our having been thrashed hitherto shall remain without compensation.

The temporal dimension characterizing Athenian decrees is, here again, achieved by the τὸ λοιπὸν in line 1423. The difference between old times, in which a man proposed a law in the first place (τὸ πρῶτον), and the need to dictate a new one (καινὸν) again (αὖ) corresponds to a translation, into Pheidippides's words, of the logic of legislative amendment. The form ἔξεστι introduces the legal possibility of drafting a new text, which is expected to replace the previous one. All the blows (the relative ὅσος is also typical of the transcription of Attic decrees, as Harris (2002) has convincingly shown) shall be erased from the record: the verb ἀφίεμεν, in this sense, clearly represents a clause against retrospective application of the law.

Finally, in the *epirrhema* of *Frogs* (represented in 405 BC at the Lenaia), the chorus recalls its didactic function and, by reproducing the language of law-making proposals, also suggests some new measures to be approved (*Ra.* 686-692):

Tὸν ἱερὸν χορὸν δίκαιόν ἐστι χρηστὰ τῇ πόλει
ξυμπαραινεῖν καὶ διδάσκειν. Πρῶτον οὖν ἡμῖν δοκεῖ
ἐξισῶσαι τοὺς πολίτας κἀφελεῖν τὰ δείματα.
Κεἴ τις ἥμαρτε σφαλείς τι Φρυνίχου παλαίσμασιν,
ἐγγενέσθαι φημὶ χρῆναι τοῖς ὀλισθοῦσιν τότε
αἰτίαν ἐκθεῖσι λῦσαι τὰς πρότερον ἁμαρτίας.
Εἶτ' ἄτιμόν φημι χρῆναι μηδέν' εἶν' ἐν τῇ πόλει.

It is right and proper for the sacred chorus to take part in giving good advice and instruction to the community. In the first place, accordingly, we think that all citizens should be made equal and their fears removed; and if someone went wrong at all through being tripped up by the wiles of Phrynichus, I say that those who slipped up at that time ought to be given the right to clear themselves of any charge and wipe out their previous errors. Secondly, I say that there ought to be no one in the city who is deprived of his rights as a citizen.

The verses of the *parabasis*, thus, suggest that citizen rights should be restored to those that had been deprived of them because of their intervention in the oligarchic revolution that had taken place in 411 BC. Once again, the vocabulary – in which certain words take us back to the nature of decrees, such as the verb δοκεῖ in v. 687 – points to future actions as opposed to previous (πρότερον) faults which need to be erased (λῦσαι). The whole discourse is logically structured (πρῶτον in v. 687, εἶτ' in v. 692) and seems to be built around the need to establish new obligations on behalf of the people: the infinitive χρῆναι (*ought to*) is mentioned twice next to the first person φημί which shows that the proposal is offered orally, just as it used to happen during the meetings in the Assembly.

Some verses later, the chorus reproduces the opposition between the current situation and the need of change for the future. In present times (vv. 718-20), it is believed that honest people are maltreated:

Πολλάκις γ' ἡμῖν ἔδοξεν ἡ πόλις πεπονθέναι
ταὐτὸν εἴς τε τῶν πολιτῶν τοὺς καλούς τε κἀγαθοὺς
εἴς τε τἀρχαῖον νόμισμα καὶ τὸ καινὸν χρυσίον.

Very often we've thought that the city is behaving in the same way towards the good upstanding citizens as it is towards the old coinage and the good gold.

Contrary to this attitude, the chorus aims at promoting an urgent amendment (Ra. 734-5):

'Αλλὰ καὶ νῦν, ὠνόητοι, μεταβαλόντες τοὺς τρόπους
χρῆσθε τοῖς χρηστοῖσιν αὖθις·

But even now, you foolish folk, change your ways and honour the honest again.

E. Final Remarks

To conclude, we may say that several passages from Old Comedy, as the ones we have included in this study, seem to show how references to juridical texts constitute a frequent strategy used by Aristophanes to achieve very specific humorous goals.

By reproducing (and distorting) lawmaking schemes on stage, the author is able to decontextualize their formalities and to draw the attention of Athenians to the most contemporary discussions on their legal system. Thus, the comic use of laws and decrees – placed within the inverted background set by the genre – reveals a critical approach to the contemporary sophistic interpretation of positive and conventional justice.

If the ordinary process of lawmaking led the Athenians from oral argumentation in the Assembly to the final inscription of legal texts in public pillars, the recovery of this juridical material by the means of comedy went precisely the opposite way. Written laws are read aloud by masked actors in a new democratic spectacle similar to the original legislative discussions. Therefore, if epigraphical documents show an ancient interest to keep legal memory alive for the generations to come, theatrical productions in the late 5th century BC, as we have seen, frequently try to update those recollections. By recalling and playing on stage with the audience's previous experience in law – through a complex interaction of written texts and dramatic speech –, Aristophanes succeeds in implementing legal allusions as a fruitful comic technique.

Physical Pain: An Ancient Legal Remedy against Oblivion

Cosmin Dariescu

A. An Overview of the Procedure Used by the Ancient Romanians for the Marking Out of Agricultural Pieces of Land

Romania, as a state, appeared in 1862, when Prince Alexandru Ioan Cuza gave this name to the United Principalities of Moldavia and Walachia which, in 1859, had both elected him as their ruler. The Romanian state managed to incorporate all the lands inhabited by the Romanian people in 1918. Unfortunately, the Second World War brought the loss of some important territories such as: Bessarabia (nowadays: The Republic of Moldova) and Northern Bukovina.

The two principalities of Walachia and Moldavia appeared as states situated south and east of the Carpathians in the 14th century A.D. In 1330, Walachia broke the vassalage connection with the Hungarian King and in 1364, Moldavia did the same. These two principalities were inhabited by speakers of a Neo-Latin language who were called "Volohs", "Olahs" or "Walachs", that is: Romanized People. They are the ancestors of the Romanians of today. After a heroic resistance in the 15th century, the two Romanian states were forced to sign treaties with the Ottoman Empire (ahd-namé) by which they were obliged to give up their external attributes of sovereignty and to pay a tribute in exchange for the preservation of their own state authorities. The Ottoman yoke was broken by the peace treaty of Berlin of July 1, 1878 (during the reign of Carol I of Hohenzollern).

The laws of Walachia and Moldavia were a mixture of written and customary rules. The written rules came from Byzantine canon and secular laws (such as the *Syntagma Canonum* by Mathew Blastares or the *Basilica* of Leon the VIth, The Wise) and, since the 17th century, from laws composed and enforced under the supervision of the princes of Moldavia and Walachia (such as: the *Romanian Book of Learning from the Imperial Laws and Other Judicial Authorities* – Iaşi,

1646; the *Guidance of the Law by God That Has All the Canon and Imperial Judicial Authorities on All the Priestly and Secular Crimes* – Târgovişte, 1652; or the *Civil Code of Moldavia* – Iaşi, 1817 etc.). The customary rules came from the *Law of the Country* (also known as the *Custom of the Land* or *Ius valachicum*). The *Law of the Country* can be defined as all the customary rules that settled the social and economic life of the agricultural and pastoral communities of the Romanian people.[1] It is an original legal creation by the Romanians, combining juridical structures of the Roman, Thracian and migratory people. The Law of the Country had so much legal power in civil and agricultural matters that even the first written acts were enforced only to complete the custom, and not to override it.

The delimitation of agricultural pieces of land was one of the most important and original branches of the *Law of the Country*. It incorporated so much popular law that it was little influenced by the Byzantine rules.[2]

The procedure of the marking out of land was one of the oldest legal procedures of the Romanian Law. It was created in an age before the establishment of the medieval centralized states in order to determine the land owned by each peasant community. After the establishment of the medieval centralized states, this procedure kept its importance. It was used in order to delimit the borders of the new states (for instance, it was used in 1520[3] and in 1539[4] to determine the border between Walachia and Transylvania or, in 1764,[5] to delimit the border between Walachia and the Ottoman possession of Dârstor) or for the marking out of the new manors or of the private real estates inside the territory owned by peasant communities.[6]

---

[1] Academia de Ştiinţe Sociale şi Politice a Republicii Socialiste România; Institutul de Istorie „N. Iorga": Instituţii feudale din Ţările Române. Dicţionar. Bucureşti 1988, p. 330.

[2] Academia de Ştiinţe Sociale şi Politice a Republicii Socialiste România; Institutul de Istorie „N. Iorga": Instituţii feudale... (as in fn. 1), p. 222.

[3] Ivaniuc, Florenţa: Instituţia hotărniciei în Ţara Românească. Secolele al XVI-lea- al XVIII-lea. Bucureşti 2003, p. 19.

[4] Academia de Ştiinţe Sociale şi Politice a Republicii Socialiste România; Institutul de Istorie „N. Iorga": Instituţii feudale... (as in fn. 1), p. 225.

[5] Ivaniuc (as in fn. 3), pp. 19-20.

[6] Giurescu, C. Constantin: Jurământul cu brazda în cap. In: Din trecut. Bucureşti 1942, pp. 192-203, in this case p.195.

The first authority to undertake the delimitation of land was that of the old men of the village or of the neighboring villages. The peasant community had complete jurisdiction in marking out the agricultural pieces of land inside its domain. A similar instance for the bounding of field existed in Loraine, where it was named "la féauté".[7]

After the establishment of the medieval centralized states, a new authority appeared in the procedure of the delimitation of land. It was the Prince, as holder of *dominium eminens (the ownership of the entire territory of the state).* Every marking out of land (even those inside the peasant communities) had to be ordered and approved by the Prince. So, after the inception of the medieval centralized states, even the old men of the village had to obtain, firstly, a princely order for the bounding of pieces of land inside the territory of peasant communities.[8] The first princely bounding orders, as known to date, were issued in the 16th century.[9]

Because the delimitation of land requires the conduct of researches in the field, and because the Prince was always a busy man, he used to send to the place a number of noblemen (in Walachia, he used to appoint 6, 12 or 24 noblemen[10]) in order to carry out the bounding of the piece of land which was subject to litigation. In cases in which both the plaintiff and the defendant were peasants, the Prince used to order the delimitation by a committee of respectable neighbors (also, peasants).[11] One of the noblemen, usually an office holder, was the Prince's agent, while the other members of the bounding committee (noblemen or commoners) were surveyors of the rightfulness of the procedure. They were at the same time judges (because they were in charge of settling the landmarks) and witnesses (because they had to testify "with their souls" about the method and the proofs they had used to set the

---

[7] Fotino, George: Obiceiuri la fixarea hotarelor. In: Pagini din istoria dreptului românesc. Bucureşti 1972, pp. 29-55, in this case p. 30, fn. 6.

[8] Giurescu (as in fn. 6), p. 105.

[9] Giurescu (as in fn. 6), pp. 195-196 and Stoicescu, Nicolae: Cum măsurau strămoşii. Metrologia medievală pe teritoriul României. Bucureşti 1971, p. 107.

[10] Six noblemen were required for the first marking out of a field, twelve were required when the first delimitation had been attacked by appeal, and so on.

[11] On June, 9, 1657, 12 neighbors of Vâlsăneşti chose the pieces of land for some heirs, as Prince Constantin Basarab had ordered. For other examples see Fotino (as in fn. 7), p. 30, fn. 7.

landmarks). In Walachia, until the 17th century the members of the bounding committee (whether noblemen or commoners) were designated only by their number (for instance: "12 boyars and land surveyor, my Esquires' boyar, jupan Vlaicu …"[12]). From the 17th century on, the names of all the members of the committee were stated in the princely order. The members of the delimitation committee, with the exception of the land surveyor (the Prince's agent), represented, in equal proportions, the interests of both the plaintiff and the defendant. Thus, prince Alexandru the IInd Mircea of Walachia, on November 7, 1570, showed how he had solved the litigation between Bistriţa monastery and a certain Ştiinţa concerning the manor Vădastra: He gave the monks 6 boyars and to Ştiinţa another 6 boyars. This bounding committee of 12 boyars was directed by Oprea, a noble office holder. In the second half of the 18th century, documents often underlined that the noblemen of the bounding committees were the agents of both parties. In order to become a member in such a committee, a nobleman needed the consent of either the plaintiff or of the defendant.[13] Because of the growing number of litigations concerning the boundaries of real estates and the relatively small number of noblemen with experience in bounding committees, in the 18th century there appeared a juridical fiction concerning the composition of such a committee. If, in a bounding committee, a nobleman was appointed who held a very important office, he was able to represent other members of the committee, approved by the same party to the litigation. Thus, on May 6, 1768, Scarlat Grigore Ghica, prince of Walachia, appointed a delimitation committee composed of 12 boyars for marking out the Soreşti and Oltina domains. But reading the document carefully it is clear that in fact the Prince appointed only 4 noblemen, 2 for each party. Prince Alexandru Ipsilanti of Walachia also appointed, on January 29, 1779, a bounding committee of only 2 boyars (one for each party), the two noblemen having the legal power of a committee of 12 boyars.[14]

[12] Ivaniuc (as in fn. 3), p. 185.
[13] Ivaniuc (as in fn. 3), pp. 190 and 191, and: Academia de Ştiinţe Sociale şi Politice a Republicii Socialiste România; Institutul de Istorie „N. Iorga": Instituţii feudale... (as in fn. 1), p. 223.
[14] Ivaniuc (as in fn. 3), p. 191.

The Prince's agent (the land surveyor) together with the other members of the delimitation committee had to reach the place where the pieces of land subject to litigation were placed. There, the Prince's agent had to gather the parties of the lawsuit, with their written proofs, along with the "old and good people" from the neighborhood. If the parties had written proofs, then the committee proceeded to the inspection of those documents. This operation could last for days. If the documents were genuine and undisputed, the bounding committee set the landmarks according to their provisions.

If the parties had no credible written proof, the bounding committee had to use witnesses (the old and good people of the neighborhood). The committee together with the relevant witnesses walked on the piece of land in litigation searching for the old landmarks. If no old boundaries could be traced then the last resort was the testimony of the old and good people under *the oath with a clod (piece of land cut with the plough) on the head or on the shoulders*.

The oath with a clod on the head or on the shoulders was taken either by the plaintiff, in an action for recovery of property, or by the old and good men from the neighborhood, in a delimitation lawsuit. In the following, we shall consider only the last use of this oath. The old and good people, gathered, as we know, by the land surveyor, took a solemn oath by putting a clod on their heads (in Moldavia) or by taking a bag filled with pieces of land on their shoulders (in Walachia). After this, the old and good men walked on the piece of land in litigation, thus showing to the bounding committee the exact lay-out of the boundaries.[15] The oath could also be made in a Christian way. First, a letter of anathema was read to all the good and old people gathered on the spot along with the parties. Such a letter, issued by the Metropolitan Bishop, invited the people who knew the lay-out of the ancient boundaries to reveal it with the threat of the most terrible mystic sanctions:

"… let you be cursed excommunicates by Our Lord, the All Maintainer and by the 318 holy fathers of Nicaea and by our devoutness. Let iron and stone melt down but your bodies, after death, let remain complete and not taken

[15] Academia de Ştiinţe Sociale şi Politice a Republicii Socialiste România; Institutul de Istorie „N. Iorga": Instituţii feudale... (as in fn. 1), p. 262.

apart … Let you be heirs to the Geezi's abscesses and let you tremble forever like Esai and until you will testify the truth, let you never be forgiven."[16]

After the reading, the good and old men who were going to show the boundaries signed the letter (thus, they made an oath). After that, they walked on the lay-out of the boundaries carrying the clod on the head or the bags filled with earth on the shoulders. Some documents reveal that the good and old people who were going to testify, after signing the letter of anathema, put it on their head and walked on the lay-out of the boundaries.[17] There are documents which show that the old and good men always had the possibility to refuse the oath, because of the mystical consequences of perjury.[18]

The punitive sanctions of perjury under the oath with the clod on the head or on the shoulders can be revealed by unveiling the magical meanings of the clod (of that piece of earth carried on the head, or in a bag on the shoulders).

In Romanian mythology, the earth was a living creature. It was named "Mother Earth". She had feelings and a high degree of morality. She did not receive in her tombs the dead bodies of villains, of oath-breakers etc. Therefore, the ancient Romanians took the earth as a witness at an oath or at a certain testimony. They said: "The Earth is my witness that I tell you the truth", or: "So we testify with our souls on the earth …" Also, when they lent something to a liar, they used to strike the earth three times with one foot because "the land remembers and it will be a loyal witness on Doomsday".[19] So, the clod carried on the head or in a bag, on the shoulders, by an old and good man or by one of the parties to the litigation was a symbol that Mother Earth was invoked to remember and punish the liar both after death (by rejecting his body) and on the Doomsday. This interpretation of the clod is sustained by later documents. One of them translated the whole ceremony of the oath with the clod on the head thus: "Let the body of the oath-breaker not rest in the

---

[16] Letter of anathema issued by Daniil, Metropolitan Bishop of Walachia, in August 1726. The entire text will be found in Giurescu (as in fn. 6), pp. 200-201.

[17] Academia de Ştiinţe Sociale şi Politice a Republicii Socialiste România; Institutul de Istorie „N. Iorga": Instituţii feudale... (as in fn. 1), p. 262.

[18] Giurescu (as in fn. 6), pp. 202-203.

[19] Vulcănescu, Romulus: Mitologie română. Bucureşti 1987, pp. 442 and 446.

land: let the sin of perjury press on the soul of the oath-breaker as the clod presses on his head."[20]

In order to understand the oath with the clod on the head, we must explain why only good and old men could be elected to make such an oath. The goal of the oath was to discover the boundaries of a certain piece of land, boundaries that could not be restored in another way. These boundaries could be set or could be modified in ancient times. Therefore, only old men from the neighborhood could remember all these important data. But not every old neighbor was able to make such an oath. Only the old neighbors with a high degree of morality could "take the land" or "take the bags with earth".

Romanian legal historians argued about the origin of this oath. Some historians considered the oath as a Roman legal remnant. Others showed that such a procedure for delimiting pieces of land could be found with other people who were not under the influence of the Roman Empire. Thus, the Alamans used to touch with their swords a clod taken from the piece of land the boundaries of which were subject to a litigation. The Saxons of Transylvania, in the 16th century, used to carry a clod on their heads and to walk barefooted on the lay-out of the old boundaries. The Slavic also knew such an oath (the Russian, the Croat) or had a special authority consisting of witnesses (12 in number) to determine the boundaries of a certain piece of land (the Czech). A very similar method to make an oath was recorded in litigations concerning landmarks of the people in the Caucasus, like the Tagorien and the Dagorien. So, the oath with the clod on the head is not a Roman remnant, but it came from a non-Roman past and, perhaps, is a compulsory creation of every ancient agricultural society.[21]

The delimitation committee followed those good and old people who had made the above-mentioned oath. The committee made signs on the lay-out of the old boundaries. If the plaintiff and the defendant were satisfied with the delimitation, the bounding committee set landmarks (pillars, stones with charcoal or ash buried beneath them, or trees marked with the glowing iron). In

---

[20] Academia de Ştiinţe Sociale şi Politice a Republicii Socialiste România; Institutul de Istorie „N. Iorga": Instituţii feudale... (as in fn. 1), p. 262.
[21] This thesis is sustained with great logic by Fotino (as in fn. 7), pp. 36-55.

every case, the committee drew up a report (*the testimony of delimitation*) to the Prince in which it described the whole procedure, the incidents occurred and the boundaries they had discovered. If none of the parties involved attacked the delimitation so made, the Prince issued *the bill of delimitation* which contained the testimony of delimitation together with the princely approval for those pieces of land to be held in the manner provided in the bill.

In the second half of the 18th century, that is after the reforms introduced by Constantin Mavrocordat in Walachia and, subsequently, in Moldavia, the bounding committee would be appointed not by the Prince but by the "Ispravnic" (the Prince's agent in every county). This bounding committee would include local noblemen. Until the end of the 18th century, the "Ispravnic" gained the power to issue bills of delimitation to the parties.[22]

B. Violence against Children – a Painful Method to Learn the Boundaries of a Certain Piece of Land

The ancient Romanian Law did not know the principle "res iudicata pro veritate accipitur". Litigations were resumed, again and again, long time after the first judgment had been made. Therefore, the owner of a newly delimited piece of land was obliged to obtain proofs about the lay-out of the boundaries.

We have shown above that the last method to discover the boundaries of a certain agricultural piece of land was the oath with a clod on the head or on the shoulders made by good and old people of the neighborhood. How did these old and good men manage to remember the boundaries of a piece of land in an age when few people knew how to read and write and when there were no drugs for enhancing human memory?

The answer is found in a legal ritual, performed when the boundary marks were set. This ritual is mentioned by some documents. Thus, a testimony from

---

[22] About the evolution of the "Ispravnic" from the local land-surveyor, appointed by the Prince to make delimitations of land in his county and to draw up reports to the Prince, to the office-holder who received the action of the plaintiff, appointed the bounding committee and gave the final approval see Ivaniuc (as in fn. 3), pp. 192-200.

April 19, 1754,[23] tells the following story: "And my father-in-law, Bogos, says that, while being a child, he was pulled by his hair by a judge of boundaries who was saying: 'You, child, always remember these boundaries!'". A document, written down on January 15, 1797, provides:

"I, Tănase Ferţul, was present at the marking out of the domain and I remember that I was pulled by my hair by Angheluţă and Ursaul Zmărăndiş in order to remember the boundaries of this above-mentioned domain and this is what we know and what we confess, fearing of God, before the judges."[24]

A testimony of delimitation for the Crăiniceşti domain, owned by the Monastery of Solca, recorded the following incident:

"And, coming into field, Preda with the abbot of Solca … and other monks of that place stood between the boundary and it was asked who knew the boundary and among those people assembled in that moment at the boundaries only Negrescu was found saying that he had been a child and he had been pulled by his wigs … in order to remember the signs. So, we didn't trust his memory and he took clods on his head, following the custom, and he walked to the boundary."[25]

A document, written in 1766, in Transylvania, ascribes the same ritual to the Romanians of the 2nd Border Regiment. Thus, when the domains of some communes of the frontier guards were delimited by boundary marks from the domains of other communes that did not belong to the 2nd Border Regiment, children from both categories of communes were pulled by the hair and were beaten until "they burst in tears". Even when it came to settling the border of the medieval state, the Romanians and their neighbors used the same ritual. A document from 1539 shows that, when Walachia and Transylvania settled part

---

[23] This document can be found in Pascu, Ştefan/Hanga, Vladimir: Crestomaţie pentru studiul istoriei statului şi dreptului R.P.R. Tome III (Feudalismul II). Bucureşti 1963, p. 509.
[24] Fotino (as in fn. 7), p. 35.
[25] Fotino (as in fn. 7), p. 35.

of their border, three young men were beaten, in order to remember the layout of that border.[26]

So, all the documents mentioned above attest that the setting of the boundary marks was always attended by violence against some children in order to make them remember the boundaries. Only children were beaten, because their life expectancy was bigger than that of an adult. So, they had more chances to protect, in future litigations, the newly established boundaries by their oath with the clod on their heads.

This procedure demonstrates that the Romanians were aware of the power of physical suffering to enhance human memory. It must not be interpreted as an extraordinary practice. Other cultures, too, used, in ancient times, bodily pain for memorizing important data. Thus, according to Pliny the Elder, in Rome the witnesses were pulled by their ears in order to retain information. There was a popular belief that the memory is to be found in man's ears. Documents of the 11th and 12th century ascribe to the German people of that time (especially to the Frank Ripuarii) the habit of pulling the children by their hair and ears in order to make them remember.[27] Even in Norse Mythology, Odin, King of Gods, discovered and memorized the spells of each rune, hanging for nine days upon the cosmic tree Yggdrasil, with his body pierced by a spear.[28] In the 17th century, in all of Europe, violence was used against children (on a regular basis) in order to make them read or write. Famous scholars like John Locke, François Fénelon and Amos Komensky (Comenius) fought, by their writings, against violent means of education. However, both John Locke and Comenius advocated the blows of ferule for religious and moral wrong doings.[29] In the 18th and 19th centuries, flogging was a common punishment in European schools. Thus, the flogging prohibition imposed by

---

[26] Academia de Ştiinţe Sociale şi Politice a Republicii Socialiste România; Institutul de Istorie „N. Iorga": Instituţii feudale... (as in fn. 1), p. 225.

[27] Fotino (as in fn. 7), pp. 35-36. In fn. 27 he quoted the Historia Naturalis, Book XI, 103 and in fn. 28 he quoted the Lex Ripuaria Tit. LX.

[28] Morogan, Elena-Maria: Mitologia Nordică. Mituri şi legende. Bucureşti 1992, pp. 15-16.

[29] Rădulescu, Sorin M.: Sociologia devianţei. Bucureşti 1998, pp. 121-122.

Pestalozzi in his schools amazed his contemporaries.[30] In the Victorian era (1837-1901), famous English schools, such as Eton or Christ's Hospital School, allowed the punishment of their pupils by the birch.[31]

The violence against children at the boundary marks could be connected with the magical powers that the landmarks had in Romanian mythology. The boundary mark had the power to influence the place where it was settled as well as the people that touched it or passed over it. There was a "folkloric" rule which said: "Do not fall asleep or do not sit down near a boundary mark, because in a minute you'll have a headache."[32] Maybe, this headache had something to do with the custom to pull the children by their wigs or by their ears. The magical powers of the landmark had their source in the fact that the boundary mark was thrust into the ground (into Mother Earth's body). The Romanians used to bring offerings to Mother Earth (such as: giving birth to a child on the ground, burying money, ring-shaped biscuits and pottery for assuring the fertility of cattle etc.).[33] So, the ritual of beating children at the boundary marks must have been the remnant of a magical offering to Mother Earth, designed to ensure the durability of that boundary.

C. The Come-Back of Testimony in the Settlement of Boundaries

The first written accounts of the oath with the clod on the head or on the shoulders date from August 1, 1634 (for Moldavia) and from July 10, 1667 (for Walachia). The last recorded traces of this type of oath stem from October 1824 (for Moldavia) and from August 5, 1792 (for Walachia).[34] The Ro-

---

[30] Smith, Mark K.: Johann Heinrich Pestalozzi on the Infed website at: http://www.infed.org/thinkers/et-pest.htm (accessed on April 18, 2006).

[31] Corporal punishment at two contrasting public schools, article on the Corporal Punishment Archive website, at : http://www.archivist.f2s.com/cpa/pubschool.htm (accessed on April 18, 2006).

[32] Academia de Ştiinţe Sociale şi Politice a Republicii Socialiste România; Institutul de Istorie „N. Iorga": Instituţii feudale... (as in fn. 1), p. 373.

[33] Vulcănescu (as in fn. 19), pp. 446-448.

[34] Academia de Ştiinţe Sociale şi Politice a Republicii Socialiste România; Institutul de Istorie „N. Iorga": Instituţii feudale... (as in fn. 1), p. 263.

manian legal historians explain the disappearance of the oath with the clod on the head by the spreading, in the second half of the 18th century and in the first half of the 19th century, of maps drawn by topographists.[35] These maps (which contained the whole lay-out of the boundaries of the pieces of land they were drawn for) induced a dramatic decline of the importance which the good and old people's testimony had had. The Constitutional Regulations (enforced in 1831, for Walachia, and in 1832, for Moldavia) provided special commissions for every county to settle the boundaries for all estates by drawing a map for each estate. One copy of this map would be given to the owner and the other would be kept by the Princely Divan (the supreme law court of the time).[36] Thus, the violent method by which Romanians used to learn the boundaries of an estate faded away.

In 2005, the Act no. 247 provided that the ownership of land could be restored, solely according to the testimonies of the neighbors (or of their heirs). Thus, the testimony is coming back in the settlement of boundaries. But the learning method of boundaries will be a much more peaceful one because, nowadays, violence against children is punished by the Romanian Law.

---

[35] Academia de Ştiinţe Sociale şi Politice a Republicii Socialiste România: Istoria dreptului românesc. Tome II (Part 1). Bucureşti 1980, p. 349.

[36] Academia Română; Institutul de Istorie „A.D.Xenopol": Regulamentul Organic al Moldovei. Iaşi 2004, pp. 327-328 and 555-556. The rules for the marking out of land were provided in Articles 391-397 of the Constitutional Regulation of Moldavia.

Illustrations

(Credits: *Discover Romania. The Romanian World in Images. XV-XIX centuries.* Interactive CD-Rom. Noi Media Print. Bucharest, 2005)

Figure 1: Alexandru Ioan Cuza, Ruler of the United Principalities (by Carol Popp de Szatmari)

Figure 2: King Carol I of Hohenzollern, 1887 (by Johann Lindner)

Figure 3: Higher rank nobleman
(boyar)
(by Monogram RGAI-I. Iakovlenko)

Figure 4: Young girl in Bucharest.:
Miss P. Denis, 1844
(by Charles Doussault)

Figure 5: Peasant with a supplica
tion (by an unknown artist)

Figure 6: Wallachian young girl,
1842 (by Janet-Lange, Ange Louis)

Figure 7: Moldavian man
(by Christian Gottlieb Geissler/
after B. Hacquet)

Figure 8: Moldavian woman
(by Christian Gottlieb Geissler/
after B. Hacquet)

Figure 9 Costumes from Wallachia. At the well, 1843
(by Ferogio/ after Michel Bouquet)

Figure 10 Costumes from Wallachia. Winter, 1843
(by Ferogio/ after Michel Bouquet)

Le fléau de Van Maanen et le salut constitutionnel. Le souvenir du Royaume-Uni des Pays-Bas et du Congrès national dans les discours sur la liberté de presse en Belgique au XIXe siècle

Bram Delbecke

Cette contribution traite de l'attitude de la Belgique vis-à-vis du Royaume-Uni des Pays-Bas, illustrant son souvenir de cette période du 19e siècle. On esquissera l'histoire du discours belge sur la liberté de la presse. La Belgique était devenue indépendante en 1830, en se détachant de ses voisins du Nord. Son discours sur la liberté de la presse était marqué par sa mémoire du Royaume-Uni, de son ministre de la Justice Cornelis-Felix Van Maanen et l'assemblée constituante de 1830-31, le Congrès national de la Belgique. Les pages suivantes expliqueront les principaux aspects de ce souvenir sur trois niveaux différents. D'abord, il s'agira de l'origine de la constitution belge et la position de la liberté de presse dans ce texte, puis on exposera de quelle manière on s'est souvenu de cette constitution et des dispositions en matière de presse et comment ce souvenir fait contraste avec la réalité judiciaire. Pour terminer, on expliquera comment on peut interpréter la fonction de ce souvenir.

1. 'À bas Van Maanen' : la position de la liberté de la presse dans la constitution belge (1831)

Pour mieux comprendre les discussions sur la liberté de la presse en Belgique dans la période 1830-1914, il faut connaître l'origine particulière de cette liberté, qui est inscrite dans la Constitution belge de 1831. Il convient de revenir aux circonstances politiques de l'indépendance de la Belgique. La Révolution de 1830 était le fruit du rapprochement de deux formations idéologiquement opposées : les libéraux et les catholiques. Cette alliance, appelée l'unionisme, s'opposait à Guillaume I, le roi du Royaume-Uni des Pays-Bas pour différentes causes.[1] Entre autres, on réagissait contre la répression sévère de la presse d'opposition dans le Sud.[2] Bien que la Constitution hollandaise garantisse la liberté de la presse,[3] le régime préférait poursuivre les publications qui critiquaient la politique en se basant sur un arrêté d'exception de 1815.[4] Cet arrêt était d'une formulation très vague, et fondait un tribunal extraordinaire avec des compétences presque illimitées. L'appel était exclu. Le système du ministre de la justice Van Maanen ne réagissait pas seulement contre les auteurs, mais aussi contre les éditeurs et les imprimeurs lesquels étaient aussi poursuivis et punis. Divers journaux qui critiquaient les démarches du souverain à propos de la législation sur l'enseignement, les cultes ou l'emploi des langues, furent condamnés. Pendant le régime du Royaume-Uni, pour plus de 50 procès de presse, il n'y en avait qu'un seul dans le Nord. Parmi les condamnés les plus célèbres, il y avait quelques prêtres renommés. Au début de l'année 1830, quelques journalistes avaient coopéré pour défendre des fonctionnaires démissionnés. Tous les responsables étaient condamnés à des peines de prison très sévères. Dans le Sud, ce régime était perçu comme très sévère et personnifié par le persécuteur principal, le ministre de la justice Van Maanen. En 1829, le projet de loi qu'il avait rédigé pour une nouvelle législation sur la presse, était tellement sévère que le peuple du sud l'appelait 'la loi de mutisme'. D'autres initiatives, comme le lancement d'un journal progouvernemental à Bruxelles, ne le rendaient pas non plus populaire. Au contraire, la persécution des journalistes qui critiquaient la politique de Van

---

[1] Les différents aspects de la Révolution belge de 1830 sont étudiés par plusieurs personnes. Les meilleurs oeuvres de synthèse récents sont: Falter, Rolf : 1830. De scheiding van Nederland, België en Luxemburg. Tielt 2005; Witte, Els : De constructie van België. In: Nieuwe Geschiedenis van België. Tielt 2005, p. 29-238.

[2] En ce qui concerne le régime de la presse pendant le Royaume-Uni des Pays-bas: De Bavay, Charles-Victor : Du régime de la presse sous l'ancien gouvernement des Pays-Bas. In : La Belgique judiciaire (1869), p. 1393-1405 ; Vermeersch, Arthur: Willem I en de pers in de Zuidelijke Nederlanden, 1814-1830. In: Staats- en Natievorming in Willem I's Koninkrijk, 1815-1830. Bruxelles 1992, p. 310-321.

[3] Art. 227 de la loi fondamentale du 24 août 1815.

[4] Arrêté du 20 avril 1815 contenant des mesures de répression contre les alarmistes et les distributeurs de bruits et nouvelles tendants à troubler la tranquillité publique. Les principes les plus néfastes pour la liberté de la presse étaient supprimés par la loi du 6 mars 1818.

Maanen excitait la population belge, ce qui s'exprimait dans un grand nombre de pétitions contre les situations intolérables du régime hollandais.

Bien que deux nouvelles lois aient apaisé la législation en matière de presse,[5] le climat de résistance restait très fort dans le Sud. Par conséquent, la vague révolutionnaire de 1830 allait aboutir à l'indépendance belge. A Bruxelles, les révoltés criaient « A bas Van Maanen ! », mettant à feu la résidence du ministre détesté. Plusieurs protagonistes de la rébellion étaient des journalistes condamnés.[6] Quelque temps après son installation, le Gouvernement provisoire promulgait un décret sur la liberté de la presse, la liberté d'expression et la liberté des cultes.[7] La Constitution du 7 février 1831, composée par le Congrès National, confirmait ces libertés. La liberté d'expression et des cultes y était inscrite, répondant ainsi à une demande spécifique des catholiques, qui ne voulaient pas d'entraves dans l'exercice public de leur culte. [8] Le texte fondamental garantissait expressément la liberté de la presse déclarant que la censure ne pourrait 'jamais' être rétablie. Toute mesure préventive était prohibée : pas de permission, pas de cautionnement. Seul un droit de timbre était permis comme mesure préventive. La responsabilité en cascade, une réaction contre le système de Van Maanen, était introduite. [9] Les audiences des tribunaux devaient être publiques.[10] En matière de délits politiques et de presse, le huis clos ne pouvait être prononcé qu'à l'unanimité. La compétence de juger des délits politiques et de presse était attribuée à un jury.[11] Cette institution symbolisait

---

[5] La loi du 16 mai 1829 remplissant quelques lacunes dans le code pénal et la loi du 1er juin 1830 sur la répression des délits d'injure et de calomnie et d'autres délits contre les autorités constituée et le repos public.

[6] Les protagonistes les plus renommés étaient: Charles Rogier, Paul Devaux, Jean-Baptiste Nothomb, François Tielemans, Joseph Lebeau, Louis Jottrand, Edouard Ducpétiaux, Alexandre Gendebien et Sylvain van de Weyer.

[7] Dans le contexte de 1830-31, la liberté d'expression et la liberté des cultes étaient basées sur le même consensus entre libéraux et les catholique, et leur tolérance mutuelle vis-à-vis de leurs idéologies. En ce qui concerne ce consensus, voir : Viaene, Vincent. Belgium and the Holy See. Gregory XVI to Pius IX (1831-1859): catholic revival, society and politics in 19th century Europe. Louvain 2001, p. 25-36.

[8] Art. 14.

[9] Art. 18.

[10] Art. 96.

[11] Art. 98.

la souveraineté populaire. Ainsi voulait-on éviter l'influence néfaste des juges professionnels, dont l'indépendance n'était pas certaine. Le dernier article prévoyait que le législateur s'occupait d'édicter des lois spéciales en matière de presse et de jury le plus vite possible.[12] En conclusion, la constituante semblait favoriser fortement la liberté de la presse. Elle concevait cette liberté comme l'antipode du système hollandais. Comme l'a dit un membre fameux du Congrès national, Devaux : « Si vous voulez des principes vrais de liberté de la presse, il faut empêcher tout retour au système Van Maanen ».[13] Non seulement Van Maanen, mais tout le régime hollandais était très impopulaire. En promulguant un décret d'exclusion éternelle de la dynastie des Nassau du trône belge,[14] le Congrés national exprimait sa peur d'une réunion éventuelle et affirmait la divergence profonde entre les provinces du Nord et celles du Sud.

Avant que le Congrès ne soit dissolu, la constituante a pris deux décrets importants. Le premier, en date du 19 juillet 1831, rétablissait le jury et formulait dans son article 8 quelques règles spéciales pour la poursuite des délits de presse.[15] Il est intéressant de mentionner les règles les plus symboliques. Dans la salle d'audience, les prévenus pouvaient prendre une place distincte, symbole du statut extraordinaire de la liberté de la presse. Les prévenus absents étaient jugés par contumace. En matière politique et en matière de presse, la détention préventive était impossible. L'abus hollandais de cette forme de détention a sans doute inspiré les membres du Congrès. Le deuxième décret, celui du lendemain le 20 juillet, organisait la législation spécifique en matière de presse.[16] Provoquer quelqu'un à commettre un méfait, attaquer la force obligatoire de la loi, injurier le roi, la dynastie ou le parlement étaient des actes punis par la loi. Toute forme de preuve était permise. La poursuite devait être initiée par une plainte, sauf pour les attaques contre le roi et sa famille, et celles contre l'autorité publique, qui pouvaient être poursuivies d'office. La respon-

---

[12] Art. 139.

[13] Huyttens, Emile. Discussions du congrès national de Belgique. Bruxelles 1844, I, p. 643.

[14] Décret du 24 novembre 1830 portant exclusion perpétuelle de la famille d'Orange-Nassau de tout pouvoir en Belgique.

[15] Décret du 20 juillet 1831 sur la presse.

[16] Décret du 19 juillet 1831 qui rétablit le jury.

sabilité en cascade et la détention préventive étaient maintenues. Le droit de réponse était établi : chaque personne qui croyait être attaquée mais qui ne voulait pas porter plainte avait le droit de faire insérer un texte avec sa réponse. Chaque journal devait porter le nom de l'éditeur responsable et les durées de prescription étaient réduites. Les lois hollandaises de 1829 et 1830 étaient abolies. Bien que beaucoup de choses fussent précisées, l'avant dernier article prévoyait que la prochaine législature devait procéder à une révision du décret. En réalité, cette révision n'a jamais été faite.[17]

En conclusion, à l'aube de l'indépendance belge, la législation en matière de presse contenait des mesures spécifiques et précises contre les abus commis à l'époque du Royaume-Uni des Pays-Bas. Le système était double : on avait créé une liberté à l'égard de la presse elle-même et une liberté à l'égard de la poursuite des abus. En fait, ce système était conçu comme l'antipode du régime de Van Maanen, ce qui révèle que ce dernier a explicitement fonctionné comme système de référence, mais d'une façon négative, c'est-à-dire comme modèle inverse. Cette caractéristique contraire est évidemment inhérente au caractère révolutionnaire de la constitution.[18]

2. 'Vive le Congrès national !' : l'abus hollandais et le sauveteur constitutionnel dans le discours sur la liberté de presse

Au 19e siècle, il y avait en Belgique un grand respect pour les mérites du législateur constitutionnel en ce qui concerne les garanties de la liberté de presse. Le Congrès national était considéré comme le sauveteur de la nation belge et en particulier le sauveteur de ses libertés. Pour les Belges du 19ième siècle, ces libertés étaient des éléments cruciaux des moeurs et des habitudes de la nation belge. La gratitude envers les législateurs constituants était énorme, parce qu'ils avaient enlevé le joug du régime hollandais et son croque-mitaine,

---

[17] Le décret était considéré provisoire, mais était renouvelé deux fois, et est resté partiellement en vigueur jusqu'à nos jours. La loi du 19 juillet 1832 renouvelait le décret jusqu'au 1er mai 1833. La loi du 6 juillet 1833 le renouvelait permanemment.
[18] Van der Tang, Ger. Grondwetsbegrip en grondwetsidee. Rotterdam 1998, p. 173-174.

Van Maanen. Dans le sentiment général des belges du 19ième siècle, ce thème était omniprésent.

Quelques participants notoires de la révolution de 1830-31 ont écrit des mémoires sur le régime hollandais et la révolution elle-même. Dans la décennie suivant la révolution, des figures de marque comme Etienne Constantin de Gerlache, le président de l'assemblée constituante, Louis De Potter, président du Gouvernement provisoire, et Jean Jacques Nothomb, secrétaire de la commission chargé de la rédaction du projet de la Constitution, ont écrit leurs mémoires du passé récent, laissant un souvenir amer du régime de Guillaume I et de son ministre Van Maanen : l'horreur absolue et la suppression totale des libertés publiques.[19] Louis De Potter, banni pour ses lettres ouvertes au roi Guillaume, était très négatif quand il s'agissait de Van Maanen. Il disait que ce ministre n'avait fait que le mal. Par ailleurs, il décrivait le roi Guillaume dans des termes beaucoup plus modérés, mais soulignant son caractère incompatible avec les mœurs des provinces belges :

« Guillaume ne voulait de la liberté pas plus que dès lors, elle ne pouvait vouloir de lui : il ne croyait pas possible de régner avec de la liberté ; et il avait raison dans un sens absolu : car *liberté* et *roi inviolable et héréditaire* sont nécessairement et éternellement incompatibles. Mais, dans un sens relatif au temps et aux hommes, si Guillaume était entré en *accomodements* avec les *faiseurs* de la liberté, il eût pu régner longtemps encore en prospérité et en paix [...], lui, ses enfants et ses petits-enfants peut-être. Il était trop franc et trop entier pour se prêter à un pareil manège. Il prit la liberté de corps à corps, et elle le terrassa. »[20]

Le discours anti-hollandais et anti-Van Maanen en matière de la liberté de presse, ne cessa pas en 1839, quand la Belgique et la Hollande s'étaient apai-

---

[19] De Gerlache, Etienne Costantin. Histoire des Pays-Bas depuis 1814 jusqu'en 1830. Bruxelles 1839; Nothomb, Jean-Baptiste. Essai historique et politique sur la révolution belge. Bruxelles 1833 ; De Potter, Louis. La Révolution belge, 1828-1839. Bruxelles 1839.
[20] De Potter, Louis. La Révolution belge, 1828-1839. Bruxelles 1839, p. 38.

sées avec le traité des XXIV articles.[21] Au contraire, bien que les protagonistes de la révolution aient déjà publié leurs écrits et mémoires, leurs successeurs politiques et judiciaires continuaient la même teneur des années 1830, en accentuant l'importance des libertés publics et de la liberté de la presse en particulier, faisant ainsi contraste avec l'oppression hollandaise de cette liberté. On peut vraiment dire que dans la période 1840-1880, il y eut un culte de la liberté de la presse et de sa protection constitutionnelle en Belgique. Bien que les Pays-Bas n'étaient plus 'l'ennemi' sur le plan international, le culte contre tout ce qui se passait outre la frontière du Moerdijck ne cessa pas. Peut-être d'autres problèmes, comme le blocage de l'Escaut, voie de communication d'une importance énorme pour la Belgique industrielle, incitaient les auteurs à continuer le blâmage de la Hollande.[22]

On peut dire que la Constitution était considérée comme couronnée par les articles qui garantissaient la liberté de la presse. Le résultat de la réaction contre le système de Van Maanen était une organisation presque parfaite de la législation en matière de presse. Suite à la pensée des penseurs libéraux français comme Benjamin Constant et Germaine de Staël, la liberté de la presse était considérée comme le seul droit dont tous les autres dépendent, comme la conséquence et en même temps comme le fondement du régime parlementaire. La mesure dans laquelle une nation permettait aux journalistes d'écrire ce qu'ils voulaient, était le meilleur indicateur du degré de liberté de cette nation. Evidemment, vu le système extrêmement libéral offert par la Constitution, la nation Belge se croyait la nation la plus libre du monde. Il va de soi que quand il fallait discuter des aspects et des principes juridiques en matière de presse, on devait tenir compte de ce statut par excellence de la liberté de la presse, et de sa place et fonction dans le discours nationaliste. Quelques exemples signifiants peuvent illustrer les aspects de cette glorification des mérites de la Révolution belge.

---

[21] Avec le Traité des XXIV Articles du 19 mars 1839, les Pays-bas ont définitivement reconnu l'indépendance belge, ainsi confirmant la scission des provinces du Nord et celles du Sud.
[22] Le gouvernement belge a racheté la douane de l'Escaut en 1863, ainsi 'libérant' le port d'Anvers.

Dans sa mercuriale de 1869, le procureur-général de la Cour d'appel de Bruxelles, Charles-Victor de Bavay, commençait son discours sur la liberté de la presse pendant le Royaume-Uni des Pays-bas avec les mots :

« De toutes les conquêtes, la plus importante, assurément, est la liberté de la presse, telle qu'elle a été décrétée et réglementée par le Congrès ».

Ensuite, il accentuait l'importance du législateur constituant comme sauveteur de cette liberté:

« Les garanties dont le Congrès a doté la presse, et qui lui donneraient, selon certaines gens, une trop grande liberté, n'étaient donc que la réparation d'une longue suite d'abus, dont la presse avait eu à souffrir pendant quinze ans[...]. Cette réparation était d'ailleurs le seul moyen de nous donner une presse véritablement libre, toujours disposée à défendre le faible contre le fort, l'opprimé contre l'oppresseur. »[23]

Dans la même période, on retrouve les mêmes idées chez le principal commentateur belge des délits de presse au 19ième siècle, le procureur Henri Schuermans. Dans son *Code de la presse,* il disait que raconter l'histoire de la liberté de presse pendant le régime hollandais était « une étude d'une utilité incontestable ».[24] Bref, la fascination pour la liberté de la presse telle qu'elle avait été établie en 1831 était totale.

D'où venait cette fascination? Pour commencer, on peut remarquer que la liberté de la presse n'était point considérée comme une nouveauté de 1830-31. Au contraire, elle était vue comme la restauration d'un droit acquis et traditionnel de la nation belge. En plus, la situation de cette liberté n'était pas unique : l'idée restauratrice était appliquée à toutes les libertés politiques et civiles

---

[23] De Bavay, Charles-Victor : Du régime de la presse sous l'ancien gouvernement des Pays-Bas. In : La Belgique judiciaire (1869), p. 1393 et 1402.
[24] Schuermans, Henri. Code de la presse. Bruxelles 1881, I, p. 41.

inscrites dans la Constitution.[25] L'amour belge pour ces libertés était un aspect des plus typiques d'un jeune état, mais aussi d'une nation beaucoup plus vieille. Les libertés arrachées dans la Constitution ont depuis des siècles caractérisé l'histoire des belges. Ainsi on créait l'idée d'une nation habituée aux libertés depuis des siècles, avec des rois et des chefs d'état qui comprenaient l'esprit du peuple belge. Dans ce discours des libertés, les mérites du législateur constitutionnel jouaient le rôle principal. Le texte fondamental du 7 février 1831 était considéré comme le plus grand don que la nation belge jamais n'avait reçu. Un fameux politicien et magistrat, Charles Faider, parlait de :

« [...] la nation belge, [...] elle qui a la gloire de posséder la Constitution la plus complète du monde en libertés garanties, la plus féconde du monde en résultats moraux et positifs ».[26]

La Constitution était vue comme la grande libération de la domination hollandaise, l'enlèvement d'un joug qui bloquait l'esprit de la nation belge et les mœurs de ses membres. Pendant toute l 19e siècle, les différentes fêtes d'anniversaire de l'indépendance belge célébraient particulièrement la Constitution et son auteur, le Congrès national. Les membres de cette assemblée constituante étaient considérés comme les vrais *founding fathers* de la Belgique et de sa liberté définitive et absolue.

A l'époque de la naissance de la Belgique, on ne voyait dans les journalistes que des commentateurs critiques du gouvernement, une garantie efficace contre tout abus du pouvoir. Sans doute la participation directe et indirecte de plusieurs journalistes aux discussions du Congrès national a favorisé cette image typique du journaliste. La liberté de la presse était aussi considérée comme la conquête la plus importante de la révolution parce qu'elle protégeait au maximum le journaliste comme chien de garde, évitant ainsi des lois néfastes et garantissant les meilleurs décisions politiques. Par conséquent, la minorité conservatrice qui se moquait de la liberté de presse ou qui la critiquait, était

---

[25] De Dijn, Annelien. In overeenstemming met onze zeden en gewoonten. De intellectuele context van de eerste Belgische constitutie (1815-1830). In: Bijdragen en Mededelingen betreffende de Geschiedenis der Nederlanden (2002), p. 25-45.
[26] Faider, Charles. La topique constitutionnelle. In : La Belgique judiciaire (1884), p. 1319.

fortement critiquée. Je cite les mots d'un fameux politicien belge, Charles Rogier, prononcés à la Chambre des Représentants pendant la séance du 23 mars 1847. Dédaigner la liberté de la presse, équivalait à dédaigner le futur splendide de la Belgique.:

« Il y a, je le sais, une espèce de parti pris, une sorte de bon ton même, de par un certain monde, à traiter aujourd'hui avec dédain et le jury et la liberté de la presse. Ces deux grandes garanties, pour lesquelles on peut dire que la révolution belge a été faite en partie, ces ceux grandes garanties qui figuraient en tête du programme de l'*Union* qui a mis fin à la domination du régime hollandais, on semble aujourd'hui assez disposé à en faire bon marché. »[27]

En plus, le journalisme était perçu comme un tremplin vers la politique. Grâce aux possibilités des journalistes, les meilleurs politiciens s'étaient formés. De nouveau, on peut se référer à la carrière de journalistes condamnés dans les années 1820, devenus des héros de la révolution et faisant ensuite de hautes carrières dans la politique et la magistrature. Leurs *curricula vitae* étaient des exemples à suivre pour tous les futurs belges concernés par le bonheur politique de la Belgique et ses libertés. Schuermans disait dans la préface de son manuel :

« Nous ne sommes qu'à l'enfance de la liberté inaugurée par l'article 18 de notre Constitution ; un jour viendra où la presse et le journalisme, qui en est l'expression la plus vivante, seront considérés comme un sacerdoce exigeant des conditions de haute moralité et des capacités hors ligne. La presse sera l'apprentissage où se formeront les futurs législateurs ; dès l'époque où le roi Guillaume proférait les étranges paroles rapportées plus haut, les 'jeunes utopistes' dont il se plaignait, n'étaient-ils pas ces Rogier, ces Lebeau, ces Van de Weyer, ces Nothomb, ces Devaux, etc. [= tous des politiciens belges fameux, protagonistes de la révolution belge qui ont, pendant leur jeunesse, hardiment critiqué le régime hollandais] à qui la Belgique dut sa rénovation politique ? Eux que le roi Guillaume traitait avec une superbe si dédaigneuse, n'est-ce pas

---

[27] Annales parlementaires (1846-47), p. 1279.

au baptême de feu des luttes de la presse qu'ils ont été éprouvés, et plusieurs, arrivés eux-mêmes au pouvoir depuis, n'y ont-ils pas fait briller toutes les qualités d'homme d'Etat de premier ordre ? »[28]

La possibilité absolue de critiquer le gouvernement devait protéger les valeurs démocratiques de la Belgique, résultant à un législateur représentatif avec la préoccupation de donner au peuple belge les meilleures lois , la plus grande liberté et la plus grande prospérité.

Grâce à ce système qui devait donner à la Belgique la législation la plus parfaite possible, le bonheur et le moral de cette nation devaient accroître sans cesse. Cette progression continue ne se révélait pas seulement sur le plan moral, mais aussi sur le plan matériel. En 1865, Charles Faider, à l'époque avocat-général près de la Cour de cassation, publiait une, dans laquelle il donnait la preuve en chiffres de la prospérité de la Belgique.[29] On ne pouvait concevoir ce progrès que comme lié aux libertés constitutionnelles, et à la liberté de la presse en particulier.

La glorification du sauvetage de la liberté de la presse par la constituante était aussi présente dans l'iconographie du jeune état.[30] L'exemple le plus illustratif de ce culte était l'érection de la colonne du Congrès au centre de Bruxelles. Au pied du monument, implanté dans le quartier où résidaient la plupart des parlementaires, quatre statues symbolisaient les quatre libertés constitutionnelles. Il faut bien remarquer que les deux groupes idéologiquement opposés, à savoir les catholiques et les libéraux, interprétaient le culte constitutionnel un peu à leur propre façon : la plupart des libéraux accentuait la liberté, la majorité des catholiques plutôt la tradition des Belges.

Pourtant, quelques auteurs et juristes semblaient être conscients de ce discours particulier et du rôle que le souvenir de Van Maanen et de la période hollandaise y jouaient. Charles Laurent, magistrat et fils de l'illustre civiliste gantois François Laurent, le faisait remarquer en 1871 dans ses *Etudes sur les délits de presse*:

---

[28] Schuermans, Henri. Code de la presse. Bruxelles 1881, I, p. 41. 18-19.
[29] Faider, Charles. Etude sur la statistique nationale. Bruxelles 1865.
[30] Plusieurs exemples sont cités dans : Janssens, Jeroen. De Belgische natie viert. De Belgische nationale feesten, 1830-1914. Louvain 2001.

« De là des orages et des tempêtes épouvantables ; la liberté de la presse était immolée ; les journalistes, traités comme des forçats libérés, étaient mis au ban de la société : pour achever le lugubre tableau des maux incalculables qui devaient fondre sur eux, on alla jusqu'à évoquer le souvenir de Van Maanen ! Cette émotion ne nous a pas étonné : nous l'avons même vue avec satisfaction ; elle prouve une fois de plus l'inaltérable attachement du peuple belge à ses institutions constitutionnelles et surtout à la liberté de la presse, la plus précieuse de nos libertés, parce qu'elle est la garantie de toutes les autres. »[31]

Bref, on peut conclure qu'au courant du 19ième siècle, on s'est souvenu du régime hollandais et du Congrès national constituant d'une manière totalement contrastive. Les quinze ans de la période hollandaise étaient décrits comme une oppression absolue, et la Révolution belge, couronnée et immortalisée par la constitution, comme la libération du joug hollandais.

3. La réalité quotidienne de la liberté de la presse en Belgique

Le souvenir du Congrès national comme sauveteur de la liberté de la presse, intégré au discours sur cette liberté considérée absolue, ne concordait pas toujours avec la réalité. Au cours du 19e siècle, on a découvert que la presse n'était pas toujours une garantie pour la politique belge et sa démocratie parlementaire, mais qu'elle pouvait aussi menacer cette société et sa position internationale. La protection de la presse politique et critique apparaît comme un couteau à double tranchant, et dans les cas où la société belge semblait être menacée, les politiciens belges n'ont pas hésité à restreindre la presse et sa liberté d'expression. Il est intéressant de raconter à vol d'oiseau les modifications principales de la législation en matière de presse dans les décennies après 1830-1831. On commence par les modifications dans la législation matérielle.

En ce qui concerne la mémoire du Royaume-Uni des Pays-Bas, on peut indiquer que déjà peu de temps après le vote de la constitution, les principes constitutionnels absolus étaient sacrifiés pour protéger la jeune Belgique

[31] Laurent, Charles. Etudes sur les délits de presse. Bruxelles 1871, p. 8.

contre l'opposition des partisans de Guillaume I. Bien que la Belgique s'était détachée du Nord, il restait de nombreux partisans d'une réunion avec les provinces du Nord, appelés les orangistes. En 1834, le gouvernement belge pensait qu'il fallait arrêter la critique de ceux qui soutenaient le retour du régime hollandais. Par conséquent, leurs publications devenaient punissables par le vote d'une loi occasionnelle, la loi du 25 juillet qui interdisait la propagande orangiste.[32] Bien que dans l'assemblée constituante, plusieurs membres du Congrès national avaient exprimé l'opinion que le législateur futur ne pourrait point créer des lois pénales rendant une opinion particulière punissable,[33] le législateur de 1834 interdisait toutes les formes de propagande hollandaise. On peut dire qu'en agissant ainsi, le gouvernement belge a voulu réglementer le souvenir du régime hollandais dans la première décennie après la révolution. Quand en 1839 la Belgique et les Pays-bas se sont réconciliés par le Traité des XXIV Articles , la loi de 1834 fut abolie.

La loi de 1834 n'était point la seule restriction matérielle de la liberté de presse. Au printemps de l'année 1847, le gouvernement belge voulut faire une nouvelle loi concernant les offenses envers la personne du roi et la famille royale. A l'occasion d'un acquittement, prononcé par la cour d'assises du Brabant, de quelques publicistes qui s'étaient moqués du roi Léopold I dans des caricatures, le gouvernement voulut restreindre la liberté d'expression et la liberté de presse sur ce point précis concernant la personne du roi et les membres de sa famille.[34]

Au début des années 1850, beaucoup d'émigrés français s'étaient domiciliés à Bruxelles, pour échapper au régime de Napoléon III. Dans leurs journaux, ces antibonapartistes critiquaient durement le nouvel empereur français, ce qui mettait le gouvernement belge dans une situation délicate. Les menaces politiques et militaires de Napoléon forcèrent le gouvernement à faire une nouvelle

---

[32] Luykx, Theo. Over de orangistische pers in België. In: Album Prof. Dr. K. Baschwitz. Amsterdam 1956, p. 12-25.

[33] Velaers, Jan. De beperkingen van de vrijheid van meningsuiting. Anvers 1990, p. 127-129.

[34] Delbecke, Bram. Verlekkerd op geitenmelk en een kalkoenhoedster. Over de ontstaansgeschiedenis van de wet van 6 april 1847. In: Pro Memorie. Bijdragen tot de rechtsgeschiedenis van de Nederlanden (2005), p. 115-131.

loi, la loi du 20 décembre 1852, relative à la répression des offenses envers les chefs des gouvernements étrangers.[35]

A la fin des années 1880, la misère sociale en Belgique industrielle posait de grands problèmes. Plusieurs ouvriers incitaient à la grève générale interdite. En 1886, une vague d'émeutes ouvrières menaçait la politique. Les politiciens ont réagi de manière répressive, par une loi occasionnelle en matière de participation criminelle, punissant ceux qui par la parole ou par des écrits incitaient à des délits. La loi occasionnelle de 1887 fut confirmée en 1891.[36]

Il est toutefois remarquable que dans les discussions parlementaires et doctrinales, bien que les initiatives avaient pour but de restreindre un aspect précis de la liberté de la presse, on se référait chaque fois à la période du Royaume-Uni et à son représentant le plus détesté, le ministre de la Justice Van Maanen de l'un côté, et aux bienfaits de la Constitution en matière de presse de l'autre. A chaque fois, on y retrouve des références aux discours des membres du Congrès national. Bien qu'on tendait à la liberté de presse, les mérites de l'assemblée nationale concernant cette liberté étaient glorifiés.

En plus, le contraste entre la répression judiciaire de la presse pendant la période hollandaise et celle depuis l'indépendance belge, ne répondait pas non plus à la réalité. Pendant le régime hollandais et le ministère du détesté Van Maanen, il y avait une cinquantaine de procès de presse. Malgré le peu de chiffres disponibles, on doit remarquer que dans les premières décennies de l'état belge, le nombre de procès de presse dépassait celui des poursuites hollandaises. Je vous cite l'exemple le plus documenté. Devant la cour d'assises de la province de Brabant, une seule donc des neuf provinces belges, il y eut pres-

---

[35] Breugelmans, Koen. Les lois belges dites 'Faider' (1852) et 'Tesch' (1858) : la liberté de la presse et les offenses envers les chefs d'états étrangers. In : Libertés, pluralisme et droit. Une approche historique. Actes du colloque d'Anvers (27-30 mai 1993). Bruxelles 1995, p. 213-225 ; Luykx, Theo. Negentiende-eeuwse pers-processen en hun invloed op de Belgische perswetgeving. In: Actuele problemen rond krant, radio en T.V. Gand 1967, p. 30-42. Ces lois sont abolies récemment par la loi du 13 février 2005.

[36] Delbecke, Bram. Les émeutes de 1886 et la participation criminelle. La provocation publique des lois du 23 août 1887 et du 25 mars 1891. Journées internationales d'histoire du droit et des institutions des pays flamands, wallons et picards. Boulogne-sur-mer, 27 mai 2006.

que quarante procès de presse pendant la période 1831-1847.[37] La divergence entre le discours sur la liberté totale de la presse et la réalité judiciaire était remarquable.

On a vu qu'au cours du 19e siècle, le législateur belge a éprouvé quelques difficultés à adapter la législation matérielle en matière de presse. Mais au niveau de la législation formelle, à savoir la législation sur la procédure en cas de délit de presse, le conflit était encore plus grand entre le souvenir du temps de la révolution et les besoins et les voeux de la pratique judiciaire. On y voit un mécanisme analogue.

Comme le stipulait la Constitution belge de 1831, les délits de presse étaient assignés aux Cours d'assises pour y être jugés par douze jurés, représentant la nation. La compétence du jury était 'la prédominance de l'opinion publique sur le sens privé du magistrat. Les dissentiments religieux ou politiques qui partagent les hommes de l'époque, rendent indispensables l'institution d'une magistrature à laquelle toutes les classes ont leur contingent à fournir. Ainsi prévaudra sur la prédilection ou l'aversion du juge ce qu'il y aura de général dans les idées individuelles des citoyens'. Les jurés incarnaient le principe salutaire de la prédominance de l'opinion publique sur l'opinion privée du magistrat. En effet, ils devaient juger des affaires qui exigent au plus haut degré, outre l'indépendance et la fermeté, la probité et la connaissance des hommes, outre les droits, les besoins de la société et de la forme de son gouvernement. Le seul juge possible du journaliste, éditeur ou imprimeur délinquant semblait être le jury populaire. Cette institution de douze jurés avait reçu du législateur constitutionnel l'auréole auguste de l'institution la plus apte à juger les affaires de presse et les affaires politiques. Inspiré par le discours de la souveraineté populaire, on concevait le jury comme l'étalon de l'opinion publique. C'était la tâche des jurés de décider si cette opinion était inquiétée ou non.[38]

Mais déjà la pratique judiciaire de la première décennie de la jeune Belgique démontrait que le jury populaire n'était pas toujours cette institution auguste. L'indépendance et l'impartialité des jurés n'étaient pas uniquement des garan-

---

[37] Debaere, Marc. De pers voor de jury. Persprocessen voor het Hof van Assisen van Brabant, 1831-1847. Louvain 1986, p. 105.

[38] Roumier, William. L'Avenir du jury criminel. Paris 2003, p. 22-88. Il faut remarquer que Roumier redoute l'aspect souverain du jury.

ties contre le despotisme. L'incompétence juridique du jury avaient rarement comme résultat un jugement conforme à l'opinion publique. On pouvait remarquer que le comportement des jurés exposés aux acrobaties rhétoriques des avocats était capricieux. En plus, la grande publicité –souvent mal venue à cause de son effet contraproductif en matière de calomnie et injures-, la lenteur de la procédure, les frais, ... étaient les autres principaux inconvénients. Ces éléments ne faisaient point de bien à la réputation du jury comme institution judiciaire. Bien qu'au Congrès national Devaux avait dit que « le jury sera toujours sévère pour les calomniateurs »,[39] les problèmes de procédure en matière de diffamation par la voie de la presse paraissaient trop grands. La solution semblait être évidente : la responsabilité aquilienne, ou les dispositions du fameux article 1382 du code civil napoléonien, avec lesquelles on pouvait exiger des dommages-intérêts. Mais dans cette matière, une question difficile se posait : le Congrès national, en assignant les cours d'assises pour les délits de presse, a-t-il exclu la compétence des tribunaux civils ? Cette question donnait lieu à de grandes discussions, aussi bien de jurisprudence que de doctrine. Finalement, la jurisprudence a reconnu la compétence du juge civil pour la première fois en 1839, la cour la plus haute, la Cour de cassation, l'a reconnue en 1863.[40]

Bien que cette évolution de la jurisprudence fut bien accueillie par l'opinion publique, la compétence exclusive du jury était fanatiquement soutenue par la doctrine et par quelques membres du parlement très combatifs. Henri Schuermans, le commentateur principal de la législation belge en matière de presse du 19ième siècle, disait qu'en publiant son étude, il avait une ambition explicite :

« Peut-être qu'un jour viendra où cette étude ne sera pas inutile et où le législateur reprendra l'oeuvre de 1831, inspiré de la même sollicitude pour la presse que celle qui animait les auteurs de la Constitution ; il se fera alors un devoir d'aplanir les obstacles, d'ôter tout prétexte à la réaction en en faisant

---

[39] Huyttens, Emile. Discussions du congrès national de Belgique. Bruxelles 1844, I, p. 657.
[40] Cass. 24 janvier 1863. Pasicrisie belge (1863) I, p. 116-117.

disparaître les causes, et de restituer au jury la juridiction exclusive et souveraine sur les matières de presse ».[41]

Comme dans les cas de la législation matérielle, cette voie considérée anticonstitutionnelle suscitait des commentaires dans lesquels la mémoire du régime hollandais et du Congrès national était omniprésente.

Après l'arrêt de la Cour de cassation, une proposition de loi fut déposée pour que la cour d'assises récupère son statut de juge exclusif en matière de presse.[42] Cette proposition était motivée comme un retour vers l'esprit de la Constitution, et dans l'exposé des motifs, on esquissait amplement cet esprit pour appuyer la compétence exclusive des cours d'assises en matière de presse. Dans les discussions parlementaires, les partisans de cette proposition se référaient exclusivement aux poursuites pendant la période hollandaise, à l'esprit des années 1830-1831 et à la réaction constitutionnelle. Un bon exemple est le discours du représentant Debaets pendant la séance de la Chambre des représentants du 2 mars 1864. Pour argumenter la proposition de loi et son retour vers l'esprit constitutionnel, il racontait amplement l'histoire des différentes poursuites et la réaction des membres du Congrès national, en citant intégralement les discussions de l'assemblée constituante.[43] De nouveau, la politique de Van Maanen et la réaction anti-Van Maanen du Congrès national fournissaient l'étalon pour organiser la liberté de la presse dans le futur.

Malgré la reconnaissance de la compétence du juge civil en matière de calomnie par la cour de cassation, la doctrine continua à lutter pour une approche plus constitutionnelle des délits de presse, c'est à dire la restauration du règne absolu du jury, même en matière civile. La constitution n'était pas adaptée à la divergence entre le journalisme politique et le journalisme satirique. Schuermans disait :

---

[41] Schuermans, Henri. Code de la presse. Bruxelles 1861, p. 410.

[42] Annales parlementaires (1864), p. 245. Une nouvelle disposition plus élaborée fut déposée en 1865, et était définitivement rejetée en 1879.

[43] Annales parlementaires de Belgique (1864), p. 311-312.

« Alors pas de faiblesse, pas de tergiversation ; que le jury n'hésite jamais. Chaque fois qu'il montrera de la fermeté en matière de calomnie bien avérée, il aura conquis de nouveaux amis à la liberté, et enlevé un prétexte d'antagonisme à ses détracteurs : la sévérité du jury, en matière de calomnie et de diffamation, doit être le vœu de tous les vrais amis de la liberté, et il n'est pas de journal sérieux qui ne réclame au nom même de la liberté .»[44]

Pour appuyer son point de vue, il ne se référait pas aux penseurs libéraux contemporains, mais exclusivement à des philosophes et politiciens des années 1820-1830 comme Benjamin Constant et Paul Devaux, qui ont eu une grande influence sur la liberté de la presse.

4. La liberté de presse, expression typique de l'identité de la nation belge comme une identité non-hollandaise

Pour terminer, je voudrais répondre à la question suivante. Comment expliquer ce caractère explicitement anti-hollandais, anti-Van Maanen et surtout, cette adhérence au souvenir de l'assemblée constituante dans le discours juridique et judiciaire en matière de presse, bien que la réalité législative et judiciaire ne concordait pas avec ce discours? Evidemment, le discours sur la liberté de la presse était très libéral, témoin d'une image très individualiste de l'homme, comme un être autonome s'exprimant selon ses propres idées pour lesquelles il était seul responsable. Ce discours hyperindividualiste était typique pour le 19ième siècle, mais n'explique pas tout. Quant au souvenir de la période 1830-1831, cette mémoire fonctionnait par excellence dans la création d'une identité belge comme un instrument pour mieux définir l'image de la Belgique. La Belgique était jeune et voulait légitimer son existence sur le plan international. Elle croyait qu'elle devait affirmer le caractère particulier de cette nation et ses mœurs et coutumes. On a vu que selon ce culte de l'identité nationale, la nation belge était, à l'époque après-Napoléonienne du 19e siècle, la nation la

[44] Schuermans, Henri. Code de la presse. Bruxelles, 1881, I, pp. 22-23

plus avancée de l'Europe parce qu'elle avait la plus grande liberté, et la perspective d'une prospérité incomparable.

Mais cette liberté de presse était une arme à double tranchant. D'une part elle était une des expressions les plus marquantes des mœurs de la nation belge, d'autre part elle pouvait mener à des situations dans lesquelles la parole imprimée était capable de menacer la société belge elle-même, au niveau national aussi bien qu'au niveau international. La presse ne pourrait fonctionner dans le système constitutionnel que si elle fonctionnait conformément à l'archétype du journaliste que le Congrès national considérait comme le seul journaliste possible: le chien de garde qui suivait la politique avec un regard critique, toujours préparé à sonner la cloche en cas d'abus de pouvoir. En réalité, les journalistes qui n'écrivaient que pour préserver le salut de la nation étaient rares. La majorité des journalistes belges au 19e siècle n'écrivaient qu'occasionnellement, ou simplement pour gagner un petit sou, dans des journaux de petite envergure et souvent très locaux, dans lesquels la politique n'occupait que peu de colonnes. Ils publiaient des faits divers, des nouvelles, des rumeurs, … Les grands principes et l'importance des libertés pour la nation ne les intéressaient que très peu.

En plus, les publications d'une minorité des journalistes n'avaient pas pour but de protéger les institutions belges, mais étaient considérées comme des vraies menaces pour la société belge. Ici, on peut se référer aux modifications occasionnelles de la législation en matière de presse citées plus haut. Toutes ces modifications avaient pour but de protéger la nation et ses intérêts, le roi belge et les chefs d'état étrangers. On devait éviter toute critique étrangère ou menace internationale. On voulait conserver l'image d'une nation parfaite, d'une société harmonieuse et heureuse qui vivait dans le meilleur des mondes possibles. La mémoire de la domination hollandaise, du régime de Van Maanen, du Congrès national et de sa constitution fonctionnait comme l'expression du culte des libertés belges et comme légitimation permanente de la Belgique.

Le souvenir du régime hollandais et de l'intervention favorable du Congrès national a disparu du discours après les années 1880. Dans cette décennie, un nouveau discours s'est manifesté, annonçant l'aube du discours de la défense sociale. Dans les discussions sur la liberté de la presse, on ne voulait plus autant sauvegarder cette liberté comme un héritage du législateur constitutionnel de l'époque révolutionnaire, mais on commençait à considérer la presse de plus en plus comme un moyen d'incitation à l'agitation. Pendant les années de la crise socio-économique et l'éruption de la vague de grèves des ouvriers wallons en 1886, l'approche de la liberté de presse se faisait plus défensive. Les lois citées de 1887 et de 1891, interdisant la provocation publique à commettre des faits qualifiés de crimes, sont les meilleurs exemples de cette évolution.

En conclusion, on peut dire qu'au dix-neuvième siècle, la Belgique s'est souvenue des quinze ans de l'union belgo-hollandaise comme l'antipode de sa propre nature. Le souvenir du Royaume-Uni, de son ministre de la Justice Van Maanen et du législateur constitutionnel belge fonctionnait non seulement comme un simple avertissement, mais en plus comme un thème nationaliste et unificateur, légitimant ainsi la nation belge elle-même. Néanmoins, en matière de presse, ce souvenir posait plusieurs problèmes, parce qu'en 1831, la liberté de presse était modelée selon l'archétype du journaliste luttant comme un chien de garde pour la préservation de la nation et de ses libertés. Les grandes évolutions socio-économiques dans la société belge du dix-neuvième siècle montraient que ces libertés n'étaient pas soutenues par tout le monde de la même façon. Le culte du souvenir du passé hollandais devait étayer les aspirations du jeune état, en légitimant son caractère propre, marqué par ses libertés, et par excellence, par sa liberté de presse.

Ne pas oublier le crime: le refus d'absolution en Catalogne (XVIe-XVIIIe siècles)

Fabrice Desnos

Veiller au maintien de l'ordre est un aspect essentiel de la fonction de juge royal. En effet, il représente le roi, dont une des missions fondamentales est d'assurer la paix et la justice entre ses sujets.[1] Les crimes ne doivent donc pas demeurer impunis, ils ne doivent pas être oubliés. La tâche qui incombe au juge s'avère délicate car, dans un système inquisitoire,[2] c'est à lui qu'appartient la réunion de preuves *luce meridiana clariores*.[3] Pour condamner, le *Ius commune* exige en effet une *plena probatio*, constituée en théorie par l'aveu de l'accusé ou par les dépositions concordantes de deux témoins idoines. A défaut d'accomplissement de l'une des conditions, l'accusé peut seulement être absous. Cette exigence se fonde sur le principe qu' « il vaut mieux laisser un coupable impuni plutôt que de condamner un innocent ».[4] Le problème est que de nombreux témoins sont reprochables en fonction notamment de leurs condition, âge, renommée ou sexe.[5] De surcroît, l'accusé n'est pas toujours

---

[1] Peguera, Lluís de : Practica criminalis et ordinis iudiciarii civilis, Barcinone, Ex Typographia Iacobi à Cendrat, 1603, f°15. Cap. IV n°6. « Rex ideo efficiendo, ut inter ista tria personarum genera pax & iustitia sint semper constituta ». Pour cela, « primum est, quod ipse Princeps curet contra Dei praecepta non peccare. Secundum est, quod peccata quae à subditis committuntur atque de iure punibilia sunt puniat, cohibeat, & de patria expellat. Tertium denique est, quod ipsam Rempublicà curet malis hominibus purgatam habere ».

[2] Sur le passage de la procédure accusatoire à l'inquisitoire, V. Esmein, Adhémar : Histoire de la procédure criminelle en France et de la procédure inquisitoire depuis le XIII° siècle jusqu'à nos jours. Paris 1882, 596 p.

[3] C., 4, 19, 25 : « Sciant cuncti accusatores eam se rem deferre debere in publicam notionem, quae munita sit testibus idoneis vel instructa apertissimis documentis vel indiciis ad probationem indubitatis et luce clarioribus expedita ».

[4] D., 48, 19, 5 : « (...) satius enim esse impunitum relinqui facinus nocentis quam innocentem damnari (...) ».

[5] Ces quatre reproches sont généralement qualifiés d'absolus. Ils se distinguent des reproches relatifs tenant notamment à la proximité avec la victime (consanguinité, domestique...). V. Schnapper,

disposé à avouer. La difficulté de l'établissement de cette *plena probatio* s'accentue encore pour certains crimes occultes,[6] ou en raison de la nécessité d'établir le *dolus malus* en plus de la constatation du corps du délit.[7] Enfin, la fréquence de certains crimes exclut l'oubli de leurs traces.[8]

Il faut alors concilier ces deux exigences antagonistes du droit pénal que sont la répression du crime et les garanties de la défense. Un allègement des modalités de preuve semble par conséquent nécessaire. Amorcé dès le Moyen Âge,[9] le processus semble s'accélérer au XVIe siècle en Catalogne.[10] Une pratique originale se développe par la mutation du système en vigueur et l'admission précoce de nouveaux moyens de preuve.[11] Progressivement, les présomptions y occupent une place plus importante et des indices *ad torturam* sont désormais utilisés *ad probandum*. Parce qu'elle purge les différents éléments de preuve qu'avait pu réunir le juge, l'absolution a pour conséquence inhérente l'oubli du crime.[12] Ainsi, pour que les crimes *ne remaneant impunita*,

---

Bernard : Testes inhabiles. Les témoins reprochables dans l'Ancien droit pénal. In: Tijdschrift voor Rechtsgeschiedenis, tome XXXIII. Bruxelles 1965, p. 580.

[6] Il est en effet peu aisé de disposer de témoins pour un homicide perpétré de nuit et au sein d'une maison.

[7] Toro Marzal, Alejandro del : El homicidio doloso en Cataluña según Cortiada. In : Revista Juridica de Catalunya 1984, pp. 741-745.

[8] Ces crimes sont alors réprimés sur le fondement de preuves plus légères, pour purger la province des « mauvais hommes ».

[9] Lévy, Jean-Philippe : La hiérarchie des preuves dans le droit savant du Moyen Âge, depuis la renaissance du droit romain jusqu'à la fin du XIVe siècle. In : Annales de l'université de Lyon III, fascicule V. Paris, 175 p.

[10] Lorsque nous parlons de Catalogne, nous prenons ici la région dans une acception large. Celle-ci comprend évidemment la principauté s'étendant au nord-est de l'Espagne, mais nous inclurons également pour cet exposé les comtés de Cerdagne et du Roussillon. Ces deux entités tombent sous domination française en 1659, comme conséquence du Traité des Pyrénées.

[11] Durand, Bernard : La détermination de la peine chez les criminalistes catalans du XVIe au XVIIIe siècle : logique juridique ou effet des mentalités. In : Recueil de mémoires et travaux de la société d'histoire du droit et des institutions des anciens pays de droit écrit, fascicule XV, Montpellier 1991, pp. 1-25.

[12] Bongert, Yvonne : Le *pro modo probationum* : intime conviction avant la lettre ? , in Revue historique de droit français et étranger, n° 1-2000, janvier-mars 2000, Paris 2000, p. 16. Selon le droit savant, l'absolution doit purger totalement les indices.

pour que les indices ne soient pas oubliés, il est nécessaire pour le juge pénal de ne pas absoudre l'accusé.

Les criminalistes catalans imaginent de nouvelles règles de procédure permettant au juge pénal d'établir la vérité. Celle-ci est nécessairement relative car c'est une vérité judiciaire, fondée sur une certitude morale. Néanmoins, elle permet de statuer et de ne pas acquitter des individus considérés comme dangereux. Nous étudierons les œuvres des criminalistes catalans du XVIe au XVIIIe siècles, généralement magistrats siégeant ou ayant siégé au Conseil criminel de Catalogne[13] ou au Conseil souverain de Roussillon[14]. Ils mettent leur expérience à disposition de leurs collègues praticiens, qu'ils soient juges ou avocats, en publiant des recueils de décisions ou des traités. Ces auteurs s'appuient sur des sources juridiques très diverses. La doctrine européenne, antérieure comme contemporaine, est connue et abondamment citée. De même, la jurisprudence des cours souveraines et les droits savants sont fréquemment allégués, tandis que le droit royal s'implante progressivement.[15]

---

[13] Le Conseil criminel est la troisième chambre de la Royale Audience, la cour supérieure de ce territoire, établie à Barcelone. Par commodité nous emploierons l'expression de « Conseil criminel » et non l'intitulé complet de « Conseil criminel royal de Catalogne ». Jaume Càncer (1559-1631) était avocat à Vilafranca de Penedés puis à Barcelone, mais ne parvint jamais à la fonction de sénateur à la Royale Audience. Pere d'Amigant de Ferrer (1645-1707) cumula différentes charges. Professeur de droit romain, il fut également assesseur au tribunal de la *Capitania general* et du *Mestre racional*, membre du conseil royal et juge au conseil criminel de Catalogne. Miquel de Calderó (XVIIe-XVIIIe siècles) était *regente* de la Royale Audience. Son opposition aux Bourbons durant la guerre de Succession entraîna la destitution de ses charges et la confiscation de ses biens. V. Peláez, Manuel J. : Diccionario crítico de juristas españoles, portugueses y latinoamericanos (hispánicos, brasileños, quebequenses y restantes francófonos) (hasta 2005), vol. I (A-L), Zaragoza 2005, 523 p. Lluís de Peguera (1540-1610) fut premier sénateur du Conseil criminel et Miquel de Cortiada († 1691) fut avocat du Fisc à la Royale Audience.

[14] Le Conseil souverain de Roussillon est la juridiction supérieure de la Cerdagne et du Roussillon, siégeant à Perpignan, après le rattachement définitif du Roussillon à la France au milieu du XVIIe siècle. Nous examinerons les opinions du conseiller Noguer, de l'avocat général de Vilar et de Jaume, tous trois écrivant au XVIIIe siècle. Ces juristes ont notamment le devoir de concilier l'ordonnance criminelle de 1670, enregistrée en 1681, avec les pratiques catalanes antérieures. V. Astaing, Antoine : Le conseil souverain de Roussillon, gardien de l'ordonnance de 1670, in Les parlements de province. Pouvoirs, justice et société du XVe au XVIIIe siècle. Textes réunis et présentés par Jacques Poumarède et Jack Thomas, Toulouse 1996, pp. 311-327

[15] Le droit coutumier n'est presque pas mentionné par les décisions nous intéressant ici.

L'oubli du crime est repoussé par le passage progressif d'une certitude légale à une certitude morale. Comment les auteurs catalans parviennent-ils alors à concilier le refus d'absolution et la présomption d'innocence de l'accusé ? Par quels moyens le juge pénal écarte-t-il l'oubli du crime lors de cette transition entre certitude légale et certitude morale ? Les divers types de sentences prononcées traduisent la volonté du juge de ne pas absoudre l'accusé (I). Or, de telles décisions ne sont possibles que par l'adaptation des moyens de garder la mémoire du crime (II).

I. Ne pas absoudre l'accusé

L'accusé dont la culpabilité n'est pas établie doit être remis en liberté, lavé de tout soupçon. D'après Peguera, la relaxe est simple, sans caution, quand on ne trouve pas de faute à reprocher au prisonnier.[16] L'absolution est encore *sine expensis* lorsqu'elle est prononcée en l'honneur d'un jour férié. Pourtant, refusant de laisser des crimes impunis, le juge écarte le principe de l'absolution à défaut de *plena probatio.* Au XVIe siècle, il est ainsi devenu très rare en Catalogne que l'accusé soit complètement absous. Outre le fait de ne pas absoudre entièrement l'accusé (A), le juge va prononcer des condamnations *pro modo probationum* (B).

A. Une absolution relative

L'accusé soumis à la torture judiciaire devrait être absous dans la mesure où il n'a rien avoué.[17] Pourtant, le juge ne croit pas toujours à son innocence et a parfois la conviction que l'individu a réellement commis l'infraction. Son silence pourrait n'être le fait que d'une endurance face aux tourments. C'est pourquoi l'absolution pure et simple n'est pas ordonnée, puisqu'elle aurait

---

[16] Peguera : Practica criminalis (cf. n. 1), f°82-83. Cap. XII §.15 n°2. « Quando captus reperitur clare, & evidenter sine culpa ; quia nulla praestita cautione, & sine expensis relaxandus venit ».
[17] Calderó, Miquel de : Sacri Regii Criminalis Concilii Cathaloniae Decisiones. Barcinone. Ex Typ. Mariae Marti Viduae, administrata per Dominicum Tallèr, 1726, pars I, p. 377. Decisio XLVII n°4. Le 14 octobre 1671, Catherina N., qui n'a pas avoué avoir tué son mari, est effectivement absoute.

pour conséquence la purge des indices ayant permis le recours à la torture. L'absolution peut en effet être assortie de contraintes. Lorsqu'il apparaît au cours du procès que l'accusé n'est pas coupable ou qu'il n'a pas produit de fidéjusseurs, Peguera explique qu'il est possible de le relaxer moyennant une caution juratoire.[18] A moins que ne surviennent de nouveaux indices, l'accusé ne pourra être remis en prison pour les mêmes faits.[19] Malgré sa remise en liberté, l'accusé demeure ainsi durant deux années sous la main du juge. En matière de crimes atroces, Jaume avoue que

« rarement le prévenu est déchargé de l'accusation mais il est élargi moyennant la caution juratoire de se représenter toutes les fois qu'il en sera requis ce qui tient lieu d'absolution du crime, s'il ne survient pas de nouvelles preuves ».[20]

On refuse donc d'absoudre l'accusé *de iure*, bien que dans la réalité de nouvelles preuves surviennent rarement. Les inconvénients pratiques tenant à l'insécurité juridique de cette situation sont évidents, en particulier pour l'accusé élargi.

Ce refus d'absoudre totalement l'accusé est une première manifestation de l'intime conviction du juge pénal. Le doute sur l'innocence entraîne une modification des effets de l'absolution. De la sorte, les éléments de preuve déjà réunis par le juge ne sont pas oubliés à défaut de *plena probatio*. Ce compromis n'est pas satisfaisant, car la possibilité d'une condamnation subsiste au dessus de l'accusé, tandis que le juge moralement convaincu de sa culpabilité doit le laisser impuni. L'évolution est inévitable.

---

[18] Peguera : Practica criminalis (cf. n. 1), f°83. Cap. XII §.15 n°4. « Quandoque etiam, deliquentes non multû gravati in processu relaxari solent cum iuratoria cautione, & praecipuè, quando nô inveniunt fideiussores ».

[19] Peguera : Practica criminalis (cf. n. 1), f°83. Cap. XII §.15 n°5-6. Cela touche également un accusé peu accablé par le procès.

[20] Archives Départementales des Pyrénées Orientales (A.D.P.O.) MS 40. Jaume, Dictionnaire des arrêts. Crimes et complices n°3. Il cite une décision du Conseil souverain de Roussillon du 31 janvier 1968 Jacques Forquet et Marguerite Aline Rostan, dans une affaire de sacrilège (de Vilar, décision 273).

B. Des condamnations pro modo probationum

Les criminalistes catalans étendent considérablement les prérogatives du juge pénal. En fonction des éléments de conviction en sa possession, ce dernier a désormais le pouvoir de prononcer une peine adaptée, extraordinaire ou ordinaire.

En principe, pour condamner à la peine de mort, « toutes les circonstances nécessaires » doivent être présentes, faute de quoi la peine prononcée est arbitraire, *infra mortem*.[21] La condamnation à une peine extraordinaire est la conséquence de l'état intermédiaire de culpabilité de l'accusé. Insuffisamment convaincu d'un crime pour mériter sa peine ordinaire, il l'est tout de même assez pour ne pas jouir de l'impunité. Calderó mentionne un grand nombre d'affaires sur cette question. Par exemple, une décision du Conseil criminel du 12 octobre 1678 condamna Iacobum N. à ramer sept années dans les galères royales. Ce cultivateur était accusé d'un meurtre *proditorius* commis par le jet d'un instrument manuel sur Ioannis Ferrer, alias *lo gollut*. Il n'existait à son encontre que deux déclarations de complices et quatre témoignages *de fama*.[22] Bien que nombreux, ces témoins ne sont pas conformes aux exigences concernant la preuve testimoniale. Cortiada fournit d'autres illustrations. Par exemple, le 8 juillet 1608, Bartholomaeus Massons fut condamné par le Conseil criminel à ramer sept années dans les galères pour avoir frappé de la fausse monnaie barcelonaise. La mort était encourue mais le délit n'était pas

---

[21] A.D.P.O. MS 40. Jaume, Dictionnaire des arrêts. Rapt n°2. De la sorte, Jacques Thorrent est condamné à cinq années de galères « convaincu d'avoir amené de nuit » une femme mariée qui n'habitait pas avec son mari par le Conseil souverain de Roussillon le 19 septembre 1681 (de Vilar, décision 11).

[22] Calderó : Sacri Regii Criminalis Concilii (cf. n. 17), pars I, p. 149. Decisio XVI n°10. L'auteur mentionne également (pars I pp. 377-378. Decisio XLVI n°7) un meurtre commandité par Anticum N., qui avait demandé à Martino N. et à d'autres *facinorosis hominibus* de tuer Guillermum Casals. Le 10 octobre 1607, la juridiction barcelonaise le condamna à sept années de galères seulement, *ex defectu probationis assassini.*

pleinement constaté, le juge ne disposant en effet que d'éléments inférieurs à une preuve : les indices.[23]

Puisque les auteurs distinguent les indices dubitables des indubitables,[24] pourquoi ces derniers ne pourraient-ils pas fonder une condamnation ? Pour sa part, Amigant estime que si deux témoignages permettent de prononcer la peine ordinaire, les dépositions d'un seul témoin doivent donner lieu à une peine extraordinaire.[25] De la sorte, certains éléments de conviction insuffisants pour justifier une peine ordinaire, car ils sont au mieux une *semiplena probatio*, vont fonder une condamnation à une peine extraordinaire, plus douce.

Puis, le juge catalan est conduit très rapidement à condamner à la peine ordinaire, même lorsque celle-ci est la mort.[26] Quelles sont alors les preuves nécessaires ? Amigant affirme qu'un seul indice indubitable fondé sur une présomption légale est suffisant pour prononcer la peine capitale.[27] Ceci ne semble pas concerner la conviction du juge puisqu'il a, le cas échéant, les « mains

[23] Cortiada, Miquel de : Decisiones Reverendi Cancellarii et Sacri Regii Senatus Cathaloniae. Barcelone 1661, pars II, p. 228. Decisio LXXXVII n°38. L'auteur cite une décision semblable du 7 février 1607 à l'encontre de Iacobum Ianer, un mineur.

[24] Les auteurs procèdent à différentes classifications en fonction de la force des indices. Certains emploient également les expressions d'adminicules, de conjectures ou encore de suspicions pour qualifier ces éléments de preuve. Noguer avoue que ces différents termes « sont pris le plus souvent pour la même chose, savoir pour toutes les circonstances qui rezultent des faits qui ont précédé, accompagné ou suivi le crime et qui peuvent servir à le constater ». Toutefois, « comme ces circonstances peuvent être plus ou moins fortes, l'on a fait trois distinctions », entre indices généraux et indices particuliers au crime, entre indices « indubités » (véhéments), et indices « dubités » et enfin entre indices prochains et indices éloignés. (A.D.P.O. MS 21. Noguer, Francesc : Traité des crimes, suivant la jurisprudence de la Cour du Conseil souverain de Roussillon, s. l., s. d., f°126. « Des preuves » article 14).

[25] Amigant i de Ferrer, Pere d' : Decisionum et enucleationum criminalium congeries seu praxis Regii Criminalis Concilii Cathaloniae curiarum inferiorum necnon aliorum tribunalium, ecclesiasticorum, et secularium. Barcinone, ex Typographia Iosephi Llopis, 1697, volumen 2, p. 133. Decisio L n°2. « ... igitur si duo testes sufficiunt pro poena ordinaria infligenda, unico tantum dato extraordinaria applicanda venit ».

[26] Durand, Bernard : Arbitraire de la peine et peine de mort en Roussillon. In : Confluence des droits savants et des pratiques juridiques, Actes du Colloque de Montpellier (12-14 décembre 1977), Milan 1979, pp. 91-120.

[27] Amigant i de Ferrer, Pere d' : Decisionum et enucleationum criminalium (cf. n. 25), volumen 2, p. 49. Decisio XLI n°33. « Posse ex praesumptione iuris, & de iure condemnationem in poenam ordinariam inferri ». L'auteur allègue Farinacius, Clarus, Tiraqueau...

pour ainsy dire liées ».[28] La présomption de l'homme ne saurait en effet contrer une présomption légale. Relativement aux délits occultes et de preuve difficile, quand la loi ne qualifie pas un indice de pleine preuve, le juge peut infliger la peine ordinaire à partir d'indices indubitables.[29] La juridiction barcelonaise n'éprouve pas davantage de difficultés à condamner à la peine ordinaire sur la base d'un seul témoin *de visu* accompagné d'autres indices *in sua specie perfectè probatis*. Franciscum Bou fut ainsi condamné à mort pour uxoricide le 27 mai 1621.[30] Ces éléments de preuve, qu'ils soient un témoignage unique ou des indices indubitables, demeurent de forts éléments de conviction.[31]

---

[28] A.D.P.O. MS 21. Noguer : Traité des crimes (cf. n. 24), f°131.

[29] Cela est non seulement vrai pour le Conseil criminel de Catalogne, mais encore pour les juges inférieurs. Cortiada : Decisiones reverendi Cancellarii (cf. n. 23), p. 307. Decisio XCIII n°37. « Nisi à lege aliquod indicium pro plena probatione qualificaretur, nam tunc non solum Senatus Supremus, verum etiam Iudices inferiores possunt ex indiciis indubitatis, in delictis occultis, & difficilis probationis poenam ordinariam imponere ». Farinacius refuse d'accorder cette compétence aux juges inférieurs : « ubi essemus in Iudicibus ordinariis, & hanc plenariam potestatem non habentibus, advertas tu Iudex, nunquam recedere a prima opinione, etiam quod delictum esset capitale, & atrocissimum » (Farinacius, Prosper : Praxis, et theoricae criminalis amplissimae, Lugduni, Sumptibus Horatii Cardon, 1613, pars III, p. 83. Quaestio 86 n°117).

[30] Cortiada : Decisiones Reverendi Cancellarii (cf. n. 23), pp. 307-308. Decisio XCIII n°38. Peguera, *Decisiones....* f°20-23. Decisio XVII. Ces auteurs allèguent Farinacius, selon qui il y a deux doctrines (Farinacius, Prosper : Praxis, et theoricae (cf. n. 29), p. 73. Quaestio 86 n°3) : « Indicia, probationes, seu praesumtiones plures diversae speciei, quarum singulae de per se ad condemnandum non sufficiunt, nec etiam coniunguntur, ut simul iunctae sufficiant » et « in criminalibus habeat locum regula, si non prosunt singula, iuvant, & sic q etiam ad condemnandum, fiat coniunctio imperfectarum probationum indiciorum, & praesumtionum ». L'auteur les concilie. Selon lui, il ne faut pas s'écarter de la première opinion, mais « nisi tamen indicia & praesumtiones, non solum sint in genere suo perfecte probatae, iuxta ea, *quae tradit Peguer in loco nunc citato*, sed etiam sint violentissime, *iuxta tradita infra numer.55* quia tunc coniunguntur, & sufficiunt ad condemnandum, ut in dictis locis, quo ad poenam pecuniariam, licet non quoad corporalem, *prout etiam dixi infra numer.78 & seq* ». Quaestio 86 n°23 (p. 75) : « ut nec semiplena probatio, ut puta unus testis de visu cum aliis adminiculis coniungatur ad effectum condemnandi » à concilier avec « semiplena probatio unius, puta testis de visu cum aliis adminiculis coniungatur, & sufficiat ad condemnandum ». Selon lui, ces deux opinions concernent respectivement les peines corporelles et pécuniaires.

[31] Contrairement à la doctrine catalane qui exige des indices forts pour prononcer une peine ordinaire, le Conseil souverain se contente régulièrement d'indices assez faibles. V. Lloansi, Bernard : La preuve en matière de fausse monnaie d'après la jurisprudence du Conseil souverain du Roussillon, in Revue historique de droit français et étranger, n° 1-1993, p. 60.

En revanche, l'utilisation d'indices dubitables, regroupés par le juge supérieur pour en former un indubitable, constitue une évolution remarquable. Déjà affirmée au XVIe siècle, cette opinion devient prépondérante à la fin du XVIIe siècle.[32] Un doute subsiste cependant relativement à la peine pouvant être prononcée. Pour Calderó, il s'agit de la peine ordinaire.[33] Cortiada acquiesce, mais seulement concernant les délits occultes et de preuve difficile. Ainsi, Petrus Barber fut condamné le 4 mai 1616 à la peine ordinaire.[34] Au XVIIIe siècle, Noguer s'accommode de la peine ordinaire, à condition cependant que ces indices dubitables soient accompagnés d'indices prochains.[35] De son côté, Jaume relate une décision condamnant à une peine extraordinaire de dix années d'exil et mille livres d'amende, pour un empoisonnement, sur le fondement de plusieurs indices dubitables. Le doute était tel que les médecins affirmaient même dans leurs rapports qu'il n'y avait aucune trace de poison dans le cadavre.[36] L'auteur facilite encore la répression en admettant, ponctuellement il est vrai, une condamnation à mort sur le fondement d'indices dubi-

---

[32] Par exemple, Iosephus N. est condamné à mort le 12 septembre 1679 « ex indiciis dubitatis, quae constituunt unum indubitatum, concurrentibus aliis probationibus, & adminiculis ». L'homicide était « proditorium ex sui natura » et était de preuve difficile « actu, & habitu » (Calderó : Sacri Regii Criminalis Concilii (cf. n. 17), p. 76. Decisio VIII n°64).

[33] Calderó : Sacri Regii Criminalis Concilii (cf. n. 17), p. 361. Decisio XLIV n°5. « Imo etiam in delictis difficilis probationis, quamvis indicia non sint omnino indubitata, sufficit quod sint plura indicia dubitata, ex quibus resultet unum indubitatum, et adsint aliae probationes, & adminicula ».

[34] Cortiada : Decisiones Reverendi Cancellarii (cf. n. 23), p. 307. Decisio XCIII n°36. « In delictis occultis, & difficilis probationis, quamvis indicia non sint omnino indubitata, sufficit, quod sint plura indicia dubitata, ex quibus resultet unum indicium indubitatum, & adsint aliae probationes, & adminicula, ut quis possit condemnari poena ordinaria delicti ». La décision du Conseil criminel est du 4 mai 1616 pour Petrum Barber et du 28 mars 1628 pour Ioannem Alzina Flassaderium. L'auteur allègue Farinacius, Xammar, Tristany, ou encore Guazzini.

[35] A.D.P.O. MS 21. Noguer, Francesc : Traité des crimes (cf. n. 24), f°135. « Des preuves » articles 25, 27 et 28. Il en est ainsi du dire ou de l'assertion du plaignant accompagné d'indices prochains et éloignés « tendant tous à la même preuve » lorsque le prévenu est contumax. Il en est de même en présence d'indices dubitables prochains et véhéments en grand nombre, chacun étant prouvé par deux témoins si le crime est grave et de preuve difficile. Enfin, cela est possible avec des indices dubitables, même légers et éloignés, mais assistés d'indices prochains s'ils sont en grand nombre et liés, bien que certains soient prouvés par un seul témoin.

[36] A.D.P.O. MS 40. Jaume, Dictionnaire des arrêts. Empoisonnement. Le Conseil souverain de Roussillon s'est prononcé ainsi le 31 octobre 1689 (de Vilar, décision 350).

tables et de preuves imparfaites. La justification réside alors dans l'atrocité du crime, sa fréquence, sa commission de nuit et « surtout le bruit qui s'était répandu d'abord après le crime ayant été pleinement prouvé ».[37]

A défaut de pleine preuve du crime, le juge peut désormais condamner sur le fondement d'indices. Cette esquisse d'un système d'intime conviction est en contradiction avec le système des preuves légales. Le refus d'absolution entraîne donc un contournement de l'ancienne procédure, devenue une gêne, et appelle l'élaboration de nouvelles règles pour garder la mémoire du crime.

II. Garder la mémoire du crime

Lorsqu'il s'agit de prouver le passé de l'accusé, le juge pénal délaisse rapidement le système des preuves légales. Des éléments de preuve contestés vont désormais forger sa conviction. Rendant le témoignage plus aisé et abandonnant la recherche systématique de l'aveu, les auteurs reconnaissent également la possibilité de transiger avec l'accusé sur l'acte commis. Le souvenir du crime s'effectue alors par un assouplissement des exigences probatoires (A) et par la collaboration de l'accusé (B).

A. L'assouplissement des exigences probatoires

La Catalogne du XVIe siècle est le théâtre d'une transition de l'objectivité à la subjectivité de la preuve. Le juge convaincu de la culpabilité de l'accusé se fonde désormais sur des éléments de preuve imparfaits pour le condamner. Cet assouplissement des exigences probatoires concerne le témoignage comme l'aveu.

En premier lieu, il y a ouverture de la recevabilité des témoignages. Peguera rappelle qu'il faut deux témoins idoines pour avoir une *probatio legitima*.[38] Dans

---

[37] A.D.P.O. MS 40. Jaume, Dictionnaire des arrêts. Indices n°2. « Quelquefois meme sur des indices douteux et des preuves imparfaites, en les comparant et combinant tous ensemble, on condamne un prévenu a mort ». La décision du Conseil souverain de Roussillon date du 16 février 1705 (de Vilar, décision 248).

les crimes, on ne conjugue pas selon lui les preuves imparfaites pour en constituer une parfaite. Il reconnaît pourtant que cette exigence reste théorique et que le juge s'est rapidement affranchi de ce carcan. Le 20 août 1582, le Conseil criminel condamna ainsi Monferratum Bertran à être suspendu par le cou à la haute fourche. Les juges disposaient à son encontre d'un témoin *de veritate facti*, soit une *semiplena probatio*, ainsi que de deux témoins *de tempore et loco contestes* spécifiant qu'il avait avoué extrajudiciairement avoir tué son père Petrum Bertran. Ces deux *semiplena probationes* conjuguées avec d'autres indices constituaient une *probatio in sua specie perfecta.*[39] L'absence de deux témoins idoines ne fut pas même mentionnée. La liberté accrue de la preuve a encore des conséquences sur les témoins inhabiles. Sans ambages, le juge prend en considération des dépositions n'obéissant pas à toutes les exigences. Jaume fait fi des doutes légitimes face aux dires d'un ivrogne. Selon lui, l'ivrognerie n'est un reproche que dans la mesure où le témoin boit « par habitude et ordinairement » et était en ébriété concomitamment aux faits relatés.[40] Càncer estime quant à lui que la pauvreté du témoin ne diminue nullement la valeur de sa déposition, s'il n'est pas une vile personne,[41] ou encore que le nombre de témoins pallie leur inhabileté. Ainsi, trois témoins domestiques peuvent former la pleine preuve d'un délit, alors qu'ils sont en théorie reprochables du fait de leur lien

---

[38] Peguera, Lluís de : Decisiones aurae civiles et criminales in actu practico frequentissimae. Augustae Taurinorum, Ioannem Dominicum Tarinum, 1613, pars I, f°23. Decisio XVII n°38. « Nam sufficiens probatio regulariter dicitur illa quae sit per duo testes ». Dans les affaires criminelles, les preuves devant être *luce meridiane clariores*, « nô sufficerêt ad huc duo testes, nisi illi essent idonei, & omni exceptione maiores : quia aliàs non diceretur legitima probatio ».

[39] Peguera : Decisiones aurae civiles (cf. n. 38), f°23. Decisio XVII n°45. « ... dictas probationes posse coniungi ad faciendâ plenam, & sufficientem probationem ad condemnandum poena ordinaria delicti ».

[40] A.D.P.O. MS 40. Jaume, Dictionnaire des arrêts. Témoins n°4. L'auteur cite une décision en matière civile du Conseil souverain de Roussillon du 11 septembre 1693, Jacob Cornet et Jean Dotras (de Vilar, décision145).

[41] Càncer, Jaume de, Variarum resolutionum iuris caesarei, pontificii et municipalis Principatus Cathaloniae, Lugduni, sumpt. Ant. Pillehotte & Ioan. Caffin, 1626, pars I, p. 207. Cap. XX n°60. « Paupertatem non diminuere testis fidem : nisi cum paupertate vilitas personae concurrat ».

avec la victime.[42] Il faut signaler que l'avocat barcelonais est sur ce point en total désaccord avec son contemporain Peguera.[43] En plus d'admettre qu'un témoignage unique soit complété par l'adjonction d'autres éléments,[44] Calderó assouplit l'exigence de concordance entre les témoignages. Pour lui, il est admissible que l'un des témoins dépose plus que l'autre, car il est possible qu'il ait vu ou entendu plus que l'autre. Le cas échéant, les témoignages ne doivent pas être considérés comme contraires.[45] Dans son *Traité des crimes*, Noguer explique pour sa part qu'il est nécessaire qu'il y ait moins de *testes inhabiles* au criminel qu'au civil.[46] La sauvegarde des intérêts de l'Etat est à ce prix.

Si les déclarations des complices ne sont généralement pas considérées, jointes à d'autres indices ou à l'infamie, elles permettent pourtant la condamnation à la peine ordinaire selon Peguera[47] et Calderó[48]. Une telle décision est envisageable sans torture, mais les complices doivent tout de même prêter serment. Cette prise en compte se justifie par leur connaissance de la vérité,

---

[42] Càncer : Variarum resolutionum iuris caesarei (cf. n. 41), p. 208. Cap. XX n°62. « Testium numerus supplet defectum inhabilium, qui tamen non sunt omnino inhabiles ». A condition que l'inhabileté ne soit pas entière.

[43] Peguera : Practica criminalis (cf. n. 1), f°59. Cap. XII §.5 n°20. En plus de Balde et Farinacius, le Digeste est allégué. D., 43, 26, 5 : « Sed si manente adhuc precario tu in ulterius tempus rogasti, prorogatur precarium : nam nec mutatur causa possessionis et non constituitur eo modo precarium, sed in longius tempus profertur. si vero praeterita die rogas, propius est, ut soluta iam causa precarii non redintegretur, sed nova constituatur ».

[44] Calderó : Sacri Regii Criminalis Concilii (cf. n. 17), pars I, p. 70. Decisio VIII n°25. L'auteur rapporte que le Fisc estime qu'il suffit de la déposition d'un témoin sur le lieu pour constituer une demi preuve car on supplée à l'idonéité du témoin par d'autres indices et adminicules. Ces derniers sont la *fama* prouvée par cinq témoins, l'aveu extrajudiciaire *per tres contestes*, la fuite immédiate du lieu du délit, la cache dans un lieu d'immunité ou encore le mensonge *in substantialibus*.

[45] Calderó : Sacri Regii Criminalis Concilii (cf. n. 17), pars I, p. 71. Decisio VIII n°33. « Et licet non dicantur testes contrarii, quando unus deposuit plus altero, cum stare possit, quod unus audierit, vel viderit, quod alter non vidit, nec audivit ».

[46] A.D.P.O. MS 21. Noguer : Traité des crimes (cf. n. 24), f°121. « Des preuves » article 7.

[47] Peguera : Decisiones aurae civiles (cf. n. 38), f°8. Decisio V n°38. « ... cum delicta quae tot in hac provincia frequentantur aliter probari nô possint, quam dictis sociorum : ideo in dicto Regio consilio est receptum, eis concurrentibus aliis adminiculis, tâtam fidem quantam aliis esse dandam : etiam ad condemnandum poena ordinaria ».

[48] Calderó : Sacri Regii Criminalis Concilii (cf. n. 17), pp. 151-152. Decisio XVI n°27. « ... in delictis, quae non sunt difficilis probationis, in quibus condemnatur ad poenam ordinariam, ex tribus sociorum dictis, concurrentibus indiciis, seu adminiculis ».

meilleure que celle de quiconque, hormis l'accusé. En outre, la preuve est parfois impossible autrement. L'argument selon lequel les complices sont infâmes à cause de leurs actes est donc écarté. Le 14 juillet 1582, Ioannem Planes, un marin, fut condamné à mort par la suspension à la haute fourche pour un *furtum magnum*[49] commis de nuit. La preuve fut établie par les dires des complices de l'accusé selon lesquels il avait l'habitude d'errer avec eux dans la région pour commettre ce genre d'exactions.[50] Pour condamner, des témoins reprochables peuvent également être joints avec d'autres indices, comme la *mala fama* de l'accusé.[51] S'il est vrai que les droits savants avaient très tôt adapté les règles relatives au témoignage,[52] il est indéniable que la percée s'élargit.

L'assouplissement concerne, en second lieu, les moyens de contourner le défaut d'aveu de l'accusé. Le juge estimant en l'espèce qu'il est probable, sinon possible, que le crime ait été commis par le patient soumis à la torture, il lui faut trouver un moyen d'utiliser à nouveau les indices. Il a alors la possibilité de « réserver » les éléments de preuve déjà établis.[53] De la sorte, la torture ne purgera pas les indices en cas d'absence d'aveu, car ce sont ces mêmes éléments qui justifieront une condamnation à une peine extraordinaire. Cette décision de réserve doit impérativement être prise avant le recours à la torture. Le juge convaincu en partie ou en totalité de la culpabilité du patient va ainsi prononcer une peine sur le seul fondement des indices, adminicules ou « semi pleines » preuves qui avaient permis la question préparatoire. Il semble alors

---

[49] Il s'agit du vol d'un *minimum* de 100 livres.

[50] Peguera : Decisiones aurae civiles (cf. n. 38), f°8. Decisio V n°39. Le condamné « erat valde malae famae et opinionis » et était en outre accusé de plusieurs délits. Decisio XXVII n°8. Peguera précise cependant que le Conseil n'accepte pas systématiquement cette preuve : « alias enim regium consilium regulariter non solet sociis criminum contra consocios fidem adhibere, ad condemnandum poena ordinaria, nisi quod sint numero tres & aliis indiciis, & adminiculis, adminiculati, & fomentati ».

[51] Calderó : Sacri Regii Criminalis Concilii (cf. n. 17), p. 70. Decisio VIII n°25. Calderó rapporte que le Fisc estime qu'il suffit de la déposition d'un témoin *super explicatione loci* pour constituer une demi preuve car on supplée aux reproches du témoin par d'autres indices et adminicules. Ces derniers sont la *fama* prouvée par cinq témoins, l'aveu extrajudiciaire *per tres contestes*, la fuite immédiate du lieu du délit, la cache dans un lieu d'immunité ou encore le mensonge *in substantialibus*. Tout cela ne prouve pourtant pas la qualité du délit.

[52] Schnapper, Bernard : Testes inhabiles (cf. n. 5), pp. 575-616.

[53] Durand, Bernard : Arbitraire du juge (cf. n. 53), p. 154.

probable que la diminution sensible de l'utilisation de la torture à partir du seizième siècle soit la conséquence de cette nouvelle pratique.[54] En effet, il n'y a dès lors pour le juge plus aucune raison d'avoir recours aux tourments, puisque les éléments lui permettant d'ordonner ce moyen d'instruction sont intrinsèquement suffisants pour condamner. Dans ces conditions, ce procédé constituerait un sadisme inutile, voire de l'inconscience dans l'hypothèse où le juge omettrait de prononcer préalablement la réserve de preuves : la seule option serait alors d'absoudre l'accusé.[55]

Désormais, certains reproches faits aux témoins et l'absence d'aveu ne sont plus un obstacle à la condamnation de l'accusé. Par ailleurs, il est parfois possible pour le juge de se reposer sur la collaboration de l'accusé.

B. La collaboration de l'accusé

Le souvenir du crime est parfois facilité par l'accusé lui-même, par son consentement à une peine. Les éléments probatoires en présence permettent ainsi une condamnation. Les criminalistes parviennent à justifier l'utilisation de ces pactes et même à les concilier avec la nécessité de ne laisser aucun crime impuni.

Des pactes avec l'accusé sont d'abord tolérés pour atténuer la peine prononcée. Peguera traite des accords passés entre le procureur fiscal et l'accusé. Ce dernier s'impose lui-même une condamnation au bannissement[56] ou à la relégation sur une île. Les deux peines sont infligées à temps et la relaxe des prisons est alors prononcée.[57] Cette solution est retenue lorsque le juge ne parvient pas à convaincre l'accusé d'un crime dont il est pourtant fortement *infamatus*.[58] Le procédé semble en contradiction avec la qualité de crime public

---

[54] Durand, Bernard : Arbitraire du juge (cf. n. 53), p. 178.

[55] V. Durand, Bernard (sous la direction de) : La torture judiciaire, Lille 2002, 2 volumes.

[56] Il peut s'agir d'un bannissement du royaume ou de la viguerie.

[57] Peguera : Practica criminalis (cf. n. 1), f°84. Cap. XII §.15 n°8. « Relaxantur à carceribus plures qui voluntariè suscipiunt bannimenta extra Regnum vel Vicariam, aut suscipiunt relegationem in insulam per aliquod tempus ».

[58] Peguera : Practica criminalis (cf. n. 1), f°84. Cap. XII §.15 n°8. « In quibus mutoties à Regio consilio audiuntur illi qui convici non possunt de criminibus pro quibus detinentur, sunt tamen de

qui interdit en principe de transiger sur des atteintes considérées comme impliquant l'ordre public. Néanmoins, ce n'est nullement une transaction privée entre l'accusé et la victime, qui reste illicite, mais une discussion de la peine menée par la partie publique.[59]

Certains crimes sont tels qu'il est préférable d'atténuer la peine de l'un des responsables, dont la culpabilité est certaine, afin de connaître l'identité d'autres auteurs de l'infraction. Selon Noguer, il est même permis de promettre l'impunité dans le pacte passé avec l'accusé. Il précise néanmoins que ceci est une prérogative des cours souveraines qui « peuvent quelques fois se dispenser de la rigueur des loix et des ordonnances par des raisons particulières ».[60] Le magistrat admet que « ces cas sont très rares et ne peuvent avoir pour objet que la tranquilité publique et le bien de l'Etat ». Ainsi, les autorités avaient découvert, durant l'année 1664, une conspiration visant à livrer Perpignan aux espagnols. La ville n'était en effet que nouvellement rattachée à la France et le Traité des Pyrénées ne s'appliquait pas sans heurts. Les tensions étaient encore grandes. L'un des conjurés, réfugié en Espagne, proposa alors aux juges du Conseil souverain de Roussillon de revenir en France afin de livrer les noms de ses complices. Son impunité fut exigée en contrepartie. La juridiction accepta car « le crime était trop énorme et les suites de trop grande conséquence[61] ». L'impunité d'un seul des responsables était préférable à celle de l'ensemble des auteurs. Le procédé est d'une efficacité remarquable. Cette pratique des pactes se retrouve notamment dans le royaume de Naples. Lorsque le nombre de détenus en attente d'un jugement est trop important, il est possible de conclure un *Truglio*. Nico Perrone explique qu'il s'agit d'un accord sur la peine à infliger, passé entre l'accusateur et l'accusé, sur la seule base des

illis multum infamati, & alias malae famae, & conditionis., ut sic Respublica malis purgetur hominibus ». La justification est donc ici encore de purger la province des « mauvais hommes ».

[59] Peguera se réfère au Digeste pour appuyer sa démonstration. D., 1, 18, 13 : « Congruit bono et gravi praesidi curare, ut pacata atque quieta provincia sit quam regit. quod non difficile obtinebit, si sollicite agat, ut malis hominibus provincia careat eosque conquirat : nam et sacrilegos latrones plagiarios fures conquirere debet et prout quisque deliquerit in eum animadvertere, receptoresque eorum coercere, sine quibus latro diutius latere non potest... ».

[60] A.D.P.O. MS 21. Noguer : Traité des crimes(cf. n. 24), f°92.

[61] A.D.P.O. MS 21. Noguer : Traité des crimes (cf. n. 24), f°93.

indices ayant conduit à l'accusation.[62] Ce procédé extraordinaire a son utilité, selon Pagano, à cause de la difficulté d'obtenir une pleine preuve au pénal.[63]

Ainsi, les criminalistes catalans ont œuvré contre l'oubli du crime, cette conséquence de la mise à l'écart de certains éléments de preuve considérés comme imparfaits. Commençant par ne pas absoudre complètement, le juge prononce par la suite des peines extraordinaires puis ordinaires. La mise en place progressive de nouvelles règles pour prouver le passé de l'accusé permet de garder la mémoire du crime. Tout est fait pour concilier le *Ius commune*, la pratique catalane et la législation royale. La doctrine catalane a démontré de grandes facultés pour appliquer avec souplesse les principes parfois opposés qui y sont contenus. Certaines exigences théoriques se sont effacées devant les nécessités de la pratique, pour que le crime soit prouvé, le criminel châtié et qu'aucun crime ne demeure impuni.

---

[62] Perrone : Il truglio. Infami, delatori e pentini nel Regno di Napoli. Palermo 2000, pp. 60-80.

[63] Pagano emploie pour sa part les termes de « transazione » ou de « concordia ». Selon lui, « par sicuro, che la transazione non sia inutile ne' criminali giudizj, soprattutto ne' stati, ove per la pubblica corruzione è malagevole acquistare intiera pruova ». Cité par Perrone : Il truglio (cf. n. 62), p. 63.

Welche Republik? Der Bezug auf republikanische Traditionen im französischen Verfassungsrecht nach dem Zweiten Weltkrieg

Thilo Engel

Die Frage „Welche Republik?“, „Quelle République?“ ist eine von drei oft zitierten Fragen, die der französische Öffentlichrechtler Jean Rivero im Jahre 1972 formulierte[1]. Ein Jahr zuvor, am 16. Juli 1971, hatte das französische Verfassungsgericht, der *Conseil constitutionnel*, eine Entscheidung gesprochen, die eine neue Epoche in der Geschichte der französischen Verfassungsgerichtsbarkeit einläutete[2]. Es war die erste Entscheidung, in der der *Conseil constitutionnel* ein vom Parlament verabschiedetes Gesetz für nicht verfassungskonform erklärte. Die Begründung war, das neue Gesetz verstoße gegen ein Grundprinzip der Republik, genauer, gegen ein „von den Gesetzen der Republik anerkanntes Grundprinzip“. Diesen Ausdruck findet man in der französischen Verfassung von 1946, in der das französische Volk sich zu den „von den Gesetzen der Republik anerkannten Grundprinzipien“ bekennt.

Der erste Absatz der Präambel lautet:

„Nach dem Sieg, den die freien Völker über die Regierungen und Staatsformen errungen haben, die versuchten, den Menschen zu versklaven und zu erniedrigen, erklärt das französische Volk erneut, dass jeder Mensch, ohne Ansehen der Rasse, der Religion oder des Glaubens, unveräußerliche und heilige Rechte besitzt. Es bekräftigt erneut feierlich die Rechte und Freiheiten des Menschen und des Bürgers, die die Erklärung der Menschenrechte von 1789

---

[1] Rivero, Jean: Les „principes fondamentaux reconnus par les lois de la République“: une nouvelle catégorie constitutionnelle? In: Recueil Dalloz Sirey (1972) Nr. 41 – chronique, S. 265-268.

[2] Décision n° 71-44 DC du 16 juillet 1971, Rec. 29.

weihte, und die von den Gesetzen der Republik anerkannten Grundprinzipien."[3]

Es gibt drei Gründe dafür, dass dieser Ausdruck der „von den Gesetzen der Republik anerkannten Grundprinzipien" (geläufige französische Abkürzung: „PFRLR") in der Präambel der im Jahre 1946 verabschiedeten Verfassung der französischen Vierten Republik auf dem europäischen Forum junger Rechtshistoriker „Erinnern und Vergessen" von Interesse ist:

1. In Frankreich blieb die Frage nach dem normativen Charakter der Präambel lange eine offene Frage. Doch das änderte sich im Jahre 1971: Das französische Verfassungsgericht, der *Conseil constitutionnel*, entschied, dass die Präambel Rechtscharakter hat. Sie sei so zu verwenden wie die gewöhnlichen Verfassungsartikel. Die Präambel kann also für ein rechtshistorisches Symposium Thema sein, weil sie Rechtscharakter hat.

2. Die Präambel von 1946 ist die Präambel der Verfassung der Vierten Republik. In der Vierten Republik gab es noch keine effektive verfassungsgerichtliche Kontrolle der Legislative. Deshalb war während der gesamten Dauer der Vierten Republik die Frage nach dem Verfassungscharakter der Präambel nicht akut. Im Jahre 1958 nahm das französische Volk eine neue Verfassung an. Seitdem spricht man von der Fünften Republik. Doch die Präambel von 1946 blieb qua Verweis ein Bestandteil der neuen Verfassung. Gleichzeitig führte die Verfassung der Fünften Republik die verfassungsgerichtliche Kontrolle des Gesetzgebers ein. Deshalb war es überhaupt möglich, dass das Verfassungsgericht 1971 die Präambel von 1946 als Grundlage für eine Entscheidung benutzte.

[3] Im französischen Original: „Au lendemain de la victoire remportée par les peuples libres sur les régimes qui ont tenté d'asservir et de dégrader la personne humaine, le peuple français proclame à nouveau que tout être humain, sans distinction de race, de religion ni de croyance, possède des droits inaliénables et sacrés. Il réaffirme solennellement les droits et libertés de l'homme et du citoyen consacrés par la Déclaration des droits de 1789 et les principes fondamentaux reconnus par les lois de la République." Der Verweis auf die Präambel der Verfassung vom 27. Oktober 1946 (Verfassung der Vierten Republik), von der hier der erste Absatz zitiert wird, findet sich im ersten Absatz der Präambel der Verfassung vom 04. Oktober 1958 (Verfassung der Fünften Republik).

3. Die Präambel von 1946 bekennt sich zu den Grundprinzipien der Vorgängerrepublik und bezieht klare Position gegen die gerade überwundene nationalsozialistische Besatzungsherrschaft und das Vichy-Régime. Sie hat also einen klaren Bezug zum Thema des diesjährigen Forums „Erinnern und Vergessen“: Es geht einerseits um die Beseitigung eines Rechts- und Herrschaftssystems und andererseits um das Erinnern an ein anderes, früheres Rechtssystem. Meine Präsentation des Stoffes nimmt sich vorrangig des Aspekts des Erinnerns an. Es geht hier um die Frage, wie eine Tradition entsteht und wie sie sich entwickelt.

Zur Entstehung der Präambel von 1946

Im Jahr 1946, nach der Befreiung von der deutschen Besatzung, mussten die Franzosen übereinkommen, welche Republik sie nun gründen wollten. Alle Mitglieder der verfassunggebenden Versammlung waren sich darin einig, dass sie die Zeit der Besatzung und des Vichy-Régimes deutlich und klar für beendet erklären wollten, und dass nun wieder eine Republik gegründet werden sollte. Doch hinter den feierlichen Erklärungen stehen zum Teil gravierende politische Differenzen innerhalb der verfassunggebenden Versammlung.

Eine strittige Frage war die des Verhältnisses des Staates zur Religion. Teile der politischen Linken hingen einem rigorosen Verständnis der Laizität an, wonach der Staat sich nicht nur passiv aus religiösen Angelegenheiten heraushalten, sondern auch aktiv gegen den Einfluss von Religion auf die Gesellschaft vorgehen solle. Die meisten französischen Privatschulen waren konfessionelle Schulen. Um den Einfluss der Kirche gegebenenfalls in engere Schranken weisen zu können, sprachen sich einige Abgeordnete der Linken gegen die Erwähnung eines Prinzips der Freiheit der Lehre in der Verfassung aus. Die Vertreter der Freiheit der Lehre waren deshalb auf die Stimmen ihrer politischen Gegner angewiesen[4]. Aus diesem Grund brachten sie den Vor-

[4] Conac, Gérard: Le préambule de la Constitution de 1946. Une genèse difficile, un itinéraire imprévu. In: Le préambule de la Constitution de 1946. Histoire, analyse et commentaires, Hrsg. von Gérard Conac, Xavier Prétot, Gérard Teboul. Paris 2001, S. 34. Conac erwähnt, dass die Zent-

schlag ein, in der Präambel allgemein auf die „von den Gesetzen der Republik anerkannten Grundprinzipien" zu verweisen. In diesen Grundprinzipien, so ihre Idee, sei die Freiheit der Lehre enthalten, die in einem Gesetz der Dritten Republik postuliert wurde. Der Verweis auf eine republikanische Tradition war also in gewisser Weise ein Trick, um eine aktuelle politische Forderung durchzusetzen[5].

Ein erster Entwurf einer Verfassung mit einem ausführlichen Grundrechtsteil wurde in einer Volksabstimmung abgelehnt. Deshalb fanden im zweiten Entwurf die Grundrechte, Grundfreiheiten und andere Grundprinzipien ihren Platz in der Präambel. Dieser zweite Entwurf wurde im Volksentscheid am 13. Oktober 1946 angenommen und wurde mit dem 27. Oktober 1946 rechtskräftige Verfassung der Vierten Republik. Die Präambel der Verfassung der Fünften Republik, vom 4. Oktober 1958, verweist in ihrem ersten Absatz auf die Präambel von 1946, die somit Bestandteil der Verfassung der Folgerepublik blieb.

Auf die Frage nach dem Rechtscharakter der Präambeln von 1946 und 1958 wird im folgenden Abschnitt eingegangen.

Zum Beginn der Verfassungsgerichtsbarkeit in Frankreich

Da die oben vertretene These, mit der Entscheidung von 1971 beginne in Frankreich die Ära der verfassungsgerichtlichen Kontrolle des Gesetzgebers, einige Irritation hervorgerufen hat, erscheint es angebracht, hier eine Erklärung einzufügen:

Die im Jahr 1875 erlassenen „Verfassungsgesetze" der Dritten Republik entwarfen skizzenhaft und in äußerster Knappheit die Organisation des Par-

---

rumspartei MRP während des Wahlkampfes für den Volksentscheid zum Verfassungsentwurf auf Kritik von Seiten der katholischen Kirche reagieren musste, weil die Freiheit der Lehre nicht explizit in der Verfassung erwähnt wurde.

[5] Zur Entstehungsgeschichte der Formulierung der „von den Gesetzen der Republik anerkannten Grundprinzipien" im ersten Absatz der Präambel von 1946: Prétot, Xavier: Principes fondamentaux reconnus par les lois de la République. In: Le préambule de la Constitution de 1946. Histoire, analyse et commentaires, Hrsg. von Gérard Conac, Xavier Prétot, Gérard Teboul. Paris 2001, S. 41-57.

laments und der Regierung. Sie wurden auch im folgenden nie ergänzt und deuten bereits an, dass das Verfassungsrecht während der 60 Jahre, die die Dritte Republik dauerte, verglichen mit der Gesetzgebungstätigkeit des Parlaments, nur eine verschwindend geringe Bedeutung hatte. Trotz der engen inhaltlichen Begrenzung des Verfassungstextes und obwohl ein eigenes Verfassungsgericht fehlte, gab es jedoch, insbesondere in den ersten drei Dekaden des 20. Jahrhunderts, wiederholte Versuche von Verfassungsrechtlern, die normative Bedeutung ihres Faches aufzuwerten und allen Gerichten das Recht zuzusprechen, ein Gesetz nicht zu beachten, welches sie für nicht verfassungskonform hielten.

Der Dekan der Juristenfakultät der Universität Paris, Henry Berthélemy, zum Beispiel, verteidigte die sogenannte *exception judiciaire d'inconstitutionnalité*, diese Möglichkeit der Kontrolle der Verfassungsmäßigkeit von Gesetzen durch die einfache Gerichtsbarkeit. Dies tat er unter anderem mit dem Verweis darauf, dass das unumstrittene Recht von Verwaltungsgerichten, gesetzeswidrige Rechtsverordnungen zu ignorieren, im Analogieschluss auch für den Umgang der Gerichte mit verfassungswidrigen Gesetzen gelten müsse. In beiden Fällen gebe es keine eigentlichen Kompetenzstreitigkeiten, sondern nur einen Konflikt zwischen zwei sich widersprechenden Normen, wobei die höher stehende Norm den Ausschlag geben müsse. „Il n'y a pas conflit de pouvoirs; il y a conflit de lois, et ce conflit de lois ne peut être raisonnablement tranché que par l'observation de la loi dont l'autorité l'emporte."[6]

Allerdings fand diese These der Möglichkeit einer dezentralisierten Kontrolle der Verfassungsmäßigkeit von Gesetzen keine Resonanz in der Rechtsprechung. Die *exception judiciaire d'inconstitutionnalité* hat sich in der Rechtsprechung während der Dritten Republik nicht durchgesetzt. Diese Beobachtung formuliert explizit Peter Ernst Goose: „Die Gerichte blieben von dieser Strömung jedoch unbeeinflusst."[7]

Am 16. September 1946 wurde in der Kommission, die den Entwurf der Verfassung der Vierten Republik vorbereitete, ein Änderungsvorschlag ver-

---

[6] Berthélemy, Henry: Les limites du pouvoir législatif. In: Revue politique et parlementaire (1925) tome 125 (=10.Oktober 1925), S. 360.

[7] Goose, Peter Ernst: Die Normenkontrolle durch den französischen Conseil constitutionnel, Berlin 1973, S. 27.

handelt und abgelehnt, mit dem die Abgeordneten Jacques Bardoux und Maurice Petsche das Institut der *exception judiciaire d'inconstitutionnalité* verfassungsmäßig festschreiben wollten[8]. Nach diesem Vorschlag hätten das oberste Verwaltungsgericht, der *Conseil d'État*, für Verwaltungsakte und Regierungsverordnungen und das oberste Gericht der einfachen Gerichtsbarkeit, die *Cour de cassation*, für Gesetze eine Nichtanwendbarkeit aufgrund eines Widerspruchs mit der Verfassung aussprechen können. Im Jahr 1946 stand eine Kontrolle der Verfassungsmäßigkeit von Gesetzen, egal in welcher Form[9], kaum zur Debatte: „ni la tradition judiciaire de respect de la loi ni le dogme rousseauiste de la loi expression de la volonté générale très vivace dans la classe politique et dans la doctrine n'allaient pas dans le sens d'une réponse affirmative“[10]. In Frankreich war und blieb die Auffassung, der Gesetzgeber verkörpere den Souverän, eine starke Tradition[11].

Dennoch kam in der Vierten Republik ein neues Verfassungsorgan auf, das *Comité constitutionnel*. Dieses war in gewisser Weise ein Vorläufer des späteren

---

[8] Conac (wie Fn. 4), S. 30.

[9] Das verfassungsrechtliche Lehrbuch von Georges Burdeau unterscheidet vier mal zwei Arten der Verfassungskontrolle. Darunter findet sich die Alternative „zentral oder dezentral“. Obwohl das Buch in seinem allgemeinen Teil zum Aufbau von Staaten auch eine historische Dimension hat, zieht es die Möglichkeit einer dezentralisierten Verfassungskontrolle für Frankreich nicht einmal in Betracht, sondern stellt zwei Rechtsräume einander klar gegenüber: In einem dezentralisierten Rechtssystem, wie dem der Vereinigten Staaten von Amerika, können und müssen die gewöhnlichen Richter sich weigern ein Gesetz anzuwenden, das sie für nicht verfassungskonform halten. „A ce système s'oppose celui qui est dit ‚centralisé', où le contrôle de constitutionnalité est réservé à une juridiction spécialement créée à cet effet ; C'est celui qui inspire le modèle européen, notamment réalisé en Allemagne, en Italie, en France et en Espagne.“
Burdeau, Georges: Droit constitutionnel. 21. Auflage. Hrsg. von Francis Hamon; Michel Troper, Paris 1988, S. 91.

[10] Conac (wie Fn. 4), S. 29.

[11] Wie lebendig die Idee der Souveränität des Gesetzgebers in Frankreich noch lange blieb, und dass sie nur mühsam von der Idee sich gegenseitig kontrollierender Staatsorgane abgelöst wurde, mag der folgende Zeitungsartikel veranschaulichen: Badinter, Robert: Le pouvoir et le contre-pouvoir. In: Le Monde (23. November 1993). Nachdruck in: Maus, Didier: Les grands textes de la pratique constitutionnelle de la Ve république. Paris 1998, S. 370-371. Der damalige Vorsitzende des *Conseil constitutionnel* sieht sich veranlasst, das Gericht gegen öffentliche Anfeindungen zu verteidigen und die Existenz eines Verfassungsgerichtes, insbesondere in seiner Funktion als Anwalt der Grundrechte im Spiel der Mächte, grundsätzlich zu rechtfertigen.

Verfassungsgerichts der Fünften Republik, des *Conseil constitutionnel*, hatte aber die entgegengesetzte Aufgabe: bei einem Zweifel über die Verfassungsmäßigkeit eines neuen Gesetzes konnte es vom Präsidenten der Republik und dem Präsidenten des *Conseil de la République* gemeinsam angerufen werden und erklären, dass es für das neue Gesetz einer Verfassungsänderung bedarf. Das Gesetz wird in diesem Fall nicht annuliert. Die Aufgabe des *Comité constitutionnel* der Vierten Republik war also weniger, die Verfassung zu schützen, als die Souveränität des Gesetzgebers zu wahren. Die Übereinstimmung von Verfassung und Gesetz sollte nicht durch eine Änderung des neuen Gesetzes, sondern durch eine Änderung der bestehenden Verfassung angestrebt werden[12]. Die Verfassung von 1946 (Art. 91) nimmt zudem ausdrücklich die Präambel von dieser Konfrontation des Gesetzes mit der Verfassung aus, womit der Rechtscharakter der ausschließlich in der Präambel enthaltenen Grundfreiheiten und Grundrechte von vornherein infrage gestellt wurde. Das *Comité constitutionnel* trat während der Dauer der Vierten Republik nur ein einziges Mal zusammen, jedoch nicht um einen Verfassungsänderungsbedarf zu erklären, sondern nur um zwischen der *Assemblée nationale* und dem *Conseil de la République* zu vermitteln[13].

Die Verfassung vom 4. Oktober 1958 und die erste Sanktion des Gesetzgebers durch den *Conseil constitutionnel* auf der Grundlage dieser Verfassung am 16. Juli 1971 markieren also durchaus einen entscheidenden Einschnitt in der Institutionengeschichte der französischen Republiken.

Der *Conseil constitutionnel* hat laut Artikel 61 der Verfassung von 1958 die Kompetenz, ein von beiden Kammern des Parlaments regulär verabschiedetes Gesetz für ungültig zu erklären. Die Entscheidung vom 16. Juli 1971 ist die erste Entscheidung, in der das französische Verfassungsgericht diese Kompetenz einsetzt und ein vom Parlament verabschiedetes Gesetz für nicht verfassungskonform und damit ungültig erklärt. Damit beginnt die Ära der verfassungsgerichtlichen Kontrolle des Gesetzgebers. Zuvor war die Legislative in

---

[12] Vedel, Georges: Manuel élémentaire de droit constitutionnel (1949). Neuauflage hrsg. von Guy Carcassonne; Olivier Duhamel, Paris 2002, S. 127. Burdeau (wie Fn. 9), S. 650 f.

[13] Goose (wie Fn. 7), S. 26 f. Goose stützt sich hier insbesondere auf Lemasurier, Jeanne: La Constitution de 1946 et le contrôle juridictionnel du législateur, Paris 1954.

ihren Entscheidungen souverän. Mit dem Einsetzen der verfassungsgerichtlichen Kontrolle der Gesetzgebung wurde der Gesetzgeber geschwächt.

Die Präambel von 1946 in der Rechtsprechung des *Conseil constitutionnel*

Am 16. Juli 1971 berief sich das französische Verfassungsgericht, der *Conseil constitutionnel*, zum ersten Mal auf die in der Präambel von 1946 erwähnten „von den Gesetzen der Republik anerkannten Grundprinzipien".

Der Gesetzgeber hatte gerade ein Gesetz beschlossen, das besagte, dass die Gründung von Vereinen genehmigungspflichtig sei. Die Gründung eines Vereins konnte laut diesem Gesetz im Vorhinein verhindert werden, bevor der Verein seine Arbeit aufnehmen konnte.

Dieses Gesetz verdrängte ein älteres Gesetz, das noch aus der Dritten Republik stammte, und das ausdrücklich die Vereins- und Versammlungsfreiheit garantierte. Der Senatspräsident übergab das neue Gesetz zur Kontrolle der Verfassungsmäßigkeit an den *Conseil constitutionnel*, und das Gericht folgte den Argumenten der Anrufung: es verkündete in seiner Entscheidung, dass das neue Gesetz nicht verfassungsgemäß sei. Laut der Entscheidung verstieß das neue Gesetz gegen das Prinzip der Vereinsfreiheit, und das Gericht erklärte, dass dieses Prinzip ein von den Gesetzen der Republik anerkanntes Grundprinzip im Sinne der Präambel von 1946 sei.

In der Folge hat der *Conseil constitutionnel* seit 1971 etwa 20 vorgeschlagene Grundprinzipien der Republik geprüft. Heute sind zehn dieser Prinzipien offiziell anerkannt, wie zum Beispiel die Unabhängigkeit der Verwaltungsgerichtsbarkeit, *indépendance de la juridiction administrative*[14], die Rechte der Strafverteidigung, *droits de la défense*[15], die Angemessenheit der Jugendstrafen[16], oder

---

[14] Décision n° 80-119 DC du 22 juillet 1980, Rec. 46.

[15] Décision n° 76-70 DC du 2 décembre 1976, Rec. 39/ JO du 07 décembre 1976, p. 7052.

[16] Décision n° 2002-461 DC du 29 août 2002, JO du du 10 septembre 2002, p. 14953. Dieses Prinzip wurde in der Entscheidung ausführlich an der republikanischen Gesetzgebung vor 1946 dargelegt, wobei auch die Einschränkungen, die in den Gesetzen zu finden sind, hier berücksichtigt werden und in das Prinzip eingang finden. Deshalb schlägt der *Conseil* keine griffige Formulierung vor. Einen Vorschlag für eine solche findet sich z.B. bei Ferdinand Mélin-Soucramanien:

weitere Grundfreiheiten, wie die Freiheit der Lehre, *liberté de l'enseignement*[17], oder die Gewissensfreiheit, die *liberté de conscience*[18].

Neben den von den Gesetzen der Republik anerkannten Grundprinzipien finden sich noch zahlreiche weitere Bestimmungen in den Präambeln von 1946 und 1958 – so zum Beispiel der Verweis auf die Erklärung der Menschenrechte von 1789, die Erklärung der Gleichberechtigung von Mann und Frau, die Verpflichtung des Staates, kostenlose Bildungseinrichtungen bereitzustellen, das Recht jedes Menschen, sich gewerkschaftlich zu organisieren, sowie das Recht auf Asyl. Die Grundrechte und Grundfreiheiten haben ihre verfassungsmäßige Begründung allein in den Präambeln, so dass diese sich zu einer wesentlichen Quelle der Rechtsprechung des *Conseil constitutionnel* entwickelt haben.

Freiheit der Auslegung oder Tradition?

1. Auslegung

Als Beispiel für die Reaktion der Fachöffentlichkeit auf die Entscheidung des *Conseil constitutionnel* von 1971 führe ich den erwähnten Artikel von Jean Rivero an[19]. Jean Rivero kritisierte die Entscheidung des *Conseil constitutionnel*, und zwar aus zwei Gründen: erstens, weil der *Conseil constitutionnel* sich überhaupt anmaßte, ein vom Parlament verabschiedetes, und also demokratisch legitimiertes Gesetz für nichtig zu erklären; zweitens, weil der *Conseil constitutionnel* sich in dieser Entscheidung auf eine Formulierung aus der Verfassung

---

„*proportionnalité des peines applicables aux mineurs*“: Constitution de la République française, Hrsg. von Ferdinand Mélin-Soucramanien, Paris 2004, S. XIV.

[17] Décision n° 77-87 DC du 23 novembre 1977, Rec. 42/JO du 25 novembre 1977, p. 5529.

[18] Wie vorangehende Anmerkung.

[19] Da der Artikel nicht nur einer der ersten war, sondern auch in vielen Veröffentlichungen zum Thema zitiert wird, ist er beispielhaft nicht nur für die direkte Reaktion der Fachöffentlichkeit auf die Entscheidung von 1971, sondern auch für die Weise, in der die Problematik der PFRLR und der verfassungsgerichtlichen Normenkontrolle im allgemeinen in der französischen Fachöffentlichkeit wahrgenommen wird. So wird auf ihn auch in den einschlägigen Handbüchern zum Verfassungsrecht verwiesen, wie z.B. bei: Burdeau (wie Fn. 9), S. 659.

stützte, die alles andere als eindeutig ist. Ein anderer Adressat der Kritik hätten freilich die Verfassungskommissionen von 1946 und 1958 sein können, die mit Texten, deren Bedeutung sich keinem Leser aufdrängt, dem kompetenten Interpreten die größtmögliche Freiheit ließ. Die in der Präambel so allgemein formulierten „von den Gesetzen der Republik anerkannten Grundprinzipien" verleiteten Jean Rivero zu diesen drei Fragen: „Welche Prinzipien? Welche Gesetze? Welche Republik?", „Quels principes? Quelles lois? Quelle République?". Der Autor wies darauf hin, dass aus der Formulierung, die der *Conseil constitutionnel* anwendete, nicht klar hervorgehe, welche Prinzipien der Verfassungsgeber im Blick hatte, als er von den „Grundprinzipien" sprach; auch nicht, um welche Gesetze es sich handelt, in denen man die Anerkennung dieser Prinzipien finden und wie man von diesen Gesetzen ausgehend zu den hinter ihnen liegenden Grundprinzipien gelangen könne. Und welche Republik meinten die Autoren der Verfassung, als sie von „der" Republik sprachen? In der französischen Geschichte gab es schon mehrere Republiken. Für Jean Rivero, der die Bedeutung dieser Entscheidung reduzieren wollte, war die Antwort klar: die Erste und die Zweite Republik lagen schon zu weit zurück, die Vierte Republik konnte nicht gemeint sein, weil die Verfassungsgeber ja gerade erst dabei waren sie zu gründen. Sie konnten, so behauptete Rivero, nur die Dritte Republik im Blick gehabt haben.

Eine eindeutige Antwort kann dem Text nicht entnommen werden, und der *Conseil constitutionnel* hat eigene Antworten gefunden. Er ist dabei nicht der Logik Riveros gefolgt, sondern hat die zeitliche Spanne auch auf Zeiten ausgedehnt, in denen es zwar keine Republik gab, in denen aber Texte verabschiedet wurden, die von einem republikanischen Geist getragen zu sein scheinen[20]. So diente die Erklärung der Menschenrechte von 1789 zur Begründung eines republikanischen Grundprinzips[21], obwohl die Erste Republik erst am 22. September 1792 begann. Das napoleonische Kaiserreich scheint

[20] Einen Überblick über diese Debatte in der verfassungsrechtlichen Literatur bietet: Champeil-Desplats, Véronique: Les principes fondamentaux reconnus par les lois de la République. Principes constitutionnels et justification dans les discours juridiques. Marseille PUAM, Paris Economica, S. 91-94.

[21] Das Prinzip der Gewissensfreiheit (liberté de conscience): Décision n° 77-87 DC du 23 novembre 1977, Rec. 42.

das republikanische Grundprinzip der Rechte der Strafverteidigung hervorgebracht zu haben, ohne dass der *Conseil constitutionnel* den napoleonischen *Code d'instruction criminelle* als Referenz jedoch explizit erwähnte[22]. Die Unklarheiten über den Beginn der Dritten Republik (Republik de facto 1870, de jure 1875, republikanischer Geist ab 1880) konnten nie endgültig behoben werden.

„Welche Republik?" Ich habe die letzte der drei Fragen Riveros an die unklare Formulierung in der Präambel von 1946 als Überschrift für diesen Vortrag gewählt, um ihr einen weiteren Sinn zu geben. Auf die Tradition welcher Republik soll das Verfassungsgericht sich beziehen? Diese ursprüngliche Frage nach den historischen Referenzen ist in der Konsequenz auch die Frage danach, welche Republik das Land in Zukunft haben soll. Selbst wenn zeitlich mit einer klar umgrenzten Dritten Republik bestimmt wäre, auf welche Republik sich die Verfassung allein bezieht, dann müsste doch erneut gefragt werden: „Welche Dritte Republik?". Die zeitliche Epoche muss qualitativ gefüllt werden. In der langen Geschichte der dritten Republik können unterschiedliche Tendenzen des Gesetzgebers ausgemacht werden. Das Herausgreifen einiger seiner Gedanken und deren historische Bewertung als „grundlegende" ist somit auch eine politische Entscheidung.

2. Tradition

Nach der Entscheidung von 1971 fragten sich – wie der Artikel von Jean Rivero belegt – Teile der Fachöffentlichkeit, ob das Verfassungsgericht von nun an immer mächtiger werde. Es wurde von Anfang an klar gesehen, dass die traditionelle Idee der Souveränität des Gesetzgebers (und damit der Schwäche der Verfassung) nun überholt war. 1971 benutzte der *Conseil constitutionnel* die Formulierung aus der Präambel von 1946, die die herausragende Bedeutung des Gesetzgebers der Dritten Republik anerkennt. Doch das Verfassungsgericht gebrauchte diese Formulierung, um die Bedeutung des zeitgenössischen Gesetzgebers zu verringern. Das Bekenntnis zu einer Tradition geschieht hier als ein Bruch mit einer anderen Tradition.

---

[22] Décision n° 76-70 DC du 2 décembre 1976, Rec. 39.

Ein Gesetz vom 1. Juli 1901 erklärte die Vereinsfreiheit. Auf dieses Gesetz berief sich das Verfassungsgericht und erklärte die Vereinsfreiheit zu einem von den Gesetzen der Republik anerkannten Grundprinzip. Indem das Gericht mit Hilfe dieses Prinzips ein Gesetz aus dem Jahr 1971 kassierte, das die Vereinsfreiheit beschränkte, sicherte das Gericht das Fortbestehen des Prinzips der Vereinsfreiheit. Doch im Jahr 1901 war es der souveräne Gesetzgeber, der die Vereinsfreiheit verkündete. Er hätte die Vereinsfreiheit im darauf folgenden Jahr wieder einschränken können. Im Jahr 1971 hatte er diese Kompetenz nicht mehr. Die Bewahrung der republikanischen Tradition der Vereinsfreiheit gelang dem *Conseil constitutionnel* durch den Bruch mit der republikanischen Tradition einer souveränen Legislative. Das Verfassungsgericht zwang also den Gesetzgeber der Fünften Republik, das Prinzip der Vereinsfreiheit aufrechtzuerhalten, das der Gesetzgeber der Dritten Republik einmal aus freien Stücken aufgestellt hat.

Doch wenn eine gesetzgeberische Tradition zur Einwendbarkeit gegen den Gesetzgeber führt und ein Rechtssatz die Stufe vom Gesetz zum Grundprinzip nimmt, dann verändert sich nicht nur die Geltungsebene und der Geltungsbereich dieses Rechtssatzes, sondern auch sein Inhalt. Wenn der *Conseil constitutionnel* sich auf die Suche nach den Grundprinzipien macht, die den Gesetzen der Dritten Republik zugrunde liegen, dann handelt es sich um normale Gesetze, die von den an ihrer Entstehung beteiligten Politikern als gewöhnliche Gesetze gedacht und verstanden wurden. Nie wurden von dem Gesetzgeber der Dritten Republik grundsätzliche und allgemeine Prinzipien formuliert. In der Praxis hat das Verfassungsgericht seit 1971 nach Gutdünken einfache Gesetze, die noch aus der Dritten Republik stammen, in Verfassungsrang erhoben. Dabei hat das Gericht allgemeine Prinzipien formuliert, die in den zugrundegelegten Gesetzen selbst während der Dritten und Vierten Republik nur mit Einschränkungen gegolten haben. Der Gesetzgeber der Dritten Republik schrieb seine Gesetze nicht mit dem Ziel langer Gültigkeit, sondern für den Tagesbedarf – nicht anders als der Gesetzgeber der Fünften Republik, der ein tradiertes Gesetz durch ein neues ersetzen will.

Die Verfassung von 1946 wollte eine Tradition begründen oder fortführen. Sie tat dies – in der Lesart des *Conseil constitutionnel* –, indem sie für den Gesetzgeber eine Zäsur setzte. Die Verfassungstexte von 1946 und 1958 haben den Grundstein zu einer republikanischen Tradition gelegt. Sie besagen, dass die Fünfte Republik sich zu der Präambel der Vierten Republik bekennt und dass die Vierte Republik sich zu den Grundprinzipien der Dritten Republik bekennt. Die Grundüberzeugungen der einen Republik sollten in der Folgerepublik aktuell bleiben. Der Text der Präambel stellt eine Basis für eine republikanische Tradition dar. Doch ohne die Rechtsprechung des Verfassungsgerichtes wäre diese Tradition ein toter Text geblieben, lettre morte, ohne praktische Relevanz. Zwei Faktoren spielen hier zusammen: erstens die Arbeit der Verfassungsgeber, das heißt der Autoren der Verfassung; und zweitens die Arbeit des Verfassungsgerichtes, also des Interpreten der Verfassung. Erst das Verfassungsgericht hat aus dem allgemeinen Bekenntnis der Verfassung zu einer republikanischen Tradition eine rechtliche Realität gemacht und den Text zu einer lebendigen Tradition entwickelt.

Doch nicht anders als die Mitglieder der Kommissionen, die die Texte entwarfen, entscheiden die Akteure der Republik bei der Anwendung dieser Texte im aktuellen Tagesgeschehen, was von dem Vergangenen bewahrt werden solle. Beständig ändert sich das Bild dessen, welcher Art die vergangene Republik war, in deren Tradition die Akteure sich sehen. Der *Conseil constitutionnel* wirkt beim Auffinden neuer von den Gesetzen der Vorgängerrepubliken anerkannter Grundprinzipien als Historiker der Republik und als rechtspolitischer Akteur. In diesem doppelten Sinn kann man sagen: Der *Conseil constitutionnel* schreibt Geschichte.

Schlussüberlegungen: Tradition als Argument

Bei den Mitreferenten Birgit Fastenmayer (bäuerliche „Sitte“ in der Agrarideologie des 19. Jhs. und im NS-Recht) und Thomas Mohr (Wiedererfindung alten keltischen Rechts in der Gründungszeit der Republik Irland) wie auch in diesem Artikel über republikanische Traditionen im französischen Verfassungsrecht wurde ein vorgebliches Anknüpfen an alte Rechtstraditionen als tatsächlich geschichtsferne Rechtfertigungsversuche aktueller politischer Ziele geschildert. Es wirkt in diesen Darstellungen so, als gebe es kein Erinnern. Und es wirkt so, als würde dort, wo es doch ein Erinnern gibt, dieses Erinnern nur ausschnitthaft sein, einem aktuellen Interesse gemäß ausgewählt, und somit in einer Diskussion ohne eigenständigen Wert. Auch in einigen anderen

Beiträgen hat das Erinnern einen schweren Stand, zum Teil aus einem ganz anderen Grund, wie zum Beispiel in Nir Kedars Bericht über religiöses Recht in der israelischen Juristenausbildung und den im politischen und juristischen Tagesgeschehen ergebnislos verhallenden Gutachten von Halacha-Experten. In diesem Bericht wurde eine seriösere Form des Erinnerns als praktisch wirkungslos beschrieben, weil sie in ihrer Traditionalität vielen juristischen und politischen Akteuren und der Öffentlichkeit als wirklichkeitsfern erscheint.

Wenn es wahr ist, dass sich hinter bewusstem und öffentlichem Erinnern oft ein aktuelles Handlungsmotiv versteckt, das wirksam ist, und es andererseits wahr ist, dass ein bewusstes Erinnern ohne ein starkes aktuelles Handlungsmotiv praktisch nicht wirksam wird, und es gar wahrscheinlich scheint, dass bewusstes und öffentliches Erinnern ohne ein aktuelles Handlungsmotiv gar nicht stattfinden würde, dann stellen sich folgende Fragen: Kann das Erinnern also aus Handlungsmotivationen herausgekürzt werden, wenn es nicht selbständig, sondern nur in Verbindung mit einem existierenden aktuellen Handlungsmotiv wirksam ist? Ist Erinnern[23] gar nicht wirksam, weil es nicht selbständig wirksam ist? Oder ist eine Verbindung aus einem Element des Erinnerns und einer aktuellen Handlungsmotivation wirksamer, als diese aktuelle Handlungsmotivation es allein wäre? In diesem Fall wäre das Erinnern dennoch wirksam, wenn auch nicht als ein selbsttragendes Argument.

Jede Tradition ist eine lebendige Tradition. Das heißt, das Fortbestehen einer Denk- oder Handlungsweise gelingt nur um den Preis der kontinuierlichen Veränderung. Wenn Tradition als Argument dient – in rhetorischer Gegenüberstellung, als Objekt, als das Andere, einer aktuellen und persönlichen Handlungsmotivation an die Seite gegeben – dann ist es doch nie das Vergangene selbst, das spricht, nie das Objekt, sondern eine je aktualisierte Erinnerung. Die Erinnerung ist genauso aktuell wie das aktuelle Handlungsmotiv. Dennoch ist es möglich, sie von diesem zu unterscheiden. Eine Erinnerung an eine historische Tatsache oder eine Tradition, die sich bewährt (oder nicht

---

[23] Gemeint ist bewusstes Erinnern. Eine ganz andere Frage wäre die, inwieweit Vergangenes – womöglich mehr als aufgrund bewussten Erinnerns – in automatisch tradierten Denk- und Handlungsweisen gegenwärtig und wirksam bleibt. Dieser Frage kann hier aber nicht nachgegangen werden, da die vorliegende Erörterung sich nur mit dem bewussten Erinnern – insbesondere in der Form des Verweises auf Althergebrachtes in der richterlichen Argumentation – beschäftigt.

bewährt) hat, können als empirische Argumente präsentiert werden und so beanspruchen, wenn schon nicht weniger aktuell, so doch weniger persönlich und weniger willensgesteuert zu sein als die rein persönliche Handlungsmotivation.

Der Versuch, eine Entscheidung oder eine Handlungsempfehlung als historisch legitimiert oder auf andere Weise empirisch oder rational begründbar vorzuweisen, lässt sich als eine Strategie interpretieren, öffentliche Zustimmung zu erreichen, die mit der Äußerung einer rein persönlichen Präferenz nicht erreicht würde. Nicht weniger als die Äußerung einer rein persönlichen Präferenz kann sich auch das Argument der Tradition einer Diskussion entziehen: das gilt für den emphatischen Gebrauch dieses Wortes, der nahelegt, Tradition sei ein eigener Wert, so dass das bloße Bestehen einer Tradition bereits ein Argument für ihr Fortbestehen sei – unabhängig von den historischen Umständen, im Zusammenhang mit diesen nur die Angemessenheit einer Handlungs- oder Denkweise nachgewiesen werden kann. Auch solch ein Bekenntnis zu einer beliebigen Tradition kann ein rhetorisches Mittel zur Erreichung von Zustimmung sein.

Als empirisches Argument dagegen wird die Angemessenheit oder fehlende Angemessenheit einer historischen Tatsache an historische Umstände oder an aktuelle Werte behauptet – dabei handelt es sich um ein Urteil, eine Verknüpfung, die von anderen Menschen, deren Zustimmung der Sprecher sucht, nachvollzogen oder überprüft werden kann. Auch wenn jeder Beteiligte ihn auf seine Weise sieht, wird mit dem historischen Argument ein gemeinsamer Gegenstand geschaffen. Wie groß der empirische Anteil an diesem tatsächlich ist, lässt sich unmöglich ermitteln. Dass die Gegenstände eines historischen Arguments immer auch einen persönlichen Anteil haben, dass sie immer geformt, immer interpretiert sind, ist selbstverständlich. Dass es aber einen empirischen Anteil gibt, bei aller Freiheit der Interpretation offensichtlich doch keine völlige Willkür herrscht, zeigt sich dann, wenn verschiedene Diskussionsteilnehmer an der Reaktion der anderen auf ihre Äußerungen erkennen, dass sie verstanden wurden, wenn sie über die öffentliche Urteilsbegründung sprechen.

Im Fall der von den Gesetzen der Republik anerkannten Grundprinzipien gibt es keinen Unterschied zwischen einer historischen und einer juristischen Herleitung einer Entscheidung, und generell haben die Interpretation von Geschichte und die Interpretation von Texten viel gemein, und das nicht nur, weil die Geschichte oft in schriftlichen Quellen vorliegt. Der Öffentlichrechtler Michel Troper vertritt in spitzem Ton die wohlbegründete These, die *motivation*, die richterliche Entscheidungsbegründung diene der Tarnung einer in Wahrheit freien und willensmäßigen Entscheidung und solle den falschen Eindruck erwecken, dass diese logisch aus dem (z.B. Verfassungs-) Text folge[24].

Wenn eine Entscheidung oder eine Handlungsempfehlung tatsächlich unabhängig ist von ihrer öffentlichen Begründung (Urteilsbegründung, Rede in der Kommission, die einen Verfassungsentwurf ausarbeitet), dann kann diese öffentliche Begründung dennoch ihren Zweck erfüllen, selbst wenn die Adressaten wissen, dass die Begründung nicht die Ursache der Entscheidung oder der Handlungsempfehlung ist. Sicher ist die Entscheidung eines Verfassungsgerichtes allein aufgrund der Macht des Gerichtes gültig. Keine Instanz ist kompetent, die Entscheidung aufzuheben. Mittelfristig jedoch ist auch eine hohe Instanz darauf angewiesen, dass ihre Entscheidungen öffentlich als legitim gelten. Auch jeder Richter an einem Gericht der ordentlichen Gerichtsbarkeit, jeder Jurist, jeder Politiker und jeder Bürger trifft eine freie Entscheidung, wenn er sich sein Urteil zu einer Entscheidung des Verfassungsgerichts bildet. Die juristische Argumentation, die sich in der Entscheidungsbegründung findet, ist dessen ungeachtet der Ort, an dem eine Kommunikation zwischen dem Verfassungsgericht und den Rechtssubjekten stattfindet, auch wenn der Verfassungstext als gemeinsamer Gegenstand mitunter ein schwer fassbarer Gegenstand ist. Der Eindruck, dass verschiedene Textstellen unterschiedlich klar sind und die Beobachtung, dass ihre Interpretation zu unterschiedlich intensiven Diskussionen Anlass gibt, sind ein Indiz dafür, dass es dennoch einen solchen gemeinsamen Gegenstand gibt.

Im Umgang mit der Vergangenheit gilt ähnliches. Erinnerungen sind wirksam. Sie sind weder nur beliebige Konventionen, noch willkürliche persönliche Gedanken. Obwohl sie einen persönlichen Anteil und einen konventionellen Anteil haben, können sie als Argumente Elemente einer Verständigung

---

[24] Troper, Michel: La motivation des décisions constitutionnelles. In: La motivation des décisions de justice. Hrsg. von Chaïm Perelman; Paul Foriers. Bruxelles 1978, S. 287-302.

über Drittes sein. Tradition ist kein Argument, sondern sie bedarf einer Begründung, die zeigt, dass tradierte Denk- oder Handlungsweisen weiterhin maßgeblichen Tatsachen oder Werten angemessen sind. Wie jede andere Entscheidung, fällt die Entscheidung zur Tradition in der Gegenwart.

La scienza giuridica italiana tra ricordo e oblio della legislazione antiebraica

Silvia Falconieri

Questo contributo si propone come una riflessione sull'atteggiamento assunto dai giuristi italiani nei confronti della legislazione antiebraica, predisposta dal governo fascista nel settembre del 1938[1] ed abrogata dal governo Badoglio che, nel gennaio del 1944, con il R.D.L. 25, stabiliva la reintegrazione "nel pieno godimento dei diritti civili e politici" dei cittadini italiani precedentemente qualificati di "razza ebraica o considerati di razza ebraica".[2]

Ricordo e oblio – o, più opportunamente, si potrebbe dire in questo specifico contesto, oblio e ricordo – individuano e riassumono queste distinte fasi e permettono, al contempo, di mettere meglio a fuoco la reazione dei giuristi italiani di fronte alla costruzione giuridica della diversità dell'ebreo. Infatti, da quanto emerge dallo spoglio di alcuni periodici giuridici in uso nella prima metà del XX secolo,[3] l'operato dei giuristi incaricati dell'interpretazione e

---

[1] Una prima stringata definizione di ebreo veniva fornita dall art. 1 del R.D.L. 1390 del 5 settembre 1938, recante le *Disposizioni per la difesa della razza nella scuola fascista.* Una più ampia e articolata formulazione venne, invece, introdotta dall'art. 8 del R.D.L. 17 novembre 1938, n. 1728, con il quale si dettavano i *Provvedimenti per la difesa della razza italiana*, dando forma legislativa alle deliberazioni assunte il 6-7 ottobre 1938 dal Gran Consiglio del Fascismo.
Nell'ambito della storiografia, oramai vastissima, che si è occupata delle vicende legate all'adozione della normativa antiebraica da parte del governo fascista, v. Michaelis, Meir: Mussolini e la questione ebraica. Le relazioni italo-tedesche e la politica razziale in Italia. Milano 1982; De Felice, Renzo: Storia degli ebrei italiani sotto il fascismo. Torino 1993; Sarfatti, Michele: Mussolini contro gli ebrei. Cronaca dell'elaborazione delle leggi del 1938. Torino 1994; Sarfatti, Michele: Gli ebrei nell'Italia fascista: vicende, identità, persecuzione. Torino 2000; Collotti, Enzo: Il fascismo e gli ebrei. Le leggi razziali in Italia. Roma/Bari 2006.

[2] R.D.L. 20 gennaio 1944, n. 25, *Disposizioni per la reintegrazione nei diritti civili e politici dei cittadini e stranieri già dichiarati di razza ebraica o considerati di razza ebraica*, art. 1.

[3] La scelta di concentrare l'attenzione sulle riviste – tanto su quelle di carattere prettamente giurisprudenziale, quanto su quelle consacrate principalmente alla dottrina – è legata alla constatazione

dell'attuazione della legislazione antiebraica appare costantemente guidato da un forte tentativo di rimozione delle categorie di *ebreo* e di *ariano*, dal desiderio di relegare le disposizioni razziali al di fuori del dibattito scientifico. Nell'Italia postfascista, invece, il ricordo delle categorie interpretative introdotte dal legislatore fascista continua a persistere nello strumentario adoperato dai giuristi italiani e guida l'operato di coloro che furono incaricati di procedere all'effettiva cancellazione della dicotomia ebreo/ariano.

A. L'oblio della legislazione razziale nelle riviste giuridiche degli anni '30

Scorrendo le pagine di alcune tra le riviste giuridiche più diffuse negli anni '30 del XX secolo, si è colpiti dalla forte sensazione che una considerevole parte della scienza giuridica italiana si sia dimostrata piuttosto restia a dedicarsi allo studio approfondito e al commento dettagliato della legislazione antiebraica e si sia quasi sforzata di mantenere il dibattito relativo alle nuove disposizioni al di fuori dei tradizionali organi di divulgazione del sapere scientifico.

Sebbene molto dipendesse dalla scelta discrezionale dei singoli comitati direttivi e dalla selezione degli argomenti da essi operata, nelle riviste nate all'inizio del secolo, ad opera di teorici del diritto – per lo più di docenti universitari di un certo rilievo – e dotate di un preciso programma ed indirizzo scientifico, la legislazione antiebraica sembra sprofondare in un completo e deliberato oblio.

---

del ruolo fondamentale da esse svolto nella diffusione e nella costruzione della cultura giuridica nel '900.

Per una ricostruzione del ruolo e della centralità assunta dalle riviste giuridiche nella costruzione e nella diffusione della cultura giuridica italiana tra il XIX ed il XX secolo, v. Quaderni fiorentini per la storia del pensiero giuridico moderno (1984) No. 13, dal titolo *La "cultura" delle riviste giuridiche italiane. Atti del primo incontro di studio. Firenze, 15-16 aprile 1983* e Quaderni fiorentini per la storia del pensiero giuridico moderno (1987) No. 16, volume interamente dedicato alle *Riviste giuridiche italiane (1865-1945).*

È questo il caso della *Rivista di diritto civile*, fondata nel 1909 da tre romanisti tra i quali spiccava il nome di Alfredo Ascoli,[4] noto giurista di origini israelitiche che, svolgendo un ruolo attivo tanto nella gestione degli incarichi redazionali quanto nella costante opera di pubblicazione di interventi dottrinali, sarebbe ben presto divenuto la vera anima del periodico.[5]

La scomparsa del nome di Ascoli dai frontespizi – avvenuta nel 1939 e legata, con ogni evidenza, all'applicazione delle disposizioni antiebraiche[6] – si andava ad inserire in un più ampio e radicale mutamento nella composizione del comitato scientifico. La nuova direzione, nella comunicazione *Ai lettori* posta in apertura del primo numero dell'annata del 1939, prendeva atto dei profondi rivolgimenti in corso nell'ordinamento giuridico italiano: "il vigoroso impulso del Governo Fascista", con la pubblicazione del I libro del codice civile, aveva operato un adeguamento del "sistema positivo del diritto privato ai principii politici e ai rapporti sociali profondamente mutati nello spazio di una generazione".[7] Di qui l'esigenza per la rivista di porsi "nuovi ardui compiti" che, nonostante la persistenza di un "collegamento ideale molto stretto" con il programma originario, mirassero a raggiungere "nuove mete", più adeguate all'avvento di "una nuova fase di attività per la scienza del diritto civile".[8]

---

[4] Su Alfredo Ascoli, v. Abbondanza, R.: Ascoli Alfredo. In: Dizionario biografico degli italiani. Roma 1962, pp. 377-379.

[5] Sulla *Rivista di diritto civile* ed il contributo ad essa fornito da Alfredo Ascoli, v. Furgiuele, Giovanni: La «Rivista di diritto civile» dal 1909 al 1931. «Un organo speciale del movimento scientifico, legislativo e pratico del più importante ramo del diritto positivo» e di «indirizzo» dello stesso nell'Italia giolittiana e del terzo decennio del nuovo secolo. In: Quaderni fiorentini per la storia del pensiero giuridico moderno (1987) No. 16, pp. 519-630.

[6] Con netto anticipo rispetto alla promulgazione dei decreti antiebraici, si era proceduto all'istituzione di una commissione incaricata di provvedere alla bonifica libraria, compilando una lista di autori "non graditi al regime". Sui lavori della commissione incaricata della bonifica libraria, v. Cesari, Maurizio: La censura nel periodo fascista. Napoli 1978. Sulla compilazione delle liste di autori da depennare e sugli ordini impartiti alle biblioteche, v. Di Benedetto, Claudio: Cataloghi di razza. In: Il linguaggio della biblioteca. Scritti in onore di Diego Maltese. A cura di Mauro Guerrini. Firenze 1994, pp. 432-438; Fabre, Giorgio: L'elenco. Censura fascista, editoria e autori ebrei. Torino 1998.

[7] La Direzione: Ai lettori. In: Rivista di diritto civile (1939) No. 1-2, pp. 1-2, qui p. 1.

[8] La Direzione, Ai lettori (nota 7), p. 2.

I primi due numeri dell'annata del 1943 si aprivano con la pubblicazione di un commosso necrologio di Alfredo Ascoli. Anche in quest'occasione l'autore, Giuseppe Osti, evitava accuratamente ogni riferimento alle ragioni che avevano costretto Ascoli ad allontanarsi dalla direzione della *Rivista di diritto civile*.[9]

Il silenzio attorno alle disposizioni antiebraiche era stato interrotto soltanto nell'annata del 1940, con la pubblicazione di una breve recensione[10] – a firma del direttore Antonio Cicu – ad un articolo con il quale il magistrato torinese Alessandro Galante Garrone aveva fornito significative indicazioni interpretative a proposito di alcune questioni sollevate dall'applicazione della nuova normativa.

L'occasione era stata offerta a Galante Garrone da un'innovativa sentenza con la quale la Corte d'Appello di Torino si era pronunciata riguardo al problema dell'attribuzione della competenza ad emettere la declaratoria di appartenenza alla razza ebraica. Si trattava, indubbiamente, di una delle questioni più dibattute nelle aule giudiziarie attorno all'attuazione dei nuovi decreti:[11] l'art. 26 del R.D.L. 1728/'38, infatti, derogando al tradizionale principio di ripartizione dei poteri tra esecutivo e giudiziario, attribuiva al Ministero dell'Interno una competenza piena ed esclusiva nella soluzione delle "questioni inerenti l'applicazione dello stesso decreto".[12]

---

[9] Osti, Giuseppe: Alfredo Ascoli (necrologio). In: Rivista di diritto civile (1943) No. 1-2, pp. 1-4.

[10] Cicu, Antonio: Recensione ad Alessandro Galante Garrone, Questioni sulla appartenenza alla razza ebraica – Competenza dell'autorità giudiziaria e amministrativa – I nati da matrimonio misto – I catecumeni. In: Rivista di diritto civile (1940) No. 2, p. 169.

[11] Per un'indicazione delle principali problematiche, connesse all'applicazione della normativa antiebraica, cfr. Fubini, Guido: La condizione giuridica dell'ebraismo italiano. Milano 1974; Fubini, Guido: Orientamenti giurisprudenziali e dottrina giuridica. In: Il Ponte (1978) No. 11-12, pp. 1412-1425; Lo Giudice, Maria Rosaria: Razza e giustizia nell'Italia fascista. In: Rivista di storia contemporanea (1983) No. 1, pp. 70-90; Fubini, Guido: La legislazione razziale nell'Italia fascista: normativa e giurisprudenza. In: La legislazione razziale in Italia e in Europa. A cura della Camera dei Deputati. Roma 1989, pp. 17-31; Camy, Olivier: La doctrine italienne. In: Le genre humain (1994) No. 30-31, pp. 477-539. Si segnala in proposito il recentissimo e prezioso contributo di Guiseppe Speciale : Giudici e razza nell'Italia fascista. Torino 2007, di cui non si è potuto tener conto, poichè apparso quando il presente articolo era in stampa.

[12] L'art. 26 del R.D.L. 1728/'38 disponeva: "Le questioni relative all'applicazione del presente decreto saranno risolte, caso per caso, dal Ministro per l'Interno, sentiti i Ministri eventualmente interessati, e previo parere della Commissione da lui nominata. Il provvedimento non è soggetto ad

La Corte d'Appello – nella controversia Rosso c. Artom, quella che sarebbe divenuta la *cause célèbre* per eccellenza – era stata chiamata a pronunciarsi sulla possibilità, per i cittadini ebrei, di procedere alla divisione di propri beni posseduti in comune con altri comproprietari, della propria razza o di razza diversa. La questione dell'appartenenza del convenuto alla razza ebraica si poneva in via pregiudiziale: la Corte ammetteva che l'autorità giudiziaria fosse fornita di giurisdizione per conoscere dell'appartenenza di un cittadino italiano alla razza ebraica ogni volta che fosse dedotto in causa un diritto civile o politico, ciò che si era verificato nel caso in questione.

Galante Garrone giudicava la sentenza meritevole di esser "segnalata e meditata", a causa della "novità e della delicatezza delle questioni toccate e per la squisita sensibilità giuridica"[13] alla base della motivazione addotta. Merito della Corte era quello di esser riuscita a mantenersi "fedele al sistema tradizionale" dei principi giuridici dell'ordinamento italiano, dissipando ogni equivoco attorno all'interpretazione dell'art. 26 e mettendo a tacere "quel significato rivoluzionario",[14] latente nella sua formulazione.

Ed è proprio a proposito di quell'intervento che il magistrato torinese, in un contributo da lui fornito ne *La Rassegna Mensile d'Israel*, in occasione del cinquantesimo anniversario della promulgazione della legislazione antiebraica in Italia, ha ricordato come larga parte dei giuristi italiani avesse avvertito nelle disposizioni razziali "una lacerazione dei principi generali (...) pacificamente riconosciuti"[15] da tutta la dottrina giuridica e ha spiegato come quella sua pub-

---

alcun gravame, sia in via amministrativa, sia in via giurisdizionale." Ulteriori precisazioni, relative all'attuazione dell'art. 26, venivano fornite dal legislatore con la L. 13 luglio 1939, n. 1024, recante le *Norme integrative del R. decreto-legge 17 novembre 1938, n. 1728, sulla difesa della razza italiana.* L'art. 1, infatti, si preoccupava di precisare: "Fermo restando il disposto degli articoli 8 e 26 del Regio decreto-legge 17 novembre 1938-XVII, n. 1728, convertito nella legge 5 gennaio 1939-XVII, n. 274, è facoltà del Ministro per l'interno di dichiarare, su conforme parere della Commissione di cui all'art. 2, la non appartenenza alla razza ebraica anche in difformità delle risultanze degli atti dello stato civile."

[13] Galante Garrone, Alessandro: Questioni sulla appartenenza alla razza ebraica – Competenza dell'autorità giudiziaria e amministrativa – I nati da matrimonio misto – I catecumeni. In: Rivista del diritto matrimoniale italiano e dei rapporti di famiglia (1939), pp. 409-418, qui p. 409.

[14] Galante Garrone, Questioni sulla appartenenza alla razza ebraica (nota 13), p. 411.

[15] Galante Garrone, Alessandro: Ricordi e riflessioni di un magistrato. In: La Rassegna mensile d'Israel (1988) No. 1-2, pp. 19-35, qui p. 19.

blicazione del '39, ben lontana dal costituire "un memorabile saggio di sapienza giuridica", volesse essere piuttosto per i colleghi avvocati e magistrati "un suggerimento e un incitamento" ad operare in maniera tale da "arginare, nei limiti del possibile, un'infinitesima parte di quell'infamia".[16] Ecco che quell'articolo, destinato ad incrementare un trend giurisprudenziale più mite che favorisse un raccordo della nuova normativa con i principi dell'ordinamento giuridico liberale, veniva presentato nelle forme di "una innocente nota a sentenza" per poi essere discretamente divulgato "nelle pieghe non sospette di una delle tante riviste giuridiche",[17] come testimoniava, appunto, l'esempio della *Rivista di diritto civile* che, scegliendo di rompere il silenzio proprio in occasione di quella sentenza e recensendo la nota di Galante Garrone, non chiariva semplicemente la propria posizione riguardo ad un particolare aspetto dell'applicazione della normativa razziale ma faceva ulteriormente risaltare il deliberato intento di collocarla al di fuori del proprio programma scientifico.

Nello stesso anno e sempre in occasione della causa Rosso c. Artom, la *Rivista di diritto privato*, giovane periodico, fondato nel 1931, utilizzava un analogo *éscamotage*.[18]

Il nuovo *status* di ebreo non aveva minimamente condizionato l'obiettivo del direttore Rotondi di dar vita ad una rivista che, trovando una "giustificazione" nel "metodo" seguito piuttosto che in uno specifico "programma", avrebbe dovuto contribuire al "progresso"[19] della scienza giuridica. Anzi, la *Rivista di diritto privato*, assumendo un atteggiamento ancor più drastico e radicale di quello manifestato dalla *Rivista di diritto civile*, si presentava come uno spazio completamente impermeabile alle disposizioni varate in "difesa della razza" e alle conseguenze da esse derivanti sul piano della disciplina privatistica. Non solo la legislazione antiebraica era palesemente ritenuta indegna di at-

---

[16] Galante Garrone, Ricordi e riflessioni di un magistrato (nota 15), pp. 30-31.

[17] Galante Garrone, Ricordi e riflessioni di un magistrato (nota 15), p. 32.

[18] Sulla *Rivista di diritto privato*, fondata da Mario Rotondi, ed i suoi rapporti con le direttive fornite dal regime, v. Santarelli, Umberto: «Un illustre (e appartato) foglio giuridico». La Rivista di diritto privato. In: Quaderni fiorentini per la storia del pensiero giuridico moderno (1987) No. 16, pp. 665-715.

[19] La Direzione: Al lettore. In: Rivista di diritto privato (1931), pp. 3-6, qui p. 3.

tenzione scientifica ma le si negava categoricamente anche ogni possibilità di esercitare un condizionamento nell'individuazione e nella scelta dei collaboratori al comitato scientifico.

Che Rotondi si curasse ben poco delle origini razziali dei propri colleghi e dell'intimazione con la quale il suo editore, il dott. Milani, gli aveva chiesto di adeguarsi alle nuove disposizioni, procedendo all'allontanamento dei giuristi ebrei dal comitato direttivo,[20] lo si può rapidamente verificare dai frontespizi della rivista nei quali, nell'infuriare della campagna razziale in Italia, continuavano a comparire nomi di noti ed apprezzati giuristi di origini israelitiche tra i quali spiccava quello dello stesso Alfredo Ascoli.

È proprio in rapporto a questo silenzio, a questa cosciente dimenticanza che, scorrendo gli indici della rivista, colpisce la comparsa della rubrica *razza* nell'annata del 1940.

Tale rubrica rinviava ad un'anonima nota con la quale venivano sapientemente raccordate due sentenze: quella pronunciata dalla Corte d'Appello di Torino nella causa Rosso/Artom e quella emessa, il 16 giugno del 1939, dal Tribunale di Roma che aveva risolto i problemi interpretativi sorti attorno all'attuazione dell'art. 26 in maniera diametralmente opposta rispetto alla corte torinese, negando categoricamente la competenza dell'autorità giudiziaria a conoscere dell'appartenenza di un cittadino italiano alla razza ebraica. L'autore della nota dimostrava di inserirsi in quel filone interpretativo, sostenuto da Galante Garrone, al cui articolo si faceva inevitabilmente riferimento.[21]
Ma quell'intervento offriva al suo anonimo autore l'occasione per assumere una posizione ancora più decisa nei confronti degli stessi presupposti sulla base dei quali era stata costruita la dicotomia ebreo/ariano: era impossibile infatti non rilevare la totale assenza di raccordo tra la nuova normativa antiebraica e le previgenti disposizioni di riordino delle comunità israelitiche, rimaste in vigore dopo il '38. Secondo l'autore, ciò rendeva difficile, quasi impossibile, in Italia poter parlare con esattezza di status di ebreo, dal momento che facilmente poteva accadere che un medesimo soggetto fosse da ritenersi

---

[20] Santarelli (nota 18).

[21] Anonimo: Nota a sent. Corte d'Appello di Torino (5 maggio 1939) e Tribunale di Roma (19 giugno 1939). In: Rivista di diritto privato (1940) No. 1-2, pp. 28-43.

ebreo alla luce delle disposizioni del 1938 e non fosse da ritenersi tale in rapporto alla legge di riordino delle Comunità israelitiche del 1930.[22] La polemica nei confronti di una legislazione che, anziché facilitare l'individuazione dell'ebreo, aveva fatto risaltare il carattere aleatorio di quella qualificazione, balza facilmente all'occhio del lettore: l'espressione *razza ebraica* era accompagnata dalle virgolette, scelta stilistica originale se rapportata agli scritti giuridici di quel tempo.

In seguito a tale intervento, la rubrica *razza* e le disposizioni antiebraiche sparivano nuovamente e definitivamente dalle pagine del periodico di Rotondi.

L'apprezzato e commentato articolo di Galante Garrone aveva trovato spazio nelle pagine della *Rivista del diritto matrimoniale italiano*, periodico che aveva visto la luce nel 1935, proprio negli anni di massimo consenso al regime fascista.

Il suo fondatore, Giovan Battista Cecchi, un avvocato milanese, aveva manifestato una posizione meno drastica nei confronti delle innovazioni legislative introdotte dal governo Mussolini nella convinzione che, in concomitanza con "le modificazioni apportate dalla nuova legislazione all'ordinamento giuridico del matrimonio", compito fondamentale del proprio periodico fosse principalmente quello di fornire "un quadro esatto e completo del movimento di pensiero che si agita intorno alla disciplina giuridica del matrimonio e dei rapporti di famiglia".[23] Nelle dichiarazioni programmatiche della direzione, la

---

[22] Il R.D.L. 30 ottobre 1930, n. 1731, recante le *Norme sulle Comunità israelitiche e sulla Unione delle Comunità medesime,* prevedeva che appartenessero "di diritto" alla Comunità tutti gli israeliti "aventi la residenza nel territorio di essa" (art. 4), lasciando supporre che l'individuazione dell'ebreo dovesse avvenire sulla base del diritto ebraico. Ne conseguiva che, alla luce del R.D.L. 1731/'30, si riteneva ebreo il nato da madre israelita.
Sulla disciplina delle comunità israelitiche, nell'Italia postunitaria, v. Capuzzo, Ester: Gli ebrei nella società italiana. Comunità e istituzioni tra Ottocento e Novecento. Roma 1999. Sui lavori preparatori e la stesura del R.D.L. 1731/'30, in particolare, nonché sul rapporto tra il riassetto disciplinare delle comunità israelitiche e la legislazione antiebraica, v. Dazzetti, Stefania: Gli ebrei italiani e il fascismo: la formazione della legge del 1930 sulle comunità israelitiche. In: Diritto, economia e istituzioni nell'Italia fascista. A cura di Aldo Mazzacane. Baden-Baden 2000, pp. 219-254.

[23] La Direzione: Ai nostri lettori. In: Rivista del diritto matrimoniale italiano e dei rapporti di famiglia (1934-1935), p. 1.

rivista si presentava come "un campo aperto anche alle più controverse opinioni" nonché come un "facile mezzo di conoscere quanto si è scritto e deciso su questi importanti e delicati argomenti"[24] e si proponeva, dunque, quale luogo privilegiato di conoscenza e di avanguardia nel campo del diritto matrimoniale italiano.

Sulla scorta di tale premessa, era inevitabile che le innovazioni introdotte dalla legislazione del 1938, con il divieto categorico di unioni miste tra ebrei e ariani,[25] non passassero del tutto inosservate nella rivista dell'avvocato Cecchi che, sin dalla promulgazione del primo decreto antiebraico, aveva prontamente dato notizia delle disposizioni razziali concernenti direttamente il regime matrimoniale.

La rubrica *razza ebraica* compariva frequentemente e costantemente negli indici e, in alcune annate, si presentava abbastanza nutrita. Del resto, la posizione assunta dalla rivista veniva enunciata chiaramente nel '42, quando, nel dare notizia dell'istituzione di un centro per lo studio del problema ebraico a Milano, si dichiarava: "La nostra *Rivista*, soprattutto in rapporto ai diritti delle persone e al diritto matrimoniale, ha già pubblicato notevoli studi in argomento (...) augurandosi che venga ripreso in serio esame il problema dei matrimoni misti, dalla legge vigente così malamente risolto."[26]

Non essendo mossa dall'obiettivo di promuovere uno specifico indirizzo scientifico, né nel campo della disciplina generale del matrimonio né tantomeno in quello della disciplina delle unioni miste, la *Rivista del diritto matrimoniale italiano*, in tema di legislazione razziale, lasciava spazio a recensioni, articoli e note a sentenza della più varia tendenza e provenienza. È così che, nello stesso anno in cui veniva pubblicato l'intervento del magistrato torinese, nella sezione dedicata allo spoglio di riviste, si annunciava la nascita de *Il diritto razzis-*

---

[24] La Direzione, Ai nostri lettori (nota 23), p. 1.

[25] Il R.D.L. 1728/'38, al capo I, dettava i *Provvedimenti relativi ai matrimoni*: il matrimonio del cittadino italiano con persona appartenente ad altra razza veniva proibito e si dichiarava nullo il matrimonio che fosse stato contratto in violazione di tale divieto (art. 1); il matrimonio del cittadino italiano con persona di nazionalità straniera veniva subordinato al preventivo consenso del Ministero per l'Interno (art. 2); si prevedeva altresì un'ammenda a carico dell'ufficiale di stato civile che avesse provveduto alla trascrizione del matrimonio celebrato in violazione dell'art. 1.

[26] Anonimo: Centro milanese per lo studio del problema ebraico. In: Rivista del diritto matrimoniale italiano e dei rapporti di famiglia (1942), p. 68.

ta, periodico fondato, nel maggio del 1939, da un gruppo di giuristi – per lo più pratici del diritto, inseriti nelle fila dell'amministrazione dello stato – che, dichiarandosi fascisti e razzisti per naturale inclinazione, avevano inteso dar vita ad una rivista specializzata esclusivamente nella trattazione e nell'approfondimento delle tematiche giuridiche connesse alla nuova legislazione razziale.[27]

Nelle parole del suo fondatore, Stefano Maria Cutelli, *Il diritto razzista* nasceva come una sorta di risentita reazione nei confronti del silenzio e dell'indifferenza manifestati da quei giuristi tradizionalisti e nostalgici che, rimasti indissolubilmente legati ai principi egualitari, si erano dimostrati del tutto incapaci di comprendere la ventata innovativa e "antisecolo"[28] racchiusa nelle nuove disposizioni dettate per la difesa della razza italiana e ne avevano accuratamente evitato lo studio ed il commento. Così, "a quel mondo tanto sensibile di studiosi che aveva sentito l'urgente bisogno di creare cento riviste per commentare e...gonfiare anche le più modeste leggine" era completamente sfuggita "l'utilità scientifica e divulgatrice di una rivista giuridica razzista"[29] la cui realizzazione si doveva, invece, all'opera di un "fascista non cattedratico, ma squadrista",[30] così come lo stesso Cutelli amava definirsi, mettendo ben in rilievo la distanza che separava le proprie convinzioni da quelle dei giuristi che continuavano a richiamarsi alla tradizione liberale.

La drasticità e la durezza delle posizioni assunte dal nuovo periodico e delle soluzioni in esso prospettate emergevano, dunque, con chiarezza sin dalle dichiarazioni programmatiche che il fondatore e direttore aveva posto in apertura al primo numero. Un esempio eclatante è rappresentato proprio dalla tanto dibattuta questione della determinazione della competenza ad emettere la declaratoria di appartenenza alla razza ebraica. Nel 1940, nella sezione dedicata

---

[27] Il ruolo e il peso assunti dalla rivista *Il diritto razzista* nella cultura giuridica italiana degli anni '30-'40 sono stati quasi completamente tralasciato dagli studi storiografici che hanno concentrato l'attenzione sul periodo della persecuzione antiebraica, fatta eccezione per il recente contributo di De Cristofaro, Ernesto: Il diritto razzista. Una rivista dell'Italia fascista. In: Rechtsgeschichte (2004) No. 5, pp. 288-292.

[28] Cutelli, Stefano Maria: Ai lettori. Come e perché nasce "Il diritto razzista" e come è accolto... In: Il diritto razzista (1939) No. 1-2, pp. 1-7, qui p. 1.

[29] Cutelli (nota 28), p. 1.

[30] Cutelli (nota 28), p. 2.

alla rassegna della giurisprudenza, anche nella rivista di Cutelli veniva segnalata e "riassunta" la celebre nota del "camerata"[31] Galante Garrone alla sentenza emessa dalla Corte d'Appello di Torino nella causa Rosso c. Artom. Da un confronto tra il testo pubblicato nella *Rivista del diritto matrimoniale italiano* e quello riportato, invece, ne *Il diritto razzista* si rileva facilmente come, più che riassunto, l'intervento originale del magistrato torinese fosse stato smussato ed aggiustato da Cutelli, desideroso di proporre la propria originale ed alternativa soluzione alle problematiche applicative sollevate dall'art. 26 del R.D.L. 1728/'38.

Nella Rivista di Cecchi, infatti, Galante Garrone aveva concluso il proprio intervento a proposito della competenza ad emettere la declaratoria di appartenenza alla razza ebraica, muovendo un'aspra critica non solo alla commistione delle competenze giurisdizionale e amministrativa ma anche nei confronti dello stesso R.D.L. 1728/'38. A questo scopo si era servito delle considerazioni di un altro giurista, il "giovane" e "valorosissimo" Allorio,[32] che aveva "giustamente" rilevato come la legge del 17 novembre 1938 divergeva dalle più "salde tradizioni giuridiche"[33] italiane. Nella versione della nota utilizzata da Cutelli tale passo veniva completamente cassato, così come si evitava accuratamente di riportare la critica mossa nei confronti del modello nazionalsocialista tedesco, chiaramente definito da Galante Garrone "un modello da non imitare".[34]

A questo punto Cutelli, con un richiamo in nota, prospettava la propria soluzione: l'istituzione della Magistratura della razza che avrebbe dovuto seguire "felicemente all'ottima Magistratura del lavoro, già creata dal fascismo".[35]

Se la rivista di Cecchi – con ogni probabilità, indice di una maggiore apertura nei confronti della normativa razziale da parte di quei periodici fondati da pratici del diritto proprio negli anni del regime fascista – si era limitata a non

---

[31] Così veniva definito il magistrato torinese dal direttore de *Il diritto razzista*. Il diritto razzista (1940) No. 2-3-4, pp. 139-158, qui p. 145.
[32] Galante Garrone si riferiva, in particolare, allo studio *Giustizia e processo nel momento presente*, pubblicato da Allorio nella *Rivista di diritto processuale civile*, nel 1939.
[33] Galante Garrone, Questioni sull'appartenenza alla razza ebraica (nota 13), p. 414.
[34] Galante Garrone, Questioni sull'appartenenza alla razza ebraica (nota 13), p. 414.
[35] Il diritto razzista (1940) No. 2-3-4, pp. 139-158, qui p. 154.

tacere la legislazione dettata in difesa della razza, Cutelli si era dimostrato convinto della necessità di far assurgere a principio dell'ordinamento giuridico italiano quello della "disuguaglianza giuridica razziale di nascita dei cittadini",[36] rivendicando al diritto razzista dignità scientifica.

La creazione di uno spazio "atipico", nel panorama delle riviste giuridiche italiane, da destinare al dibattito relativo alle questioni giuridiche sollevate dal problema della razza, rende ancor più evidente e significativo il silenzio attraverso il quale alcuni periodici – come quello di Ascoli e di Rotondi – avevano collocato la legislazione antiebraica al di fuori dei propri interessi e rivela, per contrasto, la messa a punto di una vera e propria strategia da parte dei giuristi italiani legati alle forme dello stato liberale, rivolta alla salvaguardia della purezza della scienza giuridica italiana. Tacere una specifica normativa, che spiegava inevitabilmente i suoi effetti in ogni settore della disciplina giuridica, equivaleva a dichiararne tacitamente il carattere parentetico e transitorio e a sottolinearne la totale inadeguatezza a scalfire l'edificio della scienza giuridica quale si era andato costruendo fino a quel momento.[37]

B. Il ricordo della legislazione antiebraica nell'Italia post-fascista (1944-1950)

Passando ad analizzare cosa accade all'indomani dell'abrogazione della legislazione antiebraica, sembra quanto mai indicativa la testimonianza resa dallo storico israelita Amos Luzzatto che, nel suo saggio *Autocoscienza ed identità ebrai-*

---

[36] In uno studio pubblicato ne *Il diritto razzista*, il Consigliere di Stato Michele La Torre, evidenziava come si fosse consolidata la tendenza, alla quale aderiva lo stesso direttore Cutelli, a ritenere la "disuguaglianza razziale" uno dei principi portanti del nuovo ordine giuridico instaurato dal regime fascista. V. La Torre, Michele: Effetti della condizione razziale sullo stato giuridico della persona. In: Il diritto razzista (1939) No. 1-2, pp. 32-41.
A tal proposito, Cutelli si sarebbe espresso chiaramente, nelle pagine della propria rivista, dichiarandosi a favore della codificazione del principio della razza nella *Carta del Lavoro*. V. Cutelli, Stefano Maria: Verso la dichiarazione dei principi del diritto fascista. Per l'inserimento delle nozioni di "razza" e "partito" nella Carta del "lavoro". In: Il diritto razzista (1940) No. 5-6, pp. 161-169.

[37] Sul rapporto tra memoria e costruzione del sapere scientifico, v. Rossi, Paolo: Il passato, la memoria, l'oblio. Bologna 1991.

ca,[38] ricorda come, nel 1945, al momento di varcare la frontiera di Ventimiglia, gli fosse stato ancora richiesto di indicare, tra le generalità, la propria *appartenenza razziale*: evidentissimo segno questo della difficoltà dell'Italia postfascista di rinunciare all'impiego della categoria giuridica di *ebreo*, divenuta oramai una sorta di criterio ordinatore e profondamente radicata nell'immaginario collettivo quale imprescindibile strumento di rappresentazione ed autorappresentazione.

Lo stesso legislatore del '44, nel determinare l'ambito soggettivo di applicazione del primo decreto abrogativo della legislazione razziale, non poteva fare a meno di riferirsi ai "cittadini italiani e stranieri già dichiarati di razza ebraica o considerati di razza ebraica",[39] riproducendo la formulazione con la quale, nell'ottobre del 1938, la dicotomia ebreo/ariano era stata introdotta nell'ordinamento giuridico italiano.

Quello dell'*appartenenza razziale* continuava a fungere da criterio-guida utile ed insostituibile nel processo di reintegrazione degli ebrei nella vita italiana, tanto sul piano strettamente legislativo quanto su quello dottrinale e giurisprudenziale. Sembra quasi che l'iter restitutorio sia stato interamente giocato sullo sfondo di un paradosso, in virtù del quale la cancellazione della *diversità* giuridica dell'ebreo non appariva assolutamente pensabile se non attraverso il ricorso a quella dicotomia ebreo/ariano che i decreti abrogativi avevano invece inteso rimuovere.

Dal punto di vista normativo, infatti, il rapporto con la legislazione antiebraica si articolò su due livelli distinti ma complementari:[40] da un lato, con il

---

[38] Luzzatto, Amos: Autocoscienza e identità ebraica. In: Gli ebrei in Italia. Storia d'Italia. Annali. A cura di Cesare Vivanti. Torino 1997, Vol. 11, pp. 1833-1900.

[39] R.D.L. 20 gennaio 1944, n. 25 (nota 2), art. 1.

[40] Sull'abrogazione della legislazione antiebraica e sull'elaborazione della normativa restitutoria, nell'Italia postfascista, v. L'abrogazione delle leggi razziali in Italia (1943-1987). Reintegrazione dei diritti dei cittadini e ritorno ai valori del Risorgimento. A cura di Mario Toscano. Roma 1988; Toscano: L'abrogazione delle leggi razziali. In: Il ritorno alla vita: vicende e diritti degli ebrei in Italia dopo la seconda guerra mondiale. A cura di Michele Sarfatti. Firenze 1998, pp. 59-76; Schwarz, Guri: Appunti per una storia degli ebrei in Italia dopo le persecuzioni 1945-56. In: Studi storici (2000) No. 41, pp. 791-797; Schwarz, Guri: Gli ebrei italiani e la memoria della persecuzione fascista (1945-1955). In: Passato e presente (1999) No. 47, pp. 109-130; D'Amico, Giovanna: Quando l'eccezione diventa norma. La reintegrazione degli ebrei nell'Italia postfascista. Torino 2006.

R.D.L. 25/'44, la distinzione ebreo/ariano veniva cancellata dall'ordinamento giuridico e consegnata all'*oblio*; d'altro canto, i decreti finalizzati a dar concretezza alle restituzioni presupponevano un necessario ma tacito riferimento alle categorie di *ebreo* e *ariano* che continuavano, dunque, a persistere nello strumentario di chi a quelle disposizioni era chiamato a dare attuazione.

Scorrendo gli indici delle annate di alcune riviste giuridiche successive al 1944, si è colpiti dall'impressione che, in riferimento alla cosiddetta *questione ebraica*, esistesse una sostanziale continuità con le annate del periodo compreso tra il '38 ed il '43: quei periodici che non avevano tributato alcuna importanza al *problema ebraico* continuavano a fingere che esso fosse stato inesistente, mentre in quelle riviste che avevano dedicato ad essa un seppur angusto spazio, nel rubricare gli interventi relativi alla legislazione riparatrice, si utilizzavano le voci *ebrei*, *israeliti* o *razza ebraica*, introdotte già nel 1938.

A questo proposito, appare emblematico il caso della *Rivista del diritto matrimoniale italiano* nei cui indici la rubrica *razza ebraica* è stata utilizzata fino all'inizio degli anni '50.

Nel volume del 1944, comprendente i primi sei numeri della rivista, si continuavano a seguire le vicende giuridiche degli ebrei italiani nella RSI, senza peraltro dare notizia dell'adozione del primo decreto abrogativo, ad opera del governo del sud. Difatti, la voce "razza ebraica" rinviava ad un trafiletto, inserito nella sezione *Notiziario*, con il quale si comunicava l'istituzione dell'Ispettorato generale della razza che avrebbe assunto i compiti in precedenza affidati alla Direzione generale della demografia e della razza e all'Ufficio studi e propaganda sulla razza.[41]

Soltanto a partire dal 1947, anno in cui la rivista riprendeva le sue normali pubblicazioni, dopo la conclusione degli eventi bellici, veniva registrato il passaggio dalla normativa antiebraica alla sua abrogazione. La rottura con il recente passato era sottolineata dall'impiego della rubrica *razzismo fascista*, con la quale si rinviava alla recensione di un libro di Eucardio Momigliano,[42] noto come la prima ricostruzione storica delle vicende degli ebrei italiani durante il

---

[41] Rivista del diritto matrimoniale italiano e dei rapporti di famiglia (1944) No. 1-6, p. 65.
[42] Momigliano, Eucardio: Storia tragica e grottesca del razzismo fascista. Milano 1946.

periodo fascista.[43] Per il direttore Cecchi, si trattava, con ogni probabilità, di un pretesto per chiarire, questa volta all'indomani della caduta del regime, la posizione del proprio periodico di fronte alla legislazione razziale: durante il periodo fascista, la rivista si era preoccupata di "seguire diligentemente il movimento razzista, sia in Italia che in Germania, ritenendo assai utile mettere a disposizione del futuro storico di quell'infausto periodo (...) un materiale che molti avrebbero tutto l'interesse a far sparire o dimenticare".[44] Cecchi dimostrava, peraltro, di condividere la lettura degli eventi fornita da Momigliano nella sua opera: egli insisteva, così, sull'estraneità del razzismo al fascismo, comprovata dalla adesione ad esso di "molti israeliti di primissimo piano"; sulla forte influenza esercitata sull'Italia da parte della Germania nell'introduzione di una normativa antiebraica; sulla generosità del popolo italiano, la cui reazione era esplosa "finalmente nel movimento partigiano".[45]

---

[43] Lo storico Schwarz – occupatosi di ricostruire il processo di reintegrazione degli ebrei nell'Italia postfascista – ricorda il testo di Eucardio Momigliano come la prima compiuta ricostruzione storica delle vicende degli ebrei italiani sotto il regime fascista. L'opera di Momigliano appare lo specchio della forte tendenza, dimostrata da politici e uomini di cultura, a costruire la memoria collettiva nazionale del recente passato in maniera omogenea e pacificata, così da poter essere condivisa anche da coloro che erano stati direttamente assoggettati alle disposizioni antiebraiche del 1938. La selezione degli eventi da ricordare appariva, verosimilmente, funzionale a riaccreditare la nazione italiana a livello internazionale. Ecco che nel testo di Momigliano è possibile rintracciare alcuni *topoi* ampiamente diffusi e ricorrenti nel processo di costruzione della memoria della legislazione razziale: accentuazione del ruolo giocato dalla politica nazista nei confronti di Mussolini, esclusivo tentativo di colpevolizzazione dei gerarchi fascisti, assenza di condivisione della politica antiebraica da parte della popolazione italiana ed identificazione della coscienza collettiva italiana con la Resistenza. L'esperienza nazista diveniva il termine di paragone privilegiato: da essa gli italiani intendevano prendere le distanze, mettendo in risalto la barbarie del popolo tedesco che aveva fornito appoggio e sostegno alla politica razzista del regime. V. Schwarz, Guri: Ritrovare se stessi. Gli ebrei nell'Italia postfascista. Roma/Bari 2004.
Sul rapporto tra storia e memoria, v. Traverso, Enzo: Storia e memoria. Gli usi politici del passato. In: Novecento. Fare memoria, costruire identità (2004) No. 10, pp. 9-25; Traverso, Enzo: Il passato: istruzioni per l'uso. Storia, memoria, politica. Verona 2006.
[44] Cecchi, Giovan Battista: Recensione a Eucardio Momigliano, Storia tragica e grottesca del razzismo fascista. In: Rivista del diritto matrimoniale italiano e dei rapporti di famiglia (1947) No. 1-6, p. 64.
[45] Cecchi (nota 44), p. 64.

Nei numeri successivi della rivista, gli interventi relativi all'abrogazione della legislazione razziale tornavano ad essere rubricati sotto la voce *razza ebraica*: si trattava, in prevalenza, di rinvii a sentenze, emesse in tema di reintegrazione degli ebrei nei diritti patrimoniali o relative alla riassunzione in servizio dei dipendenti licenziati per motivi razziali da imprese private.

Ma è addentrandosi nel cuore del dibattito apertosi attorno alle modalità di applicazione della normativa restitutoria che è possibile percepire che cosa e in che modo gli operatori del diritto degli anni '40 e '50 "ricordassero" dell'abrogata normativa antiebraica ed accorgersi come la maggior parte di essi fosse incapace di abbandonare gli strumenti interpretativi e classificatori forniti dal legislatore del '38, al punto da giungere a riesumare categorie ed istituti abrogati e, per giunta, non più richiamati dal dettato normativo postfascista. A tal proposito, un esempio interessante ed indicativo è costituito dalla reintegrazione degli ebrei nei propri diritti patrimoniali, una delle tematiche indubbiamente più controverse dal punto di vista applicativo.

Il 5 ottobre del 1944, con D.L.L. 252, veniva pubblicato ed entrava in vigore il R.D.L. 26/'44, recante le *Disposizioni per la reintegrazione dei cittadini italiani e stranieri già dichiarati di razza ebraica o considerati di razza ebraica nei propri diritti patrimoniali*.[46]

I problemi interpretativi ed applicativi nascevano, in particolare, con riguardo alla formulazione dell'art. 14 che, in deroga alle ordinarie disposizioni codicistiche, consentiva al "cittadino colpito dalle leggi razziali" la possibilità di esperire l'azione di annullamento per tutti quei contratti, aventi ad oggetto l'alienazione di beni immobili, che erano stati stipulati con il deliberato propo-

---

[46] La stesura del R.D.L. 26/'44 era avvenuta contestualmente a quella del R.D.L. 25/'44. La sua pubblicazione ed entrata in vigore, per considerazioni di carattere pratico e per questioni di opportunismo politico, era stata rinviata alla conclusione del conflitto con la Germania. Sull'iter di elaborazione e pubblicazione dei decreti relativi alla restituzione dei beni agli italiani di origini israelitiche, v. Levi, Fabio: La restituzione dei beni. In: Sarfatti (a cura di), Il ritorno alla vita (nota 40), pp. 77-97; Pavan, Ilaria: Gli incerti percorsi della reintegrazione. Note sugli atteggiamenti della magistratura repubblicana 1945-1964. In: Gli ebrei in Italia tra persecuzione fascista e reintegrazione postbellica. A cura di Ilaria Pavan/Guri Schwarz. Firenze 2001, pp. 83-112; Pavan, Ilaria: Tra indifferenza e oblio. Le conseguenze economiche delle leggi razziali in Italia (1938-1970). Firenze 2004.

sito di operare una riduzione della "propria quota di disponibilità" e di sottrarsi, in questo modo, all'applicazione della normativa razziale.[47]

Il testo del R.D.L. 26/'44 appare un'istantanea della transizione terminologica in atto nel linguaggio impiegato dal legislatore: dalla nozione di "cittadino già dichiarato di razza ebraica o considerato di razza ebraica", ancora riprodotta nel titolo stesso del decreto, si passava a quella di "persona colpita dalle leggi razziali" che sarebbe stata acquisita, in via definitiva, nel D.L.L. del 12 aprile 1945, con il quale venivano dettate le *Norme complementari integrative e di attuazione del R.D.L. 26/'44*, e poi impiegata anche in testi normativi non più concernenti esclusivamente la reintegrazione patrimoniale.[48]

L'art. 19 del decreto di attuazione andava a completare il quadro normativo relativo alla stipulazione dei contratti da parte degli israeliti, rendendo possibile alle "persone colpite dalle leggi razziali" l'esercizio dell'azione di rescissione di tutti quei contratti stipulati dopo il 6 ottobre 1938.[49]

Fu proprio con l'obiettivo di delimitare l'ambito soggettivo di applicazione dei decreti citati, definendo chi fosse la "persona colpita dalle leggi razziali", che i giuristi italiani riesumarono la categoria dell'"ebreo discriminato". L'istituto della "discriminazione", introdotto dall'abrogato R.D.L. 1728/'38 e non più richiamato dal legislatore degli anni '40, premiava quegli ebrei che avessero fornito un rilevante contributo alla nazione italiana e al regime fascista, consentendo loro di sottrarsi alla rigida applicazione della legislazione antiebraica.[50] Gli israeliti che avessero chiesto ed ottenuto il provvedimento della discriminazione sarebbero stati, infatti, esentati dall'obbligo di ripartire il pro-

---

[47] D.L.L. 5 ottobre 1944, n. 252, *Pubblicazione ed entrata in vigore del R.D.L. 20 gennaio 1944, n. 26, contenete disposizioni per la reintegrazione nei diritti patrimoniali dei cittadini italiani e stranieri già dichiarati o considerati di razza ebraica*, art. 14.

[48] V. ad esempio al R.D.L. 10 agosto 1944, n. 195, *Rettifica di atti di stato civile relativi a persone colpite dalle leggi razziali.*

[49] D.L.L. 12 aprile 1945, n. 222, *Norme complementari integrative e di attuazione del D.L.L. 20 gennaio 1944, n. 26, per la reintegrazione dei cittadini italiani e stranieri colpiti dalle disposizioni razziali nei loro diritti patrimoniali*, art. 19.

[50] R.D.L. 17 novembre 1938, n. 1728, *Provvedimenti per la difesa della razza italiana*, art. 14.

prio patrimonio in due quote e di destinare la cosiddetta "quota indisponibile" all'EGELI, l'ente incaricato delle alienazioni immobiliari ebraiche.[51]

La tendenza che prevaleva in giurisprudenza era quella di ritenere che la nozione di "persona colpita dalle leggi razziali" dovesse essere necessariamente esaminata in relazione all'oggetto dei decreti presi in considerazione, vale a dire, esclusivamente in rapporto agli aspetti patrimoniali della legislazione antiebraica. In quest'ottica, la formulazione impiegata dal legislatore conteneva necessariamente un qualcosa in meno rispetto alla sua omologa "cittadini già dichiarati di razza ebraica o considerati di razza ebraica". Nel momento in cui si stabiliva la necessità di riferirsi soltanto a quegli ebrei che fossero stati effettivamente lesi nei propri diritti patrimoniali, si doveva tenere in debito conto che, con il R.D.L. 126/'39, gli "ebrei discriminati" erano stati, a tutti gli effetti, equiparati ai concittadini ariani nell'esercizio dei propri diritti patrimoniali. Ne conseguiva che sarebbe stata una fortissima sperequazione ammetterli all'esercizio delle azioni di annullamento e rescissione, concesse dal legislatore.[52]

---

[51] I limiti alla proprietà immobiliare erano stati dettati dall'art. 10 del R.D.L. 1728/'38. Le modalità per procedere all'effettiva determinazione del "patrimonio immobiliare eccedente i limiti consentiti ai cittadini italiani di razza ebraica" venivano predisposte dal R.D.L. 9 febbraio 1939, n. 126, recante le *Norme relative ai limiti di proprietà immobiliare e di attività industriale e commerciale per i cittadini di razza ebraica* che, riguardo agli ebrei discriminati stabiliva, all'art. 72: "I cittadini italiani di razza ebraica, che abbiano ottenuto il provvedimento di discriminazione di cui all'art. 14 del R. decreto-legge 17 novembre 1938-XVII, n. 1728, sono equiparati, ad ogni effetto del presente decreto, ai cittadini italiani non considerati di razza ebraica."

[52] Quella basata sulla portata letterale del testo legislativo costituiva una delle argomentazioni utilizzate con maggiore frequenza dalle Corti che furono chiamate a pronunciarsi sulla legittimazione dell'ebreo ad esperire l'azione di rescissione dei contratti stipulati dopo la promulgazione della legislazione antiebraica.
Si vedano a titolo esemplificativo: Sentenza 22 febbraio 1947, Tribunale di Bologna, Passigli c. Soc. an. civile agricola San Benedetto c. Valenza c. Amministrazione delle Finanze. In: Giurisprudenza Italiana (1947), pp. 289-300; Sentenza 9 febbraio 1948, Tribunale di Modena, Castelbolognesi c. Pastorelli c. Malavasi. In: Il Foro Italiano (1948), pp. 1006-1010; Sentenza 18 luglio 1949, n. 1857, Corte Suprema di Cassazione, Finucci c. Momigliano. In: Il Foro Italiano (1949), pp. 1055-1059; Sentenza 26 giugno 1950 (che alla precedente pronuncia faceva riferimento), n. 1624, Castelbolognesi c. Pastorelli e Malavasi, Corte Suprema di Cassazione. In: Il Foro Italiano (1950), pp. 801-807.

Proprio sulla portata letterale della legge faceva leva la soluzione prospettata dall'avvocato Del Guercio in uno studio pubblicato nel 1948 sulla rivista *Temi* e divenuto ben presto termine di confronto e riferimento di ogni intervento in materia. All'autore appariva evidente come la formulazione "colpito dalle leggi razziali", nel testo dell'art. 14, si riferisse, in maniera diretta ed esclusiva, al cittadino che era stato indotto all'alienazione dei propri immobili "per sottrarsi all'applicazione delle leggi stesse": ne conseguiva che, nella determinazione dei soggetti legittimati all'esercizio dell'azione di annullamento, non si poteva assolutamente prescindere da un esame dettagliato di quei decreti – ed esclusivamente di quelli – che, nel 1938, avevano inciso sul patrimonio immobiliare dell'ebreo. Ecco che, sulla base dell'esegesi delle disposizioni varate dal governo fascista, per "colpito dalle leggi razziali" avrebbe dovuto intendersi esclusivamente l'ebreo, cittadino italiano, che non fosse stato discriminato, dato che l'ebreo discriminato non era stato colpito in nessun modo nei propri diritti patrimoniali.

Del resto – rilevava Del Guercio – un'altra forte indicazione in tal senso proveniva dall'impiego della nozione di "quota disponibile", con la quale, senza dubbio, il legislatore aveva inteso richiamare la ripartizione del patrimonio immobiliare degli ebrei in due differenti quote, quella cosiddetta "consentita" e quella "eccedente". Operando un'interpretazione "correttiva", l'espressione "quota consentita" veniva fatta coincidere con quella di "quota eccedente": ne conseguiva che gli atti di alienazione, presi in considerazione dall'art. 14, avrebbero dovuto avere ad oggetto esclusivamente i beni facenti parte della "quota indisponibile"; il che confermava l'esclusione dell'esperibilità dell'azione da parte degli ebrei discriminati, rimasti nella piena disponibilità dei propri beni immobili.[53]

Così, il dibattito che si aprì attorno alla determinazione della nozione di "persona colpita dalle leggi razziali" difficilmente prescindeva dal riferimento all'istituto della discriminazione. Si registravano, indubbiamente, delle variazioni sul tema: ad esempio, l'esistenza dell'istituto della discriminazione era considerata "rilevante" ai fini dell'applicazione della normativa restitutoria an-

---

[53] Del Guercio, Attilio: Annullamenti di alienazioni di beni immobili fatte da cittadini colpiti dalle leggi razziali. In: Temi (1948) No. 3-4, pp. 376-384.

che da Angiola Sbaiz, che però si allontanava dalla drastica posizione di Del Guercio. La Sbaiz non escludeva aprioristicamente l'applicabilità dell'art. 14 agli ebrei discriminati: "gli effetti della categoria della discriminazione non potevano evidentemente entrare in considerazione *ante litteram*",[54] ma dovevano essere necessariamente analizzati in relazione al caso concreto al quale si riferivano. In questa direzione, ciò che rilevava era esclusivamente "il fatto della discriminazione anteriore all'alienazione", con la conseguenza che la "persona colpita dalle leggi razziali" avrebbe potuto essere facilmente individuata nella figura del "non discriminato al momento dell'alienazione".[55]

Sulla stessa linea interpretativa si collocava anche uno studio di Sofo Borghese, pubblicato a commento di una singolare sentenza, emessa il 21 ottobre 1948 dal Tribunale di Milano, questa volta in tema di rescissione dei contratti stipulati, dopo il 6 ottobre 1938, da "persona colpita dalle leggi razziali". La Corte aveva inteso superare la distinzione tra discriminati e non discriminati, ritenendo di dover concedere la legittimazione attiva ad esperire l'azione di rescissione al contraente che avesse agito in "stato di bisogno"; stato di bisogno determinato dalla propria condizione di colpito dalle leggi razziali ed identificabile nel "disagio economico in cui il contraente venne a trovarsi per le leggi razziali" o nello "stato di necessità economica, direttamente connesso alle leggi repressive".[56]

Borghese commentava la decisione del Tribunale di Milano, sottolineando come la distinzione tra discriminati e non discriminati si sarebbe rivelata un'utile "guida" nella determinazione dell'effettiva sussistenza di una "situazione di pericolo" tale da indurre "gli ebrei a compiere atti giuridici che in condizioni normali non avrebbero compiuto": sarebbe stato opportuno, quindi, valutare la reale e pratica portata dell'istituto della discriminazione, allo

---

[54] Sbaiz, Angiola: Sull'annullamento e la rescissione per lesione di alienazioni immobiliari compiute da ebrei discriminati. In: Il Foro Italiano (1948), pp. 1006-1009, qui p. 1008.
[55] Sbaiz (nota 54), p. 1009.
[56] Sentenza 21 ottobre 1948, Tribunale di Milano, Foà c. Dal Lago. In: Il Foro Italiano (1949), pp. 740-747.

scopo di stabilire se esso "abbia o meno influito sulla consapevolezza da parte dell'interessato del pericolo"[57] imminente.

Dimostrandosi in sintonia con la critica mossa dalla Corte nei confronti della "affrettata" elaborazione ed imprecisa formulazione dei testi normativi con i quali erano state dettate le modalità per la reintegrazione dei cittadini ebrei nei propri diritti patrimoniali, Borghese chiariva ulteriormente la propria posizione e le considerazioni poste a suo fondamento: proprio in ragione dei molteplici inconvenienti derivanti dalla lettera stessa della legge, il compito dell'interprete avrebbe dovuto essere quello di evitare in tutti i modi di "dar facile esca a speculazioni ed abusi da parte di persone poco coscienziose che, pur rientrando formalmente fra i 'colpiti da persecuzione razziale', non hanno subito, di fatto, alcun danno dalla loro posizione". A questo scopo egli si esprimeva a favore di un'interpretazione rigorosamente restrittiva. Ogni malinteso interpretativo sorgeva, a suo dire, dalla forte sproporzione esistente tra la portata della legislazione antiebraica e quella dei testi abrogativi e restitutori che sembravano destinati "ad un paese dove l'accanimento della persecuzione avesse raggiunto gli eccessi delle uccisioni in massa, delle 'camere a gas', ed altri sistemi teutonici la cui vergogna quasi incredibile è ormai consegnata alla storia", quando era comunemente riconosciuto che "la campagna razziale non fu mai sentita in Italia, dove non è mai esistito un 'problema ebraico', e dove gli israeliti sono sempre stati considerati dalla popolazione e dal comune sentimento (…) alla pari di tutti gli altri cittadini".[58]

Simili considerazioni ricorrevano con frequenza negli interventi dei giuristi incaricati di dare effettività alle disposizioni restiturorie e, con ogni probabilità, si inserivano perfettamente in quella tendenza, manifestata negli anni immediatamente successivi alla caduta del fascismo e messa in luce da alcuni contributi storiografici,[59] a ricostruire le vicende del recente passato attraverso il ricorso ad immagini stereotipate: quella dell'italiano magnanimo e, per naturale

---

[57] Borghese, Sofo: Considerazioni in materia di leggi e anti-leggi razziali. In: Il Foro Italiano (1949), pp. 739-744, qui p. 741.
[58] Borghese (nota 57), p. 744.
[59] Bidussa, David: Razzismo e antisemitismo in Italia: fenomenologia e ontologia del bravo italiano. In: La Rassegna mensile d'Israel (1992) No. 3, pp. 1-36; Bidussa, David: Il mito del bravo italiano. Milano 1994; Schwarz (nota 43).

inclinazione, ostile ad ogni forma di razzismo e quella speculare del tedesco incivile che aveva imposto all'Italia l'adozione di una normativa razziale, sul modello nazionalsocialista.

Così, vicende giuridiche e costruzione della memoria collettiva si intrecciavano; il ricordo e l'operato dei giuristi fornivano un contributo considerevole alla costruzione e al consolidamento del mito del "bravo italiano": la rigidità con la quale veniva condotta l'esegesi dei testi abrogativi e il costante richiamo di istituti e parametri interpretativi abrogati hanno indubbiamente contribuito ad alimentare ed accreditare il mito di un *razzismo all'italiana*, dal carattere blando, che fino alle soglie degli anni '80 ha dominato tanto le pagine della storiografia politica, occupatasi delle ricostruzione delle vicende ebraiche durante il fascismo, quanto quelle della memorialistica ebraica.

Un forte contributo in tal senso è stato fornito indubbiamente dalla sensazione che l'attività svolta dai giuristi italiani, negli anni del fascismo, si sia mantenuta quasi completamente immune alla politica razziale[60] e sia stata finalizzata in prevalenza a mettere in risalto l'inadeguatezza della legislazione razziale a costituire argomento di discussione dottrinale, da un lato e ad operare un raccordo tra la nuova normativa e i principi dello stato liberale, dall'altro. Quest'ultima operazione ha permesso alla storiografia giuridica, che ha effettuato delle parziali ricognizioni delle posizioni dottrinali relative all'applicazione della legislazione antiebraica negli anni del fascismo, di insistere sul ruolo giocato dai giuristi italiani nell'attenuare il tenore delle disposizioni razziali, limitandone, per quanto possibile, il rigore al livello applicativo.[61]

---

[60] Sul rapporto tra giuristi italiani e fascismo, in generale, nonché sulla possibilità di parlare di una cultura giuridica propriamente fascista, v. Grossi, Paolo: Scienza giuridica italiana. Un profilo storico 1860-1950. Milano 2000; Mazzacane, Aldo: La cultura giuridica del fascismo: una questione aperta. In: Diritto, economia e istituzioni nell'Italia fascista (nota 22), pp. 1-19.

[61] In questo senso, v. Camy, Fubini, Lo Giudice (nota 11).

„Wohin kommen wir, wenn wir überall Gesetze machen wollen, wo Dummheiten stattfinden…“ – Praxis und Gesetz im landwirtschaftlichen Erbgang

Birgit Fastenmayer

Mit der „Bauernbefreiung“ endete der grundsätzliche Gleichlauf von bäuerlicher Hofübergabepraxis und gesetzlichem Erbrecht. Die Gesetzgebung hat seither immer wieder zu moderieren versucht: Sie appellierte an eine angebliche bäuerliche Mentalität, das Althergebrachte zu konservieren und erinnerte an eine vermeintliche vergessene „Sitte“. Ohne Erfolg. Die Grundeigentümer übergaben ihre Höfe zu Lebzeiten, weitgehend unhelligt von Sitte und Gesetz. Erst 1933 wurden Praxis und Gesetz unter dem Deckmantel der „Sitte“ zwangsweise wieder in Übereinstimmung gebracht.

Im Folgenden stehen die beiden „Gedächtnisorte“ – Vertrag und Gesetz – auf dem Prüfstand. Es soll gezeigt werden, daß es eine erinnerungsbedürftige starre „Sitte“ nicht gibt, daß hinter den bäuerlichen Vererbungsgewohnheiten vielmehr eine den jeweiligen Erfordernissen sich anpassende Praxis steht.

A. „Bauernbefreiung“: bürgerliches Erbrecht und Vertragsfreiheit auch für ländlichen Grundbesitz

Mit der „Bauernbefreiung“[1] in der ersten Hälfte des 19. Jahrhunderts in Deutschland traten die Bauern in die bürgerliche Privatrechtsordnung ein. Die

---

[1] Während man unter Bauernbefreiung im engeren Sinne die Aufhebung der Leibeigenschaft versteht, geht es im Zusammenhang dieses Textes um den dinglichen Aspekt der Reformen, die Grundentlastung, die den Bauern das Eigentum am Boden übertrug und die darauf lastenden grundherrlichen Rechte ablöste. Zu Begrifflichkeit, Durchführung und Auswirkung der „Bauernbefreiung“: Lütge, Friedrich: Geschichte der deutschen Agrarverfassung vom frühen Mittelalter bis zum 19. Jahrhundert. 2. Auflage, Stuttgart 1967, S. 201 ff.

bäuerlichen Lasten und Verpflichtungen wurden abgelöst; die Bauern erwarben vollwertiges Eigentum an dem Boden, den sie bewirtschafteten. Damit wurde auch das allgemeine bürgerliche Erbrecht anwendbar, das auf dem römischrechtlichen Grundsatz der gleichmäßigen Teilung des Nachlasses unter alle Erben beruht. Landwirtschaftlich genutzter Boden schien sich nun nicht mehr von sonstigem beweglichen oder unbeweglichen Vermögen zu unterscheiden[2]. Und dennoch: Sinnvolles Wirtschaften setzt einen gewissen Mindestbestand voraus. Es ist im Erbfall nicht gleichgültig, in welche und vor allem in wie viele Hände die zu einem Hof gehörenden Grundstücke, die Gebäude und das Inventar kommen.

I. Einzelerbfolge: Divergenz von Praxis und Gesetz

In weiten Teilen Deutschlands wurden die Liegenschaften im Erbgang nicht geteilt, sondern gingen geschlossen an einen der Erben – den „Anerben" – gegen ermäßigte Abfindung der Miterben über. Vor der „Bauernbefreiung" hatten grundherrschaftliche und landesrechtliche Ordnungen dieses Anerbenrecht festgeschrieben; Teilungsverbote verhinderten die Besitzzersplitterung, maßvolle Abfindungsregelungen beugten der Überschuldung im Erbgang vor[3].

Im Zuge der partikularen Ablösungsgesetzgebung wurden erbrechtliche Sonderregelungen nur vereinzelt aufrechterhalten[4]. Gleichwohl hielten die Bauern in den bisherigen Anerbengebieten auch ohne Zwang überwiegend an der Einzelerbfolge fest. Man bezeichnet dieses Phänomen im Agrarrecht als „Anerbensitte"[5]. Die weitgehende Kontinuität scheint die oft zitierte These des Volkskundlers Wilhelm Heinrich Riehl (1823-1897) in seinem Werk „Die

---

[2] Kroeschell, Karl: Art. Bauernbefreiung. In: Handwörterbuch des Agrarrechts (HAR). Hrsg. von Götz, Volkmar; Kroeschell, Karl; Winkler, Wolfgang. I. Band, Berlin 1981, Sp. 301 ff.; ders.: Art. Landwirtschaftliches Erbrecht. In: ebd. II. Band, Berlin 1982, Sp. 306 ff.

[3] Kurze Zusammenfassung der Hauptzüge des älteren Anerbenrechts bei Baernreither, Joseph Maria: Stammgüter-System und Anerbenrecht in Deutschland. Wien 1882, S. 5 f.

[4] Einzelheiten bei Kroeschell; Winkler: (wie Fn. 2), S. 21-258, hier S. 37.

[5] Kroeschell; Winkler (wie Fn. 2), S. 33. Das Wort steht im Folgenden ohne Anführungszeichen als feststehender terminus technicus für die Einzelerbfolge in Gebieten ohne Anerbengesetz.

bürgerliche Gesellschaft" von 1851 zu bestätigen, wonach „dem Bauern die Sitte über das Gesetz geht"[6]. Neben Christian Garve und Ernst Moritz Arndt hat Riehl sich als einer der ersten wissenschaftlich mit dem Standort der Bauern innerhalb der Gesellschaft auseinandergesetzt. Er begreift die Bauern als „beharrenden Kern in der deutschen Nation"[7], der als Gegengewicht zur städtischen Zivilisation erhalten werden müsse. Riehl gilt als typischer Vertreter einer antiaufklärerischen Reaktion auf die gesellschaftlichen und agrarischen Umwälzungen des 19. Jahrhunderts. Seine Bauerntums-Konzeption wurde zum ideologischen Bezugspunkt für die konservative agrarpolitische Strömung seiner Zeit, die sich bis ins 20. Jahrhundert fortsetzte und ihren Höhepunkt im Nationalsozialismus erreichte[8].

„Dem Bauern geht die Sitte über das Gesetz" – in die Sprache des Forums junger Rechtshistoriker übertragen, könnte das heißen: Die Bauern erinnerten sich an das Hergebrachte, das die Gesetzgebung vergessen gemacht hatte. Die Anerbensitte behauptete sich nicht gegen das Gesetz, sondern neben dem Gesetz – es war der Hofübergabevertrag, der die Einzelerbfolge lebendig hielt. Die Bauern übertrugen ihr Grundeigentum im Regelfall noch zu Lebzeiten geschlossen an eines der Kinder[9]. Übergabeverträge waren an sich nichts Neues. Schon zu Zeiten der Grundherrschaft wirtschafteten die Bauern nicht bis ans Lebensende fort. Je nach Stärke des Besitzrechts forcierte der Obereigentümer die Übergabe in jüngere Hände, denen er zutraute, die ihm zustehende Prästationen zu erwirtschaften. Neu war an den Übergabeverträgen, daß die Bauern nunmehr ohne Einmischung von außen frei verfügen konnten. Riehl erklärt die Kontinuität des geschlossenen Übergangs mit der „dem Bauern eigene(n)

[6] Riehl, Wilhelm Heinrich: Die Bürgerliche Gesellschaft. Stuttgart und Tübingen 1851, S. 47.
[7] Riehl (wie Fn. 6), S. 33.
[8] Zum Begriff „Bauerntum" bei Riehl und zu seiner Rezeption: Conze, Werner: Bauer, Bauernstand, Bauerntum. In: Geschichtliche Grundbegriffe. Hrsg. von Brunner, Otto; Conze, Werner; Koselleck, Reinhart. 1. Band, Stuttgart 1972, S. 407-439, hier S. 431-435; Achilles, Walter: Deutsche Agrargeschichte im Zeitalter der Reformen und der Industrialisierung. Stuttgart 1993, S. 299-302.
[9] Zur lebzeitigen Übergabe als Regelfall der Hofnachfolge gegenüber den selteneren Fällen der letztwilligen Verfügung oder der gesetzlichen Erbfolge: Verhandlungen des Deutschen Landwirthschaftsraths. XV. Sitzungsperiode. 1887. In: Archiv des Deutschen Landwirthschaftsraths, Band 11. Berlin 1887, S. 234-257.

zähe(n) Beharrlichkeit“[10], die ihn zum „treuesten Bewahrer väterlicher Sitte“[11] mache. Inhalt und Zweck des Übergabevertrags legen indes eine pragmatischere Erklärung für die Einzelerbfolge nahe. Drei charakteristische Elemente kennzeichnen den Übergabevertrag: Jemand übereignet seinen Hof unter Vorwegnahme der Erbfolge an einen Abkömmling. Dieser verpflichtet sich im Gegenzug einerseits, die Eltern bis an deren Lebensende auf dem Altenteil zu versorgen, und andererseits, die nicht zum Zuge gekommenen Geschwister abzufinden. Solche Verträge sind keine harmlosen Verwandtengeschäfte. Die Altersversorgung des Übergebers steht und fällt mit der vertraglichen Regelung; eine gesetzliches Altersgeld neben dem Altenteil gibt es erst seit 1957.[12] Ein Hofeigentümer, der sein Alter vor Augen hat, wird sich daher nur bedingt von familiären Gefühlen leiten lassen. Wie vormals der Grundherr die bäuerlichen Dienste und Abgaben am liebsten aus einer Hand entgegennahm, so war es auch für den Übergeber am sichersten, wenn die Altenteilsleistungen aus einem ungeteilten Hof kamen, der dieser Zusatzbelastung standhielt. Die Altenteilslast konnte erheblich sein, wie ein Beispiel aus der Provinz Ostpreußen von 1892[13] zeigt:

§ 3. Außer dem Kaufgelde verpflichtet sich der Käufer, den Verkäufern nachstehendes Ausgedinge lebenslänglich zu gewähren resp. zu liefern:

1. *freie Wohnung in den rechts vom Eingange des Wohnhauses an der Boczekschen Seite belegenen Zimmern und Kammern, sowie Benutzung des darüber befindlichen Bodenraumes und des darunter liegenden Kellers oder nach Wahl der Berechtigten jährlich 60 M;*

---

[10] Riehl (wie Fn. 6), S. 44 f.
[11] Riehl (wie Fn. 6), S. 42.
[12] Gesetz über eine Altershilfe für Landwirte vom 27. Jnui 1957, BGBl. I, 1063.
[13] Auszug aus einem Übergabevertrag vom 7. Januar 1892, verhandelt bei dem Königl. Amtsgericht Passenheim (Ostpreußen), abgedruckt bei Wenckstern, Adolf von; Böhme, Carl: Provinz Ostpreussen. In: Die Vererbung des ländlichen Grundbesitzes im Königreich Preussen. Hrsg. von Sering, Max. Berlin 1905, S. 89 f.

2. *eine eiserne*[14] *Kuh nebst freier Stallung, Sommerweide, Hütung und Winterfutter nebst Zuzucht;*
3. *vier eiserne Schafe nebst freier Stallung, Sommerweide, Hütung und Winterfutter, nebst Zuzucht und vier eiserne Hühner nebst Zuzucht;*
4. *Mitbenutzung des Backofens, Brunnens und des Abtritts;*
5. *Benutzung der beiden im Speicher am Hause belegenen Ställe;*
6. *Umgang auf dem Hofe und Grundstücke;*
7. *fünfzig Reihen von je einhundert Schritt gutgedüngtes und bearbeitetes Land zum Kartoffelpflanzen nebst der Aussaat. Das Einpflanzen und Bearbeiten der Kartoffeln ist Sache des Käufers;*
8. *die alleinige Nutzung des Gartens an der Schmiede. Der Käufer muss diesen Garten in jedem Jahre dreimal pflügen und eggen und in jedem zweiten Jahr gut düngen;*
9. *die alleinige Nutzung der beiden Obstgärten am Hause. Der Käufer ist gehalten, die Zäune dieser Gärten in gutem Zustande zu erhalten;*
10. *jährlich folgende Prästationen:*

    a) 3 Scheffel Weizen à 85 Pfd.; b) 20 Scheffel Roggen à 80 Pfd.; c) 2 Scheffel Gerste à 70 Pfd.; d) 3 Scheffel Erbsen à 90 Pfd.; e) 3 Scheffel Buchweizen à 70 Pfd.; f) 40 Scheffel Eßkartoffeln; g) 4 Scheffel Hafer à 50 Pfd.; h) 10 M zu Salz;

    i) 72 M Taschengeld in monatlichen Raten von 6 M; k) 18 Raummeter kleingemachtes Kiefern-Klobenholz nebst freier Anfuhr und 4 Klafter trockenen Torf nebst Anfuhr; l) jährlich 6 Fuhren auf eine Entfernung von 3 Meilen, jährlich 6 Fuhren zur Kirche nach Passenheim hin und zurück; m) 1 Zentner geschwungenen Flachses; n) 15 Bunde Roggenrichtstroh à 30 Pfd.;
11. *zwei bearbeitete und gedüngte Beete im Bruch von je 80 Schritt Länge und je 6 Fuß Breite;*

---

[14] Die Kuh ist als „eiserne" vereinbart, weil die Verpflichtung des Übernehmers, dem Altenteiler eine Kuh zur Verfügung zu stellen, unabhängig vom Verenden des individuellen Stücks Vieh bis zum Tod des Berechtigten fortwährend bestehen sollte („Eisern Vieh stirbt nie.").

12. jährlich zu Martini 6 Mastgänse à 12 Pfd.

13. jährlich 2 Mastschweine im Werte von je 45 M, das eine zu Ostern, das andere zu Michaeli;

14. freies Begräbnis im Werte von je 150 M, zusammen 300 M für die Verkäufer.

Die Terminologie nach Art eines Kaufvertrags entspricht der Rechtsnatur der Hofübergabe als entgeltliches Rechtsgeschäft („Kindskauf"). Das Altenteil umfasste die alltäglichen Grundbedürfnisse nach Wohnung und Verpflegung und wurde im Allgemeinen sehr reichlich und detailliert festgesetzt. Selbst wenn die Altenteilergeneration nicht voll auf ihrem verbrieften Recht beharrte: Der Hof musste den Unterhalt für sie abwerfen, ohne einen nennenswerten Nutzen von ihrer Arbeitskraft zu haben. Im Interesse der Altersversorgung galt es daher, die weiteren Übergabelasten zu minimieren. Die Abfindungsansprüche der Geschwister wurden zu Gunsten des Nachfolgers beschränkt und dieser bekam den Hof unter dem Marktpreis zum „geschwisterlichen Werte". Oder man begrenzte die Kinderzahl. Selbst die Tendenz zur Zweikinderehe will Riehl noch mit der Kraft der Anerbensitte erklären: „Um die Sitte aufrecht zu erhalten, hat man die Moral geopfert; die Gemeinden sind reich und blühend, und die Pfarrer predigen – gegen die Abtreibung der Leibesfrucht."[15]

II. Realteilung: weitgehender Gleichlauf von Praxis und Gesetz

Riehls unablässiger Rückgriff auf die „Sitte" scheint besonders fragwürdig, wenn man ihr die Gepflogenheiten in den Realteilungsgebieten[16] entgegensetzt. Auch dort war es üblich, den Besitz noch zu Lebzeiten zu übereignen. Die Praxis stimmte mit dem Gesetz insoweit überein, als grundsätzlich alle Geschwister gleichgroße Grundstücksanteile erhielten. Allerdings wurde einer

[15] Riehl (wie Fn. 6), S. 47.

[16] Traditionelle Realteilungsgebiete sind Südwestdeutschland (mit Ausnahme des Schwarzwalds), Unterfranken, Teile Hessens, das Bergische Land und das südliche Westfalen (Abel, Wilhelm: Agrarpolitik. 3. Auflage, Göttingen 1967, S. 169).

der Erbanwärter in der Regel leicht bevorzugt. Als Gegenleistung für die Versorgung der Eltern bekam er einen größeren Teil der Flächen oder die Gebäude zugeteilt[17]. Riehl geht darüber hinweg, wenn er die „Philanthropie des modernen Erbrechts“ anprangert, „welche allen Kindern alles gibt, damit keines was rechtes besitze.“[18] Für ihn gibt es nirgends ein „traurigeres Bauernproletariat, eine entsittlichtere ländliche Bevölkerung“[19] als in den Weinbaugebieten. In diesem Vorurteil verstrickt, ignoriert er die Umstände, unter denen eine Aufteilung der Grundstücke angezeigt sein konnte. In den fruchtbaren und marktangebundenen Gebieten des Rheins und seiner Nebenflüsse hat sich die Realteilung deswegen durchgesetzt, weil der arbeitsintensive Anbau von absatzstarken Handelsgewächsen auch bei kleinerem Besitz noch lohnend war. Dort, wo Realteilung zu den wirtschaftlichen und natürlichen Verhältnissen passte, hatte daher auch die Grundherrschaft keinen Anlaß, mittels Teilungsverbot einzuschreiten[20]. Der überwiegend kritischen Beurteilung in der Agrarwissenschaft hielten Kenner jener Strukturen entgegen, daß Realteilung in der Praxis nicht zwangsläufig zu Besitzzersplitterung und Verelendung führe. In Zukauf, Heirat und Pacht waren Gegenkräfte wirksam, und die freie Teilbarkeit des Bodens vertrug sich mit der Nebentätigkeit der Kleinlandwirte in Gewerbe und Industrie[21].

Mit anderen Worten: Es gibt keine alleinseligmachende „Sitte“ der Vererbung, die man auf den gesamten landwirtschaftlichen Grundbesitz übertragen könnte. Die ausschließliche Differenzierung nach Realteilung und Einzelerbfolge lenkt von den konkreten Problemen ab, die eine Übergabe zu Lebzeiten des Eigentümers aufwarf.

---

[17] Kroeschell; Winkler (wie Fn. 4), S. 57 f.
[18] Riehl (wie Fn. 6), S. 47.
[19] Riehl (wie Fn. 6), S. 60.
[20] Abel (wie Fn. 16), S. 169, 171.
[21] Ausgewogene Würdigung der Vor- und Nachteile der Realteilung durch den Präsidenten des badischen Finanzministeriums, Buchenberger, Adolf: Grundzüge der deutschen Agrarpolitik unter besonderer Würdigung der kleinen und großen Mittel. Berlin 1897, S. 91-94.

III. Der Hofübergabevertrag: bedarfsgerechtes Erinnern und Vergessen

Der landwirtschaftliche Erbgang war deshalb so störungsanfällig, weil er in der Praxis als Rechtsgeschäft unter Lebenden – durch Vertrag – vollzogen wurde. Während bei der gesetzlichen Erbfolge erst der Tod des Eigentümers Rechtsfolgen auslöste, verursachte die lebzeitige Übergabe insbesondere hinsichtlich der Altersversorgung Regelungsbedarf und eröffnete den Beteiligten einen Handlungsspielraum, dessen Ausnutzung für die Höfe existenzbedrohend werden konnte. Im 19. Jahrhundert waren insbesondere drei Tendenzen problematisch:

1. verfrühte Übergaben – denn je jünger sich ein Bauer zur Ruhe setzte, desto länger musste die nachfolgende Generation für seinen Unterhalt aufkommen;

2. überhöhte Altenteilsansprüche – die insbesondere in Kombination mit 1. drückend sein konnten und

3. als zusätzliche Belastung bei der Einzelerbfolge: unmäßige Geldabfindungen der Geschwister – weil diese den Übernehmer von vornherein in die hypothekarische Verschuldung zwangen.

Diese regional unterschiedlich ausgeprägten Mißstände hatten bereits im grundherrlich-bäuerlichen Verhältnis für Zündstoff gesorgt. Auf allzu eigenständige familieninterne Abmachungen reagierte die Provinzialgesetzgebung mit der Normierung von Altersgrenzen und mit höhenmäßiger Beschränkung der Altenteile und Abfindungen[22]. Mit der Lösung der ständischen Bindungen waren diese Dämme gebrochen und der Generationenwechsel bekam eine neue Dynamik. Nunmehr bestimmten die Bauern je nach Bedarf und eigenen Vorstellungen die Übergabemodalitäten. Die obsoleten Normen waren dem individuellen Erinnern und Vergessen überlassen.

---

[22] Zusammenstellung und Kommentierung der für das Altenteil bedeutsamen Provinzialgesetze bei Runde, Christian Ludwig: Die Rechtslehre von der Leibzucht oder dem Altentheile auf Deutschen Bauerngütern nach gemeinen und besonderen Rechten. Erster Theil. Oldenburg 1805, S. 43-261.

B. Gesetzgebung: wider das Vergessen der „Sitte"

Die Vererbung des ländlichen Grundbesitzes wurde zu einem agrarpolitischen Dauerbrennerthema des späten 19. Jahrhunderts. Insbesondere seit den 1870er Jahren musste die Freiheit des Grundstücksverkehrs als Erklärung für die zunehmende Verschuldung der Landwirtschaft und die steigende Zahl zwangsversteigerter Höfe herhalten[23]. Aus heutiger Sicht war die Agrarkrise wesentlich bedingt durch die rationeller wirtschaftende überseeische Konkurrenz, deren Getreideexporte einen Preisverfall auf den europäischen Märkten verursachten.[24] Deutschland reagierte auf den Druck des Welthandels mit einer hilflosen Schutzzollpolitik. Der Protektionismus führte nicht nachhaltig aus der Krise heraus – im Gegenteil: er zementierte die verkrusteten Agrarstrukturen[25]. Anstatt durch konsequente staatliche Förderung der Selbsthilfe – etwa des Genossenschafts- und Vereinswesens, der landwirtschaftlichen Fachschulen und naturwissenschaftlichen Versuchsstationen – die deutsche Landwirtschaft konkurrenzfähiger zu machen, steuerte die agrarpolitische Diskussion mehr und mehr in ein Fahrwasser konservativer Ideologie. Als Feindbild diente das römische Recht; es sei dem beweglichen Kapital angepasst und drohe Familiensinn und bäuerliche „Sitte" insbesondere auf erbrechtlichem Gebiet zu zersetzen[26]. Man sprach den Bauern die Fähigkeit ab, der Vertragsfreiheit aus eigener Kraft gewachsen zu sein. Die Erhaltung des Bauernstandes erfordere daher staatlichen Schutz der Landwirte nicht nur zollpolitisch nach außen, sondern mittels Intervention in den Generationenwechsel auch vor sich selbst.

---

[23] Zahlenangaben über die Hypothekenverschuldung in den einzelnen Landesteilen in Archiv des Deutschen Landwirthschaftsraths (1884). Hrsg. von Müller, Traugott. Berlin 1884, S. 109-134.
[24] Einzelheiten bei Abel (wie Fn. 16), S. 435.
[25] Zu Schutzzollpolitik und Selbsthilfe: Achilles (wie Fn. 8), S. 308-316, 354-361.
[26] Hierzu exemplarisch Jäger, Eugen: Die Agrarfrage der Gegenwart, II. Abtheilung. Berlin 1884, insbesondere Kapitel XIV. Jäger bezeichnet das „römische Recht (als) das Recht des Liberalismus", S. 99, und sieht das „Wesen der liberalistischen Auffassung" darin, daß „die strenge Verbindlichkeit der Sittengesetze, wie sie die christliche Offenbarung gegeben, wegfällt und Alles ausschließlich nach dem materiellen Nutzen beurtheilt wird.", S. 98.

I. Partikulare Gesetzgebung: vergebliches Erinnern

Diese vermeintliche Erkenntnis führte in verschiedenen deutschen Ländern zu gesetzgeberischen Leerlaufhandlungen. Man reanimierte ein bäuerliches Sondererbrecht, das der vergessenen „Sitte“ auf die Sprünge helfen sollte.

Gesetzliche Bestrebungen in diese Richtung gab es seit der Grundentlastung[27]. 1855 hatte das Königreich Bayern versucht, das Fideikommiß[28] auf bäuerlichen Grundbesitz zu übertragen[29]. Der Versuch scheiterte: Nur drei Stiftungen unveräußerlicher und unbelastbarer „Erbgüter“ waren fünfzehn Jahre nach Inkrafttreten des Gesetzes zu verzeichnen[30]. Die Bauern waren nicht daran interessiert, die jüngst erlangte Dispositionsfreiheit wieder aufzugeben und ihre Höfe für alle Zeiten der schematischen Regelung eines Gesetzes zu überlassen. Einen akzeptableren Weg schien die Gesetzgebung in den preußischen Ländern zu gehen; dort griff man das Anerbenrecht wieder auf. Die Vorreiterrolle übernahm die Provinz Hannover mit dem Höfegesetz von 1874[31]. Im Regelungsgehalt unterschied sich das Hannoversche Gesetz im Grunde nicht von den Provinzialrechten der grundherrlichen Periode: Abweichend vom bürgerlichen Erbrecht statuierte es die Einzelerbfolge und bevorzugte den Anerben vor seinen Geschwistern durch Erhöhung seines Erbteils und maßvollen Ansatz des Hofeswerts[32]. Im Gegensatz zu den älteren Anerbenrechten war die Geltung des Gesetzes aber in der freien Willenserklärung des Eigentümers begründet; nur wenn dieser seinen Hof in ein öffentliches Verzeichnis – die Höfe- oder Landgüterrolle – hatte eintragen lassen, wurde bei seinem Tod der Hof

---

[27] Zusammenstellung des neueren bäuerlichen Sondererbrechts bei Frommhold, Georg: Deutsches Anerbenrecht. Greifswald 1896.

[28] Unter Fideikommiß versteht man ein Vermögen, das durch Stiftungsakt einer bestimmten Erbfolgeordnung unterworfen ist. Um es als Familienvermögen zu erhalten, ist der jeweils Nutzungsberechtigte im Verkehr unter Lebenden durch Teilungs-, Veräußerungs- und Belastungsverbote in der Verfügung beschränkt, Abel (wie Fn. 16), S. 179.

[29] Gesetz, betreffend die landwirthschaftlichen Erbgüter. Vom 22. Februar 1855; abgedruckt bei Frommhold (wie Fn. 27), S. 87-99.

[30] Baernreither (wie Fn. 3), S. 13.

[31] Gesetz, betreffend das Höferecht in der Provinz Hannover, vom 2. Juni 1874; vgl. Frommhold (wie Fn. 27), S. 1-8.

[32] Hannoversches Höfegesetz §§ 13, 15, 16.

von der Anerbenregelung erfasst[33]. Anders als nach dem bayerischen Erbgütergesetz konnte die Eintragung allerdings jederzeit durch Übergabevertrag oder Testament wirkungslos gemacht werden[34]. Dieser Tribut an die Dispositionsfreiheit verurteilte die neuere Anerbengesetzgebung in Hannover wie in den übrigen Ländern von vornherein zum Scheitern. Der Mißerfolg lässt sich an zwei Faktoren messen: an der Anzahl der Eintragungen und an der Häufigkeit der Fälle, in denen die gesetzliche Erbfolge auch wirklich eintrat. Die Zahl der registrierten Höfe war überschaubar[35], und praktisch wirksam wurde eine Eintragung eigentlich nur dann, wenn ein Hofeigentümer in jüngerem Lebensalter überraschend starb und es versäumt hatte, durch Übergabevertrag, Ehe- und Erbvertrag oder Testament zu verfügen. Die Gesetze konnten nicht Fuß fassen, weil sie Alter und Ruhebedürfnis ignorierten und damit an der Lebenswirklichkeit der Bauern vorbeigingen. Gutsbesitzer Wilhelm Freiherr von Cetto-Reichertshausen (Bayern) brachte dieses Mißverhältnis 1887 bei den Verhandlungen des Deutschen Landwirtschaftsrats auf den Punkt:

> „Ich möchte sagen, daß die Gutsübergabeverträge im Allgemeinen, wie ich die Verhältnisse beurtheile, die regelmäßige Form der Vererbung des bäuerlichen Besitzes sind und daß jede Maßregel, die auf eine Reform dieser Übergabeverträge hinzielt, einen weit praktischeren Erfolg haben müsste, als wenn bezüglich der Erbfolge irgend eine Anordnung getroffen wird, welche die Übergabeverträge vollständig intakt läßt."[36]

Es fehlte durchaus nicht an Vorschlägen, wie den Auswüchse in den Hofübergabeverträgen entgegenzuwirken und insbesondere das Problem der Altersversorgung in der Landwirtschaft zu beheben sei. Die agrarpolitische Diskussion war jedoch so stark auf das Anerbenrecht fokussiert, daß die Reform-

---

[33] Ebd. §§ 5, 7.
[34] Ebd. §§ 1, 24.
[35] Nur in Hannover veranlasste die starke Agitation der landwirtschaftlichen Vereine und der Widerwille gegen preußische Rechtsvereinheitlichung gut 2/3 der Bauern, ihre Höfe eintragen zu lassen; verdrängt wurden die lebzeitigen Übergaben aber auch dort nicht, Abel (wie Fn. 16), S. 172.
[36] Deutscher Landwirthschaftsrath 1887 (wie Fn. 9), S. 234 f.

anregungen im Sande verliefen. Das meiste Aufsehen hatte Rittergutsbesitzer Hermann Kennemann-Klenka (Posen) 1886 im Preußischen Landes-Ökonomie-Kollegium erregt. Sei Ansinnen, man möge das Altenteil der behördlichen Kontrolle zu unterstellen, kam einem Tabubruch gleich[37]. Das Standbild des „freien Bauern auf freier Scholle" dominierte über jeden Angriff erhaben die Diskussion[38]. „Wohin kommen wir, wenn wir überall Gesetze machen wollen, wo Dummheiten stattfinden…"[39] empörte sich etwa der Entsandte des Central-Vereins für Lithauen und Masuren, Landes-Direktor von Saucken-Tarputschen. In der Überzeugung, daß Dummheit dadurch am besten bekämpft werde, daß sie Schaden leide, plädierte er dafür, die Auswüchse bei den Hofübergaben auf sich beruhen zu lassen[40].

Im Wege der Selbsthilfe und ohne gesetzlichen Zwang wollten die Verfechter einer freiwilligen bäuerlichen Lebensversicherung das Problem des Generationenwechsels in der Landwirtschaft lösen. Sie bezweckten mit ihrem Reformansatz, Altersversorgung und Geschwisterabfindungen zu einer kalkulierbaren Angelegenheit zu machen[41]. Der Sparzwang, den eine Versicherung auferlegt, war aber schwer zu vermitteln und auf freiwilliger Basis nicht durchzusetzen.

II. Bürgerliches Gesetzbuch: es bleibt bei der Privatautonomie

Die Vorarbeiten zum Bürgerlichen Gesetzbuch gaben indes der Diskussion um das Anerbenrecht neue Nahrung. Otto Gierke sprach sich auf dem 23. Deutschen Juristentag 1895 in Bremen dafür aus, das Anerbenrecht unmittel-

---

[37] Verhandlungen des Königlichen Landes-Oekonomie-Kollegiums vom 9.-11.11.1886. In: Landwirtschaftliche Jahrbücher, XV. Band, Suppl. II. Hrsg. von Thiel, Hugo. S. [37]-[39].

[38] Kritik etwa im Deutschen Landwirthschaftsrath (wie Fn. 9), S. 232, 243, 245-247, 250, 252 und bei Schneider, K.: Ueber die Nachteile des Altenteilsrechts und über einen zweckmäßigen Ersatz desselben. In: Hannoversche Land- und forstwirtschaftliche Zeitung (1887), S. 402-408, 419-425, hier S. 402 f.

[39] Landes-Oekonomie-Kollegium (wie Fn. 37), S. [128].

[40] Landes-Oekonomie-Kollegium (wie Fn. 37), S. [129].

[41] Praxisnahe Berechnungsbeispiele von Amtsrichter K. Schneider, vorgetragen im Landwirtschaftlichen Zweigverein Nienburg a. W. am 8. März 1887, Druckfassung: Schneider (wie Fn. 38).

bar im BGB zu einem gemeinrechtlichen Institut zu erheben. Der in der bäuerlichen Erbsitte verkörperte deutschrechtliche Gedanke müsse reichsgesetzlich verankert werden[42]. Der deutsche Juristenstand würde damit den Vorwurf entkräften, „daß er sich nicht loslösen könne von gewissen durch die römischen Rechtsstudien eingeimpften Schulbegriffen, und daß er nicht gerecht zu werden vermöge dem Gedanken einer neuen deutschen socialen und nationalen Denkungsart“[43]. Da auch Gierke die Dispositionsfreiheit unter Lebenden und von Todes wegen nicht antasten wollte, hätte seine Variante auf die Übergabeverträge allenfalls mittelbar als gesetzliches Leitbild einwirken können. Entgegen Gierkes Anspruch an sich und seine Kollegen kamen die Juristen eben doch nicht über „technisch-juristische Anschauungen“[44] hinaus. Die Redakteure des BGB einigten sich darauf, alles beim Alten zu belassen. Das bäuerliche Erbrecht blieb weiterhin Ländersache, jedoch mit der Maßgabe, daß die freie Verfügungsbefugnis der Grundeigentümer Vorrang vor einer gesetzlichen Regelung behalten müsse. Artikel 64 und 96 des Einführungsgesetzes zum BGB verpflichteten die Landesgesetzgebung hinsichtlich Anerbenrecht und Altenteil nunmehr ausdrücklich zur Wahrung der Privatautonomie[45].

Im Bild der Gedächtnisorte könnte man die Vererbungspraxis so umschreiben: Die Übergabeverträge erfreuten sich als flexible Erinnerungsmechanismen großer Beliebtheit. Die Anerbengesetze hingegen hegten die der Wiederbelebung harrende „Sitte“ wie ein mäßig frequentierter Friedhof seine Toten.

III. Nationalsozialistische Agrarpolitik: erzwungene Erinnerung

Nach einer Phase des Aufschwungs befand sich die deutsche Landwirtschaft seit dem Ersten Weltkrieg in einer neuerlichen Rezession[46]. Hitler nutz-

---

[42] Verhandlungen des Dreiundzwanzigsten Deutschen Juristentages. Hrsg. von dem Schriftführer-Amt der ständigen Deputation. Zweiter Band (Verhandlungen). Berlin 1895, S. 85, 87.
[43] Juristentag (wie Fn. 42), S. 89.
[44] Juristentag (wie Fn. 42), S. 85.
[45] Kroeschell; Winkler (wie Fn. 2), S. 38.
[46] Zur Lage der Landwirtschaft seit 1914: Kluge, Ulrich: Agrarwirtschaft und ländliche Gesellschaft im 20. Jahrhundert. München 2005, S. 16, 21-23.

te die krisenbedingte Unzufriedenheit der Bauern zur „Machtergreifung" auf dem Lande[47]. Hierfür bediente er sich des Agrarideologen Richard Walther Darré. Ideengeschichtlich gründete dessen um rassistische Aspekte angereicherte Theorie auf konservativen Bauerntumsvorstellungen Riehl'scher Prägung. Darré propagierte eine bäuerliche Erbfolge, bei der Blut und Boden parallel liefen, als Garantin für die Erhaltung der nordischen Rasse[48]. Dieser Gedanke wurde im Reichserbhofgesetz (REG) vom 29. September 1933[49] rechtlich verankert.

Land- und forstwirtschaftlich genutztes Grundeigentum zwischen 7,5 und 125 ha war kraft Gesetzes Erbhof und damit grundsätzlich unveräußerlich und unbelastbar[50]. Der Übergabevertrag wurde einem gerichtlichen Genehmigungserfordernis unterstellt; damit war die Kluft zwischen gesetzlichem Erbrecht und lebzeitiger Übergabe überbrückt[51]. Die Geschwister des Anerben gingen – abgesehen von Ausbildung und Ausstattung sowie dem Recht auf Heimatzuflucht – leer aus. Weibliche Erbanwärter berücksichtigte die agnatische Erbfolge des REG erst in der vierten Ordnung. Für die Ehefrau war ein Platz in der Anerbenfolge überhaupt nicht vorgesehen; sie musste sich mit einem bescheidenen Altenteil begnügen[52]. Begrüßt wurde das Erbhofrecht nur in stark verschuldeten Betrieben, insbesondere des Großgrundbesitzes, die vom Vollstreckungsverbot profitierten[53]. Aus den Realteilungsgebieten hingegen kamen erbitterte Proteste. Die Akzeptanz der Einzelerbfolge ließ sich dort nicht gegen das allgemeine Rechtsempfinden per Gesetz verordnen[54].

Die Blut-und-Boden-Ideologen waren angetreten, Übergabepraxis und gesetzliches Erbrecht mittels einer als germanisch deklarierten „Sitte" wieder zu

---

[47] Beyer, Hans: Die Agrarkrise und das Ende der Weimarer Republik. In: Zeitschrift für Agrargeschichte und Agrarsoziologie (1965), S. 62-92.
[48] Darré, Richard Walther: Das Bauerntum als Lebensquell der Nordischen Rasse. 1. Auflage, München 1929.
[49] RGBl. I, S. 685.
[50] § 37 Abs. 1 REG.
[51] § 37 Abs. 3 REG.
[52] Zu den Ansprüchen der Geschwister und der Ehefrau vgl. §§ 30, 20, 31 REG.
[53] So der Vorwurf Serings bei Grundmann, Friedrich: Die Problematik der nationalsozialistischen Erbhofpolitik. Marburg/L. 1977, S. 57.
[54] Grundmann (wie Fn. 53), S. 127-136.

vereinigen; herausgekommen ist eine Art Zwangsehe, die aus dem gestörten Verhältnis ein unerträgliches gemacht hat. Im Laufe der zwölf Jahre sahen sich die NS-Juristen daher gezwungen, die Härten dieser aufgedrängten Erinnerung nach und nach im Verordnungsweg und mittels der Rechtsprechung abzuschwächen.

C. Welcher „Sitte" zum Gedächtnis?

Spätestens bei der Thematisierung des Erbhofrechts stellt sich die Frage, auf welche Wurzeln die bäuerlichen Erbfolge tatsächlich zurückgeht und ob überhaupt von einer „Sitte" die Rede sein kann.

Nach heute herrschender Meinung war dem germanischen Rechtsbewusstsein ein Anerbenrecht fremd; diese Einsicht wurde bereits während des NS-Regimes von Agrarwissenschaftlern als historisches Argument gegen das Erbhofrecht verwandt[55]. Der Grundbesitz gehörte demnach der Hausgemeinschaft, in die man hineingeboren wurde und mit dem Tod wieder ausschied. Hierfür ist weniger der Begriff „Erbfolge" als vielmehr „An- und Abwachsung" zutreffend. Beim Ausscheiden Einzelner aus der Hausgemeinschaft wurde der Grundbesitz gleichmäßig verteilt. Kam es nicht zur Teilung, wirtschafteten die Geschwister unter der Leitung des Ältesten weiter. Daraus könnte sich mancherorts das Vorrecht eines der Söhne entwickelt haben. Zur festen Übung wurde das Anerbenrecht aber erst in den Zeiten der Grundherrschaft[56]. Das entscheidende Moment für die Einzelerbfolge muß man darin aber nicht sehen. Denn auch bei den bereits damals freien Bauern findet sich der geschlossene Hofübergang[57]. Das spricht wiederum dafür, daß praktische Bedürfnisse – etwa die Altersversorgung – maßgeblich waren.

---

[55] Diesbezügliche Kritik Serings gegen das REG: Grundmann (wie Fn. 53), S. 54-60.

[56] Zur Geschichte des landwirtschaftlichen Erbrechts: Kroeschell, Karl: Landwirtschaftsrecht. 2. Auflage, Köln [u.a.] 1966 , S. 53 f.

[57] Über die Nachfolgegepflogenheiten der altfreien Bauern in Schleswig-Holstein: Sering, Max: Erbrecht und Agrarverfassung in Schleswig-Holstein. In: Die Vererbung des ländlichen Grundbesitzes im Königreich Preussen. Hrsg. von Sering, Max. Band VII. Berlin 1908, S. 34-36.

„Wohin kommen wir, wenn wir überall Gesetze machen wollen, wo Dummheiten stattfinden…"? Ohne die eingangs gestellte rhetorische Frage letztgültig beantworten zu wollen, erscheint die gesetzliche Steuerung des landwirtschaftlichen Generationenwechsels doch bedenklich[58]. Mag sein, daß die bäuerliche Hofübergabepraxis von einer „Sitte" im Sinne von Tradition und Herkommen bestimmt ist. Die Erinnerung an diese „Sitte" ist aber immer dann dem Vergessen gewichen, wenn sie nicht in den Erfordernissen der jeweiligen Gegenwart eine neue Rechtfertigung erfuhr. Ein abstraktes Gesetz kann nicht auf die wechselhaften wirtschaftlichen und sozialen Bedürfnisse eingehen. Wenn es abweichende Disposition zulässt, bleibt es für die Praxis bedeutungslos. Generalisiert das Gesetz hingegen vereinzelte privatautonome Mißstände, gehen diese „Dummheiten" zu Lasten der Gesamtheit der Grundeigentümer. Der Rückgriff auf eine fadenscheinige „Sitte" rechtfertigt dies auf denkbar ungenügende Weise. Es erscheint mithin zweckmäßig, Erinnern und Vergessen den Betroffenen selber zu überlassen.

---

[58] Allgemein zur Wirkung des Rechts auf den menschlichen Lebenslauf und das Generationenverhältnis: Stefan Ruppert: Alter im Recht. In: Rechtsgeschichte 9 (2006), S. 138-147.

Law's Families: Conceptions of the Family in Late Eighteenth Century English Law

Adam S. Hofri-Winogradow

Why Late Eighteenth Century Family Property Law Has Been Neglected

Until 1875 the English temporal courts operated two separate jurisdictions – the common law and equity, famously described as 'a gloss on the law'.[1] As in many legal systems, family property law – the law regulating the transmission of property between family members – was one of the first areas of English law to attain a high level of sophistication. In the late eighteenth century it was still the most sophisticated branch of English law. That the existing legal historical literature about the period does not reflect this fact, concentrating mostly on those areas of law relevant to trade, such as contract, the law of bills and notes, insurance and partnership,[2] reflects the continuing baneful influence of nineteenth-century biases: research conducted using a conceptual framework assuming that 'the bourgeoisie' or 'trade' was 'rising' and that the landholding nobility was 'declining', or, what is worse, actually adopting on some level a belief-system according to which the exploitation of property for commercial or industrial purposes is 'good' or interesting and the possession and consumption of property for dynastic or other family reasons 'unproduc-

[1] The courts and the twin legal systems they operated were fused, nominally at least, by the Supreme Court of Judicature Act 1873 (36 & 37 Vict c 66); Supreme Court of Judicature Act 1875 (38 & 39 Vict c 77).

[2] The two leading works on late eighteenth century English law are Atiyah, Patrick S: The Rise and Fall of Freedom of Contract. Oxford 1979, and Oldham, James: The Mansfield Manuscripts and the Growth of English Law in the Eighteenth Century. Chapel Hill 1992, which also concentrates on Lord Mansfield's contributions to the law of trade.

tive' or bad, would tend to concentrate on those areas of the law of special relevance to trade or industry. And so the family property law of late eighteenth-century England has been curiously understudied.

Another cause for it having been understudied was the nineteenth century criticism and reform of the court of Chancery. Chancery was one of the four central English courts, the major though not the only one to operate the equity jurisdiction,[3] and increasingly in the eighteenth century the most important court for family property matters: the other three central courts, known as the common law courts, heard such matters too, but the remedies the common law had to offer, and its procedural framework, dependent on jury trial, were largely eclipsed, for complex family property suits, by Chancery's written bill procedure. However, in the nineteenth century Chancery fell victim to a massive reforming campaign, which mostly centered on the practical defects in the working of the court: the long delays experienced by suitors, the unnecessary expenses to which they were put by the court's many officers, and some features of Chancery procedure which seemed designed to multiply delays and fees.[4] The vilification necessary to drive professional opinion to reform the court has led to a very unflattering image of the late eighteenth century Chancery being imprinted on the collective memory of the English legal community. This image seems to have discouraged legal historians (with a few exceptions) from studying eighteenth-century, especially late eighteenth century, equity. It has also created some extremely long-lived path dependencies

---

[3] The equity jurisdiction was also operated by the court of the Exchequer. For the 'equity side of the Exchequer' see Macnair, Michael RT: The Court of Exchequer and Equity. In: Journal of Legal History (2001), p. 75; Bryson, William H: The Equity Side of the Exchequer (Cambridge 1975); Horwitz, Henry: Chancery's 'Younger Sister': The Court of Exchequer and Its Equity Jurisdiction, 1649-1841. In: Historical Research (1999), p. 160.

[4] For the nineteenth century criticism of the court of Chancery see, e.g., Parkes, Joseph: A History of the Court of Chancery. London 1828; and for the history of that criticism and the resulting reforms, Lobban, Michael: Preparing for Fusion: Reforming the Nineteenth-Century Court of Chancery, Part I. In: Law and History Review (2004), p. 389; id.: Preparing for Fusion: Reforming the Nineteenth-Century Court of Chancery, Part II. In: Law and History Review (2004), p. 565; and id.: "Old Wine in New Bottles": the Concept and Practice of Law Reform, c. 1780-1830. In: A. Burns, J. Innes (eds.): Rethinking the Age of Reform: Britain 1780-1850, Cambridge 2003, p. 114.

in research: most of the handful of recent articles dealing with late eighteenth century equity have dealt with the practical working of the court, asking such questions as how long did the average Chancery bill spend in Chancery from its having been filed to either a Chancery decree or its disappearance from the records.[5] The substance of late eighteenth century equity, on the other hand, has been neglected.

One more reason for our neglect of late eighteenth century equity is that the leading equity judges of the time, Chancellors Thurlow and Loughborough, have received a signally unflattering treatment at the hands of posterity. Thurlow was a unique character, the great bully Chancellor: completely disdainful of proper social manners, especially disdainful of the hereditary aristocracy, he rose from humble beginnings to being granted a Peerage and appointed Lord Chancellor by the strength of his legal skills, imposing rhetorical delivery, and friendships. Uniquely, he exercised vast clerical patronage in the Church of England while living quite openly – indeed, famously – in sin with the pretty barmaid from Nando's Coffee House in London, close to the Temple, who bore him three daughters. His total lack of courtesy and disdain for conventional religion did not endar him to Victorian England. Very soon after his death, Victorian biographers started to write that Thurlow has been overestimated by his contemporaries, who were stunned into submission by his rhetorical tactics.[6]

---

[5] See, along with the articles by Lobban in the last note, Horwitz, Henry and Patrick Polden: Continuity or Change in the Court of Chancery in the Seventeenth and Eighteenth Centuries. In: Journal of British Studies (1996), p. 24. For earlier eighteenth century equity see the important work of Michael Macnair and Henry Horwitz: Macnair, Michael RT: The Conceptual Basis of Trusts in the later 17th and Early 18th Centuries. In: Richard Helmholz and Reinhard Zimmermann, (eds.): Itinera Fiduciae: Trust and Treuhand in Historical Perspective, Comparative Studies in Continental and Anglo-American Legal History, Band 19. Berlin 1998, p. 207-36; id.: The Law of Proof in Early Modern Equity. Berlin 1999; Horwitz, Henry: Testamentary Practice, Family Strategies, and the Last Phases of the Custom of London, 1660-1725. In: Law and History Review (1984), p. 223; id.: The Mess of the Middle Class Revisited. In: Continuity and Change (1987), p. 263; id.: Chancery Equity Records and Proceedings 1600-1800. London 1995.

[6] The only modern biography of Thurlow was written for a popular audience: Gore-Browne, Robert: Chancellor Thurlow: The Life and Times of an Eighteenth-Century Lawyer. London 1953. See also Ditchfield, G.M.: Thurlow, Edward, first Baron Thurlow (1731-1806). In: Oxford Dictionary of National Biography (2004) [http://www.oxforddnb.com/view/article/27406, ac-

The sudden eclipse of Thurlow's considerable fame, on the cusp of the eighteenth and nineteenth centuries, seems to exemplify the sharp transformation which several historians of English society have noticed during the last two decades of the eighteenth century: the relatively open and secular 'masquerade society' of the eighteenth century crumbled suddenly into a rapidly rechristianised, conservative community valuing thrift, hard work and moral earnestness, reminiscent of Max Weber's ideal protestants.[7] The vilification of the late eighteenth century Chancery by nineteenth century English lawyers can thus be seen as an example of the precipitate collapse of what social historian Dror Wahrman has called 'the short Eighteenth century' into pre-Victorian society.[8] The Lord Chancellor who succeeded Thurlow, Alexander Wedderburn, Lord Loughborough, was even more clearly a scion of the 'short eighteenth century': as a Scot growing up in Edinburgh in the 1740s and 50s he was the *wunderkind* of the Scottish Enlightenment, the quintessential expression of that 'short century'. In his twenties he was the editor of the first Edinburgh Review, in the second issue of which Adam Smith published his famous essay introducing Scot and English readers to Jean Jacques Rousseau. Having quarrelled with the Edinburgh judiciary, Wedderburn retraced the steps of his better-known compatriot, Lord Mansfield, and switched to the English bar. In a political career too complex to be more than sketchily reviewed here he established himself as the great tergiversator of English politics, switching his political allegiance no less than four times, the last of which brought him to the Chancellorship in 1793.[9]

---

cessed 31 July 2006]. The key hostile Victorian biography of Thurlow is that by the Whig Chancellor, Lord Campbell: Campbell, John: Lives of the Lord Chancellors. London 1846, vol. 5, p. 473-678. Foss's biographical essay was based on Campbell: Foss, Edward: The Judges of England. London 1864, vol. 8, p. 374-85.

[7] The key source for this thesis is now Wahrman, Dror: The Making of the Modern Self. New Haven 2004; Wahrman studied with Lawrence Stone, who broached a similar thesis more briefly in his The Family, Sex, and Marriage in England 1500-1800. New York 1977, p. 667-73.

[8] Wahrman, Making of the Modern Self.

[9] There is no modern full-length biography. The best recent source is Murdoch, Alexander: Wedderburn, Alexander, first earl of Rosslyn (1733-1805), in: Oxford Dictionary of National Biography, (2004) [http://www.oxforddnb.com/view/article/28954, accessed 31 July 2006]. Adam

Wedderburn, who was a well-esteemed advocate, parliamentary debater and government minister, suffered from a truly terrible posthumous reputation. The nineteenth century saw him, even more than his predecessor Thurlow, as a 'typical eighteenth century' figure with no morals and less loyalty: this bad reputation rubbed off on his judicial work, normally condemned along with Thurlow's as of insufficient depth. Loughborough's cultured habits also rubbed his hardworking Victorian and post-Victorian successors the wrong way: Sir William Holdsworth, the author of a 16-volume 20th century *History of English Law*, cited the complaint of earlier commentators that Loughborough was too often seen in the theatre and in good society – that is, he was having a good time when he should have been home with his caseload; no wonder that the delays in Chancery were piling up.[10]

Methodology

Most of the work of Chancery was concerned with questions of inheritance law. This essay depends on the methodological premiss that through an intense engagement with the way Chancery tackled hundreds of concrete cases, one can formulate a model of the type of family relationships it saw as desireable. Formulating such a model is particularly challenging because most of what Chancery judges did was construing documents: wills and various pre- and post-nuptial agreements, known in lawyers' English as marriage settlements. Since document construction is at least ostensibly targeted at identifying the meaning the author of the document intended to convey, the normative preferences of the interpreter are not easily extractable from the record of

---

Smith's essay in the Edinburgh Review is now available in his Essays on Philosophical Subjects. Indianapolis 1982, p. 242.

[10] Lord Campbell's hostile biography of Wedderburn is in his Lives of the Lord Chancellors, vol. 6, p. 1-366; Foss' shorter version is in his The Judges of England, vol 8, p. 385-98. Another hostile nineteenth century treatment is that by Lecky, William EH: A History of England in the Eighteenth Century. London 1892, vol. 4, p. 465. Holdsworth's hostile treatment is in Holdsworth, William S: A History of English Law, vol. 12. London 1938, p. 569-76; vol. 13, London 1952, p. 578-80. The same critical narrative still recurred in the 1980s: Duman, Daniel: The Judicial Bench in England, 1727-1825: The Reshaping of a Professional Elite. London 1982, p. 89-90.

his efforts. Especially so in the case of Chancery judges, who were more often than not reticent about their normative preferences: they were never short of rhetorical strategies with which to hide them, the two most important of which were pretending that document construction was simply uncovering meanings authored by the creators of the documents construed, and pretending to blindly follow precedent.

Nevertheless, from the crabbed record of the equity proceedings of the late eighteenth century[11] I have tried to extract a model of family relationships the way equity wanted them to be. Equity dealt mostly with matters of family property, rather than with the social and emotional aspects of family relationships, but the latter are implicated in the former; especially so among social groups essentially dependent on inherited wealth, as many of those who litigated in the late eighteenth century Chancery were. While not being exclusively a court for the rich, Chancery suitors did tend to slant middle-class and up.[12] Among such social groups, inter-generational property arrangements tend to reflect the relative balance of power between the family members concerned; those family members entitled to enjoy the family's property, as well as to dispose *of* it, can and often do use the power of the purse to make those family members dependent on them behave in ways they prefer.

My distinguishing between the enjoyment of property – what we call 'having' property – and the power to dispose of it points to a key characteristic of the way family property was held by the middle and higher classes in eight-

---

[11] This research is based on the full corpus of Chancery law reports included in the English Reports for the period between Thurlow's appointment in 1778 and Loughborough's dismissal in 1801, as well as manuscript reports of the same cases preserved in Lincoln's Inn library, London, as parts of the great manuscript collections of Sargeant Hill (hereinafter: "Ms Hill") and of Charles Abbot, later Lord Colchester (hereinafter: "Ms Abbot"). Many manuscript reports added much to the printed reports: information on stages of proceedings not reported in print, comments by both court and counsel, as well as references they cited, which have been omitted from the printed reports, and variant versions of speeches by both. The practice of law reporting, consisting of taking speeches down by ear, permitted of wide variations.

[12] Information as to the social make-up of Chancery suitors during the late eighteenth century was collected by Horwitz and Polden (as in note 5), p. 48; they found that less than a third of all Chancery litigants in 1785 were "gentlemen and above", the lowest proportion of such litigants they found for any time between 1627 and 1819, and that nearly half were commercial men or artisans.

eenth century England. Family property and the powers to dispose of it in different ways were often distributed between different family members, so that, for example, a father might enjoy the right to receive the income on the family's land until he dies, at which point his son will be entitled to either the closest English equivalent of full ownership – the fee simple – or the form of tenure called 'fee tail' – the right to enjoy the income on the land yourself and to have it pass after you to your heirs in the male line, either to male descendants alone (under one form of this tenure) or to both male and female descendants (under another form). Another incident of the 'fee tail' was the power to turn it, by a technical procedure called 'common recovery', into a fee simple, the only tenure which included power to sell the land. The very complex and idiosyncratic pure theory of English property law facilitated a situation where the different powers over and entitlements to different parts of the family property tended to be distributed between several different family members. This decentralization of rights in family property contributed to the fairly non-tyrannical picture of family relationships which emerges from the late eighteenth century equity cases.

The Duty of Parents to Provide for their Minor Children

This article shall focus on a central aspect of family relationships: the intergenerational balance of power. We shall discuss four major aspects of the balance of power Chancery saw as desirable.

1. Equity considered that parents should maintain and provide for the education of their minor children, even when other funds were made available specifically for this purpose by parties outside the parental relationship.[13] In the fairly common case in which a grandfather or other relative left, by his will, a fund for his grandchildren or other young relatives, payable on their majority, Chancery nearly always directed the fund to be paid into the Bank of England immediately upon the deceased's estate having been administered,

[13] *Andrews v Partington* (1789) 3 Bro CC 60, 29 ER 408; 2 Cox 223, 30 ER 103, followed in *Prescott v Long* (1795) 2 Ves Jun 690, 30 ER 845.

and invested in one or more of a very short list of securities which were actually secure: land mortgages and government securities, known to eighteenth century investors as 'the funds'. The interest accrued on this investment was accumulated, often re-invested in the same securities, and paid to the legatee along with the capital fund, on his majority.[14] This practice was adhered to even where the testator, in giving the legacy, expressly directed that the income accrued on it during the legatees' minority was to be expended on their maintenance, education or other needs. Chancery was thus ready to interfere in the dispositions testators and non-testamentary grantors made of their family property, and indeed change them, in order to stand on the principle that minors should be provided for by their parents. Chancery's interference was moderate: it did not change the actual distribution the testator or grantor made of his property; it did change, however, the time at which he intended the interest on the property to reach his chosen donee.

Chancery in the late eighteenth century actually moved from a position of total inflexibility on this issue, subject to the single exception of parents who did not have the means to provide for their children themselves, to a more flexible position, willing to consider all of the relevant circumstances: for example, a parent having several children, some of whom could expect large legacies from non-parental sources at their majorities and some could not, might under the later regime be allowed to use the interest on the former's legacies to maintain them, based on the consideration that should he be forced to maintain all of his children out of his income, not only will it be spread more thinly on maintaining a larger number of children, but the overall distribution of his property between his children would have been distorted in an undesirable direction, giving a larger part of the fund to those children ex-

---

[14] *Green v Pigot* (1781) 1 Bro CC 103, 28 ER 1013; the rule was disapplied to legacies charged on land in *Gawler v Standerwicke* (1787-1788) 2 Cox 15, 30 ER 8; Ms Abbot vol VII 133a. For earlier stages in the development of the doctrine see *Phipps v Annesley* (1740) 2 Atk 57, 26 ER 432; *Palmer v Mason* (1737) 1 Atk 505, 26 ER 319; *Heath v Perry* (1744) 3 Atk 101, 26 ER 861; *Ferrand v Prentice* (1755) Amb 273, 27 ER 182; Dick 568, 21 ER 391. The rule received its statutory form in the Act for Repealing Certain Duties on Legacies… and for Granting Other Duties Thereon… 1796 (36 Geo 3 c 52) s 32.

pecting a gift *aliunde*, and thus perhaps contributing to the inequality of the overall provision made for each child.[15]

That even under the earlier, inflexible position, Chancery permitted impecunious parents to use the interest on legacies others gave to their children to maintain them during their minorities does not signify any tenderness in Chancery's attitude towards poor parents. Rather the opposite: insolvent fathers could lose guardianship of their children.[16] Chancery regarded maintaining your child financially as part and parcel of parenthood, at least amongst the ostensibly propertied: inability to so maintain was tantamount to a disqualification from parenthood.

By insisting that children be provided for by their parents, and that no part of any other fund which might be available for the same purpose be disbursed to the legatee until his majority, Chancery increased parents' power over their own children in the short term: children having an independent provision of their own might not have been easily restrained. Another effect of this policy, however, was to decrease the amount of free income at the father's disposal. This could be highly significant in ways which are not immediately obvious. The property of wealthy English families was often in this period settled under a sophisticated form of entail called 'strict settlement'. It was one of the fundamental quirks of early modern English property law that though on the face of the strict settlement, the family's property seemed to be settled and made inalienable for a very long time, the effective period for which land

---

[15] For the exception to the earlier inflexible position, maintained by Lord Thurlow, see *Andrews* (n 13), *Hughes v Hughes* (1784) 1 Bro CC 387, 28 ER 1193; *Hill v Chapman* (1787) 2 Bro CC 231, 29 ER 129; Ms Abbot vol IV 111b, where Thurlow refused to award money out of the interest on a child's legacy for the time before the case was referred to the Master in Chancery, despite counsel for both parties consenting to such payment; and *Fendall v Nash* (1779) 5 Ves Jun 199, 31 ER 544, where the making of such an allowance out of the interest was especially critical, as the legatees' father was reduced to absolute indigence, and the legacies were only due to be paid after both parents died. Thurlow allowed maintenance out of the interest for the time since the father's financial failure. The later, more flexible position was gradually grasped at, then reached by Lord Loughborough in *Mundy v Earl Howe* (1793) 4 Bro CC 223, 29 ER 863; *Hoste v Pratt* (1798) 3 Ves Jun 730, 30 ER 1243; *Greenwell v Greenwell* (1800) 5 Ves Jun 194, 31 ER 541. Master of the Rolls Pepper Arden contributed to the development of the new doctrine in *Cartwright v Cartwright* (1794) Ms Abbot vol XII 32b.

[16] *Wilcox v Drake* (1784) Dick 631, 21 ER 416.

could be made inalienable was only one generation. Once the eldest son of the current *paterfamilias* reached his majority, the land could be 'disentailed' and sold. In order to resettle it and make it inalienable for another generation, the *paterfamilias* needed the cooperation of his son; and it was common to achieve this cooperation by way of some fairly substantial 'sweeteners' given by father to son during the sensitive period between the latter's majority and marriage.[17] Chancery policies which cut the amount of income at the free disposal of fathers could have a negative impact on their ability to provide their sons with such 'sweeteners', and thus to encourage them to resettle the family property. Fathers less able to resettle their family property were less able to ensure their family's continuing social standing and prestige, which were a function of how much property, especially land, it held. Chancery's insistence that fathers provide for their minor children themselves thus had the effect of diverting property from being invested in the long-term stability of the family line, to ensuring that the current generation enjoys sufficient authority over its children. Current relationships were preferred to long-term stability and security.

Chancery's insistence that minors be provided for by their parents had many additional consequences in equity doctrine. It meant, for example, that in cases where the parent controlling the family property – normally, but not invariably, the father – died before his children's majority, having left them sums of money by his will, to be paid to them on their majority, the court read a gift of the interest on those sums of money, to be used by the surviving parent or guardian for the children's maintenance, education and other needs during their minorities, into the deceased's parent will, even in cases where no such gift had expressly been made.[18]

---

[17] Descriptions of the practical working of strict settlements appear in several basic works on English legal history. See, Baker John H: An Introduction to English Legal History, 4th edn. London 2002, p. 294.

[18] *Crickett v Dolby* (1795) 3 Ves Jun 10, 30 ER 866; *Tyrrell v Tyrrell* (1798) 4 Ves Jun 1, 31 ER 1; *Brown v Casamajor* (1799) 4 Ves Jun 498, 31 ER 255, in all three of which Pepper Arden emphasized that legacies directed to be paid at a future time do not generally carry interest, unless the testator was the legatee's parent. He extended the exception to legacies for wives and grandchildren. In *Carey v Askew* (1786) 2 Bro CC 58, 29 ER 31; sub nom *Cary v Askew* 1 Cox 241, 29 ER 1147 Kenyon tried to establish a rule that even where a parent gave by will a sum less than the interest on a child's portion, for his maintenance during minority, the child could still demand –

Maintaining Fathers' Power Over Their Children

2. Chancery saw as insufferable the rare situations in which children enjoyed larger rights in the family property than their fathers, putting the father at the wrong end of the power differential vis-a-vis his children. Such situations could occur, for example, where the family acquired its property through the maternal line, and settled it on the wife for life, and on the eldest son after her death. Chancery permitted a robust use of the parental 'power of restraint and correction' in order to correct such upside-down distributions of property and power: one way of correcting them was by resettling the property immediately on the eldest son's majority, increasing the father's rights in it. When some such sons asked Chancery to hold such resettlements void for undue parental influence, surprise and misrepresentation, Chancery refused to do so. It also refused to force fathers to account to their sons for the use they made of money raised by selling a part of the property in which the son had rights.[19]

Making Children's Marriage Portions Conditional on Parental Consent to their Choice of Spouse

3. The court held that during the compulsory relationship of parents and children, which lasted until the latter's majority, parents should enjoy the power to veto marital partners they considered unsuitable. At majority, however, Chancery considered that formal legal restraint should be gone: adult children were to be legally free to marry whoever they wanted, however much social and family custom and expectations narrowed their practical margin of choice.

---

and receive – the whole interest on the fund; but this extreme position, actively re-writing the will, was rejected by Arden in *Crickett*, as well as by Loughborough in *Mitchell v Bower* (1796) 3 Ves Jun 283, 30 ER 101, following Lord Hardwicke in *Hearle v Greenbank* (1749) 3 Atk 695, 26 ER 1200; 1 Ves Sen 298, 27 ER 1043. Where the sum bequeathed for maintenance during minority came not from the interest on the portion but from another fund, the child was not entitled to receive more than was bequeathed, either: *Wynch v Wynch* (1788) 1 Cox 433, 29 ER 1236.

[19] *Kinchant v Kinchant* (1784) 1 Bro CC 369, 28 ER 1183, Ms Hill vol 20 200.

This position, however, was only reached after a protracted struggle against one of those rules of Roman law which survived in equity until the late eighteenth century. Equity was influenced by both its common law normative environment and the 'learned laws', those of the civil and canon laws. Eighteenth century lawyers believed that the rules of the latter systems have reached equity by way of the Anglican church courts, which applied a version of the pre-Council of Trent canon law.[20] Recent legal historical research has pointed to a direct influence of the canon and civil laws on equity, bypassing the church courts.[21] Be that as it may, the Roman law presence in eighteenth century equity was undergoing an advanced process of attrition. If reception means the incorporation of rules of foreign origin into a certain legal system, then the Roman rules applied by equity were never actually 'received' into it: rather they were applied as acknowledgedly foreign rules, with lawyers and judges brandishing civil law authorities at each other. That this practice continued for hundreds of years shows the isolationist common law 'ancient constitution' ideology to have had less of a stranglehold on seventeenth and eighteenth century English law than some narratives of English legal and constitutional history would have us assume.

By the late eighteenth century, the number of Roman law rules *actively applied* in equity was down to three. One of these three was the rule of the Lex Papia Poppaea, that clauses making gifts to a son or daughter on their marriage (called 'marriage portions' in England) conditional on the *paterfamilias*, or a surrogate, consenting to the marriage were void, so that the gift became absolute: the recipient could claim it whether his father consented to his marriage or not.[22] As is well-known, this rule was a result of the specific demographic situation obtaining in Rome after the civil war of the first century

---

[20] A detailed rendering of this version of the history of equity was that by an important late eighteenth century lawyer and legal historian, Francis Hargrave: Juridical Arguments and Collections (London 1797), Vol. 1, p. 22, 46.

[21] Macnair: The Law of Proof in Early Modern Equity (as in note 5), p. 29-39, 289ff.

[22] D 35.1.62.2, 64, 72.4, 74, 79.4; Swinburne, Henry: A Treatise of Testaments and Last Wills, 5th edn. London 1728, p. 265-67; and on Roman pro-nuptial policy generally, Treggiari, Susan: Roman Marriage. Oxford 1991, p. 60-80; Gardner, Jane F: Family and Familia in Roman Law and Life. Oxford 1998, p. 47-55.

B.C.E. It made for an internal contradiction in Roman law, for marriage itself was still conditional, for a person in *potestas*, on the consent of his *paterfamilias* (though a magistrate could supply a consent unreasonably withheld).[23] Until 1753, the rule made more sense as part of the English system than it did at its Roman origin, for marriage could be had in England by a simple agreement to marry: parental involvement was not required. This state of English law seems extraordinarily inappropriate for the society subject to it: 16th and 17th century English families were often rigidly hierarchical, with fathers choosing conjugal partners for their children. Perhaps the fact that the law made marriage without parental consent, and even against the parents' objections, possible, and even positively encouraged it by the adoption of the Roman rule holding 'consent clauses' void, in some ways encouraged or even caused the developement of forceful styles of parenting such as were then prevalent.[24]

The propertied classes campaigned for decades to have marriage made conditional on paternal consent, and in 1753 it was so made in Lord Hardwicke's Act;[25] this made the English rules on the subject identical to those of Roman law after the Lex Papia Poppaea, with one key difference: that all English children were, in a sense, automatically emancipated at majority, which was then at 21. Automatic emancipation deprived the English father from a key instrument of correction enjoyed by his Roman predecessor. That he was also denied the power to make marriage gifts conditional on his consenting to the marriage put him in a very weak position vis-a-vis his children. Equity responded to this problem by progressively encrusting the Roman rule holding

[23] The Roman law is explained by Voet, Johannes: Commentarius ad Pandectas. The Hague 1704 23.2.7-10.

[24] On the 'forceful styles of parenting' then prevalent see Stone (as in note 7), p. 160-95; for parents' control of their children's choice of spouse see ibid., p. 180-193.

[25] An Act for the Better Preventing of Clandestine Marriages 1753 (26 Geo 2 c 33) s 11; see it discussed in two recent articles by Rebecca Probert: Probert, Rebecca: The Judicial Interpretation of Lord Hardwicke's Act of 1753. In: Journal of Legal History (2002), p. 129-151; id., The Impact of the Marriage Act of 1753: Was it Really "A Most Cruel Law for the Fair Sex"? In: Eighteenth-Century Studies (2005), p. 247-62.

consent clauses void with exceptions,[26] until at last Francis Hargrave, the most historically learned lawyer of the period who was also active in the courts, urged Thurlow in 1788 to abandon the Roman rule completely: he denied the validity of the common argument that equity should apply the same rules applied by the church courts, which had a concurrent jurisdiction with equity over legacy questions, for the sake of inter-jurisdictional harmony. Hargrave argued that since equity developed its concurrent jurisdiction over legacy questions, nobody resorted to the church courts any longer over them; and on the rare occasion when a legacy case came before them, the church courts, he said, actually follow temporal equity decisions.[27] Thurlow declined to adopt Hargrave's suggestion,[28] but Loughborough had very little patience for the application of non-English rules in the English system, and abolished the rule in 1796.[29] Hereinafter there were to be two separate legal regimes, each internally consistent: one for minor children, who had to obtain parental consent in order to marry, and marriage gifts to whom could be made conditional on parental consent to the child's choice of marriage partner; and the exact opposite for anyone over the age of majority. Some English donors tried to make marriage gifts to adults conditional on parental consent as well, but in these cases both Thurlow and Loughborough inflexibly struck down all of the conditions.[30]

Modern commentators may perhaps tend to see requirements for parental consent as tyrannically abridging the 'rights of the child'. Once one emerges from the metaphysical discussion of fundamental rights into the reality of family finances among the eighteenth century propertied classes, however, the

---

[26] See discussion of such clauses in Staves, Susan: Resentment or Resignation? Dividing the Spoils among Daughters and Younger Sons. In: John Brewer and Susan Staves (eds.): Early Modern Conceptions of Property. London 1995, p. 205-6.

[27] *Scott v Tyler* (1788) 2 Bro CC 431, 29 ER 241; 2 Dick 712, 21 ER 448; (1791) Ms Abbot vol IV 76b; and see Hargrave's argument in full in his Juridical Arguments and Collections (n 20), Vol. 1, 22, 46.

[28] His judgment was fully reported by Dickens from Thurlow's own Manuscript notes: last note.

[29] *Stackpole v Beaumont* (1796) 3 Ves Jun 89, 30 ER 909.

[30] *Jones v the Earl of Suffolk* (1782) 1 Bro CC 528, 28 ER 1278; *Hutcheson v Hammond* (1790) 3 Bro CC 128, 29 ER 449; *Crommelin v Crommelin* (1796) 3 Ves Jun 227, 30 ER 982; *Mercer and Wife v Hall* (1793) 4 Bro CC 326, 29 ER 917; *Osborn v Brown* (1800) 5 Ves Jun 527, 31 ER 717.

picture changes quite significantly: from the point of view of the parents, marriage meant making a large gift to a person towards whom they had no obligations prior to that event. What the children's freely choosing a marriage partner meant was telling their parents who to give a large gift to. Under such circumstances it is less than shocking to give the payor, not even a right to choose the payee, but merely a right to veto truly impossible ones.

It is striking that it were the outsiders who immigrated into the English legal system who were especially impatient with the presence in it of nuclei of foreign material. Loughborough, who was educated in the Scottish system,[31] had far less superstitious respect for the rules of the civil law than any of the English equity lawyers who appeared before him. He also had a rationalising ideology in true Enlightenment style, not little reminiscent of Bentham, though as an establishment figure whose career was dependent on the existing structure of the legal field, he did not use the positions of power he held for sweeping legal reforms. He was irreverent enough, however, to reject the Roman rule against 'consent clauses', noting that its adoption in a Christian country was due to the unreasoning spirit of the 'unenlightened ages', which took what they saw in the books of the civil law as rules to guide them, not caring to reason whether these rules fit either England or its legal system.[32] That this was a typical outsider's attitude is shown by the further example of Jean Louis de Lolme, a Genevan who emigrated to England and made a career out of flattering the English for their excellent constitutional principles.[33] When, in a

---

[31] For biographical material on Loughborough, see sources cited in n 9.

[32] *Stackpole v Beaumont* (n 29). Loughborough initiated other modest reforms; see, e.g., his 1794 General Order, allowing the separate creditors of each of two or more bankrupts to prove under a joint commission of bankruptcy issued out against the group without an exceptional petition to the Chancery; and requiring distinct accounts of the separate and joint estates, with separate and joint creditors having first call on those respective classes of estate and second call on any surplus of the other class of estate: General Order of the Lord Chancellor, reproduced in Christian, Edward: The Origin, Progress and Present Practice of the Bankrupt Law (London 1812-14), Vol. 2, p. 240-1. See discussion in Getzler, Joshua and Michael Macnair: The Firm as an Entity before the Companies Acts. In: Paul Brand, Kevin Costello and W. N. Osborough (eds.): Adventures of the Law. Dublin 2005, p. 267, at p. 282.

[33] See De Lolme, Jean Louis: The Constitution of England; Or, an Account of the English Government. London 1790.

rare venture into family property law, he criticised the famous will of a fellow Genevan emigré, Peter Thellusson, he also argued for a return to a mythically pure common law enshrined in Magna Carta, which gave every man his liberty and prohibited indivious schemes such as Thellusson's: Thellusson directed that most of his great property be not given to his children, but instead used for the purchase of land which shall be accumulated until the majority of his great-grandchildren. The law which permitted Thellusson to direct such a scheme was English equity, not a foreign norm such as the Roman rule against 'consent clauses', but the insistence on a pure English law is reminiscent of Loughborough's attitude, though far less knowledgable and more fanatical.[34]

Accelerating the Transfer of Family Property to Younger Family Members

4. The final characteristic of the family relationship equity saw as ideal to be mentioned here was that while parents to adult children did not labour under a formal duty to provide for them, it was expected that, absent extreme misbehaviour, substantial sums of money – much larger than those expended on the maintenance of children during their minority – should be given by parents to their children as the latter attained majority, marriage and parenthood. While such a transfer was often necessary to obtain a prestigious enough marriage, it had also to be on a scale significant enough to render adult children substantially free of the type of control parents could wield by the power of the purse, and enable them to wield something of that power over their own young children. Chancery's ideal family was a family where members of each generation enjoyed significant power over a substantial part of the family

[34] De Lolme, Jean Louis: General Observations on the Power of Individuals to Prescribe, by Testamentary Dispositions, the Particular Future Uses to be Made of Their Property (...). London 1798; see especially the second edition: id.: General Observations on Executory Devises (...). London 1800. Making up for his non-comprehension with violence, De Lolme seems to suggest, following a Rousseauian vision of the just society, that the virtues of English law should best be restored by the abolition of equity. The *Thellusson* case is reported as *Thellusson v Woodford, Woodford v Thellusson* (1798-9) 4 Ves Jun 227, 31 ER 117.

property. Perhaps more than any other attribute of the family relationship Chancery preferred, this ideal diverged from the ideal held by many parents of the property-owning classes. As is perhaps to be expected in social groups subsisting primarily on inherited wealth, many fathers distributed the family property over which they had control so as to deprive their children from either enjoying substantial parts of it or having significant powers to dispose of it themselves. Most of the property, as well as the powers of disposing of it, were sometimes postponed so as to be enjoyed only by remote generations. Peter Thellusson's above-mentioned scheme was a good example.[35]

Some of the rules which equity developed to limit such schemes of dynastic ambition are well-known, at least to common lawyers: I need only mention the rule against perpetuities[36] and the rule against accumulations. The latter was first formulated in an Act passed in 1800 on the initiative of Loughborough, fresh from having to hold Peter Thellusson's scheme valid because English law had no norm under which he could hold it to be void.[37] But the range of rules which equity developed in order to manipulate family-authored property arrangements so that every generation of young adult family members enjoyed a certain amount of property and control went far beyond the rules developed specifically to block dynastic schemes. Equity held, for example, that where a mother was given a power to appoint a fund between her seven children 'in such manner as they should deserve' – that is, was given a total discretion - each of the children could assign and sell, before his mother

[35] Text to note 34.

[36] The application of which in the late eighteenth century Chancery was quite rare; see *Robinson v Hardcastle* (1788) 2 TR 241, 100 ER 131 for Francis Buller's version of the rule; *Hay v Earl of Coventry* (1789) 3 TR 83, 100 ER 468; 86, 469 for Lord Kenyon's more permissive version; and *Routledge v Dorril* (1794) 2 Ves Jun 357, 30 ER 671 for the yet more permissive approach of Pepper Arden MR.

[37] For the rule against accumulations, see the *Thellusson* case (n 34). Loughborough's Act was An Act to Restrain All Trusts and Directions... Whereby the Profits or Produce of Real or Personal Estate Shall be Accumulated, and the Beneficial Enjoyment Thereof Postponed... 1800 (39 & 40 Geo 3 c 98). An exhaustive discussion of both the case and the Act is in Polden, Partick: Peter Thellusson's Will of 1797 and Its Consequences on Chancery Law. Lewiston, NY 2002. A case decided on the same year as *Thellusson*, where the court found itself able, unlike in *Thellusson*, to restrict a trust for accumulation without legislative reform, was Reeves v Brymer (1799) 4 Ves Jun 692, 31 ER 358; 698, 361.

executed her power, the possibility that he shall receive some property under that power.[38] So holding gave each child an asset independently of the mother's discretion, where the author of the family property arrangement clearly meant, by giving the mother such a wide discretion, to make the children dependent on her.

Even the rules of Roman law which survived in late eighteenth century equity were pressed into service in order to transfer family property to younger family members. The civil law held that 'debitum in præsenti solvendum in futuro': legacies which the testator made payable not on his death, but on a later date, vest on the death, not at the date set for payment.[39] This seemingly technical distinction received its practical import in cases where a legatee died after the testator's death, but before the time the testator set for the payment of his legacy. Holding the legacy to have vested on the testator's death meant that the entitlement descended to the legatee's heirs, while holding it not to have vested meant that the legacy lapsed, and the entitlement passed as the testator by his will directed it to pass in such a case, or, absent testamentary provisions for such a contingency, that it passed to the heirs of the testator under a partial intestacy. The application of this Roman rule thus often decided which of two groups of potential heirs took the legacy; is it therefore unsurprising that a great amount of complicated law developed on where exactly was the rule applicable.[40] The rule proved uniquely relevant to equity's

---

[38] *Musprat v Gordon and Ux.* (1792) 1 Anst 34, 145 ER 791 (a case in the Court of Exchequer).

[39] D 36.2.21; Tituli ex Corpore Ulpiani 24.31; Stein, Peter (rev): Buckland, WW: A Text-Book of Roman Law, 3rd edn. Cambridge 1966, p. 344-45. See this rule and its application by eighteenth century equity in Fonblanque, John (ed.) [Ballow?]: A Treatise of Equity, 2nd edn. London 1799, vol 2, p. 202-4, 366-368.

[40] These complexities are too intricate to be unfolded here; I hope to enlarge on them in a subsequent publication. See *Dawson v Killet* (1781) 1 Bro CC 119, 28 ER 1023; *Barnes v Allen* (1782) 1 Bro CC 181, 28 ER 1069; Ms Hill vol 20 343; *Monkhouse v Holme* (1783) 1 Bro CC 298, 28 ER 1143, Ms Hill vol 18 61, 178; *Benyon v Maddison* (1786) 2 Bro CC 75, 29 ER 42; *Gawler* (n 14); *Doe d Wheedon v Lea* (1789) 3 TR 41, 100 ER 445; *Harrison v Naylor* (1790) 3 Bro CC 108, 29 ER 438; 2 Cox 247, 30 ER 115; *May v Wood* (1792) 3 Bro CC 471, 29 ER 649; Ms Abbot vol X 26b, 27b; *Pearce v Loman, Pearce v Taylor* (1796) 3 Ves Jun 135, 30 ER 934; *Mackell v Winter* (1796) 3 Ves Jun 236, 30 ER 987; (1797) 3 Ves Jun 536, 30 ER 1144; *Batsford v Kebbell* (1797) 3 Ves Jun 363, 30 ER 1055; *Booth v Booth* (1799) 4 Ves Jun 399, 31 ER 203; *Bolger v Mackell* (1800) 5 Ves Jun 509, 31 ER 707.

effort of manipulating family property arrangements so as to transfer property to the young: where a parent gave a legacy to a child payable at the age of, for example, 25, and the child died under that age leaving children of his own, applying the Roman rule meant that the legacy was payable to the children of the deceased child, at their majorities; disapplying it normally meant that the legacy was to be divided between the siblings of the deceased child. The application of the Roman rule thus made the legacy 'jump forward' a generation. Unsurprisingly, unlike the rule against 'consent clauses', the Roman 'early vesting rule' was not abolished in the late eighteenth century, though Loughborough, ever the most flexible of the Chancery judges of the period, was quick to disapply it where its application would have frustrated the policy goal of passing family property to younger members of the testator's family.[41]

Conclusion

The ideal parents of late eighteenth century equity would provide for their children until their majorities, and transfer large sums of money to them soon after their majorities so that they could make their way in the world and enjoy some power over their own children. The ideal children of late eighteenth century equity did not exploit any power advantages they might fortuitiously have enjoyed over their parents; they gave of their own property to pull their parents out of debt, and did not marry without parental consent. Among the actual families whose affairs came before the court, most of the children seem to have measured up to the ideal fairly well. It were the parents who often came short: trying to embezzle gifts grandparents and others gave to their children, leaving property 3 or 4 generations ahead in the hope to found a dynasty, or dying while their children were still under 21 – what English law called 'infants' – leaving their children with no obvious source for maintenance during their minorities.

The conception of the family promoted by the eighteenth century court of Chancery seems equally far removed from a putative dynastic, aristocratic

[41] *Mackell v Winter* (last note).

model as from a 'laissez faire' model dedicated to the maximization of the current generation's dispository freedom. It is also – in its inter-generational dimension – a surprisingly modern model, differing from our current notions of proper inter-generational family dynamics in the single detail of requiring parental consent for marriage during minority. This revelation exposes the slow pace of social and legal change in the field of inter-generational family relations, falsifying the late-20th and early-21st century automatic assumption of continuous social and normative revolution. Many of our liberal notions of parental responsibility, if stripped of the language of rights, were already present in late eighteenth century equity.

Bibliography

1. Primary Sources (excluding Statutes and Cases)

Christian, Edward: The Origin, Progress and Present Practice of the Bankrupt Law (London 1812-14)

De Lolme, Jean Louis: The Constitution of England; Or, an Account of the English Government (London, 1790)

--. General Observations on the Power of Individuals to Prescribe, by Testamentary Dispositions, the Particular Future Uses to be Made of Their Property... (London 1798)

--. General Observations on Executory Devises… (London 1800)

The Digest of Justianian (cited as 'D'), in: Paulus Krueger and Theodorus Mommsen (eds.): Corpus Iuris Civilis, Vol. 1 (Berolini 1920)

Fonblanque, John: (ed) [Ballow?] A Treatise of Equity, 2nd edn., (London 1799)

Hargrave, Francis: Juridical Arguments and Collections (London 1797)

Parkes, Joseph: A History of the Court of Chancery (London 1828)

Smith, Adam: Letter to the *Edinburgh Review*, in W. P. D. Wightman (ed.): Essays on Philosophical Subjects (The Glasgow Edition of the Works and Correspondence of Adam Smith, Vol. 3), (Indianapolis, 1982), P. 242.

Swinburne, Henry: A Treatise of Testaments and Last Wills, 5th edn., (London 1728)

Tituli ex Corpore Ulpiani, in: Schulz, Fritz: Die Epitome Ulpiani des Codex Vaticanus Reginae 1128 (Bonn 1926).

Voet, Johannes: Commentarius ad Pandectas (Hague 1704) 23.2.7-10

2. Secondary Materials

Atiyah, Patrick S: The Rise and Fall of Freedom of Contract (Oxford 1979)

Baker John H: An Introduction to English Legal History, 4th edn. (London 2002)

Bryson, William H: The Equity Side of the Exchequer (Cambridge 1975)

Campbell, John: Lives of the Lord Chancellors (London 1846)

Ditchfield, G.M.: Thurlow, Edward, first Baron Thurlow (1731–1806), in: Oxford Dictionary of National Biography (2004) [http://www.oxforddnb.com/view/article/27406, accessed 31 July 2006]

Duman, Daniel: The Judicial Bench in England, 1727-1825: The Reshaping of a Professional Elite (London 1982)

Foss, Edward: The Judges of England (London 1864)

Gardner, Jane F: Family and Familia in Roman Law and Life (Oxford 1998)

Getzler, Joshua and Macnair. Michael: The Firm as an Entity before the Companies Acts, in: Paul Brand, Kevin Costello and W. N. Osborough (eds.): Adventures of the Law (Dublin 2005), P. 267

Gore-Browne, Robert: Chancellor Thurlow: The Life and Times of an Eighteenth-Century Lawyer (London 1953)

Holdsworth, William S: A History of English Law (London 1938-52)

Horwitz, Henry: Testamentary Practice, Family Strategies, and the Last Phases of the Custom of London, 1660-1725, in: Law and History Review (1984), P. 223

--. The Mess of the Middle Class Revisited, in: Continuity and Change (1987), P. 263

--. Chancery Equity Records and Proceedings 1600-1800 (London 1995)

--. Chancery's 'Younger Sister': The Court of Exchequer and Its Equity Jurisdiction, 1649-1841, in: Historical Research (1999), P. 160

Horwitz, Henry and Polden, Patrick: Continuity or Change in the Court of Chancery in the Seventeenth and Eighteenth Centuries?, in: Journal of British Studies (1996), P. 24

Lecky, William EH: A History of England in the Eighteenth Century (London 1892)

Lobban, Michael: "Old Wine in New Bottles": the Concept and Practice of Law Reform, c. 1780-1830, in: A. Burns, J. Innes (eds.), Rethinking the Age of Reform: Britain 1780-1850, (Cambridge 2003), P. 114

--. Preparing for Fusion: Reforming the Nineteenth-Century Court of Chancery, Part I, in: Law and History Review (2004) P. 389

--. Preparing for Fusion: Reforming the Nineteenth-Century Court of Chancery, Part II, in: Law and History Review (2004) P. 565

Macnair, Michael RT: The Conceptual Basis of Trusts in the later 17th and Early 18th Centuries, in: Richard Helmholz and Reinhard Zimmermann, (eds.): Itinera Fiduciae: Trust and Treuhand in Historical Perspective, (Comparative Studies in Continental and Anglo-American Legal History, band 19) (Berlin 1998), P. 207-36

--. The Law of Proof in Early Modern Equity (Berlin 1999)

--. The Court of Exchequer and Equity, in: Journal of Legal History (2001) P. 75

Murdoch, Alexander: Wedderburn, Alexander, first earl of Rosslyn (1733–1805), in: Oxford Dictionary of National Biography, (2004) [http://www.oxforddnb.com/view/article/28954, accessed 31 July 2006]

Oldham, James: The Mansfield Manuscripts and the Growth of English Law in the Eighteenth Century (Chapel Hill 1992)

Polden, Partick: Peter Thellusson's Will of 1797 and Its Consequences on Chancery Law (Lewiston, NY 2002)

Probert, Rebecca: The Judicial Interpretation of Lord Hardwicke's Act of 1753, in: Journal of Legal History (2002), P. 129-151

--. The Impact of the Marriage Act of 1753: Was it Really "A Most Cruel Law for the Fair Sex"? Eighteenth-Century Studies (2005), P. 247-62

Staves, Susan: Resentment or Resignation? Dividing the Spoils among Daughters and Younger Sons, in: John Brewer and Susan Staves (eds.): Early Modern Conceptions of Property (London 1995), P. 194

Stein, Peter (rev): Buckland, WW: A Text-Book of Roman Law, 3rd edn., (Cambridge 1966)
Stone, Lawrence: The Family, Sex, and Marriage in England 1500-1800 (New York 1977)
Wahrman, Dror: The Making of the Modern Self (New Haven 2004)
Treggiari, Susan: Roman Marriage (Oxford 1991)

Israeli Law as a *Lieu de mémoire (et d'oubli)*: Remembering and Forgetting Jewish Law in Modern Israel

Nir Kedar*

Law has always been an important *lieu de mémoire*.[1] Not only does it embody and preserve social conventions, but, by calling these conventions "laws", it also gives them additional validity, authority and importance. The social conventions that form the law are, of course, the product of complex political and cultural processes that accept – and thus remember and preserve – certain norms and traditions, and reject – that is, forget – others. The law, therefore, not only records the accepted social conventions but also mirrors the rejected ones. It is a *lieu de mémoire* but at the same time a *lieu d'oubli* that persuades (and sometimes even forces) us to abandon the rejected norms that are now "non-law". The establishment of the State of Israel in 1948 and formation of Israeli law involved many decisions of remembrance and abandonment. One of the most critical decisions was whether to remember or forget Jewish law, whether to turn Jewish law into the law of the land or to relegate it to oblivion.

The paper is divided into three parts. The first part briefly introduces Jewish law and *halakha* and sketches some of the problems of integrating Jewish law into modern law. The second part discusses the complex ways in which Israeli law deals with Jewish law: rejecting it in principle, but embracing it symbolically. The third part inquires into the question whether Israel really abandoned Jewish law, and concludes by showing that the dynamics of remembering and

---

* I wish to thank Ms. Lior Mishali for her research assistance.

[1] I am using here of course Pierre Nora's famous expression. See Les lieux de mémoire, sous la direction de Pierre Nora. Paris, 1997 (This three-volume edition contains the seven volumes of the original edition published by Gallimard from 1984 to 1992).

forgetting Jewish law parallels the difficulty of defining the essence of Jewish law and Judaism, and their relevant roles in Israeli social life.

I. Jewish Law and the problem of its integration into modern state law

In order to understand the problem of embracing Jewish law in modern Israel, one must first understand the nature of Jewish law and its role in Jewish history. Judaism, like Islam, but unlike Christianity, may be defined as a "legal religion" in the sense that it is a holistic system composed of countless norms that dictate the life of the believer from the moment he wakes up until the moment he goes to sleep, from birth till his death. Jewish law encompasses every aspect of private and public life. It deals with civil, commercial, and public law, and even dictates what the Jewish believer may eat, drink and wear (these are the laws of *kashrut* – the dietary laws concerning kosher food). Jews call their holistic religious-legal system *halakha* and the Moslems call theirs *shari'a*. Christianity is different. The Christian believer is supposed to accept the *credo*, basic tenets and beliefs of the Christian faith, but religious-legal rules do not dictate all aspects of his life. In this sense, even the Canonic law of the Roman-Catholic Church is very different from Jewish *halakhic* law.

What is the structure of Jewish law? The *Tora* – the first five books of the Bible – is considered by Jews to be the basic source of *halakha*. But, in spite of the central place of the Bible in Jewish faith and law, *halakha* mainly progressed through a process of "questions and answers" (in Hebrew: *she'elot u'tshuvot*, or *"shut"*), a process that recalls the Roman institution of *responsa*. People would ask the rabbis for a *halakhic* solution to a particular issue, and the rabbis would base their answer on Jewish law. *Halakha*, therefore, is a set of numerous answers – or decisions – a sort of Jewish common law. From time to time the *halakha* was codified. Some of these codes are very old. In addition to the Bible itself, the *Mishna* and *Talmud* should also be mentioned. The *Mishna* was the first compilation of Jewish oral *halakha*, codified in the early 3rd century A.D. in Palestine by Rabbi Yehuda Hanassi. The *Talmud*, which was codified around the 5th century A.D. in Palestine and in the 6th century in Persia, contained the *Mishna* and rabbinic commentaries on the *Mishna* that had been gathered in the centuries following its codification (these commentaries are known as the *Gemara*). Additional rabbinic codes were codified later – during the middle-ages and in modern times – the most famous and important of them are perhaps Maimonides' *Mishne Tora* (completed in 1180) and the *Shulkhan Arukh* by Rabbi Yossef Karo (published in 1565). The codes (and especially the *Talmud*) are heavily cited by the rabbis and considered the primary sources of *halakha*, but it is clear that over the centuries Jewish law progressed mostly through *responsa* – the answers and decisions of the rabbis.

From this definition of Jewish law, we begin to see the problem of integrating Jewish law into the law of the modern state (any modern state). An in-depth discussion on the place of religious law in modern state law lies outside the framework of this paper.[2] I will sketch only three problems that hinder the integration of Jewish law into modern state law: the scope of Jewish *halakha* and its special form; *halakha* as a holistic religious system; and the authority of the legislators and judges.

The first problem that hampers the incorporation of Jewish law into modern state law lies in the *halakha* itself, or to be more exact – in the scope and form of *halakha* which make it very difficult to transform the *halakha* into a modern legal system. This refers to three interconnected yet different problems: the scope of *halakha*, its form, and its special decentralized character. Our discussion will begin with the limitations of *halakha's* scope. *Halakha*, as mentioned, is a holistic system with jurisdiction over all aspects of private and public life. This is true in theory, but in practice there are many areas – especially in public life – that *halakha* never deals with. Of course, according to the Jewish faith, *halakha* is allowed to regulate theses areas, but this hardly ever happens. One major area where *halakha* is almost completely silent is public law, especially the laws that regulate citizenship and the modern state. *Halakhic* literature contains a wealth of discussions and norms concerning the biblical monarchies or the messianic kingdom of the future, but there is almost no discussion – let alone norms – on the modern legal-bureaucratic state, citizen-

---

[2] See Englard, Izhak: Religious Law in the Israel Legal System. Jerusalem, 1975.

ship, democracy, the rule of law, etc.[3] Likewise, *halakha* never dealt with modern civil or commercial institutions. The main reason for this is that since the emancipation and secularization of the Jewish people (beginning in the late eighteenth century) the Jews increasingly turned to the state's legal system instead of to their own autonomous legal institutions. As Izhak Englard has shown, there are no *halakhic* decisions in matters of car accidents, or other misfortunes caused by machines, or the misuse of technology; and *halakha* has nothing to say on questions of private or social insurance, corporations, securities etc. The *halakhic* position on these contemporary issues is rather passive. The rabbis do not initiate legislation or set up new legal "institutions" or arrangements in these areas. At best, they accept the existing arrangements created by the state.[4] This is not to say that the *halakha* opposes modern legal arrangements – it is probably content with them – nevertheless it was the state – not the rabbis – that developed them. To sum up, the use of Jewish law in many vital areas of living is impossible since there is simply no reference to them in *halakha*, and no central *halakhic* institution that can fill this void with legislation.

In addition to *halakha's* limited scope (by today's standards), its unique form, that is incompatible with the modern state, must also be taken into consideration. As mentioned earlier, *halakha* is composed of countless decisions and answers (*responsa*) that were adjudicated by rabbis over the last two thousand years. The Jews call this immense body of norms "the sea of *Talmud*". This form of law is very problematic for the modern centralist state, whose legal system is based chiefly on statutory law. In order to adjust Jewish law to the modern state, it must first be codified in a way that will make it viable for modern citizens and lawyers.

---

[3] See Leibowitz, Yeshaayahu: Outline for the Problem of the Jewish Religion in the State of Israel (1951). In: Leibowitz, Yeshaayahu: Judaism, Jewish People and the State of Israel. Jerusalem & Tel Aviv, 1975, pp. 85-87 (in Hebrew); Leibowitz, Yeshaayahu: The Law of the Tora as the Law of the State of Israel? In: id., pp. 192, 195-198 (in Hebrew); Englard, Yizhak: The Integration of the Jewish Law in the Israeli Legal System. In: Bazak, Jacob: The Hebrew Law and the State of Israel. Tel Aviv, 1969, pp. 110, 122 (in Hebrew); Ravitzky, Aviezer: Is a Halakhic State Possible? The Paradox of Jewish Theocracy. In: Ravitzky, Aviezer (ed.): Religion and State in Twentieth-Century Jewish Thought (in Hebrew), Jerusalem, 2005, p. 9, 29-31 (in Hebrew).

[4] See Englard, The Integration (as in note 3), p. 122.

However, the codification of Jewish law is also very problematical. Not only does it require years of hard study to be able to safely navigate in the "sea of *Talmud*", but the special decentralized character of *halakha* makes its codification an almost impossible task. Because of the geographical dispersion of the Jews, and in the absence of a Jewish centralist legislature or church, *halakha* developed as a decentralized and pluralistic system of *responsa* administered (if this word can be applied to the diffuse evolution of *halakha*) by generations of rabbis. The *responsa* are characterized by frequent disagreements among the rabbis and by *halakhic* questions that remain unresolved. It should be stressed that the decentralized and pluralistic character of Jewish law is not merely the result of historical conditions (the lack of a centralist legislature and the geographic dispersal of the Jews); rather, it evolved at a very early stage as a major feature of *halakha*. Already in the *Mishna* and the *Talmud* we find many unresolved questions and disagreements among the rabbis regarding the "correct" *halakha*. Therefore, we can say that although the creation of a centralist legislative body of *halakha* is theoretically possible, such a development is very unlikely, as it would be a major break from the Jewish legal pluralistic and decentralized tradition. This makes codification almost impossible since we do not know which norm to choose in the numerous cases of contradictory norms or unresolved questions. Furthermore, in the pluralistic and decentralized environment of *halakha* the authority of the codifier would be extremely difficult to agree on. Historically, even the great works of Maimonides and Karo were initially rejected by many rabbis and Jewish communities. Only years after their publication did they receive the imprimatur of authoritative codes.

The second problem that hinders the incorporation of Jewish law into modern state law is the nature of *halakha* as a religious holistic system. This problem can be stated in the following manner: can *halakha* be applied optionally; and if so, which parts of the *halakha* should be remembered and which forgotten? Non-observant Jews who cherish their rich Jewish heritage will be pleased to incorporate parts of Jewish law into the laws of their modern states, but they will also insist on using only those parts that are appropriate to modern life. They will agree to transplant certain rules, principles, or institutions onto modern secular laws, while rejecting other parts of *halakha* that they deem unsuitable for a modern, non-religious society.

Orthodox Jews, on the other hand, cannot accept this view of *halakha*. For them *halakha* is a hallowed, undivided, holistic system that flows from the divine wellspring. In fact, many religious Jews claim that there is no such thing as Jewish law, there is only *halakha*. Legal and non-legal parts are indistinguishable in *halakha*. We cannot choose which parts of *halakha* to follow and which to reject. Such distinctions tamper fatally with its holy character. Therefore, from the religious point of view, *halakha* cannot be "incorporated" into any other legal or normative system since it is a unified, eternal, divine system that has precedence over any earthly social legislation. The validity of a *halakhic* norm stems from its being, *ipso facto*, part of *halakha*, and not from the activity of a secular legislator or the decision of a temporal judge. At most, the integration of other norms or institutions into *halakha* may be possible – under certain conditions – but not the other way around.[5] Likewise, from the religious point of view, *halakha* cannot be integrated into a non-religious system because such an inclusion would profane its holy essence. Also from the religious perspective, the basic reason for obeying *halakhic* norms is religious in that it is linked to one's faith in the Almighty. By way of contrast, the primary purpose of secular law is regulative. At most, one can say that the law reflects political or moral principles. But it is clear that the main purpose of modern law is not religious. Therefore, the reception of Jewish law into the law of the modern state will not satisfy the religious believer, since the primary motivation behind this reception is not religious but regulatory.[6] For example, a modern parliament that embraces parts of Jewish law on negligence will probably do so in order to regulate that field. In other words, the parliament's decision to incorporate the Jewish law of negligence is most likely due to the parliament members' belief that Jewish law offers highly equitable arrangements in this domain, and not because the parliamentarians believe in the di-

---

[5] This is the opinion of the (Jewish religious) philosopher Aviezer Ravitzky. He claims that the modern Israeli legal system can be seen – in certain conditions (and as long as it does not run counter to the basic tenets of the *halakha*) – as a *halakhic* institution. This is because *halakha* always recognized the need for secular civil institutions to regulate social life. See Ravitzky, p. 23-26.

[6] Englard: The Integration (as in note 3), p.115-118; Avraham, Michael: Is the Halakha Hebrew Law? In: Akdamot (2004), No. 15, p. 141 (in Hebrew).

vine spirit of Jewish law. The very essence of *halakha* as a holistic unified religious system makes its incorporation into modern state law nearly impossible.

The third and most difficult problem that hampers the integration of Jewish law into modern state law is the problem of authority, i.e., who has the authority to legislate or interpret the law? In Judaism, *halakha* is authored by God who gave the *Tora* to Moses on Mount Sinai, but since that divine revelation *halakha* has become a human project.[7] Nevertheless, only ordained rabbis can decree *halakha*, since according to Jewish belief they are part of a continuous chain that began with Moses. If the law is not enshrined by the rabbis, then it is not part of Jewish law, even if it based upon *halakhic* material. No parliament or court of law is entitled to pronounce *halakha* unless it is recognized by ordained rabbis as a *halakhic* institution. If the state legislates norms that originate in *halakha*, religious believers will obey this law, but only because it is the law of the state and not because they accept it as Jewish law. Naturally non-religious Jews, or people of other faiths, do not accept this religious concept of authority, which is incompatible with modern ideas of democracy and the rule of law. They want their laws to be legislated by a democratic secular parliament and interpreted by independent judges, not by rabbis.

The characteristics of *halakha* and the problem of its authority make it very difficult to integrate Jewish law into the law of the modern state (any modern state). The next section examines how the first Israelis coped with this Sisyphean task, and whether Israeli law remembered or forgot Jewish law.

II. The Role of Jewish Law in Contemporary Israeli Law

The idea of making Jewish law the law of the Zionist community in Palestine was born in the early twentieth century. In this period a new term was

---

[7] Compare Mishna 1 in Tractate Avot of the Mishna: "Moses received the torah from Sinai, and he delivered it to Jehoshua, and Jehoshua to the elders, and the elders to the prophets, and the prophets delivered it to the men of the Great Synagogue". The English version of this tractate is taken from: Taylor, Charles (ed.): Mishna. Avot. Sayings of the Jewish fathers: Comprising Pirqe Aboth in Hebrew and English, 2nd edition. Cambridge UK, 1897. http://www.sacred-texts.com/jud/sjf/sjf03.htm.

coined: "Hebrew law" (*mishpat ivri*). The scholars who created this expression did not intend to discuss the law of the ancient Hebrews, but rather to distinguish between *halakha* as a whole and the body of legal norms (themselves part of *halakha*) that seemed fitting for incorporation into the future Jewish state.

The term "Hebrew law" was devised by a group of Russian Zionists in Moscow who established the "Society of Hebrew Law" (*khevrat hamishpat ha'ivri*) in late 1917. Most of the group's members were non-religious Jews, but all of them – religious and non-religious alike – believed that the national and cultural renaissance of the Jewish people must be accompanied by a legal resurgence as well, and that the growing Zionist community should use its own rich legal heritage as the basis of its laws rather than derive its inspiration solely from modern Western law – "the law of Gentiles". The group invented the term "Hebrew law" in order to emphasize that they had no desire to force *halakha* upon the new legal system but rather to take legal norms that had developed in *halakha* and that were judged suitable for modern society, and use them for the law of the future Jewish state. In other words, their idea was to revive legal norms from Jewish *halakha* and complement or amend them with norms taken from modern non-religious legal systems so that the new law would satisfy the needs of modern life.

The anarchy that followed the Bolshevik Revolution forced the "Society of Hebrew Law" to cease its activity in Russia. In the early 1920s most of the group immigrated to Palestine and continued its work, along with many new members – some of them religious but most of them not. Members of the group gave frequent public lectures in Palestine, published two legal journals (*Hamishpat* and *Hamishpat Ha'ivri*), carried out several independent studies, created bibliographies of Jewish legal sources, translated Roman legal sources (e.g. Gaius' *Institutions*) into Hebrew, and drew up plans for the incorporation of Jewish law into the future state. In addition, many of them served as judges or consultants in the "Hebrew Peace Courts" – an autonomous non-religious

Jewish court system established in 1909. Last but not least, they founded the Tel Aviv College for Law and Economics in 1934.[8]

Yet, despite their efforts, the majority of the Jewish population in Palestine and abroad found little interest in the society's work. In Palestine, most Jews used British Mandatory law and the Mandatory court system, and paid little attention to the issue of Jewish legal autonomy or revival and to the incorporation of Jewish law (be it *halakha* or Hebrew law) into the modern law of the Zionist community. Indeed, until 1948 the tension between Jewish law and secular state law was hardly felt because an independent Jewish state did not exist, and the law in Palestine was Ottoman and later British. But as the establishment of the State of Israel approached, and especially after independence, the question of Jewish law and its incorporation into Israeli law burgeoned into a source of legal, political and cultural controversy. Once it became a matter of time when the independent Jewish state would be established in parts of Palestine, Jewish lawyers began to draft laws – many of which were based on *halakha* – for the future state. Between 1938 and 1948 (and especially after 1945) over ten codes based on Jewish *halakha* were drafted by religious and non-religious lawyers. These codes dealt with all aspects of the law – from private law to penal law to constitutional law.[9]

Despite the long debates in the months prior to Israel's establishment, the political and legal elite decided that Israel would retain British Mandatory law.[10] Although the decision was intended chiefly to stave off chaos and anarchy in the fledging state, the question of Jewish law and its integration into Israeli law was also one of the reasons that affected the decision to keep British

---

[8] On the Society of Hebrew Law see Likhovsky, Assaf: The Invention of "Hebrew Law" in Mandatory Palestine. In: American Journal of Comparative Law (1998) no. 46, pp. 357-372; Shamir, Ronen: The Colonies of Law: Colonialism, Zionism, and Law in Early Mandate Palestine. Cambridge UK, 2000, pp. 30-48; Radzyner, Amihai: "Jewish Law" between "National" and "Religious". In: The Dilemma of the Religious-National Movement. Brand, Yitzhak (ed.), Forthcoming (in Hebrew).

[9] See Radzyner, Amihai: "A Scholar who was not properly eulogized" – J.S. Zuri and his Jewish Law Studies on the Background of Jewish Law Research History. In: Jewish Law Annual (2005) no. 23, p. 253, 315 note 196 (in Hebrew).

[10] See Kedar, Nir: The Establishment of the Israeli Legal System and the Rule of Law. In: Israel no. 11 (2007).

Mandatory law and not embark on the task of legislating a novel, original Israeli law (see below).

As a consequence of this decision, Jewish law plays practically no role in Israeli law today. The law of the State of Israel is completely westernized (although Israel never translated or copied the laws of another country *en bloc* as Turkey, China and Japan did, for example). Israel always drafted its own original laws according to its needs and social purposes, but its inspiration came from western laws and not Jewish law. Only one enclave of religious law took root in Israeli law: family law, which, in the period of Ottoman rule over Palestine, was considered part of religious law and not civil law. Ottoman law stated that all matters of family law would be decided according to the religious law of the faith to which a certain citizen belonged.[11] According to the Ottoman system (called *millet*), *shari'a* courts had exclusive jurisdiction over family matters among Moslems; rabbinic courts had parallel jurisdiction over Jews; and the courts of the multivarious Christian churches had a similar domain over their members. When the British conquered Palestine in 1917 they preserved this arrangement. The Israelis did the same in 1948, although Israeli law narrowed the authority of the religious courts to the area of marriage and divorce, while all other areas of family law come under the jurisdiction of civil family courts, unless the parties wish otherwise.

Family law notwithstanding, Jewish law as such was omitted from Israeli law. Not a single Israeli law is based in its entirety on Jewish law. Indeed, the Israeli Ministry of Justice has a special department for Jewish law that is supposed to suggest ways of incorporating Jewish law into modern Israeli legislation, and to add the perspective of Jewish law to all legislative debates. Although a few academics – Professor Menachem Elon is the most prominent among them – claim that Jewish law has a profound influence on Israeli legislation and jurisprudence,[12] most Israeli lawyers – both religious and non-

---

[11] In legal term we would say that the Ottoman state received by reference the religious law of family. On the reception of religious law by reference see Englard: Religious Law (as in note 2), pp. 56-77.

[12] Elon, Menachem: Jewish Law: History, Sources, Principles – *Ha-Mishpat Ha-Ivri*. Philadelphia, 1994, vol. 4; Elon, Menachem, et al.: Jewish Law (*Mishpat Ivri*): Cases and Materials. New York, 1999, pp. 420-422.

religious – agree that this influence is minimal and that Jewish law is employed mostly on the rhetorical level, and much less so on the practical level.[13] Even laws that are compatible with principles or norms in Jewish law, and that seem to be based upon Jewish law, are not really so. Israel's laws are generally drafted according to modern Western legal, political and economic principles, and only in retrospect – after the bill is completely formed – does the Justice Ministry's Department for Hebrew Law add the "Jewish perspective" – as a kind of symbolic embellishment – to the bill's statement of purpose.

But the process of legislation (described above) teaches us also about the relative importance of Jewish law's cultural function in Israeli law. Although it plays practically no role in Israeli law, Jewish law is not entirely forgotten, but is retained primarily as a symbol. The will of Israeli society to keep Jewish law as a symbol explains why the Israeli taxpayer is prepared to finance a (relatively large) special department for Jewish law in the Ministry of Justice, even though its influence on the final legislation is basically insignificant. Likewise, the desire to preserve Jewish law as a symbol also explains the tradition of a "Jewish law chair" on the Supreme Court. Since the founding of Israel, one of the judges on the Supreme Court is an expert in Jewish law, and his role is to explicate – as *obiter dicta* – Jewish law's view of the issue before the court. Here too, the part of the judicial decision that contains the Jewish law is not operative (not part of the *ratio-decidendi*), and it is usually disregarded by lawyers and law students. Yet, the convention of a "Jewish law chair" is almost never questioned. The desire to preserve Jewish law also explains its remarkable presence in the *curricula* of Israeli law schools: every law student – even non-Jews – must take at least two courses in Jewish law. And finally, the significance of Jewish law as an important part of Israeli culture explains why Israel has bequeathed names taken from Jewish law to many of its laws and legal institutions. For example the proposed new Israeli civil code is not called simply "the civil code" (*hakodex ha'ezrakhi*) even though the word "codex" is used in Hebrew; instead, it is called *khok diney mamonot* – *diney mamonot* being the *ha-*

[13] For a critique of Elon see Avraham; Englard, Yitzhak: Research on Jewish Law – Its Nature and Function. In: Mishpatim (1976) no. 7, p. 34 (in Hebrew); Englard, The Integration (as in note 3), pp. 119-120.

lakhic expression for private law. Although Jewish law played no role in the legislation of the new Israeli civil code, it is still symbolically present in its title.[14] One can say that Israelis have forgotten the content of Jewish law, but remember it as a title, an expression, a symbol.

III. Did Israel Forget Jewish Law?

The question may be posed: if Jews were so accustomed to living according to a comprehensive "legal religion" (*halakha*), and were so proud of their legal heritage, why was it so difficult for them to incorporate Jewish law into modern Israeli law? How did a people with such a rich legal heritage come to forget its past? After all, Jewish legal tradition introduced the noble principles of the biblical prophets to the world, and it is a tradition whose legal institutions in many fields were as sophisticated as those of Roman law.

We have already seen that a key to the answer lies within Jewish law itself: first, *halakha's* character as a pluralistic and decentralized system of *responsa* makes it unsuitable for the modern state; second, from a religious point of view, the *halakha* is a unified sanctified system that cannot be integrated into a non-religious legal system; and third, since it is a religious system, it forbids secular legislators or judges to expound upon and expand the *halakha*. These problems became crucial in the modern State of Israel since the majority of its population – Jews and non-Jews – were non-observant, and would never accept the enforcement of Jewish *halakha* as the country's legal system. *Halakha's* religious essence, then, explains why it was neglected in Israel: neither the religious nor the secular sectors of society – each group for its own reasons – could accept *halakha's* full integration into the law of modern-day Israel.

Even if we agree that the *halakha* cannot be enforced as the law of the land and fully integrated into the law of the state, the reason for the failure of the national-cultural project of "Hebrew law" still eludes us. What prevented modern Israelis from adopting parts of their sophisticated legal heritage to

[14] See Introduction (and Explanation) to the Bill of the Israeli Civil Code. In the web-site of the Israeli Ministry of Justice: http://www.justice.gov.il/MOJHeb/Codex/Mavo.htm. (in Hebrew).

their legal system? Why has the wisdom enshrined in the "sea of *Talmud*" had almost no effect on Israeli law? Is it acceptable that all *halakhic* laws are obsolete and incompatible with a modern state, and should therefore be forgotten?

Some scholars claim that the reason for *halakha*'s exclusion is due to historical contingency. In the first years of statehood there was simply no time to legislate; Israeli lawyers, who were mostly non-religious, stuck to what they knew best – modern Western law.[15] This explanation has a lot of truth to it. As noted, the major concern of Israel's emerging political and legal elite was to prevent chaos and anarchy. For this reason it preserved the law that had been in effect during the British Mandate. The new state's legislators feared that the creation of a novel and original legal system would be too lengthy of a process, especially since the precise meaning of the term "original Israeli law" was highly controversial. While some Israelis identified the term "original Israeli law" with *halakhic* Jewish law, others thought that this term should reflect Jewish legal heritage, the rich Jewish culture that developed over the last two centuries during which the Jews underwent secularization and emancipation, and modern Zionist culture. It is also true that most Israeli lawyers – in the 1950s as today – are non-religious who have no expertise in Jewish law. As ardent modernists some of them even conceive of Jewish law as an obsolete system belonging to the distant past, and certainly inappropriate for a modern enlightened state.[16] These lawyers are obviously incapable of navigating in the "sea of *Talmud*" in order to apply its treasures to the benefit of Israeli law and society. Expediency and ignorance explain the failure of the "Hebrew law" cultural project – the integration of parts of the Jewish law into modern Israeli law.

---

[15] Harris, Ron: Absent-Minded Misses and Historical Opportunities: Jewish Law, Israeli Law, and the Establishment of the State of Israel. In: On Both Sides of the Bridge: Religion and State in the Early Years of Israel. Bar-On, Mordechai; Zvi, Zameret (eds.), Jerusalem, 2002, p. 21 (in Hebrew); Radzyner, Amihai: The "Hebrew Law" is not *Halakhah* (Nevertheless it has Value). In: Akdamot (2005), no.16, p.81, 86-87 (in Hebrew).

[16] See for example Radzyner, Amihai; Shuki, Friedman: The Israeli Legislator and Jewish Law, Haim Cohn between "Tomorrow and Yesterday". In: Tel-Aviv Law Review (2005) no. 29, p. 167 (in Hebrew).

I believe, however, that Israeli law's attitude to Jewish law is more complex. As mentioned earlier, Israelis may have forgotten Jewish law in many senses, but they still insist on remembering it as a symbol. Therefore, we have to discover not only why Israeli law abandoned Jewish law, but why it also insisted on remembering it. I suggest that the forgetting and remembering of Jewish law is part of Israeli society's general attitude to Judaism, that is, it is part of deeper questions of culture and identity that bewilder modern Israelis. Because Israel is a society of immigrants and Jewish history is a complicated history, the construction of Israeli identity became a complex process that involved many decisions regarding remembering and forgetting, decisions that were naturally reflected in modern Israeli law.[17]

Those who advocated the integration Jewish (or "Hebrew") law demonstrated the problem of borrowing from other – Western or Eastern – legal systems. First, the new Israelis had to decide whether to remember or forget Europe. Europe was the place where most Jews emigrated from, and the place to which they were affiliated by powerful historical and cultural bonds. Most Israelis saw themselves (and still do) as Europeans, and believed that their culture and law should be European-based, especially since they perceived European law and culture as superior to other cultures and laws. The only question was which European legal tradition Israel should embrace: the Anglo-Saxon tradition or one of the continental Romano-Germanic traditions? On the other hand, Europe was also the continent of the Jews' lachrymal past, the place of exile, oppression and persecution. It was the vale of tears from which they were expelled and where they were almost annihilated during the Holocaust. For these reasons, the new Israelis wanted to forget Europe and create their own culture and law. In 1938, Moshe Silberg, a distinguished Israeli lawyer who would become a judge on the Israeli Supreme Court, rejected the idea of the German or even Swiss civil code as a model for the law of the future Jewish state, because "for us Jews, there is nothing more abominable than the German spirit".[18]

---

[17] On the problems of identity reflected in the work of the "Society of Hebrew Law" see Likhovsky, pp. 357-372.

[18] Silberg, Moshe: The Law in the Hebrew State. In: Silberg, Moshe: In Inner Harmony: Assays and Articles (in Hebrew). Tarlo, Zvi; Meir, Hovav (eds.), Jerusalem, 1981, p. 180, 198.

Likewise, the new Israelis had to decide whether to recall their ancient (or imagined) memories of the "East" or forget them. On the one hand, their return to the East was not only a return to the geographical "Zion", but also to the conceptual "Zion", the ideal of creating a model society according to the lofty principles of the biblical prophets. The East was also the cradle of Western civilization. The great civilizations of Egypt and Mesopotamia, and later the great Moslem empires, possessed sophisticated legal systems, and gave humanity science and technology, the monotheistic idea, and biblical morality. The East, then, was a veritable treasure house of symbols and laws. On the other hand many European Zionists held orientalist views, which saw the East as a backwater and Moslem and Ottoman law as non-rational, chaotic, and generally unsuited to the Jewish state-in-the-making. The formation of Israeli law forced the Israelis to confront problems of identity related to Israel's locus on the East-West axis. But this was only one problem of identity that bewildered the first Israelis.

Another major problem, which is reflected in the Israeli law and is directly related to our subject, is the complex relations between Israel and Judaism. The Zionist movement was, of course, the Jewish national movement, and as such it emphasized Jewish cultural and collective identity – often in a chauvinistic manner. On the other hand, Zionism – like all national movements – was a revolutionary movement that sought to break with the past and revolutionize all aspects of Jewish public life. Thus, Zionism developed a complicated – not to say schizophrenic – attitude towards Judaism: it was a national movement that wished to remind the Jews of their individual and collective identity, and at the same time it sought to forget – or at least revitalize – Judaism. Israel suffers from the same schizophrenia. It depicts itself (even in its laws) as a Jewish and democratic state. However, it is not clear what Jewishness means, i.e., what it means to be Jewish in Israel. Religious Jews claim that to be Jewish means to be a religious Jew, a Jew who believes in the tenets of the Judaism and lives according to *halakhic* commandments. Most Israeli Jews, however – like most Jews all over the world – do not see themselves as religious people though they identify themselves as Jewish. So the question the Zionists, and later the Israelis, asked was how to remain Jewish while abandoning Judaism – both the religious faith and the traditional way of Jewish life. This question has confounded modern Jewry for the last two hundred and fifty years and is still a major source of cultural and political controversy in Israel.[19] The article makes no attempt to solve the conundrum; first, because it is a Herculean task beyond the scope of this article, and second because it is probably an insoluble issue. Most modern Jews – in Israel and abroad – have "solved" the problem by simply avoiding it. They are secular Jews who consider themselves Jewish. They speak Hebrew (or have at least learned one of the Jewish languages: Hebrew, Yiddish, Ladino and their like); they celebrate Jewish holidays, honor Jewish rituals, and revere Jewish symbols, yet they do so without being committed to the Jewish faith or to the principles of *halakha*. Many religious Jews regard this behavior as hypocritical, cowardly, or irrational, as do many avowedly secular or atheistic Jews (who refer to themselves as being "of Jewish origin" at the most).[20] Some label this approach "Judaism as culture" or "Judaism as civilization" – two terms that aim to demonstrate that Judaism is broader in scope than mere liturgy or *halakha*. But the truth of the matter is that most secular Jews act the way they do without giving much thought to the exact definition of their identity or Jewishness. As opposed to the dogmatic, "black or white" approach of religious or atheistic Jews, Israeli society defines itself as Jewish by its remembrance of Jewish symbols and traditions, despite its forgetting of many other attributes of religious Judaism.

Israeli law's relationship to Jewish law corresponds, then, to the complex relationship between Israeli society and Judaism; both sets of relationships correspond to the efforts to forge a new Jewish-Israeli identity that relies on a rich Jewish heritage, and at the same time seeks a new pattern for it. In the

---

[19] Among the many books and article in this subject, see Neher, André: Clef pour le Judaisme. Paris, 1977; Herman, Simon: Jewish Identity: A Social Psychological Perspective. Jerusalem, 1979 (in Hebrew); Rash, Yehoshua (ed.): Regard and Revere – Renew Without Fear: The Secular Jew and his Heritage. Tel-Aviv, 1986; Zucker, David: We the Secular Jews: What is a Secular Jewish Identity? Tel Aviv, 1999; Sagi, Avi: A Critique of Jewish Identity Discourse. Ramat-Gan; Bar-Ilan University, 2002 (in Hebrew); Friedlander, Yehuda et al.: The Old Shell Be Reviewed and the New Sancified: Essays on Judaism, Identity and Culture. Tel-Aviv, 2005 (In Hebrew). For the contemporary Israeli discourse in this subject see also the many writings of Eliezer Schweid, Aviezer Ravitzky, Ruth Gavison and Yedidiya Z. Stern.

[20] See Frumann, Ram: What to do on the Holidays? Secular People and the Jewish Holidays. In: Kleinberg, Aviad (ed.): Hard to Believe: Rethinking Religion and Secularism in Israel. Tel Aviv, 2004. p. 205-263.

same manner, Israeli law simultaneously remembers and abandons the past. It has forgotten Jewish law as a viable legal system, and re-invented it as a symbol.

IV. Conclusions

Since its establishment in 1948, Israel has been engaged in an ongoing debate over its Jewish identity. Part of this debate concerns Jewish law: Israeli legislators and judges are blamed for forgetting Jewish law and refusing to use it as the law of the state. My aim in this paper has been to demonstrate how cultural processes of remembrance and forgetting are preserved in the law. I have tried to show that the attitude of Israeli law toward Jewish law reflects, in essence, the general process of redefining Jewish identity in Israel. Redefinition is a process of remembrance and forgetting. Israeli culture has abandoned many attributes of Judaism (mainly religious aspects), yet at the same time it has preserved other attributes as symbols of Jewish identity. Jewish law is one of these symbols, and in that sense, Israeli law is a *lieu d'oubli* but at the same time also a *lieu de mémoire* of Jewish law.

Institutionen und Ursprung der juristischen Schriftlichkeit in Ungarn im 12.-13. Jahrhundert

László Komáromi

A. Einführende Bemerkungen

Die ersten Jahrhunderte des mittelalterlichen ungarischen Staates weisen verschiedene Formen auf, mit Hilfe derer die Staatsgewalt und Privatpersonen ihre Rechtsakte von dem Vergessen zu bewahren versuchten. Sowohl die Schriftlichkeit des königlichen Hofes als auch die für die Festsetzung von privaten Rechtsakten verantwortlichen Institutionen wurden in der ungarischen Geschichtswissenschaft tiefgehend erforscht, und mehrmals unter dem Gesichtspunkt eines eventuellen ausländischen – westlichen oder byzantinischen – Einflusses untersucht. Dabei wurden vermutliche Vorbilder sowohl aus dem lateinischen als auch dem griechischen und slawischen Teil Europas in Betracht gezogen. Für die Anlehnung an byzantinische Muster spricht insbesondere, daß die ungarische juristische Schriftlichkeit gerade unter der Herrschaft von Bela III. (1172-1196) aufblühte. Dieser wurde am kaiserlichen Hof in Konstantinopel als möglicher Thronfolger des byzantinischen Kaisers Manuel I. Komnenos erzogen, jedoch kehrte er nach zehn Jahren nach Hause zurück und führte ein Vierteljahrhundert lang in Ungarn als König die Regierung.[1] In

---

[1] Hinsichtlich des Aufschwungs der höfischen Schriftlichkeit unter Bela III. betont die byzantinische Erziehung des Königs Kumorovitz, L. Bernát: A magyar pecséthasználat története a középkorban [Der Gebrauch von Siegeln in Ungarn im Mittelalter]. 2. Auflage, Budapest 1993, S. 50.; ders.: A középkori magyar magánjogi írásbeliség első korszaka [Die erste Epoche der mittelalterlichen ungarischen privatrechtlichen Schriflichkeit]. In: Századok (1989) Nr. 123, S. 397 und Zlinszky, János: Römisches Recht in Ungarn. In: Iurisprudentia universalis, Festschrift für Theo Mayer-Maly zum 70. Geburtstag. Hrsg. von Martin J. Schermaier et al. Köln 2002, S. 951. Hinsichtlich der Praxis der „Petitionen" Mezey, László: A pécsi egyetemalapítás előzményei (a deákság és a hiteles-hely kezdeteihez) [Die Vorgeschichte der Universitätsgründung in Pécs (zu den

dem vorliegenden Text soll auf die Frage eingegangenen werden, inwieweit der Aufbau und die Praxis der königlichen Kanzlei und die Tätigkeit der Institutionen der privaten Schriftlichkeit von äußeren Vorbildern beeinflußt wurden.

B. Die ungarische königliche Kapelle und die zeitgenössischen europäischen Herrscherkanzleien

Die überwiegende Mehrheit der überlieferten Urkunden aus dem 11.-12. Jahrhundert sind in Ungarn königliche Urkunden. Die meisten von ihnen enthalten Spenden, Stiftungen und Urteile des Herrschers. Sie sind in Stil und Form vielfältig. Manche sind den Urkunden der deutschen und italienischen kaiserlichen Kanzlei ähnlich, andere scheinen französischen, manchmal dalmatinischen oder venezianischen Mustern zu folgen.[2] Wir kennen sogar eine griechische Gründungsurkunde von Stephan I., deren Original zwar verloren ging, aber zu Beginn des 12. Jahrhunderts (1109) von König Koloman kopiert und erneuert wurde und den einfachen Stil der zeitgenössischen byzantinischen Privaturkunden widerspiegelt.[3] Privatpersonen ließen ihre Rechtsakte damals nur selten schriftlich festsetzten, aber auch in diesen wenigen Fällen

---

Anfängen der klassizistischen Bildung und der glaubwürdigen Orte)]. In: A pécsi egyetem történetéből [Aus der Geschichte der Universität in Pécs]. Hrsg. von Andor Csizmadia. Pécs 1967, S. 62-63; ders.: A hiteleshely a közhitelűség fejlődésében és III. Béla szerepe [Der glaubwürdige Ort in der Entwicklung der Glaubwürdigkeit und die Rolle von Bela III.]. In: Középkori kútfőink kritikus kérdései [Kritische Fragen unserer mittelalterlichen Quellen]. Hrsg. von János Horváth und György Székely. Budapest 1974, S. 331-332; ders.: Deákság és Európa. Irodalmi műveltségünk alapvetésének vázlata [Klassizistische Bildung und Europa. Abriss der Grundlagen unserer literarischen Kultur]. Budapest 1979, S. 132-133 und Érszegi, Géza: Oklevéltan [Urkundenlehre]. In: A történelem segédtudományai [Die Hilfswissenschaften der Geschichte]. Hrsg. von István Kállay. Budapest 1986, S. 23. Hinsichtlich der sogenannten glaubwürdigen Orte: Mezey, A hiteleshely, S. 332.

[2] Zu den Urkunden dieser Periode siehe Szentpétery, Imre: Magyar oklevéltan [Ungarische Urkundenlehre]. 2. Auflage. Budapest 1995, S. 36-77; Györffy, György (Hrsg.): Árpád-kori oklevelek [Urkunden aus der Arpadenzeit] 1001-1196. Budapest, 1997, S. 5-16.

[3] Text und Literatur: Györffy, György (Hrsg.): Diplomata Hungariae antiquissima. Budapest 1992, S. 81-85.

handelte es sich um königliche Urkunden, da man meistens über vom König stammenden Güter verfügte und deshalb, zur Unanfechtbarkeit des Rechtsgeschäftes, auch seine Erlaubnis notwendig war. Vom 12. Jahrhundert an erfolgte die königliche Ratifikation immer häufiger durch Besiegelung. Die Urkunde wurde vom Schreiber der an der Sache interessierten Partei – meistens der Kirche – verfaßt. Erst gegen Mitte des 12. Jahrhundert tauchen solche Urkunden auf, die darauf hinweisen, dass sich mit der Abfassung – oder mindestens mit der Besiegelung – der Urkunde ein neben dem König angestelltes, ständiges Personal beschäftigte, dessen Mitglieder unter den Namen *scriptor* und *sigillator* (manchmal auch *notarius* oder *cancellarius*) erschienen.[4] Langsam entfaltete sich demnach am Hof ein zentrales Amt, das sich unter Geisa II. (1141-62) und Stephan III. (1162-72) zu einer aus Klerikern (Kaplanen) bestehenden Organisationseinheit, zur sogenannten königlichen Kapelle (*capella regia*) entwickelte. Ihr Haupt war der *comes capellae*, der Vertraute des Graner Erzbischofs. Er besiegelte die vom Notar oder von den Parteien verfaßten Urkunden. Sowohl er als auch die anderen Angestellten waren angesehene kirchliche Persönlichkeiten (Domherren oder Pröpste), die später häufig zur Bischofswürde gelangten.[5]

Wenn man die zeitgenössischen westlichen Herrscherkanzleien vergleichend betrachtet, sind als mögliche Vorbilder vor allem die päpstliche, die deutsche kaiserliche und die französische königliche Kanzlei zu erwähnen. Die älteste war wahrscheinlich die päpstliche, die bereits im 9. Jahrhundert als konstante und gut entwickelte Einrichtung funktionierte, aber auch die deutsche und französische Kanzlei bildeten im Laufe des 11. und 12. Jahrhunderts ihre ständige Organisation, Urkundenpraxis und Ämter aus.[6] Die Bezeichnun-

---

[4] Szentpétery, Magyar oklevéltan (wie Fn. 2), S. 47-48, 52-56; Kumorovitz: A magyar pecséthasználat (wie Fn. 1), S. 43-46.

[5] Kubinyi, András: Királyi kancellária és udvari kápolna Magyarországon a XII. század közepén [Königliche Kanzlei und höfische Kapelle in Ungarn in der Mitte des 12. Jh.]. In: Levéltári Közlemények (1975) Nr. 46, S. 60, 91-98, 101, 106.

[6] Zur päpstlichen Kanzlei siehe Giry, Arthur: Manuel de diplomatique. 2. Auflage. Paris 1925, S. 671, 674-676, 683, 685.; Bresslau, Harry: Handbuch der Urkundenlehre für Deutschland und Italien. Band I, 3. Auflage. Berlin 1958, 5. und 6. Kap.; Érszegi, Oklevéltan (wie Fn. 1), S. 18-20; zur fränkischen kaiserlichen und französischen königlichen Kanzlei: Giry, S. 724, 737-742,

gen der Würdenträger erinnern an die erwähnten ungarischen Titel, besonders die Namen der französischen Funktionäre scheinen an der ungarischen Kanzlei üblich gewesen zu sein. Auch in Frankreich nannte man im 9. Jahrhundert die Zentralstelle der höfischen Schriftlichkeit *capella*, unter der Leitung des *archicapellanus*, später *archicancellarius*, der fast immer ein Kleriker war. Die ihm unterstellten Personen wurden *capellani* und *notarii* genannt.

Die älteste, tief in der römischen Antike wurzelnde Tradition findet sich jedoch bei der byzantinischen Herrscherkanzlei. Sie bestand bereits im 5. Jh. aus verschiedenen Abteilungen. Der *quaestor sacri palatii* war für die Vorbereitung und Gegenzeichnung der kaiserlichen Dekrete zuständig. Das Büro der *magistri scriniorum* bearbeitete und beantwortete die von anderen Behörden und Bürgern zum Kaiser geschickten Eingaben und an das kaiserliche Gericht eingereichten Klagen. Ferner erledigte es auch die vom Herrscher auf die Gesuche geschriebenen Bemerkungen und übersetzte gewisse Dokumente ins Griechische. Zur Kanzlei gehörte noch die von Konstantin dem Großen gegründete *schola notariorum*, deren Vorsteher, der *primicerius*, vor allem für die Ausbildung der Notare verantwortlich war. In den nächsten Jahrhunderten wurde diese Organisation mehrmals geändert und die lateinischen Namen wurden durch griechische Titel ersetzt. Seit dem Ende des 11. Jahrhunderts überwachte und koordinierte die verschiedenen Büros der λογοθέτης τῶν σεκρέτων, dessen Funktion am Ende des 12. Jahrhunderts bereits der *μέγας* λογοθέτης ausübte. Seine Aufgaben übernahm jedoch in der Folgezeit der μεσάζων, der zuerst als Mittler zwischen dem Kaiser und Anderen, später als wichtigster Berater des Herrschers zum Leiter der Kanzlei, Vorbereiter und zum letzten Überprüfer der kaiserlichen Urkunden wurde. Allein er durfte die für den Kaiser vorbehaltene rote Tinte benutzen und damit die Urkunden mit roten Beglaubigungszeichen versehen.[7]

747-752; Bresslau, S. 352 ff.; Érszegi, Oklevéltan (wie Fn. 1), S. 20; zur deutschen Herrscherkanzlei: Bresslau, 7. Kap.; Érszegi, Oklevéltan (wie Fn. 1), S. 20.

[7] Zur byzantinischen Herrscherkanzlei siehe Dölger, Franz/Karayannopulos, Johannes: Byzantinische Urkundenlehre. München 1968, S. 57-67; Oikonomidès, Nicolas: Les listes de préséance byzantines des IXe et Xe siècles. Paris 1972, S. 310 ff.; ders.: L'évolution de l'organisation administrative de l'empire byzantin au XIe siècle (1025-1118). In: Travaux et Mémoires (1976) Nr. 6,

C. Die „Anordnung“ Belas III. und ähnliche ausländische Arengen

Was hat der aus Byzanz nach Ungarn zurückkehrende Bela III. als neues, byzantinisches Element an der ungarischen Herrscherkanzlei eingeführt? Seine ‚Reform‘ wurde mehrmals mit einer von ihm im Jahre 1181 ausgegebenen Urkunde erklärt, in der Bela die Veräußerung des Landbesitzes von Frau Froa bestätigte. In der Arenga traf der König die folgenden Anordnungen:

„Da wegen der Hinfälligkeit der menschlichen Natur sich im Laufe der Zeit an die Stelle der Erinnerung an vergangene Ereignisse sich die Vergessenheit leicht einschleicht, ist es notwendig alles schriftlich niederzulegen, was die vertragschließenden Parteien vereinbarten, damit dies sowohl durch die schriftliche Bestätigung als auch durch das Zeugnis von geeigneten Männern unverletzbar und unerschütterlich sei. Ich, der vorzügliche König von Ungarn habe diese Sachen überlegt und für die Zukunft für meine Majestät vorsorgend – damit keine der vor mir verhandelten und abgeschlossenen Angelegenheiten ungültig sei – es für erforderlich gehalten, daß alle in der Anwesenheit meiner Majestät erledigte Sachen schriftlich bestätigt werden (...)“[8]

Diese Maßnahme wurde in der Fachliteratur oft als eine allgemeine Vorschrift interpretiert, mit der Bela die Schriftlichkeit in der Zentralverwaltung obligatorisch eingeführt haben soll.[9] Diese Auffassung wurde jedoch in der

---

S. 125-152; ders.: La chancellerie impériale de Byzance du 13e au 15e siècle. In: Revue des Études Byzantines (1985) Nr. 43, S. 167-194; zum *μεσάζων*: Beck, Hans-Georg: Der byzantinische „Ministerpräsident“. In: Byzantinische Zeitschrift (1955) Nr. 48, S. 309-338.

[8] „Quoniam ex defectu nature humane in memoriam rerum preteritarum per temporum successus de facili surrepti obliuio, dignum est scripto supportari et confirmari, quod inter legitimas contractum est personas. Quatinus et scripti confirmatione et uirorum idoneorum testificatione inuiolabiliter constet inconcussum. Quod ego Bela illustrissimus rex Hungarie considerans et in futurum mee regie maiestati precauens, ne aliqua causa in mei presentia uentilata et definita in irritum redigatur, necessarium duxi, ut negotium quodlibet in audientia celsitudinis mee discussum scripti testimonio confirmetur...“ Györffy, Árpád-kori oklevelek (wie Fn. 2), S. 82.

[9] z.B. Hóman, Bálint/Szekfű, Gyula: Magyar történet [Ungarische Geschichte], Band I, 2. Auflage. Budapest 1935, S. 406; Fejérpataky, László: III. Béla király oklevelei [Die Urkunden von König Bela III.]. Sonderausdruck aus: III. Béla magyar király emlékezete [Zum Gedenken des ungarischen Königs Bela III.]. Hrsg. von Gyula Forster. Budapest 1900, S. 4, 12, 18; Bónis, György: A

letzten Zeit dadurch entkräftet, daß diese Einleitung in der Tat eine sogenannte *oblivio-memoria* Arenga ist, welche auch in der westlichen Urkundenpraxis häufig verwendet wurde.[10] Ähnliche Texte sind beispielsweise in zeitgenössischen, 1171 in Lüttich und 1181 in Altenburg ausgestellten, Urkunden zu finden. Die ‚Anordnung' kann deshalb auch auf die Kenntnisse eines wallonischen Klerikers oder eines aus der deutschen kaiserlichen Kanzlei stammenden Notars zurückgeführt werden, der diese Sätze einfach als solche Stilelemente benutzte, die er früher in seiner ausländischen Praxis erlernt hatte.[11] Eine Formulierung gleicher Art taucht auch in einer anderen, von Bela III. 1181 ausgestellten Urkunde auf, in welcher der König den Zagreber Domherren ihr verlorenes Grundstück zurückgab:

„Da im Laufe der Zeit vieles, was als milde Gabe gespendet wurde, nach einigen Tagen in die undankbare Vergessenheit gerät, ist es meine feste Absicht, mit königlicher Autorität und durch Privilegien jene [Gaben] zu bekräftigen, die die Kirchen Gottes von unserer Majestät und Freigiebigkeit, oder von adeligen Männern oder von unseren unterworfenen Gläubigern bekommen haben."[12]

---

jogtudó értelmiség a Mohács előtti Magyarországon [Der Juristenstand in Ungarn vor Mohács (1526)]. Budapest 1971, S. 17; Mályusz, Elemér: Királyi kancellária és krónikaírás a középkori Magyarországon [Königliche Kanzlei und Chroniken im mittelalterlichen Ungarn]. Budapest 1973, S. 9.

[10] Kubinyi (wie Fn. 5), S. 108; Érszegi, Géza: III. Béla kancelláriai reformjáról [Über die Kanzleireform von Bela III.]. In: Magyar Herold (1984) Nr. 1, S. 74.

[11] 1171 Lüttich: „Quecumque instituta vel conventiones inter diversas personas sollempniter contrahuntur, dignum reputamus, ut scripto diligenter annotentur, ne per successiones temporum transeant in oblivionem mentium et a memoria hominum deleantur." 1181 Altenburg: „Equum et rationi censemus consentaneum, ut contractus, qui in nostra fiunt audientia, nostre auctoritatis pragmatica sanctione roborentur." Kubinyi (wie Fn. 5), S. 109-110.

[12] „Quoniam diuturnitate temporum benefactorum sepius olbiteratur memoria et quod pie devotionis geritur officio, post paucos admodum dies ingrata celat oblivio, idcirco que tam a nostra regia maiestate et munificentia quam ab illustribus viris sive quibuscunque Dei fidelibus sub nostra potestate degentibus Dei ecclesie sunt collata, regia auctoritate firmare et privilegiis perpetuare proposui." Érszegi, III. Béla kancelláriai reformjáról (wie Fn. 10), S. 79, Fn. 7.

Die Ähnlichkeit zwischen den ungarischen und ausländischen Arengen steht außer Zweifel, die ungarischen formulieren jedoch etwas klarer und kategorischer. Obwohl eine allgemeine und normative Anordnung aus ihnen nicht herauszulesen ist, geht aus ihnen doch eine konkrete königliche Absicht hervor.[13]

Es ist weniger bekannt, aber ähnliche Topoi wurden auch in byzantinischen kaiserlichen Urkunden verwendet. Herbert Hunger publizierte aus einem in Heidelberg aufbewahrten griechischen Kodex zwanzig solche Prooimien-Muster, die um 1300 aus früheren kaiserlichen Goldbullen zusammenstellt wurden. Das unter Nummer 4 stehende Prooimion enthält das Klischee, im Sinne einer Vorlage und Formel, für die Beglaubigung von alten Goldbullen und anderen Urkunden:

„Es gehört zu den Aufgaben der Kaisermacht, nicht nur die Waffen gegen die Feinde zu erheben, gegen die Widersacher ins Feld zu ziehen und die von ihrer Seite den Untertanen drohenden Schädigungen und Gewalttaten abzuwehren und von ihnen fernzuhalten, sondern auch der Zeit entgegenzuwirken, welche den Untertanen schweres Unrecht und Schaden zufügt. Denn viele Vorteile, deren sie sich erfreuen, erfahren durch den unaufhörlichen Fluss der Zeit Bewegungen und Veränderungen, manches lässt sie (die Zeit) veralten, anderes völlig verblassen, dem Abgrund der Vernichtung anheim fallen und entzieht ihm so den mit ihm verbundenen Nutzen. N. N. hat an meine Majestät eine Eingabe gerichtet, daß die seinen Vorfahren von den früheren Kaisern verliehenen Chrysobulle, die durch Erbschaft auf ihn übergingen und sich auf seine bewußten Immobilien beziehen, teils die lange Zeit und das zerstörende Alter, teils der leicht verderbliche Beschreibstoff der Chrysobulle, das Papier, aufzulösen und zu vernichten drohen. Von daher erwachse ihm eine große Gefahr, nämlich die Auflösung seiner Existenzgrundlagen und seiner fundamentalen Stützen. Da nun der Obenerwähnte meine Majestät dringend bat, es mögen Kopien dieser Chrysobulle von Seiten meiner Majestät angefertigt, in die Register eingetragen und die Gültigkeit der Originale in allen beglaubigt

---

[13] Érszegi, III. Béla kancelláriai reformjáról (wie Fn. 10), S. 76-77.

werden, so geht meine Majestät auf seine Bitte ein und gewährt dies und das."[14]

Der byzantinische Kaiser fühlte sich also berufen, die von seinen Vorgängern gewährten Privilegien vor dem Zahn der Zeit und dem Dunkel der Vergessenheit zu bewahren und schriftlich niederzulegen. Ein ähnlicher Gedanke findet sich, wenn auch noch allgemeiner gefaßt, auch in den Prooimien von manchen byzantinischen kaiserlichen Novellen. Die Unbeständigkeit der Menschen und der rasche Wechsel der Verhältnisse kann auch die Ordnung der Gesetze verletzen, doch der Herrscher soll das Durcheinander bekämpften, indem er die Gesetze überprüft und die altbewährten und zweckentsprechenden Anordnungen bestätigt.[15] Inwieweit sich Bela dieses Element der byzantinischen Kaiseridee zu eigen machte, ist nicht leicht zu beurteilen. Die zitierten byzantinischen Texte sind den ungarischen nur in ihrem Grundgedanken ähnlich. Es handelt sich nicht um eine wörtliche Übernahme. Jedenfalls ist zu bemerken, dass der spätere ungarische König seine vielleicht empfänglichste Lebensperiode – vom 13. bzw. 15. bis zum 22. bzw. 24. Lebensjahr – neben dem Kaiser, Manuel Komnenos verbrachte, der, auch selbst ein Wissenschaftler, seinen offiziellen Thronfolger wahrscheinlich gut ausbilden wollte und deshalb den jungen Despoten zur Leitung der staatlichen und kirchlichen Angelegenheiten hinzuzog.[16] Es stellt sich jedoch die Frage, ob der König diese Kenntnisse nun in Ungarn anwenden konnte.

---

[14] Hunger, Herbert: Prooimion. Elemente der byzantinischen Kaiseridee in den Arengen der Urkunden. Wien 1964, S. 220-223 (Text und Übersetzung).
[15] Siehe die Prooimien von Nov. 49 und 107 Justinians und der Novellensammlung von Leo VI., Hunger (wie Fn. 14), S. 171-173.
[16] Kristó, Gyula/Makk, Ferenc: III. Béla emlékezete [Erinnerung an Bela III.]. Budapest, 1981, S. 10-13. Laut Synodalaufzeichnen aus dem Jahre 1166 saß der junge Alexios (Bela) Despotes an einer Synode in Konstantinopel neben dem präsidierenden Kaiser, im Kreise von Lukas, Athanasios und Nikophoros, Patriarchen von Konstantinopel, Antiochia und Jerusalem, ebd. S. 52.

D. Die Modernisierung der königlichen Kapelle

Nachdem Bela zurückkehrte und 1172 den ungarischen Thron bestieg, fand er völlig andere Verhältnisse vor als am byzantinischen Hof. Es gab bereits eine ständige Herrscherkanzlei, aber ihr Personal war viel geringer, ihre Tätigkeit viel einfacher als in Konstantinopel. Ihre Leiter und Angestellten waren eher die Mitglieder des königlichen Gefolges als die Notare eines geschlossenen Amtes.[17] Hinzu kam, daß es keinen festen Ort für die Arbeit der Kanzlei gab. Der *notarius* begleitete den König auf seinen Fahrten durch das Land und schrieb die Anordnungen seines Herrschers am Ort der Handlung nieder. Dies geht beispielsweise aus der Urkunde von Caba aus dem Jahre 1177 hervor, in welcher der König an einem Sonntag im Haus von Gespan Ssene unter einem Eichenbaum sitzend die Spende seines Getreuen bestätigte.[18] Andere königliche Urkunden aus dem ersten Jahrzehnt der Herrschaft Belas III. zeigen ferner keine einheitliche Textur, auch ihr Aussteller war nicht derselbe. Anzeichen für eine bedeutende Neuerung tauchen erst zwischen 1181 und 1183, unter der Kanzlerschaft von Kalan auf. Er ist der erste, der sich konsequent mit Kanzler (*aule regie cancellarius*) tituliert, und seine Urkunden weisen bereits alle Elemente auf (Invokation, Intitulation, Arenga, Narration, Disposition, Corroboration, Datierung und Unterfertigung), die auch in den Urkunden der nächsten Jahrhunderte regelmäßig vorkommen.[19] Nach einer zweijährigen Übergangsperiode (1183-1185) lief die Ausfertigung der Urkunden auf den von Kalan gelegten Grundlagen weiter. Seine Nachfolger – Adrian, Saul und Katapan (1185-1197) – hielten sich an die neue Praxis.[20]

Es hat also den Anschein, daß mit der Thronbesteigung von Bela III. die Amtshandlung und Organisation der ungarischen Hofkanzlei nicht sofort und radikal geändert wurde, auch nicht nach seiner oben erwähnten Urkunde aus

---

[17] Bónis: A jogtudó értelmiség (wie Fn. 9), S. 17.

[18] „...Tale uotum et oblationem meam rex et omnes principes qui aderant approbarunt et ut perhenniter ratum esset, rege iubente per manum Pauli prepositi et eiusdem regalis notarii presenti scripto confirmatum est et sigillo regali roboratum. Quando rex ista fieri precepit, in die dominico in domo Ssene comitis sub quadam quercu sedebat..." Györffy : Árpád-kori oklevelek (wie Fn. 2), S. 81.

[19] Érszegi : III. Béla kancelláriai reformjáról (wie Fn. 10), S. 75.

[20] Kubinyi (wie Fn. 5), S. 114-115; Érszegi: III. Béla kancelláriai reformjáról (wie Fn. 10), S. 77.

dem Jahre 1181, in welcher er angeblich die schriftliche Abfassung der durch die königliche Majestät entschiedenen Angelegenheiten oder der mit seiner Zustimmung entstandenen Verträge und Spenden anordnete. Die Neuerungen sind eher auf die Arbeit der Kanzler zurückzuführen. Manche von ihnen, wie beispielsweise Adrian und Katapan, studierten in Paris.[21] Sie wandten ihre dort erworbenen Kenntnisse später sicherlich auch in Ungarn an. Dies kann sowohl durch den Vergleich des Schriftbildes von zeitgenössischen ungarischen und französischen Urkunden[22] als auch durch verschiedene Stilelemente, wie auch die in Frankreich übliche *datum per manus*-Formel,[23] bewiesen werden. Es ist deshalb kein Wunder, wenn man in der Organisation und Praxis der ungarischen Herrscherkanzlei oder in den Titeln der Würdenträger die Elemente und Fachausdrücke der viel weiter entwickelten byzantinischen Hofkanzlei nicht finden kann. Obwohl Bela sie wahrscheinlich kannte, arbeiteten jedoch bei ihm Kleriker mit einer westlichen Ausbildung, er konnte deshalb mit ihnen keine Herrscherkanzlei nach byzantinischem Muster aufbauen. Vielleicht wollte er das auch nicht tun, da es nicht nötig war. Die Grundsteine wurden bereits früher gelegt und es gab keinen Bedarf für eine völlig neue Struktur.

E. Die Praxis der Petitionen

Trotzdem gibt es ein weiteres Element in der Praxis der ungarischen Hofkanzlei, das in mehreren Quellen der Anordnung von Bela zugeschrieben wurde. Sowohl die im 14. Jahrhundert aus früheren Aufzeichnungen zusammenstellte Chronikkomposition, deren diesbezüglicher Teil bereits um 1270 niedergeschrieben wurde, als auch eine etwa zehn Jahre später entstandene andere Chronik, die sogenannte *Gesta Hungarorum* von Simon Kézai berichten

---

[21] Bónis: A jogtudó értelmiség (wie Fn. 9), S. 22; Kubinyi (wie Fn. 5), S. 115-117.
[22] Hajnal, István: Írástörténet az írásbeliség felújulása korából [Schreibgeschichte aus der Zeit der Erneuerung der Schriftlichkeit]. Budapest 1921, S. 135. und im Anhang Tafel VII. (12. A + B) und Tafel VIII. (13. A + B); Hajnal, István: Vergleichende Schriftproben zur Entwicklung und Verbreitung der Schrift im 12.-13. Jahrhundert. Budapest 1943, Anhang V. 5. und VIII. a).
[23] Szentpétery: Magyar oklevéltan (wie Fn. 2), S. 64-65.

ganz kurz darüber, daß Bela III., bei Kézai als der griechische Bela bezeichnet, die Diebe und die Schurken verfolgte und Petitionen einführte, wie dies am römischen und kaiserlichen Hof üblich sei.[24] Der römische Hof kann hier die antike römische Kurie bedeuten,[25] wo die schriftlichen Ersuche, in denen man den Kaiser in einem Streitfall um persönliche Fällung des Urteils bat, seit dem Prinzipat *supplicatio* nannte.[26] Die Supplikation verwandelte sich jedoch in Byzanz in eine allgemeine Möglichkeit, sich mit einer Bitte (δέησις), nicht nur in Prozeßfällen, sondern auch in anderen Angelegenheiten, an den Kaiser zu wenden. Für die Erledigung solcher Ersuchen war ein besonderer Beamter, der ἐπὶ τῶν δεήσεων verantwortlich.[27] Diese Praxis findet sich auch im mittelalterlichen Rom bei der päpstlichen Kurie und später auch an den königlichen Höfen von mehreren westeuropäischen Herrschern.[28] Wenn die Supplikation aber in Ungarn durch Bela III. eingeführt wurde, liegt es natürlich näher, an

---

[24] Chronici Hungarici compositio saeculi XIV: Scriptores rerum Hungaricarum tempore ducum regumque stirpis Arpadinae gestarum (SRH), Band I. Hrsg. von Emericus Szentpétery. Budapest 1937, S. 462: „Postea regnavit Bela frater eius, qui fures et latrones persecutus est et petitionibus loqui (sic) traxit originem, ut Romana habet curia et imperii...“; Simonis de Keza Gesta Hungarorum: „Sed post hunc regnavit Bela Graecus, quem Becha et Gregor apud imperatorem Graecorum diutius tenuerunt. Hic quidem fures et latrones persecutus est petitionibusque loqui (sic) traxit originem, ut Romana habet curia et imperii...“, ebd. S. 183.

[25] Deshalb wird die Praxis der Petitionen als Einfluss des römischen Rechts erwähnt bei Zajtai, Imre: Sur le rôle du droit romain dans l'évolution du droit hongrois. In: L'Europa e il diritto romano. Studi in memoria di Paolo Koschaker. Milano 1954. Band II, S. 190-191; Bónis, György: Einflüsse des römischen Rechts in Ungarn. In: Ius Romanum medii aevi V, 10. Mailand 1964, S. 22; auch Gerics denkt an das römische Recht: Gerics, József: Az írásbeli petíciók bevezetéséről szóló krónikahely magyarázatához [Zur Erklärung der Chronikstelle über die Einführung der Petitionen]. In: Egyház, állam és gondolkodás Magyarországon a középkorban [Kirche, Staat und Denken in Ungarn im Mittelalter]. Hrsg. von István Zombori. Budapest 1995, S. 242.

[26] Zur römischen Praxis der Petitionen siehe Kaser, Max: Das römische Zivilprozessrecht. 2. Auflage, neu bearb. von Karl Hackl. München 1996, S. 540-542, 623; Dölger/Karayannopulos (wie Fn. 7), S. 58-59.

[27] Dölger/Karayannopulos (wie Fn. 7), S. 61; Oikonomidès: Les listes de préséance (wie Fn. 7), S. 322; Oikonomidès: La chancellerie impériale (wie Fn. 7), S. 174.

[28] Giry (wie Fn. 6), S. 701-702; Érszegi, Oklevéltan (wie Fn. 1), S. 18; Gerics (wie Fn. 24), S. 242; Györffy, György: A magyar krónikák adata a III. Béla kori petícióról [Die Angabe der ungarischen Chroniken über die Petition unter Bela III.]. In: Középkori kútfőink kritikus kérdései [Kritische Fragen unserer mittelalterlichen Quellen]. Hrsg. von János Horváth und György Székely, Budapest 1974, S. 335. p.

seine byzantinischen Erfahrungen als motivierende Faktoren zu denken. Die von den Chroniken von Kézai als Vorbild erwähnte kaiserliche Kurie könnte deshalb den byzantinischen Hof bezeichnen.[29]

Diese Folgerung steht jedoch nicht auf festem Grund. Ein anderer Geschichtsschreiber, Rogerius, der Erzbischof von Spalato, der in der zweiten Hälfte des 13. Jahrhunderts als Diplomat mehrmals nach Ungarn kam, erzählt in seinem „Carmen miserabile“ (1243) viel ausführlicher, dass die Praxis der Petitionen in Ungarn erst von Bela IV. (1235-1270), dem Enkel von Bela III., eingeführt wurde. Laut Rogerius trug diese Anordnung dazu bei, daß das Verhältnis zwischen dem König und dem Adel sich verschlechterte. Die Adligen waren daran gewöhnt, mit dem König ihre Angelegenheiten mündlich zu besprechen. Es wurde viel komplizierter und teuerer, mit ihm durch schriftliche Petitionen in Kontakt zu treten.[30] Es ist deshalb möglich, daß die zwei späteren und wortkargen Chroniken die Verantwortung für diese unpopuläre Anordnung einfach auf einen früheren König, Bela III., abwälzen wollten.[31]

F. Festsetzung von privaten Rechtsakten: *pristaldus* und *cartula sigillata*

Kehren wir jetzt zurück zur schriftlichen Festsetzung von privaten Rechtsakten, Verträgen oder einseitigen Handlungen. Wie oben schon erwähnt, wurden diese zuerst von dem König bestätigt, beurkundet oder jedenfalls besiegelt. Diese Methode war natürlich nicht bei allen Rechtsakten des Volkes anwendbar. Die Gewohnheit bildete deshalb andere Institutionen aus. Die erste dieser Institutionen war der Häscher. Wann er in Ungarn zuerst auftauchte, ist unklar, weil über seine Tätigkeit – aus der Natur der Sache – ursprünglich keine Aufzeichnungen entstanden. Seine Aufgabe war nur die mündliche Bezeugung der vor ihm geschehenen Ereignisse. Sein ungarischer Name *poroszló* (auf

[29] Dafür: Érszegi: Oklevéltan (wie Fn. 1), S. 23; dagegen: Gerics (wie Fn. 24), S. 241-242 und Györffy: A magyar krónikák adata (wie Fn. 28), S. 335.

[30] SRH II, S. 556, 559.

[31] Mit anderen Vermutungen aus der früheren Literatur Györffy. A magyar krónikák adata (wie Fn. 28), S. 335-336.

Latein *pristaldus*) weist darauf hin, daß es sich hier um eine Institution (süd-) slawischer Herkunft handelt, in der slawischen Sprache wird er *pristav* (anwesende Person) genannt. Die Häscher führten ihre Tätigkeit im Dienste zentraler oder lokaler Behörden, Gerichte oder kirchlicher Persönlichkeiten durch. Als deren Abgesandte nahmen sie an Prozeßverfahren und anderen Handlungen teil, wie beispielsweise an der Festsetzung von Grundstücksgrenzen, an Besitzübertragungen und verschiedenen Vertragsabschlüssen. Danach kehrten sie zum Sender zurück und erstatteten einen mündlichen Bericht.[32] Diese Methode erwies sich jedoch unvollkommen, weil die Häscher von den Parteien bezahlt wurden, und so bot sich ein weites Feld für Mißbräuche. Die Goldene Bulle von Andreas II. schrieb deshalb 1231 vor, daß die Zeugnisse der „betrügerischen Häscher" nur dann gültig seien, wenn sie auch von dem Bischof oder dem kirchlichen Kapitel bestätigt wurden.[33]

Fortschrittlicher erscheint es daher, die Rechtsakte nicht nur mündlich zu bezeugen, sondern sie auch schriftlich niederzulegen. Der erste Versuch, dies bei Privathandlungen allgemein üblich zu machen, war die Anordnung von König Koloman (1095-1116), der Ende des 11. Jahrhunderts vorschrieb, die Kauf- und Darlehensverträge zwischen Juden und Christen in Form eines mit Siegel versehenen Schriftstückes (*cartula sigillata*) abzuschließen.[34] In der *cartula sigillata* sollte die Ware, der Preis und die Namen der anwesenden jüdischen

---

[32] Érdujhelyi, Menyhért: A közjegyzőség és hiteles helyek története Magyarországon [Die Geschichte des öffentlichen Notariats und der glaubwürdigen Orte in Ungarn]. Budapest 1899, S. 57-62; Bónis, György: A közhitelűség szervei Magyarországon és a magyar hiteleshelyi levéltárak [Organe der Glaubwürdigkeit in Ungarn und die Archive der ungarischen glaubwürdigen Orte]. In: Levéltári Szemle (1964) Nr. 1-2, S. 125-126. (Auf französisch: Les autorités de „foi publique" et les archives des loci credibiles en Hongrie. In: Archivum (1962) Nr. 12); Zlinszky, János: Az ügyvédség kialakulása Magyarországon és története Fejér megyében [Die Herausbildung der Rechtsanwaltschaft in Ungarn und ihre Geschichte im Komitat Fejér]. Székesfehérvár 1976, S. 10-13.

[33] „...Et quia multi in regno leduntur per falsos prestaldos, citationes vel testimonia eorum non valeant, nisi per testimonium diocesis episcopi vel capituli..." Decreta Regni Mediaevalis Hungariae. Hrsg. von János M. Bak, György Bónis und James Ross Sweeny. 2. Auflage. Idyllwild 1999, S. 38.

[34] Závodszky, Levente: A Szent István, Szent László és Kálmán korabeli törvények és zsinati határozatok forrásai [Die Quellen der Gesetze und Synodalbeschlüsse unter Stephan dem Heiligen, Ladislaus dem Heiligen und Koloman]. Budapest 1904, S. 195-196.

und christlichen Zeugen niederschreiben und die Schrift mit dem Siegel beider Parteien besiegelt werden. Diese Form war nur bei Geschäften über einem bestimmten Wert verpflichtend. Die kleine Anzahl von Quellen, die von solchen mit Siegeln versehenen Schriftstücken berichten, weist jedoch darauf hin, daß sich diese Form in der Praxis nicht durchsetzen konnte.[35]

G. Die „glaubwürdigen Orte" in Ungarn und ähnliche Institutionen in Europa

Bei der Forderung nach schriftlicher Festsetzung von Privatgeschäften, ist erst mit der Wende des 12. zum 13. Jahrhundert ein Aufschwung festzustellen. Dies führte zu einer neuen Institution, die während des ganzen ungarischen Mittelalters, sogar bis zum 19. Jahrhundert, für die Beurkundung von privaten Rechtsakten in Gebrauch blieb: die so genannten glaubwürdigen Orte (*loca credibilia*). Zu ihnen gehörten kirchliche Kapitel und klösterliche Konvente, demnach kirchliche Körperschaften, die die gleiche Funktion erfüllten wie die öffentlichen Notare in Westeuropa und Byzanz. Sie stellten authentische Urkunden von verschiedenen Rechtsangelegenheiten aus und bewahrten ihre Duplikate auf. Wenn sie dies für Privatpersonen taten, hieß die Urkunde *fassio*, wodurch die Parteien meistens ihre privatrechtlichen Rechtsgeschäfte, ein- oder beiderseitige Erklärungen, beglaubigen ließen, wie beispielsweise die Übertragung, den Tausch, die Aufteilung oder Verpfändung von Landgütern, außerdem Testamente, Freilassungen von Sklaven, Zahlungsaufforderungen und Proteste gegen Rechtsverletzungen. Die glaubwürdigen Orte wurden aber auch von Behörden damit beauftragt, verschiedene Prozeßhandlungen zu bestätigten, wie etwa Vorladungen, Zeugnisse, Schwüre oder die Vollstreckung von Gerichtsentscheidungen. Darüber wurde die Behörde durch eine Urkunde, die *relatio*, informiert. Für die Abfassung war bei kirchlichen Kapiteln der Lektor, bei klösterlichen Konventen der Prior verantwortlich. Seit dem 14. Jahrhundert gab es jedoch neben den meisten glaubwürdigen Orten auch

---

[35] Die einzige Urkunde, die beweist, dass diese Form benutzt wurde, ist das Testament von Gespan Márton (12. Jh.). Kumorovitz: A magyar pecséthasználat (wie Fn. 1), S. 36-38; Kumorovitz: A középkori magyar magánjogi írásbeliség (wie Fn. 1), S. 386-388.

fachkundige Notare. Zur Authentizität der Urkunde war nicht nur die Besiegelung, sondern auch die Anwesenheit von mehreren Klerikern, Domherren und Siegelbewahrern, bei Konventen das Beisein von mehreren Mönchen nötig, denn nicht eine einzelne Person, sondern die Körperschaft selbst hatte den Rechtsakt zu bestätigen. Das Duplikat wurde am glaubwürdigen Ort aufbewahrt oder der Text der Urkunde, oder lediglich ein Auszug dessen, wurde in ein Register eingetragen.[36]

Die Nutzung von kirchlichen Körperschaften als Urkundenaussteller und Beglaubiger weicht von der westlichen und byzantinischen Praxis sowie von der Tätigkeit der – von der römischen Tradition geprägten – öffentlichen Notare wesentlich ab, da dort eine einzelne, sogar eher weltliche Person (Notar, *Tabellio*) diese Funktion ausübte.[37] Trotzdem wurde auch in diesem Fall nach ähnlichen ausländischen Institutionen geforscht. Aus dem westlichen Teil Europas könnte man die Urkundenpraxis der Offiziale heranziehen.[38] Der Offizial (*officialis*) war eine Amtsperson in der kirchlichen Verwaltung, ein Stellvertreter des Bischofs in der geistlichen Jurisdiktion, der deshalb auch ein authentisches Siegel hatte und zu dessen Personal, neben anderen Funktionären, auch Notare und Siegeler gehörten. Die Aufbewahrung der Urkunden und die Ausfertigung von Kopien war Aufgabe des *receptor actorum*. Seit dem 12.-13. Jahrhundert wandten sich nicht nur streitende Parteien, sondern auch Perso-

---

[36] Zu den ungarischen glaubwürdigen Orten siehe Eckhart, Franz: Die glaubwürdigen Orte Ungarns im Mittelalter. In: Mitteilungen des Instituts für österreichische Geschichtsforschung, IX. Ergänzungsband, 2. Heft. 1914, S. 395-558. Zur Zusammenfassung oben: Szentpétery: Magyar oklevéltan (wie Fn. 2), S. 121-138, bes. 126-129; Stolcz, Alfonz: A hiteles helyek és azok jelentősége a középkorban Magyarországon [Die glaubwürdigen Orte und ihre Bedeutung im Mittelalter in Ungarn]. Újvidék 1912, S. 25-66; Érdujhelyi (wie Fn. 32), S. 80-85; Mezey: A pécsi egyetemalapítás előzményei (wie Fn. 1), S. 73-83.

[37] Zu den römischen und byzantinischen Tabellionen siehe Sachers, E.: Tabellio, tabularium, tabularius. In: Paulys Realencyclopädie der classischen Altertumwissenschaft. (Neue Bearb. begonnen von Georg Wissowa). Reihe 2, Halbband 8, Stuttgart 1932, S. 1847-1868, 1962-1969, 1969-1984; Ankum, Hans: Les tabellions romains, ancêtres directs des notaires modernes. In: Atlas du notariat. Hrsg. von Elisabeth M. van der Marck. Deventer 1989, S. 5-44; zum öffentlichen Notariat in Westeuropa: Wolf, Armin: Das öffentliche Notariat. In: Handbuch der Quellen und Literatur der neueren Europäischen Privatrechtsgeschichte, Bd. I, Mittelalter (1100-1500). Hrsg. von Helmut Coing. München 1973, S. 505-514.

[38] Bónis: Einflüsse (wie Fn. 25), S. 23; Bónis: A közhitelűség szervei (wie Fn. 32), S. 126.

nen, die einfach ihre Privathandlungen beurkunden lassen wollten an den Offizial.[39] So kam dem Offizial eine ähnliche Funktion wie den glaubwürdigen Orten in Ungarn zu. Als wichtiger Unterschied ist jedoch zu bemerken, daß der Offizial die Privaturkunden immer in seinem Namen und mit seiner Autorität ausstellte, im Gegensatz zu den glaubwürdigen Orten, die dies als Körperschaften taten.[40]

Auch die ähnlichen Institutionen der östlichen Praxis weichen in diesem Punkt von der ungarischen Entwicklung ab. Auch in Byzanz war es üblich, Privaturkunden von hohen kirchlichen Persönlichkeiten – Bischöfen oder Vorstehern der Mönche – beglaubigen zu lassen, wobei als Zeugen häufig auch andere Kleriker anwesend waren, die die Urkunde auch unterzeichneten. Diese Methode hatte jedoch Ausnahmecharakter und auch hier handelte es sich nicht um eine körperschaftliche Bestätigung. Die Parteien wollten einfach ihre Rechtsakte durch rechtskundige und hochgeachtete kirchliche Würdenträger bestätigen lassen.[41]

Wenn also die glaubwürdigen Orte ihre Tätigkeit als Urkundenaussteller und Beglaubiger gerade unter Bela III. begannen, konnten diese auf kein fertiges Muster, weder aus dem Westen noch aus dem Osten, zurückgreifen. Elemente ihrer Praxis waren natürlich auch bei anderen ähnlichen Institutionen des zeitgenössischen Europas zu finden. Es weist jedoch nichts darauf hin, daß diese als Vorbilder bewußt beachtet und übernommen wurden. Der Beginn dieser Tätigkeit ist im Übrigen auch hier nicht auf eine königliche Anordnung zurückzuführen. Obwohl die ersten, von glaubwürdigen Orten ausgestellten Urkunden aus dem Jahre 1181 tatsächlich während der Regierungszeit von Bela entstanden, sind diese eher nur vereinzelte Beispiele einer späteren, in der ersten Hälfte des 13. Jahrhundert verbreiteten und aufblühenden Praxis, die erst unter Andreas II. (1205-35) oder Bela IV. (1235-1270) regelmäßig und einheitlich wurde.[42]

---

[39] Giry (wie Fn. 6), S. 837-841; Balogh, Elemér: Középkori bajor egyházi bíráskodás [Geistliche Gerichtsbarkeit im mittelalterlichen Bayern]. Budapest 2000, S. 36-55; 286-295.

[40] Mezey: A pécsi egyetemalapítás előzményei (wie Fn. 1), S. 68.

[41] Saradi-Mendelovici, Hélène: La ratification des actes privés byzantins par une autorité civile ou ecclésiastique. In: Revue des Études Byzantines (1988) Nr. 46, S. 167-180.

[42] Szentpétery: Magyar oklevéltan (wie Fn. 2), S. 122-125.

Diese Entwicklung ist deshalb wahrscheinlich mit einheimischen Gegebenheiten zu erklären. Seit dem Ende des 12. Jahrhunderts war es üblich, daß die erwähnten kirchlichen Körperschaften – Kapitel und Konvente – an der Beweisführung in Prozessen bzw. bei Gottesurteilen teilnahmen und über das Ergebnis eine Urkunde für das Gericht ausstellten.[43] Analog zu dieser Gewohnheit bot sich die Möglichkeit, daß sie auch in anderen Fällen eine authentische Bestätigung geben konnten, die auch ohne einen Prozeß von anderen Behörden als gültige Rechtsakte angenommen werden konnte. Zu dieser Idee trug sicherlich auch das Ansehen der Kirche und ihrer rechtskundigen Kleriker bei. Diese zuerst nur an manchen Stellen übliche Praxis breitete sich allmählich weiter aus und wurde so zu einer landesüblichen Sitte. Die glaubwürdigen Orte fungierten dann in Ungarn bis zur Mitte des 19. Jahrhunderts als wichtigste und offizielle Einrichtung zur Erinnerung privater Rechtsakte.

[43] Szentpétery: Magyar oklevéltan (wie Fn. 2), S. 121-122.

Die französische Vergangenheitsbewältigung des Zweiten Weltkriegs durch die Rechtsprechung am Beispiel des „Oradourprozesses“

Henning Meyer[1]

Der französische Jurist Denis Salas begann seinen Aufsatz mit dem Titel *La justice entre histoire et mémoire*, der im Jahr 2002 in einem Sammelband über die französischen Nachkriegsprozesse erschienen ist, mit folgender Bemerkung:

„Un nouveau rapport à la mémoire est né de l'époque la plus noire de l'histoire européenne. Le tribunal de Nuremberg en fut le symbole ... aux crimes de la barbarie nazie qui ont endeuillé l'Europe doit correspondre une sanction exceptionnelle.“[2]

Die Nürnberger Prozesse waren demnach für Salas der Auftakt und das Symbol für eine Reihe von Gerichtsverfahren zur Aufarbeitung der Weltkriegsgeschichte. Die dafür empfundene Notwendigkeit führte er auf die kriminelle Spezifität dieser Geschichte zurück. Er fügte seiner Bemerkung allerdings eine Frage an, die für den in diesem Referat behandelten Nachkriegsprozess paradigmatisch ist:

„A quoi servent ces procès si loin de la guerre ? Sont-ils organisés seulement pour juger un homme ? Ou ont-ils, plus largement, un but politique, pédagogique ou mémoriel ?“[3]

---

[1] Der Autor dankt Horst Meyer für seine Anregungen und für das Korrekturlesen dieses Textes.

[2] Salas, Denis: La justice entre histoire et mémoire, In: Barbie, Touvier, Papon... Des procès pour la mémoire. Hrsg. von Jean-Paul Jean und Denis Salas. Paris 2002, S. 20-34, hier S. 20.

[3] Salas (wie Fn. 2), S. 21.

Die französische Justiz hat sich wiederholt mit der Geschichte der Besatzungszeit befasst. Ich werde hier aus Platzgründen nur auf die sogenannten „großen" Nachkriegsprozesse eingehen. Die ersten zwei Prozesse dieser Art fanden noch vor den Nürnberger Prozessen statt und betrafen Philippe Pétain (23. Juli – 15. August 1945) und Pierre Laval (9. Oktober 1945), die führenden Personen des Vichy-Regimes. Im November 1946 und Mai 1950 fanden zwei Verfahren gegen René Hardy statt, dem vorgeworfen wurde, den Widerstandskämpfer Jean Moulin verraten zu haben, der in der Folge von der Gestapo zu Tode gefoltert worden war. Im Frühjahr 1953 folgte der „Prozess von Bordeaux" in Sachen des Massakers von Oradour-sur-Glane, mit dem ich mich in diesem Beitrag hauptsächlich befassen werde. Carl Oberg und Helmut Knochen, die in der Besatzungszeit die beiden obersten Angehörigen der SS in Paris gewesen waren, wurden im Oktober 1954 verurteilt. 1979 stand Jean Leguay vor Gericht, der frühere Repräsentant des Generalsekretärs der französischen Polizei bei den deutschen Besatzungsbehörden. Nach dem Prozess gegen den ehemaligen Chef der Gestapo in Lyon, Klaus Barbie, vom 11. Mai bis zum 4. Juli 1987 wurde auch der damalige Generalsekretär der Vichy-Polizei und Vorgesetzte Leguays, René Bousquet, im März 1989 angeklagt. Der Prozess, der seine Rolle in den Razzien und Deportationen französischer Juden nach Deutschland aufzeigen sollte, konnte aufgrund seiner Ermordung am 8. Juni 1993 nicht stattfinden. Vom 17. März bis zum 20. April 1994 fand ein Verfahren gegen Paul Touvier statt, einen ehemaligen Verantwortlichen der französischen Miliz in der Rhone-Region. Maurice Papon, der in der Besatzungszeit Generalsekretär der Präfektur in Bordeaux gewesen war und dem die Beteiligung an der Deportation von 1560 Juden aus der Region um Bordeaux zur Last gelegt wurde, stand vom 8. Oktober 1997 bis zum 2. April 1998 vor Gericht. Am 2. März 2001 wurde Aloïs Brunner, der von Juni 1943 bis August 1944 das Durchgangslager von Drancy geleitet hatte, in Abwesenheit zu einer lebenslangen Haftstrafe verurteilt.[4]

Der französische Zeithistoriker Henry Rousso hat die französischen Nachkriegsprozesse in zwei „Wellen" unterteilt. Die erste Welle von „historischen

[4] Vgl.: Jean, Jean-Paul: Repères, In: Barbie, Touvier, Papon... Des procès pour la mémoire. Hrsg. von Jean-Paul Jean und Denis Salas. Paris 2002, S. 12-17.

Prozessen" (*procès historiques*[5]) fand im direkten Anschluss an die Ereignisse statt und trug zu einer ersten Aufklärung des Geschehenen bei. Die zweite Welle begann erst lange Zeit nach dem Ende des Zweiten Weltkriegs mit dem Prozess gegen Jean Leguay im Jahr 1979 und konnte nur noch auf der Basis der Unverjährbarkeit von Verbrechen gegen die Menschlichkeit durchgeführt werden, die 1964 vom französischen Parlament kodifiziert worden war.[6]

Der „Prozess von Bordeaux" oder „Oradourprozess" [7], der vom 12. Januar bis zum 13. Februar 1953 vor dem Militärgerichtshof in Bordeaux abgehalten wurde, ist chronologisch gesehen ein verspäteter Prozess der ersten Welle. Er sollte die Gründe für das Massaker von Oradour-sur-Glane ermitteln und die Verantwortlichen identifizieren und bestrafen. Über acht Jahre waren seit den Ereignissen vergangen, weil ungeklärte Zuständigkeitsfragen und langwierige Ermittlungsverfahren den Prozessbeginn verzögert hatten.

Der Vorsitzende Nussy Saint-Saëns begann den Prozess am 12. Januar mit den Worten: „Le véritable procès que nous avons à juger est, et demeure, celui de l'hitlerisme."[8] Diese sehr verallgemeinernde Bemerkung sowie der Prozessverlauf und die Prozessfolgen zeigen aber auch Elemente der zweiten Welle auf, wie im Folgenden gezeigt wird. So gesehen scheint der Oradourprozess an der Schnittstelle der zwei Prozesswellen zu liegen.

Deshalb soll zunächst die Vorgeschichte des Prozesses skizziert werden, bevor ich auf den Prozessverlauf und die Prozessfolgen eingehe. Zum Abschluss soll dann dieser Ansatz wieder aufgenommen werden und der Oradourprozess in den Kontext der anderen Nachkriegsprozesse eingeordnet und die Bedeutung solcher Verfahren für die Vergangenheitsbewältigung diskutiert werden.

---

[5] Rousso, Henry: La hantise du passé. Entretien avec Philippe Petit. Paris 1998, S. 96.

[6] Rousso (wie Fn. 5), S. 110-112. Vgl. auch: Rousso, Henry: Vichy. L'événement, la mémoire, l'histoire. Paris 2001, S.678-710.

[7] In einem Artikel, der am 15. Januar 2003 in *L'Alsace* erschienen ist, wird unterstellt, dass der Prozess im Limousin „*Procès de Bordeaux*" und im Elsass „*Procès d'Oradour*" genannt wird. Siehe: Boeglin, Edouard: 12 janvier 1953 : le procès, enfin, In: L'Alsace, 15. Januar 2003.

[8] Théolleyre, Jean-Marc: Procès d'après-guerre : « Je suis partout », René Hardy, Oradour-sur-Glane, Oberg et Knochen. Paris 1986, S. 114.

Vorgeschichte

Oradour-sur-Glane ist ein kleines Dorf in Zentralfrankreich, ungefähr 20 Kilometer nordöstlich der Stadt Limoges in der Region Limousin. Vier Tage nach der Landung der Alliierten in der Normandie marschierte am 10. Juni 1944 eine Einheit der 2. SS-Panzerdivision „Das Reich" nach Oradour und umzingelte den Ort. Die Division war aus Südfrankreich gekommen und befand sich auf dem Marsch an die Normandiefront. Die Bevölkerung Oradours wurde auf dem Marktplatz zusammengetrieben. Die Männer wurden von den Frauen und Kindern getrennt, in Gruppen aufgeteilt und in Garagen und Scheunen des Ortes erschossen. Die Frauen und Kinder wurden in der Dorfkirche eingesperrt und mit Gewehr- und Maschinengewehrschüssen, Rauch- und Handgranaten getötet. Im Anschluss wurde im gesamten Ort Feuer gelegt.

Der Ablauf dieses Massakers ist relativ genau bekannt, es hatte Überlebende bei den Erschießungen der Männer gegeben und eine Frau war aus der Kirche entkommen. Unklar sind hingegen die Gründe geblieben, die zu dem Massaker geführt hatten. Eine Annahme lautete, dass es sich um eine Repressalie für die Entführung eines Offiziers der Division durch französische Widerstandskräfte gehandelt haben könnte. Eine zweite Annahme beruhte auf einem Irrtum: Die Einheit hätte Oradour-sur-Glane mit dem nahe gelegenen Ort Oradour-sur-Vayres verwechselt, der mitten im Partisanengebiet lag. Alle Quellen stimmen überein, dass es in Oradour-sur-Glane keine Widerstandstätigkeit gegeben habe. Eine weitere Annahme beruhte schließlich noch auf der divisionseigenen Logik der Abschreckung. Durch solche Maßnahmen sollte verhindert werden, dass sich die Bevölkerung dem Widerstand anschloss oder diesen unterstützte.

Gerichtliche Untersuchungen über die Täter wurden gleich nach dem Ende der deutschen Besatzungszeit aufgenommen. Die Grundlage eines Prozesses sollte eine Ordonnanz der provisorischen französischen Regierung vom 28. August 1944 bilden, welche die Verfolgung und Bestrafung von Kriegsverbrechen ermöglichte, die feindliche militärische Kräfte auf französischem Boden begangen hatten.[9] Jedoch stieβ die französische Justiz auf einige Hindernisse, die einen gerichtlichen Prozess über Jahre hinaus verzögern sollten:

Die Offiziere der SS-Einheit, die am 10. Juni 1944 in Oradour-sur-Glane gewesen waren, befanden sich nicht mehr in Frankreich und deren Auslieferung konnte nicht erreicht werden, obgleich sie die Hauptverantwortlichen des Massakers waren. Zweitens waren unter den Personen, die als Mitglieder der SS-Einheit und somit als potentielle Täter identifiziert und verhaftet worden waren, französische Staatsangehörige, auf die die Ordonnanz vom 28. August 1944 nicht angewendet werden konnte. Hierbei handelte es sich um die im Rahmen der allgemeinen Wehrpflicht im annektierten Elsass-Lothringen in die SS zwangsrekrutierte Elsässer.[10]

So erklärte der Untersuchungsrichter, der bisher die Ermittlungen in der „*Affaire d'Oradour*" am Zivilgerichtshof von Limoges geleitet hatte, diesen am

---

[9] Vgl.: Moisel, Claudia: Les procès pour crimes de guerre allemands en France après la Seconde Guerre mondiale, In: Bulletin de l'IHTP (2002) Nr. 80, S. 91 f.; Fouché, Jean-Jacques: Oradour : la politique et la justice. Saint-Paul 2004, S. 71-73.
Für den Gesamtkontext der französischen Gerichtsverfahren gegen deutsche Besatzungsvergehen siehe auch: Moisel, Claudia: Frankreich und die deutschen Kriegsverbrecher. Politik und Praxis der Strafverfolgung nach dem Zweiten Weltkrieg. Göttingen 2004.

[10] Zur Geschichte der zirka 130000 „*Incorporés de force*" oder „*Malgré-nous*" siehe u.a.: Herberich-Marx, Geneviève; Freddy Raphaël: Les incorporés de force alsaciens : deni, convocation et provocation de la mémoire, In: Vingtième Siècle (April-Juni 1985) Nr. 6, S. 83-102; Rigoulot, Pierre: La tragedie de Malgré-nous. Tambow, le camp des Français. Paris 1990; Riedweg, Eugène: Les « Malgré Nous » : Histoire de l'incorporation de force des Alsaciens-Mosellans dans l'armée allemande. Mulhouse 1995.
Ursprünglich war die Waffen-SS eine reine Freiwilligenarmee gewesen, doch der durch den Krieg hervorgerufene Personenbedarf ließ sich so schon bald nicht mehr decken. Mit der Wehrmacht wurde daraufhin vereinbart, dass die eingezogenen Rekruten wählen konnten, ob sie in der Waffen-SS oder in der Wehrmacht Dienst tun wollten. Als auch diese Maßnahme nicht mehr ausreichte, um die Soll-Stärken in den Einheiten der Waffen-SS aufrecht zu erhalten, wurden ganze Jahrgänge oder Teile davon direkt in die Waffen-SS eingezogen. Vgl. dazu: Wegner, Bernd: Hitlers politische Soldaten: die Waffen-SS 1933-1945. Paderborn 1997, S. 263-295. Im Elsass ließ Gauleiter Wagner am 25. August 1942 die allgemeine Wehrpflicht für alle „Deutschrassigen" verkünden, da bis dahin nicht im ausreichenden Maße Freiwillige angeworben worden waren. In den darauf folgenden Jahren wurden die Jahrgänge 1906-1928 teilweise oder vollständig eingezogen. Zur Waffen-SS kamen Oktober 1942 der Jahrgang 1924, Februar 1944 der halbe Jahrgang 1926 und April 1944 die Jahrgänge 1908-1910. Vgl. dazu: Rigoulot, Pierre: La tragedie de Malgré-nous. Paris 1990, S. 81-107.

25. November 1944 für nicht zuständig und verwies die Frage an den Militärgerichtshof von Bordeaux. Dieser Initiative folgte der französische Justizminister am 30. Januar 1945. Allerdings sollte der Prozess gegen die deutschen Beschuldigten von dem der Beschuldigten mit französischer Staatsangehörigkeit getrennt werden. Dagegen bestimmte im Februar 1945 der Inhaber der Militärgewalt für die Region von Limoges, Colonel Rousselier, dass der Fall der angeklagten Elsässer abgeschlossen sei. Als Begründung führte er an, dass die Beschuldigten in die SS zwangseingezogen und somit Opfer eines Kriegsverbrechens gewesen wären. Demzufolge könnten sie nicht des Begehens eines Kriegsverbrechens im Rahmen ihres Zwangsdienstes beschuldigt werden.

Im September 1945 wurde in Straßburg ein Elsässer ausfindig gemacht, von dem angenommen wurde, dass er aktiv am Massaker beteiligt gewesen war. Obwohl auch er ein Zwangsrekrutierter war, wurde am 12. März 1946 am Gerichtshof von Limoges ein Verfahren gegen ihn eröffnet. Der Angeklagte bekannte, am 10. Juni 1944 in Oradour-sur-Glane zwei Frauen erschossen zu haben und aktiv an der Zerstörung des Ortes beteiligt gewesen zu sein. Zudem wurde ihm zur Last gelegt, Oradour als Flüchtling vorher gekannt und somit der SS als Führer gedient zu haben. Der Prozess endete mit dem einstimmigen Urteil der fünf Richter und der Verurteilung des Angeklagten zum Tode. Doch bereits am 22. März hob das Berufungsgericht von Limoges das Urteil auf und erklärte, dass der Angeklagte zur Tatzeit minderjährig gewesen sei und die Uniform des Feindes getragen hätte. Auch dieses Verfahren wurde an den Militärgerichtshof von Bordeaux verwiesen. Dieser übergab die Frage dem Zivilgericht von Toulouse, welches sich ebenfalls für nicht zuständig erklärte und eine Empfehlung an die französische Regierung schickte, das Verfahren durch eine Amnestie zu beenden.

Als im April 1947 in einem Kriegsgefangenenlager in Großbritannien ein Elsässer gefunden wurde, der als Freiwilliger in der 2. SS-Panzer-Division „Das Reich" gedient hatte, der am 10. Juni 1944 den Rang eines Stabsunteroffiziers bekleidet und sich an diesem Tag in Oradour befunden hätte, lag die Sachlage anders als bei den Zwangsrekrutierten. Über diesen Elsässer konnte gerichtet werden. Für die Letzteren schien sich das Problem der Strafverfolgung durch die Einstellung des Verfahren und den Ausschluss weiterer gerichtlicher Verfolgung durch eine richterliche Ordonnanz vom 17. August 1948 gelöst zu haben.[11]

Ein Gesetz des französischen Parlaments vom 15. September 1948 sollte einen Ausweg aus dieser „Doppelten Nichtzuständigkeit" (*double incompétence*[12]) der Militär- und Zivilgerichtsbarkeit bieten. Der erste Artikel dieses Gesetzes lautete:

„Lorsqu'un des crimes prévus par l'ordonnance du 28 août 1944 sur la répression des crimes de guerre est imputable à l'action collective d'une formation ou d'un groupe faisant partie d'une organisation déclarée criminelle par le tribunal militaire international agissant en vertu de l'acte du 8 août 1945, tous les individus appartenant à cette formation ou à ce groupe peuvent être considérés comme co-auteurs, à moins qu'ils n'apportent la preuve de leur incorporation forcée et de leur non-participation au crime."[13]

Dieses sogenannte „Lex Oradour" beinhaltete Brüche mit der Rechtstradition und wurde deshalb schon in seinem parlamentarischen Entstehungsprozess angefochten: Erstens war das Gesetz rückwirkend und widersprach dem Rechtsgrundsatz *nulla poena sine lege*. Des Weiteren belastete es den Angeklagten damit, seine Unschuld zu beweisen, was eine Umkehr der Beweislast darstellte. Drittens ersetzte es das Prinzip der individuellen Schuld durch eine Kollektivschuld und widersprach somit auch den Vorstellungen des Internationalen Militärgerichtshofs von Nürnberg, auf den in dem Gesetzestext Bezug genommen wurde.[14] Trotzdem sollte auf der Grundlage dieses Gesetzes in

---

[11] Zu den Vorverfahren vgl. u. a.: Fouché, Jean-Jacques: Oradour. Paris 2001, S. 224-227; Fouché (wie Fn. 9), S. 33-126.

[12] Fouché, Oradour (wie Fn. 11), S. 226; Fouché, Oradour : la politique et la justice (wie Fn. 9), S. 94.

[13] „Loi n° 48-1416 du 15 septembre 1948 modifiant et complétant l'ordonnance du 28 août 1944 relative à la répression des crimes de guerre", Artikel 1. In: Journal Officiel de la République Française (1948), S. 9138.

[14] „Le Tribunal International de Nuremberg s'était déclaré contre la responsabilité collective". In: L'Aurore, 7. Januar 1953.
Das Gesetz wurde das erste Mal in dem Ascq-Prozess im Jahr 1949 in Lille angewendet und vehement angegriffen. Dabei ging es um ein Massaker an 86 Franzosen in der nordfranzösischen Stadt Ascq am 1. April 1944. Auf Grundlage der „Lex Oradour" wurde am 6. August 1949 gegen

Bordeaux im Januar 1953 der Prozess gegen alle Schuldigen des Massakers vom 10. Juni 1944 stattfinden.

Außenpolitisch fand der Prozess vor dem Hintergrund des Ost-West-Konfliktes und des Koreakrieges statt. Zur gleichen Zeit wurden die Gründung einer europäischen Verteidigungsgemeinschaft und die Wiederbewaffnung Deutschlands diskutiert. Der französische Indochinakrieg befand sich in der Endphase und in Algerien kündigte sich ein weiterer Dekolonialisierungskonflikt an.[15] Innenpolitisch befand sich die Vierte Republik nach einem knappen Jahr unter Antoine Pinay Ende 1952 vor einem neuen Regierungswechsel. Im Januar 1953 übernahm René Mayer für wenige Monate die Regierungsgeschäfte. Im Kontext dieser innenpolitischen Instabilität entwickelte sich um den Oradourprozess eine „Politische Schlacht" (*bataille politique*), die von den elsässischen Abgeordneten ausging.[16] Zu dieser politischen Mobilisierung trugen auch die für die erste Jahreshälfte 1953 anstehenden Kommunalwahlen bei.[17]

Der Prozess

Auch am Vorabend des Prozesses[18] hatte sich nichts daran geändert, dass nur wenige ehemalige Mitglieder der verantwortlichen SS-Einheit gefunden

---

acht Angehörige der für das Massaker verantwortlichen Aufklärungsabteilung der 12. SS-Division die Todesstrafe verhängt. Vgl. dazu: „Ascq. Das Gesetz ist Mord". In: Der Spiegel (1950) Nr. 24.

[15] Vgl. dazu: Rioux, Jean-Pierre: Le procès d'Oradour. In: L'Histoire (Februar 1984) Nr. 64, S. 14; Fouché, Oradour : la politique et la justice (wie Fn. 9), S. 127-129.

[16] Fouché, Oradour : la politique et la justice (wie Fn. 9), S. 131.

[17] So: Fouché, Oradour : la politique et la justice (wie Fn. 9), S. 436.

[18] Der Ablauf des Oradourprozesses ist ausführlich im Archiv des 1999 in Oradour gegründeten Erinnerungszentrums dokumentiert. Eine weitere Quelle ist der Beitrag von Jean-Marc Théolleyre, der als Berichterstatter von der französischen Tageszeitung *Le Monde* dem Prozess beigewohnt hat und im Jahr 1986 eine Sammlung seiner dazu abgefassten Artikel veröffentlicht hat: Théolleyre (wie Fn. 8).
Zudem sind in den letzten Jahren verschiedene Veröffentlichungen zu dem Prozess entstanden: Fischbach, Bernard: Oradour, l'extermination. Straβburg 2001; Vonau, Jean-Laurent: Le Procès de Bordeaux. Les Malgré-Nous et le drame d'Oradour, Straßburg 2003; Fouché, Oradour : la politique et la justice (wie Fn. 9); Moisel, Frankreich und die deutschen Kriegsverbrecher (wie Fn. 9). Ebenfalls erwähnt sei eine universitäre Arbeit: Javerliat, Guillame: L'affaire d'Oradour de 1953: une crise nationale. Unveröffentlichte „Mémoire de Maîtrise", Université de Limoges 2004.

worden waren und für den Prozess zur Verfügung standen. Der Aufenthaltsort des Divisionskommandeurs der 2. SS-Division „Das Reich“, Heinz Lammerding, war bekannt. Allerdings befand er sich am Ende des Krieges in der britischen Besatzungszone und die Briten verweigerten eine Auslieferung an Frankreich. Die Einstellung der Briten zur Auslieferung Lammerdings wurde von der Bundesrepublik übernommen.[19] Als das Verfahren am 12. Januar 1953 begann, saßen einundzwanzig Personen auf der Anklagebank: Ein Stabsfeldwebel, ein Stabsunteroffizier und neunzehn Soldaten, kein Offizier. Von den neunzehn Mannschaftsdienstgraden waren dreizehn zwangsrekrutierte Elsässer.

So plädierten die Verteidiger der elsässischen Angeklagten bereits am ersten Sitzungstag für eine Trennung des Verfahrens ihrer Mandanten von dem der deutschen Angeklagten. Dabei wurde nicht versäumt, das „Lex Oradour“ vom 15. September 1948 anzufechten, dessen dritter Artikel die Grundlage für die Anklage der Elsässer bilden sollte. Des Weiteren verwiesen die Verteidiger auf die Minderjährigkeit einiger Mandanten zur Tatzeit und auf die bereits ergangenen Urteile. Die Diskussionen darüber dauerten auch den folgenden Tag an. Dann erfolgte jedoch die Antwort des Gerichts, dass der Prozess wie geplant fortgesetzt werde. Zur Begründung dieses Entschlusses hieß es, dass das Gesetz vom 15. September 1948 eine politische Entscheidung gewesen wäre und vor diesem Gericht nicht diskutiert werden könne. Des Weiteren erklärte sich das Gericht in den Fragen der Minderjährigkeit und der bereits ergangenen Entscheidungen für zuständig. Auf dieser Grundlage konnte der Prozess jedoch nur bis zum 28. Januar weitergeführt werden. An diesem Tag war die französische Abgeordnetenkammer einem von den elsässischen Abgeordneten eingebrachten und mit Nachdruck propagierten Antrag nachgekommen und hatte der Änderung des Gesetzes vom 15. September 1948 zugestimmt. Die Änderungen beinhalteten die Außerkraftsetzung der Artikel 1 und 2 sowie die Aufhebung des Begriffs der Kollektivschuld.

Die Verfahren mussten nun formal getrennt werden, der Vorsitzende lehnte jedoch eine Auslagerung des Verfahrens gegen die elsässischen Angeklagten

---

[19] Siehe dazu: Fouché, Oradour : la politique et la justice (wie Fn. 9), S. 487-490.

ab und stellte es vielmehr auf eine neue Rechtsgrundlage, dem „gemeinen“ Recht des *Code pénal*.

Am 13. Februar 1953 erging der Urteilsspruch im Oradourprozess: Die abwesenden Angeklagten wurden fast ausschließlich zum Tode verurteilt. Über die beiden anwesenden ehemaligen Unteroffiziere erging das gleiche Urteil. Fünf der sechs deutschen Angeklagten im Range einfacher Soldaten erhielten zwischen zehn und zwölf Jahren Zwangsarbeit oder Gefängnis, ein einziger wurde freigesprochen. Die dreizehn Elsässer wurden alle zu Zwangsarbeit oder Gefängnisstrafen zwischen fünf und acht Jahren verurteilt.

Das Urteil wurde in beiden Regionen mit Entsetzen aufgenommen, das in massiven Reaktionen seinen Ausdruck fand. Im Elsass hingen z. B. die Fahnen auf Halbmast, das Gefallenendenkmal von Straßburg wurde mit einem schwarzen Netz überhängt, es kam zu Streiks und zu Demonstrationen. Die Vertreter des Opferverbunds von Oradour hatten sich aufgrund des Prozessverlaufs schon vorzeitig aus dem Gerichtssaal entfernt. Im Namen der Opfer fanden Demonstrationen in Bordeaux und Limoges statt.[20] Während man sich im Elsass kollektiv verurteilt fühlte[21], herrschte in Oradour-sur-Glane Unverständnis über die Milde der Urteile. Gemäss der amerikanischen Historikerin Sarah Farmer, die im Jahr 1994 das vielbeachtete Buch mit dem Titel *Oradour: Arrêt sur mémoire* veröffentlicht hatte, wäre für die Opfergemeinschaft Oradours als einzig denkbarer Prozessausgang nur die Todesstrafe für alle Angeklagten akzeptabel gewesen.[22]

---

[20] Siehe dazu: Barral, Pierre: L'affaire d'Oradour, affrontement de deux mémoires. In: Mémoire de la Seconde Guerre mondiale, Actes du colloque de Metz 6-8 octobre 1983. Hrsg. von Alfred Wahl. Metz 1984, S. 243-252, hier S. 248 f.; Fouché, Oradour : la politique et la justice (wie Fn. 9), S. 436-445.

[21] Vgl. dazu einen Text, der nach der Urteilsverkündigung öffentlich im Elsass ausgehängt wurde: „*Nous n'acceptons pas. Toute l'Alsace se déclare solidaire des treize enfants condamnés à tort à Bordeaux et des 130 000 incorporés de force. Lâchement abandonnée entre les mains des nazis et sacrifiée par les gouvernements de l'époque, notre population souffre atrocement avec ses fils et leurs familles. Elle restera avec eux dans la peine. L'Alsace française s'élève avec véhémence contre la carence gouvernementale et se révolte contre l'incompréhension dont ses fils sont les malheureuses victimes*“. Zitiert nach: Gatti, Armand: Le jugement de Bordeaux n'a pas effacé le drame d'Oradour. In: Le Parisien Libéré, 14. Februar 1953.

[22] So: Farmer, Sarah: Martyred village : commemorating the 1944 massacre at Oradour-sur-Glane. Berkeley, Los Angeles, London 1999, S. 163. Hierbei handelt es sich um die englische Ausgabe

Die Amnestie

Jean-Jacques Fouché, der als Projektleiter und erster Direktor des Erinnerungszentrums in Oradour-sur-Glane sowie als Autor des Werkes *Oradour* viel über dieses Thema gearbeitet hat, veröffentlichte 2003 eine Arbeit über den Prozess. Darin stellte er folgende rhetorische Frage: „*Le chaos politique aurait-il pu déboucher sur autre chose qu'un désastre judiciaire ?*"[23]

Diese politisch-rechtliche Chaossituation wurde vervollständigt, indem die französische Legislative nur kurze Zeit nach dem Prozessende am 20. Februar 1953 diesmal mit einem „Aufruf zur Einheit" (*Appel à l'unité*[24]) intervenierte. Der erste Artikel dieses Gesetzes, das die in Bordeaux verurteilten Elsässer mit sofortiger Wirkung amnestierte, lautete:

„Amnistie pleine et entière est accordée aux Français incorporés de force dans l'armée allemande, pour tout fait qualifié crime ou délit commis au cours d'une action criminelle accomplie par l'unité dans laquelle ils avaient été versé".[25]

Während sich im Elsass die Lage entspannte, wurde in Oradour-sur-Glane auf zwei Arten auf die Amnestie reagiert: Die kommunistische Partei, die im

---

des 1994 erschienenen und 2004 neu aufgelegten Buches: Farmer, Sarah: Oradour : Arrêt sur mémoire, Paris 1994; Farmer, Sarah: Oradour 10 juin 1944 : Arrêt sur mémoire, Paris 2004. Ein weiterer Beitrag Sarah Farmers in Bezug auf Oradour ist: Farmer, Sarah: samedi 10 juin 1944, 14 heures… In: Farmer, Sarah; Serge Tisseron. Parlez-moi d'Oradour. Paris 2004, S. 12-17.

[23] Fouché, Oradour : la politique et la justice (wie Fn. 9), S. 448.
Weitere Beiträge Jean-Jacques Fouchés sind: Fouché, Jean-Jacques: La Déception des témoins. Le conflit des récits du massacre à Oradour-sur-Glane. In: Le Génocide des Juifs entre procès et histoire 1943-2000. Hrsg. von Florent Brayard. Brüssel 2000, S. 189-212; Fouché, Jean-Jacques: Das „Centre de la mémoire" in Oradour. In: Die Zukunft der Vergangenheit: Wie soll die Geschichte des Nationalsozialismus in Museen und Gedenkstätten im 21. Jahrhundert vermittelt werden? Hrsg. von Museen der Stadt Nürnberg. Nürnberg 2000, S. 137-142; Fouché, Jean-Jacques: Oradour et les « malgré nous ». In: Le mrap (September 2004) Nr. 128, S. 2-4.

[24] Barral (wie Fn. 20), S. 250.

[25] „Loi n° 53-112 du 20 février 1953 portant amnistie en faveur des Français incorporés de force dans les formations militaires ennemies". In : Journal Officiel de la République Française, 21. Februar 1953.

Gemeinderat Oradours die Mehrheit ausmachte, versuchte die Situation durch spektakuläre Protestaktionen für die anstehenden Kommunalwahlen zu nutzen. So gründete sie z. B. ein Aktionskomitee und organisierte Massendemonstrationen.[26] Die Vereinigung der Opfer und Hinterbliebenen demonstrierte hingegen durch symbolische Akte seine Ablehnung: Das Kreuz der Ehrenlegion Oradours wurde an der Präfektur von Limoges abgegeben, der Verein ließ ein neues Grabmal für die sterblichen Überreste der Opfer bauen und das von staatlichen Mitteln erbaute leer stehen und in Zukunft sollten keine staatlichen Vertreter mehr zu den jährlichen Gedenkfeierlichkeiten eingeladen werden. Schließlich wurden an den Eingängen zu den Ruinen des am 10. Juni 1944 abgebrannten und seitdem in diesem Zustand der Zerstörung konservierten Ortes Tafeln angebracht, die die Namen all derjenigen Abgeordneten und Senatoren aufführten, die für das Amnestiegesetz gestimmt haben.[27] Die Opfergemeinschaft führte eine Trennung von Politik und Gedenken ein und baute damit die künftige Distanz zu Paris auf. Das Gedenken an das Massaker wurde in Oradour-sur-Glane „privatisiert", ein Umstand, der nicht ohne Konsequenzen für den Aufarbeitungsprozess der Geschichte des Massakers blieb: „*Les hésitations de la justice ont retardé le travail de mémoire*"[28], so hieß es zum 50. Jahrestag des Prozessendes in einer Regionalzeitung des Limousin. Es sei noch angemerkt, dass die in Bordeaux verhängten Todesstrafen nicht vollstreckt worden sind und der letzte im Prozess von Bordeaux Verurteilte Anfang der Sechzigerjahre aus der Haft entlassen worden ist.[29]

Die Bewohner des in unmittelbarer Nähe zu den Ruinen neuerbauten Oradours versanken in Trauer und Isolation: Die Häuser wurden in einheitlichem Grau gestrichen, die Strassen erhielten keine Namen und in dem Ort gab es weder Blumen noch Feste. Es sollte bis zu Beginn der Neunzigerjahre dauern,

---

[26] Vgl.: Ministère de l'Intérieur, Direction Générale de la Sureté Nationale: Renseignements généraux de la Haute-Vienne, Nr. 150, Betreff: „Réaction de la population à la suite du procès d'Oradour-sur-Glane". Limoges, 28. März 1953. In: Archives Départementales de la Haute-Vienne, Limoges, 986 W 483.

[27] So: Desourteaux, André; Robert Hébras: Oradour / Glane : Notre village assassiné. Montreuil-Bellay 1998, S. 184.

[28] Catus, Bertrand: Cinquante ans après la plaie reste ouverte. In: L'Echo, 17. Februar 2003.

[29] Vgl.: Farmer, Martyred village (wie Fn. 22), S. 169; Fouché (wie Fn. 11), S. 232 f.

bis sich die Lage in Oradour normalisierte und mit ihr auch die Beziehung zum französischen Staat. Der entscheidende Schritt wurde im Jahr 1982 gemacht, als Staatspräsident François Mitterrand Oradour besuchte, der 1953 für das Amnestiegesetz gestimmt hatte. Nachdem die französische Regierung bei den Feierlichkeiten des 40. Jahrestags des Massakers von seinem „Ministre des Anciens Combattants“, Jean Laurain, vertreten worden war[30], bemühte sich die Gemeindeleitung Oradours um die Aufnahme des 50. Jahrestags in das Programm der nationalen Gedenktage.[31] In der Folge nahmen Staatspräsident Mitterrand und Premierminister Balladur an der Gedenkveranstaltung teil. Am 16. Juli 1999 besuchte mit Jacques Chirac erneut ein französischer Staatschef Oradour, um das neugebaute Erinnerungszentrum einzuweihen.

Schwieriger scheint sich die Normalisierung der Beziehung Oradour-sur-Glanes zum Elsass gestaltet zu haben und ist ausschließlich auf den Willen des 1995 ins Amt gekommenen Bürgermeisters, Raymond Frugier, zurückzuführen. Aufgrund seiner Vermittlungsversuche konnte am 10. Juni 1998, also 45 Jahre nach dem Prozess von Bordeaux, eine elsässische Delegation unter der Führung des Straßburger Bürgermeisters Roland Ries an den Gedenkfeierlichkeiten in Oradour teilnehmen. Im Zentrum dieser Annäherung scheint die gegenseitige Anerkennung eines Opferstatus gestanden zu haben, die den seit 1953 andauernden „Opferkonflikt“ (*conflit de victimes*[32]) als Nährboden für die Unnachgiebigkeit der Betroffenen beendete. So bemerkte der Bürgermeister Oradours in einer Rede:

„L'Alsace et la Moselle, sacrifiées en 1870, ont été à nouveau abandonnées, annexées à l'Allemagne en 1940, avec ses 130 000 jeunes contraints d'endosser l'uniforme Allemand. Oradour, détruite, martyrisée, avec un raffinement déconcertant de cruauté. Des deux côtés, chacun a souffert des mêmes doctri-

---

[30] So: Beaulieu, C.: Association Nationale des Familles des Martyrs. In: Le petit radounaud, November 1984, S. 30.

[31] Lapuelle, Robert: 10 juin 1994. In: Le Radounaud, Juli 1994 (ohne Seitenzahlen). „*Le petit radounaud*“ und „*Le Radounaud*“ sind die Gemeindenachrichten von Oradour.

[32] Fouché, Oradour et les « malgré nous » (wie Fn. 23), S. 4: „*Le pardon serait la seule possibilité de mettre fin à un conflit de victimes. Jusqu'à aujourd'hui on a assisté à un conflit pour la reconnaissance de la place de « première victime » devant la communauté nationale.*“

nes, et des mêmes hommes, chacun a subi le totalitarisme d'un régime abhorre. Ces faits doivent être connus, évoqués, accepté par tous, c'est à ce prix que les plaies pourront enfin se cicatriser."[33]

Trotz einiger individueller Initiativen bestehen noch heute keine offiziellen Beziehungen zwischen Oradour und Deutschland.

Fazit

In einem Artikel der Frankfurter Allgemeinen Zeitung vom 3. Februar 1953 wurde der Oradourprozess mit folgenden Titeln umschrieben: „Umstrittene Vorgeschichte ... Umstrittenes Verfahren ... Umstrittenes Urteil ... Das unlösbare Problem".[34] Dieses Zitat spiegelt wieder, wie wenig Aussicht auf Erfolg dem Verfahren in Bordeaux in zeitgenössischen Betrachtungen schon vor Prozessende zugeschrieben wurde.

In der Vorstellung des Europäischen Forums junger Rechtshistoriker 2006 in Frankfurt am Main hieß es: „Ein Urteil oder Vergleich soll einen Streit dem Vergessen überlassen." Ein solches Vergessen konnte im Oradourprozess nicht erreicht werden, trotz des zusätzlichen Amnestiegesetzes. Vielmehr war das Gegenteil der Fall: Der Prozess hinterließ in Oradour wie auch im Elsass offene Wunden, die erst sehr spät zu heilen begannen und vielleicht bis heute noch nicht vollständig verheilt sind.

Der Straßburger Rechtswissenschaftler und Historiker Jean-Laurent Vonau hat in seiner 2003 erschienenen Arbeit über den Prozess von Bordeaux versucht die Gründe für den Misserfolg des Verfahrens zusammenzufassen[35]: An erster Stelle nennt Vonau die Abwesenheit der Offiziere der 2. SS-Division, die an dem Befehl zum Massaker beteiligt gewesen waren und die den Krieg überlebt hatten. Auf der Anklagebank saßen nur Soldaten niederen Ranges,

---

[33] „Discours de M. Raymond Frugier, Maire d'Oradour-sur-Glane", In: Le Radounaud, Edition spéciale, November 1999, (ohne Seitenangaben).
[34] „Welchen Weg nimmt der Oradour-Prozeß?". In: Frankfurter Allgemeine Zeitung, 3. Februar 1953.
[35] Vonau (wie Fn. 18), S. 196-198.

die sich auf die Befolgung von Befehlen berufen und somit ihre Verantwortlichkeit an den Ereignissen mindern konnten. Zweitens habe nach Vonau keine ausführliche wissenschaftliche Untersuchung der Vorfälle in Oradour, z. B. durch Gerichtsmediziner, stattgefunden. Schwerwiegender sei noch das Versäumnis gewesen, dass während des Verfahrens der Ort des Verbrechens nicht besucht worden ist, weder mit den Angeklagten, wogegen Sicherheitseinwände gesprochen hätten, noch von den Verantwortlichen der Urteilsfindung. Schließlich stelle die „Einmischung" des Gesetzgebers in ein Gerichtsverfahren eine Ursache für dessen Misserfolg dar, was Vonau als eine Seltenheit für die französische Strafrechtsgeschichte bezeichnet:

„Cette immixtion flagrante du législateur dans le judiciaire constitue un fait rarissime dans l'histoire du droit répressif en France. De même, il est exceptionnel qu'une amnistie générale mette un terme à un procès retentissant et détruise, en un temps record, un jugement pourtant bâti à grand-peine."[36]

Der Oradourprozess verlief im Spannungsfeld der öffentlichen Meinung, der Rechtsprechung und der Politik. Die vehementen Einwirkungen der öffentlichen Meinung und der Politik haben dem Prozessverlauf geschadet. Das Problem der Zwangsrekrutierungen der Elsässer und Mosellaner war vor dem Prozess nicht politisch geregelt worden.[37] Es handelte sich aber doch um ein politisches Problem, das später zugunsten der nationalen Einheit entschieden wurde. Der Wunsch der Opfer Oradours nach Gerechtigkeit wurde hintangestellt.

Zum Abschluss sei nun noch auf die Gemeinsamkeiten eingegangen, die der Oradourprozess, obgleich schon 1953 stattgefunden, mit der zweiten Welle französischer Nachkriegsprozesse hat.

Henry Rousso hat die zweite Welle als eine „zweite Säuberung" (*seconde épuration*[38]) bezeichnet. Wie im Oradourprozess seien die Erwartungen an diese Prozesse immer weitergegangen als nur der einer Suche nach Gerechtigkeit. In

---

[36] Vonau (wie Fn. 18), S. 198.
[37] Vgl.: Vonau (wie Fn. 18), S. 198-203.
[38] Rousso (wie Fn. 5), S. 112.

den Prozessen gegen Barbie, Touvier und Papon habe nicht die Verurteilung individueller Schuld im Vordergrund gestanden, sondern die Verarbeitung der Verbrechen einer Epoche. Besonders im Prozess von Bordeaux, aber auch in den späteren Verfahren hätten die Nachkriegsprozesse mehr Probleme verursacht als gelöst. Gleich ist auch, dass in diesen Fällen Recht unter außergewöhnlichen Bedingungen gesprochen worden sei, teilweise in rechtlich und verfahrenstechnisch bedenklichen Situationen.[39]

Diese Prozesse lassen sich als Erinnerungsprozesse bezeichnen. Die Opfer suchen darin Erklärung, Erleichterung, Unterstützung ihrer Trauerarbeit und Aufarbeitung und schließlich auch Reparation. Dazu hat Henry Rousso bemerkt:

„Ce que la France a aujourd'hui du mal à affronter, ce n'est pas tant son passé que le fait de devoir vivre avec une fracture qu'aucun procès, aucune commémoration, aucun discours ne viendra réparer. Affronter et accepter l'irréparable, tel est à mon sens le véritable enjeu de notre génération et celui des générations futures."[40]

In diesen Prozessen standen Individuen vor Gericht, seien es ehemalige Soldaten oder Beamte der Vichy-Regierung. Doch die Erwartung ein ganzes Regime zu richten, den Nationalsozialismus im Fall des Oradourprozesses oder die französische Verwaltung in ihrer Verwicklung in die Deportierungen im Paponprozess, konnte sicherlich nicht erfüllt werden. Denis Salas schrieb dazu: „*En voulant donner une leçon d'histoire, ces procès manqueraient à leur fonction du jugement.*"[41] Diese Verfahren standen immer unter dem Druck oder dem Einfluss der öffentlichen Meinung, der Politik und miteinander konkurrierenden kollektiven Erinnerungen. Eine Erklärung dafür ist, dass die Zeitzeugen in den Erinnerungsprozessen eine zentrale Position einnahmen.[42]

Dieser Punkt stellt einen Unterschied zwischen dem Prozess von Bordeaux 1953 und den Nachkriegsprozessen der zweiten Welle dar. Während im Jahr

[39] Vgl.: Rousso (wie Fn. 5), S. 95-97.
[40] Rousso (wie Fn. 5), S. 118.
[41] Salas (wie Fn. 2), S. 30.
[42] Vgl.: Salas (wie Fn. 2), S. 21. Vgl. dazu auch: Wieviorka, Annette: L'ère du témoin. Paris 1999.

1953 die Zeitzeugen vor Gericht aussagen konnten, fanden die Prozesse der zweiten Welle ausschließlich auf der Grundlage der Verbrechen gegen die Menschlichkeit statt, da nur diese Verbrechen noch nicht verjährt waren. Ende der Siebzigerjahre und vor allem am Ende des 20. Jahrhunderts hatten die Zeitzeugen ein hohes Alter erreicht oder waren verstorben. Da für ein Gerichtsverfahren Zeugen benötigt werden, geriet die Rechtsprechung durch die Unverjährbarkeit in eine ungewöhnliche Situation außerhalb ihres zeitlichen Erfahrungswerts.[43] In den Prozessen gegen Barbie, Touvier und Papon wurde versucht, dieses Dilemma durch die Beteiligung von Historikern zu lösen, eine Maßnahme, die nicht unumstritten ist.[44]

---

[43] Die verspätete Regelung dieser Verbrechen war notwendig, da es sich bei der Erinnerung daran um das kollektive Gedächtnis der Franzosen okkultierter Erinnerungen handelte. Diese Verbrechen waren somit in der Vergangenheitsbewältigung, die dem Krieg folgte, nicht berücksichtigt worden. Vgl. dazu u. a.: Rousso, Henry: Le syndrome de Vichy. De 1944 à nos jours. Paris 1990; Conan, Eric; Henry Rousso: Vichy, un passé qui ne passe pas. Paris 1994; Rousso (wie Fn. 5).

[44] Zu dieser Problematik vgl. u. a.: Rousso (wie Fn. 5); Ory, Pascal: Du rôle des historiens dans des procès récents. In: Travail de mémoire 1914-1998. Une nécessité dans un siècle de violence. Hrsg. von Jean-Pierre Bacot. Paris 1999, S. 53-55; Rousso, Henry: Justiz, Geschichte und Erinnerung in Frankreich. *Überlegungen zum Papon-Prozeß*. In: Geschichte vor Gericht. Historiker, Richter und die Suche nach Gerechtigkeit. Hrsg. von Norbert Frei, Dirk van Laak und Michael Stolleis. München 2000, S. 141-163; Ricœur, Paul: Les rôles respectifs du juge et de l'historien. In: Esprit (August-September 2000) Nr. 266-267, S. 48-71; Rousso, Henry: L'expertise des historiens dans les procès pour crimes contre l'humanité. In: Barbie, Touvier, Papon… Des procès pour la mémoire. Hrsg. von Jean-Paul Jean und Denis Salas. Paris 2002, S. 58-70; Salas (wie Fn. 2); Fleury, Béatrice; Jacques Walter: Le procès Papon. Médias, témoin-expert et contre-expertise historiographique. In: Vingtième Siècle (Oktober-Dezember 2005) Nr. 88, S. 63-76.

Law in a Gaelic Utopia: Perceptions of Brehon Law in Nineteenth and early Twentieth Century Ireland

Thomas Mohr

1. The Utopia

It is well known that the term "utopia" was invented by a lawyer. The word was used by Sir Thomas More as the title of his famous work describing an ideal commonwealth situated on a fictitious island in the New World. "Utopia" literally means "nowhere" or "no place" in Latin but since the publication of More's book in 1516 the word has acquired a different meaning in the English language. It is now generally understood to mean "good place" or "ideal place" with connotations of impracticality and unattainability.

Yet, in a broad sense the word "utopia" can mean much more than an imaginary idyllic land. In many ways a utopia represents an expression of desire on the part of its author. Following this reasoning, one might say that utopia is little more than a means of expressing ideal dreams of human happiness. Taken in this context, a utopia need not be a place at all. Alternatively, a utopia can be defined in terms of time. For many people this means an ideal future. Much of the genre of science fiction is dependent on utopias of this sort. For other people utopia lies in the past, in the idea of the Golden Age, a concept that is probably common to most cultures.

In Ireland the Golden Age is traditionally taken to be the early medieval period, the time before invasions of the mid-twelfth century that created political links, for better or for worse, with the neighbouring island. Irish school children are still taught that early medieval Ireland was known as the "island of saints and scholars". For Irish people living in the nineteenth and early twentieth centuries, a period in which many Irish people feared that their country was losing its identity, pre-invasion Ireland was the "Gaelic utopia".

Returning for a moment to the subject of utopias in general, just as the nature of a utopia can vary to large degree so too can the means of achieving it.

Commonly advocated means of achieving utopia include the use of science to free humankind from want, the direct application of religious and philosophical ideals, a process of universal social conditioning, the provision of complete sexual freedom and the discovery of means of living in harmony with nature. Yet, anybody who takes even a passing interest in utopian literature will quickly discover that law is seldom advocated as means of achieving an ideal society or state of being. Indeed, it is fair to say that there is a powerful anti-legal element inherent in much utopian literature. Although Thomas More was himself a lawyer he made clear that his ideal commonwealth would have very little law. He wrote that:

"They [the Utopians] have very few laws, because, with their social system, very few laws are required. Indeed, one of their great complaints against other countries is that, although they've already got books and books of laws, they never seem to have enough. For, according to the Utopians, it's quite unjust for anyone to be bound by a legal code which is too long for an ordinary person to read right through, or too difficult for him to understand."[1]

Not only would More's "Utopia" have a minimum of law, it would also be bereft of a legal profession. As More set out:

"[T]hey have no barristers to be over-ingenious about individual cases and points of law. They think it better for each man to plead his own cause, and tell the judge the same story as he'd otherwise tell his lawyer. Under such conditions, the point at issue is less likely to be obscured, and it's easier to get at the truth – for, if nobody's telling the sort of lies that one learns from lawyers, the judge can apply all his shrewdness to weighing the facts of the case and protecting simple-minded creatures against the unscrupulous attacks of the clever ones."[2]

---

[1] More, Thomas: Utopia. London, 1965, p. 106.
[2] *Ibid.*

One of the most intriguing aspects of "Utopia" is that it is difficult to know when More is being serious or when, as a man with a lively sense of humour, he is simply having a laugh. Whatever of More's motives, few people would be surprised to learn that the total absence of lawyers is an extremely common feature in utopian literature.

The perception of early medieval Ireland as a "Gaelic utopia" goes completely against this trend. Law is one of the vital supporting pillars of the Gaelic utopia. This article concerns popular perceptions in nineteenth and early twentieth century Ireland of what is sometimes called "early Irish law". The popular name for this ancient legal system is "brehon law", a term derived from the word *brithemain* meaning "judges" or "jurists" in the Irish language. This article will examine why the brehon law provided such fertile soil for utopian visions in nineteenth and early twentieth century Ireland. Having done this, it will examine the utopian elements in the works of a number of selected scholars and contrast such perceptions with the reality of the brehon law as revealed by later scholarship. This article will also attempt to examine the significance of these utopian visions in relation to the law of the independent Irish state that emerged in the aftermath of the treaty signed by Irish representatives and members of the British government in 1921. However, before proceeding any further, it is necessary to set out the nature of brehon law for those who are unfamiliar with this ancient legal system.

2. Early Medieval Ireland and the Brehon Law

Ireland was never incorporated into the Roman Empire. Roman law and Roman ideas of a centralised and urban-based system of administration were never extended to the island. One of the notable features of early medieval Ireland was the extent to which it was politically fragmented. The country was divided into approximately 120 petty kingdoms or *tuathta*. However, another notable feature of early medieval Ireland was that, in spite of such political divisions, there was a surprising degree of cultural homogeneity.

The politically divided island had a common language that was recorded in one of the earliest examples of vernacular literature to arise in medieval Europe. It is worth noting that the language used in this literature shows almost no traces of variation of dialect, a surprising feature when considering the politically fragmented nature of early Irish society. An even more surprising feature of early medieval Irish society, taking these political divisions and the absence of a single centralised state into account, is that the entire island of Ireland had a single system of law. How this state of affairs came to pass remains an unsolved mystery. One might, however, speculate that a sense of solidarity amongst the aristocratic and learned elite, a class known as the *nemed*, together with the rights of free movement throughout the island enjoyed by such persons were influential factors in allowing a single system of law to develop in the absence of a centralised state.

Our knowledge of early Irish legal system has come down to us by means of a number of scattered law texts. The brehon law was recorded in written form, always in old Irish rather than in Latin, from the seventh century AD onwards. Many of these texts were collected into large collections such as the *Senchas Már* or "Great Tradition" or the *Bretha Nemed* or "Judgments of Privileged Persons". Nevertheless, there was never any attempt at codification as occurred with respect to Roman law. The brehon law texts that have survived the ravages of time have, unfortunately, often survived in fragmentary form. While it is impossible to estimate the overall loss with complete confidence there is abundant evidence to show that it is quite considerable.

The surviving evidence reveals a legal system that seems quite unusual to modern eyes. Concepts of crime and punishment were not primary concerns under the brehon law. Instead, the system was mostly what a modern lawyer would call "tort", a form of law concerned with civil wrongs. The brehon law seems to have focused on keeping the peace by ensuring that wrongdoers were held liable to compensate the victims of their transgressions.

In the mid-twelfth century the invasion of a number of land-hungry barons from England and Wales brought the English common law to many parts of Ireland. From this time onwards the brehon law was largely relegated to those regions of Ireland, mostly in the north and west, which remained under native control. At the beginning of the seventeenth century the entire island of Ireland came under the control of the English Crown. Consequently, the jurisdiction of the brehon law was finally extinguished and was entirely replaced with the common law system that remains the basis of the Irish legal system to this day.

The above account should be considered as little more than a "whistle stop tour" of the brehon law. Limitations of space militate against a more comprehensive account. Yet, in truth this article is not really concerned with examining the reality of the brehon law. Instead, the focus of this article is on examining what the brehon law was perceived to be in nineteenth and early twentieth century Ireland. In this period the perception of brehon law was often heavily distorted and proved to be ripe territory for the imposition of utopian visions.

3. The Foundations of the Gaelic Utopia

There are a number of reasons why the brehon law provided such fertile soil for utopian thought in nineteenth and early twentieth century Ireland. First, there were formidable obstacles that impeded the discernment of what the brehon laws actually provided. As mentioned earlier, many brehon law texts have been lost while others have only survived in fragmentary form. Consequently, there are great gaping holes in our knowledge that inevitably results in a somewhat disjointed view of brehon law. For example, although a law text dedicated to legal disputes concerned with bee keeping has survived[3] no equivalent text specifically dedicated to the law of homicide remains extant. It is also worthy of note that no records of court procedure or of decisions in particular cases have survived. Finally, it must also be admitted that the original translations of the surviving brehon law texts from old Irish into English in the nineteenth and early twentieth centuries have since been revealed as badly flawed. Such limitations on the available knowledge concerning brehon law ensured that there was plenty of scope for interested persons in this period to fill the sizeable gaps with their own dreams as to how they believed the brehon law should have been. It might also be added that the rise of Irish cultural and political nationalism in the late nineteenth century militated against attempts at achieving a dispassionate view of subject matter of this nature.

---

[3] This is the well-known brehon text *Bechbretha* or "Bee Judgments". See Charles-Edwards, Thomas and Fergus Kelly (eds.): *Bechbretha*. Dublin, 1983.

A further incentive to create a utopian picture of the brehon law was that such visions provided a useful means of criticising the current state of law in Ireland. The common law system introduced by the English was often condemned as an alien imposition and as an instrument of oppression by many Irish nationalists. Draconian legislation on matters of public order embodied in numerous "Coercion" Acts did little to improve the image of law in nineteenth and twentieth Ireland.[4] Indeed, it has been estimated that between 1800 and 1921, dates that roughly correspond with the existence of the "United Kingdom of Great Britain and Ireland", some 105 public order statutes dealing with Ireland were brought into force.[5] This period also saw frequent suspensions of *habeas corpus*. In such a context it is little wonder that W.T. Cosgrave, the first Irish Prime Minister[6], wrote the following words in 1923 to the committee charged with creating a system of courts for the newly created Irish state:

"In the long struggle for the right to rule in our own Country, there has been no sphere of the administration lately ended which impressed itself on the minds of our people as a standing monument of an alien government more than the system, the machinery and the administration of law and justice which supplanted in comparatively modern times the laws and institutions till then a part of the living national organism."[7]

It is often claimed that the draconian public order measures passed in the nineteenth and early twentieth centuries combined with a popular equation of law with foreign rule to create a psychological gulf between law and the peo-

---

[4] On this subject see Townshend, Charles: Political Violence in Ireland: Government and Resistance since 1848. Oxford, 1983; Strauss, E.: Irish Nationalism and British Democracy. London, 1951; Broeker, Galen: Rural Disorder and Police Reform in Ireland, 1812-36. London, 1970; and Harrington, T.: A Diary of Coercion. Dublin, 1888.

[5] Farrell, Michael: Emergency Legislation: The Apparatus of Repression. Derry, 1986, p. 5.

[6] Cosgrave's official title as head of government was "President of the Executive Council of the Irish Free State".

[7] University College Dublin Archives, Kennedy Papers P4/1090.

ple in Ireland. It is also often argued that this gulf has still not been entirely bridged even in the context of an independent Irish state.[8]

4. The "Visionaries"

In describing the utopian visions of the brehon law that existed in nineteenth and twentieth century it would be easy to focus on the writings of a few extreme nationalists or obscure eccentrics. For the purposes of this article I have decided not to concentrate on such sources. The main authors of the utopian visions examined in this article were certainly Irish nationalists and may also have possessed certain eccentric qualities. Yet, they could hardly be termed extremists and would enjoy positions of some note in the early years of the independent Irish state that emerged in the 1920s. By focusing on more "respectable" intellectual figures I hope to illustrate the pervasiveness of utopian ideas of brehon law which were not limited to the febrile dreams of a lunatic fringe.

This article will focus primarily on the works of three individuals; Eoin MacNeill, Darrell Figgis and Hugh Kennedy. Limitations of space do not allow a full account of the career of Eoin MacNeill (1867-1945) who has been given the epithet of "scholar revolutionary" by his biographers.[9] MacNeill was the driving force behind the creation of a nationalist militia known as the "Irish Volunteers" in 1913, played a controversial role in the events that led up to the nationalist uprising in Dublin at Easter 1916 and became the first Minster for Education in the Irish state established in 1922. For our purposes his most important attribute was that he was a well-known scholar of Gaelic civilisation and was considered to be the leading authority on brehon law in the early twentieth century. Darrell Figgis (1882-1925) was a prominent writer

---

[8] An example of this oft-repeated argument can be seen in one legal commentator's use of the impression "that the Irish do not respect law … as a result of having been a marginal minority in the United Kingdom" to support an argument for that natural rights should continue to be enforced by the Irish courts. Phelan, Diarmuid Rossa: Natural Law and Popular Sovereignty. In: Studies, vol. 86 (1997), p. 221.

[9] Martin, F.X. and Byrne, F.J. (eds.): The Scholar Revolutionary, Eoin MacNeill, 1867-1945, and the making of the new Ireland. Dublin, 1973.

and nationalist politician whose red beard earned him the nickname of *an fear feasógach* or "the bearded man". He is worthy of note to scholars of modern Irish history because he was the effective chairman of the committee that drafted the first Irish constitution.[10] Hugh Kennedy (1879-1936) was a respected lawyer who was to enjoy the distinction of being appointed the first Attorney General of the Irish Free State and later the first Chief Justice of the Irish Supreme Court. He was known amongst certain friends and colleagues as "the Brehon".[11] All three of these men were considered reputable figures and held varying public offices in the early years of the Irish state. To a certain extent this article will also look at the works of Laurence Ginnell (1852-1923), a lawyer, scholar and a member of parliament. What is important for our purposes is that all of these men wrote or spoke publicly about the brehon law before or immediately after the achievement of Irish independence.

5. Utopian Visions of Brehon Law

Having introduced our main commentators it is now my intention to give a quick overview of some of the main utopian traits in their perceptions of brehon law. Such impressions were shared by many of their contemporaries and it could be argued that they still have still not been entirely erased from the popular consciousness in Ireland. Having examined these utopian views of brehon law it is my intention to examine how closely these impressions corresponded with reality.

The brehon law was often perceived as upholding egalitarian values. Differences of social class in early Ireland were seen as being of much less significance than elsewhere in contemporary Europe and were also considered to be less rigid than under the feudal system that was introduced in post-conquest

[10] The official chairman of the constitution committee was Michael Collins, a major figure in the Irish secessionary movement and Minister for Finance in the Irish rebel government. Other duties ensured that Collins had little time to devote to the creation of the draft constitution and he only chaired two meetings of the committee. Consequently, Figgis, as deputy chairman and the only paid member of the committee, chaired almost all of the sessions. Farrell, Brian: The Drafting of the Irish Free State Constitution: I, In: Irish Jurist, vol. 5 (1970), p. 117.

[11] Holland, Ailsa C.: The Papers of Hugh Kennedy. In: Irish Jurist, vol. 24 (1989), p. 290.

Ireland. It was often claimed that the great majority of the population in early Ireland were not only free and but were also landholders.[12]

Closely related to such ideals of social equality was the perceived centrality of popular sovereignty in early Ireland. Early medieval Ireland was politically fragmented into a patchwork of petty states. This factor, together with elective nature of kingship was seen as ensuring that the free population had considerable control over their own political affairs. The great annual assemblies on the sacred hills of Tara, Uisneach and Tailteann were sometimes put forward as popular legislative assemblies.[13] As for the position of the kings of the petty states or *tuathta*, Laurence Ginnell went as far as claiming that "the office resembled as much that of president of a republic as it did that of a modern king".[14]

In such a context it was perceived that the brehon law not only embodied principles of popular sovereignty but, in the absence of a centralised state, the enforcement of the law was also seen as being based entirely on the will of the people. Laurence Ginnell noted that brehon law was enforced by "the inherent equity of the particular judgment itself, by the force of an immemorial law universally obeyed, by public opinion informed by the general prevalent love of justice".[15] Darrell Figgis argued that it would be difficult to find a system so "soundly based on a people's will while compact in itself" and that "It was at

---

[12] Figgis believed that the unfree classes in Ireland were made up of a foreign and transient minority. Figgis, Darrell: The Gaelic State in the Past and Future. Dublin, 1917, pp. 17-18. Eoin MacNeill, a scholar of far greater weight on the subject of brehon law than Figgis, claimed that "the freeholders were numerous" and that "the freeman element in an Irish *tuath* [petty state] consisted chiefly of landed freeholders". MacNeill, Eoin: Early Irish Laws and Institutions. Dublin, 1935, pp. 32-3.

[13] Ginnell, Lawrence: The Brehon Laws. Dublin, 1917, chapter 4 "Legislative Assemblies"; and MacNeill, Eoin: Early Irish Laws and Institutions. Dublin, 1935, chapter 6.

[14] Ginnell, Lawrence, The Brehon Laws. Dublin, 1917, p. 41

[15] *Ibid.* at p. 52. Sir John Davies (1569-1626), a poet and lawyer who was certainly no friend of the brehon law, is said to have admitted that "There is no nation of people under the sun that doth love equal and indifferent justice better than the Irish, or will rest better satisfied with the execution thereof, although it be against themselves as they may have protection and benefit of the law when upon just cause they do desire it." MacNeill, Eoin: Early Irish Laws and Institutions. Dublin, 1935, p. 152. On this topic see also Figgis, Darrell: The Gaelic State in the Past and Future. Dublin, 1917, p. 23.

once both aristocratic and democratic".[16] The popular enforcement of brehon law was even put forward as confounding the theory of the great British legal theorist John Austin who saw law as the command of a sovereign who would also enforce sanctions.[17]

As mentioned earlier, crime and punishment were not central concerns for the brehon law. For the most part brehon laws adhered to a system based on the payment of compensation. It was often pointed out that there was no centralised state in early medieval Ireland to enforce sanctions such as imprisonment or execution. It was also asserted that torture and trial by ordeal, a common feature of medieval law across Europe, were unknown to the brehon law.[18] The apparent humanity of brehon law was one of most useful means to attack the state of law in Ireland in the nineteenth and early twentieth centuries. The lack of emphasis on criminal sanctions in the brehon law led many scholars to believe that capital punishment was rarely if ever used in medieval Ireland. Laurence Ginnell argued that in this period "There is ample evidence of various kinds that the whole public feeling of Ireland was opposed to capital punishment".[19]

The position of women in early Ireland proved to be particularly fertile ground for utopian visions of brehon law. According to Eoin MacNeill "The status of women in ancient Irish law and the social prominence of women in ancient Irish literature, have been found remarkable." MacNeill believed that the advanced status of women in early Ireland was the result of the influence of a Pictish social order that existed in pre-Celtic times.[20] Darrell Figgis went further than MacNeill in this respect when describing what he termed the "Gaelic State":

---

[16] Figgis, Darrell: The Gaelic State in the Past and Future. Dublin, 1917, p. 34.

[17] Ginnell, Lawrence: The Brehon Laws. Dublin, 1917, pp. 52-3.

[18] According to Ginnell: "The odious system of torture called the *ordeal*, so common in the Middle Ages, by which evidence was roasted or boiled, according to taste, out of unwilling witnesses, and confessions of guilt wrung often from persons perfectly innocent; this was never known in Ireland, except possibly in the Pale. There is not a word about it in the Brehon Laws." Ginnell, Lawrence: The Brehon Laws. Dublin, 1917, p. 142.

[19] Ginnell, Lawrence: The Brehon Laws. Dublin, 1917, p. 121.

[20] MacNeill, Eoin: Early Irish Laws and Institutions. Dublin, 1935, pp. 63-6.

"Not the least excellence of the State was the equal dignity it gave to women. … [I]n the social and economic spheres they took their place as the equal of men … Never once do we find the law of the Irish State recognising any inequality between the sexes."[21]

Before examining the accuracy of such exalted, but by no means untypical, claims I want to examine the popular perception of brehon law with respect to property. It was often asserted that rights of private property were minimal under the brehon law and that property as a whole was largely held in common. Even hostile sources seemed to take this perception of early Irish society for granted. A brief and unflattering sketch of Irish history written by the Earl of Midleton, a man of strong unionist principles, condemned the "chaos" of medieval Irish society which he believed was based on a "system of communal ownership".[22]

The distinguished nineteenth century British jurist Sir Henry Maine commenced his own study of the brehon laws expecting to find evidence of primitive customs of tribal communism. However, his examination of brehon law seems to have disillusioned him to a certain extent on this point and he came to the conclusion that early Irish lawyers "seem to have a bias towards private as distinguished from collective property".[23] Eoin MacNeill strenuously denied this claim and argued in favour of the prevalence of the "custom of collective ownership" under the brehon law.[24]

The belief that the brehon law protected a form of primitive communism had a certain impact on scholarship outside Ireland. The prevalence of such beliefs led the well-known French historian P. Boissonade to write that "the clans held the land in common" and that "no man held individual property save his household goods". Boissonade even went so far as to state that "in each district of Ireland the free population lived communistically in immense

---

[21] Figgis, Darrell: The Gaelic State in the Past and Future. Dublin, 1917, p. 26.

[22] Earl of Midleton: Ireland – Dupe or Heroine. London, 1932, pp. 5-6.

[23] Maine concludes on the issue of private property in early Ireland that "No doubt it was then, as always, the great source of legal business". Maine, Henry: Lectures on the Early History of Institutions. London, 1875, p. 105.

[24] MacNeill, Eoin: Early Irish Laws and Institutions. Dublin, 1935, p. 87.

wooden buildings … they lived and fed in common, seated on long benches, and all the families of the district slept there upon beds of reeds".[25] Marxist scholars also seized upon such conceptions of brehon law. Friedrich Engels believed that in pre-conquest Ireland "the soil had been the collective property of the *gens* or the clans".[26] The Irish socialist James Connolly, a leader of the nationalist uprising of 1916, wrote of the "Gaelic principle of common ownership by the people of their sources of food and maintenance".[27] Notwithstanding the revelations of later scholarship, works written in more recent times continue to describe the prevalence of a system of "Celtic Communism" in early medieval Ireland.[28]

Perceptions of brehon law as a system that protected communal property rights were widely held both by those, such as Engels, who felt it was a good thing and by those, such as the Earl of Midleton, who perceived it as a sign of barbarism. In the early years of the independent Irish state such perceptions proved to be so strong that they decisively influenced the outcome of a number of important court cases.[29]

---

[25] Boissonade, P.: Life and Work in Medieval Europe. Translated by Eileen Power, New York, 1964, pp. 78-9.

[26] Engels, Friedrich, The Origin of the Family, Private Property and the State. London, 1977, p. 194.

[27] Connolly, James: Labour in Irish History. 1910, Foreword. http://www.marxists.org/archive/connolly/1910/lih/index.htm

[28] For example see Berresford, P. Ellis: A History of the Irish Working Class. London, 1972, chapter 1. Berresford accuses Eoin MacNeill of setting out to "destroy" the ideas of James Connolly and those of P.W. Joyce whose "Social History of Ancient Ireland" (London, 1903) has been widely condemned as inaccurate. Berresford also condemns MacNeill as occupying a place "to the right of the Irish political spectrum". In fact, contrary to the impression given by Berresford, MacNeill had his own, admittedly more moderate, views that extensive communal property rights had prevailed in early Ireland.

[29] For a more detailed treatment of these cases see Mohr, Thomas: Salmon of Knowledge: Brehon Law before Twentieth Century Courts. In: Peritia, Journal of the Medieval Academy of Ireland, vol. 16 (2002), p. 352.

6. The Erne Fishery Case

A new form of popular protest took hold in parts of the newly created Irish Free State in the 1920s and 1930s. Such protests did not focus on rights relating to land but on rights relating to water. Small inland fishermen resented the exclusive fishing rights for salmon owned by consortiums of landlords on the tidal estuaries of the western seaboard. These fishermen usually confined their protests to small-scale acts of poaching. However, on a number of occasions certain fishermen went so far as to challenge these controversial exclusive fishing rights in the courts. One such challenge took place in County Donegal in the 1920s when a group of fishermen challenged the exclusive fishing rights for salmon on the river Erne. This legal challenge resulted in a case called *Moore v. The Attorney General* which was popularly known as the "Erne fishery case". [30] This case is interesting to legal historians because, in a scarcely believable turn of events it was substantially decided on the basis of the brehon law, a legal system that had been dead for over three centuries. In order to assist them in the interpretation of this ancient legal system the fisherman called upon the assistance of Professor Eoin MacNeill a man who was then considered the greatest living authority on the brehon law. MacNeill was assisted by Professor Daniel Binchy, another leading legal scholar and ambassador to Germany between 1929 and 1932.

The people who owed the exclusive fishing rights could trace the title to their fishery back over three centuries to the time when the jurisdiction of the English common law was finally extended to northwest Ireland. As for the fishermen, their case was largely reliant on the interpretation of Chapter 16 of that hallowed English medieval legal document the Magna Charta. Translated into English that portion of the Great Charter declares that:

[30] *Moore v Attorney General* [1929] I.R. 191 and [1934] I.R. 44.

"No banks shall be defended from henceforth, but such as were in defence in the time of King Henry our grandfather, by the same places and the same bounds, as they were wont to be in his time."[31]

In the late 19th Century, this passage was interpreted as meaning that after the creation of the Magna Charta the Crown could no longer create an exclusive fishery on tidal waters unless those waters had already been appropriated as an exclusive fishery before King Henry II's death in the year 1189.[32] However, the influence of the English Crown and the common law had not been extended to County Donegal by this date. Such jurisdiction was not expanded to northwest Ireland until the early seventeenth century. Nevertheless, the Irish courts held that there was nothing in the terms of Chapter 16 of the Magna Charta or in any other source that said that the original act of appropriation had to have been made by the Crown itself.[33] As long as somebody, anybody, had created an exclusive fishery on the tidal area of the river Erne before the year 1189 the title to the exclusive fishery remained valid. It was held that the burden of proof lay upon the fishermen since they were challenging such a long-established title. At first glance the legal challenge facing these fishermen seemed insurmountable. In essence they had to prove that nobody had or could have claimed an exclusive fishery on the river Erne before 1189. This was certainly no easy task. After all, it is a far more difficult task for a person to prove on the balance of probabilities that a particular institution *did not* exist at a certain point in time than to prove that such an institution actually *did* exist, especially when dealing with a period of history as remote as the twelfth century.

While the fishermen's case under the common law seemed weak at this point the brehon law held out considerable promise of salvation. The brehon

[31] In Latin: "Nullae ripariae defendantur de caetero, nisi illae quae fuerunt in defenso tempore Henrici regis avi nostri, per eadem loca et eosdem terminos, sicut esse consueverunt tempore suo". *Moore v Attorney General* [1929] I.R. 191, at 213.

[32] *Malcomson v. O'Dea* 10 H.L.C. 593 and *Neill v. Duke of Devonshire* 8 A.C 135. This interpretation of Chapter 16 of the Magna Charta has since been questioned. Murphy, Bryan: The Lawyer as Historian: Magna Charta and Public Rights of Fishery. In: Irish Jurist vol. 3 (1968), p. 131.

[33] *Moore v Attorney General* [1929] I.R. 191 at 233.

law was, after all, the legal system that applied to County Donegal in the twelfth century and it was contended that the brehon law protected a system of common fishing rights. Consequently, it was argued that it was not possible for anybody to have appropriated an exclusive fishery in twelfth century Ireland because, quite simply, the brehon law would not have permitted it. Such arguments were supported by such leading authorities as Eoin MacNeill and Daniel Binchy who appeared as expert witnesses for the fishermen.

To support his claims that common fishing rights had pre-dominated in early Ireland Eoin MacNeill drew the court's attention to a passage taken from the brehon tract of *Do fastad cirt ocus dligid* or "Of the confirmation of right and law". MacNeill argued that this passage listed a number of items that were considered to be common property under the brehon law.

"How many things have been established as the inherent rights of every territory and which are equally due to every person?[34] The salmon of every place [*aé áite*]; wild garlic; the "*andach*" property of each water; the quick drawing [of a net] from each stream; the sufficiency for a night of faggots of each wood which has not the tripartite division of [trees]; cooking fuel in each wood; the mast [nuts] of each wood ... ."[35]

Eoin MacNeill was satisfied that the reference to the *aé áite,* translated as "the salmon of the place", refuted any assertion that individuals could claim exclusive fishing rights, at least not for salmon, under the brehon law.[36]

MacNeill's arguments seem to have impressed the Irish Supreme Court, headed by Chief Justice Hugh Kennedy, which heard the case in 1933. Kennedy noted in his judgment that he was "clearly of the opinion that the Bre-

---

[34] MacNeill gave his own translation of this sentence which was "How many things have been established as the full right of every Tuath which are of equal right to every condition". National Archives of Ireland, CSS Papers, CO 3412, Oral Evidence, Book 2, p. 65, para. 1213.

[35] [1929] I R 191, at 239. Extract is from Trinity College Dublin Library, Manuscript E. 3. 5.

[36] National Archives of Ireland, CSS Papers, CO 3412, Oral Evidence, Book 2, pp. 65-66, paragraph 1219-1226.

hon Law of the twelfth century did not incorporate the feudal notion of the ownership of fishing in tidal waters."[37] He concluded that:

"It is perfectly clear that as in Roman Law, the right of fishery was *publici juris,* so in Brehon Law the right of fishery for salmon was vested in the inhabitants of the Tuath and an effort was made to secure equality for all by allowing each person to take one salmon."[38]

The fishermen won their case and private fishing rights that had been recognised for over three centuries were struck down. A common fishery was resurrected on the mouth of the river Erne that supposedly reflected the position that had existed under the auspices of the brehon law.

7. The Moy Fishery Case

As might be expected, the decision of the Supreme Court in the Erne fishery case was followed by a rush by fishermen all over Ireland trying to declare that particular stretches of rivers should now be declared common fisheries. The Erne fishery case had a sequel a mere three years after the final decision in the Supreme Court. On this occasion fishing rights on the river Moy, once again in the west of Ireland, were the subject of dispute. The resulting case of *Little v. Cooper*[39], popularly known as the "Moy fishery case", was finally heard in the High Court in 1936. However, an important change had taken place since the conclusion of the Erne case. In the intervening three years Professor Binchy had completely revised his opinion on the question of private fishing rights under the brehon law. Binchy had the courage to admit that further study of the brehon law had convinced him that the evidence he had provided in the Erne fishery case had been given in error. Contrary to his previous opinion, he now believed that the brehon law had sanctioned the existence of extensive private fishing rights in early Ireland. Binchy had extensive evidence

---

[37] [1934] I.R. 44 at 69.
[38] [1934] I.R. 44 at 68.
[39] [1937] I.R. 1.

to support his new position. In particular, he pointed to following passage found in the *Senchas Már*:

"If he owns the bank on both sides (literally on this side and on that) he has his choice whether he will dam one-sixth on each side of it, or one third on one side only. If he only owns one side, he shall dam one-sixth on the side which belongs to him and if he do more than that amount (that is if he dam more than that amount) two-thirds of the extra amount are due by him to the owners of the weirs (literally up and down) above and below whichever way the fish pass."[40]

This passage of brehon law seemed to provide that a person who owned the land on one side of a river was entitled to build a privately owned weir, a barrier containing nets to catch fish, which could span one-sixth of the width of the river. If a person owned the land on both sides of the river the above passage allowed them to cover one-third of the width of the river with a privately owned fishing weir. If these limits were broken the passage provided for compensation that had to be paid to the other owners of private weirs who might be adversely affected.

Binchy had other evidence suggesting that the brehon law did indeed recognise private fishing rights which, for reasons of space, cannot be detailed. However, it included linguistic evidence that pointed to the strong possibility that the reference to "the salmon of the place" in the text "Of the confirmation of right and law", which had proved so important in the earlier Erne fishery case, was in fact a mistranslation.[41] Such evidence pointed to a conclusion that was difficult for many Irish people to accept. It seemed that the brehon

---

[40] Trinity College Dublin Library, Manuscript-Book H. 5. 15 P. 16, Column 1. Quoted in National Library of Ireland, MSS. 995, Book 2, Part II, pp. 173-174 paragraph 1376.

[41] Professor Osborn Bergin suggested in the later case of *Foyle and Bann Fisheries and Irish Society v. Attorney General and Others* (unreported) that the words *aé áite* previously given as "the salmon of the place" were intended to refer to a plant known in English as "liverwort" which may have been believed to have medicinal uses. National Archives of Ireland, Supreme Court, Case No. 8/1949, Part III of President's Report, 21st Day (Forenoon) p. 1-3, paragraphs 1-4.

law had not only recognised private fishing rights but had extended legal protection and regulation to such rights of private property.

8. Reality

For many people such revelations were the first of many "terrible truths" revealed by modern scholarship in relation to the brehon law. Those who believed that the brehon law reflected an egalitarian society in which differences of social class were minimal would soon be presented with considerable evidence to the contrary. In fact, the brehon laws go into great detail to divide the population into a myriad of social classes. All the way from the rank of slave, in old Irish *mug* or *cumal*, to various grades of small farmer, for example an *ócaire*, to a big farmer or *bóaire*, to the noble freeman or *mruigfer* and on to varying grades of kingship. Moreover, the amount of compensation a person was entitled to receive in event of a legal wrong was based entirely on a person's "honour price" which was determined on the basis of their social position.

As mentioned earlier, scholars in the early twentieth century frequently made significant claims as to the rights enjoyed by women under the brehon law. In fact, by the standards of the early middle ages the brehon laws *could* be considered relatively benign with respect to the rights of women. For example, numerous brehon texts make it clear that it was possible for a woman to divorce her husband, a position that was not always provided by contemporary systems of law elsewhere in Europe. While a husband could strike his wife to correct her, a blow that left a lasting blemish was a ground for the woman to seek a divorce.[42] By the standards of their time these were impressive provisions. Yet all too often the commentators who praised the position of women under the brehon law insisted on applying the standards of the twentieth century to a medieval law code. In this context, the claims made in relation to the rights of women under the brehon simply do not correspond with reality.

---

[42] Kelly, Fergus: A Guide to Early Irish Law. Dublin, 1995, p. 74; and Ó Cróinín, Dáibhí: Early Medieval Ireland 400-1200. Harlow, 1995, pp. 129-30.

It may be recalled that Darrell Figgis went as far as to claim that "Never once do we find the law of the Irish State recognising any inequality between the sexes".[43] In reality, early Ireland was very much a patriarchal society and in many respects the brehon law reflected this position. Scholars writing in the latter half of the twentieth century have noted that the brehon law texts expressed similar sentiments with respect to women as the Indian Law of Manu. This law code provided that a woman's "father protects her in childhood, her husband protects her in youth, and her sons protect her in old age; a woman is never fit for independence".[44] Under normal circumstances a woman could not make a valid contract under the brehon law without the permission of her male guardian, usually her husband or her father.[45] Save in exceptional circumstances evidence given by women was inadmissible on basis that it was considered inherently "biased and dishonest".[46] The brehon laws also allowed for polygamy and termed the principal wife the *cétmuinter* and the secondary wife the *adaltrach*, a word openly derived from the Latin *adultera*. While it was true that the brehon laws allowed a woman certain grounds for obtaining a divorce, her husband had far more extensive grounds to divorce her. Among these grounds was general incompetence. A man could divorce a woman who *bé loites cach rét* or a woman who "makes a mess of everything".[47]

Those aspects of brehon law which did not accord with the values of nineteenth and twentieth century Ireland often caused difficulties for those who sought to paint a picture of a "Gaelic utopia". For example the provision of divorce in early Ireland was difficult to accept for many Irish catholics. Laurence Ginnell suggested that the word "divorce" was a mistranslation of what was intended by the brehon law and that a separation in which the marriage

---

[43] Figgis, Darrell: The Gaelic State in the Past and Future. Dublin, 1917, p. 26.

[44] Compare this to the following provision from a brehon law tract: "her father has charge of her when she is a girl, her husband when she is a wife, her sons when she is a [widowed] woman with children, her kin when she is a "woman of the kin" (i.e. with no other guardian), the Church when she is a woman of the Church (i.e. a nun). She is not capable of sale or purchase or contract or transaction without the authorization of one of her superiors". Kelly, Fergus: A Guide to Early Irish Law. Dublin, 1995, pp. 76.

[45] Kelly, Fergus: A Guide to Early Irish Law. Dublin, 1995, pp. 75-6.

[46] Ibid. at pp. 207-8.

[47] Ó Cróinín, Dáibhí, Early Medieval Ireland 400-1200. Harlow, 1995, pp. 129.

was not considered completely dissolved was intended. Whatever of the truth or otherwise of such speculation on matters of divorce, Ginnell's conclusion on the subject says a great deal about the preoccupations that underpinned his study his brehon law:

> "I am convinced that the law on this subject must not be taken as presenting a true picture of ancient Irish life ... [and] that singular purity characterised the Irish in the past as in the present."[48]

Claims concerning the apparent humanity of the brehon law, in particular the absence of trial by ordeal, proved particularly unfortunate. Brehon texts contain numerous references to such ordeals as "trial by hot metal" and "trial by cauldron". There are even references to ordeals by means of drinking poisonous substances. Another form of ordeal recognised by the brehon law was settling a dispute by means of fighting a duel. In such instances justice was held to lie with the victor of the combat.[49]

It has already been mentioned that crime and punishment were not central concerns of the brehon law. Yet this is not to say that such concepts were entirely ignored. Certain brehon law texts provide for the amputation of body parts including hands, fingers, feet, eyes, ears, noses, tongues, testicles and even breasts for certain offences.[50] Contrary to the claims of many commentators in the early twentieth century, there were numerous instances in which the brehon law demanded the penalty of death. The means by which capital punishment was imposed included hanging, execution by axe or sword and an obscure method called *góla* or "the pit" which may have involved exposure or starvation.[51] There are also texts that mention the punishment of setting a person adrift on the sea in a small boat with an offshore breeze. Lawrence Ginnell sought to explain away this unenviable form of punishment in terms that clearly illustrate his discomfiture with the reality that the brehon law seemed to sanction capital punishment:

---

[48] Ginnell, Lawrence: The Brehon Laws. Dublin, 1917, pp. 125-6.
[49] Kelly, Fergus: A Guide to Early Irish Law. Dublin, 1995, pp. 209-211.
[50] Ibid. at p. 221.
[51] Ibid. at pp. 216-221.

"One of the many punishments mentioned incidentally [by the brehon law texts] was that of placing a man on the open sea, on some small punt or wicker basket presumably. This was rather exposing a man to death than putting him to death. I cannot but think that some of the kindly Gael would be on the look-out for an unfortunate man to be exposed, and, deeming his punishment sufficient, as soon as the coast was clear would come to his relief."[52]

Finally, with respect to property, Sir Henry Maine seems to have been correct in asserting that the early Irish lawyers did "seem to have a bias towards private as distinguished from collective property".[53] As has already been seen with respect to fishing rights, the brehon law often went into meticulous detail in defining rights of private property. Indeed, if twentieth century commentators required any further evidence that contradicted the suggestion that common fishing rights had prevailed under brehon law they were provided with a powerful practical example. This was the common fishery created in County Donegal as a consequence of the Erne fishery case.

The common fishery created on the river Erne, following the supposed example of the brehon law, was an unmitigated disaster. Any member of the public was entitled to fish on the common fishery and large numbers of people took full advantage of this position. This ensured that the local fishermen who had taken the case found it impossible to make a living. Many of these fishermen came to the conclusion that they should have been given exclusive fishing privileges on the estuary in return for having taken the case against the former owners of the private fishery. They were either unaware or chose to ignore the obvious irony of such a position. As might be predicted, a few years of over-fishing brought fish stocks to the brink of collapse. In the end, the State had to intervene and take over the management of the fishery. This process included the payment of large sums of money to compensate the original owners of the private fishing rights on the river.[54]

---

[52] Ginnell, Lawrence: The Brehon Laws. Dublin, 1917, p. 121.

[53] Maine, Henry: Lectures on the Early History of Institutions. London, 1875, p. 105.

[54] National Archives of Ireland, Office of the Attorney General, File 2000/10/305. For a treatment of the wider political consequences of the Erne fishery case see Mohr, Thomas: Law with-

9. Volksgeist

At the beginning of this paper it was asserted that utopias tend to represent expressions of desire on the part of their authors. It was also noted that a utopia need not be set in an imaginary place but can also be located in terms of time. In the case of popular perceptions of brehon law it might be assumed that the idyllic utopia was seen as existing in the realm of the past. However, such a view would not be entirely accurate. In truth, the utopia envisioned by the commentators examined by this paper lay not in the past but in the future. In this context it is of little importance that the utopian visions of brehon law had little in common with the realities of medieval Ireland. The values expressed in these utopian visions reveal the hopes and dreams of persons in the nineteenth and early twentieth centuries as to the state of affairs in a future independent Irish state. In particular, they reflect desires to remake Irish law in such a way that the law would no longer be seen as an alien imposition. These utopian visions reflected aspirations that sought to recast Irish law in such a way as to finally reconnect with the values and spirit of the Irish people and, in this manner, finally bridge the great psychological gulf between the law and the Irish people.

Such desires manifested themselves during the negotiations between Irish representatives and members of the British government in the summer of 1922. These negotiations concerned the drafting of the constitution whose adoption would herald the creation of the new "Irish Free State". Hugh Kennedy, a lawyer of some years standing, came to the following conclusion with respect to the system of the law that had been the study of his life:

"The great body of law, institutions and forms, called the "English Common Law"... is not in Ireland a Common Law at all. It is an alien structure imposed by statute, an exotic from which a cutting has been artificially fostered in Ireland but which has not taken root or become acclimatised in any real sense. ... The institutions, forms and ceremonials of the English Com-

out Loyalty: The Abolition of the Irish Appeal to the Privy Council. In: Irish Jurist, vol. 37 (2002), p. 187.

mon Law have never been absorbed by the Irish People or become in any true sense their own. They have remained... the features of a foreign system and of alien rule."[55]

These words reveal a deep-seated desire to radically reform Irish law on the part of a man who would become the first Chief Justice of the Irish Supreme Court. They reveal a desire to reform the law in such a way as to create a distinctly Irish form of law that was more in accord with the values and the spirit of the Irish people. Those interested in the field of historical jurisprudence might consider such aspirations to have been based on a desire to connect with the *Volksgeist* of the Irish people.

Irish commentators did not use the term *Volksgeist* with its association with the ideas of Karl Friedrich von Savigny. Instead, commentators such as Darrell Figgis tended to speak of creating a law in tune with the "intuition" or "hereditary mind" of the Irish people.[56] Yet the parallels with the preoccupations of Savigny and other members of the historical school of jurisprudence are obvious. Like Savigny, many of the commentators mentioned in this paper looked to the past to provide an example for the future. However, rather than looking to Roman law they looked to the brehon law, or at least what they perceived the brehon law to be. The conclusion of Darrell Figgis' account of the brehon law in "The Gaelic State in the Past and Future" provides a good example of the desire to use early Irish law as means to reconnect with the spirit of the Irish people in the twentieth century. Figgis concluded his examination of the brehon past by stating that "from that past the answer must be found for its future, for the past has stored up instincts and intuitions, old

---

[55] The National Archives/Public Record Office (United Kingdom) CAB 23/30, SFB 60. Almost identical sentiments were expressed by W.T. Cosgrave in his letter of 29 January 1923 to the committee charged with creating a system of courts for the Irish Free State:
"The body of laws and the system of judicature so imposed upon this Nation were English (not even British) in their seed, English in their growth, English in their vitality. Their nomenclature were only to be understood by the student of the history of the people of Southern Britain. A remarkable and characteristic product of the genius of that people, the manner of their administration prevented them from striking root in the fertile soil of this Nation." University College Dublin Archives, Kennedy Papers, P4/1090.
[56] Figgis, Darrell: The Gaelic State in the Past and Future. Dublin, 1917, p. 84.

memories of the blood and desires of the national mind, that are waiting to burst into the future."[57]

10. Old Wine into New Bottles

Just as there were those in the early twentieth century who wished to revive the fortunes of the Irish language as part of an Irish national resurrection there were those, albeit far fewer in number, who wanted to resurrect a distinctly Irish form of law. Such ideals manifested themselves in a number of different ways. Between 1919 and 1921, a time of secessionary conflict with the forces of the British Crown, the Irish rebel authorities set up their own court system known as the "Dáil courts". Amongst other sources, these courts were encouraged to use brehon law in determining cases.[58] As might be guessed from the obstacles mentioned earlier, the modern application of brehon law did not prove to be a practical proposition in the great majority of cases.[59]

Hugh Kennedy's attempt to do away with the wigs and gowns so closely associated with the established legal system in Ireland represents a more colourful manifestation of the desire to recast Irish law. Kennedy attempted to redesign the dress of the Irish judiciary in order to reflect the dress worn by the brehons. His objective was, however, hampered by the considerable disability that nobody was entirely sure what the dress of the brehons had actually constituted. The new judicial uniforms that were eventually created were the product of pure fantasy and, in the long run, were not successful.[60]

---

[57] Ibid. at p. 5

[58] The Dáil Courts were permitted to make use of citations from "the early Irish Law Codes or any commentary upon them in so far as they may be applicable to modern conditions". Macardle, Dorothy: The Irish Republic. Dublin, 1951, p. 376.

[59] Dorothy Macardle does, however, mention one instance in which James Creed Meredith gave judgment in favour of an unmarried mother claiming medical expenses by applying the brehon law. According to Macardle: "This created an interesting link with old Irish principles of justice and preserved continuity between the old Brehon Law of Ireland and the Republican courts". Macardle, Dorothy: The Irish Republic. Dublin, 1951, p. 376.

[60] University College Dublin Archives, Kennedy Papers, P4/1163-9. Another possible manifestation of a desire to resurrect the Gaelic past in Irish law might be seen in the pleas of Professor

11. Legacy and Conclusion

When the time came to create an independent Irish state it was obvious that the brehon law could not be revived as the basis of a new Irish legal system. The first rudimentary draft constitution produced by the constitution committee in 1922 provided for the continuance of the established system of law.[61] Yet, this is not to say that the values that brehon law was seen as embodying, accurately or otherwise, were not without influence. At this point it is necessary to remember the commentators on which this paper has chosen to focus. It may be recalled that Darrell Figgis was the effective chairman of the committee that drafted the first Irish constitution. Hugh Kennedy, who became the first Attorney General of the Irish Free State and the first Chief Justice of the Supreme Court, was also a member this constitution committee.[62] Eoin MacNeill, who was later made a minister in first Irish government, was an external adviser on the drafting of the constitution and a member of the

---

William Magennis of University College Dublin for university representation in the lower house of the Irish parliament. Magennis expressed his disappointment in the debates of the 1922 constituent assembly that Darrell Figgis, the author of "The Gaelic State" had not placed more "traces of Gaelic civilisation" into his draft constitution. This allowed Magennis to make use of his own utopian views of the Gaelic past in order to support his position. He declared that "In the old Gaelic days *an t-ollamh* – the professor – was next to the King" and used this perception to argue in favour of marking "the Gaelic spirit's desire to honour education". *Dáil Debates*, vol. 1 col. 1109, 4 October 1922. The Irish provisional government eventually acceded to this request although it seems more likely that this concession was actually motivated by a desire to ensure minimal protestant representation, in the form of representatives from Trinity College Dublin, than any desire to honour the Gaelic past.

[61] "Article X" of this first rough draft provided for the continuance of existing laws subject to compatibility with the constitution. University College Dublin Archives, Kennedy Papers, P4/339. Similar provisions were enacted in Article 73 of the 1922 Constitution and Article 50 of the 1937 Constitution.

[62] Kennedy did not seem have a high regard for Figgis as evidenced by correspondence between Kennedy and James Douglas, another member of the constitution committee. University College Dublin Archives, Kennedy Papers, P4/315. When the committee reported to the Provisional Irish Government on 7 March 1922 Kennedy was one of those who supported an alternative draft constitution to that put forward by Figgis. National Archives of Ireland, Department of the Taoiseach, S8953.

constituent assembly that brought it into force.[63] Thus, it is fair to say that these persons can be numbered among the architects of the first Irish constitution. The ideals and values that they had expressed through the medium of the brehon law were now manifested in tangible form in the first optimistic drafts of the constitution for an embryonic Irish state with their considerable emphasis on popular sovereignty, social equality, a desire to put an end to capital punishment and a desire to promote the equality of women.[64]

Sadly, not all of the above ideals survived contact with the realities of government or with the series of tense negotiations with the British in the summer of 1922.[65] Many of these ideals were cruelly parodied in the bloody civil war into which the first Irish constitution was born. A substantial minority refused to accept the new constitution meaning that the gulf between law and people was not entirely eliminated. Those who refused to accept the new constitution included our fourth commentator, Laurence Ginnell. Although elected to sit on the constitutional assembly that would approve the constitution, Ginnell chose to vent his opposition by heckling and disrupting the proceedings. Consequently, one of the very first actions of the Irish constituent assembly was to secure Ginnell's expulsion.[66]

It is also fair to conclude that with the passage of time a certain amount of disillusion with the new legal order began to prevail even among many of those who had initially supported the Irish constitution of 1922. Such sentiments became more apparent as civil liberties were repeatedly sacrificed by an Irish state that felt itself under serious threat from its internal opponents. A draconian system of military courts created by "Amendment No. 17" to the constitution led one Irish judge to openly declare his disappointment with the

---

[63] MacNeill's comments on the draft constitution can be seen in National Archives of Ireland, Department of the Taoiseach, S8953. MacNeill may have had some familiarity with the work of the constitution committee even before its formal report of 7 March 1922 since his brother James MacNeill was a full member of that body.
[64] National Archives of Ireland, Department of the Taoiseach, S8953.
[65] Mohr, Thomas: British Involvement in the Creation of the Constitution of the Irish Free State. In: Proceedings of the XVIIth British Legal History Conference. Lewis A.D.E. (ed.), to be published by Round Hall Press, Dublin in 2007.
[66] *Dáil Debates,* vol. 1, col. 8-13, 9 September 1922.

new legal order.[67] Mr. Justice FitzGibbon expressed his disenchantment in the form of biting sarcasm declaring that "we find the Briton's conceptions of liberty and justice set forth in his Magna Charta and his Bill of Rights; those of the American in his Declaration of Independence and his Constitution; while those of the Gael are enshrined in Amendment No. 17".[68] Such disillusion with the new Irish political and legal order might suggest that the subject-matter of this article reflects a story that is all too familiar in world history, that of the utopia betrayed.

Yet, such a negative conclusion may not be entirely appropriate in the Irish context. The independent Irish state managed to pull off the road to dictatorship followed by so many of its European counterparts in the 1920s and 1930s. Less than a decade after the conclusion of the Irish civil war the victors peacefully handed over power to the losers in the aftermath of a general election. This transition ensured that a new Irish constitution was drafted that was inspired by ideals which, if not identical to those of Figgis, Kennedy and MacNeill, were certainly inspired by a similar spirit. Some at least of the values that they had expressed were replicated in the new constitution of 1937 which, once again, sought to recast the Irish legal order and bridge the gap between Irish law and the Irish people. In later years the assignment of priority to certain natural law values over written law by the Irish courts when interpreting the 1937 constitution might also be seen as an attempt to bridge this gap between law and people.[69] This has been a distinctive feature of Irish jurispru-

---

[67] Constitution (Amendment No. 17) Act, 1931.

[68] *State (Ryan v. Lennon)* [1935] I.R. 170 at 235.

[69] Possible examples of such preoccupations behind the application of natural rights might be seen in the frequent assertions that the legal order should reflect the religious values of the Irish people. For example Mr. Justice Declan Costello has written that "By proclaiming the Christian beliefs of the people who enacted the Constitution, an assertion is being made that the legal order established by it should be informed by the values which Christians hold. … A relationship between moral law and positive law is established which requires in important respects that positive law should accord with moral law or otherwise be invalid." Costello, Declan: Aspects of a Judicially Developed Jurisprudence of Human Rights in Ireland. In: Understanding Human Rights: An Interdisciplinary and Interfaith Study, Falconer, Alan D. (ed.), Dublin, 1987, p. 150.

dence since the 1960s with certain antecedents in the 1930s.[70] Ironically, in recent years the application of these natural values in the Irish courts has clashed with concepts of popular sovereignty which also remain a central aspect of the Irish legal order as expressed in the aspirations of many of our commentators on brehon law.[71]

Much more recently, in early 2004, the Irish government announced its intention to carry out a major overhaul of Irish statutory law. This important project involves the complete abolition and replacement of all legislation applicable to Ireland that was passed before independence in 1922. In this way, the Irish government has declared its intention to sweep away over 700 years of legislative history. All legislation passed from the thirteenth century to the early 1920s, in other words all legislation passed in the period of foreign rule, is to be swept away in order that Irish statutory law be based entirely on measures passed since independence. While there are practical reasons put forward for carrying out this ambitious project there is also a powerful ideological background. This is reflected in the words of Bertie Ahern, the Irish Prime Minister or *Taoiseach*, when he declared that:

"My objective is simple, I will ensure that the Irish statute book comprises only laws passed by the Oireachtas [the Irish parliament] under the authority of the Irish people. Ancient laws passed by foreign parliaments in the name of the British monarchy have no place in our modern democracy."[72]

---

[70] See *Ryan v Attorney General* [1965] I.R. 294, *McGee v. Attorney General* [1974] I.R. 284 and Kennedy CJ's dissenting judgment in *State (Ryan) v. Lennon* [1935] I.R. 170.

[71] *In re Article 26 Regulation of Information (Services Outside the State for Termination of Pregnancies) Bill, 1995* [1995] 2 I.L.R.M. 81. On this point see the prophetic remarks of Murnaghan J in *State (Ryan) v. Lennon* [1935] I.R. 170 at 240. In this context it is worthy of note that in the last decade the Irish courts have confined the enforceable sources of natural rights to those that are expressly or implicitly recognised by acknowledged sources of law. Other sources of natural rights have been likened by one judicial authority to utopian thought and have been declared unenforceable by the Irish courts. See Murphy J in *W. O'R. v. EH.*: "What are described as "natural rights" whether arising from the circumstances of mankind in a primitive but idyllic society postulated by some philosophers but unidentified by any archaeologist, or inferred by moral philosophers as the rules by which human beings may achieve the destiny for which they were created, are not recognised or enforced as such by the courts set up under the Constitution." [1996] 2 I.R. 248 at 294.

[72] The Nation (newsletter of the *Fianna Fáil* political party), Autumn 2005, p. 7.

Although this initiative marks a new departure for Irish law, it represents the continuation of an old theme. It is a modern manifestation of an old desire to recast Irish law in order to make it more acceptable to the perceived spirit and values of the Irish people. It is an ambition that has been expressed through the media of two Irish constitutions. It is a dream that was once expressed through utopian visions of brehon law.

When to Remember and When to Forget? The Masovian Gentry's Court *petita* in the Vasa Period (1587-1668)

Adam Moniuszko

A. Introduction

What are *petita*? To explain this, it is necessary to write a few remarks about the specific political system of the Polish-Lithuanian Commonwealth, especially about the place of the parliament in it. The Polish gentry (or nobility – none of these terms reflects the exact meaning of the Polish term *szlachta*) obtained at the end of 15th century a right to choose its representatives for the parliament – the so-called diet. The diet soon became a central institution of the political system – no new law could be passed without its consent.[1] It had also certain competences within the administration of justice. The most significant one was a diet court, which dealt with the most serious cases like the *crimen laese maiestatis,* betrayal, where a nobleman was endangered by capital punishments such as the death sentence, infamy (a sort of civil death) or banishment. The diet court from the end of the 16th century consisted of the king,

[1] A crucial role in that process was played by a law, passed by the parliament (all laws enacted by the parliament were called constitutions) in 1505, which stated: "[...] statuimus, ut deinceps futuris temporibus perpetuis, nihil novi constitui debeat per nos et successores nostros sive communi consiliariorum et nuntiorum terrestrium consensu, quod fieret in praeiudicium gravamenque Reipublicae, et damnum atque incommodum cuiuslibet privatum, ad innovationemque iuris communis et publicae libertatis", Grodziski, Stanisław/Dwornicka, Irena/Uruszczak, Wacław (eds.): Volumina Constitutionum, vol. 1, part 1 (1493-1526). Warszawa 1996, p. 138. This constitution is regarded as one of the stepping stones in the Polish parliamentary system in the Early Modern period, even though the changes in political practice in the 1560s, influenced by the gentry's *executio iuris* movement, were more significant. See Uruszczak, Wacław: The Crown and the Seym in Poland under the rule of the last Jagiellonian Kings. In: Cała historia to dzieje ludzi...Studia ofiarowane profesorowi Andrzejowi Wyczańskiemu w 80-tą rocznicę urodzin i 55-lecie pracy naukowej. Ed. by Cezary Kuklo/Piotr Guzowski. Białystok 2004, pp. 74-75.

members of senate and deputies from the house of representatives. Another right of the parliament was to annul condemnation sentences, especially in a case of banishment or infamy.[2] The members of the house of representatives were chosen by the gentry in special local assemblies, called dietines *(sejmik).* In Masovia, they gathered in each territory (*ziemia, terra)*, and an additional general Masovian dietine was assembled in Warsaw.[3] Apart from electing their representatives, the local gentry prepared instructions for them concerning matters which should be discussed during the diet. A wide variety of things could be included in the instruction – from issues of international politics to local problems like the renovation of the nearest bridge. These instructions are regarded as highly valuable sources for the study of the public opinion, the mentality and the political culture of the gentry.[4] A very specific element of them were the *petita* – requests in individual cases addressed to the king or to the parliament. One of the most significant parts of these consisted of petitions which focused on the administration of justice, i.e. demands for a quicker trial or annulment of a sentence in definite cases. These were the court *petita* of the gentry which form the subject of the following analysis.

A remark about the territorial scope of this research should also be added. Masovia was one of the regions of the Polish Crown bordering with Lithuania and Prussia, which became central after Sigismund III had moved the capital from Cracow to the Masovian city of Warsaw. It was unique due to its settlement of a great number of petty gentry. It is estimated that about 20% of population in that area (25'000 families) belonged to that privileged estate.[5] The sources on which this research is based are the pre-diet dietines instruc-

---

[2] Bardach, Juliusz (ed.): Historia państwa i prawa Polski, vol. 2: Od połowy XV wieku do r. 1795. Warszawa 1966, p. 126.

[3] An exception was the dietine in Płock which was held for two territories. Altogether, there were 14 territorial dietines and a general one in Masovia, Choińska-Mika, Jolanta: Sejmiki mazowieckie w dobie Wazów. Warszawa 1998, pp. 23-25.

[4] Maciszewski, Jarema: Polska a Moskwa 1603-1618. Opinie i stanowiska szlachty polskiej. Warszawa 1968, pp. 25-27.

[5] Gieysztorowa, Irena: Od Jagiellonów do Sobieskiego 1526-1696. In: Cztery wieki Mazowsza. Szkice z dziejów 1526-1914. Ed. by Irena Gieysztorowa/Andrzej Zahorski/Juliusz Łukaszewicz. Warszawa 1968, pp. 23-27.

tions preserved as 19th century copies by Adolf Pawiński in his files[6] and the ones published by Eugeniusz Barwiński in the materials for the 1592 and 1597 diets.[7] This means that about a quarter of all Masovian instructions for that period (about 250 out of over 1000) were included as sources into the research. The quantitative data, thus, cannot be treated as absolute. They may only indicate certain tendencies.

B. Formation of *petita*

Petitions were mainly addressed to two institutions. The first one was a diet and diet court. Participation in a diet included the right to put forward – through the house of representatives – requests to the king and to the king's courts, which represented the second recipient institution. Within the realm of the king's power was also the issuing of a safe conduct, which suspended the execution of a sentence.[8] In general, the gentry's court petitions were not interested in other institutions, with the exception of the treasure tribunal. This indicates that the Masovian gentry was well informed about the system of the judiciary and that their requests were put forward to those institutions which were able to solve the problem. The model of communication between periphery and centre led from the gentry through the dietnes to the diet and the monarch.[9] It was used not only in political affairs, but also regarding the judi-

---

[6] Pawinski's files are stored in the Biblioteka Polskiej Akademii Nauk w Krakowie (Library of Polish Academy of Sciences in Cracow). Therefore, when referring to them, I will use the abbreviation BPAN Kr. and the appropriate signature of the respective unit. Additionally, information about the place and year of a dietine will be included in brackets.

[7] Barwiński, Eugeniusz (ed.): Dyaryusze sejmowe r. 1597. Kraków 1907, pp. 355-365; Barwiński, Eugeniusz (ed.): Dyaryusze i akta sejmowe 1591-1592. Kraków 1911, pp. 129-155.

[8] Bardach (as in fn. 2), p. 113.

[9] For Polish research regarding communication between the king, the government and the gentry in the 17th century see: Choińska-Mika, Jolanta: Między społeczeństwem szlacheckim a władzą. Problemy komunikacji społeczności lokalne – władza w epoce Jana Kazimierza. Warszawa 2002; Choińska-Mika Jolanta: The Diet (Sejm) as a forum of communication between locality and the center during the rule of John Casimir Vasa (1648-1668) in the light of contemporary parliamentary documents. In: 53 Conference of the International Commission for the History of Representative and Parliamentary Institutions, vol. 2. Barcelona 2003, p. 1093-1105.

ciary system. Convincing participants of a dietine to include a particular petition in the instruction for their representatives created a possibility for the local inhabitants to present it to a monarch or to a diet. The best way to obtain support from a dietine was the personal attendance during its deliberation and the appropriate presentation of a case. The instructions mentioned "mournful" or "plaintive" requests and complaints. This may suggest that they were presented in a moving way.[10] Another method was to send a letter of request to a dietine. The author had to be well known to the local gentry – for example, he had to be an inhabitant of a neighbouring territory – or he had to have a supporting group among them. This way was popular among magnates who could count on their clients in the process of acquiring the local gentry's backing. However, the gentry did not always support the requests. Sometimes, the refusal was so firm that it was put in the instruction. For example, in 1668 the Czersk dietine received a letter of request from one of the biggest magnates, the future king of Poland, John Sobieski, who was a grand *hetman* of the Crown (commander in chief of the Polish army) by that time. The letter was read and the gentry did not agree with the petitions. They even instructed their dietine speaker to write a reply including a reminder of the damages caused by Sobieski's soldiers and expectations of compensation.[11] In another case, which was refused, an instruction gave an explanation for that action:

"Za panem Szymakowskiem iż po różnych sejmikach są intercesje aby był do czci przywrócony ich[mość] panowie posłowie pozwalać na to nie mają, bo tam w braterskiej krwi brodzić, aby tedy do takowych *tyrannides* zakryć swawolnym drogę choćby wszystkiej Rzeczypospolitej na to zgoda była nie mają na to pozwalać." [12] (As Mr Szymakowski spilt the brotherly blood, our repre-

[10] BPAN Kr. 8319, f. 32 (Czersk 1601); f. 307 (Czersk 1667), f. 311 (Czersk 1667), f. 328 (Czersk 1667); BPAN Kr. 8353, f. 67 (Zakroczym 1644); BPAN Kr. 8337, f. 63v.-64 (Różan 1624); BPAN Kr. 8350, f. 57 v. (Wizna 1613); BPAN Kr. 8335, f. 50v.-51 (Nur 1666); BPAN Kr.8336 (II), f. 37 v. (Płock 1600).
[11] BPAN Kr. 8319, f. 335v.-336 (Czersk 1668).
[12] BPAN Kr. 8336, f. 178 (Płock 1643). Sources are quoted in original old-Polish language with an English summary in brackets.

sentatives, in order to prevent others from committing such horrendous crimes, must not allow his restitution under any circumstances.)

It is interesting to see that the very same dietine in Płock earlier and later on put forward petitions in favour of Szymakowski's restitution.[13] How should such a contradiction be explained? Presumably, during the dietine of 1643 his enemies or victims gained a majority and blocked his request. This example shows what factors might come into play during proceedings of dietines. Evidently, a petition, which did not find the appreciation of the public opinion, could barely succeed.

Besides generally being handed over to the representatives, the dietine instruction, often including petitions, was also inscribed in widely accessible court books. Everyone could go to the court office and, after paying a minor fee, check the instruction or have a copy of it. This was a simple and efficient technique of memorising the decisions of dietines. As far as *petita* are concerned, this was a very useful tool to preserve a collective legal memory. It was done in a very specific aspect of remembering and supporting individual cases. *Petita* provided information – a necessary element in constructing a tradition[14] – often with expressed legal values standing behind it. The case of the Prażmowskis family provides a fine example of how long that memory could last. They were sued in 1597 in the king's court for illegal possession of the king's village Nieporęt. Although their defence argued on the basis of privileges regarding that village and given to them by Masovian dukes in the times when Masovia was a Polish fief, the decision was handed against them. The gentry from their home territories of Czersk and Warsaw first demanded liberation from citation.[15] They regarded the sentence as unjust and continuously demanded its annulment or, alternatively, compensation for the Prażmowskis family.[16] Even 70 years later, in 1667 one among the points of the instruction

[13] BPAN Kr. 8336, f. 163 (Płock 1639); f. 187 (Płock 1646); f. 192 (Płock 1647).
[14] Patrick, Glenn H.: Legal traditions of the world. Oxford 2004, pp. 13-15.
[15] BPAN Kr. 8319, f. 15v.-16 (Czersk 1597).
[16] BPAN Kr. 8319, f. 41v.-42 (Czersk 1606), f. 46 (Czersk 1608), f. 50 (Czersk 1611), f. 52 (1613), f. 56 (Czersk 1616), f. 181 v. (Czersk 1647), BPAN Kr. 8348, f. 42 (Warszawa 1632), f. 81 (Warszawa 1646), f. 90v. (Warszawa 1648), f. 102 (Warszawa 1649).

dealt with that case, supporting efforts of Czersk *podkomorzy* (*succamerarius*) Albrecht Prażmowski:

"I co tym niemniejsze ponosi tenże Pan Podkomorzy czerski ukrzywdzenie w *haereditas* Jegomości *avisa* dóbr Nieporętu dobrotliwej JKM PNM szczodrobliwości zostaje dotychczas *in recompensa* aby tedy miłościwy uznać mógł Jegomość od Pana Świątobliwego tak za te odjęte dobra jako i za obustronne które *pro integritatem publicam* Białej Rusi Carowi Jegomości odeszły włości respekt pokorny do Pańskiego majestatu wniosą prośbę."[17] (The dietine instructed its representatives to humbly ask His Majesty the King to show generosity and to compensate Prażmowski for unjustly taken estates.)

C. Subjects of *petita*

Two main groups of petitions may be distinguished. The first one demanded quicker litigation or a condemnation sentence, which seemed just in the eyes of the gentry. The second group of court *petita* was mainly concerned with banishment or infamy convictions. They usually represented a punishment for criminal offences, *crimen peculatus* or blocking execution. The gentry requested the diet to annul these or other severe convictions in individual cases. This implied that a local society was ready to forget about crimes committed by the convict and to accept him again as an equal member. Sometimes, it was not an annulment of the sentence that was demanded, but rather a lessening of its rigour. The question arises why in some cases, the gentry was keen to remember some harmful illegal actions and wanted them to have legal consequences, meanwhile in other cases, it was ready to forgive and forget.

The first factor worth analysing relates to the subjects of the requests. What was the social status of the people in favour of whom the *petita* were stipulated?

---

[17] BPAN Kr. 8319, f. 328v. (Czersk 1667).

Table 1. Subjects of *petita*[18]

Social status:	1588 -1607	1608 -1627	1628 -1647	1648 -1668
Senatorial and dignitary's elite (including Masovian)[19]	1 (1)	–	5 (1)	27 (6)
Local elites (including outside Masovia)	9 (–)	4 (–)	20 (–)	13 (3)
Tax collectors	1	1	1	10
The rest of the gentry (including outside Masovia)	18 (–)	13 (1)	23 (1)	20 (7)
Others:				
– clergy	–	1	1	1
– burghers	–	–	–	1

The list indicates that a vast part of the requests was in favour of the local gentry. An overrepresentation of its higher and medium classes, which formed the local elites, can be noticed. This becomes clearer when we acknowledge that it consisted of circa 300 persons out of the 25'000 gentry's families in Masovia. It was, to a great extent, this part of the gentry which was politically active and participated in the dietines.[20] This means that the gentry in the dietines was keen to support individual requests of their well-known and respect-

[18] Source of all tables: own research based on BPAN Kr. 8319 (Czersk), BPAN Kr. 8322 (Liw), BPAN Kr. 8331 (Łomża), BPAN Kr. 8334 (general Masovian dietine), BPAN Kr. 8335 (Nur), BPAN Kr. 8336 (Płock), BPAN Kr. 8337 (Różan), BPAN Kr. 8346 (Sochaczew), BPAN Kr. 8348 (Warszawa), BPAN Kr. 8350 (Wizna), BPAN Kr. 8352 (Wyszogród), BPAN Kr. 8353 (Zakroczym), Barwiński, Dyaryusze i akta (as in fn. 7), pp. 129-155.

[19] The separation of the first two categories is based on the formal criterion of the performing office. In the first category are the highest officials ranked in accordance with criteria used in the prosopography of that group: secular senators (excluding the minor castellans), ministers and dignitaries. See: Chłapowski, Krzysztof: Elita senatorsko – dygnitarska za czasów Zygmunta III I Władysława IV. Warszawa 1996, pp. 15-16; Ciara, Stefan: Senatorowie i dygnitarze koronni w drugiej połowie XVII wieku. Wrocław/Warszawa/Kraków 1990, pp. 9-11. In the second group (local elites) I have decided to include minor castellans, all local officials and persons who had been chosen by the gentry as their representatives for the diets. Tax collectors are taken into consideration as a separate group due to specific petitions in their cases.

[20] Choińska-Mika (as in fn. 3), p. 56.

able members. Other estates' cases were rare. Promoting cases of the gentry from other regions was not a usual thing to do, either. The situation changed in the period between 1648 and 1668, but the seven respective requests were in fact connected to only two cases. The first referred to the Lithuanian colonel Stephan Niewiarowski who was accused – with a group of other officers – of the murder of Wincenty Gosiewski, a Lithuanian field *hetman* (one of the head commanders of the Lithuanian army). They were imprisoned in Malbork, and Niewiarowski's wife asked for his liberation and for giving him a better chance to prove his innocence. This postulate was supported by some of the Masovian dietines.[21] However, this attempt was not successful. Instead of taking Niewiarowski's part, the Masovian general dietine insisted: "Także y *occisores* nieboszczyka Pana Gosiewskiego aby sądzeni byli nieodwłocznie"[22] (assassins of deceased Mister Gosiewski must be judged instantly). In the end, he was sentenced to death with others accused of that crime by the diet court, and he was executed in the beginning of 1665. The second case was a demand to sentence Titus Boratini and Andrew Tymf who were – in the eyes of the gentry – responsible for the devaluation of the zloty by issuing a great number of coins with a lowered silver content.[23] Since these were cases of a countrywide dimension and, hence, interesting for the public opinion in the whole Polish-Lithuanian Commonwealth, it is not surprising that they found a place in the instructions of Masovian dietines, too.

There is, however, one exception from the rule of supporting local cases, which can be observed around 1650, i.e. an increase in numbers of senatorial and dignitary's elite's cases supported in *petita* by the Masovian dietines. Whereas in the 40 years between 1588 and 1627 this happened only twice, it occurred 27 times in the period between 1648 and 1668. Various causes of that process may be distinguished. One of them was definitely a sharp political crisis in the 1660s during which the grand marshal and *hetman* of the Crown George Sebastian Lubomirski was sentenced for banishment by the diet court

---

[21] BPAN Kr. 8331, f. 211v. (Łomża 1664), BPAN Kr. 8346, f. 35 (Sochaczew 1664), BPAN Kr. 8350, f. 272v. (Wizna 1664).

[22] BPAN Kr. 8334, f. 165v. (Masovian general dietine 1664).

[23] BPAN Kr. 8331, f. 217v. (Łomża 1665), BPAN Kr. 8334, f. 169v., f. 169v. (Masovian general dietine 1665), BPAN Kr. 8322, f. 88v.-89 (Liw 1666), BPAN Kr. 8319, f. 324v. (Czersk 1667).

in a political trial. Although Masovia was known as a terrain which supported the monarch in that conflict,[24] there were petitions addressed to the king and asking him to show his royal mercy and annul this sentence against Lubomirski.[25] Almost half of the 27 requests concerned a heritage quarrel, after the death of John Zamoyski, over one of biggest estates in the Commonwealth. Due to the great importance and the high value of the quarrel's object, this case had to be resolved by the diet court. Therefore, both sides searched for support from the dietines, hoping for it to prove useful during a trial. Most of the Masovian dietines backed princess Gryzelda Wiśniowiecka, a sister of John Zamoyski.[26] It seems that the major reason for this support was the popularity of her deceased husband, prince Jeremy Wiśniowiecki, who was acknowledged as a hero of the war against the uprising Cossacks. The Masovians backed her case, even though it was against the letter of law. Zamoyski's estate had been established as *ordiantio*, so that it could neither be divided nor inherited by a woman. Thus, the most zealous adherents of princess Wiśniowiecka treated it as contrary to public law and proposed its annulment: "Taż *ordinatio* jako *successionem naturalem* JO Księżnej jejm. *extirpans et iuri publico contraria et praejudiciosa* skasowana była."[27] Among the Polish gentry, succession by women in case of a lack of closer male successors was common and, as can be noticed, other solutions were treated as contrary to the tradition.

The rise in numbers of the petitions backing the country's elite seems to confirm the thesis of an increase in influence of the grand magnates' families upon the Masovian gentry in the second half of 17th century.[28] It may also indicate a slow process of establishing a clientary system. One example could be significant. In 1637, Stanislaw Koniecpolski, the highest ranked senator and

---

[24] Nagielski, Mirosław: Rokosz Jerzego Lubomirskiego w 1665 roku. Warszawa 1994, pp. 144-145.

[25] BPAN Kr. 8319, f. 293v.-294 (Czersk 1666), BPAN Kr. 8322, f. 91 (Liw 1666), BPAN Kr. 8335, f. 58-58v. (Nur 1666), BPAN 8350, f. 275v. (Wizna 1665).

[26] BPAN Kr. 8319, f. 296v. (Czersk 1666), f. 308-308v., f. 327v.-328 (Czersk 1667), f. 347-347v. (Czersk 1668), BPAN Kr. 8322, f. 95-95v. (Liw 1666), BPAN Kr. 8331, f. 242v. (Łomża 1667), BPAN Kr. 8337, f. 114v. (Różan 1667), f.124-124v. (Różan 1668) BPAN Kr. 8346, f. 51-51v. (Sochaczew 1667), BPAN Kr. 8350, f. 309-309v. (Wizna 1667), BPAN Kr. 8353, f. 97 (Zakroczym 1666), f. 101v.-102 (Zakroczym 1667).

[27] BPAN Kr. 8353, f. 101v.-102 (Zakroczym 1667).

[28] Choińska-Mika (as in fn. 3), p. 15.

the biggest magnate in the country, bought some premises in Masovia in order to obtain political influence in the region.[29] A few years later – in 1644 – his son Alexander Koniecpolski entered into a conflict with prince Jeremy Wiśniowiecki over the Ukrainian property Rumno. Albeit the place of conflict was thousand kilometres away from Masovia, its dietines supported Koniecpolski and demanded a court litigation as well as a sentence in his favour.[30]

Another interesting point is provided by a comparison between the ten requests of annulling sentences upon tax collectors in the period between 1648 and 1668 and the one request in every previous period. 20 years of continuous wars against Cossacks, Tatars, Russia and Sweden had had its impact in this situation. Levying high taxes in a country destroyed by military action and by unpaid soldiers was not the easiest of tasks for the collectors who were elected in the dietines by and from the local gentry. Therefore, delays in collecting taxes occurred. Not delivering them on time meant that collectors could be convicted for the embezzling of public funds. Apart from the local solidarity with their tax collectors, there were also practical reasons for the dietines' help. A *petitum* of a dietine in Wizna from 1654 provided a very significant one:

"A że *malo exemplo* na Komisjej przeszłej lwowskiej *ex delatione* thesauri na urodzonym p. Tomaszu Grądzkim poborcy naszym stanęła wprzód *poena peculatus* niśli się on pieniędzy Rzeczypospolitej tknął, jako *ex iuramento super exactionem praestito patet,* starać się mają pp. posłowie nasi, aby ta kondemanta z niego zniesiona była i napotem aby takowe kondemnaty nie stawały, gdyż przez to i poborstwa na się przyjmować nie chcą."[31] (As our tax collector Tomasz Grądzki was sentenced for having embezzled public funds before he even touched them, the representatives should try to annihilate this condemnation. This case sets a bad example and that sort of condemnations should be prevented in the future, because, due to them, the collection of the taxes is not carried out.)

---

[29] Choińska-Mika (as in fn. 3), p. 87.
[30] BPAN Kr. 8319, f. 166v. (Czersk 1645), BPAN Kr. 8348, f. 73v.-74 (Warszawa 1645), BPAN Kr. 8350, f. 161v. (Wizna 1645), BPAN Kraków 8353, f. 66v. (Zakroczym 1644).
[31] BPAN Kr. 8350, f. 184v. (Wizna 1654).

The presentation of the social status allows for the assumption that – besides other reasons – the local medium class gentry had the best chance of getting support in their cases. Just like the senatorial and dignitary's elite from the middle of the 17th century onwards, they could count on the local society demanding justice for them, either by remembering their situation and reminding the courts of it, or by trying to enforce the legal forgetting of their past. However important it may be, the social status was not the only condition in obtaining the support of the dietines.

D. *Petita's* Axiology

A number of *petita* also included arguments for a proposed solution. These were all but highly sophisticated philosophical considerations. Generally, they consisted of a short practical justification. Nevertheless, its analysis can result in finding the core of a system of legal values and the mentality which stood behind the definite proposals. There were cases in which the gentry remembered what happened and demanded to pursue these cases in the court. They refer to two main situations: crimes awaiting punishment and unjust sentences (or such which were given in violation of the legal procedure). Hence, these petitions could also be in favour of the sentenced person.

Table 2. Arguments for pursuing the case

Sort of crime or scope of harm	15
Inequity of legal action	15
Formal defects of legal action	12
(including fraud)	3
Common good / harm	4
Preventing from impunity	4
General prevention	3
Long wait for litigation	2
Just right of the plaintiff	1
Loss of court books	1

The gentry especially demanded punishment of exceptionable crimes which shook the local society. Such demands could be stressed directly in the petition:

"Żałosna Jegomości Pana Franciszka Sochy Chomentowskiego Łowczego Czerskiego *querimonia* o zabicie jedynego syneczka swego w szkołach ojców Jezuitów *in spem domus sua* uczącego się przez okazyję Pana Duklesa Majora Regimentu Jegomości Pana Chełmskiego który przypomniawszy Boiaźni Bożej *saerit* strzelaniem do obrazu Świętch Bożych *in honorem Dei* musiało nas słusznie *movere* abyśmy zlecili Ichmościom PP Posłom naszym aby ta sprawa słuszną otrzymała i boskiego *contemptu* i ućcziwego zabicia *vindictam*."[32] (Request for justice on behalf of Mr Franciszek Chomentowski in a deeply moving case of crimes committed by major Dukles and his company – i.e. homicide of Chomentowski's son at a Jesuits' school and shooting sacred paintings.)

Sometimes, however, we can read that reason from between the lines. The use of a suitable descriptive adjective could provide a proof – "cruel homicide", "great violence" or "disgraceful *excess*" may be given as examples.[33] Likewise, giving the details of a crime in *petita* – like the place where it was commited[34] – or stressing close family relations between a victim and an offender could indicate that feeling. A short request by a Czersk dietine may serve as an example: "For Mister Florian Rudziński, so that the case of killing his brother by the own daughter and son-in-law be instantly judged."[35] It is quite interesting that arguments for a prevention from impunity and for a general prevention were seldom used. The idea of retributive justice, where a

---

[32] BPAN Kr. 8319, f. 324 (Czersk 1667).
[33] BPAN Kr. 8319, f. 16 (Czersk 1597), BPAN Kr. 8336, f. 178 (Płock 1643), BPAN Kr. 8353, f. 67 (Zakorczym 1644), BPAN 8337, f. 63v.-64 (Różan 1624).
[34] It concerned places with special safety regulations like public roads, dietines proceedings or court sessions. In spite of sharpened restrictions, serious crimes occurred in those places, which is reflected in the gentry's court petitions, BPAN 8350, f. 26v. (Wizna 1597), f. 32 (Wizna 1598), BPAN Kr. 8331, f. 117v. (Łomża 1616).
[35] BPAN Kr. 8319, f. 82v. (Czersk 1628).

crime needs public punishment, was not so popular among the gentry. Other frequently used arguments for pursuing the case were put forward against an unjust conviction. The sense of equity of law was deeply rooted in the legal culture of the gentry. Evidence for this proposition is provided by the high number of equity and just arguments used in petitions. They were often based on the belief that a particular person was innocent and did not commit the crimes he or she was accused of or sentenced for. This belief was rooted in the fact that the accused person was known in the local society and that the neighbours could attest that he or she was innocent. As an illustration, one *petitum* of a dietine from 1616 may be quoted: "For Łomża *subdapifer* Stanislaw Iłowski, whose virtues and modesty are well recommended to us, to judge his case, on which he is inequitably engaged."[36] It is also characteristic that, quite often, dietines demanded issuing of a safe conduct, which enabled the party to appear in court. They were certain that the party would be able to easily prove its innocence: "For Jeziorkowski Adam, innocently and *ad male narrata* was inculpated and sentenced for infamy, in which, after receiving a safe conduct, his innocence will be shown."[37] Apart from equity, the gentry paid attention to the formal side of trials. In case of defects, they demanded the annulment of the sentence or a *restitutio in integrum*. The grounds for this could be: impossibility of attending the trial or unawareness of citation.[38]

The second branch of Masovian petitions concerned situations, where the local gentry asked for the annulment of sentences, which – even in their opinion – were just and legal. Despite this, the gentry decided to forget about the past and promote the cases hoping to obtain positive results. Reasons of this action are shown in table 3.

---

[36] BPAN Kr. 8331, f. 117v. (Łomża 1616).

[37] BPAN Kr. 8331, f. 117 (Łomża 1616).

[38] BPAN Kr. 8322, f. 63v. (Liw 1638), BPAN Kr. 8350, f. 60v.-61 (1616), BPAN Kr. 8319, f. 328v.-329 (Czersk 1667).

Table 3. Arguments in favour of forgetting the past

Reconciliation and compensation to the party	14
Merits / service for the country	9
(including military service)	5
Appeal to king's mercy	6
Common good	5
Aiding widows and orphans	2
Intercession of king and states	2
Denunciation of leaders	1

The most frequently used argument was reconciliation with the harmed party and compensation for the committed crime. A typical example of this way of thinking is provided by a *petitum* for Peter Grodzicki, Różan *podkomorzy* (*succamerarius*):

"Po wotach senatorskich za jmp. Piotrem Grodzickim podkomorzym różańskim pp posłowie prośbę gorącą wnieść mają, aby *tandem intercedente authoritate* Jego Królewskiej Mości mógł *ad pristinum honoris statum* przyjąć, ponieważ już *cum parte transegit*, mając ten i na zasługi w rzeczpospolitej wzgląd, pilne staranie pp. Posłowie uczynić mają." [39] (Our representatives should make heartily request asking for Mr Piotr Grodzicki's restitution because he has reconciled with the harmed party and due to his merits for the country.)

Moreover, there are instances where the dietines refused their support because the malefactor had not satisfied the victim of a crime. In 1662 the gentry of the Czersk territory protested against the annihilation of sentences against Alexander Chołoniewski explaining that it was done "in unawareness and without conciliation with the party and against protests of representatives of our Czersk territory."[40] Therefore, it may be assumed that this was one of the absolutely central values for the gentry and their feeling of justice. The crime was a concept of harming another party and a local society. It is only after

[39] BPAN Kr. 8336, f. 191v.-192 (Płock 1647).
[40] BPAN Kr. 8319, f. 279v.-280 (Czersk 1662).

reconciliation that the neighbours could forget about the past and promote petitions to annul a conviction.

People known for their merits and services for the country, especially after the military service, could also count on the support by the dietines. In the system of the gentry's values, service for the country was very highly estimated and, by means of this social capital, one might compensate for one's guilt. A very good illustration for this is a case of Samuel Łaszcz, possessor of the dignity of the guard of the crown. He was a very good officer, but also a person with a shocking record of well over a hundred convictions for crimes on his account. Despite this, in 1648, after an uprising by the Cossacks, the dietine in Czersk asked for his restitution, justifying its request by his past and present *merita* for the country.[41]

E. Conclusions

Court *petita* of the gentry helped to preserve a common legal memory on the level of individual cases. An analysis of the subjects of the *petita* indicated that mostly the beneficiaries were persons belonging to local middle and well-off gentry as well as, from the middle of 17th century onwards, senatorial and dignitary's elites. The dietines preserved the legal memory in a specific way, by reminding the courts of cases to judge or of unjust and illegal sentences to annul. Unfortunately, it is all but possible to ascertain the efficiency of these petitions. It may be assumed that many were acknowledged. Still, many were constantly repeated, which clearly indicates a lack of effect in those cases. One of the reasons for this situation was that the diets simply did not always have enough time to deal with the *petita* of all territories. A proposal of the gentry to assign one day in each week of a diet for the considering of petitions might be a sign for that.[42]

There were different motives of supporting requests by a dietine. Some were based on the political situation or on social boundaries; others on commonly shared feelings of justice. An examination of the system of values

---

[41] BPAN Kr. 8319, f. 202 (Czersk 1648).
[42] BPAN Kr. 8336 (II), f. 31v. (Płock 1600).

which was used in the *petita* leads to interesting conclusions. With respect to the feeling of justice, the prior value was equity. Without constructing any doctrine of equity of law, the local gentry sensed the situation when the administration of justice did not fulfil its expectations. In those situations, it wanted changes and expressed that in their petitions. The members of the gentry who suffered an unjust or illegally obtained sentence could count on constant support for their requests by the dietine. The Prażmowskis family is the best example of that. On the one hand, the gentry was keen not to forget about extraordinary crimes and the punishment for them. On the other hand, court *petita* indicate when they were ready to forget. A reconciliation with and compensation to the harmed party was almost *conditio sine qua non.* However, the first step on this way had to be taken by the malefactors. A service for the country and for the common good had a great importance, too. It is only after fulfilling one of these conditions that a person could count on the benefit of forgetfulness and on the support of the dietine.

Contested Memories of the Revolution. The Remembrance of Revolutionary Suffrage Laws (1848/49) as Political Arguments in German Discussions on Constitutional Reform, 1860-1875

Christian Müller

Prof. Dr. Eike Wolgast zum 70. Geburtstag am 8. September 2006

"We demand our right, nothing but our right, but our whole right, unchanged and unchallenged!"[1] Discussions about constitutional reforms in the 1860s and early 1870s in the German federal states were often staged in a language of well-acquired rights of 1848/49. Liberals and Democrats frequently used this rhetoric to press for democratising federal constitutions in those states in which governments had staged a breach of constitution in the political reaction after 1849 to illegally abandon the suffrage legislation of 1848/49.

Not much research has been done on the legacy of the 1848/49 revolutions as legal "reforms" in Germany. Recent publications on the German national movement have emphasised the tantamount meaning of remembering legal and constitutional frameworks of the revolutionary years as a means to form political alliances and shape political movements.[2] The political potential of instrumentalised memories of the 1848/49 laws during the 1860s and 1870s has been characterised as an era of "ordered silence".[3] This article argues in

---

[1] Petition of a Delegation of Plauen citizens to re-introduce the suffrage law of 1848, Plauen/Saxony 4.12.1866. In: Sächsisches Hauptstaatsarchiv [SächsHStA] Dresden, Ständeversammlung, no. 5920, fol. 15.

[2] Cf. Siemann, Wolfram: Gesellschaft im Aufbruch. Deutschland 1849-1871. Frankfurt am Main 1990; Biefang, Andreas: Politisches Bürgertum in Deutschland 1857-1868. Nationale Organisation und Eliten. Düsseldorf 1994.

[3] Hettling, Manfred: Nachmärz und Kaiserreich. In: 1848. Revolution in Deutschland. Ed. by C. Dipper/U. Speck. Frankfurt am Main/Leipzig 1998, pp. 11-24, pp. 13f.; Baumgart, Franzjörg: Die

contrast that the political and legal heritage of the revolution in public discussions was not generally "forgotten" or "silenced" but rather vividly "remembered" until the 1870s.

However, nothing is purposely remembered or forgotten without reasons. This articles will address three questions to show how and for which purposes the memories of the legally instituted suffrage laws were used in the discussions about and claims for political reform during the formation phase of a German nation state. Which party formations applied the imagined and commemorated legal traditions of 1848? Which purposes served constitutional remembrance in the 1860s and early 1870s? How were these commemorations in political thought and action forgotten during the 1870s?

It will be argued that remembering the suffrage could be and was used for several purposes. Instrumentalised memories were tools for party strategies to indicate compromise and conflict positions towards government policies. They were utilized as weapons among the forming parties to unite or distinguish themselves in their political aims in federal and regional constitutional politics and national concepts. This essay will also show how remembrance of common political strivings succeeded or failed to form collective party identities. Looking at the political coalitions which supported the suffrage compromises in 1848/49, one can trace different strategies of memory after 1859. It was vital to the political instrumentalisation of suffrage memory whether it could be memorised both in form (as healing of a breach of law and constitution) and content (the suffrage concept being still the ideal of the remembering parties), or just in form. Thus, the different strategies in commemorating the revolutionary laws offer a framework for evaluating the potentials and chances for democratising German constitutions after 1849/50 and the integrative and splitting effects on political movements and parties striving for such reforms.[4]

---

verdrängte Revolution. Darstellung und Bewertung der Revolution von 1848 in der deutschen Geschichtsschreibung vor dem Ersten Weltkrieg. Düsseldorf 1976.

[4] For the general and more complex argument cf. Müller, Christian: Das Wahlrecht als Waffe. Die Wahlrechtsdiskussionen in Deutschland zwischen Revolution und Reichsgründungszeit (1848-1881). Phil. Diss. MS, Heidelberg 2006.

Drawing from recent historical research which has been occupied mainly with the commemoration of the past as a political weapon and as a revolutionary tactics to "march backward into battle" (Skinner),[5] the article compares the legal revolutionary tradition in Saxony and Mecklenburg-Schwerin in contrasting and generalising views. In 1848/49, suffrage concepts were essential parts of the "political confession" of both democrats and liberals.[6] In both states, the obvious breach of constitutional law and the quarrels over electoral legislation in 1850 made the suffrage issue central to the relations of parties and governments until the 1870s. In the analysis, Electoral Hesse and Württemberg will be compared additionally with regards to the effects of a memorised revolutionary past in suffrage discussions.

Different political techniques of remembering and forgetting have to be placed in their political and social contexts to evaluate their arguments, forms and meanings. Thus, the suffrage conflicts of 1848/50 will be sketched briefly to show what could be remembered. The politicisation of memory and oblivion in the German lands will be analysed in three distinct periods: the advent of an instrumentalised revolutionary memory 1859-66, the revolutionary memory as a political weapon in the processes of nation-state building and constitutional reform 1866-70, and the subsequent oblivion of revolutionary laws in the inner nation-building processes in the 1870s.

A. Origins of Memory: Revolutionary Suffrage Laws and Breaches of Constitutions 1848/50

In 1848, a double crisis of modernity gained momentum all over Europe. In the German lands in particular, liberal and democratic movements pressed for

---

[5] Skinner, Quentin: Some Problems in the Analysis of Political Thought and Action. In: Political Theory (1974) vol. 23, pp. 277-303, p. 283; Koselleck, Reinhart: Einleitung. In: Geschichtliche Grundbegriffe, vol. 1. Ed. by Otto Brunner/Werner Conze/Reinhart Koselleck. Stuttgart 1972, pp. XIII-XXVII; Wolfrum, Edgar: Geschichte als Waffe. Göttingen 2001; Winkler, Heinrich August (ed.): Griff nach der Deutungsmacht. Göttingen 2004; Zimmer, Oliver: A Contested Nation. History, Memory and Nationalism in Switzerland, 1761-1891. Cambridge 2003, pp. 1-16.

[6] Langewiesche, Dieter: Liberalismus und Bürgertum in Europa. In: Liberalismus und Sozialismus. Ed. by idem. Bonn 2003, pp. 41-69, p. 50.

a broadening of political participation to the estate assemblies and for a new basis of government legitimacy.[7] Suffrage laws were central to these initiatives for constitutional reform. In Saxony the separation of elections in estate categories and the indirect mode and the census should be abandoned. In Mecklenburg-Schwerin, the old estate Diet jointly held with the Duchy of Strelitz should be replaced by an elected parliament. The democratic electoral laws for the national assembly at Frankfurt emphasised the urgent need for suffrage reforms in the German lands.[8]

Democrats in Saxony and Mecklenburg argued for a single chamber elected by direct universal manhood to introduce a republic in which the people as a community of equal citizens could participate directly in the process of legislation. The Liberals responded differently to the democratic reform concepts. In Saxony, they accepted a broad direct suffrage only for the second chamber. It should embrace all men with own income ("Selbständigkeit"). On these grounds the suffrage law of July 1848 came about as a compromise between these two parties.[9] This resembles the suffrage compromise achieved in Württemberg in 1849.[10] In Mecklenburg, the model of a single chamber was advocated by liberals who wanted to transform the old estate assembly into a modern parliament. Accepting a single chamber representation, however, liberals asked for a separate representation of merchants and landed interest within it. Like Electoral Hesse, the only compromise to combine universal elections and

---

[7] Cf. Langewiesche, Dieter: Republik, Konstitutionelle Monarchie und „Soziale Frage" – Grundprobleme der deutschen Revolution von 1848/49. In: Historische Zeitschrift (1980) vol. 230, pp. 529-548, pp. 529f.; Wehler, Hans-Ulrich: Modernisierungstheorie und Geschichte. Göttingen 1975, pp. 36f.

[8] For 1848/50 cf. among others: Neemann, Andreas: Landtag und Politik in der Reaktionszeit. Sachsen 1849/50-1866. Düsseldorf 2000; Pogge von Strandmann, Hartmut: The German Revolutions of 1848-1850 and the Sonderweg of Mecklenburg. In: The Revolutions in Europe 1848-1849. From Reform to Reaction. Ed. by idem/R.J.W. Evans. Oxford 2000, pp. 99-134.

[9] The Saxon suffrage law of 1848 gave the active vote to every male Saxon citizen who would be "selbständig" (financially liable and independent in personal status). Elections to the second chamber should be direct and held in uniform constituencies. Cf. for the details Diersch, Victor Camillo: Die geschichtliche Entwicklung des Landtagswahlrechts im Königreich Sachsen. Jur. Diss., Leipzig 1918, pp. 107-115.

[10] Langewiesche, Dieter: Liberalismus und Demokratie in Württemberg. Düsseldorf 1974, pp. 166-179.

a representation of interests was provided by the government.[11] Liberals accepted this complicated electoral mode furthered in the constitutional assembly during the discussions on the 'Staatsgrundgesetz' in 1849 as favourable to their interests. Most democrats voted against it but accepted it as legitimate basis for general elections in 1849. The differences in establishing the suffrage laws – on the one hand a liberal-democratic compromise and on the other hand a forced government solution – determined in part the possibilities of instrumentalising the law as a political means of remembrance.

Conservatives both in Saxony and Mecklenburg severely rejected the legal reform of the constitution. In their eyes, governments had been forced to abandon the legitimate order in 1848. They argued that revolutionary legislation lacked legitimacy and advocated a return to the old representational order and their ancient estate rights.[12] Saxon and Mecklenburg governments were eager to follow this interpretation when the revolutionary impetus ebbed away in 1849/50. However, to conservatively reform electoral legislation according to constitutional law, governments would have to come to terms with liberal-democratic parliaments in the orderly process of legislation. Therefore governments used several means to circumvent this process. At the same time they tried to hide an open breach of constitution by doubtful legal arguments. While conservatives looked upon the restoration of the pre-revolutionary legal order as legitimate, liberals and democrats considered governmental methods illegal and illegitimate and could thus exploit them for political protest. Breaking and stretching constitutional law, the governments provided democrats

---

[11] The Mecklenburg-Schwerin suffrage law of 1849 divided elections into two processes. 2/3 of the deputies should be elected by universal suffrage, divided into two tax classes (half of the deputies be elected by the highly taxed, the other half by the rest of the constituency), 1/3 of the deputies should be elected by landed interest and merchants. Cf. Raabe, H.F.W. (ed.): Gesetzsammlung für die Meklenburg-Schwerin'schen Lande, 2. series. Wismar/Ludwigslust 1852, vol. IV, pp. 684-689.

[12] To give just a brief selection: Freimüthige Sachsen-Zeitung nos. 81, 83, 139 from 25.3., 27.3., 5.6.1850; Dresdner Journal nos. 153-158, 2.6. to 7.6.1850; Norddeutscher Correspondent (Neue Rostocker Zeitung) nos. 25, 46, 62, 63 from 10.8., 4.9., 22.9., 23.9.1849 and no. 218, 17.9.1850; Urthel des Schiedsgerichts zur Entscheidung über die Rechtsbeständigkeit des unter dem 11. October 1849 für das Großherzogthum Mecklenburg-Schwerin publicirten Staatsgrundgesetzes, Schwerin 1850.

and liberals with an argumentative basis on which they could press for constitutional reform after 1850.[13]

The potential use of memory differed according to the political context: in Saxony and Württemberg suffrage laws had been a common success of liberals and democrats and could serve as a common basis of remembering the revolution. Mecklenburg and Electoral Hesse had seen bitter disputes over the electoral legislation between democrats and liberals. There was no common legal compromise to be remembered after 1850 unless some tactical need asked for a contest of rivalling memories. Thus, in Saxony and Württemberg both the electoral concept and its legal form could be remembered jointly, while in Electoral Hesse and Mecklenburg only the form of unconstitutional abandonment could be remembered in common. The content of revolutionary suffrage laws remained highly contested.

B. Remembering the Revolution: Suffrage Reforms and Contested Revolutionary Heritage 1859-1866

Remembering the revolutionary laws and the breach of constitutions became a prevalent issue in the early 1860s when the National Association put the 'Reichsverfassung' and its suffrage law on its political agenda. In addition, this national movement put pressure on the German governments by remembering the suffrage conflicts in Electoral Hesse, Saxony, Mecklenburg and Württemberg.[14] Remembering the revolution was applied to promote the re-

---

[13] Cf. for Saxony: Biedermann, Karl: Die Wiedereinberufung der alten Stände in Sachsen aus dem Gesichtspunkte der Rechts und der Politik. Leipzig 1850; Idem: Mein Leben und ein Stück Zeitgeschichte, vol. 2. Breslau-Leipzig 1887, pp. 26-28; Neues Dresdner Journal nos. 65-72, 5.6.-12.6.1850. For Mecklenburg: Protest of 25 liberal deputies. In: Mecklenburgisches Landeshauptarchiv Schwerin [MLHA] 5.12-1/1, Staatsministerium Schwerin, no. 441, fol. 1; Rostocker Zeitung nos. 225 and 230, 19.9. and 25.9.1850.

[14] Flugblätter des deutschen Nationalvereins VI und VII, Coburg 1862. Cf. Biefang (as in fn. 2), pp. 248-287; Gagel, Walther: Die Wahlrechtfrage in der Geschichte der deutschen liberalen Parteien 1848-1918. Düsseldorf 1958, pp. 20-37; Biefang, Andreas (ed.): Der Deutsche Nationalverein 1859-1867. Vorstands- und Ausschußprotokolle. Düsseldorf 1995: Ausschusssitzung 4./5.10.1862, no. 39, pp. 197-203.

turn to the reforming processes of 1848/49 and to argue for national unity and political freedom both in the national and the federal spheres.

Liberal and democratic movements in the German states turned towards the issue of electoral reform in the early 1860s. For Saxony and Mecklenburg, the success in Electoral Hesse to stage the 1849 electoral law as a common liberal-democratic issue of political remembrance functioned as a guiding example for their own arguments. In 1861/62, Prussia had backed the liberal-democratic movement in Electoral Hesse in their fight against Friedrich Wilhelm to symbolically announce a reversal of the Olmütz punctation of 1850 and a shift in power within the German Confederation.[15] The success of revolutionary memory as a political argument in the German lands was intimately connected with the larger scale of national politics. While in Electoral Hesse national liberals had succeeded in joining the reforming forces under the symbol of 1849 as the means of conflict against the government, in Saxony and Mecklenburg-Schwerin this task turned out to be rather difficult due to different national and federal political settings and lines of conflict.

In Saxony the quest for electoral reform was taken up again in 1860. Arguing for a revision of the suffrage, the Leipzig 'Generalanzeiger' promoted a return to the "basis of law". Turning to the conflict in Electoral Hesse, it asked for the "reinstitution of the completely legal compromise law of 1848".[16] In the discussions on the government bill in 1861, however, neither liberals nor democrats argued for a complete return to the 1848 law so as not to endanger the compromise day-to-day politics in the Saxon Diet.[17] Only in 1863 when the Saxon government openly rejected claims for an elected assembly in the German Confederation did the Saxon "Fortschrittsverein" turn to the law of

---

[15] Cf. analysis and documents in: Seier, Hellmut (ed.): Akten und Dokumente zur kurhessischen Parlaments- und Verfassungsgeschichte 1848-1866. Marburg 1987, pp. XIX-LXXVIII, pp. 305-376; Huber, Ernst Rudolf: Deutsche Verfassungsgeschichte seit 1789, vol. 3. 3rd ed., Stuttgart 1988, pp. 410f.; Müller, Jürgen: Deutscher Bund und Deutsche Nation 1848-1866. Göttingen 2005, pp. 333-342.

[16] Leipziger Generalanzeiger no. 272, 12.11.1860, Constitutionelle Zeitung no. 258, 4.11.1860. Cf. Neemann (as in fn. 8), p. 220.

[17] Neemann, Andreas: Models of Political Participation in the Beust era: The State, the Saxon Landtag, and the Public Sphere, 1849-1864. In: Saxony in German History. Ed. by James Retallack. Ann Arbor/MI 2000, pp. 119-134; Neemann (as in fn. 8), pp. 493f.

1848.[18] The democrats initialised an extra-parliamentary petition movement to back their parliamentary claim against the legitimacy of the 1850 breach of constitution. The suffrage law of 1848 was considered the only legitimate means to reconcile the people with the government and to heal the constitutional conflict. "Only the reform which holds the consecration of law could generally suffice and appease."[19]

In contrast to the concerted agitation in Saxony, remembering the revolutionary law in Mecklenburg was more difficult. There was no elected diet in which discussions on the constitution could be held freely. The old estate assembly rejected every motion even before it could be discussed. In addition, liberal-conservative landed interest was reluctant to promote the 1849 suffrage law as it would not mirror their concerns properly.[20] They tried to convince the Grand Duke to transform the old estate assembly into an elected parliament without referring to the despised 1849 suffrage law.[21] Democrats and left liberals would not count on a compromising position with both government and conservative landed interest and played the card of political conflict by remembering the revolutionary law since 1859. Although they had voted against it in 1849, for them it was the only concrete means whose legal form could be remembered. "You have to promote the just law even if you don't like it."[22] The example of Electoral Hesse guided this strategy of conflict.[23] The old suffrage law should be the "flag under which the law-loving and oath-

---

[18] Wilhelm Schaffrath to Heinrich Wuttke, Dresden 25.4.1863. In: Stadtarchiv Dresden, Wuttke papers; Schulthess Europäischer Geschichtskalender (1863) vol. 4, pp. 39f.; Crimmitschauer Anzeiger und Wochenblatt no. 34, 29.4.1863; Neemann (as in fn. 8), p. 460.

[19] Mittheilungen über die Verhandlungen des sächsischen Landtags [MVL Sachsen], II. Kammer, 1863/64, p. 3836; SächsHStA Dresden, Ständeversammlung, no. 5599, fols. 15-22.

[20] Wiggers, Julius: Aus meinem Leben. Leipzig 1901, pp. 180f.

[21] Petition of 82 liberal Ritterschaft members. In: MLHA 3.1-1, Landstände, no. 25.515.13, fol. 292 adhib.

[22] Sievers, J.H.: Was ist zu thun? Leipzig 1861, p. 9.

[23] Richthofen to Schleinitz, Hamburg 6.2.1861. In: Geheimes Staatsarchiv Preußischer Kulturbesitz, Berlin-Dahlem [GStA PK], III. HA., 2.4.1., MdAA, no. 3577/3, fols. 71-74; Manecke-Duggenkoppel to the Engere Ausschuß, Schwerin 1.8.1862. In: MLHA 3.1-1 Landstände, no. 25.515.13, fols. 316 and 316 adhib.

abiding people of Mecklenburg should gather, trusting in its well-acquired right".[24]

Comparing these developments with Prussia and its three-class suffrage, one can trace a distinct tactic to forget suffrage traditions of 1848 in the liberal-democratic movements. Unlike the quest of the Prussian-dominated National Association for the re-introduction of revolutionary electoral laws in the other federal states, the inner-Prussian suffrage discussion was dominated by purposeful oblivion. Memories of the Prussian democratic suffrage of 1848 had remained vivid among democrats and National Association activists well into the 1860s.[25] Adhering to the compromising principle based on the 1850 constitution, Prussian liberals made the democratic wing in the "Fortschrittspartei" set aside memories of the 1849 suffrage octroi as reforming arguments within liberalism.[26] Facing Bismarck's threat to use democratic suffrage concepts for conservative ends in a "Bonapartist" way, the democratic wing could not convince their liberal brothers in arms to instrumentalise the revolutionary memory.[27]

Opposition movements in the early 1860s argued for a constitutional reform by remembering the revolutionary laws when no compromise with governments could be found. This can be seen in Saxony and Württemberg after 1864 as well as in Electoral Hesse and Mecklenburg from 1859 onwards. However, the instrumentalisation of the 1848/49 laws could not only unite, but also split the opposition movements. While Prussian foreign policy per-

---

[24] Wiggers (as in fn. 20), p. 181; Idem: Die Reform der Landesvertretung. Berlin 1860, p. 12; Idem: Das Verfassungsrecht im Großherzogtum Mecklenburg-Schwerin. Berlin 1860; Sievers (as in 22), pp. 9f.

[25] Cf. Correspondence between Theodor Müllensiefen and Louis Berger, June 1860. In: Westfälisches Wirtschaftsarchiv Dortmund, F4 (Müllensiefen papers), no. 42.

[26] Cf. Biefang, A.: National-preußisch oder deutsch-national? Die deutsche Fortschrittspartei in Preußen 1861-1867. In: Geschichte und Gesellschaft (1997) vol. 23, pp. 360-383, p. 378.

[27] Comment of the liberal deputy in the Prussian Landtag Heinrich Beitzke to his wife, Berlin 15.6.1865. In: Ein Gegner Bismarcks: Dokumente zur Neuen Ära und zum preußischen Verfassungskonflikt aus dem Nachlaß des Abgeordneten Heinrich Beitzke; 1798-1867. Ed. by Horst Conrad. Münster 1995, no. 97, pp. 325f. Cf. also Fehrenbach, Elisabeth: Bonapartismus und Konservatismus in Bismarcks Politik. In: Idem: Politischer Umbruch und gesellschaftliche Bewegung. Ausgewählte Aufsätze zur Geschichte Frankreichs und Deutschlands im 19. Jahrhundert. München 1997, pp. 367-380.

suaded reluctant liberals and democrats in Electoral Hesse to assemble under the complicated suffrage law of 1849, no such success was in sight in Mecklenburg. Therefore the use of the 1849 law split reforming forces.

C. Contested Memories: The Suffrage as a Rhetorical Weapon during the Formation of a German Nation-State 1866/70

In 1866, the coordinates for suffrage discussions in Germany changed dramatically. Bismarck used the national suffrage law of 1849 as a "weapon" to split the German Confederation and to reconcile part of the bourgeois national movement with his policies of forming a small-German nation-state with the North German Bund.[28] Liberals and democrats in the German states were forced to taking sides for or against Bismarck's concept of a nation-state. The suffrage question changed into an open space of discussion in which constitutional reform could be argued as the means either to nationalise politics or to pursue reforms in contrast to constitutional politics in the nation-state nucleus. Remembering the 1848/49 revolutionary laws subsequently served as a means to oppose nationalising policies and to divide national-liberals, federalist liberals and democrats.

The democratic legitimacy of the North German Reichstag and the war of 1866 re-staged the dual crisis of political participation and government legitimacy prevalent in 1848 in the framework of nation-state building. Firstly, against the Reichstag, the federal diets fell short of democratic legitimacy so that suffrage reform movements set off immediately after the war to press for broader political participation in the federal states. Saxony and Mecklenburg-Schwerin faced this problem in late 1866. Secondly, the states which were defeated in the 1866 war saw themselves under the pressure of diminishing political legitimacy. Saxon and Württemberg governments alike tried to broaden the popular legitimisation of their policies and to appease the still dwelling

---

[28] Cf. Bismarck, Otto von: „Der Norddeutsche Bund". In: Bismarck, Die Gesammelten Werke, vol. 15. Berlin 1928, p. 287; Pollmann, Klaus Erich: Parlamentarismus im Norddeutschen Bund 1867-1870. Düsseldorf 1985, pp. 66-92. For the general argument, cf. Müller (as in fn. 4), passim.

constitutional conflicts. A central tool would be a suffrage settlement which consoled at least liberals and left liberals.

Between 1866 and 1870, remembering the revolutionary suffrage laws served two political functions. On the one hand the traditions of 1848/49 could be used as a direct point of reference both in form (legality and legitimacy) and content (suffrage concept) to revive claims for constitutional reform. On the other hand the federal states' traditions set an argumentative counterpoint against the nationalising discourse of constitutional reform and could thus be formed as the means to distinguish between small-German and greater-German, and between national-liberal and left-liberal/democratic parties.

In Saxony, the national liberals furthered the 1848 law as a nationalising argument. During the early days of the Prussian occupation of Saxony in the summer of 1866, the Leipzig liberal Karl Biedermann asked Max Duncker whether he would promote the re-introduction of the Saxon suffrage law of 1848 among Prussian court circles.[29] With this means it would be easy to convince Saxon liberalism to wholeheartedly join a unitarian nation-state lead by Prussia. While Bismarck and the Prussian civil administrator in Saxony von Wurmb could not agree on this project, the intermediary Saxon "Landeskommission" announced general elections after the old electoral system.[30] The new Saxon government under Richard von Friesen thus kept its chances of introducing a moderate suffrage reform to end the constitutional conflict and appease the country. Although von Friesen had announced some reform for the new Diet, political movements and parties in the country uniformly asked for a strict return to the 1848 suffrage law: "We demand our right, nothing but our right, but our whole right, unchanged and unchallenged!"[31]

---

[29] Karl Biedermann to Max Duncker, Leipzig 20.7.1866. In: GStA PK, VI. HA., Max Duncker papers, no. 25, fols. 70-71.

[30] Bismarck to von Wurmb, Berlin 17.6. and 4.9.1866. In: GStA PK, III. HA., MdAA, 2.4.1., no. 3923/2, fol. 1 and no. 3923/3, fol. 19.

[31] Friesen, Richard von: Erinnerungen aus meinem Leben, vol. 2. Dresden 1880, p. 288; MVL Sachsen, I. Kammer, 1866/68, vol. 1, p. 9; Plauen Petition of 4.12.1866. In: SächsHStA Dresden, Ständeversammlung, no. 5920.

The revolutionary suffrage law and its party political instrumentalisations moved to centre stage of Saxon suffrage reform contests.[32] On a common meeting in Dresden in early November 1867, national liberals, democrats and socialists failed to achieve a cross-party consensus on the use of its remembrance.[33] The working class movement rejected the law because it would have barred some of the working-class electorate from the polls due to the "Selbständigkeit" clause. Julius Vahlteich, leader of the Dresden workers' association, argued for the principles of the Reichstag electoral system and allowances. This vigorous refutation of revolutionary traditions furthered the split between socialist and bourgeois democracy in Saxony in 1869.[34]

The old Saxon democracy urged for the political use of a common memory of the 1850 breach of constitution and its only healing by the 1848 suffrage law. With this argument they wanted to form a united agitation movement which would put the Saxon government under political pressure from within.[35] Some democrats which proposed an appeal to the Bundesrat (Art. 76 II Bundesverfassung BV) to re-introduce the 1848 suffrage law were set aside. National liberals called for a more pragmatic use of reform arguments in the Saxon Diet. They argued more pragmatically that the Reichstag electoral mode would have nationalising effects on Saxony. As German and Saxon electoral laws of 1848/49 were based on similar principles, one should further the Saxon legal memory of 1848 as a side argument for the suffrage reform. Karl

---

[32] Cf. Retallack, James: Suffrage Reform, Corporatist Society, and the Authoritarian State: Saxon Transitions in the 1860s. In: Saxony in German History. Ed. by idem. Ann Arbor/MI 2000, pp. 199-214.

[33] Meeting report by an anonymous government agent, Dresden 1.11.1867. In: SächsHStA Dresden, Ministerium des Innern, no. 11039, fols. 169-183.

[34] Crimmitschauer Anzeiger und Wochenblatt nos. 30 and 31, 11.3. and 13.3.1869, Demokratisches Wochenblatt no. 11, 13.3.1869, p. 120f.; Constitutionelle Zeitung nos. 56 and 58, 11.3. and 13.3.1869. Cf. Wieczoreck, R.: Zur Trennung der proletarischen von der bürgerlichen Demokratie. In: Demokratie und Emanzipation zwischen Elbe und Saale. Ed. by Helga Grebing et al. Essen 1993, pp. 26-39.

[35] Cf. MVL Sachsen, II. Kammer, 1866/68, vol. 3, pp. 2626, 2631, 2636, 2647f., 2664.

Biedermann argued on a party meeting in Leipzig in 1867 that one "should not throw the ancient right over board!"[36]

Although Saxon democrats pressed for the 1848 suffrage law, they were eager to cooperate with national liberals in the legislative process. They supported the liberal argument as long as deputy allowances were not abandoned. Both liberals and democrats would accept the suffrage reform of 1868 only as a partial success in a process of piecemeal reform which had to be expanded in subsequent years. The new Saxon suffrage granted direct suffrage, but only citizens who paid one "Taler" a year of direct taxes qualified for the active vote. Thus, both parties urged for further reform in the 1869/70 Diet. While national liberals and parts of the democrats asked for adapting the Saxon electoral mode to the Reichstag, the greater German Saxon democrats held on to the 1848 law: "It just needs the courage to re-install the insulted right [...] to appease and reconcile our Saxon fatherland."[37] With this argument, the democrats subsequently lost their stand with their voters.

In Mecklenburg-Schwerin, the conservative government and the Grand Duke would not reconcile the legitimacy gap between the Reichstag and the old estate assembly after 1866. Bismarck backed their neglect of popular claims to introduce a uniform suffrage in the North German states as well as a re-introduction of the 1849 suffrage law. Thus, both federal initiatives by the Mecklenburg liberal-national movement were doomed to fail: the enlargement of legislative competences by the Reichstag for the political rights of citizens (Art. 78 and Art. 4 Sentence 1 BV) and the complaint before the Bundesrat to settle constitutional conflicts within federal states (Art. 76 II BV).[38] The Rostock liberal Julius Wiggers tried to convince at least the Reichstag that their claims were just. He objected against the principles of the 1849 suffrage

---

[36] Nationalzeitung no. 484, 16.10.1867; Constitutionelle Zeitung nos. 247 and 265, 23.10. and 14.11.1867; Treitschke, Heinrich von: Zur Charakteristik des öffentlichen Geistes in Sachsen. In: Preußische Jahrbücher (1867) vol. 20, pp. 195-215.

[37] MVL Sachsen, II. Kammer, 1866/68, vol. 3, p. 2649.

[38] Cf. Stenographische Berichte des Reichstags 1867, Anlagen vol. 2, no. 140, pp. 215f., and ibid. 1869, pp. 599-601; [Freydorf, Rudolf von]: Die mecklenburgische Verfassungsfrage. Leipzig 1877, pp. 54-61; [Prosch, C.F.W.]: Die Competenz des Norddeutschen Bundes aus Art. 78 der Bundesverfassung. Berlin 1870, pp. 115f.; Idem. In: Rostocker Zeitung no. 216, 31.8.1867.

law but promoted it as the only legitimate means to reform the Mecklenburg constitution.

"With the 'Staatsgrundgesetz' a suffrage law is offered which is abundantly stocked with census and estate elements that the conservative party cannot ask for more. It will grant them a majority in the future legislative from which they will benefit when revising the 'Staatsgrundgesetz'. The Liberal party on the other hand has more reasons to take offence at the mode of elections."[39]

Wiggers tried to convince liberals and democrats of the formal function of remembrance, as the formal re-introduction of the legal order and the legitimate constitution would serve as a means to reconcile Grand Duke, government, liberal-democrats and the people. Although the leftist 'Volkspartei' in Mecklenburg argued along the same lines, they would only accept the law of 1849 but otherwise abstain from any compromise favoured by the liberal Reichstag members. They would obstinately rather stick to the old estate constitution.[40] Thus, the leftist political spectre put the fragile coalition of liberals and democrats under pressure and contributed to undermining the standing of the 1849 suffrage law among the liberal landed interest even further.

The Bundesrat failed to accept this argument for a case along the lines of Art. 76 II BV due to Bismarck's intervention. The Mecklenburg deputy to the Bundesrat Bernhard von Bülow wrote triumphantly to Schwerin that the "rush for the 'Staatsgrundgesetz'" had been averted. However, he warned the Mecklenburg governments not to be too optimistic that the "democratic principle had been barred" from any reform initiative.[41] The left liberal part of the Mecklenburg opposition pressed for a political remembrance in the country as the national initiatives had failed so far. After 1870, they advocated a reform

---

[39] Wiggers, Julius: Die Mecklenburgische Verfassungsfrage. Berlin 1869, p. 18.

[40] Demmler, G.A.: Public Lecture in 1867. In: MLHA, 5.12-3/1, Ministerium des Innern Schwerin, no. 21184, fols. 265, 275-277.

[41] Bernhard von Bülow to Jasper von Oertzen, Berlin 13.5.1869 and Hammerstein to Oertzen, Neustrelitz 18.5.1869. In: MLHA 5.12-2/3, Gesandtschaft Berlin, no. 949, fols. 71-74; ibid. 5.12-1/1, Staatsministerium Schwerin, no. 443, fol. 72.

both in the Reichstag and in Mecklenburg but the 1849 memory was only staged on the federal state level.

In comparison, governments in Saxony and Württemberg tried to broaden their legitimacy by a suffrage reform which should open the electorate along the lines of the Reichstag suffrage.[42] Thus, they could reconcile the national liberals with their politics. The national liberals soon dropped their instrumentalised remembrance of the 1848/49 laws as a means of conflict. Only the democrats insisted on remembering the revolutionary laws as a quest for indemnity against governments. The situation in Mecklenburg differed from this. While the Schwerin government was reluctant to give in to any constitutional reform, the liberal-national party could not agree on a coherent strategy to reconcile the different suffrage quests. The all-encompassing Mecklenburg liberals failed to unite under the suffrage law of 1849 as the central political argument due to the diverse ideal concepts of political representation and to the contested memory of the revolutionary law even among liberals. The electoral mode of the 1849 law was difficult to communicate to the political public because its complicated mode did not resemble the national suffrage by any means. The formal quest for healing the breach of the constitution in 1850 was the only way to pursue the 1849 law. This line of argument was heavily contested among Mecklenburg liberal-democrats. Revolutionary remembrance rather divided than united political opposition in Mecklenburg.

D. Sinking into Oblivion: The Revolutionary Suffrage Laws in the 1870s

Agitation for the commemorated right of the revolution ebbed away soon after the formal 'Reichsgründung' in 1871 when it became obvious that the

---

[42] For Württemberg cf. Der Beobachter nos. 279 and 303, 28.11. and 27.12.1867; Verhandlungen der Württembergischen Kammer der Abgeordneten, 1866/68, vol. 3, pp. 1683, 1688, 1691; Menzinger, Rosemarie: Verfassungsrevision und Demokratisierungsprozeß im Königreich Württemberg. Stuttgart 1969, pp. 69-85; Runge, Gerlinde: Die Volkspartei in Württemberg von 1864 bis 1871. Stuttgart 1970, pp. 129f.; Gawatz, Andreas: Wahlkämpfe in Württemberg. Landtags- und Reichstagswahlen beim Übergang zum politischen Massenmarkt (1889-1912). Düsseldorf 2001, pp. 38f.

new mass parties, political Catholicism and Social Democracy, would benefit from a broader suffrage. The electoral outcomes of the Reichstag suffrage and the changing political conditions within the federal states finally ended the active memory of the revolutionary suffrage laws among liberals and democrats. The processes of revolutionary remembrance fading out in the 1870s were intimately connected to the constitutional and party frameworks in the federal states.

In Saxony, election turnouts after 1871 showed an ever-growing strength of the Social Democrats. In addition, conservative politics tried to split liberalism by both tactically aligning with Social Democracy in the Reichstag elections and by loosening the bonds between liberalism and democracy in the Saxon Diet. The national liberals were content with the reform of 1868. For them, the reform had healed the breach of constitution of 1850 as the government had de facto asked for an indemnity. Therefore they forgot the ancient right as a means of conflict to ask for constitutional reforms. Instead they established themselves as a majority and compromise party with the government to influence and further legislative projects which had long been delayed. Being under pressure from both left and right wing politics, liberals held on to the 1868 suffrage compromise which seemed to secure them a parliamentary majority for the time being. On the 1869/70 Diet only the Democrats would use the memory of law to press for further constitutional reform. By associating with Social Democracy in the 1870s, the Democrats subsequently dropped this argument to align with the more pragmatic claims.[43] In Saxon politics, remembering the revolutionary law of 1848 could not serve a tactical purpose and sank into oblivion.

In Mecklenburg this process was delayed as liberals and democrats still tried to gain a representative constitution. Until 1875, memory was kept alive by the left wing of the Liberal-Nationals to form a legalistic argument which could be used on the Reform Diets in 1874 and 1875. Remembering the 1849 law had been fruitful in the town election campaigns to the Reichstag in late 1873, so they argued that remembering the form of the 1849 constitution and suffrage

[43] Dresdner Nachrichten nos. 286-291, 13.10. to 18.10.1875.

law would meet the claims of the people.[44] In both form and content the instrumentalisation was highly controversial among the Liberal-National movement in Mecklenburg.[45] Democrats and left liberals like Julius Wiggers would have loved to claim the Reichstag election mode but used the legal memory as a line of argument "not because I like it, but because it is our lawful right".[46] However, they failed to convince the liberal spectre, both because the form of remembered memory of 1849 and because the suffrage concept expressed in it would not match liberal-conservative ideals.[47] With the failure of the 1875 Reform Diet to introduce a constitution based on elections and the liberal majority in the Reichstag being contested in 1877, reform arguments which concentrated on the memory of the 1849 law soon ebbed away. As a tactical means, remembering the revolutionary suffrage became obsolete.

E. Conclusion: Remembering and Forgetting Revolutionary Laws as Political Weapons 1860-1875

In the German states, the memory of revolutionary suffrage laws could be formed as a political weapon between 1860 and 1875. This memory was used by liberals and democrats alike. However, standing and context of revolutionary memories differed according to party political use and purposes. Framing the suffrage reforms of 1848/49 was highly determined by regional and party

---

[44] Rostocker Zeitung no. 300, 22.12.1873.

[45] Rostocker Zeitung nos. 270, 284, 287, 288, 290, 299, 16.11. to 21.12.1873; ibid. no. 35, 11.2.1874; Pamphlets and Meeting Report of the „Liberal-National Party" 14.2., 21.2. and 20.6.1874. In: MLHA 5.12-1/1, Staatsministerium Schwerin, no. 442, additional private papers of the National Liberal Westphal; Karge, Wolf: Liberale Demokraten oder demokratische Liberale? In: Modernisierung und Freiheit. Beiträge zur Demokratiegeschichte. Ed. by Michael Heinrichs/Klaus Lüders. Schwerin 1995, pp. 673-685, pp. 679f.

[46] Wiggers, Julius. In: Rostocker Zeitung no. 2, 3.1.1873.

[47] For the variety of suffrage concepts on the Reform Diet of 1874, cf. Düberg, Christian (ed.): Der außerordentliche Landtag von 1874. Wismar-Rostock-Ludwigslust 1874, pp. 169-177; John, Anke: Die Entwicklung der beiden mecklenburgischen Staaten im Spannungsfeld von Landesgrundgesetzlichem Erbvergleich und Bundes- bzw. Reichsverfassung vom Norddeutschen Bund bis zur Weimarer Republik. Rostock 1997, pp. 160-183; Wiese, René: Orientierung in der Moderne. Großherzog Friedrich Franz II. von Mecklenburg in seiner Zeit. Bremen 2005, pp. 234-243.

lines of conflict. In the early 1860s, the national movement figured as a prominent guiding example to claim for constitutional reforms in the federal states on the basis of well-acquired rights in the form of an illegally and illegitimately abandoned law. However, the 1848/49 tradition was only vividly remembered in those federal states and political contexts in which fruitful legal compromises with governments were no longer possible.

In instrumentalising memory as political arguments, the parties that realigned in Germany in the 1860s faced the problem which particular aspect of the revolutionary suffrage should be memorised and instrumentalised. Two main aspects could be used to press for legal reforms: the concept of political representation expressed in the laws, and the mode of legislative compromise and governmental breach of constitutional ways of legislation. Thus, memories of the revolution involved a dual process of remembering: the concept aspects of representation as political content and the form aspects as healings of illegitimate government measures. The form of constitutional conflict lay at the basis of instrumentalised memory as one could urge for the "legitimate law" as an ancient and well-acquired right. However, concrete uses of this argument were highly contested between liberals and democrats as they meant a positioning towards government policies. Democrats tended to stress the formal aspect of a healing of constitutional conflicts to contradict government claims of legitimacy of their policies. In contrast, liberals stressed this formal aspect only as a side argument for suffrage reform. In Saxony, the split of liberal and democratic reform agitation sprang from the different instrumentalisation of the formal side of the 1850 constitutional conflict. In Mecklenburg-Schwerin, the position of the memorised constitutional conflict of 1850 was internally contested in an encompassing liberal-democratic movement. In this context, the search for a common symbolic memory as a political argument hampered rather than furthered a coherent agitation for constitutional reform.

The content of the revolutionary suffrage laws also influenced their functions in reform discussions. Remembering a suffrage law as an actualised concept for constitutional reform was easier in those states in which the federal suffrage principles of 1848/49 and the Reichstag suffrage of 1866/67 resembled each other. In Saxony, liberals and democrats could merge both arguments with slight variations (deputy allowances, "Selbständigkeit" clause) for a reform agitation. In Mecklenburg-Schwerin, the 1849 suffrage mode included general, tax class and professional interest elections. It was almost impossible to reconcile this complicated mode with a nationalising argument for the Reichstag suffrage. Furthermore, liberals and democrats had to decide whether to keep their tactical alliance or split over different suffrage concepts. Thus, remembering the revolutionary suffrage in Saxony could serve to illustrate party nuances in popular representation concepts. In contrast to this, in Mecklenburg the goal to include all reform elements into a common opposition movement prevented an open contest for the ideal suffrage concept and made a compromise agitation on the basis of the 1849 law impossible.

Memories of the 1848/49 legal traditions were highly contested because they depended on the intensity and goals for which the legal traditions should be memorised. Conflict tactics were pursued by the democrats after 1866 to express their discontent with the nation-state building process dominated by Prussia and Bismarck's politics. To oppose the North German constitution as the leading example, Democrats in Saxony and Mecklenburg-Schwerin held on to the own federal traditions of 1848/49 against a nationalising suffrage politics pursued by national liberals. Remembering the revolution also served as a means to keep up the constitutional conflict with Saxon government. National Liberals in Saxony could well use the memory of 1849 as a side argument for their suffrage claims. However, they would not stretch this argument to follow a strategy of political compromise with the government. In Mecklenburg-Schwerin, the umbrella movement of Liberals, small-German Democrats and Liberal-Conservatives could not agree on a coherent strategy to remember form and content of the 1849 law. Being highly contested, revolutionary memory in Mecklenburg-Schwerin split the liberal movement rather than uniting it under a leading symbol for constitutional reform.

Forgetting revolutionary laws was a process dominated by German liberals between 1869 and 1878. The formation phase of the German nation state between 1866 and 1870/75 was interpreted by contemporaries as a genuine process of catching up with the reforms of 1848/49. The piecemeal and compromising legislation between governments and liberals was seen as the German form of "revolution".[48] Liberals welcomed any moderate reform pro-

[48] Cf. Die Grenzboten (1868) vol. 27,1, p. 310.

posal which seemed to secure their parliamentary majority for pursuing legislative projects that had been postponed since 1849. The potential of remembering revolutionary suffrage laws for a further democratisation of federal constitutions diminished in those contexts where and when a reform settlement was achieved. The advent of modern "mass politics" and new types of mass parties favoured by a democratic suffrage on the national level after 1871 also put an end to liberal openness for democratising reforms of federal suffrage laws.[49] The commemorations of the 1848/49 suffrage laws could not be used for political purposes anymore and were forgotten.

[49] Cf. the comments by Otto von Camphausen to his brother Ludolf, Berlin 31.10.1884. In: Historisches Archiv der Stadt Köln, Camphausen Papers (Best. 1023), L 1437: "The universal suffrage puts us [the national liberals] ever so much under pressure in fighting with the Catholics and Socialists that every statesman should consider if and how the [Reichstag] universal suffrage could be altered. The man [i.e. Bismarck, C.M.] who brought us the universal suffrage and who condemned the three tax classes Prussian suffrage by all means in the constitutional Reichstag [in 1867] is the only person who might easily liberate us from the lot of his suffrage coup d'état [of 1866]."

Coming to Terms with the Past: The Mexican Juncture between Remembrance and Forgetfulness

Jaime Olaiz González

A. Introduction

It is well known that Mexico is currently passing through a democratization process after more than three-quarters of a century of being ruled by an authoritarian regime which monopolized and controlled the whole political system. The subordination of the legislative and judiciary branches under the agenda and interests of the President was clear and it undermined significantly the spread and consolidation of democratic institutions in Mexico until the last decade of the past century.

Right after the fall of the former Soviet Union, like in the rest of the world, Mexico faced the need of adjusting its political, economic and social structures to the new waves of democracy in an exceptional context, so the government had no other choice than to gradually undertake a series of reforms that would establish the foundation of democratic institutions on a long term basis. With such an aim, the former administrations of the presidents Salinas (1988-1994) and Zedillo (1994-2000) devoted themselves to enabling the transition from a closed economic and political system into a democratic regime with full openness at home and towards the world. This was and still is a task of the most grievous kind.

The economic reforms were implemented before those of political nature. The calculation of the government was that the former would not provoke as much reaction as the latter. However, nowadays it is clear that the political reform – even with the risks at hand at that time – was as imperative as the other reforms, and still is an unfulfilled issue in the Mexican democracy.

Part of these political reforms concerns the way by which the Mexican state and its society are willing to face the large legacy of crimes and systematic violations of human rights committed by the authoritarian regime, particularly those that came after 1968. Such an endeavor is still an issue and it seems that the current political actors do not have even a minimum of interest to face it.

We all are aware that most of the modern democracies, such as the Argentinean, the Chilean, the South African or the Eastern European, had to pass through a process of coming to terms with their respective legacies of massive violations of human rights, unveiling the historic truth about those illegal actions and implementing adequate reparations and guarantees that such would not happen again so as to finally restore the failed democracies on the foundations of truth, justice, peace and reconciliation. These transitions to democracy can only be understood through the lens of the modern concept of transitional justice.

Such an itinerary has not been adopted in Mexico, and it is my belief that if we do not do it in the next decade, our fragile democratic institutions will fail since they will be useless in a society confronted with a false or ignorant perspective of its recent past. In this respective, we are dealing with the relationship between remembrance and forgetfulness.

B. Particularities of the Mexican Transition

1. Authoritarian regime with democratic appearance; 2. Absence of military predominance in government; 3. Absolute control over media and press; 4. Control over the judiciary; 5. The Mexican transition has been focused on two issues: changeover of power and gradual evolution of democratic institutions

Several particularities made the Mexican transition to democracy so different from many other democratization processes which were all characterized by, among others, access to power by force, military predominance on all levels of government, isolation from the rest of the world, intermittent state of war or conflict within the territory and large proliferation of radical groups.

Such did not occur in Mexico. However, most scholars and experts agree that Mexico experienced an authoritarian regime for almost seven decades, and more emphatically, over the 60's, 70's and 80's.

The Mexican political system was considered as authoritarian for two specific characteristics: (a) the predominance of the executive power over the other two branches of government; (b) the absence of minimal democratic conditions, which undermined the civil, social and political rights of all citizens.

Authors like Víctor Flores[1] Olea or Lorenzo Meyer[2] have agreed that it was adequate to speak about a "transition" in Mexico even if it did not come strictly from a military or dictatorial regime, because the old regime had authoritarian characteristics such as verticality, centralism, corruption, inexistence of political plurality, state control over elections, media and press, as well as an absolute absence of democratic checks and balances to the president.

The key to the functionality of this authoritarian regime, for almost three quarters of a century, was the systematic use of coercion to strengthen the predominance of the hegemonic party – Partido Revolucionario Institucional, aka PRI – and the extensive endurance of the system. This arbitrary use of force allowed the perpetration of numerous human rights violations for more than three decades. In this period, known as "Dirty War", it was the carefully designed policy of the state to persecute and eliminate groups of dissidents and government's critics in order to secure stability and order in the nation, even if it required to disregard elementary rights.

It is clear then that the particularities of the Mexican authoritarian regime, which lasted from 1928 to 2000, are quite different from those that characterized the other authoritarian regimes in the second half of the last century. However, it is now that the nation is facing its recent past with objective criticism.

Like all authoritarian regimes, the Mexican system cultivated a democratic appearance towards the international community, but used autocratic methods at home. Even though the military did not have a relevant position in the government, their submission and loyalty to the executive assured its permanence in power. However, it was not the military that carried out the strategy of murder, torture and massive disappearing, but the "Dirección Federal de

---

[1] Flores Olea, Víctor: ¿Qué democracia? In: Los Compromisos con la Nación. México 1996, pp. 375-397.

[2] Meyer, Lorenzo: El presidencialismo. Del populismo al neoliberalismo. In: Revista Mexicana de Sociología, published by the Instituto de Investigaciones Sociológicas de la Universidad Nacional Autónoma de México, April-June 1993, pp. 57-83.

Seguridad" and paramilitary groups created alongside the government and its *apparatus* for such purposes. These two cells deployed, for almost thirty years, a repressive action which was undertaken and allowed by those in power.

Absolute control over the media and the press was established at that time. All newspapers, television and radio programs were previously reviewed and authorized by the Ministry of the Interior. The public opinion only knew what the state wanted it to know. No more, no less. This was the strategy of propaganda which inspired the 1930's totalitarian regimes.

Elections were organized, settled and qualified by the Ministry of the Interior. Electoral fraud was a popular and unchallengeable practice and the use of social programs with electoral purposes was a frequent tool employed by the government to gain votes for the official party.

As has been said, the executive fully dominated the other two branches of government. The legislative body used to approve, without any analysis or discussion, all pieces of legislation presented by the president. Opposition parties with a representation in the congress were not taken into account or listened to by the overwhelming official majority. But the longest lasting and most harmful control was the one over the Supreme Court and the rest of the judiciary, where the principles of legality and due process of law were just principles and not practices. The judiciary ruled according to the economic, political and ideological interests of the current administration. Justices and judges were appointed for their political loyalty instead of for their legal qualifications and prestige. The positive law was usually adjusted to the interests of the so-called *nomenklatura*.[3]

In the light of this, there is a consensus that the Mexican political system had been seized, for almost eight decades, by an authoritarian regime which managed to create a democratic appearance to other nations while undermining at home civil, political, economic and social liberties, and even deploying a

---

[3] Salinas de Gortari, Carlos: México un paso difícil a la modernidad. México 2000, p. 1393. The former Mexican president defines nomenklatura as a net of social and political agents that emerged in the 1930s when the corporative structure of the Partido Revolucionario Institucional was created. This net was consolidated in the 1940s and 1950s merging great political influence, economic power and social control over unions and corporative organizations. The nomenklatura had a particular control over the police corps and national security agencies.

state strategy to eliminate all possibilities of democratization.

Until today, the Mexican transition to democracy has been defined by two predominant aims: (1) the changeover of power which occurred in 2000 when – for the first time – an opposition party was democratically elected for the Presidency and the results were recognized even by the hegemonic party; (2) the gradual reform and evolution from authoritarian to democratic institutions, in order to achieve an open system which fulfills the minimum requirements of modern western democracies.

These two aims must be seen as answering to the transitional and systematic democratization problems that Samuel Huntington explains in his *Third Wave*.[4] According to this author, the new democratic institutions have to face, when they get into power, the different challenges and problems implied in a process of democratization. Such problems can be divided into three categories: (a) transitional; (b) contextual; and (c) systematic.

Transitional problems are those directly related with the sudden change of regime: restoration of failed democratic institutions, creation of autonomous offices to organize elections, dismantling of the repressive apparatus, the secret police and paramilitary groups, enactment of different mechanisms of democratic participation such as referendum or plebiscite, drafting and discussing a new constitution, and recognition and protection of human rights, among others. In this category, and qualified as highly important, Huntington speaks about the transitional problem which concerns the legacy of past human rights violations committed by an authoritarian regime. This problem can be divided into two types: (a.1.) the problem of torture which is directly related to the dichotomy of *trials and punishment versus forgetfulness and forgiveness,* that we will discuss later on; and (a.2.) the *praetorian problem,* which concerns the gradual evolution from military predominance in government into civil roles trying to calmly reinsert into the society those who previously were the hegemonic class.

Contextual problems are those customs and traditions that shape the idiosyncrasy of a nation. Such problems are present from the beginning of any so-

[4] Huntington, Samuel: The Third Wave. Democratization in the Late Twentieth Century. Oklahoma 1991, pp. 190-250.

ciety and are components that have to be taken into account in every democratization process.

Systematic problems finally are those that appear as a natural or necessary result of democratic restoration. These problems do not belong to democratization, but are consequences of it and surpass the strict challenges of democratization.

It is clear then that in the Mexican transition, some structural transitional problems have been taken care of, but a fundamental problem has not yet been faced. This is the question of what to do with the human rights violations legacy. The great issue in Mexico is that we transited so suddenly from the structural transitional problems to the systematic problems and forgot to face the dichotomy of *trials and punishment versus forgetfulness and forgiveness.*

C. Fundamental Importance of Facing the Past to Consolidate a Democratic Transition

1. The dilemmas of facing the past; 2. Ultimate aim: the Moral Reconstruction of a nation; 3. The itinerary of truth, justice, reparation, forgiveness and reconciliation; 4. The Pedagogy of Peace in the thought of John Paul II; 5. International criminal justice; 6. The debate between Carlos S. Nino and Diane F. Orentlicher

For the last thirty years, scholars, practitioners and human rights activists have devoted themselves to establishing a framework that would enable different societies to face the legacies of mass violence and human rights violations in order to morally rebuild a nation.

Most transitions to democracy in this period have faced as a key issue the way by which each nation had to come to terms with its own past. The way chosen by a society has defined the final outcome of its democratization process.

Experiences, such as the South African, Chilean, Argentinean, Eastern European, Greek, Uruguayan and Brazilian, have contributed to creating this framework thereby making clear right from the beginning that the democratization processes and the ways of facing the past are necessarily different. Thus, there are no absolute rules or recipes to undertake a task of this nature.

However, there is a common ground among them: the dilemma of whether or not to face the past; the dilemma of jeopardizing the renewed stability by opening forgotten wounds; the dilemma of building a future without memory in order to preserve peace; the dilemma of seeking the truth, bringing justice and forgiving past violations that are not easily pardoned; the dilemma of vengeance or forgiveness.

Martha Minow, professor at Harvard Law School, considers that "perhaps there simply are two purposes animating societal responses to collective violence: justice and truth".[5] While this is true, it has to be faced under a broad perspective: Indeed, there are legitimate demands of justice and truth, but these two cannot come alone if we are trying to restore a moral and legal order that has been broken. Thus, forgiveness is a third element that enables, together with the other two, moral and social reconciliation.

Professor José Zalaquett explains clearly the need for Moral Reconstruction in the wake of past human rights violations.[6] Zalaquett thinks that "past human rights violations and other crimes with a political motif were the expression of force's empire and the absence of a moral order ... How to face such violations as a part of a Moral Reconstruction process is an endeavor that *prima facie* is traditionally solved by criminal justice. But such alternative – as professor Zalaquett warns – enforces an existing legal order but not necessarily serves to rebuild one after a period of mass violence ... the true challenge is to adopt viable measures to reconstruct a failed moral order. For such a task, forgiveness and reconciliation – along with truth and justice – are complementary elements to do so."

As legal historians, we are perfectly aware that truth is absolutely necessary to reach a fair and objective analysis of the past, bringing justice to any spe-

---

[5] Minow, Martha: Between Vengeance and Forgiveness. Facing History after Genocide and Mass Violence. Boston 1998, p. 9.

[6] Roth-Arriaza, Naomi: The Need for Moral Reconstruction in the Wake of Past Human Rights Violations: An Interview with José Zalaquett. In: Human Rights in Political Transitions: Gettysburg to Bosnia. Ed. by Carla Hesse/Roberto Post. New York 1999. See also Zalaquett, José: Balancing Ethical Imperatives and Political Constraints: The Dilemma of New Democracies Confronting Past Human Rights Violations. In: Hastings Law Journal (1992) vol. 43, p. 1425.

cific situation. Authors like Diane Orentlicher[7] or Priscilla Hayner[8] are advocates of the importance of Truth Commissions, trials and punishments for perpetrators of human rights violations, as well as of reasonable compensations for victims and their relatives. But truth and justice are not the only components of this endeavor. Having Moral Reconstruction as the ultimate aim of facing the past, forgiveness and reconciliation are key elements to reach that goal.

On the one hand, forgiveness – as professor Zalaquett indicates[9] – is a mechanism designed to restore the moral order so as to enforce the validity of those rights that were violated. On the other hand, reconciliation requires that those who did wrong admit it and settle differences in a framework of mutual tolerance. Moreover, perpetrators are compelled not only to admit their crimes but also to recognize that they did wrong. With such a *mea culpa* from perpetrators, the distance to social reconciliation gets shorter.

For the above mentioned, there is a consensus on the importance of facing the past through the lenses of truth, justice, compensation, forgiveness and reconciliation, in order to achieve a Moral Reconstruction of a nation after its period of violence. In the thought of John Paul II, this itinerary was named "Pedagogy of Peace".[10] By such a pedagogy, the former Pope tried to explain the necessary steps to enabling national reconciliation in those countries that, by the third quarter of the past century, evolved from an authoritarian regime to a democratic system. John Paul II explained it in the following terms: "There is no justice without truth, there is no forgiveness without justice and there is no peace without forgiveness and reconciliation."

Pedagogy of Peace is a useful methodology in coming to terms with the past. It prevents young democracies from the failure of facing the past just by

---

[7] Orentlicher, Diane: Settling Accounts: The Duty to Prosecute Human Rights Violations of a Prior Regime. In: Yale Law Journal (1991) vol. 100, p. 2537.

[8] Hayner B., Priscilla: Ensayos sobre la justicia transicional. International Center for Transitional Justice, New York 2003, pp. 117-137.

[9] Roth-Arriaza (as in fn. 6), p. 3.

[10] Quezada Toruño, Rodolfo: Verdad, Justicia y Perdón en el Pensamiento del Papa Juan Pablo II. Inaugural Address at Universidad Rafael Landivar. Guatemala, January 29, 2002. See also: La Iglesia y las culpas del pasado. Memoria y Reconciliación. Documentos Pontificios 71, Comisión Teológica Internacional, Editorial Basilio Núñez, 2000, p. 71.

the means of criminal justice or legal forgiveness through amnesties. It enables them to overcome the dilemma which the former Uruguayan president Julio María Sanguinetti indicated as *fear and impatience*[11] in transitions to democracy. Sanguinetti suggested that in these situations it is always "better" to face the past with enough distance to assure objectiveness and with enough memory to avoid forgetfulness.

However, there is a remarkable exception in this struggle between remembrance and forgetfulness, and it concerns the catalogue of crimes which were defined, after the Nuremberg Trials, as crimes which cannot be the object of an amnesty or of forgiveness: genocide, war crimes and crimes against humanity.[12] Nuremberg showed that the punishment of these crimes was justified not only because it prevents their repetition in the future, but also because its punishment is a legal and moral obligation since such crimes violated the most precious principles and rights of humankind. However, the punishment of these crimes is not in conflict with the concurrent presence of forgiveness after the legitimate enforcement of justice and law, in order to contribute to the Moral Reconstruction that we spoke about in the paragraphs above.

It must be said that forgiveness does not inhibit the empire of justice in this endeavor, but contributes to the full achievement of justice and equity in a society the moral and legal foundations of which were broken by violence and systematic denials of the Rule of Law.

All these concepts have created for decades an intense debate about the relative advantages of facing the past, unveiling the truth or forgetting the facts of massive violations and torture. I believe that we all agree that it is imperative to the state in any circumstances to seek, unveil, protect and live the truth in order to build a legitimate historic legacy. On such common ground,

---

[11] Sanguinetti, Julio María: El temor y la impaciencia. Ensayo sobre la transición democrática en América Latina. Fondo de Cultura Económica. Buenos Aires 1991, pp. 7-12, 69.

[12] Ambos, Kai/Guerrero Peralta, Oscar: El Estatuto de Roma de la Corte Penal Internacional. Universidad Externado de Colombia. Bogotá 1999. See also Roth-Arriaza (as in fn. 6), p. 5. Clark, Roger: Codification of the Principles of the Nuremberg Trial and the Subsequent Development of International Law. In: "The Nuremberg Trial and International Law". Ed. by George Ginsburg/V.N. Kudriavtsev, pp. 195-197.

there was a remarkable debate between the professors Carlos S. Nino[13] and Diane F. Orentlicher[14] – in 1991 – about the advantages of prosecuting human rights violations of prior regimes, particularly after the Argentinean experience. Professor Orentlicher attributed much importance to prosecuting such crimes as an international obligation of all nations. Professor Nino tried to explain – after his own experience in the first democratic government in Argentina after the fall of the military regime – that punishment to all perpetrators is quite difficult in an environment of democratic restoration. As professor Nino warned: "There was too much at stake." Therefore, professor Nino – as has happened in Nuremberg, Tokyo, the former Yugoslavia and Greece, among others – advocated the "selective" trials to avoid further attempts to break young democracies.

Both were right. Particularly today, Orentlicher's theses are sound and convenient, and actually binding under International Law (cf. Statute of the International Criminal Court, 1998; Convention on the Non-Applicability of Statutory Limitations to War Crimes and Crimes against Humanity, 1968). But also Carlos Nino's arguments are extremely important in order to establish as much justice as possible under the political and social circumstances. It is all about the exercise of "Ethics of Responsibility" suggested by Max Weber in his famous speech "Politics as a Vocation" in 1919. The great issue in facing the past is to adequately apply all these theories to the specific context of each transitional process. Still, international and comparative law – nowadays – make such an endeavor much easier.

D. A Hope to Overcome the Mexican Juncture of Facing the Past

1. Blocking truth and justice in Mexico; 2. Tools in international law and jurisprudence to prosecute past human rights violations; 3. Failures of the Special Prosecutor Office in Mexico

---

[13] Nino, Carlos S.: The Duty to Punish Past Abuses of Human Rights Put into Context: The Case of Argentina. In: The Yale Law Journal (1991) vol. 100, pp. 2619-2640.
[14] Orentlicher, Diane F.: A Reply to Professor Nino. In: The Yale Law Journal (1991) vol. 100, pp. 2641-2643.

There are a few arguments in Mexico which are carefully designed to block justice and punishment against perpetrators of past human rights violations.

First of all, there is the constitutional principle of non-retroactivity – article 14 of the Mexican Constitution – which deactivates any possibility of enforcing the United Nations Convention on the Non-Applicability of Statutory Limitations to War Crimes and Crimes against Humanity. Even though this convention states that statutory limitations cannot be applied to such crimes in any circumstance or context by reason of the capital nature of the human rights in question, the Mexican congress embraced and ratified this Convention back in 2001, considering that "statutory limitations of the Convention will be enforceable only on those crimes committed after 2001, but not on those committed before". It seemed that the principle of non-applicability of statutory limitations to these crimes was justified not for their nature, but for the generosity of the state. A similar thing happened with the Statute of the International Criminal Court that was ratified by the Mexican Senate in 2005 submitting its application in Mexico to the approval of the President and the Senate in any given case. Such reserves are – under international law of course – locks to deactivate any initiative to bring to justice perpetrators of past human rights violations.

From my point of view, urgent constitutional reforms in these matters are imperative. It is clear that such ratifications were legal but not fair. It is here that the "Radbruch Formula" taken into account by the Supreme and Constitutional German Courts,[15] serves well to provide an answer to when there is such a tension between legality and justice that "codified law would not be binding if it is in conflict with justice in such intolerable way that law would become unfair, and it has to surrender before justice". This principle was used by the German Supreme Court to rule in the trials of the Berlin Wall Shootings.

---

[15] Alexy, Robert: Der Beschluβ des Bundesverfassungsgerichts zu den Tötungen an der innerdeutschen Grenze vom 24. Oktober 1996. Hamburg (Joachim Jungius-Gesellschaft der Wissenschaften) 1997. Translated into Spanish, under the name "Derecho Injusto, Retroactividad y Principio de Legalidad Penal", by Daniel Oliver-Lalana, with the authorization of Scientific Society Joachim-Jungius, Hamburg. Pro manuscripto.

After Nuremberg, several rulings establishing the non-applicability of statutory limitations to war crimes, genocide or crimes against humanity[16] provide a large catalogue of legal arguments to defend the seeking of truth and justice. All these contributions have been ignored in Mexico. The ruling political class still consists predominantly of members from the former authoritarian regime who are unwilling to concede any possibilities of prosecuting them or their colleagues for those illegal actions committed in the past.

It seems that for a great number of Mexicans, nothing happened in the last quarter of a century. For a great number of Mexicans, past human rights violations are part of a "left-wing" discourse that has nothing to do with reality. Systematic denial from the government has contributed to enlarging a culture of forgetfulness in Mexico. This situation enjoyed a limited progress back in 2000, when President Fox was elected. Originally, he promised a Truth Commission as an adequate instrument to seek and unveil the truth. Once in office, he reconsidered and created a Special Prosecutor Office to investigate those crimes committed in the past.

From 2001 until today, the performance of this Office has been legally deficient, and, in the public opinion, its moral authority is very low. The great failure is that the Special Prosecutor Office has not faced the problem of past human rights violations as an issue of Moral Reconstruction of the nation, but just as a task of criminal justice, and even in this, it has significantly failed.

The failures of the Special Prosecutor Office for Social and Political Movements of the Past can be summarized as follows:

a. the mistake of focusing its work only in the area of criminal justice, instead of primarily seeking the truth in order to enable not only trials and punishments for perpetrators, but also compensations for victims and their relatives. The aim of unveiling the truth would be a remarkable effort that has not yet been undertaken by the Special Prosecutor Office.
b. the inadequate and deficient legal argumentation of the actions filed by the Special Prosecutor Office before the Mexican judiciary. Actions were filed for genocide – which clearly did not occurred in Mexico – in-

[16] Cf. Cases Priebke & Hass, Argentinean Supreme Court; Case Klaus Barbie, French Court of Appeal.

stead of being filed for crimes against humanity.

c. the ignorance about comparative law and jurisprudence in international criminal law, international human rights law and international humanitarian law left the Special Prosecutor Office with the sole possibility of elaborating its charges with an internal or domestic law perspective only.
d. the absence of any dialogue with experts on past human rights violations and transitions to democracy, at home and abroad. It has been a lost opportunity to learn – through the work of the Special Prosecutor Office – from the experiences and legacies of analogous situations in other countries.
e. the lack of political willingness to inform victims and society about the final outcome of the Special Prosecutor Office's work, as has happened in Chile, Argentina, Brazil, Peru, South Africa, etc.
f. the reluctance to reconsider the benefits of creating a Truth Commission, which would guarantee objectiveness, impartiality, distance from the power structures, moral authority of its members and social support.
g. the lack of placing the victims and their relatives in the center of the procedures in order to contribute, with their consent and satisfaction, to further Moral Reconstruction.

E. Conclusion: There Is a Chance for Moral Reconstruction in Mexico

Recent denials from the Mexican Supreme Court of Justice regarding prosecutions against members of the former regime that ordered or committed violations of human rights, under misinterpreted principles of law such as non-retroactivity or statutory limitations, have shown a poor Mexican knowledge about different international codifications, customs and rulings that have created a path against impunity and forgetfulness. Such denials hinder the Mexican effort to face its past.

There is a great need for Moral Reconstruction in Mexico. We have not yet passed through a process of facing our recent past and investigating those human rights violations that occurred in the authoritarian regime. As we are experiencing a transition to democracy, we must come to terms with our past. This is unavoidable. But the government or the political parties will not take such effort. It has been clear that it is an initiative that requires advanced citizenship and support from the international community, as has happened in many Latin American, European, Asian and African countries.

We still have a chance of undertaking a Moral Reconstruction in Mexico. Experiences of comparative law, international law conventions, a well spread human rights culture around the globe and, more emphatically, a legitimate desire of truth, justice and reconciliation are sufficient elements for such an undertaking. In the meantime, we still regard the German *Vergangenheitsbewältigung* and many other successful transitional experiences as paradigmatic examples of nations restoring themselves by facing their past.

Juridical Memory Making and the Transformation of Historical Expert Witnessing: Contextualizing the Eichmann Case and the Frankfurt Auschwitz Trial

Vladimir Petrović

A conference on legal remembrance and forgetting seems a proper ground for thematizing the link between the juridical memory making and the transformation of the expert witness role of professional historians. Both in historical and legal scholarship, recent discussions on the merits of historical expert witnessing are characterized by heated comments expressed under unusually dramatic titles. Can historians perform the role of expert witnesses in legal proceedings? And should they? Quick and determinate responses are offered, with historians either being perceived as useful expert witnesses, or not. The persistence of such a counter-intuitive normative stance calls for empirical scrutiny. Therefore this article aims to contribute to the understanding of historical expert witnessing by converting the question of whether historians could and should testify into the question of why, when and how they actually testified. The article therefore examines the contributions of historians to the Eichmann trial (1961) and the Frankfurt Auschwitz trial (1963). It tracks a dramatic shift in the expert role of historians from the role of authentication of documents to the role of contextualization of cases, as experienced in the course of those proceedings. This shift is brought in connection with the change in the relationship between law and history, expressed in the advent of juridical memory making in the aftermath of the Nuremberg trial. The developments in juridical memory making are perceived as neglected, yet important, influence on the transformation of historical expert witnessing in the sixties as well as on its proliferation at the end of the 20th century. Connecting the developments in juridical memory making with the debate on the merits of the forensic contribution by professional historians and social scientists is seen as an important precondition for the creation of a viable genealogy of historical expert witnessing.

A. Juridical Memory Making and its Discontents

What is juridical memory making? It has been frequently noted that prominent trials make history, not only by rendering important judgments and influencing societal development, but also by offering a powerful account which captures the attention of the public and affects the way societies remember and forget. From the Dreyfus case, Stalin's show trials, the Nuremberg proceedings, Brown vs. Board of Education and Eichmann trial to the Klaus Barbie, Slobodan Milošević or Saddam Hussein cases, the historical relevance of such high-profiled proceedings and their impact on the collective memory have been observed, albeit very differently interpreted. It was apparent that those trials operate in a complex context in which law, politics, memory and history intertwine in a memorable public event, producing a particular outlook on the past. However, it was less apparent what to make out of this confusing cocktail and whether these aspects of the trial should be, or indeed could be disentangled.

The issue of juridical memory making was therefore ignored or deplored by theoreticians for a long time, mainly because such extralegal effect of the trial was equated with the politization of justice.[1] This traditional negative stance, embedded in legal positivism, is well reflected in Hannah Arendt's critique of the conduct of the Eichmann trial: "The purpose of the trial is to render justice, and nothing else."[2] Her dictum, no matter how influential, remained clouded by a strong sensation that, whether one likes it or not, there are cases with virtually unavoidable extralegal potential, including the impact on collective memory. As the concept of apolitical justice was shaken in works by such

---

[1] Scholarly interest in collective memory grew fairly recently. It took more than six decades for the scattered works of Maurice Halbwachs (who coined the term in 1925) to find serious resonance in the social sciences. Seminal readings on the issue of collective memory and its making: Connerton, Paul: How Societies Remember. New York 1989; Hobsbawm, Eric/Ranger, Terence (eds.): The Invention of Tradition. New York 1992. The connection between collective memory, history and politics was dealt with at length in an ambitious project launched by Nora, Pierre (ed.): Les Lieux de mémoire I-VII. Paris 1984-1993.

[2] Arendt, Hannah: Eichmann in Jerusalem. London 1963, p. 232.

different authors as Otto Kircheimer and Judith Shklar, the idea of using such cases in pursuing wider political and social agendas gained modest legitimacy.[3]

Huge incentive in this direction came with the collapse of communism and the global transition towards democracy. It was accompanied by the legal reaction on the crimes of past regimes, placing the topic of juridical memory making in the center of attention of the growing body of literature dealing with transitional justice, as the trials were rediscovered as powerful 'vectors of memory'.[4] Ruti Teitel described them as "long-standing ceremonial forms of collective history making" which "enable vivid representations of collective history through the recreation and dramatisation of the criminal past".[5] Further elaboration on the ways to strengthen liberal consensus by means of judicial activity was offered by Mark Osiel, who fully embraced the idea that "criminal trials must be conducted with these pedagogical purposes in mind".[6]

---

[3] The political aspect of criminal justice in democratic societies was thematized in Kircheimer, Otto: Political Justice. Princeton 1961. The topic is further elaborated in Becker, Theodore L. (ed.): Political Trials. New York 1971. Judith Shklar went even beyond, concluding that "it is not the political trial itself but the situation in which it takes place and the ends that is serves which matter. It is the quality of the politics pursued in them that distinguishes one political trial from another." Shklar, Judith: Legalism: Law, Morals, and Political Trials. Cambridge, Mass. 1986, p. 45.

[4] The expression was coined by Rousso, Henry: Le Syndrome de Vichy (1944-198...). Paris 1987. Trials were further thematized as important carriers of memories in Wood, Nancy: Vectors of Memory: Legacies of Trauma in Postwar Europe. New York 1999. The seminal readings on transitional justice (Kritz, Neil: Transitional Justice. Washington, D.C. 1995; Borneman, John: Settling Accounts: Violence, Justice and Accountability in Postsocialist Europe. Princeton, N.J. 1997; McAdams, A. James (ed.): Transitional Justice and the Rule of Law in New Democracies. Notre Dame 1997; Teitel, Ruti: Transitional Justice. Oxford 2000; Elster, Jon: Closing the Books: Transitional Justice in Historical Perspective. New York 2004) are all noting the paramount importance of trials in the transition towards the new societal consensus. Within this body of literature, the impact of legal actions on collective memory is empirically most extensively covered in Aigullar, Paluma et al.: The Politics of Memory: Transitional Justice in Democratizing Societies. Oxford 2001 and analyzed in depth by Osiel, Mark: Mass Atrocity, Collective Memory and the Law. Brunswick and London 2000. Interdisciplinary contributions to the topic in Sarat, Austin/Kearns, Thomas (eds.): History, Memory and the Law. Ann Arbor 2002; also in Bacot, Jean-Pierre (ed.): Travail de mémoire 1914-1998. Paris 1999.

[5] Teitel (as in fn. 4), pp. 72-73.

[6] Osiel (as in fn. 4), p. 2.

This pedagogical aspect is treated as unavoidable asset by Lawrence Douglas, who put to question the Arendtian minimalist approach:

"No one, I believe, would deny that the primary responsibility of a criminal trial is to resolve the question of guilt in a procedurally fair manner. And certainly one must appreciate the potential tension between the core interest of justice and the concerns of didactic legality. To insist, however, as Arendt does, that the sole purpose of a trial is to render justice and nothing else, presents, I will argue, a crabbed and needlessly restrictive vision of the trial as legal form."[7]

Still, the same authors reflect upon "a complicated relationship between transitional justice, truth and history".[8] Judith Shklar noted that for the purposes of the Nuremberg trial, "history had to be tortured throughout in order to reduce the events to proportion similar to those of a model criminal trial within a municipal system".[9] This issue is perceived as one of the major stumbling blocks of the concept, and is considered "problematic in myriad ways".[10] Doubts in the truth produced in the course of the trial are deeply rooted in the idea that, apart from the Last Judgment, there can be no infallible man-made court of law, and much in the accordance with Hegel's famous understanding of *Weltgeschichte als Weltgericht*, history is frequently invoked as a more elaborate, accurate and impartial judge.

Worrisomely, this *topos* was frequently invoked by the defendants in various courtrooms in order to delegitimate the court by calling upon the superior judgment of History, God, Destiny or Nation. In Nuremberg, Albert Speer was asked by his attorney: "In assuming a common responsibility, did you want to acknowledge measurable guilt or co-responsibility under the penal law, or did you want to record a historical responsibility before your own

---

[7] Douglas, Lawrence: The Memory of Judgment. Making Law and History in the Trials of the Holocaust. New Heaven and London 2001, p. 27.

[8] Teitel, Ruti: Transitional Justice Genealogy. In: Harvard Human Rights Journal (2003) vol. 16, p. 86.

[9] Shklar (as in fn 3), p. 147.

[10] Osiel (as in fn. 4), p. 79.

people?" Speer replied: "That question is very difficult to answer." The answer was seemingly found by the Argentinean General Leopoldo Galtieri, who proclaimed, after being found guilty by the Argentinean court, that only history can render judgment upon his deeds. His colleague, Emillio Masseri, was even blunter: "My critics may have the chronicle, but History belongs to me". [11]

The concern about the ability of the court to pursue mnemonic goals was also voiced by the less self-interested observers. Tina Rosenberg claimed that "trials, in the end, are ill suited to deal with the subtleties of facing the past".[12] Ian Buruma concluded similarly: "Just as a belief belongs in church, surely history education belongs in school. When the court of law is used for history lessons, then the risk of show trials cannot be far of. It may be that show trials can be good politics – though I have my doubts about this too. But good politics don't necessarily serve the truth."[13] Much blunter was the historian of Holocaust Michael Marrus: "My own view is that trials cannot and should not

[11] Speer's statement in: The Nizkor Project: The Cross-examination of Albert Speer, The Trial of German Major War Criminals, Friday, 21. June 1946, <http://www.nizkor.org/hweb/imt/tgmwc/tgmwc-17/tgmwc-17-160-12.shtml> (accessed on 30.6.2006), p. 91. The Argentinean generals are quoted in Osiel (as in fn. 4), p. 108. The Serbian ex-president Slobodan Milošević approached the problem from the other side, claiming that the International Criminal Tribunal for the former Yugoslavia was not rendering justice upon him but was instead judging history by "accusing … Serb intelligentsia and the Academy of Arts and Sciences and the Vidovdan battle of Kosovo". International Criminal Tribunal for the former Yugoslavia, Cases and Judgments, The Milosevic case, Transcripts, Defense's opening statement, 14.2.2002, <http://www.un.org/icty/transe54/020214IT.htm> (accessed on 30.6.2006), pp. 246-248. After his death, media comments in a sense echoed this dichotomy, repeatedly pronouncing that he escaped justice and that it was up to history to render him a judgment. „Should the four years of the Slobodan Milosevic trial now be considered a failure? As far as history is concerned, the former President of Yugoslavia has already been condemned by a large section of public opinion." Maupas, Stéphanie: The Legacy of an Unfinished Case, <http://www.crimesofwar.org/onnews/news-milosevic7.html> (accessed on 30.6.2006). The opportunity given to the accused to expose their views in history is analyzed in Simpson, Garry: Didactic and Dissident Histories in War Crimes Trials. In: Albany Law Review (1997) vol. 60, pp. 833-839.

[12] Rosenberg, Tina: The Haunted Land. London 1995, p. 258.

[13] Buruma, Ian: The Wages of Guilt: Memories of War in Germany and Japan. London 1995, p. 142.

be expected to do the job of historians – to teach history."[14] Various authors advanced a number of important epistemological, methodological and procedural arguments challenging the legal reading of the past as provided by the courts.[15] The crux of the problem was neatly captured by Gerry Simpson: "The performance of a war crimes trial is both situated in history and yet seeks to transcend it."[16]

Amidst such strong controversy, the division of labor between history and law remains blurred both inside and outside the courtroom. The tension is well reflected in a confusing palette of interchangeable terms used to describe this sensitive junction – prosecuting history (Aurora Voiculescu) and judicial historiography (Erich Haberer) to denote the law's interest in history; judicization of history (Richard Evans) and judicial reading of history (Henry Rousso) to stand for the historiographical interest in legal matters.[17] However, despite the semantic closure, the key issues remain unresolved. Are the courts sup-

---

[14] Marrus, Michael: «History and the Holocaust in the Courtroom». In: Lessons and Legacies V. The Holocaust and Justice. Ed. by Ronald Smelser. Evanston 2002, pp. 215-229, p. 216.

[15] Theories of incompatibility of historical and legal narratives are systematized in Wilson, Richard Ashby: Judging History: The Historical Record of the International Criminal Tribunal for the former Yugoslavia. In: Human Rights Quarterly (2005) vol. 27, no. 3, pp. 908-925. Sets of similarities and differences between the tasks of a historian and a judge are enumerated in Wildt, Michael: Differierende Wahrheiten. In: Geschichte vor Gericht. Historiker, Richter und die Suche nach Gerechtigkeit. Ed. by Norbert Frei et al. München 2000, pp. 51-57. The same issue is tackled by Ginzburg, Carlo: The Judge and the Historian. London 1999. On more specific issues, Kitson, Clarck: The Critical Historian. New York 1967, pp. 13-18 dwells on different standards of proof in historiography and in the court of law. Different understandings of causality in law and history are demonstrated in Shklar (as in fn. 3), pp. 194-200. On different notions of the truth in law and history see Sheleff, Leon: Four Thruths – Legal and Political, Judicial and Historical. In: Legal Semiotics and Sociology of Law. Ed. by B. S. Jackson. The Onati International Institute for the Sociology of Law, Onati 1994, pp. 73-88.

[16] Simpson (as in fn. 11), p. 826. A similar dichotomy is neatly phrased as the difference between "einer Geschichte *vor* Gericht und der Geschichte *als* Gericht" by Van Laak, Dirk: Widerstand gegen die Geschichtsgewalt. In: Frei et al. (eds.) (as in fn. 15), pp. 7-15, p. 14.

[17] Voiculescu, Aurora: Human Rights and Political Justice in the Post-Communist Eastern Europe: Prosecuting History. London 2000; Haberer, Erich: History and Justice: Paradigms of the Prosecution of Nazi Crimes. In: Holocaust and Genocide Studies (2005) vol. 19, no. 3, p. 502; Evans, Richard J: "History, Memory, and the Law: The Historian as Expert Witness". In: History and Theory (2002) vol. 41, p. 326; Rousso, Henry: The Haunting Past. Pennsylvania 2002, p. 48.

posed to render judgments on history? Are the historians allowed to question the decisions of the courts? Do those two social practices and realms of experience exclude each other or do they meet? And if they meet, is it on a collision course or in a common endeavor? What is the relationship between the verdict of the court and the judgment of history? What is the verdict of history, and who exactly is the agent of this verdict? Against such confused background, the appearance of historians in the capacity of expert witnesses – seemingly logical aspirants to such an agency by the virtue of their position – was likely to trigger further controversies.

B. Developments in Historical Expert Witnessing

Historians were in a sense always indirectly engaged in the advancing of the cause of justice. The famous mottos of the craft, from Tacitus' *sine ira et studio* to Ranke's *wie es eigentlich gewesen* are unmistakably echoing the historian's commitment to truthful and just interpretation of the past. Historians have therefore provided numerable services by using their skills to reveal false documents and to authenticate legal evidence. (The iconic venture in this respect was Lorenzo Valla's discrediting of the *Donatio Constantini*). Such a role seemed appropriate for historians turned to the constant scrutiny of the authenticity of documents and striving to get the most out of them. This is what they did anyhow, as observed by Marc Bloch: "A document is a witness; and like most witnesses, it does not say much except under cross-examination."[18] As both legal practice and history writing underwent thorough professionalization in the course of the 19th century, this kind of assistance became formalized with first appearances of historians as expert authenticators in various courts, including trials as important and controversial as the Dreyfus case.[19]

---

[18] Bloch, Marc: A Contribution towards a Comparative History of European Societies. In: J.A. Anderson (ed.): Land and Work in Medieval Europe. Berkeley 1967, p. 48.

[19] On the entangled development of the practices see Firedrich, Carl: Law and History. In: Vanderbilt Law Review (1961) vol. XIV, pp. 1027-1048; Kelley, Donald R.: Foundations of Modern Historical Scholarship. Language, Law, and History. New York 1970; Kelley, Donald R.: The Human Measure, Social Thought in the Western Legal Tradition. Cambridge 1990. On the role of

However, this coexistence was eroding in the course of the 20th century. On one hand, historians got more and more engaged in commenting and passing judgments on legal matters, and, on the other hand, the law spread to regulate ever larger domains of human experience. A visible example of divergences between legal and historical logic was the historiographical debate on the responsibility for the outbreak of the First World War.[20] Perhaps because of the heated tone of those debates, the legal aftermath of the Second World War – the Nuremberg trials, styled by Robert Kempner as "the greatest historical seminar ever held" – was a seminar held in the absence of historians.[21] Nevertheless, the Nuremberg trials were a landmark in juridical memory making. Its importance for the reconfiguration of the relationship between history and law was observed by Shoshana Felman:

"Until the middle of the twentieth century, a radical division between history and justice was in principle maintained. The law perceived itself either as ahistorical or expressing a specific stage in society's historical development. But law and history were separate. The courts sometimes acknowledged they were part of history, but they did not judge history as such. This state of affairs has changed since the constitution of the Nuremberg tribunal, which (through the trial of the Nazi leaders as representatives of the historical regime and the historical phenomenon of Nazism) for the first time called history itself into a court of justice … In the wake of Nuremberg, a displacement has occurred in relationship between history and trials. Not only has it become thinkable to put history on trial, it has become judicially necessary to do so."[22]

---

historians in the Dreyfus case see Dumoulin, Olivier: Le rôle social de l'historien: De la chaire au prétoire. Paris 2003.

[20] As the Versailles treaty was bluntly delegating the responsibility solely to the German side, more precisely to the Emperor Wilhelm and the Generalstaff, it intruded upon the traditional realm of historiography, and many historians (not only Germans) retorted by launching a decade long debate about the causes of the First World War. Interesting contributions about the historians' taking on the matter in Wilson, Keith (ed.): Forging the Collective Memory. Oxford 1996.

[21] Robert Kempner, one of the prosecutors in the Nuremberg trials, is quoted in Douglas (as in fn. 7), p. 2.

[22] Felman, Shoshana: The Juridical Unconscious: Trials and Traumas in the Twentieth Century. Cambridge 2002, pp. 11-12.

Such a strong intrusion of the idea that high-profile trials might be utilized to influence the collective memory and history was making utterly unclear what should be a historian's legitimate position on such a venture. The reading of the history of the Second World War, provided both by the indictment and the judgment, haunted historiography for quite some time. Many currents in postwar contemporary historiography – as different as the revisionist movement, the debate between intentionalists and functionalists, and the remoralisation of historiography – could be plausibly linked with the impact of Nuremberg.[23] Among the less observed aspects of the advent of juridical memory making was a visible transformation in the realm of historical expert witnessing. It took about fifteen years after the Nuremberg trials for it to materialize, as historians stepped out of the traditional role of authentication of documents and assumed the much wider function of contextualization of the cases. The debut of the new type of historical expert witnessing could hardly have happened in a more dramatic legal context. It occurred in two generically similar and practically coinciding proceedings paradigmatic for the practice of juridical memory making – the Eichmann trial and the Frankfurt Auschwitz trial.

---

[23] About the influence of the Nuremberg trials on the development of a "conspiratorial view of history", caused by the stress on the responsibility of a handful of accused top Nazi executives, see Shklar (as in fn. 3), pp. 172-173; Osiel (as in fn. 4), pp. 97-100. "The trials succeeded quite well in fixing the public mind that the sole responsibility for the war rested with Hitler." Smith, F. Bradley: The Road to Nuremberg. New York 1981, p. 251. Introduction to various aspects of the debate between intentionalists and functionalists in Kershaw, Ian: The Nazi Dictatorship, Problems and Perspectives. Oxford 2000. In the decades after the trial, historians got in a position to render judgments not just about the war, but also about the proceedings, as is obvious from the title of Bosch, William: Judgment on Nuremberg. Chapell Hill 1970. Many aspects of Nuremberg were subject to criticism. The law, however, retaliated. One of the fiercest critiques of the Nuremberg proceedings, the revisionist David Irving (Nuremberg: The Last Battle. London 1996), is currently serving a prison sentence in Vienna on the grounds of "denying genocide by the National Socialists or other National Socialist crimes against humanity". Turkishpress: Austrian Court Jails British Historian for Holocaust Denial, <www.turkishpress.com/news.asp?id=108907> (accessed on 30.6.2006).

I. The Eichmann Trial

In 1961, in a Jerusalem courtroom, Adolf Eichmann was read 15 counts of indictment, including crimes against Jewish people, crimes against humanity and membership in hostile organizations. In effect, he stood accused of organizing, overseeing and perpetrating the Holocaust. The importance of the trial, and particularly its educational potential, was publicly announced by the Israeli Prime Minister, David Ben Gurion, who considered it an indispensable opportunity "that our youth remember what happened to the Jewish people". The prosecutor, Gideon Hausner, shared this outlook by preparing a trial that would "bring the youth closer to the nation's past".[24] The trial was indeed meant to repeat the Nuremberg judicial memory making venture, but also to revise much of it by stressing the uniqueness of the Holocaust as the crime of crimes of the Nazi regime.

To such an end, the prosecution, in the course of this single criminal trial, embarked on the large task of revealing the development of the anti-Semitic policies in Germany and the mechanism of the annihilation of the Jews. A prominent place in this venture was reserved for a historian from the University of Columbia, Professor Salo Baron, the founder of Jewish studies in the United States.[25] This choice was made in consultations among Ben Gurion, Hausner, the foreign minister Golda Meir and other high ranking government officials, which is very indicative of the importance attached to Baron's intended role.[26] This role was very different from the historians' customary

---

[24] Ben Gurion quoted in: Arendt (as in fn. 2), p. 8; Hausner quoted in: Douglas (as in fn. 7), p. 3. Pedagogical and theatrical aspects of the Eichmann trial are discussed in Felman, Shoshana: Theaters of Justice: Arendt in Jerusalem, the Eichmann Trial, and the Redefinition of Legal Meaning in the Wake of the Holocaust. In: Critical Inquiry (2001) vol. 27, no. 2, pp. 201-240.

[25] More on Baron's life in Liberles, Robert: Salo Wittmayer Baron: Architect of Jewish History. New York 1995. His activity on the trial in ibid., pp. 322-337.

[26] The choice of Baron was bold since his approaches to Jewish history were known as innovatory and nonconformist: Schorsch, Ismar: Chancellor's Parashah Commentary, <http://www.jtsa.edu/community/parashah/archives/5757/behukkotai.shtml> (accessed on 30.6.2006). Ben Gurion noted his concerns in a diary entry: "Concerned about his testimony. I told him that it is important to show to the younger generation (and also to the rest of the world) how great was the qualitative loss in the destruction of six millions …", Quoted in Liberles (as in fn. 25), p. 330.

function as authenticators. Baron was contacted and advised to compile in secrecy no less than the report on the state of European Jewry before and after the Second World War. He came to Jerusalem from his university in an equally secretive manner, waiting for the trial to commence. Baron appeared among the first witnesses for the prosecution, testifying through two lengthy sessions. Being aware of the uniqueness of his role, he began his testimony with a methodological justification of his position:

"I appear here as a witness, not an eye-witness or a jurist, but as a historian. It is known that a historian who studies contemporary history is always confronted with a double problem. The first problem is: Does one already have a historical perspective? Generally, one does not, until the passing of several decades, at least. The second problem is: Does one have documents? These are usually locked away and not available and one does not know about events that happened until 50 years later or more. It seems to me that precisely in this regard, there is a difference. The period before the Second World War is so remote from this generation, and sometimes so forgotten even by people who lived through it, that already, it seems to me, we have a historic perspective which usually is lacking in such cases. And with regard to documents, perhaps we are fortunate in that many of the German archives were captured by the Allies and many of them have already been published. Also many of the participants in these events wrote diaries, autobiographies and so on and the material accumulated at such a pace that there is perhaps need for a vast bibliography, merely to have on record the large number of these manifestations."[27]

This statement of methodological optimism regarding both the heuristic problems and the issue of scholarly distance was followed by the first session of his testimony dedicated to the milieu in which the interwar European Jewry lived. Baron testified with respect to economic conditions, demographical

---

[27] Transcripts of Baron's testimony are available at The Nizkor Project, The Trial of Adolf Eichmann, Session 12 and Session 13, <http://www.nizkor.org/hweb/people/e/eichmann-adolf/transcripts/Sessions/Session-012-03.html> (accessed on 26.6.2006). They were subsequently published in Baron, Salo W.: European Jewry before and after Hitler, Responses at the Eichmann Trial. In: American Jewish Yearbook (1962) vol. 63.

tendencies, cultural contribution and political diversity in various Jewish communities in Europe, underlining "the exceptionally vital and creative force of the Jewish world in Europe of that time".[28] He was also testifying about the pressure under which European Jewry was at the time, providing historical examples of the development of anti-Semitism in Europe, with special emphasis on its extreme emanations in Germany in the thirties. He both stressed the continuity of the anti-Semitic sentiments in the European culture and determined murderous novelties brought about by Nazism.

In the second session, Baron contrasted the previous account with the chilling description of the destruction of the European Jewish communities. He calculated both the factual and the demographic loss in the course of the Holocaust (the factual loss estimated to be 6-7 million and the demographic 8 million people), dramatically claming that "the Jewish people would have now totaled about 20,000,000 souls or more. Instead of 20,000,000 there are 12,000,000."[29] He concluded the testimony by tracking the dynamics of the Nazi conquest of much of Europe and the consequent spillover of their policy of extermination.

Eichmann's name was not mentioned in Baron's account. His purpose was to provide the general context in which the individual criminal responsibility of the accused was to be situated. This prompted one of the observers of the trial, the Dutch writer Harry Mulisch, to comment: "It was longwinded and interesting and professor-like, but I fail to see what does it have to do with Eichmann."[30] The other, more elaborate critical account was offered by no other than Hannah Arendt, otherwise Baron's junior colleague and long-lasting friend. It was given within the overall frame of her criticism of the trial in which, according to her, "it was history that, as far as the prosecution was concerned, stood in the center of the trial". She deplored this for, in her view, it was "bad history and cheap rhetoric. Worse, it was clearly at cross-purposes

---

[28] The Nizkor Project (as in fn. 27), Session 12, Part 4.

[29] The Nizkor Project (as in fn. 27), Session 13, Part 1.

[30] Mulisch, Harry: Criminal Case 40/61, The Trial of Adolf Eichmann: An Eyewitness Account. Philadelphia 2005, pp. 63-64. More favorable eyewitness account: Pearlman, Moshe: The Capture and Trial of Adolf Eichmann. New York 1963, pp. 227-233.

with putting Eichmann on trial …"[31] She concluded that putting Baron on the stand allowed the defense to redirect the attention from Eichmann's individual criminal responsibility to the murky issues of philosophy of history.

And indeed, such a broad contextualization opened up a space for unpleasant lines of questioning in cross-examination, carefully used by Eichmann's lawyer, Dr Robert Servatius. In a protracted conversation with Baron, not deprived of scholarly overtones, filled with references to authors such as Hegel, Spengler, Marx and others, Servatius was dwelling on the subject of agency in history. He attempted to point out, and on occasions even got Baron's support for his views, that large historical events such as the Second World War or genocide cannot be seen exclusively through the lenses of human agency. He was even trying to put forward the idea that, in phenomena such as anti-Semitism, "irrational motives are at the root of the fate of this people, something beyond the understanding of a human being".[32] By implication he also asserted that no single human (not even Eichmann) can bear full responsibility for such dramatic, all-comprising events which are to be seen as history at work. Baron's response exemplified the confused division of labor between the judges and historians:

Witness Baron: "This is not a historical question, but more a legal question. To what extent an individual person who is not a leader is also responsible in the historical sense – there is no doubt that sometimes insignificant people have much more influence on the course of history than their importance to the state warrants."

Presiding Judge: "Why do you refer to this as a legal problem? This is not clear to me."

Witness Baron: "I thought that here there was a question whether there is a distinction between a leader and an ordinary person as to whether he is responsible for changes in history or not."

---

[31] Arendt (as in fn. 2), p. 16.
[32] The Nizkor Project (as in fn. 27), Session 13, Part 2.

Presiding Judge: "Let us perhaps leave that to the jurists."
Witness Baron: "Quite right."[33]

Although such an intervention was of no great relevance for Eichmann's faith (he was sentenced to death and executed), it did point out the dangers of the broad contextualization of the case against an individual perpetrator, and the necessity of balancing the need for a broader background of the case with the issue of legal relevance of such a background for a given case. The judgment was echoing this confusion. It was also reflecting the need of the judges to maintain a clear borderline between the tasks of historians and jurists, mixed with the awareness of the exceptionality of the case at stake:

"The desire was felt – understandable in itself – to give, within the trial, a comprehensive and exhaustive historical description of events which occurred during the Holocaust … There are also those who sought to regard this trial as a forum for the clarification of questions of great import … In this maze of insistent questions, the path of the Court was and remains clear. It cannot allow itself to be enticed into provinces which are outside its sphere. The judicial process has ways of its own, laid down by law, and which do not change, whatever the subject of the trial may be. Otherwise, the processes of law and of court procedure are bound to be impaired, whereas they must be adhered to punctiliously, since they are in themselves of considerable social and educational significance, and the trial would otherwise resemble a rudderless ship tossed about by the waves."[34]

However, despite these restraints, and despite barely mentioning Baron by name, the judgment did introduce much of the context he brought into the courtroom, particularly his findings on the scope of the genocide. His report was, however, used selectively, as the judges could not have been expected to consciously subscribe to the memory making. However, even if his report was

[33] Ibid.
[34] The Nizkor Project, The Trial of Adolf Eichmann, Judgment, <http://www.nizkor.org/hweb/people/e/eichmann-adolf/transcripts/Judgment/Judgment-001.html> (accessed on 30.6.2006).

to be omitted completely, having in mind the publicity the trial gained, its didactic impact would be secured by his mere appearance and the delivery of the testimony. It was this impact Hannah Arendt feared, noting that the "justice demands that the accused be prosecuted, defended and judged, and that all the other questions of seemingly greater importance – of 'How could it happen?' and 'Why did it happen?', of 'Why the Jews?' and 'Why the Germans?' … be left in abeyance".[35]

II. The Frankfurt Auschwitz Trial

Arendt's critical account of the Eichmann trial was published in 1963, which was too late for the Attorney General of Hessen, Fritz Bauer, to read it, as in that year a team working under his supervision completed investigations and presented an indictment against 20 officers and guards of the infamous Auschwitz concentration camp. However, even if he had that chance, he would hardly be influenced by her standpoint, as exactly those questions Arendt was brushing aside were at the center of his attention. Dissatisfied with a stalemate in legal reactions to the crimes against humanity committed in Nazi Germany, he was for some time launching a set of initiatives towards the prosecution of Nazi war criminals. Bauer was not only a persistent promoter of the Eichmann trial in Germany, but he also provided the Israeli government with information on his whereabouts in and requested from the FRG government to demand his extradition to Germany.[36]

As those initiatives were stumbling over the unwillingness of Adenauer's government to open a debate about the recent past, he grew determined to reopen it through a trial he could influence, which came to be known as the Frankfurt Auschwitz trial.[37] "Bauer's intentions were not strictly judicial but

---

[35] Arendt (as in fn. 2), p. 232.

[36] Wojak, Irmtrud: Fritz Bauer: Stationen eines Lebens, <http://www.fritz-bauer-institut.de/texte/essay/07-98_wojak.htm> (accessed on 26.6.2006).

[37] Basic details about the trial in: Renz, Werner: 40 Jahre Auschwitz-Prozess: Ein unerwünschtes Verfahren, <http://www.fritz-bauer-institut.de/texte/essay/12-03_renz.htm> (accessed on 26.6.2006); Wittmann, Rebecca: Beyond Justice. The Auschwitz Trial. Cambridge, Mass. 2005; Pendas, Devin: Frankfurt Auschwitz Trial, 1963-1965: Genocide, History, and the Limits of the

more broadly historical as well. Quite explicitly, beyond his concern with individual cases, Bauer wanted to bring to task a whole era, an entire ideology."[38] Such a motivation, being similar to the ones of Ben Gurion and Hausner, brought about a similar result – the prosecution commissioned expert reports, as early as 1961, from historians of the Institute for Contemporary History in Munich.[39] Not just the idea, but also the very scope of the initiative was a novelty, and it was not by chance that the Institute for Contemporary History provided the experts. The Institute was among the new scholarly institutions (formed in 1949) dedicated exactly to the research of the Nazi period.

The reports were presented in the Frankfurt Auschwitz trial by Helmut Krasunik (*The Persecution of the Jews*), Hans Buchheim (*The SS – Instrument of Domination* and *Command and Compliance*), Martin Broszat (*The Concentration Camps 1933-1945* and *National-socialist Policy towards the Poles*) and Hans-Adolf Jacobsen (*The Commisionars Order and Mass Executions of Soviet Russian Prisoners of War*).[40] In another analogy with Baron's testimony, the reports did not mention the accused at all. In the introduction to the subsequent volume, the authors explained why, by defining the role of a historian as an expert witness in the following way:

Law. New York 2005. On the historians' contribution in the Auschwitz trial: Wojak, Irmtrud: "Die Verschmelzung von Geschichte und Kriminologie. Historische Gutachten im ersten Frankfurter Auschwitz-Prozess". In Frei et al. (eds.) (as in fn. 15), pp. 29-45.

[38] Wittmann (as in fn. 37), pp. 64-65. Although Bauer was not the prosecutor in this case, his role in it cannot be underestimated. The full list of the judges, prosecutors, advocates, accused and witnesses in: Fritz Bauer Institute: Register zum Frankfurter Auschwitz-Prozess, <http://www.fritz-bauer-institut.de/auschwitz-prozess/pdf/auschwitz-prozess.pdf> (accessed on 26.6.2006).

[39] It remains to be confirmed whether Baron's performance at the Eichmann trial gave Bauer this idea. The chronology opens up the possibility that it might have been the other way around. It is also possible that there was no direct influence and that the outcome was directly conditioned by the pedagogical purposes of both prosecutors. Also, Bauer could have been influenced by a less noted precedence to the practice in Germany. Hans-Günther Seraphim made a report on the inner structure of the SS and its cleansing actions in the Ulm Einsatzkommando trial. Wittmann (as in fn. 37), p. 79.

[40] All of the reports were subsequently published and still present a seminal historiographical reading: Buchheim, Hans et al., Anatomie des SS-Staates, I-II. München 1967. Quotations are taken from the English version: Krausnick, Helmut et al.: Anatomy of the SS State. New York 1968.

"The case of an accused who took part in these crimes can only be judged rightly if the whole moral, political and organizational background leading to his actions is surveyed. The task of historical expert is to assist the Court by painting as clearly as possible a picture of this background. He is not there to concern himself with the case of any particular accused … It is for the expert to provide a picture of the historical and political landscape in which each individual occurrence took place …"[41]

Hence, similar to the Eichmann trial, the historians assumed the role of providing the context. They were also aware that they took part in a rare venture: "For this reason during these trials of the National Socialist criminals, it has been thought advisable, contrary to normal Court procedure, to hear experts *before* the witnesses."[42] They justified such an elevated position by stressing a cautious methodological optimism:

"When presenting the history of National Socialist period to the Court of Justice, a special effort must be made to do so rationally and dispassionately, for the facts presented are not merely the subject of an historical analysis which commits no one, but may have a decisive influence on the fate of the accused."[43]

How decisive was this influence in reality? The Frankfurt court, just as the Jerusalem one, was forced to balance the broadness of the historical approach, no matter how desired by the prosecution, with the duty to render justice to individual perpetrators. The issue of the relevance of the historical contribution reappeared in a dilemma summarized by Rebecca Wittman:

"One could argue that the entire historical background given in the indictment was irrelevant to the charges, and in many ways, it was; however, it

[41] Krausnick (as in fn. 40), p. xiii
[42] Krausnick (as in fn. 40), pp. xiii-xiv.
[43] Krausnick (as in fn. 40), pp. xiv-xv.

makes sense that the courts decided that some form of explanatory overview was necessary for trying crimes of this nature."[44]

The court took the middle way, admitting and commending all the reports as "well-founded and convincing" but not reflecting much on them in the core of the judgment. More general reports, as Broszat's The Concentration Camps and Buchheim's The SS – Instrument of Domination, served as a basis for the short opening part of the judgment. The elements of other reports were sporadically used in its second part, related to the Auschwitz extermination camp. However, the degree of the responsibility of the individual accused, dealt with in the central, third part of the judgment, was assessed in the light of material evidence and the testimonies of eye-witnesses.[45]

Although, in the German legal context, some of Arendt's concerns were irrelevant, as there was no cross-examination of witnesses which might challenge the views or findings of the experts, the exposure of this group of historians brought their work to the attention of the public. Some of the reports were crushing entrenched myths of postwar German society. The murderous mechanism of the concentration camps and the diabolic role of the SS was exposed in Broszat's and Buchheim's report, restating much of what was already known and accepted in German public, presented through the activity of the Nuremberg trials, in Eugen Kogon's book *The SS State* and in other works.[46] However, some of the reports were presenting new findings: Krausnick's report outlined the scope, extent and uniqueness of the Nazi extermination campaign against the Jews. Jacobsen's report was tracking the practice of the killing of prisoners of war by the Wehrmacht as well as by the SS. The other Buchheim report was delivering the decisive blow to the "obeying orders" defense, by stressing the readiness of soldiers to comply with criminal commands.

---

[44] Wittmann (as in fn. 37), p. 108.

[45] Auschwitz-Process-Urteil, <http://www.idgr.de/texte/dokumente/justiz/auschwitz-urteil.php> (accessed on 30.6.2006). Such an approach was disappointing to many. Bauer was criticizing the lack of connection of the accused to the mass murder, and Kogon was criticizing the lack of readiness to plunge into the contemporary history of Germany.

[46] Kogon, Eugen: Der SS Staat. Stockholm 1947.

Such spotlight was prone to attract criticism in which methodological concerns were hard to disentangle from political disapproval. The legal scholar and jurist Ernst Forsthoff particularly addressed the issue, critically labeling historical expert witnessing as an example of "forensic historicism". He asserted that, as the historiography is subject to changes introduced by new research, it is unsuitable for the courtroom purposes. Forsthoff claimed that such utilization of contemporary historiography amounts to its politization.[47] Interestingly enough, his criticism was methodologically echoing Arendtian concerns with a completely different political agenda in mind. In one of the recent reassessments, on the contrary, the reports have been criticized exactly for shielding behind scholarly objectivity.[48] However, despite the criticism, the reports exceeded their courtroom purpose and still stand for seminal readings on the history of the Third Reich, most probably because they were more limited and targeted than Salo Baron's forensic contribution to the Eichmann trial.

C. From Authentication to Contextualization: Towards the Genealogy of Historical Expert Witnessing

The resemblances between the engagement of historians in the Eichmann trial and the Frankfurt Auschwitz trial are striking, and their connection with

---

[47] Forsthoff, Ernst: Der Zeithistoriker als gerichtlicher Sachverständiger. In: Neue Juristische Wochenschrift (1965) vol. 13, pp. 574-75. On Forsthoff's position and motivation Van Laak, Dirk: Widerstand gegen die Geschichtsgewalt. In: Frei et al. (eds.) (as in fn. 15), pp. 16-25.

[48] Berg, Nicolas: Der Holocaust und die westdeutschen Historiker: Erforschung und Erinnerung. Göttingen 2003. Berg was examining, among other things, the political standpoints of the experts themselves, suggesting that the reports were lacking sensitivity towards the uniqueness of the program of annihilation of the Jews. The debate between Berg and Hans Buchheim, one of the expert witnesses, over the ways to approach the crimes against humanity and the relationship between historical research and remembrance in: Buchheim, Hans: Zur öffentlichen Auseinandersetzung mit dem Verbrechen gegen die Menschheit, < http://www.fritz-bauer-institut.de/texte/essay/10-02_buchheim.htm> (accessed on 30.6.2006.); Berg, Nicolas: Gedächtnis und Perspektivität. Auch das Nachdenken über Nationalsozialismus und Holocaust ist nicht anders als historisch zu verstehen. Eine Antwort auf Hans Buchheim, <http://www.fritz-bauer-institut.de/ texte/essay/04-03_berg.htm> (accessed on 30.6.2006).

juridical memory making seems obvious. In both cases the prosecution was striving towards a landmark historical trial supposed to send a powerful message to the world. In both cases, such a task was calling for a wide assessment of the political context in which the crimes of the accused occurred – in effect, for a comprehensive history of the Third Reich. Both prosecutors estimated that the appropriate way to provide such a context was an expert opinion, and they called upon historical scholarship to produce it. In both cases reputed historians came forth with expert reports, providing the overall background for the case, leaving out entirely the activities of the accused. In both cases, the reports were taken as evidence and were selectively incorporated into the judgments. Finally, in both cases this practice drew considerable attention as well as sharp criticism. The historians left their auxiliary role of authenticators of documents and moved into the spotlight of the courtroom.

How can this transformation be interpreted? Going back to the entangled relationship between law and history offers a promising avenue. The transformation occurred in a sensitive junction between the postwar advent of juridical memory making and the developments in contemporary historiography. Pursuing the pedagogical effect of the trials, the prosecutors in Jerusalem and Frankfurt were reaching out for the historical context provided by specialists. Whereas the Nuremberg trials were held in the absence of historians, two decades after the start of the Second World War, there were already solid results of historical scholarship on the issue. It is not an accident that both Baron and the experts of the Institute for Contemporary History emphasized the heuristic uniqueness in this field. The idea that historians could legitimately explore their own epoch was enabled by the unprecedented availability of historical sources, disclosed on the Nuremberg trial, published in various government-sponsored editions, printed in memoirs of the protagonists or seized and made available by the victorious Allied forces. The creation of new institutions to facilitate this interest provided the necessary infrastructure for the new role of historians.[49] More importantly, the atrocities of the Second

[49] Among surprisingly rare overviews of this development: Watt, Donald Cameron (ed.): Contemporary History in Europe. London 1969; Seldon, Anthony (ed.): Contemporary History. Practice and Method. New York 1988.

World War prompted the remoralisation of historiography and have contributed to the collapse of the implicit theory of distance in historical scholarship. In the light of an unprecedented horror, the responsibility of the historian was redefined. The prosecutors used this opportunity to introduce historians into the venture of juridical memory making. The established cooperation was a good example of what Erich Haberer called "the Nuremberg paradigm in prosecuting war crimes".[50] The Eichmann case and the Auschwitz trial are indispensable examples of the influence of judicial memory making on the shift in the courtroom role of historians.

It is tempting to extend this conclusion to contemporary legal developments. After all, as Shoshana Felman notes,

> "Nuremberg did not intend, but has in fact produced, this conceptual evolution that implicitly affects all later trials, and not only the tradition of war crimes and of international criminal law. In the second half of the twentieth century, it has become part of the function of trials to repair judicially not only private but also collective historical injustices."[51]

And indeed, in the last two decades historians participated in a number of prominent trials (the Zündel case in Canada, Sears vs. EEOC in the United States, the cases of Barbie, Touvier and Papon in France, David Irving vs. Deborah Lipstadt in United Kingdom, the Jaruzelski trial in Poland, the Milošević trial and other cases at the ICTY), causing a set of disconnected, yet very telling debates about the merits of the practice.[52] The connection between their role, the revival of public interest in the Second World War and

[50] Haberer (as in fn. 17), p. 1.

[51] Felman (as in fn. 22), p. 12.

[52] They have been equally active in a number of governmental or non-governmental commissions and restitution or rehabilitation initiatives. One of the recent reviews of the transformation: Fink, Carole: A New Historian? In: Contemporary European History (2005) vol. 14 I, pp. 135-147.

the increased sensitivity towards human rights violations is aptly noted both by proponents and opponents of the practice of historical expert witnessing.[53]

However, although the proliferation of historical expert witnessing in recent years could plausibly be connected to the spreading of transitional justice concepts and the growing legitimacy of juridical memory making ventures, establishing a straight line between the Nuremberg and Eichmann cases, the Frankfurt Auschwitz trial and recent legal developments would not do full justice to the complexity of the phenomenon. It has to be taken into account that the practice proliferated to an extent which makes it increasingly difficult to track its various emanations. Historians appear both for the prosecution and for the defense, in criminal and civil trials, in national and international courts, in common law and continental law jurisdictions, delivering testimonies on very different topics. In such a rich landscape, there is no easy way to give meaning to the changes of the role of forensic historians. What is at stake is not writing a comprehensive history of historical expert witnessing. It is necessary to form a dialogue capable of maintaining the integrity of the phenomenon, while remaining sensitive to the different contexts in which it emerges, as well as perceptive towards the mutual influences. Such an approach could be a starting point for a viable genealogy of historical expert witnessing, lending it the necessary cohesion, yet providing it with the flexibility needed.

---

[53] Evans (as in fn. 17), p. 326 notes: "Since the beginning of the 1990's there has been a widespread recovery of public memory." Rousso (as in fn. 17), p. 50 echoes: "This judicialization of the past very much belongs to the 'age of memory'."

Steuerung des Erinnerns und Vergessens?Archivische Bewertung von Schriftgut der Justiz

Nicolas Rügge

A. Einführung

Die Justiz organisiert ihr Erinnern und Vergessen nicht zuletzt mit Hilfe von Fristen.[1] Während des Geschäftsgangs bringen Fristsetzungen das Verfahren voran und sorgen für die Wiedervorlage der Akten. Ist das Verfahren erledigt, wird die Akte „weggelegt"; sie wandert von der Geschäftsstelle in die „Altregistratur" und tritt damit in ein Zwischenstadium von Erinnern und Vergessen ein: Der Vorgang ist aus dem aktuellen Justizgedächtnis getilgt, kann aber bei Bedarf neu erinnert werden. Wie lange die Akte jetzt noch verwahrt wird, bestimmt wiederum eine Frist, deren Dauer sich im Wesentlichen nach der Verjährung richtet. Daher müssen zum Beispiel, wenn die Masse der Zivilprozeßakten schon nach fünf Jahren vernichtet wird, die vollstreckbaren Titel, Urteile usw. entnommen und in Form einer Urteilssammlung 30 Jahre lang aufbewahrt werden. Mit Hilfe ihres Fristensystems kann die Justiz also präzise angeben, wann sie ein Verfahren dem Vergessen anheimgeben kann. An diesem Punkt kommen die zuständigen staatlichen Archive ins Spiel und entscheiden, ob tatsächlich das Vergessen eintritt oder aber die Verfahrensakte – und damit die Einzelheiten des Verfahrens – dauerhaft erinnerbar bleiben.

Diese Rollenverteilung ist noch relativ jung. Zwar kannten auch das ältere deutsche und erst recht das römische Recht bereits Fristen und Verjährungen.[2] Doch zumindest im „Heiligen Römischen Reich Deutscher Nation" mit

---

[1] Dank für kritische Lektüre an Stephanie Haberer, Martina Wiech und Karl H. L. Welker.

[2] Vgl. nur die zahlreichen Artikel zur Verjährung in Zedlers Universal-Lexicon Bd. 47. Leipzig, 1746 Sp. 854-922; allgemein geläufig ist aus dem deutschen Recht die Wendung von „Jahr und Tag", nach deren Ablauf ein ursprünglich eigenbehöriger Stadtbewohner als frei zu gelten hatte.

seinem komplizierten Rechtsgefüge behielten traditionale Vorstellungen und partikulares Privilegienrecht ein hohes Gewicht. Ansprüche gründeten sich nicht selten auf das Herkommen und ererbte Besitztitel, daher taugten selbst – und manchmal gerade – die ältesten Dokumente als Beweismittel. Weil man nicht vorhersehen konnte, wann die Urkunden und Akten ihre rechtliche Relevanz verloren[3], hob man sie eben auf[4] und bildete daraus „Archive" als Arsenale der wahrgenommenen oder beanspruchten rechtlichen, sozialen und politischen Stellung.

Diese vormoderne Rechtsordnung wurde in Deutschland im Lauf des 19. Jahrhunderts beseitigt. Zunächst verschwanden wesentliche Institutionen, die das bisherige Recht konstituiert hatten: das Alte Reich und das Reichskammergericht, auch viele Territorialstaaten und kleinere Herrschaften mit ihren Gerichten und Universitäten. Die Bestrebungen zur Rechtseinheit im Zivilrecht mündeten schließlich erst 1900 in die Einführung des Bürgerlichen Gesetzbuches. Schon zuvor hielten in den Städten die Gewerbeordnung und allgemeine Einwohnerrechte Einzug, auf dem Land wurde die tausend Jahre alte Grundherrschaft abgebaut. Die bis dahin gehüteten Dokumente der vergangenen Ordnung wurden nun wertlos. Genauer gesagt, büßten sie ihre praktische hoheitliche und rechtliche Bedeutung ein, gewannen dafür aber (wenigstens zum Teil) einen neuen „historischen" Wert hinzu.

In genau diesem Sinn läßt sich ein fundamentaler Funktionsverlust – oder eben: Funktionswandel – der damaligen „Archive" feststellen: von der herrschaftlichen Schatzkammer zum Fundus historischer Erfahrungen. Was z.B.

---

[3] Schwer kalkulierbar war nicht nur das Gewirr von Rechtsnormen, sondern auch die Macht der Parteien. Vgl. als Fallbeispiel Bei der Wieden, Helge: Grundherrliche Ansprüche auf den Nachlaß eines ehemals leibeigenen Bürgers der Stadt Lübeck im Ausgang des 17. Jahrhunderts. In: Das Gedächtnis der Hansestadt Lübeck. Festschrift für Antjekathrin Graßmann zum 65. Geburtstag. Hrsg. von Rolf Hammel-Kiesow und Michael Hundt. Lübeck 2005, S. 361-370. Der preußische König Friedrich II. nahm um 1770 die absolutistisch-zentralistischen „Ratsreformen" seines Vaters teilweise zurück und ließ zu diesem Zweck die westfälischen Städte – zu deren Überraschung – ihre alten, teils noch niederdeutsch verfaßten Privilegien einreichen; vgl. Rügge, Nicolas: Im Dienst von Stadt und Staat. Der Rat der Stadt Herford und die preußische Zentralverwaltung im 18. Jahrhundert. Göttingen 2000, S. 117 f.

[4] Nur weil sich die Frage nach Aufbewahrungsfristen nicht stellte, sind überhaupt zahlreiche ältere Protokoll- und Prozeßserien bis heute erhalten geblieben.

ein Landadliger in seinem Gutsarchiv aufbewahrte, um die Rechte über seine eigenbehörigen Bauern zu wahren, war noch 1848 von deren gewaltsamem Zugriff und symbolträchtiger Vernichtung bedroht.[5] Nach Abwicklung der Grundherrschaft jedoch schienen viele Dokumente nur noch ‚Muster ohne Wert' zu sein[6] – erst später sollten Historiker darin wertvolle sozial- und rechtsgeschichtliche Quellen entdecken.

Mit dieser Zäsur sind die Archive in ihrer heutigen Bedeutung erst entstanden. Ganz verschwunden ist die ältere Funktion damit allerdings nicht. Denn neben dem Schriftgut, das „nur noch" historischen Wert hat, hüten sie auch solche Dokumente, die für ihren Träger – im Fall der staatlichen Archive in Deutschland: den Bund und die Länder – von dauerhafter Bedeutung sind. Das können z.B. ältere Staatsverträge sein, die man kaum noch zur Hand nehmen muß, die aber weiterhin wirksam sind und staatliche Rechtsansprüche begründen, oder Vorläufe zu beschlossenen Gesetzen, die die Rechtmäßigkeit des Verfahrens dokumentieren und die zu bedenkenden Gesichtspunkte für den Fall späterer Novellen festhalten. Dazu gehören auch die Grundbücher und Grundakten: Der Rechtsanspruch auf Grundbuchberichtigung verjährt nicht, daher gewährleisten diese Unterlagen Rechtssicherheit auf nicht absehbare Zeit und sind von Justiz wegen „dauernd aufzubewahren". Insofern haftet den Staatsarchiven doch noch ein wenig von der fürstlichen Schatzkammer an. Doch was ihre spezifisch moderne Funktion angeht, verfolgt die Archive das Problem der „Bewertung": Welche Unterlagen sind die mühsame und teure Anstrengung wert, nach Erledigung ihres Entstehungszwecks nicht vernichtet, sondern dauerhaft aufbewahrt zu werden?

---

[5] Vgl. zum Überblick Wehler, Hans-Ulrich: Deutsche Gesellschaftsgeschichte Bd. 2. München, 1987 p. 709.

[6] So trug im 19. Jh. der Archivar des Guts Hünnefeld im Osnabrücker Land bezüglich eines „Convolut(s) enthaltend: alte, unleserliche Kaufbriefe, Obligationen und dergleichen, auch Freibriefe, Eigengebungsbriefe (...)" in eine der aktuellen rechtlichen Bedeutung gewidmeten Bemerkungsspalte ein: „Alles ohne Werth! Allenfalls zur Nachricht, wie solche Documente früher ausgefertigt worden, aufzubewahren" (Niedersächsisches Landesarchiv – Staatsarchiv Osnabrück, Dep 24 b I, Findbuch S. 287 f.).

B. Archivische Bewertung: vom Altpapier zur Quelle

Die Notwendigkeit der Bewertung bedarf keiner langen Begründung. Wer die Masse und Aussagekraft moderner Akten kennt, kann schwerlich dafür plädieren, die gesamte Schriftgutproduktion der Verwaltung und Justiz zu archivieren. Dagegen spricht übrigens auch der Datenschutz, der die Archive dazu verpflichtet, alle Unterlagen, denen nicht mit gutem Grund ein bleibender Wert zugeschrieben werden kann, der Vernichtung und also dem Vergessen anheimzugeben – insofern kann geradezu von einem (Grund-) ‚Recht auf Vergessen' gesprochen werden.

Doch erst allmählich haben die Archivare bemerkt, welche praktische und theoretische Herausforderung das Bewertungsproblem darstellt. Im 19. Jahrhundert wandelte sich mit der Funktion auch das Berufsbild. Hatten anfangs fast ausschließlich Juristen die staatlichen Archive geleitet, etablierte sich der Beruf zunehmend als historischer, im engeren Sinn als mediävistischer. Zum bevorzugten Tätigkeitsfeld wurden Urkundeneditionen, dagegen verwendete man auf die laufenden Übernahmen jüngeren (Massen-) Schriftguts aus der „lebenden" Verwaltung weniger Zeit und Gedanken. Vorherrschend blieb noch lange Zeit das Selbstbild des Historiker-Archivars, der die Archivwürdigkeit einer jüngeren Akte ohne besondere Reflexion aus seiner Erfahrung und seinem „Fingerspitzengefühl" heraus zu erkennen meinte.

Ganz so theoriefeindlich ist das archivische Denken inzwischen nicht mehr. Im Rahmen dieses Beitrags kann die internationale Diskussion leider nicht angemessen dargestellt werden, erst recht wäre ein Vergleich der Bewertungspraxis unterschiedlicher Länder ein Forschungsthema für sich. Es gibt ein mehrsprachiges Handbuch der Archivterminologie,[7] das nationale Besonderheiten ahnen läßt, und wahrscheinlich wird man sich auf dem Weg zu einer künftigen europäischen Archivgesetzgebung eingehend mit diesen Fragen beschäftigen müssen.[8] An dieser Stelle genüge der Hinweis, daß international e-

---

[7] Menne-Haritz, Angelika: Schlüsselbegriffe der Archivterminologie. Lehrmaterialien für das Fach Archivwissenschaft. 3. Aufl. Marburg 2000.

[8] Ansätze zu einer europäischen Normierung sind derzeit v.a. auf dem Gebiet der Datenzugangs- oder Informationsgesetze zu erkennen. Vgl. Rumschöttel, Hermann: Das allgemeine Informationszugangsrecht zwischen Datenschutz, Archivgesetzen, Amtsgeheimnis und Verwaltungseffi-

her Modelle einer Kontinuität der Datenverwendung in Verwaltung und Archiven vorherrschen,[9] während die deutsche Tradition eine scharfe Zäsur zwischen beiden postuliert. Den Zwischenschritt der praktischen ,Wertlosigkeit' sehen andere Länder so radikal nicht – vielleicht mit bedingt durch eine kontinuierlichere Verfassungs- und Rechtsgeschichte?

Nach der in Deutschland prägenden Vorstellung werden die ins Archiv gelangenden Akten für ihren neuen Zweck geradezu „umgewidmet".[10] Auf den Begriff gebracht hat diese Lehre der einflußreiche amerikanische Archivar Theodore Schellenberg (1903-1970): Er unterschied grundlegend zwischen dem „Primärwert" (primary value) der Akten für die Entstehungsbehörde und ihrem „Sekundärwert" (secondary value) für andere Nutzer, der erst die Ar-

---

zienz. In: Der Zugang zu Verwaltungsinformationen – Transparenz als archivische Dienstleistung. Hrsg. von Nils Brübach. Marburg 2000, S. 199-207; Schäfer, Udo: Die deutsche Gesetzgebung im Sog nationaler und supranationaler Transparenzregelungen in Europa. Ebd., S. 209-225; Polley, Rainer: Die gesetzgeberische Entwicklung zum dem Akteneinsichts- und Informationszugangsgesetz in Brandenburg und zu den Informationsfreiheitsgesetzen in Berlin und in Schleswig-Holstein. Ebd., S. 227-243; Klein, Michael: Informationsgesetze und Archive – Das Beispiel Berlin. In: Archivgesetzgebung in Deutschland – Ungeklärte Rechtsfragen und neue Herausforderungen. Hrsg. von Rainer Polley. Marburg 2003, S. 99-114, hier 112 f.; Riemann, Frank: Die Transparenz der Europäischen Union. Das neue Recht auf Zugang zu Dokumenten von Parlament, Rat und Kommission. Berlin 2004.

[9] Dem entsprechen vor allem die Konzepte des „life-cycle" (,Lebenslauf' der Akten mit ,Ruhestand' im Archiv) und zuletzt des „records continuum" (nicht einmal Phasenfolge, sondern gleichbleibende Qualität der Aufzeichnungen). Die unscharfe Grenze zwischen Verwaltung und Archiv macht diese Ansätze attraktiv für die Beschreibung der Herausforderungen, die der Einsatz digitaler Systeme für die Zusammenarbeit im ,vorarchivischen' Feld bedeutet. Vgl. Metzdorf, Jens: Aufgeweckte Wächter. Die internationale Diskussion um elektronische Aufzeichnungen, Postkustoden und archivarische Verantwortung. In: Der Zugang zu Verwaltungsinformationen – Transparenz als archivische Dienstleistung. Hrsg. von Nils Brübach. Marburg 2000, S. 29-39. Zum internationalen Überblick: Shepherd, Elizabeth: Theories of appraisal (1997), online unter http://www.ucl.ac.uk/~uczcw09/appraisl/level1.htm; Cook, Terry: What is Past is Prologue: A History of Archival Ideas Since 1898, and the Future Paradigm Shift. In: Archivaria 43 (1997/98), S. 17-63; Craig, Barbara: Archival Appraisal. Theory and Practice. München 2004.

[10] Menne-Haritz, Angelika: Archivische Bewertung. Der Prozess der Umwidmung von geschlossenem Schriftgut zu auswertungsbereitem Archivgut. In: Schweizerische Zeitschrift für Geschichte 51 (2001), S.448-460.

chivwürdigkeit begründe.[11] Unter den sekundären Werten, d.h. den Bewertungsmaßstäben, trennt Schellenberg wiederum die „evidential values",[12] die als Nachweise über Existenz und Aufgabenerledigung der Entstehungsbehörde dienen, von den sachlichen „Informationswerten" (informational values) unterschiedlichster Art. Mit dieser Dichotomie[13] – zwischen der Überlieferung der Behördentätigkeit vs. der relevanten Inhalte – hat es jeder Archivar bei seiner Bewertungsaufgabe zu tun, die im Folgenden bezogen auf die Justiz konkreter betrachtet werden soll.

C. Aussonderung von Schriftgut bei der Justiz

Ob eine Justizakte als Archivgut ins Staatsarchiv übernommen wird oder nicht, entscheidet sich in der Regel zum Zeitpunkt der „Aussonderung" nach Ablauf der Aufbewahrungsfrist. Der Zeitraum, den das Schriftgut nach Erledigung noch „abliegen" muß, steht in den bundesweit geltenden Aufbewahrungsbestimmungen der Justiz verzeichnet.[14]

---

[11] Schellenberg, Theodore R.: Akten- und Archivwesen in der Gegenwart. Theorie und Praxis. Übers. von Gudrun Banzhaf, durchges. von Ernst Posner u. Georg Winter, München [1960], S. 16, 28-31, 131 ff. Der Abschnitt über die Bewertungsmaßstäbe (S. 131 ff.) wurde neu übersetzt und herausgegeben von Angelika Menne-Haritz unter dem Titel: Die Bewertung modernen Verwaltungsschriftguts. Marburg 1990. Die Unterscheidung von „primär" und „sekundär" drückt nach Schellenberg nur die zeitliche Abfolge aus, keineswegs einen Rangunterschied.

[12] Über die Interpretation und Gewichtung dieses Begriffs ist unter deutschen Archivaren viel diskutiert und gestritten worden. Die deutsche Fassung von 1960 spricht vom „Beweiswert", während A. Menne-Haritz den Terminus „Evidenz(wert)" wählte und mit weitergehender theoretischer Bedeutung auflud (Evidenz als Niederschlag der Entscheidungsprozesse und Entstehungszusammenhänge, die, ins Zentrum der Bewertungsüberlegungen gerückt, für eine auswertungsoffene Quellenüberlieferung sorge, während eine auf inhaltlichen „Informationswerten" beruhende Bewertung die Archivbestände zu Dokumentationen bekannter Tatsachen degradiere).

[13] Dazu neuerdings anregend aus systemtheoretischer Perspektive: Pilger, Andreas und Kathrin: Die Bewertung von Verwaltungsschriftgut als Beobachtung zweiter Ordnung. In: Der Archivar 56 (2003), S. 111-118.

[14] Bestimmungen über die Aufbewahrungsfristen für das Schriftgut der ordentlichen Gerichtsbarkeit, der Staatsanwaltschaften und der Justizvollzugsbehörden (in der geltenden Fassung von 2004, dazu gibt es einen Erlaß für die Fachgerichte außer der Arbeitsgerichtsbarkeit).

An Vorschriften sind außerdem die länderspezifischen Archivgesetze zu nennen, die den Archiven den Rahmen ihrer Arbeit definieren, und die ebenfalls von den Bundesländern erlassenen Aussonderungsbestimmungen, die der Justiz konkreter das Verfahren vorgeben, wie mit ihren Unterlagen nach Ablauf der Fristen umzugehen ist. Nach dem niedersächsischen Archivgesetz[15] ist „Archivgut ... das Schriftgut, das von bleibendem Wert für die Erfüllung öffentlicher Aufgaben, für die Sicherung berechtigter privater Interessen oder für die Forschung ist" (§ 2 Abs. 2). Weitere inhaltliche Vorgaben werden der Bewertung nicht gemacht, klargestellt wird allein die Entscheidungskompetenz: „Das zuständige Staatsarchiv stellt fest, welches Schriftgut Archivgut ... ist" (§ 3 Abs. 4). Die Behörden „bieten" die Unterlagen nur „an".

Dieses Anbietungsverfahren ist in den Aussonderungsbestimmungen der niedersächsischen Justiz näher geregelt.[16] Für die Bewertungsfrage ist vor allem interessant, auf welche Weise die Justizbehörden den Archiven bei der Vorauswahl des Schriftguts helfen sollen. Archivwürdiges Schriftgut ist demnach insbesondere zu finden in:

a) Verfahren, die für die Rechtsverhältnisse oder die Verwaltung der öffentlich-rechtlichen Anstalten und Körperschaften von wesentlicher Bedeutung sind
b) Rechtsvorgängen mit bedeutsamen Unterlagen über die Entwicklung von Wissenschaft, Kunst, Literatur, Massenmedien und Sport
c) Rechtsvorgängen von Bedeutung für die Geschichte der politischen Parteien, Gewerkschaften, Arbeitgebervereinigungen usw.
d) Verfahren, an denen natürliche oder juristische Personen beteiligt waren, die im Gerichtsbezirk oder darüber hinaus von Bedeutung waren oder sind,

---

[15] Niedersächsisches Archivgesetz vom 25. Mai 1993 (Nds. Gesetz- und Verordnungsblatt Nr. 18/1993, S. 129-131). Die Archivgesetze der Bundesländer weichen in Einzelheiten voneinander ab, lehnen sich aber in den Grundsatzfragen an das erste, das Bundesarchivgesetz vom 6. Januar 1988 an. Vgl. zu den unterschiedlichen Bestimmungen über die Bewertung: Polley, Rainer, Die archivische Bewertung als Gegenstand einer komparativen Normenanalyse – Ein programmatisches Anliegen. In: Neue Perspektiven archivischer Bewertung. Hrsg. von Frank M. Bischoff und Robert Kretzschmar. Marburg 2005, S. 145-188.
[16] Veröffentlicht in: Niedersächsische Rechtspflege 51 (1997), S. 3-5.

Verfahren, an denen bekannte Persönlichkeiten des öffentlichen Lebens beteiligt waren sowie Verfahren, die öffentliches Aufsehen erregt oder zu parlamentarischen Erörterungen geführt haben
e) Strafverfahren mit politischem Bezug sowie Strafverfahren, die Umweltdelikte, Wirtschaftskriminalität, organisierte Kriminalität, Kapitalverbrechen oder Probleme spezifischer Bevölkerungsgruppen betreffen.

Nach diesen Kriterien soll jeder Sachbearbeiter nach Erledigung eines Verfahrens dessen Archivwürdigkeit beurteilen und auf dem Aktendeckel ankreuzen: „archivwürdig ja/nein".[17] Allerdings wird allzu selten „ja" gekennzeichnet, sicher auch aus Unsicherheit hinsichtlich der erwünschten Vorauswahl. Zwar weiß ein Richter, Staatsanwalt oder Rechtspfleger, ob er es mit „Prominenten" zu tun hat und ob sein Fall in der Zeitung steht. Fraglich ist hingegen, ob er die übrigen Kriterien beurteilen kann und wird – wer beispielsweise in Asyl- oder Jugendstrafkammern arbeitet, hat unentwegt mit „Probleme(n) spezifischer Bevölkerungsgruppen" zu tun. Dennoch bleiben die Archive auf die Vor- und Mitarbeit der Justizbehörden angewiesen, gerade weil die großen Fallaktenserien insbesondere der Zivil- (Registerzeichen C bzw. O) und Strafverfahren (Js/UJs) schwieriger zu bewerten sind als die in anderen Verwaltungszweigen überwiegenden, nach Aufgabengebiet und Federführung analysierbaren Sachakten. Im beiderseitigen Interesse arbeiten daher Staatsarchive und Justiz daran, ihre Kommunikation zu intensivieren und zu effektiveren Verfahren zu gelangen.[18]

[17] Ebd., Nummer 2. Die Kennzeichnung und Anbietung ist nicht erforderlich bei einer Reihe von Aktentypen, für welche die Staatsarchive von vornherein erklärt haben, daß dort keine archivwürdigen Unterlagen zu erwarten sind (diese sog. Verzichtskataloge ebd. S. 7 als Anlagen 2-5).
[18] So können Mitarbeiter(innen) der betreuten Stellen zu „Behördentagen" oder Führungen ins Archiv eingeladen werden und umgekehrt Archivar(inn)e(n) für ihre Anliegen in Dienstbesprechungen oder Fortbildungsveranstaltungen werben. Vgl. Kluttig, Thekla: Strategien und Spielräume archivischer Behördenberatung. In: Der Zugang zu Verwaltungsinformationen – Transparenz als archivische Dienstleistung. Hrsg. von Nils Brübach. Marburg 2000, S. 147-154, hier 149 f.

D. Bewertung von Justizschriftgut

Der Umgang der deutschen Staatsarchive mit den Justizakten basiert auf den Ergebnissen einer Arbeitsgruppe von staatlichen Archivaren, die sich in den 1990er Jahren intensiv mit dieser Überlieferung beschäftigt hat und deren Abschlußbericht im Druck erschienen ist.[19] Dieses für die Praxis grundlegende Werk fungiert sozusagen als archivischer Kommentar zu den Aufbewahrungsbestimmungen der Justiz. Auf Grundlage einer Analyse der einzelnen Aktentypen werden Empfehlungen ausgesprochen, z.B. komplette Archivierung, komplette Vernichtung oder (häufiger): Archivierung in Auswahl, etwa weniger Beispiele, der Berufungs- oder Revisionsfälle oder eines Samples in Höhe einer bestimmten Prozentquote. Methodisch kann die Durchsicht des gesamten Bestandes sinnvoll sein (sog. Autopsie), es kann eine inhaltliche Vorauswahl (z.B. Beschränkung auf bestimmte Tatbestände oder Prozeßbeteiligte wie in den Kriterien der Aussonderungsbestimmungen) oder ein schematisches Vorgehen empfohlen sein (z.B. Ziehung jeder n-ten Akte, Auswahl nach einem Buchstabenmodell oder statistische Zufallsauswahl).

Insgesamt bemühen sich die Archive zum einen um die „besonderen Fälle", die allgemeines Aufsehen erregten: den mysteriösen Fernsehfall aus „XY", den Massenmord, den Terroristenprozeß, die Korruptionsaffäre, die umstrittene Abschiebung. Gleiches gilt im Prinzip für den Bereich der freiwilligen Gerichtsbarkeit, hier wäre etwa zu denken an spektakuläre Konkurse und Zwangsversteigerungen, an die Handelsregisterakten bedeutender und alteingesessener Firmen, an Testamente und Adoptionen von Prominenten. Diese Überlieferung zu erkennen ist relativ einfach, die Vorauswahl der Gerichte und Staatsanwaltschaften erfaßt diese Fälle noch am ehesten, und zusätzlich werten die Archivare selbst die Presse aus.

---

[19] Stahlschmidt, Rainer (Red.): Empfehlungen zur Archivierung von Massenakten der Rechtspflege. Abschlußbericht der Bund-Länder-Arbeitsgruppe zu Fragen der Bewertung und Archivierung von Massenakten der Justiz in Deutschland. Düsseldorf 1999. Vgl. den Tagungsbericht von Martina Wiech, Moderne Justizakten als zukünftige Quellen historischer Forschung – Workshop zur Archivierung von Unterlagen der Justiz [Juni 2005], http://hsozkult.geschichte.hu-berlin.de/tagungsberichte/id=826.

In der Regel komplett in die deutschen Staatsarchive gelangt sind z.B. die Strafverfahrensakten über die Verfolgung nationalsozialistischer Gewaltverbrechen (NSG-Verfahren). Sie geben nicht nur Auskunft über in der NS-Zeit begangenes Unrecht, sondern werden von der Forschung zunehmend als Quelle für die Justizgeschichte der Nachkriegsjahrzehnte entdeckt.[20] Sie sind – mit Schellenberg gesprochen – zugleich Information über ermittelte Tatbestände und Evidenz erfolgreicher, gescheiterter oder unterlassener Strafverfolgung.

Schwieriger zu fassen sind die zeittypisch besonderen Fälle, wie sie die Aussonderungsbestimmungen zu definieren versuchen: die epochenspezifische Jugend-, Wirtschafts- und Umweltkriminalität, die zeittypischen zivilgerichtlichen Auseinandersetzungen, Scheidungsprozesse usw. Und erst recht diffizil gestaltet sich die Frage, in welchem Maß „alltägliches" Schriftgut ohne erkennbare Besonderheit oder Zeittypik archiviert werden soll. Heute sind wir froh, daß der Historischen Kriminalitätsforschung reiche Bestände auch über „Bagatellkriminalität" früherer Jahrhunderte zur Verfügung stehen.[21] Heute ist jedes Staatsarchiv stolz auf die Prozeßakten des Reichskammergerichts, obwohl von deren Archivwürdigkeit anfangs nicht alle überzeugt waren.[22] Von den umfangreichen Prozeßserien der territorialen bzw. Land- und Amtsgerichte sind häufig nur Bruchstücke erhalten – aus der Frühen Neuzeit und erst

---

[20] Vgl. aus der großen Zahl neuerer Literatur den Ausstellungskatalog Auschwitz-Prozess 4 Ks 2/63 Frankfurt am Main. Hrsg. vom Fritz-Bauer-Institut. Köln 2004; Miquel, Marc von: Ahnden oder amnestieren? Westdeutsche Justiz und Vergangenheitspolitik in den sechziger Jahren. Göttingen 2004; Bialystok in Bielefeld. Nationalsozialistische Verbrechen vor dem Landgericht Bielefeld 1958 bis 1967. Hrsg. von Freia Anders u.a. Bielefeld 2003.

[21] Vgl. Schwerhoff, Gerd: Gerichtsakten und andere Quellen zur Kriminalitätsgeschichte. In: Aufriß der Historischen Wissenschaften. Bd. 4: Quellen. Hrsg. von Michael Maurer. Stuttgart 2002, S. 267-301.

[22] So urteilte der fürstlich lippische Archivrat Clostermeier 1823 rein nach dem rechtlichen Wert, die RKG-Akten könnten „ohne allen für Lippe daraus entspringenden Nachtheil ihrem Schicksal überlassen werden", während sein Nachfolger Falkmann 1852 die historische Bedeutung sehr wohl erkannte (Bender, Wolfgang: Salzufler Betreffe vor dem höchsten Reichsgericht. Akten des Reichskammergerichts als genealogische und heimatgeschichtliche Quelle. In: Jahrbuch Bad Salzuflen 1999, Bielefeld 1998, S. 62 f.). Vgl. aus der neueren Forschung: Prozessakten als Quelle. Neue Ansätze zur Erforschung der Höchsten Gerichtsbarkeit im Alten Reich. Hrsg. von Anette Baumann, Siegrid Westphal, Stephan Wendehorst u. Stefan Ehrenpreis. Köln 2001.

recht aus der jüngeren Vergangenheit. Bei der Rekonstruktion von Lebensläufen des 20. Jahrhunderts „unterhalb“ von Prominenz und großer Devianz lassen den Forscher die rechtsgeschichtlichen Quellen leicht im Stich.[23]

Ein anderes Beispiel: Den erhaltenen Testamenten aus dem Mittelalter und der Frühen Neuzeit wird allgemein ein hoher Quellenwert zugesprochen.[24] Auch Testamente aus dem 19. Jahrhundert werden noch gelegentlich von Familienforschern und Sozialhistorikern eingesehen. Die Überlieferung des 20. Jahrhunderts gilt aber weitgehend nicht mehr als archivwürdig.[25] Darüber ließe sich sicher streiten: Das genealogische Interesse an diesen Unterlagen besteht ohnehin fort, und daß die aktuellen Testamente generell weniger aussagekräftig sein sollten als ihre unmittelbaren Vorläufer, müßte wohl erst bewiesen werden.[26] Bereits im 19. Jahrhundert hat die Justiz Unmengen von Akten produziert, die einen erheblichen (vielleicht zu hohen) Teil der heutigen Archivbestände ausmachen: Als seltene Zeugnisse einer weitgehend schriftlosen Epoche braucht man diese Quellen keineswegs aufzuheben, ja klugen Zeitgenossen schien bekanntlich schon das 18. ein „tintenklecksendes Säkulum“ zu sein.[27]

---

[23] Vgl. Lampert, Tom: Ein einziges Leben. Geschichten aus der NS-Zeit. München 2003, S. 256: „Nach dem Krieg wurden zum Beispiel Strafprozeßakten wegen Diebstahls und Betrugs [...] routinemäßig vernichtet, weil die zuständigen Behörden sie als ‚nicht archivwürdig‘ einstuften.“

[24] Vgl. z.B. Queckenstedt, Hermann: Geseke Vysevase und ihre Erben. Ein Testament aus dem spätmittelalterlichen Osnabrück. In: Osnabrücker Mitteilungen 96 (1991), S. 45-82 (mit weiterer Literatur) und jüngst den Tagungsbericht von Sylvie Tritz, Seelenheil und irdischer Besitz: Testamente als wirtschafts-, rechts- und sozialhistorische Quellen für den Umgang mit den „letzten Dingen“ [Nov. 2005], http://hsozkult.geschichte.hu-berlin.de/tagungsberichte/id=926.

[25] Stahlschmidt (wie Fn. 19), S. 36: „Das in früherer Zeit herausragende sozialgeschichtliche Interesse rechtfertigt für das 20. Jahrhundert nur noch die Archivierung eines kleinen Anteils“.

[26] Umfangreiche Anbietungen sind abzusehen, da seit 2004 Testamente, Erbverträge usw. nicht mehr dauernd, sondern nur noch 100 Jahre aufzubewahren sind; vgl. Rügge, Nicolas: „Fristenlösung“ statt dauernder Verwahrung. Anmerkungen zu den neuen Aufbewahrungsbestimmungen der Justiz. In: Archiv-Nachrichten Niedersachsen 8/2004, S. 81-86.

[27] Friedrich Schiller in den „Räubern“ (1781).

E. Strategien der Risikovermeidung

Wird das Alter der Überlieferung zum Bewertungskriterium erhoben, droht die Gefahr, daß künftigen Forschergenerationen die angeblich in den Akten kaum Spuren hinterlassenden „kleinen Leute" der Frühen Neuzeit weit plastischer vor Augen stehen werden als wir und unsere Zeitgenossen. Daher hat es seinen guten Sinn, daß das Berufsbild des Archivars neben dem Hüten der älteren Überlieferung auch die Bildung von Archivbeständen aus erst jüngst geschlossenen Akten umfaßt. Dadurch sollte der Irrglaube zu vermeiden sein, daß die „früheren" Zeiten grundsätzlich mehr Interesse verdienten als die scheinbar vertrauten gegenwärtigen; daß man vor allem „ältere" Quellen bewahren müsse, während für die jüngste Vergangenheit und die scheinbar offen zutageliegende Gegenwart genügend Zeugnisse zur Verfügung stünden. Nein: Kein Argument für den Quellenwert ist so relativ und vergänglich wie das Alter, und trotz der allgegenwärtigen Informationsflut scheint keineswegs ausgemacht, auf welches Material sich die Archive konzentrieren sollten – konkreter gesagt: auf welches heute in den Justizbehörden vorhandene Schriftgut die staatlichen Archivare ein besonderes Augenmerk haben müssen, damit sich die Nachwelt ein treffendes Bild von unserer Zeit machen kann. Jeder Historiker weiß: Für die Zeitgenossen ist nur schwer zu erkennen, welche Dokumente die Besonderheiten ihrer Epoche am besten widerspiegeln; spätere Generationen werden ihre Fragen an die Quellen richten, und dann werden womöglich bisher ungeahnte Aspekte der Überlieferung („latente Inhalte"[28]) wichtig erscheinen.

Diesem Dilemma ist schwerlich zu entkommen, wenn man nicht alles archivieren will; man kann die Risiken aber zu mildern versuchen. Weitgehend durchgesetzt hat sich der minimale Konsens, jede Bewertungsentscheidung – wie sie auch immer ausfiel – schriftlich zu vermerken und damit transparent

---

[28] Siegfried Büttner verwendet diesen Terminus für „Fakten und Zusammenhänge, für die unsere Zeit ein Sensorium noch nicht entwickelt hat", die aber z.B. als Spuren und Muster Eingang in Aktenserien gefunden haben können: Büttner, Siegfried; Robert Kretzschmar; Rainer Stahlschmidt: Der archivische Umgang mit großen Fallaktenserien. Bericht der Arbeitsgruppe „Archivierung großer Fallaktenserien" der Archivreferentenkonferenz des Bundes und der Länder. Marburg 2001, S. 3.

zu halten. Im übrigen bedarf es vor allem einer fortgesetzten professionellen Selbstreflexion über die gesellschaftlichen Ziele und Grenzen der archivischen Tätigkeit heute. Diese eigentlich banale Einsicht hat sich nur mühsam bei einer Berufsgruppe durchgesetzt, die sich langen Zeiträumen verpflichtet weiß und mit Hinweis darauf Veränderungen traditionell eher skeptisch betrachtet. Inzwischen ist aber ein breites Interesse am fachlichen Austausch bemerkbar und eine neue Offenheit gegenüber Anregungen aus der Geschichtswissenschaft und anderen Bereichen der Gesellschaft.[29] Der hohe Anspruch an die Ausbildung der wissenschaftlichen Archivare dürfte dazu beitragen, daß eine Bewertungsentscheidung von Fachpersonal getroffen wird, das mit vielfältigen historischen Fragestellungen und Methoden vertraut ist. Daß der Kontakt zur Forschung nicht mit der Dissertation enden darf, wenn ein Archivar Quellenüberlieferung bilden, Besucher und Anfragende beraten soll, müßte sich von selbst verstehen.

In der guten Absicht, ausgetretene Bewertungspfade zu verlassen, haben sich viele Staatsarchive von den sozialwissenschaftlichen Methodendiskussionen der 1970er und 1980er Jahre dazu anregen lassen, große Aktenmengen mit Hilfe repräsentativer Querschnitte einzudampfen. Man hat z.B. schematisch jede 50. oder 100. Strafakte übernommen, alle Personalakten der Anfangsbuchstaben D, O und T oder bestimmter Geburtsjahrgänge in Zehnerschritten. Von solchem „Sampling“ kommt man inzwischen wieder ab, weil die so gebildeten Bestände gewaltig anwachsen, aber kaum oder gar nicht benutzt werden – und weil man inzwischen festgestellt hat, daß eine statistisch wirklich valide Zufallsauswahl schwer herzustellen ist und eine (abhängig von der Grundgesamtheit) oft unvertretbar hohe Übernahmequote erfordert.[30]

---

[29] Vgl. Archive und Forschung. Referate des 73. Deutschen Archivtags 2002 in Trier. Hrsg. vom VdA. Siegburg 2003; Pilger, Kathrin und Andreas: Das www.forum-bewertung.de. Erfahrungen und Perspektiven. In: Neue Perspektiven archivischer Bewertung. Hrsg. von Frank M. Bischoff und Robert Kretzschmar. Marburg 2005, S. 81-99. Umgekehrt entdeckt die Geschichtswissenschaft ihrerseits die Archive als Gegenstand (statt Ort) ihrer Forschung: Auch mit Fragen der Steuerung von Wissen durch Bildung von Archivbeständen beschäftigt sich gegenwärtig das Graduiertenkolleg „Archiv Macht Wissen“ an der Universität Bielefeld: http://www.uni-bielefeld.de/geschichte/gk1049/forschungsprogramm.html.

[30] Zur Methodik grundlegend: Buchholz, Matthias: Überlieferungsbildung bei massenhaft gleichförmigen Einzelfallakten im Spannungsverhältnis von Bewertungsdiskussion, Repräsentativität

Daher gewinnen in den letzten Jahren die qualitativen Auswertungsmöglichkeiten gegenüber den quantitativen wieder an Gewicht, jedoch ohne zwangsläufig den Rückfall in eine reine Auswahl nach Inhalten und Informationswerten zu provozieren. Als Anhaltspunkte zur Bewertung dienen demnach weniger inhaltliche Vorgaben (wie bei Justizakten z.B. das verfolgte Delikt, die Höhe des Streitwertes, das Herkunftsland eines Asylbewerbers oder der Ausgang seines Verfahrens) als vielmehr formale Erkenntnismöglichkeiten: das Vorhandensein substantieller Schriftsätze, ausführlicher Verhörprotokolle oder Zeugenaussagen, detaillierter Inventare oder Nachlaßverzeichnisse, psychologischer Gutachten usw.[31] Auf solche Art von Quellen stützen sich z.B. jüngere Forschungsarbeiten, die anwaltliche Argumentationen in Zivilprozessen der NS-Zeit untersuchen oder Vernehmungsstrategien zur Erwirkung von Geständnissen nachgehen.[32] Ein solches Vorgehen trägt dazu bei, die qualitative Auswertbarkeit der Bestände zu erhöhen, ohne ihnen bewußt eine inhaltliche Richtung zu geben. Es mindert somit die Gefahr, Archivgut als Belegstücke für vermeintlich bekannte Entwicklungen auszusuchen und damit Geschichte dokumentieren zu wollen, statt der Forschung Quellen möglichst auswertungsoffen bereitzustellen.

---

und Nutzungsperspektive. Eine Fallstudie am Beispiel von Sozialhilfeakten der oberbergischen Gemeinde Lindlar. Köln 2001. Zur Kritik Büttner/Kretzschmar/Stahlschmidt (wie Fn. 28), S. 4 f. und 57-64, dazu wiederum Buchholz S. 147 u. 150 ff.: Umstritten ist insbesondere, inwieweit sich die Quotenberechnung nur auf vordefinierte Merkmale beziehen kann und daher der (auswertungs-) offenen Datengesamtheit und erst recht den „latenten Inhalten" nicht gerecht wird.

[31] Diese Tendenz äußert sich schon in einigen Empfehlungen der Stahlschmidt-Arbeitsgruppe (wie Fn. 19). Um die Aussagekraft der Akten in diesem Sinn zu evaluieren, empfiehlt sich eine Analyse des normativen Verwaltungs-„Programms" einerseits und der jeweils unterschiedlichen Entscheidungsspielräume der Bearbeiter andererseits, die sich in den Akten als Formen von Varianz und Redundanz widerspiegeln: Vgl. dazu Büttner/Kretzschmar/Stahlschmidt (wie Fn. 28) und Pilger/Pilger (wie Fn. 13).

[32] Schröder, Friedo: Die anwaltliche Tätigkeit während der nationalsozialistischen Herrschaft. Eine Analyse der anwaltlichen Argumentation in Zivilprozessen anhand der vorhandenen Prozessakten der Landgerichte Frankenthal, Wiesbaden, Limburg und Frankfurt und der Handakten der jüdischen Konsulenten des OLG-Bezirks Frankfurt. Frankfurt/M. 2001; Niehaus, Michael; Norbert Schröer: Geständnismotivierung in Beschuldigtenvernehmungen. Zur hermeneutischen und diskursanalytischen Rekonstruktion von Wissen. In: sozialer sinn 1/2004, S. 71-93.

F. Aktuelle Herausforderungen

In der Sondersituation Deutschlands nach der Vereinigung der beiden Teilstaaten 1990 und der Öffnung des vormaligen „Ostblocks“ konnten sich die Archive, nicht zuletzt in Unterstützung der Justiz, in mehrfacher Hinsicht bewähren: bei der Klärung offener Vermögensfragen, bei Rehabilitationen und bundesweit bei der Entschädigung von Zwangsarbeitern.[33] Große Beachtung fand und findet noch das Sonderarchiv der Bundesbeauftragten für die Unterlagen des Staatssicherheitsdienstes der ehem. DDR.[34] Die Archive haben damit über ihre traditionelle Rolle hinaus unerwartet eine erhebliche gesellschaftliche Bedeutung gewonnen. Diese Erfahrungen machen aufmerksam auf ihren Beitrag zur Rechtssicherheit und werden sicher auch Auswirkungen auf Bewertungsfragen haben.[35]

Außerdem liegt in dem Vordringen elektronischer Systeme mit dem Ziel eines „papierlosen“ oder „papierarmen Büros“ eine aktuelle Entwicklung von besonderer Tragweite, die selbst in den deutschen Amtsgerichten inzwischen zur Einführung des elektronischen Grundbuchs und Handelsregisters geführt hat und die an analoge Akten gewöhnten Archive vor neue Herausforderungen der Übernahme, Benutzung und Konservierung stellt. Darüber gibt es seit Jahren eine intensive Debatte und allmählich auch erste Erfahrungen.[36] Die „Langzeitarchivierung“ ohne Papier ist für die Verwaltungen kein Selbstläufer mehr, ebensowenig wie für die Archive die herkömmlichen Verfahren der Anbietung, Bewertung und physischen Verwahrung von Archivalien. Was die

---

[33] Vgl. die Beiträge der Sektion „Archive und Wiedergutmachung“ des 72. Deutschen Archivtags in Cottbus, abgedruckt im Tagungsband: Archive und Herrschaft (Der Archivar, Beiband 7). Siegburg 2002, S. 223-347.

[34] Die spätere Abgabe der (bewerteten?!) Akten an das Bundesarchiv wird derzeit diskutiert.

[35] In den neuen Bundesländern ging es zunächst vor allem darum, Bewertung und Aktenvernichtung auszusetzen, für bestimmte Schriftgutgruppen der ehemaligen DDR-Justiz sind längere Aufbewahrungsfristen verfügt worden. Die Stahlschmidt-Arbeitsgruppe (wie Anm. 19, S. 14-18) empfiehlt für zahlreiche Aktengruppen, bis zum Abschluß der Rehabilitierungsverfahren (Nach-) Kassationen in den Staatsarchiven nur mit Zustimmung der zuständigen Gerichte vorzunehmen.

[36] Vgl. bes. die Veröffentlichungen des Arbeitskreises „Archivierung von Unterlagen aus digitalen Systemen“, zuletzt: Digitale Archivierung. Wirtschaftlichkeit und pragmatische Lösungen. Hrsg. von Christoph Popp und Harald Stockert. Mannheim 2005.

Kriterien der Bewertung angeht, sind allerdings elektronische Daten grundsätzlich nicht anders zu behandeln als analoges Schriftgut.

Diese Maßnahmen sind nicht vom Himmel gefallen, sondern Teil einer umfassenderen Rationalisierung, die wiederum als Reaktion auf den Kosten- und Leistungsdruck zu verstehen ist, dem auch die öffentliche Verwaltung und Justiz ausgesetzt ist.[37] Zumal unter den jüngeren Archivaren wächst das Bewußtsein dafür, daß archivierte Unterlagen Kosten verursachen: Sie beanspruchen Lagerungsfläche, müssen erschlossen und großenteils auf längere Sicht konservatorisch behandelt[38] werden. Auch daher rührt das allgemeine Unbehagen an Samplebildungen und einer großzügigen Übernahmepraxis.

Es wird sich zeigen, ob den Archiven eine grundsätzliche Wende zu erheblich geringeren Übernahmequoten bevorsteht, zu Nachkassationen (d.h. nachträglicher Vernichtung früher einmal übernommener Unterlagen) und gar zu Ersatzverfilmungen und -digitalisierungen (d.h. Verfilmen bzw. Einscannen von Archivgut und Vernichtung der Originale).[39] Der Rationalisierungsdruck kann heilsam sein, wenn er professionelle Standards nicht verletzt, sondern im Gegenteil zur Konzentration darauf zwingt und eine kritische Selbstreflexion in Gang setzt, deren Ergebnisse dann guten Gewissens selbstbewußt vertreten werden können.[40] Speziell bei der Justizüberlieferung darf der hohe „Primärwert" der Rechtssicherheit nicht gefährdet werden. Die Archive haben mit der Justiz zusammenzuarbeiten, um sie von überflüssigem Ballast effektiv zu entlasten und die wirklich dauerhafte Verfügbarkeit insbesondere digitaler Daten

---

[37] Seit Jahren haben Staatsarchive und Datenschutzbeauftragte dafür plädiert, die für viele Gruppen von Justizakten verfügte dauernde Aufbewahrung durch lange, aber begrenzte Fristen zu ersetzen (vgl. Stahlschmidt, wie Fn. 19, S. 9). Daß die Justiz dem 2004 weitgehend nachgekommen ist (dazu Rügge, „Fristenlösung", wie Fn. 26), mag auch inzwischer stärker ins Gewicht fallenden Kostenerwägungen geschuldet sein.

[38] Eindringlich dargestellt bei Bender, Wolfgang: Kampf dem Papierzerfall? Die Massenentsäuerung von Archivgut als ein Mittel der Bestandserhaltung. In: Der Archivar 54 (2001), S. 297-302.

[39] Kluttig, Thekla: Aufgeweckte Archivare? Anmerkungen aus dem Sächsischen Hauptstaatsarchiv Dresden zur gegenwärtigen Situation der Überlieferungsbildung. In: Neue Perspektiven archivischer Bewertung. Hrsg. von Frank M. Bischoff und Robert Kretzschmar. Marburg 2005, S. 51-70; Wiech, Martina: Strategische Herausforderungen an das Landesarchiv Nordrhein-Westfalen auf dem Bereich der Überlieferungsbildung – Probleme und Lösungsansätze. Ebd., S. 71-79.

[40] Schneider, Gerd: „Archivare aufgewacht!" Anmerkungen eines Externen zur gegenwärtigen Situation im deutschen Archivwesen. In: Der Archivar 57 (2004), S. 37-44.

von herausragendem Wert mit zu gewährleisten. Insofern, in Bezug auf ihren Träger nämlich, helfen die Archive tatsächlich mit, dessen Erinnern und Vergessen zu steuern.[41]

Was aber ihre „sekundären", erst in der Moderne errungenen (Forschungs-) Funktionen angeht, haben die Archive mehr denn je mögliche Konkurrenzen zu beachten, den spezifischen Wert ihrer Quellen und deren Grenzen zu berücksichtigen. Welche Art von Information ist bereits (in je auf die eigenen Bedürfnisse verknappter Form) hinreichend gesichert: in amtlichen Veröffentlichungen und der juristischen Literatur[42] publiziert und „verewigt", in den Medien bekanntgegeben und analysiert? Und auf welchen Feldern kann demgegenüber die archivalische Überlieferung ihre Stärken ausspielen? In welchen Fällen lohnt sich also das in der Tat mühsame und teure Unterfangen, Papierstapel und Dateien, die nicht für die Ewigkeit gemacht sind, ewig aufheben zu wollen?

Um in dieser Richtung weiterzukommen, bedürfte es wohl einer interdisziplinären „Quellenkunde der Neuzeit", die sich intensiv um die Sichtung und Gewichtung der jüngeren, schwer überblickbaren Vielfalt von Hinterlassenschaften mit möglichem historischem Wert bemüht.[43] An einem solchen Ziel könnten die Archive, die Rechtsgeschichte und andere Forschungsrichtungen gemeinsam arbeiten. Sicher kommt den Archiven dabei eine besondere Verantwortung für die künftige Quellenüberlieferung zu. Damit leisten sie einen spezifischen Teilbeitrag zu dem komplexen Phänomen gesellschaftlicher Erinnerung – nicht weniger, aber auch nicht mehr. Das in diesem Sinn historische Erinnern und Vergessen zu steuern sind sie weder willens noch fähig.

---

[41] Menne-Haritz, Angelika: Prozessgedächtnis und Überlieferungsbildung. In: Digitale Archive – ein neues Paradigma? Hrsg. von Andreas Metzing. Marburg 2000, S. 283-308. Vgl. das viel zitierte Schlagwort vom Archiv als „Gedächtnis der Verwaltung". Dazu ebenfalls anregend: Haas, Stefan: Erinnerung in administrativen Systemen. Gedächtnisstrukturen der preußischen Verwaltung in Westfalen im 19. Jahrhundert. In: Westfälische Forschungen 51 (2001), S. 39-57.

[42] Einschließlich der schnell vordringenden elektronischen Informationssysteme, deren dauerhafte Verfügbarkeit allerdings zu gewährleisten bleibt.

[43] Reininghaus, Wilfried: Quellenkunde und Quellenkritik aus der Sicht der Archive und der neueren Geschichte. In: Archive und Forschung. Referate des 73. Deutschen Archivtags 2002 in Trier. Hrsg. vom VdA. Siegburg 2003, S. 91-98.

„Nicht Erinnern“ und „Übles vergessen“: Zum Amnestiebegriff im klassischen Griechenland

Philipp Scheibelreiter

A. Einleitung?

Die Suda, ein byzantinisches Konversationslexikon,[1] enthält einen Eintrag zur Amnestie. Hier steht zu lesen: Ἀμνηστία: ἡ λήθη. καὶ ὄνομα κύριον. – „Amnestie: Vergessen (und ein Eigenname).“ Anders wird im 6. Jh. n. Chr. bei Hesych Amnestie negativ formuliert[2]: ἀμνηστία· τὸ μὴ μιμνήσκεσθαι – „Amnestie: Das (sich) nicht Erinnern.“ Ältere Definitionen fehlen leider, da erst ab dem Hellenismus und dem wissenschaftlichen Wirken der Alexandriner die Lexikographie gepflegt wird[3]. Aber auch Hesych und die Suda – und deswegen werden sie hier, trotz der zeitlichen Distanz herangezogen – überliefern das begriffliche Material der Klassik, mit dem – modern formuliert – der Tatbestand der Amnestie beschrieben werden konnte. Gerhard Thür definiert Amnestie als:

„…der gesetzmäßig festgesetzte Verzicht auf Anklage, Wiederaufnahme von Verfahren, Urteilsvollstreckung und Strafvollzug als Mittel, die streitenden Parteien nach internen und externen Kriegen zu versöhnen.“[4]

---

[1] Suda α 1613; das Wörterbuch wird um 1000 n. Chr. datiert. Die Abkürzung antiker Autoren und Werke erfolgt nach Der neue Pauly. Realenzyklopädie der Antike. Hrsg.: Hubert Cancik und Helmuth Schneider. Stuttgart-Weimar 1996.

[2] Hesych. s.v. ἀμνηστία.

[3] Die ältesten Lexika sind Schulwörterbücher im 5. Jh., die alte Ausdrücke aus Homer oder Solon erklärten. Erst auf Grundlage des Sophistik brachten es die alexandrinischen Gelehrten des Hellenismus zu der Ausformung des eigenen Genus Wörterbuch.

[4] Thür, Gerhard: Amnestia. In: Der Neue Pauly Bd. 1, Sp. 602-603, hier Sp. 602.

Damit ist eine wichtige Einschränkung auf die staats- und völkerrechtliche Ebene erfolgt. Geregelt werden Amnestien somit in innerstaatlichen normativen Akten wie Gesetzen oder Volksbeschlüssen[5] und in zwischenstaatlichen Vereinbarungen. Die Konsequenzen einer Amnestie sind aber vor allem privat- und strafrechtlicher Natur. Die Amnestie steht oft am Ende eines Konfliktes und dient der Neudefinition der Beziehungen der Konfliktparteien zueinander. Der Konflikt oder dessen Auswirkungen sollen ganz oder teilweise dem Vergessen anheim fallen. Der Gegenstand des Vergessens ist zumeist ganz generell gehalten: Man wolle nicht mehr an das denken, „… was früher zwischen zwei Staaten anderes passiert ist" (εἴ τι πρότερον γέγονεν ἀλλότριον ταῖς πόλεσι πρὸς ἀλλήλας),[6] an das, „...was damals passiert ist" (περὶ τῶν τότε γεγενημένων),[7] oder an das, „...was früher war" (τῶν ἔμπροσθεν).[8] Die „vorangegangenen Übel" sind es, die nun aus dem kollektiven Gedächtnis gestrichen werden sollen.

In der Folge soll untersucht werden, ob, und wenn, wie im klassischen Griechenland der Tatbestand einer Amnestie bezeichnet wurde. Danach soll ein kursorischer Überblick über staats- und völkerrechtliche Amnestien des 5. Jhs. das theoretische Ergebnis praktisch unterlegen.

Einen entscheidenden Impuls für diese Fragen gibt Mommsen: Das Wort ἀμνηστία als klassischer staatsrechtlicher Begriff sei von den Römern als solcher übernommen und mit oblivio übersetzt worden:[9] „ἀμνηστία oder ἄδεια sind griechische Rechtsbegriffe; den Römern fehlt die Sache nicht ganz, aber das technische Wort."[10] Zu dieser Annahme veranlasste Mommsen eine Formulierung aus der ersten philippischen Rede Ciceros, die auf die athenische Amnestie von 403 v. Chr.[11] – das antike Paradigma einer Amnestie schlechthin – anspielt:[12]

---

[5] Das kann für den griechischen Rechtskreis als gesichert gelten, vgl. Waldstein, Wolfgang: Untersuchungen zum römischen Begnadigungsrecht. Innsbruck 1964.

[6] Demosth. or. 18,184.

[7] Isokr. or. 14,14; And. 1,81. 108.

[8] Antiph. 1,6.

[9] Mommsen, Theodor: Römisches Strafrecht. Leipzig 1899, S. 458 Anm. 1.

[10] Mommsen (wie Fn. 9), S. 458.

[11] Dazu siehe unten.

[12] Cicero: Phil. I 1.

Nec vero usquam discedebam nec a re publica deiciebam oculos ex eo die quo in aedem Telluris convocati sumus. In quo templo, quantum in me fuit, ieci fundamenta pacis Atheniensiumque renovavi vetus exemplum; Graecum etiam verbum usurpavi quo tum in sedandis discordiis usa erat civitas illa, atque omnem memoriam discordiarum oblivione sempiterna delendam censui.

„Niemals habe ich den Staat verlassen und habe die Augen abgewandt von dem Tag an, an dem wir in den Tempel der Tellus zusammengerufen worden waren. In diesem Tempel habe ich, soweit es mir möglich war, die Fundamente für den Frieden gelegt und das alte Beispiel der Athener erneuert; auch habe ich das griechische Wort übernommen, das damals jene bedeutende Polis bei der Beilegung von inneren Konflikten gebraucht hatte. Und ich habe dafür gestimmt, dass jede Erinnerung an die Zwistigkeiten durch ewig andauerndes Vergessen auszulöschen sei."

Ist dieses „Graecum verbum", der Begriff, den Cicero mit oblivio übersetzt, notwendiger Weise das griechische ἀμνηστία?[13] Oder verbirgt sich dahinter ein anderer genereller Terminus?[14] Immerhin bezeichnet Plutarch die Amnestie von 403/2 v. Chr. als Volksbeschluss über die Amnestie (τὸ ψήφισμα τὸ τῆς ἀμνηστίας).[15] Auch wenn Plutarch ἀμνηστία verwendet oder vor ihm schon Cicero einen griechischen Terminus seiner Zeit übernimmt, besagt das noch nicht, dass es sich dabei um den originalen Wortlaut aus dem 5. Jh. v. Chr. handelt. Was also hat Cicero mit oblivio gleichgesetzt, vielleicht sogar übersetzt? Tatsächlich ist ἀμνηστία als zumindest politischer Begriff erstmals

[13] Waldstein (wie Fn. 5), S. 22 - 32.

[14] z.B. ὁμονοία (Übereinkunft), ἄδεια oder μὴ μνησικακεῖν (zu diesen Termini sogleich) vgl. Cicero: Philippics I & II. Edited with Introduction and critical notes by John D. Denniston. Oxford 1926 (repr. 1978), hier: Cic. Phil. I 1,1,1 ad locum; Canfora, Luciano: Studi di storia della storiographia Romana. Bari 1993, S. 307-309.

[15] Plut. mor. 814b; ebenso Plut.Cicero 42,3: ...(sc. Κικέρων) ἔπεισε τὴν σύγκλητον Ἀθηναίους μιμησαμένην ἀμνηστίαν τῶν ἐπὶ Καίσαρι ψηφίσασθαι, νεῖμαι δὲ τοῖς περὶ Κάσσιον καὶ Βροῦτον ἐπαρχίας.

im 2. Jh. v. Chr. überliefert[16] – "…the word is not found in any classical Greek."[17] Der zweite von Mommsen vorgeschlagene Begriff, ἄδεια (wörtlich Furchtlosigkeit), beinhaltet als „Aussetzen des staatlichen Strafverfolgungsanspruches"[18] nur einen Teilbereich der Rechtsfolgen einer Amnestie und scheidet so als genereller Begriff aus.[19] Wie also werden Sachverhalte, die von Amnestie berichten, in den griechischen Quellen anstelle von ἀμνηστία/ἄδεια bezeichnet?

B. μὴ μνησικακεῖν – ein Terminus technicus?

Eine Vielzahl von Quellen (allen voran jene aus dem 4. Jh. v. Chr., die die athenische Amnestie von 403/2 v. Chr. beschreiben)[20], benutzen dafür ein verneintes Verbum: μὴ μνησικακεῖν – „nicht an Übles erinnern". Kann das als staatsrechtlicher Begriff angesehen werden oder dient es nur zur Umschreibung?

Wörtlich übersetzt mit ‚nicht an Übles Erinnern/nicht nachtragen'[21] oder „not recall the past wrongs",[22] weist μὴ μνησικακεῖν zumindest semantisch eine Nahebeziehung zur ἀμνηστία auf. Die schon eingangs zitierte Definition

---

[16] Waldstein (wie Fn. 5), S. 27; Cicero: Philippics I-II. Edited by John T. Ramsey. Cambridge 2003, 1, 1,1 ad locum.

[17] Denniston (wie Fn. 14), Cic. Phil. I 1,1,1 ad locum. Die frühesten Belege finden sich bei Heraklit (Herakl. 2. Brief) und einer umstrittenen Stelle aus dem Menexenos des Platon (Plat. Mx. 239c). Erstmals in juristischem Kontext erscheint der Begriff in zwei Inschriften aus Milet: SIG 588,9 (198 v. Chr.) und SIG 633,5 (180 v. Chr.), vgl. zu alledem die Untersuchung von Waldstein (wie Fn. 5), S. 27ff.

[18] vgl. Thür, Gerhard: Adeia. In: Der Neue Pauly, Bd. 1, Sp. 105-106, hier Sp. 105.

[19] vgl. die Belege bei Demosth. or. 24,45; And. 1,12.15.77; Lys. 13,55; IG I^3 52B16; 370, 31+33; 370, 64. Bei Thukydides ist darunter das „freie Geleit" zu verstehen (Thuk. 8,76. 81).

[20] Aristot. Ath. Pol. 39,6; Andoc. 1 90; Isokr. or. 18,3; Aischin. leg. 2,176. 3, 208; Xen. hell. 2,4,23.

[21] So Nippel, Wilfried: Bürgerkrieg und Amnestie: Athen 411-403. In: Amnestie oder die Politik der Erinnerung in der Demokratie. Hrsg. von Gary Smith und Avishai Margalit. Frankfurt am Main 1997, S. 103-119, hier S. 111.

[22] Carawan, Edwin: The Athenian Amnesty and the scrutinity of the laws. In: JHS (2002) Nr. 122, S. 1-23, hier S. 2 Anm. 5; vgl. weiters Atkinson, John: Truth and reconciliation the Athenian way. In: Acta Classica (1999) Nr. XLII, S. 5-13, der hierfür "being proscribed the raising of any malicious references to past offences" (hier: S. 5) übersetzt.

von Hesychs – ἀμνηστία als τὸ μὴ μιμνήσκεσθαι – ist auch der Wortbildung nach eine Tautologie: Vom gleichen Wortstamm μνα-/μνη- gebildet, enthalten beide eine Negation – hier ein Substantiv mit Alpha privativum (ἀ-μνηστία), da ein verneinter Infinitiv. μὴ μνησικακεῖν hat allerdings noch den Zusatz κακά – „Schlechtes" ist es, das vergessen werden soll. Ist μὴ μνησικακεῖν deshalb aber genauer determiniert? Oder verhält es sich gerade umgekehrt und lässt sich Amnestie im technischen Sinne bloß auch unter den weiten Begriff des Nicht-Erinnerns subsumieren?

Auch im Griechischen entstammt jeder Rechtsbegriff ursprünglich einem weit gefassten Wortfeld[23]. Erst die wiederholte, effiziente Verwendung in juristischem Kontext bildete aus dem vom allgemeinen Sprachgebrauch eines Wortes einen rechtlich relevanten Terminus aus. Bederman beschreibt diesen Prozess der Herausbildung einer Fachterminologie wie folgt:

> "Within each political culture, treaty terminoloy and ceremony began in a rudimentary condition and quickly became more systematized and predictable."[24]

Gerade für das (μὴ) μνησικακεῖν ist dieser Weg leicht nachvollziehbar.[25] Begriffsdefinitionen sind weniger in Lexika[26] denn in den sogenannten Scholien, ab dem Hellenismus gebräuchlichen, erklärenden Randbemerkungen zu klassischen Texten, zu finden.

---

[23] Waldstein (wie Fn. 5), S. 32.

[24] Bederman, David J.: International Law. Cambridge 2001, S. 146.

[25] Natürlich sind mit μὴ μνησικακεῖν auch Sachverhalte beschrieben, die keinen rechtlichen Hintergrund aufweisen – so Carawan (wie Fn. 22), S. 4 skeptisch. Das heißt aber nicht umgekehrt, dass Amnestie nicht auch so beschrieben wurde – gerade aufgrund der vielen Bedeutungen wird es ja notwendig, die Entwicklung vom allgemeinen zum rechtlich konnotierten Sprachgebrauch nach zu untersuchen!

[26] Diese erscheinen ergiebiger als Hesych. s. v. ἀμνησικακία · τὸ μὴ μιμνήσκεσθαι κακῶν – „Amnesikakia: Das nicht an die Übel erinnern" oder der Eintrag in der Suda, der auf die geringe Bedeutung des Terminus bei den Römern rekurriert (Suda, s.v. Μνησικακεῖν· δοτικῇ. Πολύβιος τοῦ μνησικακεῖν ἐπὶ τοῖς γεγονόσιν οὐδ' ἥντιναοῦν ἔμφασιν ἐποίουν οἱ Ῥωμαῖοι.).

In den Wolken des Aristophanes rät der so genannte „Anwalt der guten Sache“ dem missratenen Sohn Pheidippides, seinem Vater zu verzeihen und auch die Schläge zu vergessen, die er von ihm erhalten hat:[27]

> „Und nicht dem Vater zu widersprechen (auch nicht ihn Iapetos zu nennen) und nicht übel sich zu erinnern an die Jugend, in der Du wie ein Kücken im Nest aufgezogen wurdest.“

Die Scholien geben für die Wendung der ersten Hälfte des zweiten Verses μηδ' μνησικακῆσαι τὴν ἡλικίαν mehrere Erklärungen: ἐπὶ κακῷ μνησθῆναι τῆς ἡλικίας[28] – „sich nicht an das Schlechte erinnern“, εἰς μνησικακίαν ἐμβαλεῖν – „nicht schlecht machen“ oder ἔχθραν ποιήσας ἢ μισήσας[29] – „Feindschaft erzeugen oder hassen“.

Eine zweite Stelle entstammt der Lysistrata des Aristophanes: Hier verbietet ein athenischer Ratsherr der Lysistrata, davon zu sprechen, dass – in der angespannten Kriegssituation des peloponnesischen Krieges – auch Kinder in den Krieg geschickt werden (müssen):[30] „Schweig und erinnere nicht an das Übel!“ (σίγα, μὴ μνησικακήσῃς). Μνησικακήσῃς stehe nach den Scholien[31] hier „… anstelle von erinnere nicht an die Übel, indem du davon sprichst, dass sie nun noch jüngere Kinder in den Krieg schicken!“ (ἀντὶ τοῦ μὴ μνησθῇς τῶν κακῶν λέγουσα ὅτι τοὺς παῖδας ἔτι νεωτέρους ὄντας ἐκπέμπουσιν εἰς πόλεμον)

Eine dritte Interpretation des μνησικακεῖν enthält ein Scholion zur Rede des Demosthenes gegen Aristokrates[32]. Konkret wird die Frage formuliert ‘τί ἐστι τὸ μνησικακεῖν’ – „Was ist mnesikakein?“ Der Scholiast gibt die Ant-

---

[27] Aristoph. Nub. 998-999. μηδ' (ἀντειπεῖν τῷ πατρὶ μηδὲν μηδ' Ἰαπετὸν καλέσαντα) μνησικακῆσαι τὴν ἡλικίαν ἐξ ἧς ἐνεοττοτροφήθης.

[28] Scholia vetera in Nubes. Edidit Douwe Holwerda, Groningen 1977.

[29] vgl zu beiden Einträgen Scholia recentiora in Nubes. Edidit Willem J. W. Koster, Groningen 1974.

[30] Aristoph. Lys. 590.

[31] Scholia Graeca in Aristophanem. Edidit Friedrich Dübner, Paris 1862.

[32] Demosth. or. 23,100.

wort[33]: Der, der nach Ungerechtigkeiten von einem sucht und diesen dann zu strafen und ihm schaden sucht, ist einer, der μνησικακεῖ.

Von diesen drei unterschiedlichen Definitionen für eine Phrase ließe sich allein die Stelle aus der Lysistrata in einen politischen Kontext stellen[34]: Die rebellische Athenerin Lysistrata wird durch ein Organ der Polis dazu angehalten, nicht schlecht über die Kriegspolitik Athens zu sprechen, diese nicht zu erwähnen.

μνησικακεῖν ist in Grundbedeutung eine schlechte Charaktereigenschaft, typischer Weise von Barbaren wie den Persern.[35] Demosthenes definiert es auch als das Gegenteil der Vernunft[36]. Abgeschwächt als „nachtragend" verstanden, findet μνησικακεῖν Eingang in die Rechtssprache: So mahnt Demosthenes, man solle sich einzelnen Personen gegenüber, die sich gegen den Staat schlecht verhalten hatten, nun aber die Freunde Athens sind, nicht nachtragend verhalten[37] – οὐ δὴ δεῖ μνησικακεῖν – oder man solle dem Volk der Rhodier nicht nachtragen, dass sie einst von Athen abgefallen sind[38] – φημὶ δὴ χρῆναι ... μὴ μνησικακεῖν. Gerade in den attischen Gerichtsreden, also im juristischen Kontext, wird häufig die Formel angewendet: οὐ δὴ δεῖ μνησικακεῖν.[39] Und das kann sich auch direkt auf den Wortlaut ältere Amnestiegesetze beziehen.[40]

Der Gebrauch des Infinitivs μνησικακεῖν anstelle des später davon abgeleiteten Substantivs μνησικακία ist als Indiz für das Alter und die Authenzität der Formel zu werten. Staats- oder völkerrechtliche Terminologie entwickelt sich in einer Zeit, da zwischen dem Normsetzenden und dem von ihm repräsentierten Staat noch nicht differenziert wird, also hierin noch keine Abs-

---

[33] Scholia in Demosth. or. 23,100 ὁ ἐρωτῶν τὰ τινὸς ἀδικήματα, ὥστε τι βλάπτειν καὶ ἀμύνεσθαι αὐτόν, μνησικακεῖ, (...).

[34] Bei Aristophanes gibt es aber auch an prominenter Stelle einen Verweis auf die große Amnestie von 403 v. Chr. – vgl. Aristoph. Plut. 1147.

[35] Plut. Artaxerxes. 6,9. Themistokles. 28,3.

[36] Demosth. or. 23,93,8. 23,100,4.

[37] Demosth. or. 23,191.

[38] Demosth. or. 15,16.

[39] Demosth. or. 15,16; 23,191; Isokr. or. 14,14; Aristeid. Leuktrikos 457; Symmachikos 483.

[40] zB. And. 1,90.

traktion stattgefunden hat.[41] In frühen völkerrechtlichen Verträgen des späten 6., frühen 5. Jhs. v. Chr. schwört der Vertragspartner die Einhaltung der Vertragspflichten, und dies wird mit einem Infinitiv in Abhängigkeit zu einem verbum iurandi ausformuliert. So wurde etwa auch das Gebot der Vertragstreue – nicht abzufallen – mit dem verneinten Infinitiv μὴ ἀποστήσεσθαι bezeichnet und nicht mit dem Verbot des Austritts, der ἀπόστασις.[42] Abstrakte Begriffe prägen sich erst später aus, sind somit – für die Frühzeit – nur in deskriptiven Quellen, nicht aber den originalen Dokumenten in Gebrauch.[43]

Es kann also davon ausgegangen werden, dass mit dem οὐ/μὴ μνησικακεῖν ein solcher Terminus technicus vorliegt, eine Formel, die eben durch den Gebrauch in juristischem Kontext Eingang in völkerrechtliche Verträge oder Gesetze gefunden hat,[44] um generell Amnestie zu regeln.[45] Da man Normen verbal ausgedrückte, bedarf es gar keiner Erklärung für den synonymen Gebrauches von μὴ μνησικακεῖν und ἀμνηστία[46]: Die verneinte Verbal-

---

[41] vgl. Siewert, Peter: Der Eid von Plataiai. München 1972, S. 24-26.

[42] Zu der so genannten Loyalitätsklausel siehe Scheibelreiter, Philipp: Untersuchungen zur vertragsrechtlichen Struktur des delisch-attischen Seebunds. Wien 2005, S. 151-163.

[43] Neben Infinitiven werden Verpflichtungen mit Imperativen in der 3. Person oder Indikativen des Futurums ausgedrückt: Die Partei soll sich an nichts Schlechtes erinnern – die Partei wird sich an nichts Schlechtes erinnern.

[44] vgl. z.B. die Amnestie in Megara 424 v. Chr. (Thuk. 4, 74,2).

[45] Allgemein vgl. dazu Lenger, Marie-Thérès: Décret d´Amnestie et lettres aux forces armées de Chypre. BCH (1956) Nr. LXXX, S. 437-461, hier S. 447. Ein weiteres berühmtes Beispiel ist die Amnestie für die rückberufenen Exilanten aus Tegea 324 v. Chr., IPArk 8 (IG V^2 262), Ze 54. Carawan (wie Fn. 22) betont den Unterschied zwischen ἀμνηστία und οὐ/μὴ μνησικακεῖν: Der Infinitiv, der in Gesetz und Vertrag an genauer determinierte Amnestiefolgen anschließt bzw. diese summarisch bezeichnet, verstärkt deren Rechtswirkungen. Andererseits folgt die „Zusammenfassung“ der Regeln oft in einem Besicherungseid – hier ist Carawan (wie Fn. 22), S. 5 und S. 9 auch beizupflichten. Für ihn ist Amnestie „the guarantee of political forgiveness in the hellenistic period“. Auch dem ist zu zu stimmen. Funktional aber kommt den beiden Möglichkeiten einer Formulierung in chronologischer und sogar synchroner Reihung die gleiche Bedeutung zu: Sie determinieren staatlich verordnetes Vergessen in abstrakter Weise. Denn auch eine ἀμνηστία musste – hinsichtlich ihrer Rechtsfolgen – erst in Gesetz oder Vertrag genauer ausformuliert werden. Somit ist – funktional betrachtet – kein Unterschied zwischen dem älteren οὐ/μὴ μνησικακεῖν und der jüngeren ἀμνηστία gegeben.

[46] So Waldstein (wie Fn. 5), S. 28 Anm. 28; aA Carawan (wie Fn. 22), S. 3 Anm. 9; dazu Anm. 45.

form, die vom selben Wortstamm wie das jüngere Substantiv gebildet wird, entspricht der im 6/5. Jh. v. Chr. gebräuchlichen Art, Normen generell zu formulieren.

Dass später neben das „Übel Vergessen“ die „Nichterinnerung“ tritt, ist kein Widerspruch dazu, dass hier ein und derselbe Tatbestand vorliegt. Die beiden Begriffe decken sich ab der Zeit, da ἀμνηστία rechtlich konnotiert wird, auch insofern, als μνησικακεῖν absolut stehen kann, sich zumeist aber auf einen im Genetiv stehenden Unrechtssachverhalt bezieht,[47] wodurch der Zusatz κακά an Bedeutung verliert.[48] Für den Rechtsbereich tritt die ἀμνηστία erst später neben οὐ/μὴ μνησικακεῖν; die davon gebildete μνησικακία hat primär die unjuristische Bedeutung von Rachsucht – so vor allem bei Plutarch.[49] Die gebräuchliche Form, politische Amnestie zu bezeichnen, ist das μὴ μνησικακεῖν τῶν παρεληλυθότων[50] – so belegt es auch die Athenaion Politeia des Aristoteles.[51] Und diese Phrase werden Cicero[52], aber auch andere Autoren wie Cornelius Nepos[53] oder Justin[54] mit oblivio übersetzt haben.

---

[47] Eine Ausnahme stellt die oben erwähnte Stelle aus Aristoph. Nub. 999 dar, wo das Bezugswort τὴν ἡλικίαν im Akkusativ steht, vgl. Aristophanes: Clouds. Edited with Introduction and Commentary by Kenneth James Dover, Oxford 1968, Aristoph. Nub. 999 ad locum.

[48] vgl. Carawan (wie Fn. 22), S. 2 A 5: μνησι- bezieht sich zumeist auf ein Partizip wie γεγενημένων/παρεληλυθότων, -κακεῖν verstärkt dies bloß.

[49] vgl. so vor allem bei Plutarch: Plut. Artaxerxes 6,9. Coriolan12. 27,6. 30,3. 36, 2-3. Gracchen 30,7. mor. 272c3. 481d. 567b. 728b. 859d. 860a. 966b. Und Plutarch ist es ja, der für 403 v. Chr. erstmals von dem ψήφισμα ἀμνηστίας spricht.

[50] vgl. Aristotele: La costituzione degli Athenesi, a cura di Giuseppe Lozza, Milano 1991, Ath. Pol 39,6 ad locum: “Questa è la formula consueta per indicare un´amnistia politica”. Ebenso spricht Rhodes, Peter J.: A Commentary on the Aristotelian Athenaion Politeia. Oxford 1981, Ath. Pol. 39,6 ad locum von der “regular formula for an amnesty”.

[51] Aristot. Ath. Pol. 39,6.

[52] So auch Thalheim, Otto: Amnestia. In: RE I 1870-1871, 1871; Thür (wie Fn. 4), 603.

[53] C. Nep. 8 Thrasybulus. 3,2: ne qua disensio ex ante actis nasceretur, omnes iure iurando obstringuntur discordiarum oblivionem fore.

[54] Iustin 5: Thrasybulus legem tulit, ne quis ante actorum rerum accusaretur neve multaretur, eamque illi oblivionis appellarunt.

C. Die Rechtsfolgen einer Amnestie

Konkret sind es zwei Konsequenzen, die in den Quellen immer wieder synonym für die Amnestie gebraucht werden: Die Wiederverleihung des Bürgerrechtes und die Wiederaufnahme verbannter Bürger einer Polis.

I. Die Wiederverleihung des Bürgerrechts – τοὺς ἀτίμους ἐπιτίμους ποιῆσαι

Die ἀτίμια war Strafe für die unterschiedlichsten Delikte[55] (wie Fahnenflucht, Misshandlung der Eltern oder dreimaliges falsches Zeugnis bei Gericht[56], Unterschlagung, Bestechung, Diebstahl). Auch Staatsschuldner verfielen bei Säumnis oder Uneinbringbarkeit der Schulden der ἀτίμια. Die Überprüfung des Vollbürgerrechts, der ἐπιτιμία, wie sie bei Magistraten der athenischen Polis zu Amtsantritt regelmäßig – in der so genannten Dokimasie – vorgenommen wurde, konnte ebenfalls in der Entziehung des Bürgerrechts resultieren – etwa wegen Verlustes der Einsichtsfähigkeit eines Kandidaten, seiner Verschwendungssucht oder wegen Prostitution.

Die ἀτίμια musste durch Gerichtsurteil ausgesprochen werden, um in Rechtskraft zu erwachsen, Rechtsfolge war – wie Ruschenbusch es formuliert[57] – die „bürgerliche Zurücksetzung“:[58] Ein ἄτιμος konnte weder eine Funktion als Soldat oder Beamter übernehmen, noch an der Legislative (Volksversammlung) und Judikative (Gerichte) der Polis teilhaben. Ferner waren ἄτιμοι vom Besuch auf dem Markt und von Heiligtümern ausgeschlossen. Unberührt davon blieb freilich das Aufenthaltsrecht in der Polis.[59]

Durch Beschluss der Volksversammlung konnte es zu einer Amnestie der Entrechteten und Wiedereinsetzung in den Status eines Bürgers kommen, aus

[55] vgl. Ruschenbusch, Eberhard: Untersuchungen zur Geschichte des athenischen Strafrechts. Köln 1968, S. 22-23.
[56] Thür, Gerhard: Atimia. In: Der Neue Pauly, Bd. 2, Sp. 215, hier Sp. 215.
[57] Ruschenbusch (wie Fn. 55), S. 17.
[58] Zur Entwicklung aus dem Institut der „Friedlosigkeit“ in der Gemeinde, der man sich zum eigenen Schutz nur durch Auswanderung entziehen konnte, vgl. Ruschenbusch (wie Fn. 55), S. 19ff.
[59] Xenophon: Hellenika. Hrsg. von Gisela Strasburger. Tübingen 1970, 2,2,12 ad locum; ausführlicher dazu Ruschenbusch (wie Fn. 55), S. 18.

den ἄτιμοι werden ἐπίτιμοι. Diese wesentliche Konsequenz einer Begnadigung ist für die Amnestie Solons für säumige Darlehensschuldner belegt[60], ebenso für die beiden athenischen Amnestiegesetze, die im Angesicht schwerer äußerer Bedrohung beantragt wurden: 481/80 v. Chr. von Themistokles wegen der Persergefahr,[61] 405 v. Chr. von Patrokleides vor der Belagerung durch die Spartaner.[62] Letztere mündet in der Kapitulation Athens und dem Friedensvertrag von 404 v. Chr.,[63] der die gleiche ἀτιμία – Klausel zum Inhalt hat. Die attischen Redner Lysias,[64] Andokides[65] und Aischines[66] belegen die Klausel ebenfalls.

II. Die Aufnahme Verbannter – τούς τε φεύγοντας καταδέχεσθαι

Eine weitere typische Konsequenz der Amnestie ist die Wiederaufnahme Exilierter. Die strafweise erzwungene Flucht aus dem Gebiet der Polis konnte verschiedene Ursachen haben – Platon nennt exemplarisch Mord,[67] Misshandlung der Eltern[68] und Beherbergung Verbannter.[69] Zwar beinhaltete die ἀτίμία nicht automatisch auch die Verbannung, umgekehrt aber definiert Ruschenbusch[70] Verbannung mit „dem Entzug des Rechtsschutzes für den Fall des Betretens athenischen Staatsgebietes“,[71] also mit der Androhung der ἀτίμία, sollte ein Exilierter wider das Urteil verstoßen und in die Stadt zurückkehren.

---

[60] Plut. Solon 19,4.
[61] And. 1,107.
[62] Xen. Hell. 2,2,10; Lys. 25,27.
[63] And. 1,80. 109.
[64] Lys. 6,24ff.
[65] And. 1,73-76.
[66] Aischin. Ctes. 19ff. 28ff.; 3,175f.
[67] Plat. leg. 871a =§ 21nach Ruschenbusch, Eberhard: Ein altgriechisches Gesetzbuch. München 2001.
[68] Plat. leg.881b =§ 27 Ruschenbusch (wie Fn. 67).
[69] Plat. leg.955b =§ 64 Ruschenbusch (wie Fn. 67).
[70] vgl. Plut. Solon 19,4 = T 70 nach Ruschenbusch, Eberhard: ΣΟΛΩΝΟΣ ΝΟΜΟΙ. Wiesbaden 1966.
[71] Ruschenbusch (wie Fn. 55), S. 12.

Neben der generellen Bestimmung, Verbannte wieder in den Staat einzugliedern (so in den athenischen Amnestien von 481/80,[72] 405[73] und 404 v. Chr.[74]) ist für 481/80 v. Chr. das Gesetz belegt, aufgrund des Scherbengerichtes – des Ostrakismos – Verbannte wieder rückzuführen.[75]

Wenn die Quellen des 5. und 4. Jhs. v. Chr. von Amnestiebeschlüssen sprechen, so wird das einerseits mit einer Formel dargestellt: οὐ/μὴ μνησικακεῖν. Damit kann sowohl der Wortlaut einer Norm als auch – etwa im bekräftigenden Eid – deren wesentlicher Inhalt wiedergegeben werden. Dies untermauert auch die epigraphische Evidenz.[76] Andererseits werden konkrete materielle Rechtswirkungen der Amnestie herangezogen, um diese zu definieren. Einzelne berühmte Beispiele für staats- und völkerrechtliche Amnestiebeschlüsse sollen diese Erkenntnis etwas plastischer erscheinen lassen.

E. Staatsrechtliche Amnestien

I. Solon

Der athenische Staatsmann und Dichter Solon berichtet in einer berühmten Elegie davon, dass er viele Athener wieder in die Heimat geführt habe, auch solche, die vor der Not der Schulden geflohen waren.[77]

Bei Plutarch wird die gesetzliche Bestimmung dazu tradiert[78]:

'ἀτίμων ὅσοι ἄτιμοι ἦσαν πρὶν ἢ Σόλωνα ἄρξαι, ἐπιτίμους εἶναι, πλὴν ὅσοι ἐξ Ἀρείου πάγου ἢ ὅσοι ἐκ τῶν ἐφετῶν ἢ ἐκ πρυτανείου καταδικασθέντες ὑπὸ τῶν βασιλέων ἐπὶ φόνῳ ἢ σφαγαῖσιν ἢ ἐπὶ τυραννίδι ἔφευγον ὅτε ὁ θεσμὸς ἐφάνη ὅδε.'

---

[72] And. 1,107.
[73] Lys. 25,27.
[74] And. 1,80. 109; Xenophon: Hellenika 2,2,20; Plutarch: Lysander 14,4.
[75] Aristot: Ath. pol. 22,8.
[76] vgl. etwa IG II/III^2 1 111 Ze 58-62. 82-82 (Dekret der Athener für die Insel Keos 363/62 v. Chr.); IPArk 5 §8 Ze 57-61 (Gesetz aus Tegea über die Rückkehr von Exilanten 324 v. Chr.) und Ditt. Syll. 588, Ze 85 (Friedensvertrag von Milet mit Magnesia 196 v. Chr.).
[77] Sol. fr. 24,8 D (36, 8-15).
[78] Plut. Solon 19,4 = T 70, Ruschenbusch (wie Fn. 70). Der bei Plutarch tradierte Wortlaut wird hier als authentisch angenommen.

„Von den atimoi sollen diejenigen, die es gewesen waren, ehe Solon Archon war, nun epitimoi sein, außer denen, die vom Areopag oder von den Ephetengerichten oder dem Prytaneion unter dem Vorsitz der Könige verurteilt worden sind wegen Mordes, Totschlags oder wegen Strebens nach Tyrannis, und fliehen mussten, als dieses Gesetz erlassen wurde."

Das Gesetz normiert eine Amnestie in Form der Atimie-Klausel, nimmt aber bestimmte Personengruppen davon aus: Von dem Areopag verurteilte Mörder, von den Ephetengerichten verurteilte Totschläger und Mörder an Nichtbürgern und von den Archontengerichten (die ihr Amtslokal in dem Prytaneion, dem Rathaus hatten) verurteilte Staatsverräter[79]. Alle anderen ἄτιμοι sollten nun ἐπίτιμοι sein, also ihr volles Bürgerrecht erlangen. Darunter fallen also auch die in der Elegie genannten Staatsschuldner[80]. Da die Atimie nicht auch Verbannung implizierte, ist keine Rückberufung Verbannter intendiert[81]. Die dafür gebräuchliche Formel ist für die solonische Amnestie auch nicht belegt.

II. Amnestiegesetz aus Athen 480 v. Chr.

Im Zuge der Perserkriege beschloss die athenische Volksversammlung eine Amnestie für verbannte athenische Bürger. Die innenpolitische Geschlossenheit sollte so demonstriert[82], aber auch die Gefahr des Überlaufens eigener Bürger zum Feind gebannt werden[83]. Wieder waren Gewaltverbrecher und Staatsverräter[84] davon ausgeschlossen[85].

---

[79] Stahl, J. Michael: Über athenische Amnestiebeschlüsse. In: RhM (1891) Nr. 46, S. 250-286, hier S. 250-253.

[80] T 70, Ruschenbusch (wie Fn. 70) ad locum.

[81] Stahl (wie Fn. 79), S. 250-253.

[82] Welwei, Wilhelm: Das klassische Athen. Darmstadt 1999, S. 56.

[83] Daneben vermutet Baltrusch, Ernst: Symmachie und Spondai. Berlin 1991, S. 35 dass dieser innenpolitische Frieden in Erfüllung der Gründungsbedingungen des Hellenenbundes, der griechischen Symmachie, die zur Perserabwehr geschlossen worden war, erlassen wurde

[84] So aus konkretem Anlass die Familie der gerade überwundenen Tyrannen, der Peisistratiden.

Explizit als Normadressaten werden die durch Ostrakismos Verbannten genannt. Die Quellen gehen unterschiedlich konkret darauf ein. Herodot berichtet nur, dass der 482 v. Chr. ostrakisierte Aristeides[86] zum athenischen Feldlager kommt[87] - und das ist nur auf Basis einer Amnestie möglich. Aristoteles verbindet die Formel zur Wiederaufnahme mit dem Ostrakismos[88]: (τετάρτῳ δ' ἔτει) κατεδέξαντο πάντας τοὺς ὠστρακισμένους (ἄρχοντος Ὑψηχίδου), διὰ τὴν Ξέρξου στρατείαν· – „...sie nahmen (...) alle die Ostrakisierten wieder auf, wegen des Feldzuges des Xerxes." Nach Plutarch

„lösten die Athener das (Ostrakismos-) Gesetz auf und entschieden per Volksbeschluss die Rückkehr der Ausgewanderten" – λύσαντες τὸν νόμον ἐψηφίσαντο τοῖς μεθεστῶσι κάθοδον[89].

Diese Formulierung mit dem Terminus μεθίστασθαι (sich fortbewegen), der in diesem Kontext erstmals in einer unter dem Namen des Andokides überlieferten Schrift aus dem 5./4. Jh. v. Chr. belegt ist[90], ist zu modern für ein Psephisma aus 480 v. Chr.[91] Näher am möglichen Wortlaut eines Amnes-

---

[85] Welwei (wie Fn. 80), S. 56.

[86] 114 Ostraka gegen Aristeides sind bekannt, vgl. dazu Rhodes, Peter J.: Arist. Ath. Pol. 22,7 ad locum.

[87] Hdt. 8,79,1.

[88] Aristot. Ath. Pol 22,8.

[89] Plut. Aristeides 8,1.

[90] [And.] 4,5. Zur Datierung dieser Rede siehe Heftner, Herbert: Der Ostrakismos des Hyperbolos, RhM 2000 (Nr. 143), S 32-59, hier S 33 Anm. 6 und S 46 Anm. 42, wo das Jahr 395/94 v. Chr. als terminus ante quem angeführt wird. Für den Ostrakismos ist der Terminus μεθιστάναι (fortgehen, medial: sich fort bewegen), erst im 4.Jh. v. Chr. belegt. Und auch hier kann ihm keine rechtliche Konnotation sondern nur eine deskriptive Funktion zugesprochen werden, vgl. dazu die Testimonien T 18 ([And.] 4,5), T 34 (Arist. Pol. 3,1284a17-37) und T 35 (Arist. Pol. 3, 1284b15-30), zit. nach: Ostrakismos: Testimonien I. hrsg. von Peter Siewert u.a. Stuttgart 2002. Weiters zu μεθιστάναι vgl. Arist. Ath. Pol 22,6 (T 39 Siewert) und [Demosth. or.] 26,6.

[91] Ebenso der Wortlaut aus Plut. Themistokles 11,1, wo zu lesen ist, dass es den auf Zeit Ausgewanderten möglich sein solle, zurück zu kehren – τοῖς ἐπὶ χρόνῳ μεθεστῶσιν ἐξεῖναι κατελθοῦσι

tiegesetzes aus 480 v. Chr. ist Andokides[92], der neben der Atimie-Klausel auch die Wiederaufnahmeklausel tradiert: ἔγνωσαν τούς τε φεύγοντας καταδέξασθαι καὶ τοὺς ἀτίμους ἐπιτίμους ποιῆσαι.

Darunter lassen sich auch die Opfer des Ostrakismos subsumieren, die ja ihre Heimat auf Zeit verlassen hatten müssen und ansonsten sofort der Atimie verfallen wären[93].

III. Amnestiegesetz auf Antrag des Patrokleides 405 v. Chr.

In einer vergleichbaren Situation wie 480 v. Chr. befand sich Athen nach der den peloponnesischen Krieg entscheidenden Niederlage gegen die Spartaner bei Aigospotamoi 405 v. Chr.: Wieder drohte eine Belagerung der Stadt. In Nachahmung des Verhaltens zur Zeit der Angriffe des Xerxes[94] wurde eine Amnestie erlassen, deren Inhalt Xenophon mit der Atimie-Klausel wiedergibt[95]: διὰ ταῦτα τοὺς ἀτίμους ἐπιτίμους ποιήσαντες ἐκαρτέρουν.

Andokides überliefert das ganze Psephisma, das in der Volksversammlung von Patrokleides beantragt worden sein soll[96]: Rechtskräftig verurteilte Staatsschuldner sollten ebenso begnadigt werden wie Schuldner, deren Prozesse gerade anhängig waren. Auch Rechenschaftsprozesse bezüglich der Amtsführung staatlicher Organe sollten niedergeschlagen, ebenso aus Bürgschaftsverträgen für Staatsschuldner Verurteilte begnadigt werden. Schließlich fallen Sympathisanten der Umsturzbewegung des Jahres 411. v. Chr. unter die Amnestie, nicht jedoch die 400 Oligarchen selbst. Es werden alle Personen ausgenommen, deren Strafausmaß über die Atimie hinausgeht, also zum Tode oder zur Verbannung Verurteilte[97]. Die Amnestie umfasste also nicht automatisch

---

92 And. 1,107.

93 vgl. Aristoteles: Der Staat der Athener, übersetzt und erläutert von Mortimer Chambers, Darmstadt 1990, Aristot. Ath. pol. 22,8 ad locum.

94 Meyer, Eduard: Geschichte des Altertums IV/2. Stuttgart 1953, S. 360.

95 Xen. hell. 2,11.

96 And. 1,77-79.

97 Erst 404 v. Chr., im Rahmen des Friedensschlusses mit den Persern, dürfen diese wiederkehren (And. 1,80; Lys. 12,77).

alle ἄτιμοι[98], sondern primär Staatsschuldner, die schon verurteilt worden oder deren Prozesse anhängig gewesen sind[99]. Das Psephisma stellt schließlich die Nichteinhaltung des staatlich verordneten Vergessens unter Strafe[100]:

μὴ κεκτῆσθαι ἰδίᾳ μηδενὶ ἐξεῖναι μηδὲ μνησικακῆσαι μηδέποτε – „es soll nicht erlaubt sein, privat die Listen der nun Begnadigten zu erwerben noch ihnen jemals Übles nachzutragen."

Wer dagegen verstieße, solle vom Areopag in das Exil geschickt werden. Während sich die deskriptiven Quellen auf die Atimie-Klausel beschränken, gibt Andokides den Wortlaut des Psephismas wieder: Neben der taxativen Aufzählung, wer zu begnadigen, wer davon ausgenommen sein müsse, fallen zwei rechtliche Begriffe auf: Einleitend die ἄδεια, abschließend das μηδὲ μνησικακῆσαι.

IV. Ausführung des Friedens von 404 v. Chr.

Am Ende des peloponnesischen Krieges steht der Athen von Sparta diktierte Friedensvertrag. Die wesentlichen Bedingungen des Vertrages tradiert Xenophon[101]:

... ἀλλ' ἐποιοῦντο εἰρήνην ἐφ' ᾧ τά τε μακρὰ τείχη καὶ τὸν Πειραιᾶ καθελόντας καὶ τὰς ναῦς πλὴν δώδεκα παραδόντας καὶ τοὺς φυγάδας καθέντας τὸν αὐτὸν ἐχθρὸν καὶ φίλον νομίζοντας Λακεδαιμονίοις ἕπεσθαι καὶ κατὰ γῆν καὶ κατὰ θάλατταν ὅποι ἂν ἡγῶνται.

---

[98] Andokides: On the mysteries. Ed., with introduction, commentary and appendixes by Douglas MacDowell. Oxford 1962, 77-79 ad locum.

[99] περὶ δὲ τῶν ἐγγεγραμμένων εἰς τοὺς πράκτορας ἢ τοὺς ταμίας τῆς θεοῦ καὶ τῶν ἄλλων θεῶν ἢ τὸν βασιλέα vgl. dazu McDowell: Andokides, De mysteriis 1, 78 ad locum.

[100] And. 1,79.

[101] Xen hell. 2,2,20.

Neben den typischen Unterwerfungsbedingungen, der offensiven (Herausgabe aller Schiffe bis auf 12) und defensiven (Schleifen der Mauer zum Piräus) Entwaffnung und dem Symmachie – Versprechen Athens an Sparta[102] verpflichtet sich Athen dazu, die Flüchtlinge – das sind vor allem die nach dem Putsch von 411 v. Chr. exilierten Oligarchen – aufzunehmen: τοὺς φυγάδας καθέντας. Davon berichtet auch Plutarch[103]: καὶ τοὺς φυγάδας ἀνέντες. Lysias referiert dazu noch die Atimie-Formel[104]: ὥστε τοὺς μὲν φεύγοντας κατεδέξασθε, τοὺς δ' ἀτίμους ἐπιτίμους ἐποιήσατε. In Anspielung auf den Gesetzesantrag des Patrokleides[105] belegt Andokides schließlich ebenfalls beide Amnestieregelungen[106]: ἠξιώσατε γὰρ τούς τε φεύγοντας καταδέξασθαι καὶ τοὺς ἀτίμους ἐπιτίμους ποιῆσαι.

V. Die Amnestie von 403/2 v. Chr.

Nach innenpolitischen Unruhen in Athen, ausgelöst von einem oligarchischen Umsturz, kam es dank dem Einschreiten des spartanischen Königs Pausanias 403 v. Chr. zu einem Vertrag zwischen den Bürgerkriegsparteien[107]: In Athen sollten alle Oligarchen begnadigt werden (ἀπιέναι δὲ ἐπὶ τὰ ἑαυτῶν

[102] Dies erfolgt in Form der Freund-Feindklausel (τὸν αὐτὸν ἐχθρὸν καὶ φίλον νομίζοντας Λακεδαιμονίοις – man wolle die gleichen Freunde und Feinde haben wie Sparta) und der Hegemonieklausel (ἕπεσθαι καὶ κατὰ γῆν καὶ κατὰ θάλατταν ὅποι ἂν ἡγῶνται – man wolle Sparta folgen zu Land und zu Wasser, wo immer es hinführe).

[103] Plut. Lysandros 14, 4.

[104] Lys. 25, 22.

[105] And. 1, 80: Κατὰ μὲν τὸ ψήφισμα τουτὶ τοὺς ἀτίμους ἐπιτίμους ἐποιήσατε· τοὺς δὲ φεύγοντας οὔτε Πατροκλείδης εἶπε κατιέναι οὔθ' ὑμεῖς ἐψηφίσασθε.

[106] And. 1, 109.

[107] Vgl. dazu die Rekonstruktion von Loening, Thomas Clark: The reconciliaton agreement in Athens of 403/02 B.C., Wiesbaden 1987, S. 30-58; vgl. weiters Atkinson (wie Fn. 22), S. 8-9. Zum politischen Hintergrund vgl. Thiemann, William: Cause in History and the amnesty at Athens: An Introduction. In: TAPhA (2002) Nr.132, S. 63-69; Quillin, James M.: Achieving Amnesty: The role of events, institutions and ideas. In: TAPhA (2002) Nr.132, S. 71-107; Wolpert, Andrew: Lysias 18 and the Athenian memory of Civil war. In: TAPhA (2002) Nr.132, S. 109-126; Ober, Joshua: Social Science History, Cultural history, and the amnesty of 403. In: TAPhA (2002) Nr.132, S. 127-137. Einen guten Überblick über den historischen Kontext, der hier nicht näher dargestellt werden kann, liefert W. Nippel (wie Fn. 21).

ἕκαστον), wobei es ihnen frei stünde, nach Eleusis auszuwandern und sich dort gleichsam in einer oligarchischen Kolonie Athens anzusiedeln.[108] Dieser Vergleichsvertrag sah auch Ausnahmen vor, so die so genannten 30 Tyrannen und ihre 10 Stellvertreter, die der Oligarchenpartei Athens angehörten, und deren Exekutivorgane, die ἕνδεκα (11-Männer). Aber auch diese konnten in Rechenschaftsverfahren versuchen, sich zu rehabilitieren[109].

Die eidliche Besicherung des Vergleiches ist mehrfach belegt[110], direkt berichten davon nur Lysias[111] – παρεληλυθότων ἄδειαν ποιήσειν („die Immunität bezüglich dessen, was an Übeln voran gegangen ist") und Aristoteles[112]

τῶν δὲ παρεληλυθότων μηδενὶ πρὸς μηδένα μνησικακεῖν ἐξεῖναι, πλὴν πρὸς τοὺς τριάκοντα καὶ τοὺς δέκα καὶ τοὺς ἕνδεκα καὶ τοὺς τοῦ Πειραιέως ἄρξαντας, μηδὲ πρὸς τούτους, ἐὰν διδῶσιν εὐθύνας.

Andokides aber kennt den gesamten Eid[113]:

καὶ οὐ μνησικακήσω τῶν πολιτῶν οὐδενὶ πλὴν τῶν τριάκοντα καὶ τῶν δέκα καὶ τῶν ἕνδεκα οὐδὲ τούτων ὃς ἂν ἐθέλῃ εὐθύνας διδόναι τῆς ἀρχῆς ἧς ἦρξεν.

Auf die generelle Amnestieformel folgen also die Ausnahmen und darauf deren Möglichkeit, sich durch ein Verfahren (εὐθύνη) zu rehabilitieren. Ein weiterer Eid auf die Amnestie ist bei Xenophon belegt[114]: καὶ ὀμόσαντες ὅρκους ἦ μὴν μὴ μνησικακήσειν

Nippel fasst den Inhalt der Amnestie prägnant zusammen als

---

[108] Xen. hell. 2, 4,38.
[109] Nippel (wie Fn. 21), S. 111.
[110] Xen. hell. 2,4,42; Lys. 12,53; 13,80; 25,23.34; 6,39; Isokr. or. 18,25.29.
[111] Lys. 25,28.
[112] Aristot. Ath. Pol. 39,6.
[113] And. 1,90.
[114] Xen. hell. 2,4,43.

„…das Verbot für Anklageerhebung für Bürger und ein Gebot an Gerichtsmagistrate und Geschworene, eine Anklage in den durch das innerstaatliche Friedensabkommen geregelten Punkten nicht zuzulassen bzw. keine Verurteilung vorzunehmen."[115]

Alle Verfahren, die nicht in der Demokratie vor 403 v. Chr. anhängig geworden sind, alle Prozesse aus der oligarchischen Zeit, die einen politischen Hintergrund haben, sollen außer Kraft gesetzt sein – ἄκυρα εἶναι[116].

Die Quellen der eben kurz skizzierten fünf berühmten Amnestiefälle aus Athen benutzen immer die gleiche Terminologie: Trotz unterschiedlichen Regelungsgehalts wird Amnestie entweder durch das οὐ/μὴ μνησικακεῖν oder anhand ihrer typischen Rechtsfolgen determiniert.

F. Völkerrechtliche Amnestien

Auch Quellen des Völkerrechts bedienen sich dieser beiden Möglichkeiten: Wenn im Rahmen der Perserabwehr die in der Not gebildete griechische Symmachie des Jahres 482 v. Chr. innerstaatliche Streitigkeiten aussetzt, so wird das mit dem „Beseitigen" oder „Aufschieben/Aussetzen" interner Kriege beschrieben[117]. Die Thessaler versichern den Phokern für den Fall, dass sie mit ihnen auf die Seite der Perser wechseln wollten, zu, dass man erlittenes Unrecht vergessen wolle[118]: οὐ μνησικακέομεν

Der Friedens- und Wiedereingliederungsvertrag der nordgriechischen Bottiaier in den delisch-attischen Seebund 421 v. Chr. sieht auch vor, dass diese Gemeinden, die 432 v. Chr. von Athen abgefallen waren[119], nun unter der wechselseitigen Zusicherung, dass man erlittenes Unrecht vergesse, wieder Aufnahme in die Symmachie fände[120]:

---

[115] W. Nippel (wie Fn. 21), S. 113.
[116] Dem. or. 24,56; vgl. dazu auch And. 1,87.
[117] Hdt. 7,145; Plut. Themistokles 6,5.
[118] Hdt. 8,29, 2.
[119] Thuk. 4,57; 58,1.
[120] IG I^3 1-2 76 Z 16-21.

[Βοττιαῖοι δὲ ὀμν]υόντον κατὰ [τάδε]·
φίλοι ἐσόμε[θα Ἀθεναίοις καὶ χσύμ[μαχοι πιστὸ[ς] κα[ὶ]
ἀδόλος καὶ τ[ὸς αὐ]τὸ[ς φίλος καὶ ἐχθ]ρὸς νομιôμε[ν] *h*όσ-
περ ἂν Ἀθενα[ῖοι], καὶ ο[ὐκ ὀφελέσο τὸ]ς ἐχθρὸς τὸς Ἀθεν-
αίον οὔτε χρ[έμα]σιν οὔτε *h*απλôς οὔτε δυνάμει οὐδεμιᾶι ο
ὐδὲ μνεσικ[ακέσο] τôν [παροιχομέν]ον ἕνεκα.

"Die Bottiaier aber sollen zu diesen Bedingungen schwören: Wir werden Freunde der Athener sein und Bundesgenossen treu und ohne Falsch und wir werden die gleichen für Freunde und für Feinde halten wie die Athener und ich werde den Feinden der Athener nicht von Nutzen sein, weder einfach mit Geldmitteln noch mit irgendwelcher Kraft und ich werde nicht Übel denken wegen der Dinge, die früher passiert sind.“

Die Reihe der vor allem aus epigraphischer Evidenz bekannten Amnestiebestimmungen im völkerrechtlichen Kontext ist lang – auch die Beispiele aus der Zeit des zweiten attischen Seebunds (Rhodos[121], Keos[122]) oder der Frieden Milets mit Magnesia aus 196 v. Chr.[123] gebrauchen das μὴ μνησικακεῖν[124] – die Formel wurde also auch noch weit über die griechische Klassik hinaus verwendet.

121 Pseudo-D. 15,14.

122 IG II/III² 1 111 Ze 58-62. 82-82 (Dekret der Athener für die Insel Keos 363/62 v. Chr.)

123 Ditt. Syll. 588, Ze 85 (Friedensvertrag von Milet mit Magnesia 196 v. Chr.)

124 Carawan (wie Fn. 22), S. 6-7 definiert die Formel wieder als in einem Eid zusammengefasste Generalklausel für das genauer Bedungene. Das steht nicht im Widerspruch zur Annahme, dass damit Amnestie-Inhalte ausgedrückt wurden – ganz im Gegenteil: Der Eid fasst die Rechtswirkungen einer Amnestie zusammen – genauso wie ein genereller Begriff die konkreten Konsequenzen.

G. Conclusio

Der Begriff ἀμνηστία ist als staatsrechtlicher Terminus relativ jung. Das frühe 5. Jh. v. Chr., in dem sich eine griechischrechtliche Begrifflichkeit ausprägt, kennt zwei Möglichkeiten, den Tatbestand des „Vergessens vorangegangenen Unrechts“ zu umschreiben:

Einerseits wird Amnestie anhand ihrer Rechtsfolgen beschrieben, der Wiederverleihung bürgerlicher Rechte (τοὺς ἀτίμους ἐπιτίμους ποιῆσαι) und der Wiederaufnahme von Verbannten (τούς τε φεύγοντας καταδέχεσθαι).

Andererseits ist die negative Konträraussage zum „Vergessen“[125], das „Nicht-Erinnern“, worunter sich viele Sachverhalte subsumieren lassen, in Gebrauch. Der wesentliche Sinngehalt der Norm ist das Neudefinieren von zwischenstaatlichen/innerstaatlichen Beziehungen durch verordnetes Vergessen der Vergangenheit. Dass dies mitunter nicht gleichzeitig die Negierung der Vergangenheit implizierte, hat Nippel aufgezeigt[126]. Ganz im Gegenteil: Das Verbot, „zu erinnern“, wirkt zwar stärker als das Gebot „zu vergessen“, setzt aber ein historisches Bewusstsein dafür voraus, was ganz wertfrei mit „das Vergangene“ oder „das Frühere“ bezeichnet wird. Dem stehen die oft genau determinierten Zielsetzungen und Konsequenzen, die genau formulierten Ausnahmetatbestände einer Amnestie gegenüber.

In der Enge einer Polis ist es nicht denkbar, dass politische Umwälzungen so schnell vergessen wurden, werden konnten. Sowohl wegen der Zweckmäßigkeit einer knappen Zusammenfassung wesentlichen Normgehalts durch eine dem Eid nahe stehende Formulierung als auch aufgrund der historischen Entwicklung staatsrechtlicher Begrifflichkeit lässt sich die Frage τίς μὲν ἐστι ἡ ἀμνηστία; für das klassische Griechenland wohl nur so beantworten: τὸ δὲ μὴ μνησικακεῖν.

---

[125] Zur negativen Konträraussage und ihrer Funktion vgl. Siewert (wie Fn. 39), 22.

[126] Nippel (wie Fn. 21), S. 118.

„Wiewohl von alters her, wie Ihr wißt, ye und ye verboten ist ...“: Gesetzgebung als Erinnern an Normen im Ancien Régime

Martin P. Schennach

A. Einleitung

In den Jahren 1570, 1575, 1576 und 1579 erließ die ‚oberösterreichische', d. h. für Tirol und die österreichischen Vorlande zuständige Regierung im Namen des Landesherrn Erzherzog Ferdinand II. von Österreich jeweils inhaltlich identische Gesetze mit einem räumlich auf die Residenzstadt Innsbruck und die Vorstadt beschränkten Geltungsbereich.[1] Darin wurde Bürgern und Inwohnern (d. h. Bewohnern minderer Rechtsqualität) der Stadt, Angehörigen des Hofgesindes und der in Innsbruck angesiedelten Verwaltungs- und Justizbehörden sowie Fremden gleichermaßen das Mitführen und Abfeuern von Schußwaffen innerhalb der Stadtmauern und in der Vorstadt bei Strafe untersagt. Die Publikation erfolgte auf den Adressatenkreis abgestimmt auf verschiedenen Kanälen: Der Hofmarschall hatte das Verbot den Angehörigen des Hofstaats zu publizieren, Bürgern und Inwohnern sowie Fremden war es durch den Stadtrichter bekannt zu machen – wobei die Wirte zusätzlich die bei ihnen Einkehrenden auf das Verbot hinzuweisen hatten –, und für die Kundmachung an die Angehörigen der Regierung sowie der Kammer hatten die jeweiligen Behörden selbst Sorge zu tragen. Auf diese Weise sollten sämtliche, unterschiedlichen jurisdiktionellen Zuständigkeiten unterstehenden Personengruppen der Stadt möglichst vollzählig erreicht werden.

---

[1] Vgl. Tiroler Landesarchiv (zukünftig abgekürzt: TLA), An die Fürstliche Durchlaucht 1570, fol. 356^{v}-258^{r}, 4. Aug. 1570; TLA, An die Fürstliche Durchlaucht 1576, fol. 325^{v}-326^{r}, 30. April 1575; TLA, An die Fürstliche Durchlaucht 1576, fol. 394, 4. Mai 1576; TLA, Von der Fürstlichen Durchlaucht 1579, fol. 182^{v}, 4. Juni 1579.

Schon bei der Kenntnisnahme des Verbotsinhalts mag der Rechtshistoriker stutzig geworden sein. Ist ein derartiges Verbot aufgrund seiner Selbstverständlichkeit nicht völlig überflüssig? Es gehört schließlich zum rechtshistorischen Handbuchwissen, daß die frühneuzeitliche wie die mittelalterliche Stadt einen Bezirk erhöhten Friedens konstituierte, in dem das Führen von Waffen strengen Restriktionen unterlag, vom Abfeuern von Schußwaffen ganz zu schweigen.[2] Dieser Befund gilt auch für die damals zwischen 4000 bis 5000 Bewohner zählende Stadt Innsbruck, wo das Verbot des Schußwaffenführens und -abfeuerns bereits unter Kaiser Ferdinand I. 1558 durch ein Gesetz betont worden war und ebenfalls in die 1568 erlassene „Ordnung guter Mannszucht" Eingang gefunden hatte.[3]

Die ausgezeichnete archivalische Überlieferungslage erlaubt es uns, die Motive zu erschließen, welche die Regierung innerhalb eines Jahrzehntes zur viermaligen Wiederholung einer inhaltlichen Selbstverständlichkeit veranlaßten. Dabei handelte es sich um konkrete Vorfälle, die seitens des Gesetzgebers als Anlaß zur Erneuerung des längst bestehenden Verbots benutzt wurden. 1570 war eine Gewehrkugel in der Regimentskanzlei eingeschlagen, über die Köpfe des dort tätigen Schreibpersonals hinweggesaust und in den Ofen eingeschlagen. Nachforschungen ergaben, daß der Schuß fahrlässig aus einem Fenster des gegenüberliegenden Gasthauses abgegeben worden war. Ähnlich spektakuläre Begebenheiten ereigneten sich fünf Jahre später: Innerhalb der Stadt waren von Unbekannten fünf bis sechs Schuß abgegeben worden, wobei sich eine Kugel in ein Zimmer der Finanzbehörde verirrte. Das landesfürstliche Placet zur neuerlichen Kundmachung war noch nicht eingelangt, als vier Monate später von der Regierung die rasche Neupublikation der Vorschrift urgiert wurde: Nächtens war eine Gewehrkugel in das Sitzungszimmer des Regierungsrates eingeschlagen und in der Täfelung stecken geblieben. In den

---

[2] Vgl. nur allgemein Bader, Karl Siegfried; Dilcher, Gerhard: Deutsche Rechtsgeschichte. Land und Stadt – Bürger und Bauer im alten Europa (Enzyklopädie der Rechts- und Staatswissenschaft; Abteilung Rechtswissenschaft). Berlin u.a. 1999, S. 642-645; Dilcher, Gerhard: Gewalt, Friede und Recht – in der mittelalterlichen Stadt und außerhalb. In: Festschrift für Gert Kleinheyer zum 70. Geburtstag. Hrsg. von Franz Dorn und Jan Schröder. Heidelberg 2001, S. 95-106.

[3] TLA, Buch Tirol 1558, fol. 392, 5. Dez. 1558; TLA, Kopialbuch oö. Hofrat, Ausgegangene Schriften in Regimentssachen, Bd. 4 (1568), fol. 1^v-4^v, 2. Jan. 1568.

Jahren 1576 und 1579 wiederum stellte das Abfeuern von Gewehren durch Angehörige des Hofstaates in unmittelbarer Nähe der Regierung den Anlaß für die wiederholte Kundmachung dar.

Dieses viermalige „Erinnern“ an eine Rechtsnorm sagt nur bedingt etwas über die Implementation der entsprechenden Bestimmung aus. Die Regierung schloß aus sie unmittelbar betreffenden Einzelfällen auf potentiell weiter verbreitete Mißstände. Ob diese tatsächlich gegeben waren, läßt sich nicht zuverlässig beurteilen, wenngleich bezweifelt werden darf, daß sich in der Residenzstadt regelmäßig „Wildwestszenen“ abgespielt haben. Rekonstruieren läßt sich nur, daß das Abfeuern von Gewehren bei Festlichkeiten wie beispielsweise bei Hochzeiten als Freudenbekundung durchaus verbreitet war.[4]

B. Recht und Gesetz im Mittelalter

Das einleitende Beispiel, bei dem der Gesetzgeber den Normadressaten eine seit langem bestehende Vorschrift durch deren neuerliche Publikation ins Gedächtnis zu rufen versucht, führt mitten in das Thema des vorliegenden Beitrags, das jedoch aufgrund seiner Breite nach einer Fokussierung verlangt.

Gerade das Mittelalter bietet überreiches Untersuchungsmaterial für das Ausloten des Beziehungsdreiecks „Verschriftlichung – Recht – Gesetz“. So konnte das schriftliche Festhalten von Rechtsnormen in einer weitestgehend oralen Gesellschaft in den verschiedensten Kontexten – im Rahmen einer Dorf- oder Stadtgemeinde, im Rahmen einer Grundherrschaft, in ursprünglich privaten und später gewohnheitsrechtlich Geltung erlangenden Kompilationen – unter anderem auch dem Sicherstellen von Erinnerung dienen.[5] Doch schon die Frage nach der Abgrenzung von „Gesetzgebung“ einerseits und „Recht“ andererseits zeigt die sich für das Mittelalter eröffnende Problematik. Im weltlichen Bereich wurde im Mittelalter die Gesetzgebungsbefugnis nicht als selbständiges Herrschaftsrecht verstanden, sondern als Annex und Ausfluß

---

[4] Vgl. nur TLA, CD 1617, fol. 65^{v}-66^{r}, 7. Juni 1617; CD 1596, fol. 16^{r}-17^{r}, 17. Febr. 1596.

[5] Allgemein Schmidt-Wiegand, Ruth: Recht und Gesetz im Spannungsfeld zwischen Schriftlichkeit und Mündlichkeit im Mittelalter. In: Frühmittelalterliche Studien 27 (1993), S. 147-166.

der Jurisdiktionsgewalt.[6] Zu einer tiefgreifenden Änderung kam es auf dem Gebiet des Heiligen Römischen Reichs erst in der Frühneuzeit im Gefolge der Rezeption von Jean Bodin: Erst jetzt wurde die *potestas legislatoria* als eigenständiges, ja als zentrales Herrschaftsrecht verstanden.[7] Und während im Kirchenrecht schon im 12. Jahrhundert die Überzeugung von der intentionalen Gestalt- und Wandelbarkeit der Rechtsordnung durch die beim Papst konzentrierte Gesetzgebung Platz griff,[8] setzte sich diese Vorstellung im weltlichen Bereich nur ganz allmählich durch.[9]

Aufgabe des mittelalterlichen Herrschers war primär die Rechtswahrung bzw. allenfalls die Rechtsbesserung, das heißt die Beseitigung von Unklarheiten, Widersprüchen oder wahrgenommenen Lücken, nicht die bewußte und autoritative Schaffung neuen Rechts.[10] In diesem Kontext wird man rasch mit der Themenstellung „Gesetzgebung als Erinnerung an Rechtsnormen" kon-

---

[6] Vgl. Schlosser, Hans: Rechtssetzung und Gesetzgebungsverständnis im Territorialstaat Bayern im 16. Jahrhundert. In: Zeitschrift für bayerische Landesgeschichte 50 (1987), S. 41-61, hier S. 45.

[7] Vgl. zuletzt Mohnhaupt, Heinz: Grundlinien in der Geschichte der Gesetzgebung auf dem europäischen Kontinent vom 16. bis 18. Jahrhundert. Ein experimenteller Überblick, in: Zeitschrift für Neuere Rechtsgeschichte 28 (2006), S. 124-174, hier S. 133-135; Mohnhaupt, Heinz: Potestas legislatoria und Gesetzesbegriff im Ancien Régime. In: Ius Commune 4 (1972), S. 188-239, hier S. 189-190; Stolleis, Michael: Condere leges et interpretari. Gesetzgebungsmacht und Staatsbildung in der frühen Neuzeit. In: Ders.: Staat und Staatsräson in der frühen Neuzeit. Frankfurt a. M. 1990, S. 167-196, hier S. 170-175; Ebel, Wilhelm: Geschichte der Gesetzgebung in Deutschland (Göttinger rechtswissenschaftliche Studien 24). Göttingen [2]1958, S. 69-70.

[8] Vgl. Fransen, Gérard: Art. „Gesetzgebung, kirchliche". In: Lexikon des Mittelalters, Bd. IV. München/Zürich 1989, Sp. 1392-1394, hier Sp. 1393.

[9] Vgl. Krause, Hermann: Dauer und Vergänglichkeit im mittelalterlichen Recht. In: Zeitschrift der Savigny-Stiftung für Rechtsgeschichte, Germ. Abt. 75 (1958), S. 206-251, hier S. 242-243; Kroeschell, Karl: Deutsche Rechtsgeschichte. Bd. 1: Bis 1250. Köln/Weimar/Wien [12]2005, S. 315-316; Dilcher, Gerhard: Zeitbewußtsein und Geschichtlichkeit im Bereich hochmittelalterlicher Rechtsgewohnheit. In: Hochmittelalterliches Geschichtsbewußtsein im Spiegel nichthistoriographischer Quellen. Hrsg. von Hans-Werner Goetz. Berlin 1998, S. 31-54, hier S. 53-54; Grawert, Rolf: Historische Entwicklungslinien des neuzeitlichen Gesetzesrecht. In: Der Staat 11 (1972), S. 1-25, hier bes. S. 3-4; Gagnér, Sten: Studien zur Ideengeschichte der Gesetzgebung. Uppsala 1960; Wolf, Armin: Gesetzgebung in Europa 1100-1500. Zur Entstehung der Territorialstaaten. München [2]1996.

[10] Vgl. Dilcher, Gerhard: Der Gedanke der Rechtserneuerung im Mittelalter. In: Geschichte der Zentraljustiz in Mitteleuropa. Festschrift für Bernhard Diestelkamp zum 65. Geburtstag. Hrsg. von Friedrich Battenberg und Filippo Ranieri. Weimar u.a. 1994, S. 1-16, hier S. 13-14.

frontiert – vorausgesetzt, daß man einer entsprechenden Untersuchung einen der Komplexität historischer Verhältnisse Rechnung tragenden, weit gefaßten Gesetzesbegriff zugrunde zu legen bereit ist.

Überblickt man rechtshistorische wie historische Gesetzesdefinitionen, lassen sich mehrere konstitutive Elemente extrahieren, über die breiter Konsens besteht: erstens der Erlaß durch eine übergeordnete und legitimierte Autorität; zweitens der Geltungswille; drittens der generell-abstrakte Charakter. Gewisse Merkmale können ergänzend angeführt werden, beispielsweise wenn auf die äußere Form abgestellt und zusätzlich zur implizit stets vorausgesetzten Schriftlichkeit eine Urkundenform oder urkundenähnliche Form verlangt wird.[11] Der seitens des Gesetzgebers zu fordernde Geltungswille scheint freilich für das Mittelalter schon diskutabel, ‚galt' doch Recht im Mittelalter „kraft einer den Normen immanenten Autorität, nicht allein deshalb, weil sie förmlich in Kraft gesetzt worden sind."[12] Für die Geltung einer Norm war in der Tat im Mittelalter die Observanz, das heißt die faktische Anwendung, ungleich wichtiger als der in einem Anwendungsbefehl zum Ausdruck kommende Herrscherwille.[13] Solange ein Gesetzgebungsakt vorhandene Rechtsgewohnheiten[14] wiedergab, denen die Oberservanz *per definitionem* zukam, stellte sich dieses Problem ohnehin nicht. Virulent wurde es nur, wenn ein Gesetz „neues

---

[11] Vgl. nur die Definition bei Schlosser, Hans: Rechtsgewalt und Rechtsbildung im ausgehenden Mittelalter. In: Zeitschrift der Savigny-Stiftung für Rechtsgeschichte, Germ. Abt. 100 (1983), S. 9-52, hier S. 30; Pauser, Josef: Landesfürstliche Gesetzgebung (Policey-, Malefiz- und Landesordnungen). In: Quellenkunde der Habsburgermonarchie (16.-18. Jahrhundert). Ein exemplarisches Handbuch. Hrsg. von Josef Pauser, Martin Scheutz und Thomas Winkelbauer (Mitteilungen des Instituts für Österreichische Geschichtsforschung, Ergänzungsband 44). Wien/ München 2004, S. 216-256, hier S. 216-217.

[12] Willoweit, Dietmar: Hofordnungen als Zeugnisse des Rechtsdenkens. In: Hof und Theorie. Annäherungen an ein historisches Phänomen. Hrsg. von Reinhardt Butz u.a. Köln/Wien/Weimar 2004, S. 165-178, hier S. 168; nunmehr auch Herchert, Gaby: Recht und Geltung. Zur bildungsgeschichtlichen Deutung des Begriffs der Geltung im Mittelalter. Würzburg 2003, bes. S. 133-136.

[13] Simon, Thomas: Geltung. Der Weg von der Gewohnheit zur Positivität des Rechts. In: Rechtsgeschichte 7 (2005), S. 100-137.

[14] Auf die terminologische Diskussion „Gewohnheitsrecht versus Rechtsgewohnheiten" kann an dieser Stelle nicht weiter eingegangen werden. Einen Überblick bietet Kannowski, Bernd: Rechtsbegriffe im Mittelalter. Stand der Diskussion. In: Rechtsbegriffe im Mittelalter. Hrsg. von Bernd Kannowski und Albrecht Cordes (Rechtshistorische Reihe 262). Frankfurt a. M. u.a. 2003, S. 1-27.

Recht" schuf. Dies führt mitten in eine für unsere Fragestellung prekäre Frage rund um den mittelalterlichen Gesetzesbegriff: Ist für diesen die Setzung „neuen Rechtes" eine *conditio sine qua non*, wie dies zum Beispiel Hermann Krause deutlich postuliert: „Rechtssetzung dagegen enthält das Element des Willens zur verbindlichen Geltung von Regeln, die bisher nicht galten oder dunkel oder strittig waren [...]"[15]. Oder genügt auch die Konfirmation und allenfalls Besserung vorgefundenen Rechts (die Rechtsdarstellung), um den Kriterien eines Gesetzes Genüge zu tun? Reiner Schulze forderte dementsprechend nachdrücklich, historische Gesetzgebung „nicht allein als Rechtsetzung – im Sinne einer Schaffung neuer Normen – sondern auch als Rechtsdarstellung – im Sinne der Fixierung und Ordnung bestehenden Rechts – durch eine übergeordnete Autorität zu verstehen."[16]

Das inhaltliche Postulat nach der bewußten Schaffung „neuen Rechts" setzt als Prämisse die grundsätzliche Überzeugung von der Gestaltbarkeit der Rechtsordnung voraus, die – wie bereits angedeutet – im weltlichen Bereich in größerem Umfang erst im 15. Jahrhundert Fuß faßte. Das Zugrundelegen eines derart restringierten Gesetzesbegriffes würde für das Mittelalter nicht nur zu einer signifikanten Einengung des Untersuchungsgegenstandes führen, sondern wirft zugleich erhebliche methodische Schwierigkeiten auf: In einer vorwiegend oralen Gesellschaft ist die Rekonstruktion der vor einer schriftlichen Fixierung geltenden Rechtsgewohnheiten problematisch. Ferner wäre zu erörtern, welche inhaltlichen Kriterien überhaupt zu fordern sind, um von „neuem Recht" sprechen zu können: Muß dieses ausdrücklich bisherige Rechtsgewohnheiten kassieren, genügt die Besetzung bisher nicht normativ erfaßten Raums oder ist gar schon die Rechtsbesserung und Systematisierung ausreichend? Zumeist findet man Lösungsansätze, die explizit oder implizit

---

[15] Krause, Hermann: Art. „Gesetzgebung". In: Handwörterbuch zur deutschen Rechtsgeschichte. Hrsg. von Adalbert Erler und Ekkehard Kaufmann. Bd. 1, Berlin 1971, Sp. 1606-1620, hier Sp. 1607.

[16] Schulze, Reiner: Geschichte der neueren vorkonstitutionellen Gesetzgebung. Zu Forschungsstand und Methodenfragen eines rechtshistorischen Arbeitsgebietes. In: Zeitschrift der Savigny-Stiftung für Rechtsgeschichte, Germ. Abt. 98 (1981), S. 157-235, hier S. 165-167, Zitat S. 166; vgl. auch Diestelkamp, Bernhard: Einige Beobachtungen zur Geschichte des Gesetzes in vorkonstitutioneller Zeit. In: Zeitschrift für Historische Forschung 10 (1983), S. 385-420, hier S. 390.

eine Gesetzgebung ‚im modernen Sinn', eine ‚echte Gesetzgebung', für welche die Setzung neuen Rechts konstitutiv sei, vom mittelalterlichen Gesetzesverständnis abgrenzen, wo dies zumeist nicht zutreffe[17] – wenngleich das Sicherstellen von „Erinnerung" im Sinne von rechtswahrender und rechtsbessernder Gesetzgebung durchaus auch noch in der Frühneuzeit eine gewisse Rolle spielt.[18]

Die Problematik kann an dieser Stelle nicht weiter entwickelt werden. Die Ausführungen dürften aber deutlich gemacht haben, daß eine sowohl zeitliche als auch inhaltliche Fokussierung der Fragestellung unabdingbar ist. Im folgenden wird eine zeitliche Beschränkung insofern vorgenommen, als unter Berücksichtigung spätmittelalterlicher Entwicklungstendenzen der Schwerpunkt der Untersuchung auf die Frühe Neuzeit gelegt wird, wobei inhaltlich vorwiegend (aber nicht ausschließlich) die Gesetzgebung zur ‚guten Policey' im Mittelpunkt stehen soll.

C. Gesetzgebung und ‚gute Policey' im Ancien Régime

Die Bedeutung der Policeygesetzgebung, die quantitativ die legislative Tätigkeit frühneuzeitlicher Territorien stark dominierte, für die Herausbildung moderner Staatlichkeit ist spätestens seit der grundlegenden Untersuchung von Hans Maier[19] bekannt und wird von der neueren Forschung *una voce* her-

---

[17] Vgl. Brauneder, Wilhelm: Österreichische Verfassungsgeschichte. Wien [10]2005, S. 44; Härter, Karl: Entwicklung und Funktion der Policeygesetzgebung des Heiligen Römischen Reiches Deutscher Nation im 16. Jahrhundert. In: Ius Commune 20 (1993), S. 61-141, hier S. 62; Lieberich, Heinz: Die Anfänge der Polizeigesetzgebung des Herzogtums Baiern. In: Festschrift für Max Spindler zum 75. Geburtstag. Hrsg. von Dieter Albrecht. München 1969, S. 307-378, bes. S. 308; Schlosser, Rechtsgewalt und Rechtsbildung (wie Fn. 11), bes. S. 34 und 51; Dilcher, Rechtserneuerung (wie Fn. 10), S. 14.

[18] Pointiert bringt die Vorbehalte gegenüber dem Gesetzesbegriff der deutschen Rechtsgeschichte (vor allem in der Nachfolge von Wilhelm Ebel) auf den Punkt Fögen, Marie Theres: Morsche Wurzeln und frische Früchte. Notizen zum Gesetzesbegriff der deutschen Rechtsgeschichte, in: Rechtshistorisches Journal 6 (1987), S. 349-360, bes. S. 356-360.

[19] Maier, Hans: Die ältere deutsche Staats- und Verwaltungslehre. München [2]1980.

vorgehoben.[20] Dabei stand die Gesetzgebung zur ‚guten Policey' bis vor kurzem im Schatten einerseits der privatrechtlichen Kodifikationen der Frühneuzeit, die insbesondere unter dem Blickwinkel der Rezeption des römisch-gemeinen Rechts die Aufmerksamkeit auf sich zogen, andererseits der Strafrechtsgeschichte.[21] Erst in den letzten Jahren verzeichnen Untersuchungen zur ‚guten Policey' sowohl unter Historikern als auch Rechtshistorikern einen signifikanten Aufschwung.[22] Die lange Zeit stiefmütterliche Behandlung der Policeygesetzgebung lag wohl nicht zuletzt in der schwierigen und disparaten archivalischen Überlieferungslage begründet. Hier verspricht inzwischen das ambitionierte, am Max-Planck-Institut für Europäische Rechtsgeschichte in

[20] Vgl. nur stellvertretend Willoweit, Dietmar: Deutsche Verfassungsgeschichte. Vom Frankenreich bis zur Wiedervereinigung Deutschlands. Ein Studienbuch (Kurzlehrbücher für das juristische Studium). München [5]2005, hier S. 162-163; Fried, Johannes: Überlegungen zum Problem von Gesetzgebung und Institutionalisierung im Mittelalter. In: Institutionen und Geschichte. Theoretische Aspekte und mittelalterliche Befunde. Hrsg. von Gert Melville (Norm und Struktur 1). Köln/Weimar/Wien 1992, S. 133-136, hier S. 133-134; Pauser, Josef: „sein ir Majestät jetzo im werkh die polliceyordnung widerumb zu verneuern". Kaiser Maximilian II. (1564-1576) und die Landstände von Österreich unter der Enns im gemeinsamen Ringen um die „gute policey". In: Recht und Gericht in Niederösterreich. Die Vorträge des 17. Symposions des Niederösterreichischen Instituts für Landeskunde. Stift Ardagger, 30. Juni bis 4. Juli 1997. Hrsg. von Willibald Rosner (Studien und Forschungen aus dem Niederösterreichischen Institut für Landeskunde 31). St. Pölten 2002, S. 17-66, hier S. 18; Klippel, Diethelm: Zur Geschichte der Gesetzgebung in der Frühen Neuzeit. Eine Einführung. In: Gesetz und Gesetzgebung im Europa der Frühen Neuzeit. Hrsg. von Barbara Dölemayer und Diethelm Klippel (Zeitschrift für Historische Forschung, Beiheft 22). Berlin 1998, S. 7-16, hier S. 7.

[21] So schon Schlosser, Hans: Zum Rechtsquellencharakter der bayerischen Polizeimandate des 16. Jahrhunderts. In: Archivalische Zeitschrift 75 (1979), S. 225-232, hier S. 226; ähnlich noch Schildt, Bernd: Die frühneuzeitlichen Policey- und Landesgesetzgebung am Beispiel von Dorf- und Landesordnungen der Grafschaft Schwarzburg aus dem 16. Jahrhundert. In: Recht – Idee – Geschichte. Beiträge zur Rechts- und Ideengeschichte für Rolf Lieberwirth anläßlich seines 80. Geburtstages. Hrsg. von Heiner Lück und Bernd Schildt. Köln/Weimar/Wien 2000, S. 229-248, hier S. 248.

[22] Stellvertretend seien nur genannt: Härter, Karl: Policey und Strafjustiz in Kurmainz. Gesetzgebung, Normdurchsetzung und Sozialkontrolle im frühneuzeitlichen Territorialstaat (Studien zur europäischen Rechtsgeschichte 190). 2 Teilbde. Frankfurt a. M. 2005; Holenstein, André: „Gute Policey" und lokale Gesellschaft im Staat des Ancien Régime. Das Fallbeispiel der Markgrafschaft Baden(-Durlach) (Frühneuzeit-Forschungen 9/1-2). 2 Teilbde. Tübingen 2003. Verwiesen sei zudem auf die von Michael Stolleis herausgegebene Reihe „Studien zu Policey und Policeywissenschaft".

Frankfurt am Main angesiedelte Projekt „Repertorium der Policeyordnungen der Frühen Neuzeit“ Abhilfe.

Materiell war dabei der Policeybegriff umfassend. Die ‚gute Policey' bezeichnete die gute Ordnung des Gemeinwesens im allgemeinen sowie in Zusammenhang hiermit sämtliche Maßnahmen, die der Bewahrung oder (Wieder-)Herstellung dieses Zustandes dienten. Der Begriff hatte sich Mitte des 15. Jahrhunderts im urbanen Bereich entwickelt und wurde bald zu einer Leitkategorie frühneuzeitlicher Gesetzgebung.[23]

I. „Wiewohl von alters her, wie Ihr wißt, ye und ye verboten ist ...“: Policeygesetzgebung als Fortschreibung traditionalen Rechts[24]

Dabei dominiert die Einschätzung, daß mit dem Einsetzen der Policeygesetzgebung auf Ebene der Territorien Mitte des 15. Jahrhunderts und mit ihrem nahezu exponentiellen Wachstum ab dem 16. Jahrhundert – in deutlicher Abgrenzung vom Mittelalter – ein fundamental neues Rechtsverständnis einherging, das Recht nicht mehr als unveränderliche Größe und Konstante, sondern als gestaltbare Variable auffaßte. Zudem bot die Policeygesetzgebung die Möglichkeit zur legislativen Durchdringung von rechtlich bislang nicht normierten Lebensbereichen, was eine Kompetenzausweitung für den Gesetzgeber, der die Inhalte der ‚guten Policey' definierte, nach sich zog.[25] Damit harmonieren zwei theoretische Modelle, die zur Erklärung des plötzlich rapiden Anwachsens der Gesetzgebungstätigkeit im ausgehenden Mittelalter entwickelt wurden und die man etwas plakativ als „Krisentheorie“ und „Verdich-

---

[23] Vgl. Simon, Thomas: „Gute Policey“. Ordnungsleitbilder und Zielvorstellungen politischen Handelns in der Frühen Neuzeit (Studien zur europäischen Rechtsgeschichte 170). Frankfurt a. M. 2004, S. 111-120; Härter, Policey und Strafjustiz (wie Fn. 22), bes. S. 118-123; Pauser, Maximilian II. und die Landstände (wie Fn. 20), S. 17-18 (alle mit weiteren Literaturhinweisen).

[24] Zitat: TLA, Kopialbuch Ältere Reihe, Lit. Qq, Nr. 42, S. 234, 11. Aug. 1522. Dieses auch für den Titel herangezogene Quellenzitat wurde – im Gegensatz zu den übrigen Quellenauszügen – leicht normalisiert.

[25] Stolleis, Michael: Geschichte des öffentlichen Rechts in Deutschland. Bd. 1: Reichspublizistik und Policeywissenschaft 1600-1800. München 1988, S. 369-370.

tungstheorie" umschreiben könnte.[26] Diese besagen, daß im Spätmittelalter und in der beginnenden Frühneuzeit der Gesetzgeber auf krisenhafte Erscheinungen von Wirtschaft und Gesellschaft bzw. auf die zunehmenden Komplexität („Verdichtung") des menschlichen Zusammenlebens reagieren und durch neue legislativen Maßnahmen steuernd eingreifen mußte.

Demgegenüber führt die „Insuffizienztheorie" deutlich besser die zumindest partielle Verankerung der Policeygesetzung im traditionalen Recht vor Augen. Diese stellt die These auf, daß der sich entwickelnde frühmoderne Staat in zunehmendem Maße regulative Aufgaben übernahm, die zuvor ausschließlich oder überwiegend zuständige Institutionen wie die ländliche und städtische Gemeinde oder die Kirche nicht mehr zufriedenstellend wahrnehmen konnten. In der Tat betreten bei weitem nicht alle Teile der Policeygesetzgebung rechtliches Brachland oder greifen gestaltend in die Rechtsordnung ein, sondern pochen auf die Einhaltung längst vertrauter, traditionaler Normen. Das einleitende Beispiel des wiederholten Verbots des Abfeuerns von Schußwaffen im Stadtgebiet, das eine Selbstverständlichkeit städtischen Lebens einschärft, ist nur ein Exempel unter vielen. Fastenmandate, mit denen der Landesherr seine Pflichten als christlicher Herrscher wahrnimmt, indem er die Einhaltung des christlichen Fastengebotes einmahnt, bringen ein kirchliches Gebot in Erinnerung und bedrohen dessen Nichtbefolgung mit weltlichen Strafen.[27] In Einklang hiermit steht der Befund, daß das landesfürstliche Gesetzgebungsrecht wenngleich nicht gänzlich, so doch zumindest partiell im spätmittelalterlichen Gebots- und Verbotsrecht verankert ist, das seinerseits stark im alten Herkommen verwurzelt war und keinesfalls eine unbeschränkte rechtliche Gestaltungsbefugnis einräumte.[28] Ein vergleichbares Bild ergibt sich bei näherer Analyse des sogenannten Landgebots, das Hans Schlosser als Be-

---

[26] Simon, Thomas: Krise oder Wachstum? Erklärungsversuche zum Aufkommen territorialer Gesetzgebung am Ausgang des Mittelalters. In: Wirkungen europäischer Rechtsgeschichte. Festschrift für Karl Kroeschell zum 70. Geburtstag. Hrsg. von Gerhard Köbler und Hermann Nehlsen. München 1997, S. 1201-1217, hier bes. S. 1206-1210.

[27] Vgl. z. B. TLA, Causa Domini 1550, fol. 43^{v}-44^{r}, 1. März 1550.

[28] Vgl. Willoweit, Dietmar: Gebot und Verbot im Spätmittelalter – vornehmlich nach südhessischen und mainfränkischen Weistümern. In: Hessisches Jahrbuch für Landesgeschichte 30 (1980), S. 94-130.

sonderheit des bayerischen Rechts ausgemacht und als unmittelbaren Vorläufer der Landesordnungen bezeichnet hat. Dabei zeigt sich, daß die Landgebote nicht auf systematische Rechtsänderung und Rechtsgestaltung abzielten. „Einen breiten Raum beanspruchen dagegen die wiederholenden Bestätigungen alter Landrechtssätze, des Herkommens und der alten Gewohnheiten.“[29]

Derartige Rechtsetzungsakte wollen eine als bedroht wahrgenommene Ordnung sichern oder wiederherstellen, indem sie traditionale Gebote bzw. Verbote wieder einschärfend in Erinnerung bringen und allenfalls adaptieren.[30]

Wie stark Teile der Policeygesetzgebung hergebrachte Normen aufgreifen und so die „Erinnerung“ an Normen sicherstellen, deren Implementation als ungenügend perzipiert wurde, zeigt nicht zuletzt die in vielen Policeygesetzgebungsakten ausdrücklich zu findende Berufung auf das „alte Herkommen“ und vorhandene Rechtsgewohnheiten.[31] Natürlich ist Vorsicht angebracht, von derartigen Behauptungen in den Narrationes der Gesetzestexte nicht einfach stringent auf das Bestehen entsprechender Rechtsgewohnheiten schließen zu wollen; es kann sich im Einzelfall um einen Legitimationstopos des Gesetzgebers handeln, um die Akzeptanz einer Neuregelung bei den Normad-

---

[29] Schlosser, Rechtsgewalt und Rechtsbildung (wie Fn. 11), S. 18.

[30] Vgl. auch Härter, Policey und Strafjustiz (wie Fn. 22), S. 188; Weber, Matthias: Ständische Disziplinierungsbestrebungen durch Polizeiordnungen und Mechanismen ihrer Durchsetzung – Regionalstudie Schlesien. In: Policey im Europa der Frühen Neuzeit. Hrsg. von Michael Stolleis (Ius Commune, Sonderheft 83). Frankfurt a. M. 1996, S. 333-375, hier S. 353-355; Weber, Matthias: Die schlesischen Polizei- und Landesordnungen der Frühen Neuzeit (Neue Forschungen zur schlesischen Geschichte 5). Köln/Weimar/Wien 1996, S. 172-176; Schulze, Reiner: Die Polizeigesetzgebung zur Wirtschafts- und Arbeitsordnung der Mark Brandenburg in der frühen Neuzeit (Untersuchungen zur deutschen Staats- und Rechtsgeschichte, Neue Folge 22). Aalen 1978, S. 125-129; Janssen, Wilhelm: „... na gesetze unser lande ...“. Zur territorialen Gesetzgebung im späten Mittelalter. In: Gesetzgebung als Faktor der Staatsentwicklung. Tagung der Vereinigung für Verfassungsgeschichte in Hofgeismar am 21./22. März 1993. Redigiert von Dietmar Willoweit (Der Staat, Beiheft 7). Berlin 1984, S. 7-40, hier S. 32-33; Stolleis, Geschichte des öffentlichen Rechts (wie Fn. 25), S. 371.

[31] Vgl. z. B. TLA, Kopialbuch Ältere Reihe, Lit. C, Nr. 4, fol. 340^{v}, 26. Jan. 1482; Kopialbuch Ältere Reihe, Lit. D, Nr. 5, fol. 146^{v}, 25. April 1483; Kopialbuch Ältere Reihe, Lit. W, Nr. 24, fol. 48^{v}-49^{r}, 9. Jan. 1501; TLA, Buch Tirol 1532, fol. 99, 15. Jan. 1532; ebd., fol. 351^{v}-352^{r}, 9. Dez. 1532.

ressaten zu erhöhen. Doch ist auch eine solche Schlußfolgerung sicherlich nicht zu generalisieren.

So stammen die ersten Tiroler Policeygesetze gegen den preistreiberischen Aufkauf und Vertrieb von Lebensmitteln und gegen den Getreide- und Viehexport aus den Jahren 1453, 1474, 1482 und 1489. Unter Maximilian I. nehmen die einschlägigen Bestimmungen nochmals rasant zu (1491, zwei Mandate 1496, 1497, 1501, 1502 etc.).[32] Dies besagt aber keineswegs, daß der ‚Fürkauf' in den Jahrzehnten vor der Überlieferung der frühesten Normen ein sozial und rechtliches akzeptiertes Verhaltensmuster war.[33]

In einigen Fällen lassen sich sogar die Interessenslagen und Initiativen erschließen, die bei Policeybestimmungen zur gesetzlichen Fixierung bestehender Normen geführt haben. Es war beispielsweise im Sinn der Schonung der für die Salz- und Edelmetallproduktion eminent wichtigen Holzbestände, wenn 1522 mit Hinweis auf die bisherige Rechtslage betont wird, daß die Harzgewinnung nur bei vorheriger Genehmigung durch die lokalen Obrigkeiten erlaubt sei.[34] Deutlich wird überdies der Nutznießer greifbar, wenn im Jahr 1501 unter Verweis auf die Regierungszeit Erzherzog Siegmunds sämtlichen Fischern auf dem Innfluß eingeschärft wird, das dem Innsbrucker Hof zukommende Vorkaufsrecht zu respektieren.[35] Anders verhält es sich bei zwei Beispielen aus dem Jahr 1492: Wenn Richter und Pfleger in einem Mandat Maximilians I. nachdrücklich angewiesen wurden, es bezüglich der Inhaftie-

---

[32] Vgl. nur Steinegger, Fritz: Die Münz- und Wirtschaftsordnung von Herzog Sigmund dem Münzreichen für Tirol vom 7. und 8. Oktober 1453. In: Tiroler Heimat 58 (1994), S. 43-55, hier S. 52; TLA, Codex 195, fol. 19^r-21^v, 29. Juni 1474; TLA, Ältere Kopialbuchreihe Nr. 4, Lit. C, fol. 382^r; ebd., Nr. 10, Lit. L, fol. 59, 5. Juni 1489; TLA, Verhandlungen der Landschaft, Bd. 1, fol. 130, 25. Okt. 1491; TLA, Ältere Kopialbuchreihe, Lit. S, Nr. 19, S. 296-297, 6. Mai 1496; ebd., S. 378-379, 5. Dez. 1496; ebd., Lit. T, Nr. 20, S. 265, 16. Aug. 1497; ebd., Lit. W, Nr. 24, fol. 68^v-69^r, 1. Nov. 1501; ebd., Lit. X, Nr. 25, fol. 30^r, 2. Dez. 1502.

[33] Vgl. nur die auf Drängen der Landstände in die Landesfreiheiten von 1404 und 1451 aufgenommenen entsprechenden Bestimmungen: Schober, Richard: Die Urkunden des Landschaftlichen Archivs zu Innsbruck (1342-1600) (Tiroler Geschichtsquellen 29). Innsbruck 1990, S. 11-15 und S. 25-27.

[34] TLA, Kopialbuch Ältere Reihe, Lit. Qq, Nr. 42, S. 234, 11. Aug. 1511.

[35] Ausgewählte Regesten des Kaiserreichs unter Maximilian I. (1493-1519) (Regesta Imperii XIV). 3. Bd., 1. Teil. Bearbeitet von Hermann Wiesflecker u.a. Wien/Köln/Weimar 1996, Nr. 15032, 11. März 1501.

rung ‚angesessener', über Grund und Boden verfügender Untertanen „beleiben [zu] lassen wie von alter herkomen", geht diese Verordnung auf eine Beschwerde von Vertretern des Bürger- und Bauernstandes auf dem unmittelbar zuvor abgehaltenen Landtag zurück.[36] Dort war, wie im übrigen mehrmals zuvor und danach, bemängelt worden, daß die lokalen Obrigkeiten aufgrund von finanziellen Motiven auch ‚angesessene' Untertanen nicht nur wegen des Verdachts peinlicher Straftaten festnehmen würden, sondern ebenso bei nur mit bürgerlichen Strafen bedrohten Vergehen. In einem am selben Tag erlassenen Mandat wurde auf Begehren der Tiroler Landstände das Importverbot für italienische Weine erneuert,[37] das schon seit dem 14. Jahrhundert dem Schutz der regionalen Weinproduktion diente, Eingang in die Landesfreiheiten gefunden hatte und regelmäßig durch Einzelgesetze bekräftigt und eingeschärft wurde. Gerade die Forschungen Peter Blickles haben im übrigen deutlich gemacht, wie sehr Gravamina die spätmittelalterliche und frühneuzeitliche Gesetzgebung in Tirol beeinflußt haben, wobei es nicht nur um die Abwendung bestehender Mißstände, sondern auch im Bereich der ‚guten Policey' um die Bewahrung und Fortschreibung alten Herkommens ging.[38]

Auch Einzelpersonen bzw. Personengruppen und -verbände konnten im Supplikationswege beim Landesherrn vorstellig werden und um die Bekräftigung geltender, jedoch als in der Durchsetzung gefährdet wahrgenommener Rechtsgewohnheiten durch einen Gesetzgebungsakt ersuchen. Ein Musterbeispiel hierfür ist die Tiroler Leprosenordnung („Sondersiechenmandat") von 1554, die die Modalitäten der Almosensammlung durch die Kranken eingehend regelte und auf die Bitte einiger Betroffener hin erlassen wurde, da manche Leprösen diese „alten gepreuch" nicht mehr einhalten würden, weshalb sie nunmehr mit landesfürstlicher Autorität neu kundgemacht wurden.[39] Ge-

---

[36] TLA, Kopialbuch Ältere Reihe, Lit. O, Nr. 15, fol. 74^r-75^r, 18. Aug. 1492.

[37] TLA, Kopialbuch Ältere Reihe, Lit. O, Nr. 15, fol. 75^r, 18. Aug. 1492.

[38] Vgl. zuletzt Blickle, Peter: Beschwerden und Polizeien. Die Legitimation des modernen Staates durch Verfahren und Normen, in: Gute Policey als Politik im 16. Jahrhundert. Die Entstehung des öffentlichen Raumes in Oberdeutschland. Hrsg. von Peter Blickle, Peter Kissling und Heinrich Richard Schmidt (Studien zu Policey und Policeywissenschaft). Frankfurt a. M. 2003, S. 549-568.

[39] Vgl. hierzu auch Schennach, Martin P.: Gewohnheitsrecht, Einzelgesetzgebung und Landesordnungen in der Grafschaft Tirol in Spätmittelalter und Frühneuzeit. In: Landesordnungen und

rade hier zeigt sich allerdings auch, daß eine Verschriftlichung des Gewohnheitsrechtes dessen Ergänzung oder Veränderung nach sich ziehen konnte. So konzedierte die Leprosenordnung zwar, daß ein Zuwiderhandeln grundsätzlich von den Betroffenen selbst „wie von alter herkomen" mit Strafen geahndet werden dürfe; in einigen Fällen jedoch wurde die Strafkompetenz nunmehr den lokalen Obrigkeiten zugewiesen.

Die derzeitige *communis opinio*, wonach die Policeygesetzgebung durch die normative Erfassung bislang nicht geregelter Lebensbereiche zu einer Ausdehnung der legislativen und in der Folge administrativen Tätigkeit des frühmodernen Staates führte, sei damit nicht in Frage gestellt. Allerdings darf man nicht vergessen, daß auch die Policeygesetzgebung in einem zwar schwer quantifizierbaren, jedenfalls aber nicht vernachlässigbaren Ausmaß der Fixierung und Fortschreibung des alten Herkommens diente.[40] Hier ist jeweils eine einzelfallspezifische Untersuchung vorzunehmen. Dabei zeigen sich rasch materienspezifische Differenzen: So waren Landesherren gerade im Bereich der Forstgesetze – deren Zuordnung zum Bereich der ‚guten Policey' seit den Untersuchungen von Christoph Ernst außer Frage steht[41] – deutlich eher bereit, legislative Maßnahmen in bewußter Abkehr von Rechtsgewohnheiten zu setzen und so gestaltend einzugreifen, wohingegen in anderen Bereichen die Ordnungsvorstellungen von Obrigkeit und Untertanen stärker harmonierten und ein legislatives Anknüpfen an den traditionalen Rechtsbestand eher möglich war. Dies hatte verständlicherweise erhebliche Auswirkungen auf den

---

Gute Policey in Bayern und Österreich. Hrsg. von Hans-Joachim Hecker, Hans Schlosser und Reinhard Heydenreuter (Studien zu Policey und Policeywissenschaft). Frankfurt a. M. (im Erscheinen).

[40] Insofern zu relativieren Brauneder, Wilhelm: Der soziale und rechtliche Gehalt der österreichischen Polizeiordnungen des 16. Jahrhunderts. In: Ders.: Studien I: Entwicklung des Öffentlichen Rechts. Frankfurt a. M. u.a. 1994, S. 473-487, hier S. 477-478 (Erstveröffentlichung 1976).

[41] Ernst, Christoph: Den Wald entwickeln. Ein Politik- und Konfliktfeld in Hunsrück und Eifel im 18. Jahrhundert (Ancien Régime, Aufklärung und Revolution 32). München 2000; Ernst, Christoph: Forstgesetze in der Frühen Neuzeit. Zielvorgaben und Normierungsinstrumente für die Waldentwicklung in Kurtrier, dem Kröver Reich und der Hinteren Grafschaft Sponheim (Hunsrück und Eifel). In: Policey und frühneuzeitliche Gesellschaft. Hrsg. von Karl Härter (Ius Commune, Sonderheft 129). Frankfurt a. M. 2000, S. 341-381.

Implementationsprozeß, der im Fall eines intentionalen Abweichens von Rechtsgewohnheiten konfliktanfällig war.

II. „Damit sich niemand der Unwissenheit zu entschuldigen habe...“: Normwiederholung als Sicherstellung von Erinnerung

Die frühneuzeitliche Policeygesetzgebung erlaubt nicht nur durch ihre partielle Verankerung im traditionalen Recht, sondern auch aus einem weiteren Blickwinkel einen direkten Brückenschlag zum Themenkomplex „Sicherstellen von Erinnerung“. In diesem Zusammenhang kann ebenfalls auf das einleitende Beispiel verwiesen werden: So wie es der Gesetzgeber für nötig erachtete, ein altbekanntes Verbot binnen eines Jahrzehnts viermal in nahezu identer Form neuerlich kundmachen zu lassen, präsentiert sich die regelmäßige Normeinschärfung und Normwiederholung insgesamt als ein integraler Bestandteil der Policeygesetzgebung im Ancien Régime.

Wie selbstverständlich die Wiederverlautbarung von Policeygesetzen schon kurz nach der einsetzenden Intensivierung der landesherrlichen Gesetzgebung war, zeigt ein repräsentatives Beispiel aus dem Tiroler Raum. Die Reglementierung und Beschränkung der Tätigkeit auswärtiger Krämer, die abseits der Märkte ambulant und in Konkurrenz zu einheimischen Händlern ihre Waren anboten, schien unter mehreren Gesichtspunkten angebracht: Sie beeinträchtigten die Tätigkeit der ‚Angesessenen', ohne durch Abgaben ihren Dienst zum Gemeinwohl beizutragen; zudem wurden sie in den Narrationes der einschlägigen Mandate diskursiv pauschal als potentielle Hinterzieher von Mauten und Zöllen sowie Betrüger ihrer Kundschaft dargestellt, indem ihnen die Verwendung gefälschter Maße und Gewichte und der Verkauf minderwertiger Ware unterstellt wurde. Der Erlaß entsprechender Normen war ein Erfolg der städtischen Händler, die es durch Beschwerden und Supplikationen verstanden hatten, ihre Partikularinteressen geschickt mit dem Hinweis auf den anzustrebenden „gemeinen Nutzen“ zu verbinden, was sich unter Maximilian I. auch quellenmäßig nachweisen läßt.[42] Schon sein Vorgänger hatte 1489 eine

[42] TLA, Landschaftliche Landtagsakten, Fasz. 1, Pos. 15.

erste einschlägige Regelung publizieren lassen.[43] Fünf Jahre später betonte Maximilian nachdrücklich, daß „solher ordnung und bevelhen, die wir hiemit vernewt und bestätt haben wellen, in allen iren punckhten und articklen gelebt und nachgangen“ werden solle.[44] In Reaktion auf Landtagsgravamina wurden die Mandate im März und November 1507 und nochmals 1514 mit geringfügigen inhaltlichen Adaptionen wiederholt.[45]

1. Normwiederholung als Ausdruck mangelhafter Normdurchsetzung?

Im Zuge des bereits erwähnten Aufschwungs der Forschung zur ‚guten Policey' wurde auch den vielfältigen Publikationsformen frühneuzeitlicher Gesetze erhebliches Augenmerk zugewandt.[46] Bevor an eine Norm erinnert werden kann, muß sie zunächst den Adressaten zur Kenntnis gelangen, um ihre verhaltenssteuernde Wirkung entfalten zu können. Dabei herrschte im Ancien Régime das sogenannte materielle Publikationsprinzip: Der Normgeber ergriff konkrete Maßnahmen, um die möglichst umfassende Kenntnisnahme des Norminhaltes durch die Adressaten sicherzustellen. Das formelle Publikationsprinzip setzte sich demgegenüber erst seit dem ausgehenden 18. Jahrhundert von Frankreich aus durch. Hier beschränkt sich der Gesetzgeber auf die Setzung eines bestimmten formellen Aktes, der grundsätzlich allen Normad-

---

[43] TLA, Kopialbuch Ältere Reihe, Lit. L, Nr. 10, fol. 72^r (ohne nähere Datierung).

[44] TLA, Kopialbuch Ältere Reihe, Lit. Q, Nr. 17, S. 81-82, 1. Aug. 1494.

[45] TLA, Kopialbuch Ältere Reihe, Lit. Aa, Nr. 28, fol. 51^r-52^r, 10. März 1507; ebd., fol. 49, 27. Nov. 1507; Kopialbuch Ältere Reihe, Lit. Hh, Nr. 34, fol. 6, 17. Jan. 1514.

[46] Vgl. zum Beispiel Weber (wie Fn. 30), S. 164-172; Dehesselles, Thomas: Policey, Handel und Kredit im Herzogtum Braunschweig-Wolfenbüttel in der Frühen Neuzeit (Studien zu Policey und Policeywissenschaft). Frankfurt a. M. 1999, S. 54-59; Dubach, Philipp: Gesetz und Verfassung. Die Anfänge der territorialen Gesetzgebung im Allgäu und im Appenzell im 15. und 16. Jahrhundert (Oberschwaben. Geschichte und Kultur 6). Tübingen 2001, S. 262-277; Härter, Karl: Gesetzgebungsprozess und gute Policey. Entstehungskontexte, Publikation und Geltungskraft frühneuzeitlicher Policeygesetze (PoliceyWorkingPapers. Working Papers des Arbeitskreises Policey/Polizei in der Vormoderne 3), 2002 [Online: http://www.univie.ac.at/policey-ak/pwp/pwp_03.pdf]; Holenstein, „Gute Policey“ und lokale Gesellschaft (wie Fn. 22), S. 191-233; Härter, Policey und Strafjustiz (wie Fn. 22), S. 221-244.

ressaten die Möglichkeit eröffnet, sich selbst vom Norminhalt Kenntnis zu verschaffen. Im Zuge der materiellen Publikation, die pointiert als eine „Bringschuld des Staates“[47] umrissen werden kann, bediente sich der Gesetzgeber unterschiedlicher Techniken, um die effektive Kenntnisnahme sicherzustellen, insbesondere der mündlichen „Berufung“ (des Ausrufens an öffentlichen Orten wie Kirchen- und Marktplätzen bzw. der Verlesung von der Kirchenkanzel oder auf öffentlichen Versammlungen) sowie des Anschlagens der gedruckten Mandate an Kirchen- oder Stadttoren.[48]

Im Zuge der Analyse der vielfältigen Publikationstechniken gelangte man rasch zur Erkenntnis, daß die Wiederholung von Normen in identischer oder zumindest weitgehend übereinstimmender Form ein Charakteristikum der legislativen Tätigkeit des frühmodernen Staates im Bereich der ‚guten Policey’ darstellte. Hieraus zog die ältere Forschung die Schlussfolgerung offensichtlich insuffizienter Normimplementation im Ancien Régime, was vor allem mit den beschränkten Machtmitteln und dem noch nicht entwickelten Herrschaftsapparat des Staates begründet wurde.[49] Nur allzu gut schien sich das Bonmot von Christian Thomasius, wonach die „Policey=Ordnungen von niemand als von den Kirchthüren und anderen Örtern, daran sie wegen der Publikation angeschlagen und feste gemacht werden, gehalten“ würden, in dieses Bild einzufügen.[50] Der Befund wenn nicht fehlender, so doch stark de-

---

[47] So auch Pauser, Josef: Die österreichischen gesamtstaatlichen Gesetzblätter, e-text auf http://anno.onb.ac.at/info_g.htm [Zugriff am 7. Nov. 2006].

[48] Vgl. hierzu nun ausführlich auch Schennach, Martin Paul: Zuschreiben von Bedeutung. Publikation und Normintensität frühneuzeitlicher Gesetze. Paper, präsentiert auf der 9. Diskussionsrunde des Arbeitskreises „Policey/Polizei im vormodernen Europa“ am 22.Juni 2006 in Stuttgart-Hohenheim.

[49] Siehe zum Beispiel Raeff, Marc: The well-ordered police state. Social and institutional change through law in the Germanies and Russia 1600-1800. New Haven/London 1983, bes. S. 50-53.

[50] Hier zit. nach Unruh, Georg-Christoph von: Polizei, Polizeiwissenschaft und Kameralistik. In: Deutsche Verwaltungsgeschichte. Bd. I: Vom Spätmittelalter bis zum Ende des Alten Reiches. Hrsg. von Georg-Christoph von Unruh, Kurt G. A. Jeserich und Hans Pohl. Stuttgart 1983, S. 388-427, hier S. 397, Anm. 11 mit Verweis auf Thomasius, Christian: C. Melchiors von Osse Testament auf Hertzog Augusto [...]. Halle 1717, Note 256; entsprechende Zitate auch bei Winkelbauer, Thomas: Sozialdisziplinierung und Konfessionalisierung durch Grundherren in den österreichischen und böhmischen Ländern im 16. und 17. Jahrhundert. In: Zeitschrift für Historische Forschung 19 (1992), S. 317-339, hier S. 324; Stolleis, Michael: Was bedeutet „Normdurch-

fizitärer Normdurchsetzung wurde auf den ersten Blick zudem durch die *verba legalia* bestätigt.[51] Die Narrationes zahlreicher Mandate bringen nach dem Hinweis auf die bislang zu einer Materie ergangenen Gesetze wortreich zum Ausdruck, daß deren mangelhafte Normdurchsetzung den Anlaß für die – allenfalls modifizierende – neuerliche Kundmachung darstelle.[52] Dieses gängige Argumentationsschema mag partiell als rhetorischer Legitimationstopos für die Ausweitung der legislativen Tätigkeit des Landesherren fungiert haben,[53] doch ist dieser Befund nicht zu generalisieren. In der Tat lassen sich entsprechende Klagen auch im behördeninternen Schriftverkehr regelmäßig finden. So begründete beispielsweise die oberösterreichische Regierung im Jahr 1567 die neuerliche Kundmachung einer Fischereibeschränkung in einem Schreiben an Erzherzog Ferdinand II. mit der bislang ungenügenden Befolgung der entsprechenden Anordnungen der Tiroler Landesordnung von 1532, eines Fischereigesetzes von 1556 sowie eines unmittelbaren Vorgängermandats: „Unnd als wir hernach befunden, das ob derselben nit gehalten unnd gelebt worden, haben wir volgenndts [...] von newen ernnstliche bevelch ausgeen lassen."[54] In einer grundsätzlichen Stellungnahme hob die Regierung 1586 speziell die Nachlässigkeit der lokalen Obrigkeiten als Grund für die frequenten Normeinschärfungen hervor. Es sei demnach zu konstatieren, daß,

„wann Eur Durchlaucht schon ainsmals in ainer sachen offne mandata oder bevelch in dis Eur Durchlaucht lanndt der Fürstlichen Grafschafft Tyrol ausferttigen unnd darinnen mit ernnst schaffen unnd gebieten lassen, das doch demselben durch die für- unnd nachgeseczten obrigkhaiten khain zeit nit, wie sich gebürte, gehorsame oder würckhliche volziehung gelaist würdet, sonnder

---

setzung" bei Policeyordnungen der frühen Neuzeit? In: Grundlagen des Rechts. Festschrift für Peter Landau zum 65. Geburtstag. Hrsg. von Richard H. Helmholtz (Rechts- und staatswissenschaftliche Veröffentlichungen der Görres-Gesellschaft, Neue Folge 91). Paderborn u.a. 2000, S. 739-757, hier S. 744.

[51] So argumentiert auch noch Schildt, Policey- und Landesgesetzgebung (wie Fn. 21), S. 238.

[52] Beispielhaft sei verwiesen auf TLA, Buch Tirol, Bd. 5, fol. 258, 5. Mai 1545; TLA, Ambraser Memorabilien V/72, Beilage; TLA, Buch Tirol, Bd. 11, fol. 696, 15. März 1585; Tiroler Landesmuseum Ferdinandeum, Dipauliana 1091, Nr. 210, 20. März 1657.

[53] Vgl. nur Härter, Policey und Strafjustiz (wie Fn. 22), S. 245.

[54] TLA, An die Fürstliche Durchlaucht 1567, Teil 2, fol. 1188^{r}-1189^{r}, 20. Sept. 1567.

sich darinnen ainsthails gannz ungehorsame unnd farlässig halten unnd erzaigen. Daraus dann ervolgt, das erforderter notturfft nach bald hernach über das jar und schier gleich von jar zu jar umb ainer yeden sachen willen so vilmalen offne mandata unnd bevelch ausgeferttigt werden müessen."[55]

Würden die Obrigkeiten ein Mandat pflichtgemäß vollziehen, so könne man sich Aufwand und Kosten sparen, zumal aus dem derzeitigen Zustand offenkundiger Mißachtung ergangener Gesetze durch die zur Vollziehung berufenen Organe „nit geringer schimpff und verclainerung" für das Ansehen des Landesfürsten resultierten.

Auch derartige Ausführungen sind nicht vorbehaltlos zu übernehmen, sondern kontextabhängig und kritisch zu interpretieren. Es ist ein durchaus gängiger Bestandteil einer behördlichen Entschuldigungs- und Entlastungsstrategie, tatsächliche oder vermeintliche Mängel auf das Versagen anderer Stellen zurückzuführen. Wie gefällig diese Exkulpierungsmöglichkeit war, zeigt sich am Umstand, daß die Regierung mit exakt denselben Worten wie 1586 fast zwei Jahrzehnte später die angeblich insuffiziente Durchsetzung der Policeygesetze gegenüber dem neu bestellten Gubernator der oberösterreichischen Ländergruppe, Erzherzog Maximilian III. von Österreich, zu begründen versuchte.[56]

Das stete Erinnern an bereits erlassene Verordnungen, das die Policeygesetzgebung des Ancien Régime prägte, erscheint somit vorderhand als klarer Ausweis und Beleg ihrer fehlenden oder mangelhaften Umsetzung. Von dieser Prämisse ausgehend entwickelte der Historiker Jürgen Schlumbohm die Theorie einer primär symbolischen Gesetzgebung im Ancien Régime: Da die ständige Normwiederholung demnach vermeintlich keine oder nur sehr beschränkte Auswirkungen auf die Lebenswirklichkeit gezeitigt habe, müßten andere Erklärungsmodelle gefunden werden. In diesem Zusammenhang betonte Schlumbohm, daß die demonstrative Selbstdarstellung und rituelle Selbstinszenierung des Staates ein wichtiges, wenn nicht sogar das wichtigste Motiv des frühneuzeitlichen Gesetzgebers gewesen seien. Die „allgemeine Be-

---

[55] TLA, An die Fürstliche Durchlaucht 1586, fol. 131^{v}-136^{v}, hier fol. 135^{v}, 20. Febr. 1586.
[56] TLA, An die Fürstliche Durchlaucht 1604, fol. 7^{r}-9^{v}, 7. Jan. 1604.

folgung der verkündeten Norm zu erreichen gehörte weniger zwingend dazu als im modernen Verständnis von staatlicher Gesetzgebung."[57]

Der Rechtshistoriker Hans Schlosser hatte die Frage einer allfälligen symbolischen Gesetzgebung im Ancien Régime freilich schon ein Jahrzehnt früher gestellt und unter Verweis auf den eindeutig auf Durchsetzung und Einhaltung abzielenden Willen des Policeygesetzgebers verneint.[58] Dem ist zuzustimmen. Es wäre „schimpflich, mandata außgeen ze lassen und ob derselben volziehung nit zu halten", wie die oberösterreichische Regierung der ihr unterstellten vorderösterreichischen Regierung 1550 einschärfte.[59] In der Tat würde sich die Theorie einer vor allem symbolischen Gesetzgebung kaum mit der zeitgenössischen Sichtweise vereinbaren lassen, die Mandate als Emanationen des landesfürstlichen Willens ansah. Diesen Willen einfach beiseite zu schieben, wäre wohl auf entschiedenen Widerstand gestoßen und als „verkleinerung irer Fürstlichen Durchlaucht lantsfürstlichen hocheit undt reputation" gerügt worden.[60] Auch die moderne Rechtssoziologie hatte schon vor Schlumbohm nachdrücklich auf die methodischen Schwierigkeiten im Zusammenhang mit behaupteter symbolischer Gesetzgebung hingewiesen: Wie wolle man den Nachweis antreten, daß es dem Gesetzgeber nicht um die im Gesetz enthaltenen Gebote und Verbote gehe, sondern ‚eigentlich' um etwas anderes? „Wer hier nicht auf äußerste methodische Sorgfalt bedacht ist, öffnet haltlosen Spekulationen und ideologischen Zuschreibungen Tür und Tor. Apodiktische Urteile sollten ohnehin unterlassen werden."[61]

---

[57] Schlumbohm, Jürgen: Gesetze, die nicht durchgesetzt werden – ein Strukturmerkmal des frühmodernen Staates? In: Geschichte und Gesellschaft 23 (1997), S. 647-663, hier S. 659; ähnlich der Tenor bei Dinges, Martin: Normsetzung als Praxis? Oder: Warum werden die Normen zur Sachkultur und zum Verhalten so häufig wiederholt und was bedeutet dies für den Prozeß der „Sozialdisziplinierung"? In: Norm und Praxis im Alltag des Mittelalters und der frühen Neuzeit. Internationales Round-table-Gespräch Krems an der Donau 7. Oktober 1996 (Österreichische Akademie der Wissenschaften, philosophisch-historische Klasse; Forschungen des Instituts für Realienkunde des Mittelalters und der frühen Neuzeit. Diskussionen und Materialien 2). Wien 1997, S. 39-53, bes. S. 52.

[58] Schlosser, Rechtssetzung und Gesetzgebungsverständnis (wie Fn. 6), S. 59-60.

[59] TLA, Von der Königlichen Majestät 1550, fol. 49v-50r, 14. Juli 1550.

[60] TLA, Verhandlungen der Landschaft, Bd. 5, S. 582 (1590).

[61] Kindermann, Harald: Alibigesetzgebung als symbolische Gesetzgebung. In: Symbole der Politik. Politik der Symbole. Hrsg. von Rüdiger Voigt. Opladen 1989, S. 257-273, hier S. 266-267.

Dementsprechend skeptisch bis ablehnend fielen die sowohl seitens der Geschichtswissenschaft wie der Rechtsgeschichte geltend gemachten Einwände gegen die Schlumbohm'sche These aus, der jedoch – wenngleich sie inzwischen als überholt gelten muß – der große Verdienst einer nachhaltigen Stimulierung der Forschungsdiskussion zukommt. Die formulierten Bedenken können folgendermaßen zusammengefaßt werden:[62]

Man dürfe nicht simplifizierend von einer vermeintlich heutzutage reibungslosen Normimplementation ausgehen und diese mit der vorgeblich unzureichenden früherer Jahrhunderte kontrastieren, zumal einer solcher Sichtweise ein unzulässiges binäres Denkschema „effektive Normdurchsetzung" versus „(weitgehende) Wirkungslosigkeit" zugrunde liege. Zudem wurde herausgearbeitet, daß auch die Prämisse einer vermeintlichen Wirkungslosigkeit der Policeygesetzgebung methodisch äußerst schwierig zu belegen sei und in generalisierender Form überhaupt nicht aufrechterhalten werden könne. Es fehle an einem sinnvollen Kriterium zur historisch zuverlässigen Verifikation „effektiver" Normdurchsetzung. „Normabweichung ist vielmehr eine Existenzbedingung staatlicher Normsetzung und Normdurchsetzung", wie Karl Härter prägnant ausdrückte.[63] Für vergangene Jahrhunderte gilt dies umso mehr, fanden doch nur deviante Verhaltensweisen in den Schriftquellen ihren Niederschlag, während die Normbefolgung im allgemeinen nicht eigens registriert wurde. Klagen über die fehlende Implementation von Verordnungen seien zudem in ihrem Zusammenhang zu interpretieren und unter Umständen zu relativieren, können sie doch – wie bereits angedeutet – beispielsweise auch als Legitimation für die Entfaltung und den Ausbau der legislativen Tätigkeit dienen oder aber Ausdruck behördeninterner Konfliktlinien sein. Selbst häufige Quellenbelege von Normübertretungen müssen nicht notwendigerweise auf die „Unwirksamkeit" eines Gesetzes hinweisen, sondern können verschiedene Ursachen haben, zum Beispiel eine intensivierte Verfolgung oder eine tatsächliche Zunahme devianten Verhaltens.

---

[62] Vgl. v. a. Härter, Karl: Sozialdisziplinierung durch Strafe? Intentionen frühneuzeitlicher Policeyordnungen und staatlicher Sanktionspraxis. In: Zeitschrift für Historische Forschung 26 (1999), S. 365-379; Stolleis, „Normdurchsetzung" (wie Fn. 50); Landwehr, Achim: Die Rhetorik der „guten Policey". In: Zeitschrift für Historische Forschung 30 (2003), S. 251-287.

[63] Härter, Sozialdisziplinierung (wie Fn. 62), S. 370.

2. Motive für Normwiederholungen

Im Zuge der Diskussion über die vermeintliche symbolische Gesetzgebung im Ancien Régime wurde der häufigen Einschärfung von Gesetzen durch neuerliche Kundmachung besondere Beachtung eingeräumt, da gerade diese einen integralen Bestandteil der Argumentation Schlumbohms darstellte. Hierbei wurde darauf aufmerksam gemacht, daß die Wiederholung und Einschärfung einer Norm in einer primär oralen Gesellschaft wesentliche Geltungsvoraussetzung waren. Erst sie stellten das „Erinnern" sicher.[64] Damit stehen landesherrliche Policeygesetze im Ancien Régime nicht alleine da, wobei man zur Illustration nicht einmal auf die regelmäßige Verlesung verschriftlicher Weistümer hinweisen muß. Auch Dorfordnungen – egal, ob diese von der Herrschaft gesetzt[65] oder von der Gemeinde selbständig in Form einer Einung bzw. Willkür erlassen – wurden regelmäßig verlesen und erneuert.[66] So heißt es in der Ordnung des Tiroler Dorfes Silz von 1683:

„Damit sich nunn auch der unwissenheit, sonderlich auf dem fahl der ybertretung, niemand entschuldigen oder außhalftern kinne, hat ain ersambe gmein dise ehehaft und ordnung allwegen an maienabent *(30.VI.)* – als daselbs die ganze gmain und nachperschaft versamblet – offenlichen vor- und ablesen zu lassen."[67]

---

[64] Vgl. Dubach, Gesetz und Verfassung (wie Fn. 46), S. 276-277.

[65] Vgl. nur Trauchburg, Gabriele von: Ehehaften und Dorfordnungen. Untersuchungen zur Herrschafts-, Rechts- und Wirtschaftsgeschichte des Rieses anhand ländlicher Rechtsquellen aus der Grafschaft Oettingen (Materialien zur Geschichte des Bayerischen Schwaben 23). Augsburg 1995, S. 16; Willoweit, Gebot und Verbot (wie Fn. 28), S. 111.

[66] Blickle, Peter: „Coniuratio". Die politische Karriere einer lokalen Gesellschaftsformation. In: Stadt – Gemeinde – Genossenschaft. Festschrift für Gerhard Dilcher zum 70. Geburtstag. Hrsg. von Albrecht Cordes, Joachim Rückert und Reiner Schulze. Berlin 2003, S. 341-360, hier S. 347; Schildt, Bernd: Bauer – Gemeinde – Nachbarschaft. Verfassung und Recht der Landgemeinde Thüringens in der frühen Neuzeit (Regionalgeschichtliche Forschungen im Verlag Hermann Böhlaus Nachfolger Weimar). Weimar 1996, S. 88.

[67] Tirolische Weistümer. 6. Teil: 2. Ergänzungsbd.: Oberinntal. Gerichte Hörtenberg und St. Petersberg. Zusammengestellt und redigiert von Karin Greiffenhagen. Hrsg. von Nikolaus Grass und Hans Constantin Faussner (Österreichische Weistümer, Bd. 19). Innsbruck 1994, S. 170.

„Damit sich niemand der Unwissenheit zu entschuldigen habe" – die Zielsetzung der Normwiederholung ist mit diesen Worten konzis ausgedrückt. Sie stellt, nicht nur in Tirol, ein häufig wiederkehrendes Element des Formulars frühneuzeitlicher Policeygesetze dar[68] und wird in der angeführten Dorfordnung von den Gemeindegenossen aufgegriffen – wobei dieser Beleg durchaus nicht einzigartig ist.[69] Fallweise läßt sich so feststellen, daß auf den jährlichen Ehafttaidingen in Tirol, auf denen sämtliche angesessenen Männer einer (Dorf- oder Gerichts-)Gemeinde zu erscheinen verpflichtet waren, während der gesamten Frühen Neuzeit ein ganzes Bündel von Normen unterschiedlicher Provenienz periodisch eingeschärft wurden. Dazu zählen jene Ordnungen, die sich die Gemeinde selbst gegeben hatte, die im alten Herkommen verankerten Ge- und Verbote der (Gerichts-)Herrschaft sowie schließlich von Seiten der Obrigkeit als wichtig eingestufte Inhalte von landesfürstlichen Mandaten sowie der Tiroler Landes- bzw. Policeyordnung. Schon quantitativ konnten die auf diese Weise periodisch einzuschärfenden Normen beträchtliche Ausmaße annehmen. In der Nordtiroler Herrschaft Kufstein wurden beispielsweise im 17. Jahrhundert 82 Bestimmungen aus landesfürstlichen Gesetzgebungsakten und Ge- und Verboten der Gerichtsherrschaft verlesen, hinzu kamen noch lokale Dorfordnungen.[70]

Bei dieser Fülle präsent zu haltender Normen war eine gewisse mnemotechnische Aufbereitung unerläßlich, wollte man den durch die Normwiederholung intendierten Erinnerungs- und Verinnerlichungseffekt erreichen. In der Tat wurden beim erwähnten Kufsteiner Beispiel nicht wörtliche Passagen aus Einzelgesetzen oder ganze Bestimmungen (‚Titel') der Landesordnung respektive der Policeyordnung verlesen, sondern nur deren Inhalte wiedergege-

---

[68] TLA, Causa Domini 1528, fol. 178, 24. Febr. 1528; TLA, Buch Tirol 1550, fol. 128r-129r, 10. Okt. 1550; TLA, Buch Jägerei 1, fol. 61, 15. März 1565; TLA, Causa Domini 1578, fol. 106, 8. Okt. 1578; TLA, Causa Domini 1584, fol. 82, 22. Okt. 1584; TLA, Causa Domini 1585, fol. 244, 5. Juni 1585; vgl. auch Holenstein, „Gute Policey" und lokale Gesellschaft (wie Fn. 22), S. 213-214.

[69] Vgl. nur Tirolische Weistümer, 6. Teil, 2. Ergänzungsbd. (wie Fn. 67), S. 229: „Und damit sich keinner der unwissenheit umbso weniger ursach suechen kinne: Soll dise ordnung in may iehrlich publiciert werden."

[70] Die tirolischen Weisthümer. I. Theil: Unterinnthal. Hrsg. von Ignaz von Zingerle und K. Theodor von Inama-Sternegg (Österreichische Weisthümer 2/I). Wien 1875, S. 15-35.

ben. Schon bei der erstmaligen mündlichen Verkündung eines Mandats läßt sich im Einzelfall feststellen, daß keine Verlesung „von Wort zu Wort" erfolgte (die *expressis verbis* vorgeschrieben werden konnte), sondern vielmehr der Gesetzesinhalt für den Berufungsvorgang aufbereitet und dem Normadressaten möglichst verständlich dargeboten wurde.[71]

Nicht nur die Notwendigkeit, Normen angesichts einer weitgehend oralen Gesellschaft präsent zu halten, bedingte ihre Wiederholung. Gerade Michael Stolleis forderte auch eine materienspezifische Betrachtungsweise, trafen frühneuzeitliche Policeygesetze doch auf ein breites Spektrum möglicher Reaktionen der Normadressaten.[72] Wo Policeygesetze Rechtsgewohnheiten fest- und allenfalls fortschrieben oder wo die Ordnungsvorstellungen von Obrigkeiten und Untertanen weitgehend harmonierten, war die Ausgangslage für die Gesetzesimplementation eine gänzlich andere als in Bereichen, in denen landesherrliche Gesetze mit dem alten Herkommen brachen oder dem Rechtsverständnis der Bevölkerung diametral entgegenstanden. Dementsprechend unterschiedliche Zielsetzungen konnten der Normwiederholung zukommen. Über die Notwendigkeit und Sinnhaftigkeit von Feuerordnungen bestand so zweifellos breiter Konsens zwischen städtischer und landesfürstlicher Obrigkeit einerseits und den Untertanen andererseits. Wenn folglich der Bürger- und Inwohnerschaft der Handelsstadt Bozen jährlich am Dreikönigstag die städtische Feuerordnung vorgehalten wurde, diente dies tatsächlich ausschließlich der Aufrechterhaltung von „Erinnerung": Jeder sollte die ihn und die Gemeinschaft treffenden Verhaltensregeln möglichst präsent haben, um im Ernstfall einen reibungslosen und raschen Ablauf der Löschmaßnahmen sicherzustellen.[73] Ganz anders lag der Fall bei jenen Mandaten, welche die freie Jagd auf die landesfürstlichen Wildbestände nach dem Tod eines Tiroler Landesherrn untersagten.[74] Sie kollidierten mit der rechtsgewohnheitlich begründeten Rechtsposition der ländlichen Bevölkerung, die diese Befugnis für

---

[71] Vgl. auch Holenstein, „Gute Policey" und lokale Gesellschaft (wie Fn. 22), S. 221-223.
[72] Stolleis, „Normdurchsetzung" (wie Fn. 50), bes. S. 751-752.
[73] Stadtarchiv Bozen, Archivkiste 219, 21. März 1629 (samt Beilagen).
[74] Hierzu ausführlich Schennach, Martin P.: Jagdrecht, Wilderei und „gute Policey". Normen und ihre Durchsetzung im frühneuzeitlichen Tirol (Studien zu Policey und Policeywissenschaft). Frankfurt a. M. 2007, S. 121-142.

sich in Anspruch nahm und sie zugleich als Schutzmaßnahme gegen übermäßige Wildhegung durch die landesherrliche Jagdverwaltung verstand. Nachweislich seit dem Tod Maximilians I. bis in das 18. Jahrhundert ergoß sich folglich nach jedem Ableben eines Herrschers ein Strom von Verbotsmandaten über das Land, auf welche die Bevölkerung mit aktivem Widerstand und bewußter Mißachtung reagierte. Dennoch verzichtete der Gesetzgeber nicht auf das regelmäßige Einschärfen der Verordnungen, die teilweise in Monatsabständen erlassen wurden, selbst wenn an eine vollständige Umsetzung nicht im Entferntesten zu denken war. In einem derartigen Fall sollte nicht primär die Erinnerung an die Norm aufrechterhalten werden. Ein Verzicht auf ihre immer wieder erfolgende Einschärfung hätte jedoch bedeutet, nicht nur von vornherein auf jede noch so geringe Durchsetzungschance zu verzichten, sondern vor allem auch den eigenen Regelungsanspruch aufzugeben.

Gerade bei Gesetzen, bei denen mit dem latenten oder gar offenen Widerstand der Adressaten zu rechnen war, kam der Normwiederholung die Funktion eines nachdrücklichen „Einprägens“ der obrigkeitlichen Gebote und Verbote mit dem Ziel einer zumindest langfristigen Verhaltenssteuerung zu. Ob diese jeweils erreicht wurde, ist dabei einzelfallspezifisch zu untersuchen. Daß ein Bruch mit lang eingespielten, sozial akzeptierten Verhaltensweisen nicht über Nacht möglich war, liegt jedenfalls auf der Hand: „Repetition thus became part of a process of education.”[75]

Auch äußere Anstöße oder verwaltungsorganisatorische Ursachen konnten zu einer Wiederholung von Gesetzen Anlaß geben.[76] Bei der neuerlichen Ausfertigung und Publikation eines Mandats wurde 1582 als Begründung angegeben, daß nicht sichergestellt sei, daß die entsprechende Vorgängerregelung an der Peripherie noch vorhanden sei, da

„dergleichen Mandat und Bevelch auß ursachen / das etwo die Herrschaft und GerichtsInnhaber / dann auch Pfleger unnd Richter sich offtmals veren-

[75] Raeff, Police state (wie Fn. 49), S. 54.
[76] Vgl. Härter, Policey und Strafjustiz (wie Fn. 22), S. 239-240.

dern / und dardurch aintweders verlegt oder gar verloren / oder sonst an ort und enden / da sy offenlich auffgeschlagen / zerrissen werden".[77]

Bei der Neuauflage von „Laster"- bzw. Sittenmandaten, die eine den christlichen Geboten entsprechende Lebensführung sicherstellen sollten, ist in den oberösterreichischen Landen der Zusammenhang mit äußeren Ereignissen frappant. Sie stellen nahezu immer eine Reaktion auf Türkenkriege oder Naturkatastrophen dar, was häufig im Gesetzestext angeführt wird[78] und ansonsten aus dem vorbereitenden Schriftverkehr zu erschließen ist.[79] Der Zusammenhang war für die Zeitgenossen evident: Die genannten Ereignisse waren Strafen Gottes und somit Ausdruck des göttlichen Zorns für die menschlichen Verfehlungen, der durch Gebete und Tugendhaftigkeit besänftigt werden muß. Gott straft die sündenbehaftete „Unordnung", und der Gesetzgeber muß zur Abwendung der göttlichen Strafen zur Wiederherstellung der Ordnung beitragen. Dieser Konnex wurde in den Normtexten zumeist ausdrücklich hervorgehoben[80] und war den Normadressaten geläufig und eingängig. Schließlich fanden sich auf Ebene der Gemeinden ganz parallele Muster. Örtliche Gemeinschaften reagierten auf lokale Ereignisse, die als Strafe Gottes aufgefaßt werden mußten (Epidemien, Naturkatastrophen), indem sie sich unter anderem in Form der *coniuratio* Satzungen gaben, die ebenfalls der (Wieder-)Herstellung einer christlichen Lebensführung dienen sollten.

---

[77] TLA, Causa Domini 1582, fol. 432, 14. Febr. 1582.

[78] Vgl. nur beispielsweise TLA, Buch Tirol 1529, fol. 112^r, 12. Juli 1529; ebd., fol. 114^v-115^r, 3. Aug. 1529; Buch Tirol 1544, fol. 168^r, 28. Jan. 1544; ebd., fol. 196, 26. April 1544.

[79] Vgl. TLA, Von der Königlichen Majestät 1529, fol. 416, 16. Juli 1529; ebd., fol. 473^v, 26. Sept. 1529; TLA, Von der Königlichen Majestät 1530, fol. 48^r-50^r, 28. März 1530; TLA, Von der Königlichen Majestät 1551, fol. 269, 14. Sept. 1551; TLA, An die Fürstliche Durchlaucht 1566, fol. 254^r-257^r, 8. Aug. 1566; TLA, Von der Fürstlichen Durchlaucht 1571, fol. 646^v-647^r, 13. Jan. 1571. Auf den engen Konnex zwischen Policeygesetzgebungsaktivitäten und Türkenkriegen in den habsburgischen Ländern macht aufmerksam Pauser, Josef: „für etwas guets neus". Die Policeyordnung der niederösterreichischen Ländergruppe von 1542 und 1552. In: Landesordnungen und Gute Policey (wie Fn. 39). Dort finden sich auch umfangreiche Literaturangaben zur „Vergeltungstheologie".

[80] Geradezu exemplarisch TLA, Causa Domini 1562, fol. 673, 1. Sept. 1562.

In diesen Fällen stellten Normwiederholungen eine Reaktion auf vermeintliche Vollzugsdefizite dar. Wenngleich eine Vielzahl von Kommunikationskanälen existierte, welche die oberösterreichische Regierung mit Informationen von der Peripherie versorgten – beispielsweise Supplikationen, Visitationsergebnisse oder die Berichte lokaler Obrigkeiten –, verfügte die Zentralbehörde zu keinem Zeitpunkt über eine auch nur annähernd ausreichende Datengrundlage, um zuverlässige Aussagen über die tatsächlich landesweit sanktionierte Devianz in Policeybereichen wie „Ehebruch", „Gotteslästerung" oder „Zutrinken" treffen zu können. Gerade in Zusammenhang mit den Sittenmandaten erschien dies aber auch gar nicht notwendig. Allein der Umstand, daß das Land durch offensichtlich göttliche Strafen heimgesucht worden war, mußte aus Sicht der Regierung das große Ausmaß nicht geahndeten strafbaren Verhaltens belegen. Insofern spiegelt die Normwiederholung die obrigkeitliche Wahrnehmung von Devianz wider, ohne daß dies *ex post* Aussagen über die tatsächlichen Verhältnisse erlauben würden. Ähnliches gilt für jene (allenfalls spektakulären) Einzelfälle, die zur Kenntnis der Regierung gelangten und von deren Vorliegen diese auf die Existenz weiterverbreiteter Mißstände schloß, auf die durch das Einschärfen der entsprechenden Mandate reagiert werden mußte. Geradezu prototypisch läßt sich dies anhand eines Vorfalls aus dem Jahr 1585 nachweisen. Erzherzog Ferdinand II. hatte damals in der Residenzstadt und deren Umgebung mehrere beschäftigungslose, umherziehende Landsknechte („Gartknechte") wahrgenommen und dies der Regierung zur Kenntnis gebracht.[81] Diese sah sich verständlicherweise zur Entfaltung von Aktivitäten veranlaßt und fertigte prompt ein früheres Gesetz neuerlich aus, das in seiner Narratio die vielfältigen Verstöße gegen vorangegangene Normierungen anführte.[82] Allerdings hatte die Regierung im Vorfeld keine weitergehenden Erhebungen angestellt, indem sie beispielsweise Berichte lokaler Obrigkeiten eingefordert hätte. Ob der einleitend im Mandat geschilderte Zustand daher zutraf und tatsächlich entsprechender Regelungsbedarf bestand, bleibt rückblickend unklar.

---

[81] Vgl. TLA, Von der Fürstlichen Durchlaucht 1585, fol. 23^{v}-25^{r}, 15. Mai 1585.
[82] Vgl. TLA, Causa Domini 1585, fol. 244, 5. Juni 1585.

Ähnliches kann zumindest partiell für jene Gesetzeswiederholungen gelten, mit denen Landesfürsten auf landständische Beschwerden reagierten. Der nicht zu unterschätzende Einfluß der Gravamina auf die territoriale Gesetzgebung in der Frühneuzeit ist im letzten Jahrzehnt eingehend dargestellt worden.[83] Wenngleich Gravamina und die in der Folge wiederverlautbarten Mandate natürlich konkrete Mißstände und Implementationsdefizite widerspiegeln können, ist dies nicht zwangsläufig der Fall. Die Verhandlungssituation auf Landtagen war gekennzeichnet durch landesherrliche Steuerpostulate einerseits und landständische Abwehrstrategien andererseits. In diesem Kontext kam auch den Gravamina eine gewisse Rolle zu, konnten sie doch unter Umständen zur Illustration der beschränkten ständischen Finanzkraft herangezogen werden.[84]

Bei einigen Fällen von Normwiederholung kam ferner ein Charakteristikum der Policeygesetzgebung zum Tragen: ihre Flexibilität, die ein rasches Reagieren auf sich wandelnde Rahmenbedingungen ermöglichte. Ein Musterbeispiel hierfür bietet die Tiroler Getreidepolitik in der Frühneuzeit. Zwar bestand zur Sicherstellung der Getreideversorgung ein grundsätzliches Exportverbot, das jedoch in Jahren mit ausreichenden Ernten nicht exekutiert bzw. durch sehr freigiebige Vergabe von Dispensationen unterlaufen wurde.[85] War dagegen die Versorgungslage im Land prekär oder herrschte ein signifikantes Preisgefälle zwischen Tirol und den oberitalienischen Märkten, reagierte der Gesetzgeber mit der neuerlichen Publikation des Exportverbots und mit einem erheblichen

---

[83] Einen rezenten Überblick bietet Würgler, Andreas: Bitten und Begehren. Suppliken und Gravamina in der deutschsprachigen Frühneuzeitforschung. In: Bittschriften und Gravamina. Politik, Verwaltung und Justiz in Europa (14.-18. Jahrhundert). Hrsg. von Cecilia Nubola und Andreas Würgler (Schriften des Italienisch-Deutschen Historischen Instituts in Trient 19). Berlin 2005, S. 17-52.

[84] Diese Möglichkeit der Instrumentalisierung von Gravamina im Verhandlungsverlauf war den Zeitgenossen durchaus bewusst und wurde fallweise sogar ausdrücklich thematisiert: Vgl. nur TLA, Verhandlungen der Landschaft, Bd. 12, S. 10 (11. März 1619), S. 199-200 (11. April 1620), S. 429 (25. Mai 1626).

[85] Vgl. allgemein Fischer, Josef: Tirols Getreidepolitik von 1527-1601 (Forschungen zur inneren Geschichte Österreichs 13). Innsbruck 1919; ferner TLA, Kopialbuch Ältere Reihe, Lit. Rr, Nr. 43, S. 5-6, 4. Jan. 1523; TLA, Von der Königlichen Majestät, fol. 376^{r}-378^{r}, 4. Sept. 1555.

Ressourceneinsatz, um dessen Durchsetzung zu fördern.[86] Ein regelmäßiges „Erinnern“ an das Exportverbot war nicht notwendig, vielmehr musste direkter Handlungsbedarf gegeben sein.

Der enge Konnex zwischen dem Sicherstellen von Erinnerung an bestimmte Normen und deren wiederholter Publikation ist somit deutlich. So vielfältig jedoch die Motive für die Gesetzeswiederholung im Einzelfall sein können, so vielgestaltig präsentieren sich die dem Gesetzgeber zu Gebote stehenden Techniken der Normwiederholung. So konnte der Publikationsbefehl die lokalen Obrigkeiten anweisen, das Mandat während eines bestimmten Zeitraumes in periodischen Abständen immer wieder von neuem durch Berufung kundzumachen. Eine zahlenmäßig kleine Gruppe von Mandaten war von vornherein dazu bestimmt, dauerhaft (zum Beispiel einmal jährlich) und ohne neuerliche Aufforderung seitens der Zentralbehörde publiziert zu werden. Ferner bestand die Option, ein Mandat in identischer oder modifizierter Form im Bedarfsfall neu zu drucken und zu erlassen. In den oberösterreichischen Ländern läßt sich nachweisen, daß als zentral erachtete Mandate im Extremfall im Jahresabstand neu aufgelegt und den Obrigkeiten zur Publikation zugesandt werden. Die Wahl der Publikationsform und die Wiederholungsfrequenz eines legislativen Aktes dürfen somit nicht isoliert vom Implementationsprozess betrachtet werden. Die jährliche Verlesung oder gar Neuausfertigung von Mandaten ist nicht zuletzt Ausdruck einer spezifischen Bedeutungszuschreibung durch den Gesetzgeber, die Signalwirkung für die zur Vollziehung berufenen Organe wie für die Normadressaten hatte. Diese Vorgehensweise wurde daher nur bei einem geringen Prozentsatz aller Normsetzungsakte angewandt.[87] Dabei zeigt sich eine gewisse Schwerpunktsetzung bei jenen Mandaten, deren Durchsetzung zwar einerseits große Relevanz zugemessen wurde, bei denen aber andererseits mit dem latenten oder sogar aktiven Widerstand der Adressaten zu rechnen war. Dies lässt sich besonders anhand

---

[86] Vgl. TLA, Buch Tirol 1527, fol. 134^{v}-135^{r}, 20. Febr. 1527; Buch Tirol 1538, fol. 261^{r}-262^{r}, 19. Dez. 1538; Buch Tirol 1559, fol. 412, 9. März 1559; Buch Tirol 1560, fol. 44^{r}-45^{r}, 9. April 1560; TLA, An die Königliche Majestät, 1560, fol. 13^{r}-16^{r}, 9. Jan. 1560; Buch Tirol 1561, fol. 249^{v}-250^{r}, 17. Juni 1561; TLA, Buch Tirol 1570, fol. 88^{r}-92^{v}, hier fol. 89, Aug. 1570 (ohne nähere Datierung).

[87] Vgl. Dubach, Gesetz und Verfassung (wie Fn. 46), S. 272-275; Landwehr, Rhetorik (wie Fn. 62), S. 264.

von Forst- und Jagdgesetzen nachweisen, bei denen die Interessensgegensätze zwischen der Landesherrschaft und der ländlichen Bevölkerung regelmäßig scharf hervortraten.

Nicht zuletzt ausgehend von dem Befund eines breiten Spektrums möglicher Publikationsformen wurde jüngst das Konzept der variablen Normintensität frühneuzeitlicher Policeygesetze entwickelt.[88] Demnach wurde unterschiedlichen Rechtssetzungsakten trotz Gleichrangigkeit auf formaler Ebene vom Gesetzgeber eine unterschiedliche Bedeutung zugemessen, was sich anhand mehrerer inner- wie außerrechtlicher Kriterien deutlich festmachen lässt, wobei der Publikationsweise erhebliche Aussagekraft zukommt.

D. Normwiederholung und Kodifikation

Die Policeygesetzgebung ergänzte auf vielfache Weise das traditionelle peinliche Strafrecht, indem es weitere deviante Verhaltensweisen festschrieb und Zuwiderhandlungen mit Strafen sanktionierte. Aber während die Normwiederholung für die Policeygesetzgebung charakteristisch ist, wird man sie im Bereich des peinlichen Strafrechts weitgehend vergeblich suchen. Nicht ohne Grund: Die Rechtswidrigkeit der Tötung eines Menschen beispielsweise mußte man nicht wiederholt in Erinnerung bringen. Anders verhält es sich nur in jenen quantitativ nicht ins Gewicht fallenden Tatbeständen, bei denen normativ statuiertes Sollen und Rechtsbewußtsein der Normadressaten auseinanderklafften. Dies läßt sich zum Beispiel anhand der Regulierung der bäuerlichen Fehdeführung im 15. Jahrhundert illustrieren.[89]

Ebenso wird man im privatrechtlichen Bereich Normwiederholungen und -einschärfungen weitgehend vergeblich suchen (wobei man sich allerdings des behelfsmäßigen Charakters der Trennung von Privatrecht und Policeyrecht in

---

[88] Vgl. Schennach, Publikation und Normintensität (wie Fn. 48).

[89] Für Tirol z. B. Stolz, Otto: Geschichte der Verwaltung Tirols. Teilstück des 2. Bandes der Geschichte des Landes Tirol (Forschungen zur Rechts- und Kulturgeschichte XIII). Innsbruck 1998, S. 113-114; allgemein Reinle, Christine: Bauernfehden. Studien zur Fehdeführung Nichtadliger im spätmittelalterlichen römisch-deutschen Reich, besonders in den bayerischen Herzogtümern (Vierteljahrschrift für Sozial- und Wirtschaftsgeschichte, Beihefte 170). Stuttgart 2003.

der Frühneuzeit bewußt sein muß, da fallweise auch privatrechtliche Materien wie beispielsweise erb- oder vormundschaftsrechtliche Fragen unter der Leitvorstellung einer guten Ordnung des Gemeinwesens normativ geregelt wurden): Zwar kam es im ausgehenden Mittelalter und in der Frühneuzeit in zahlreichen Territorien zu Kodifikationen des Privatrechts in „Landrechten" oder in (Teilen von) Landesordnungen.[90] Landesherrliche Einzelgesetze, mittels derer den Gerichten oder gar den Normadressaten wieder und wieder die Befolgung des kodifizierten Landrechts eingeschärft wurde, fehlen jedoch. Wo eine Kodifikation geltende Rechtsgewohnheiten wiedergibt, erübrigte sich eine solche Vorgehensweise von vornherein. In der Tat findet der mittelalterliche Gedanke der Rechtswahrung und Rechtsdarstellung, allenfalls der Rechtsbesserung auch noch in den erwähnten Landrechten und Landesordnungen in unterschiedlicher Intensität und Ausprägung seinen Niederschlag.[91] So beschwört die Präambel der Tiroler Landesordnung von 1526 mit Verweis auf die Unbeständigkeit nicht verschriftlichter Rechtsnormen und auf die Notwendigkeit der Anpassung des Rechts an sich ändernde Zeiten Rechtswahrung und Rechtsbesserung als Leitmotive der Kodifikation. In der Narratio führt Erzherzog Ferdinand I. unter anderem aus:

„Haben wir gnedigklichist betracht vnd erwegen [!]/ das guette Recht vnd gepreüch / so die nit in schrifft verfaßt / mißbraucht / vnd zuzeiten in abgang vnd vergessen kumen / das auch durch langwirige zeit der Rechten vnd gepreüch / in Stetten / vnd Gerichten / der menschen merckliche verändrung beschicht / vnd khain Recht noch geprauch dermassen begründt / das mit der zeit nit durch mercklich notdurfft / Endrung vnd besserung / auch einsehung zuthun nutzbarlichen geacht wirdet."

---

[90] Auf die Problematik der Abgrenzung von „Landesordnung" und „Landrecht" kann hier nicht eingegangen werden. Zeitgenössisch wurden die beiden Termini „weder terminologisch noch inhaltlich unterschieden": vgl. Weber, Polizei- und Landesordnungen (wie Fn. 30), S. 56.

[91] Vgl. auch Willoweit, Dietmar: Die Gleichzeitigkeit des Ungleichzeitigen: Rationales und traditionales Rechtsdenken im ausgehenden Mittelalter. In: Recht und Verfassung im Übergang vom Mittelalter zur Neuzeit. Teil 2: Bericht über Kolloquien der Kommission zur Erforschung der Kultur des Spätmittelalters 1996 bis 1997. Hrsg. von Hartmut Boockmann u.a. (Abhandlungen der Akademie der Wissenschaften in Göttingen. Historisch-Philologische Klasse, 3. Folge, 239). Göttingen 2001, S. 369-385, hier S. 381-383.

Eine Präambel ist isoliert jedoch nur bedingt aussagekräftig, zumal wenn sie toposartige Formulierungen aufgreift und abwandelt. Im Fall der Tiroler Landesordnung bestätigt sich jedoch die These einer weitgehenden Festschreibung der geltenden Rechtsgewohnheiten.[92] Dieser Befund ist jedoch nicht zu generalisieren. Die gesetzgeberischen Intentionen, die zu den privatrechtlichen Kodifikationen des 16. und 17. Jahrhunderts führten, decken ein breites Spektrum ab.[93] Am einen Ende des Spektrums finden sich Beispiele wie die Tiroler Landesordnung von 1526, die weitgehend bestehendes Recht sammelten, verschriftlichten und vereinheitlichten. Auf diese Weise fügen sie sich in die vornehmlich rechtsbewahrende und rechtsbessernde Tradition des Mittelalters ein, die schon im Oberbayerischen Landrecht Ludwigs des Bayern von 1346 ein prominentes Beispiel fand.[94] Am anderen Ende des Spektrums findet man privatrechtliche Kodifikationen mit stark romanisierenden Tendenzen, die partiell ausdrücklich entgegenstehende Rechtsgewohnheiten kassieren. Ähnliche Entwicklungslinien wie bei den Landrechten bzw. Landesordnungen lassen sich im übrigen im 15. und beginnenden 16. Jahrhundert bei den Stadtrechtskodifikationen bzw. -reformationen festmachen.[95]

Bei derartigen Privatrechtskodifikationen, die nicht nur der Rechtsbewahrung, Systematisierung und „Besserung" dienten, sondern mit romanisierender Stoßrichtung das vorgefundene Recht abänderten oder sogar explizit aufhoben, mag das Fehlen von einschärfenden Gesetzgebungsakten verwundern.

---

[92] Wesener, Gunter: Einflüsse und Geltung des römisch-gemeinen Rechts in den altösterreichischen Ländern in der Neuzeit (16. bis 18. Jahrhundert) (Forschungen zur neueren deutschen Privatrechtsgeschichte 27). Wien/Köln 1989, S. 28-30.

[93] Vgl. hierzu allgemein Wieacker, Franz: Privatrechtsgeschichte der Neuzeit unter besonderer Berücksichtigung der deutschen Entwicklung. Göttingen [2]1996 (unveränderter Nachdruck der 2. Auflage 1967), S. 195-200; ferner Schiemann, Gottfried: Usus modernus und Gesetzgebung. In: Gesetz und Gesetzgebung (wie Fn. 20), S. 157-170, hier bes. S. 161-162; Ebel, Geschichte der Gesetzgebung (wie Fn. 7), S. 51-53.

[94] Oberbayerisches Landrecht Kaiser Ludwigs des Bayern von 1346. Edition, Übersetzung und juristischer Kommentar. Hrsg. von Hans Schlosser und Ingo Schwab. Köln/Weimar/Wien 2000; Das Landrecht von 1346 für Oberbayern und seine Gerichte Kitzbühel, Kufstein, und Rattenberg. Kritische Edition der Georgenberger Handschrift Ms. 201. Hrsg. von Ingo Schwab (Fontes rerum Austriacarum; Fontes iuris 13). Köln/Wien/Weimar 2002. Ergänzende Beispiele bei Ebel, Geschichte der Gesetzgebung (wie Fn. 7), S. 51-53.

[95] Vgl. Wieacker, Privatrechtsgeschichte (wie Fn. 93), S. 189-195.

Angesichts des ausgeprägten „usualen Rechtsgeltungsverständnis"[96] der frühneuzeitlichen Justiz, das der Observanz einer Norm, mithin ihrer Anwendung in der Praxis deutlich größere Bedeutung zumaß als der *voluntas legislatoris*, wäre dies ein durchaus naheliegendes Instrumentarium gewesen, um die Durchsetzungschancen der entsprechenden Bestimmungen zu erhöhen. Da dies jedoch nicht der Fall war, erscheint es nicht einmal so überraschend, wenn die Wirkung der Gerichtsordnung Landgraf Wilhelms III. von 1497 sowie die Vermehrte Marburgische Hofgerichtsordnung Landgraf Philipps des Großmütigen von 1524 hinsichtlich des darin geregelten Ehegüter- und Erbrechtes sowie des Retraktrechtes auf das Gewohnheitsrecht selbst nach 75- bzw. 50-jähriger Geltungsdauer nur marginal war. Zu Recht zog Bernhard Diestelkamp daraus den Schluß, daß derartige Rezeptionsgesetze nicht auf konsequente Durchsetzung unter Verdrängung bewährten Gewohnheitsrechtes ausgerichteten waren, sondern vor allem der Schaffung eines *ius certum* im Fall von Widersprüchlichkeit, Unklarheit oder Lückenhaftigkeit des Gewohnheitsrechtes dienten.[97]

Gerade das konsequenterweise hieraus resultierende nahezu vollständige Fehlen von einschärfenden Mandaten und Reskripten ist ein fundamentaler Unterschied zum Hauptbetätigungsfeld der frühneuzeitlichen Gesetzgebung im materiell umfassenden Bereich der ‚guten Policey'. Dementsprechend langsam – wenn überhaupt – fand regionalen oder lokalen Rechtsgewohnheiten widersprechendes gesatztes Privatrecht Eingang in die Justizpraxis: Hagen Wend konnte so anhand des Trierer Landrechts von 1668 illustrieren, wie sich dessen Eingang in die Praxis durch ein ganz allmähliches, sich über Jahrzehnte hinziehendes Einsickern vollzog, wobei dieser Prozeß bei den früh professionalisierten Obergerichten einsetzte und die lokalen Gerichte und die außerstreitige Gerichtsbarkeit zuletzt erreichte.[98]

---

[96] Simon, Geltung (wie Fn. 13), S. 102-103.

[97] Diestelkamp, Bernhard: Das Verhältnis von Gesetz und Gewohnheitsrecht im 16. Jahrhundert – aufgezeigt am Beispiel der Oberhessischen Erbgewohnheiten von 1572. In: Ders.: Recht und Gericht im Heiligen Römischen Reich. Frankfurt a. M. 1999, S. 443-479 (Erstveröff. 1977).

[98] Wend, Hagen: Die Anwendung des Trierer Landrechts von 1668/1713 im rechtsrheinischen Teil des Kurstaates und in benachbarten Gebieten. Frankfurt a. M. 1973.

Was tun mit den Dekretalen Papst Gregors IX.? Zum nachreformatorischen Schicksal der Normen des kanonischen Rechts

Renate Schulze

A.

Was tun mit den Dekretalen Papst Gregors IX.? Diese Frage klingt auf den ersten Blick salopp, ja fast zu einfach – und doch verweist sie deutlicher auf den Kern des Beitrags, als es zunächst den Anschein haben mag. Er wird sich dem Erinnern und Vergessen am Beispiel des evangelischen Kirchenrechts widmen, wie es im *Ius Ecclesiasticum Protestantium* Justus Henning Böhmers[1] Ausdruck gefunden hat. Dieses zwischen 1714 und 1736 entstandene epochemachende Werk des Hallenser Gelehrten und ersten großen evangelischen Kirchenrechtlers hatte sich, wie die Passage *iuxta seriem decretalium ostendens* im vollständigen Titel *Ius Ecclesiasticum Protestantium, usum modernum iuris canonici iuxta seriem decretalium ostendens, & ipsis rerum argumentis illustrans*[2] zeigt, zum „roten Faden" der Darstellung eben die Dekretalen Papst Gregors IX. (1227-1241) gewählt. Mit der schlichten Bezeichnung Dekretalen gemeint war der *Liber canonum extra Decretum vagantium* oder – kurz gefaßt – *Liber extra*, der spä-

[1] Zu Justus Henning Böhmer vgl. beispielsweise Schubart-Fikentscher, Gertrud: Böhmer, Just Henning. In: Handwörterbuch zur deutschen Rechtsgeschichte [HRG]. Hrsg. von Adalbert Erler/ Ekkehard Kaufmann. Berlin 1971. Band 1, Sp. 484, 485; Landau, Peter: Böhmer, Justus Henning. In: Juristen. Ein biographisches Lexikon. Von der Antike bis zum 20. Jahrhundert. Hrsg. von Michael Stolleis. München 2001, S. 93; Liermann, Hans: Böhmer, Justus (Jobst) Henning. In: Neue Deutsche Biographie [NDB]. Hrsg. von der Historischen Kommission bei der Bayerischen Akademie der Wissenschaften. Band 2 (1955), S. 392.

[2] Böhmer, Justus Henning: Ius Ecclesiasticum Protestantium. Band 1. Halae (Halle, Saale) 1714. In deutscher Übersetzung lautet der Titel: Kirchenrecht der Protestanten, den zeitgenössischen Gebrauch des kanonischen Rechts gemäß der Ordnung der Dekretalen darstellend und mit den aus der Sache selbst kommenden Argumenten erläuternd.

ter als zweites Buch in das *Corpus Iuris Canonici* von 1582 eingehen sollte. In päpstlichem Auftrag zusammengestellt hatte den *Liber extra* der Dominikaner Raimund de Pennaforte und ihn auch in die fünf Teile gegliedert, deren Inhalte markant durch die Begriffe *iudex* (päpstliche Regierung), *iudicium* (Verfahrensrecht), *clerus* (geistliches und Vermögensrecht), *sponsalia* (Eherecht) und *crimen* (Straf- und Strafprozeßrecht) wiedergegeben werden können.[3]

Was tun mit den Dekretalen Papst Gregors IX.? Das ist zugleich die Frage nach dem Umgang mit den Normen des kanonischen Rechts. Wie sollten sich die neu entstandenen protestantischen Landeskirchen verhalten, die sich doch im Zuge der Reformation von der Kirche des römischen Papstes getrennt hatten und sich nun vor die Frage gestellt sahen, ob sie das päpstliche kanonische Recht überhaupt noch anwenden konnten oder durften.

Martin Luthers Position in dieser Frage war unmißverständlich: Er lehnte das kanonische Recht kategorisch ab.[4] Nicht umsonst wird von ihm immer wieder die berühmte Szene vom 10. Dezember 1520[5] am Wittenberger Elstertor erzählt, im Rahmen derer er – nebst der gegen seine Lehre gerichteten Bannandrohungsbulle Papst Leos X. – das *Corpus Iuris Canonici*[6] den Flammen überantwortet hatte. Eindeutiger konnte Luther kaum demonstrieren, daß er,

---

[3] Erler, Adalbert: Kirchenrecht. Ein Studienbuch. München [5]1983, S. 29.

[4] Böhmer, Ius Ecclesiasticum Protestantium (wie Fn. 2), Tit. 2, § 64, S. 128: „auctoritas LVTHERI, iuris Canonici hostis infensissimi" – „des kanonischen Rechts unversöhnlichster Feind".

[5] Luther spricht vom Montag nach St. Nicolai als dem Tag des Geschehens. St. Nicolai, der 6. Dezember, fiel im Jahre 1520 auf einen Donnerstag, so daß die Bücherverbrennung also am 10. Dezember 1520 stattfand, Luther, Martin: Warum des Papstes und seiner Jünger Bücher von D. Martin Luther verbrannt sind. 1520. In: D. Martin Luthers Werke. Kritische Gesamtausgabe. Teil 1, 7. Band. Weimar 2003 (Unveränderter Nachdruck der Ausgabe von 1897), S. 152-186, hier S. 161 Fn. 2.

[6] Dies darf allerdings nicht als amtliche Bezeichnung verstanden werden. Vielmehr benutzte man die Bezeichnung *Corpus Iuris Canonici* bereits im Mittelalter als Parallelbegriff zum *Corpus Iuris Civilis*, Wolter, Udo: Ius canonicum in iure civili. Köln Wien 1975, S. 3. Offiziell als *Corpus Iuris Canonici* benannte man im Jahre 1582 die das *Decretum Gratiani*, die Dekretalen Gregors IX., den *Liber Sextus*, die Clementinen, die Extravaganten Johannes' XXII. und die *Extravagantes communes* vereinende Sammlung des kanonischen Rechts, vgl. Erler, Adalbert: Kirchenrecht. Ein Studienbuch, S. 30.

nachdem er „dem Ansehen desselben einen erschrecklichen Stoß“[7] versetzt hatte, das kanonische Recht dem Vergessen anheimfallen lassen wollte. Und daß er dieses Exempel ganz bewußt statuierte, zeigt nicht zuletzt seine noch im Jahr 1520 das Geschehen rechtfertigende Schrift „Warum des Papstes und seiner Jünger Bücher von D. Martin Luther verbrannt sind“.[8]

Die Juristen betrachteten das kanonische Recht allerdings – auch schon zu Luthers Zeiten – mit anderen Augen.[9] Denn sie kannten diese Materie aus dem Studium und wußten um deren Praktikabilität, so daß sie das kanonische Recht oftmals schon aus reiner Gewohnheit weiter anwendeten. Zudem bedurften die neu entstandenen protestantischen Landeskirchen rechtlicher Regelungen. Doch hatten die im 16. Jahrhundert geschaffenen evangelischen Kirchenordnungen nicht jegliche Frage beantwortet, so daß sich bald – jedenfalls sofern man sich auf systematische Erwägungen einließ – die Frage der subsidiären Anwendung des kanonischen Rechts stellte.

Seit dem denkwürdigen Ereignis am Elstertor sollten schließlich fast 200 Jahre vergehen, bis dem kanonischen Recht und seiner Anwendung in der evangelischen Kirche eine feste wissenschaftliche Basis gegeben wurde. Justus Henning Böhmer widmete sich als erster und zugleich umfassend der Frage, in welcher Form eigentlich das „alte“ kanonische Recht in den protestantischen Landeskirchen erinnert wurde und weiterlebte. Erste Ergebnisse dieser Analyse eines *usus modernus iuris canonici* legte er 1701 im *Ius Parochiale* vor – einer systematisch aufgebauten, allerdings auf ausgewählte Materien des dritten Buchs der Dekretalen beschränkten Untersuchung.[10] Umfassend behandelte er die Fragestellung in den fünf Bänden des *Ius Ecclesiasticum Protestantium.* Hierin untersuchte Böhmer jeden einzelnen Titel der – den ganz überwiegen-

---

[7] Mosheim, Johann Lorenz von: Allgemeines Kirchenrecht der Protestanten. Helmstädt 1760, Einleitung S. 4.

[8] Luther (wie Fn. 5), S. 161-182.

[9] Liermann, Hans: Das kanonische Recht als Gegenstand des gelehrten Unterrichts an den protestantischen Universitäten Deutschlands in den ersten Jahrhunderten nach der Reformation. In: Der Jurist und die Kirche. Ausgewählte kirchenrechtliche Aufsätze und Rechtsgutachten von Hans Liermann. Hrsg. von Martin Heckel/ Klaus Obermaier/ Dietrich Pirson. München 1973, S. 108-131, hier S. 114.

[10] Zu diesem frühen Werk Schulze, Renate: Auf dem Weg zum Ius Ecclesiasticum Protestantium – Justus Henning Böhmers Ius Parochiale. In: ZRG 123 Kan. Abt. 92 (2006), S. 660-686.

den Teil des kanonischen Rechts ausmachenden – Dekretalen und erörterte, ob und gegebenenfalls inwieweit die jeweiligen Inhalte in den evangelischen Bereich übertragen werden konnten. Dies tat er sorgfältig und kenntnisreich,[11] so daß man ihm weit und breit Anerkennung zollte und seinen Ausführungen maßgebliches Gewicht zumaß. So legte Böhmer die Basis für die Beantwortung der entscheidenden Frage, ob man sich in den protestantischen Landeskirchen durch fortzusetzende Anwendung weiterhin der Regelungen des kanonischen Rechts – hier in Gestalt der Dekretalen – erinnern sollte oder ob diese mangels Gebrauch langsam, aber sicher aus dem protestantischen Gedächtnis verschwinden und so in Vergessenheit geraten konnten. Wie dies geschah, soll nun an einem ausgewählten Beispiel im Einzelnen gezeigt werden.

B.

Dieses Beispiel bietet der neunte Titel des ersten Buchs der Dekretalen. *De renunciatione* überschrieben, behandelt er den Themenkomplex des Verzichts auf ein Amt, der dem lateinischen Synonym *resignatio* entsprechend auch als freie Resignation bezeichnet wird. Es geht dabei um die Frage, ob ein Kleriker auf sein geistliches Amt (*officium sacrum*) beziehungsweise auf die damit verbundene Pfründe (*beneficium ecclesiasticum*) verzichten kann oder sogar völlig den geistlichen Stand (*ordo ecclesiasticus*) verlassen und damit „ins weltliche Leben zurückkehren" darf.

Blickt man zunächst auf den Dekretalentitel *De renunciatione*, so unterteilt sich dieser in fünfzehn Kapitel, die jeweils eine päpstliche Antwort auf eine konkrete Frage überliefern, und zwar immer in derselben charakteristischen

[11] Ohne Grund jedenfalls dürfte das von der Hallenser Fakultät nach Böhmers Tod verfaßte Elogium unter Zuhilfenahme der Trias *thesaurus, museum ambulans, Bibliotheca vivens* nicht davon gesprochen haben, daß Justus Henning Böhmer einem wandelnden Lexikon vergleichbar war: „Omnibus, qui abdita quaererent, thesaurus fuit, nec quicquam erat, quod non statim sciret, adeo vt museum ambulans viuentemque dixisses Bibliothecam." – „Für alle, die entlegene Dinge suchten, war er eine Schatzkammer, und es gab nichts, was er nicht sogleich wußte, so daß du ihn ein wandelndes Museum oder eine lebende Bibliothek genannt hättest." Das Elogium ist abgedruckt bei Böhmer, Justus Henning: Exercitationes ad Pandectas. Band 6. Hanoverae et Gottingae (Hannover und Göttingen) 1764, S. XVIII.

Ordnung: der – juristisch gesprochen – Tenor der päpstlichen Entscheidung wird vorangestellt, darauf folgen die Namen des betreffenden Papstes und des Empfängers des päpstlichen Schreibens, schließt sich die Schilderung des Sachverhalts an.[12] Somit finden sich fünfzehn aneinandergereihte und nur nach dem Entstehungsjahr geordnete entscheidungserheblich gewordene Fragen mit den als Antwort gegebenen päpstlichen Dekreten.

Justus Henning Böhmer stellt dem in seinem *Ius Ecclesiasticum Protestantium* eine in sich geschlossene Abhandlung entgegen und erörtert das Thema *De renunciatione* im Zusammenhang. Wie auch sonst klärt Böhmer als erstes die Begrifflichkeiten und führt Differenzierungen ein, die er für seine folgende Erörterung der „vniuersa[13] doctrina de *munerum sacrorum abdicationibus*“[14] – der allgemeinen Lehre von der Niederlegung geistlicher Ämter – benötigt, die drei Aspekte beinhaltet: „Praeterea renunciatio est vel tantum *officii sacri* aut *beneficii ecclesiastici*; vel etiam praeterea *ordinis*.“[15] Es geht also zum einen um die Niederlegung des Amts (*officium*) in den möglichen Varianten der Niederlegung des Diensts als Priester beziehungsweise Pfarrer (*officium sacrum*) oder der Pfründe (*beneficium ecclesiasticum*) bei gleichzeitigem Verbleib im geistlichen Stand, zum anderen um das zum Verzicht auf das Amt hinzutretende Verlassen des geistlichen Stands (*ordo ecclesiasticus*). Diesen Aspekten widmet Böhmer die folgenden Ausführungen, wobei er in jeder Konstellation klärt, ob und inwieweit sie den protestantischen Bereich betrifft, so daß das Erinnern sehr unterschiedlich ausfallen kann.

Beginnend mit der *renunciatio ordinis* schildert Böhmer den geschichtlichen Werdegang der Regelungen und zeigt damit auf, wie bestimmte Inhalte über die Jahrhunderte behandelt worden sind. Besonders umfangreich werden die Ausführungen stets, wenn Böhmer sie bei der Urkirche beginnen läßt. Zum

---

[12] Gregorii Papae IX. Decretales. Augustae Taurinorum (Turin) 1745, Lib. I. Tit. IX., Sp. 79-90.

[13] So schreibt Böhmer das Wort „universa“ und damit wie stets am Wortanfang den Buchstaben „v“ statt „u“.

[14] Böhmer, Ius Ecclesiasticum Protestantium (wie Fn. 2), Tit. 9, § 1, S. 363.

[15] Böhmer, Ius Ecclesiasticum Protestantium (wie Fn. 2), Tit. 9, § 1, S. 363: „Außerdem umfaßt die Amtsniederlegung entweder nur die Tätigkeit als Geistlicher oder die Pfründe; oder fernerhin auch das Verlassen des (geistlichen) Standes.“

Anknüpfungspunkt wählt er aber ebenso Konzilien[16] oder das römische Recht – etwa die Novellen Iustinians, in denen zum Teil kirchliche Vorschriften übernommen worden sind.[17] Auf diese Weise arbeitet Böhmer gegebenenfalls heraus, daß manche Unterscheidung – im vorliegenden Fall diejenige zwischen *renunciatio ordinis & officii* – erst ein Kind späterer Zeiten war.

Mit dem erwähnten Gang durch die Kirchengeschichte verbindet Böhmer regelmäßig die inhaltliche Erläuterung des Dekretalentitels, im Rahmen derer die Einzelheiten des kanonischen Rechts aus sich heraus, bei Bedarf unter Beifügung von Belegstellen aus der kanonistischen Literatur dargestellt werden. So erfährt der Leser, daß das kanonische Recht die *renunciatio ordinis*, die auch unter dem Begriff *desertio ordinis ecclesiastici* (Abfall vom kirchlichen Stand) vorkommt, mißbilligt und, sollte sie tatsächlich vorkommen, als zu ahndendes *delictum ecclesiasticum* begreift.

Ist der Regelungsinhalt damit erläutert, spannt Böhmer den Bogen zu den protestantischen Kirchen und fragt, ob es dort ebenfalls Regelungen diesen Inhalts gibt und, wenn ja, in welcher Form. Böhmer bleibt indes nicht bei der Schilderung des Rechtszustands stehen, sondern prüft weiter, ob es das betreffende Rechtsinstitut bei den Protestanten eigentlich geben darf oder ob diese Regelung im Widerspruch zum evangelischen Bekenntnis steht. Stets geht es Böhmer darum, die Regelung des kanonischen Rechts genauestens zu analysieren und zu ergründen, worauf sie beruht: „*fundamentum* decisionis ante omnia eruendum est.“[18]

So arbeitet er heraus, daß die Protestanten ein absolutes Verbot der *desertio ordinis* deshalb nicht akzeptieren dürfen,[19] weil dieses im kanonischen Recht

---

[16] *Concilium Triburiensis*, Böhmer, Ius Ecclesiasticum Protestantium (wie Fn. 2), Tit. 9, § 2, S. 363; *Concilium Tridentinum*, Böhmer, Ius Ecclesiasticum Protestantium (wie Fn. 2), Tit. 9, § 4, S. 364.

[17] Böhmer, Ius Ecclesiasticum Protestantium (wie Fn. 2), Tit. 9, § 3, S. 364.

[18] Böhmer, Ius Ecclesiasticum Protestantium (wie Fn. 2), Tit. 9, § 8, S. 366: „Die Entscheidungsgrundlage muß vor allem anderen ermittelt werden.“

[19] Böhmer, Ius Ecclesiasticum Protestantium (wie Fn. 2), Tit. 9, § 7, S. 366. Das ändere jedoch nichts daran, daß einige Protestanten – Böhmer nennt hier Schilter und zitiert aus dessen Institutiones iuris canonici lib. I. tit. 14 §. 6 – dennoch die päpstliche Sichtweise der Dinge verträten. Um dessen aus Böhmers Sicht irrige Ansichten nicht unkommentiert stehenzulassen, verfaßte Böhmer schon 1712 eine Bearbeitung der Institutiones Schilters, Böhmer, Justus Henning: Schilterus illustratus, seu emendationes et additamenta ad Io. Schilteri Institutiones iuris canonici. Halae

verankerte Verbot auf der Doktrin beruht, daß einem Mann mit Aufnahme in den Klerikerstand ein fortan unauslöschlicher klerikaler Wesenszug (*character indelebilis*) eingeprägt werde – mit der Konsequenz, daß er das mit Exkommunikation zu ahndende Verbrechen der Apostasie begeht, wenn er den geistlichen Stand verläßt. Folglich betrachtet das protestantische Kirchenrecht, das mit der Ordination zum Pfarrer keine Verleihung eines unauslöschlichen Wesenszugs verbindet, die *desertio ordinis* lediglich als Unterfall der aber auch nur ausnahmsweise und unter bestimmten Voraussetzungen gestatteten einfachen *resignatio* oder *renunciatio*. Das ist zudem der Grund, warum das protestantische Kirchenrecht den Resignierenden nicht verpflichtet, Kleriker zu bleiben, so daß dieser durchaus „ins weltliche Leben zurückkehren" kann:

> „planum est, nulla lege Protestantes post resignationem obligari, vt maneant clerici, habitu, clericis proprio, incedant, vsu gladii abstineant, & consistorio adhuc subiecti maneant."[20]

Dieser Einordnung der *desertio ordinis* als ein Fall der *renunciatio* schließt sich die Erörterung der Bedingungen an, unter denen eine solche Niederlegung des Amts wirksam erklärt werden kann. Hauptvoraussetzung ist ein schwerwiegender, zumeist in der Person des Resignierenden liegender Grund – eine *iusta causa*. Betrachtet man diese Gründe genauer, ist das Erinnern auf Seiten des protestantischen Kirchenrechts nicht zu übersehen, denn Böhmer schildert die nach kanonischem Recht eine *resignatio* rechtfertigenden, bei Innozenz III. genannten Gründe und prüft sie der Reihe nach auf ihre Kompatibilität mit

---

Magdeburgicae (Halle, Saale) 1712, S. [12] im Rahmen der Vorrede Ad Lectorem: „Plura scitu necessaria omisit Auctor, in pluribus etiam incaute secutus est principia Pontificiorum, quae non adeo commode nostris applicari possunt ecclesiis, adeoque de his emendandis & supplendis laboraui." – „Vieles grundsätzlich Notwendige läßt der Autor [Schilter] aus, in vielen Dingen ist er unvorsichtigerweise den Prinzipien der Päpstlichen gefolgt, die eben nicht so leicht auf unsere Kirchen angewandt werden können, und deshalb habe ich [Böhmer] mich bemüht, diese Bereiche von Fehlern zu befreien und zu ergänzen."

[20] Böhmer, Ius Ecclesiasticum Protestantium (wie Fn. 2), Tit. 9, § 9, S. 367: „Klar ist, daß die Protestanten nach dem Amtsverzicht durch kein Gesetz verpflichtet werden, Kleriker zu bleiben, nach wie vor die Kleidung der Kleriker zu tragen, sich vom Gebrauch des Schwertes fernzuhalten und weiterhin Untergebene des Konsistoriums zu bleiben."

dem Kirchenrecht der Protestanten.[21] So konstatiert er beispielsweise die Anwendung des Grunds der körperlichen Gebrechlichkeit oder Altersschwäche (*debilitas corporis* vel *senium*) auch bei den Protestanten, während er die Resignation *ob personae irregularitatem* für den protestantischen Bereich ablehnt.[22] Dieser nach kanonischem Recht anerkannte Grund sei auf die Protestanten nicht anzuwenden, weil er auf der von diesen abgelehnten päpstlichen Doktrin der in der Person liegenden Irregularität beruhe, die von der Möglichkeit eines dauernden Weihehindernisses ausgehe, also durch das kanonische Recht festgesetzte, beständige Hindernisse kenne, die entweder den Empfang der Weihe oder die Ausübung einer Weihe unerlaubt machen.

Diese Ausführungen zeigen, daß Böhmer das Kirchenrecht und die kirchliche Praxis in den protestantischen Ländern in den Mittelpunkt stellt, beides aber nichtsdestotrotz aus dem kanonischen Recht heraus erläutert, das stets den Bezugspunkt darstellt: „Atque hoc ipsum quidem de iure canonico certum exploratumque est."[23] Oder wie er sich an anderer Stelle ausdrückt: „vt[24] tamen ex iure canonico fundamenta eius & rationem praemittam."[25]

Doch zieht Justus Henning Böhmer zur Erklärung des nach der Reformation eingetretenen Zustands nicht allein das – also oftmals das Fundament bildende – kanonische Recht heran, sondern stützt sich zudem auf die in den Territorien vorhandenen Kirchenordnungen und auf die Werke der kanonistischen Literatur sowie protestantischer Autoren. Dabei setzt sich Böhmer mit abweichenden Auffassungen auseinander und spart Kontroversen keineswegs aus, sondern stellt die divergierenden Ansichten unter Anführung von Belegstellen zunächst dar, um danach die verschiedenen Positionen zu diskutieren und schließlich zu einer Entscheidung zu kommen. Eine Illustration erfährt die Entscheidung der für die Praxis bedeutenden Fragen oftmals durch thema-

---

[21] Böhmer, Ius Ecclesiasticum Protestantium (wie Fn. 2), Tit. 9, § 10, S. 368 ff.

[22] Böhmer, Ius Ecclesiasticum Protestantium (wie Fn. 2), Tit. 9, § 10, S. 370.

[23] Böhmer, Ius Ecclesiasticum Protestantium (wie Fn. 2), Tit. 9, § 13, S. 371: „Und besonders das ist ja nach dem kanonischen Recht unzweifelhaft und feststehend."

[24] Hier schreibt Böhmer am Wortanfang erneut „u" statt „v".

[25] Böhmer, Ius Ecclesiasticum Protestantium (wie Fn. 2), Tit. 10, § 1, S. 410: „Auf daß ich dennoch aus dem kanonischen Recht heraus dessen (des protestantischen Kirchenrechts) Grundlagen und Beweggrund vorausschicke."

tisch geeignete *Responsa* (Rechtsgutachten) insbesondere der Hallenser Spruchfakultät,[26] der Böhmer selbst angehörte.

Denn Böhmer bleibt nicht bei der Erörterung der prinzipiellen Fragen zur *renunciatio* stehen, sondern widmet sich nach deren Klärung den in der Praxis hinsichtlich dieses Rechtsinstituts immer wieder auftretenden Streitfällen. Wichtig zu klären war beispielsweise, wie die Protestanten mit der Resignation zugunsten einer dritten Person (*renunciatio* beziehungsweise *resignatio in fauorem tertii*) umgehen sollten, bei der stets der Verdacht bestand, daß hier geistliche Würden gegen Geld verkauft wurden, also ein Fall von Simonie vorlag. Obgleich Böhmer diese Art der *resignatio* deshalb für weniger ehrenhaft (*minus honesta*) hält,[27] bleibt ihm nichts anderes übrig, als zu konstatieren, daß diese aus der katholischen Kirche bekannte Fallgestaltung auch in den protestantischen Kirchen Einzug gehalten hat, insbesondere mit Blick auf die Pfründe der Mitglieder der Ordens- oder Klerikerkapitel (*beneficia ecclesiastica capitulorum*), die nach wie vor regelmäßig anhand des früheren, also kanonischen Rechts beurteilt würden.[28] Doch fand ganz pragmatisch eine Anpassung an die protestantischen Gegebenheiten statt, so daß eine *resignatio in fauorem tertii* zu ihrer Wirksamkeit nun konsequenterweise nicht mehr das Einverständnis des Papstes, sondern – je nach Zuständigkeit – dasjenige des Patrons, des Konsistoriums oder des Landesherrn voraussetzte. Ein neuerliches Zeichen dafür, daß das protestantische Kirchenrecht mit überkommenen Instituten umgehen und sich daher mit den diesbezüglichen Regelungen des kanonischen Rechts schon aus praktischer Notwendigkeit heraus auseinandersetzen mußte, diese also jedenfalls erinnerte. Die Resignation zugunsten eines Dritten ließ man einstweilen zu, vermutlich weil man dieses Institut zur Bewältigung der Lebenswirklichkeit in den Klöstern und Stiften brauchte, wie die zahlreichen von Böhmer angefügten *Responsa* zu damit verbundenen Einzelproblemen zeigen.

Die Magdeburger Spruchfakultät hatte sich beispielsweise im August 1704 mit der Frage zu befassen, ob derjenige, zu dessen Gunsten die *resignatio* statt-

---

[26] Zur Spruchfakultät in Halle (Saale) weiterführend Schubart-Fikentscher, Gertrud: Hallesche Spruchpraxis. Consiliensammlungen Hallescher Gelehrter aus dem Anfang des 18. Jahrhunderts. Weimar 1960.

[27] Böhmer, Ius Ecclesiasticum Protestantium (wie Fn. 2), Tit. 9, § 14, S. 372.

[28] Böhmer, Ius Ecclesiasticum Protestantium (wie Fn. 2), Tit. 9, § 15, S. 373.

gefunden hatte, den Platz des Resignierenden einnehmen darf oder nur auf die letzte Stelle im Kollegium des Stifts S. Gangolph einrückt, was die Spruchfakultät folgendermaßen beschied:

„So erscheinet hieraus so viel/ daß der resignatarius K. als vltimus inter maiores sich der halben praebende so lange vergnügen muß/ bis einer von denen vorhergehenden mit Tode abgehet."[29]

Ein anderes *Responsum* veranlaßte der Fall mehrerer sich gleichzeitig ereignender *resignationes in fauorem tertii*,[30] während ein Erfurter *Responsum* vom März 1712 zu klären hatte, ob eine *resignatio* nur zu einem bestimmten Zeitpunkt im Jahr möglich ist.[31]

C.

Diese wenigen Mosaiksteine des Erinnerns und Vergessens auf Seiten des evangelischen Kirchenrechts sollen genügen. Schon sie zeigen, daß die eingangs gestellte Frage: „Was tun mit den Dekretalen Papst Gregors IX.?" nicht pauschal zu beantworten ist. Weit entfernt von der generellen Abneigung und kategorischen Ablehnung eines Martin Luther hat sich Justus Henning Böhmer im einzelnen mit den Inhalten der Dekretalen auseinandergesetzt und differenzierte Lösungen entwickelt, in denen beides vorkam: die Beibehaltung der überkommenen Normen des kanonischen Recht, sofern diese dem protestantischen Bekenntnis nicht widersprachen, sowie im Falle eines solchen Widerspruchs die Ablehnung dieser Normen. Oder anders und unter Bezugnahme auf das Tagungsthema gewendet: Böhmer gestattete das Erinnern oder empfahl das Vergessen.

---

[29] Böhmer, Ius Ecclesiasticum Protestantium (wie Fn. 2), Tit. 9, § 18, S. 376.
[30] Böhmer, Ius Ecclesiasticum Protestantium (wie Fn. 2), Tit. 9, § 20, S. 379 f.
[31] Böhmer, Ius Ecclesiasticum Protestantium (wie Fn. 2), Tit. 9, § 21, S. 380 ff.

Gnade und Vergessen im 19. und 20. Jahrhundert: ein „Einschlafen“ des Prinzips der Gewaltenteilung?

Monica Stronati

A. Mildtätigkeit in Verfassung, Gesetzbüchern und Lehre – eine Wortkunde

„Der König kann Gnade gewähren und die Strafen abändern“: dieser Art. 8 des *Statuto albertino* aus dem Jahre 1848 umreißt ebenso wenig wie andere europäische Verfassungen die Bedeutungen der königlichen Mildtätigkeit, sondern gibt nur zu verstehen, daß Inhaber der Mildtätigkeit in all ihren Formen der König ist.

Überdies trägt die Zweideutigkeit[1] des Wortes Gnade eine Bedeutung von „Begnadigung“[2] weiter, die der Auffassung des *ancien régime*[3] nahe kommt, das

---

[1] Requejo Pagés, Juan Luis: Amnistia e indulto en el constitucionalismo histórico español. In: Historia Constitucional, Revista Electrónica de Historia Constitucionale (2001) n. 2, http://hc.rediris.es/o2/Numero02.html, Paragraph 3: „A la perplejidad que resulta de la constitucionalización de un *derecho* de gracia le sigue una confusión en los términos más que notable.“, zum Begriff Straferlaß: „puede calificarse como *general* o *particular*, siendo así que en Italia, por ejemplo, al indulto particular se le conosce con el nombre de *gracia*, esto es, con el que entre nostros se utilizza para referirse a la clemencia en cuanto género.“

[2] Gemäß Tommaseo ist *rimettere in grazia* (wieder die Gunst zuteil werden lassen) mehr als *fare grazia* (Begnadigung gewähren), „questo è perdono, nel senso d'indulto o amnistia; il Rimettere in è almeno un principio dell'antico favore.“ Tommaseo, N./Bellini B.: Dizionario della lingua italiana, volume secondo, parte seconda. Torino 1869. In der französischen Rechtssprache war das Recht der Begnadigung das „Privilège de remettre la peine à un criminel légalement condamné par les tribunaux du pays. *grâce* ne peut appartenir qu'au monarque au nom duquel se rende la justice. Pour ne pas discréditer le droit de *grâce*, il ne faut l'exercer que dans le cas où la clémence royale ne peut déconsidérer l'oeuvre de la justice.“ Bescherelle, Louis-Nicolas: Dictionnaire national ou Dictionnaire universel de la langue française. Paris 1856, S. 58.

[3] Der erste italienische König, Vittorio Emanuele II, schwur „far rendere a ognuno, secondo le sue ragioni, piena ed esatta giustizia“, er verpflichtete sich so zu einer Handhabung der Mildtätig-

heißt hauptsächlich als Mitleid und Barmherzigkeit des Königs. Dennoch gibt die Verfassung, zusammen mit den aus der Vergangenheit überkommenen Bestandteilen, die Linien für eine neue juristische Konstruktion der Mildtätigkeit vor. Im Kontext betrachtet waren der „Mildtätigkeit"[4] Schranken gesetzt,

---

keit, die in Einklang stand mit der damals vorherrschenden Idee, dass das Ziel der Begnadigung sei: „Gerechtigkeit zu stiften". Der König „stiftet Gerechtigkeit", da er jedem gemäß seinem Verdienst und Stand vergibt und die „Begnadigung" erteilt. Nicht anders funktionierte die spanische *mercede*, die an den Begriff der ausgleichenden Gerechtigkeit gebunden ist: „Quizá la principal aproximación entre gracia y justicia se produzca por el concepto originario de merced, entendida ésta como justicia distributiva, mas en oposición a la justicia commutativa [...]. Ententiendo por justicia distributiva, remuneratoria o distintiva, discriminatoria y desigualitaria por tanto, aquella que conviene al príncipe para galardonar los trabajos y servicios prestados a favor de los reyes y de la causa pública de los reinos, otorgada a las personas según la calidad de éstas, sus linajes u estados. Mientras la justicia commutativa la referían a la debida ‚entre un hombre y otro', entre personas o partes singulares, particularmente en razón de los contratos." De Dios, Salustiano: Gracia, merced y patronazgo real. La Camara de Castilla entre 1474-1530. Madrid 1993, S. 277-278. Die spanischen *Las Partidas* kennen eine Unterscheidung zwischen „Barmherzigkeit", *mercede* und „Begnadigung": „la misericordia es concedida por el Rey por espontaáneo sentimiento de piedad para con el que ve ‚cuytado o mal andante, o por piedad que ha de sus fijos o de su compañia'. La merced seria un acto de perdón por servicios prestados al Rey por el beneficiario o por sus ascendiente, mientras que la gracia se diferencia de los anteriores conceptos que entrañan *perdón*, en que su concesión es gratuita y volontaria 'como manera de gualardón que con derecho (el Rey) se puede excusar de lo facer, si quisiere'. Es decir, que mientras que los perdones tienen alguna motivación en su concesión, la gracia goza de plena liberalidad." Linde Paniagua, Enrique: Amnistia e indulto en España. Madrid 1976, S. 31-32. Wenn es sich also auch um Begriffe handelt, die juristisch getrennt sind, tendiert man in der Praxis zu einer verschwommenen, nicht unterscheidenden Anwendung: „De antender a criterios de rigor, la gracia y la merced aparecerían como ámbitos no sólo distintos sino casi antagónicos [...]. Mas esto no lo debemos considerar excesivamente indicativo, ya que no es nada extraño contemplar las dos palabras de gracia y merced utilizadas en las fuentes de forma acumulativa, o bien de modo alternativo [...]. En definitiva, como conclusioón, que entre las ideas de gracia y merced se había producido en la prática un uso indistinto, si non confusión [...]", de Dios Salustiano, merced y patronazgo real (siehe zuvor), S. 274-277.

[4] Der Gesetzgeber des Jahres 1865 legt die Verfassungsvorschriften (Art. 67 Statut: „I ministri sono responsabili. Le leggi e gli atti del Governo non hanno vigore se non sono muniti della firma d'un ministro.", Art. 6: „Il Re nomina a tutte le cariche dello Stato: e fa i decreti e regolamenti necessarii per l'esecuzione delle leggi, senza sospenderne l'osservanza, o dispensarne") folgendermaßen aus: Art 825 c.p.p.: „Le suppliche per grazia di pene pronunziate, dovranno essere dirette al Re e presentate al ministro di grazia e giustizia: esse saranno sottoscritte dal supplicante o da un avvocato o procuratore esercente. Le suppliche per grazia, presentate come sopra o in qualsiasi

beispielsweise hatte der König nicht das Recht, Begnadigungen im Alleingang zu erlassen.

Die Verkündung des *Statuto albertino* erfolgt in einem Klima, in dem Zugeständnisse unausweichlich waren. Der kurze Zeitraum zur Ausarbeitung des Textes zwang dazu, das Augenmerk hauptsächlich auf die französische Erfahrung zu richten, wobei der Eindruck entsteht, daß sich die italienische Verfassung wesentlich derjenigen jenseits der Alpen angeglichen hat. Auch wenn diese Anschauung nicht ganz der Wahrheit entspricht, bedingt sie doch das Verständnis des Instituts der Mildtätigkeit.

Die italienische Verfassung wird vor allem aus zwei Gründen als Statut bezeichnet, einerseits um von der politischen[5] Bedeutung des Wortes „Verfassung" Abstand zu nehmen, das für sich unannehmbar für die sabaudische Monarchie[6] war, und andererseits, um die Behauptung der Konstitutionsgebenden zu unterstreichen, kein bestehendes Modell[7] zu „imitieren", sondern

---

altra forma, non sospenderanno l'esecuzione della sentenza, salvo che venga altrimenti ordinato dal Re per mezzo del ministro di grazia e giustizia. Il decreto di grazia non può riguardare che una condanna passata in cosa giudicata." Art. 831: „L'indulto si accorda per decreto reale, col quale sono determinati i reati e le condanne che vi sono comprese, e le condizioni per l'ammissione [...]"; Art. 830: „L'amnistia si concede per decreto reale, sopra proposta del Ministro di grazia e giustizia, udito il Consiglio dei ministri [...]".

5 „Quindi, la denominazione di 'Statuto' aveva innanzitutto un significato di 'raffreddamento' istituzionale, di 'moderazione' giuridica, di riconduzione ad un modello costituzionale riformato ma non sovvertito, conseguentemente assumeva una valenza politica ben precisa". Lo Statuto albertino illustrato dai lavori preparatori. Hrsg. von Luigi Ciaurro. Roma 1996, S. 45.

6 „All'idea costituzionale di straordinaria e multiforme accezione Re Carlo Alberto non opponeva un'assoluta incomprensione, ma un programma suo da lungo tempo meditato, che tuttavia ancora non s'era risolto ad attuare, col quale doveva concludere l'opera, veramente grandiosa, di restaurazione integrale dello Stato [...]." Crosa, Emilio: La concessione dello Statuto. Carlo Alberto e il ministro Borelli „redattore" dello Statuto. Torino 1936, S. 11.

7 Vor allem der König: „ordina di occuparsi di un progetto nel quale si avesse cura di non imitare pedissequamente le altre nazioni [...]", aber auch die Minister, wie beispielsweise Graf Gallina: „Crede che non sia conveniente copiare letteralmente gli stranieri per ciò che si vorrà fare nel paese. Ma adottando principi di diritto e di giustizia generalmente riconosciuti, pensa che non dovrebbe essere difficile appropriarsene e farne un insieme veramente nazionale, modificato secondo la posizione, le circostanze, i mezzi, le opinioni che ci sono proprie." Siehe Negri, G./Simoni, S.: Lo statuto albertino e i lavori preparatori. Roma 1992, S. 209 und S. 219.

vielmehr eine eigenständige Verfassungsrichtung[8] ins Leben zu rufen. Zu diesem Zweck nahmen die Mitglieder des Konferenzrats fast alle verfassungsmäßigen Erfahrungen, sowohl die italienischen aus der Zeit vor der staatlichen Einheit als auch die ausländischen in Augenschein, um schließlich als Bezugspunkt die französische Verfassung aus dem Jahre 1814 zu wählen. Diese wurde dann in wesentlichen Punkten den italienischen Gegebenheiten und Anforderungen unterworfen. Die eigentliche strategische Schwierigkeit bestand für die italienischen Verfassungsgeber in der Notwendigkeit, die Folgen der Einführung des Prinzips der Gewaltenteilung[9] zu umgehen, das mittlerweile vom Begriff Verfassung unabtrennbar geworden war.[10] In Bearbeitung der repräsentativen Mechanismen, d.h. „in der Verbesserung der bereits funktionstüchtigen Institutionen",[11] zielten sie darauf ab, eine gemischte Regierungsform zu schaffen, in der zwar die öffentlichen Angelegenheiten vom Gleichgewicht der Gewalten geregelt würden, aber ohne „auf die Ordnungsgrundsätze der Monarchie" zu verzichten.

Die italienische Lösung war im Grunde geradlinig. Man gab keine genaue Definition der Gewalten und verwirklichte eine Aufteilung der Befugnisse, in-

---

[8] Die Absicht bestand darin, das monarchische Prinzip zu schützen, wie es in der Wiener Schlußakte (Art. 57) gemeint war und im Süden Deutschlands akzeptiert wurde: Bayern 1818, Absatz II § 1; Baden 1818, § 5; Württemberg 1819, § 4; Hessen 1820. (Siehe Crosa, Emilio: La Monarchia nel diritto pubblico italiano. Fratelli Bocca, Editori, Torino 1922, S. 4) Jedoch „Il Piemonte non presentava un assetto sociale che potesse compararsi in alcuna maniera a quello germanico, né corporazioni con privilegi o diritti consacrati dal tempo, né una nobiltà stabilita legalmente [...] per cui ad una rappresentanza per classi non era in alcuna maniera da pensare. L'assetto sociale era, cioè, assai più progredito che non in Germania, e tale da prestarsi alle forme più evolute di organizzazione statuale d'inspirazione britannica, quali s'erano attuate colla restaurazione francese." Crosa, La concessione dello Statuto (wie Fn. 6), S. 14.

[9] Ein Prinzip, das auch Anerkennung fand, wie der Cav. Des Ambrois anläßlich des Konferenzrates am 3. Februar 1848 erklärt: „Qualunque siano gli inconvenienti della tripla divisone dei poteri, questa forma ha tuttavia il grande vantaggio di stabilire fra di loro un equilibrio, di prestare forza all'ordine pubblico, di aiutare il Governo con i suoi lumi e la sua saggezza." Negri/Simoni, Lo Statuto albertino (wie Fn. 7), S. 207.

[10] Erklärung der Rechte des Menschen und des Bürgers, Versailles, 26. August 1789, Art. „Toute société dans laquelle la garantie des droits n'est pas assurée ni la séparation des pouvoirs déterminée, n'a point de Constitution.»

[11] Erklärung des Graf Gallina während des Konferenzrates am 7. Februar 1848, in: Negri/Simoni, Lo Statuto albertino (wie Fn. 7), S. 219.

dem man sie von den „Gewalten", die dem Monarchen zustanden, ableitete, da man letzteren *ab origine* als den eigentlichen Kern der verfassungsmäßigen Ordnung[12] betrachten mußte.

B. Vergessen und Amnestie: europäische Erfahrungen im Vergleich

Das *Statuto albertino* bleibt also hinsichtlich des Problems der Gewaltenteilung bewußt lakonisch, derart, daß am 9. Juli 1856[13] der Staatsrat ohne Schwierigkeiten eine Ausnahme von diesem Prinzip bestätigen konnte. Der Rat äußerte sich dabei zur Erweiterung der „Begnadigung" und insbesondere zur Frage, wem die Kompetenz zukomme, eine Amnestie auszuüben.

---

[12] Die italienischen Verfassungsgeber zielten nicht darauf ab, ein neues System zu gründen, sondern beabsichtigen, im Hinblick auf eine Kontinuität mit den bereits auf Anregung des Staatsoberhaupts unternommenen Reformen, einer Ordnung repräsentativen Charakters, jedoch in ‚offener' Form, den Vorzug zu geben, um so einer möglichen Entwicklung der Regierung in parlamentarischer Richtung nicht im Wege zu stehen. Siehe: Manca, Anna Gianna: Il Sonderweg italiano al governo parlamentare (a proposito delle acquisizioni della più recente storiografia costituzionale italiana). In: Quaderni fiorentini per la storia del pensiero giuridico moderno (2004/2005) n. 33/34, T.II, S. 1285-1333; Parlament und Verfassung in den konstitutionellen Verfassungssystemen Europas. Hrsg. von A. G. Manca/L. Lacchè. Berlin 2003 (insbesondere Colombo, Paolo: Una questione mal posta a proposito del regime statutario: le prerogative regie in campo legislativo, S. 237-254); Mazzonis, Filippo: La Monarchia e il Risorgimento. Bologna 2003; Martucci, Roberto: Storia costituzionale italiana. Dallo Statuto albertino alla Repubblica (1848-2001), Roma 2002; Colombo, Paolo: Storia costituzionale della monarchia italiana. Roma-Bari 2001; Colombo, Paolo: Il re d'Italia. Prerogative costituzionali e potere politico della Corona (1848-1922). Milano 1999; Executive and Legislative Powers in the Constitutions of 1848-49. Hrgs. von Horst Dippel. Berlin 1999, darin insbesondere Ullrich, Hartmut, The Statuto Albertino, S. 129-161; Verfassungswandel um 1848 im europäischen Vergleich. Hrsg. von M. Kirsch/ P. Schiera. Berlin 2001; Kirsch, Martin: Monarch und Parlament im 19. Jahrhundert. Der monarchische Konstitutionalismus als europäischer Verfassungstyp. Göttigen 1999.

[13] „(...) il diritto di concedere amnistie debba appartenere al potere esecutivo incaricato di provvedere, sotto la responsabilità dei Ministri, alle quotidiane emergenze dello Stato, anziché al potere legislativo, cui spetta stabilire norme generali alle quali ed il governo ed i magistrati giuridici debbono attenersi, ciascuno nella cerchia in cui si esercita la propria azione." Der vollständige Text der Meinung des Staatsrates findet sich bei: Levi, Abramo: Amnistia – Indulto. In: Digesto Italiano, Bd. III, Teil I. Torino 1895, S. 93-94.

Die beratende Versammlung räumte ein, daß das Verfassungsprinzip der Gewaltenteilung die Legislative als das zuständige Organ bezeichne, dennoch sei eine „Ausnahme von dieser Regel“[14] ratsam, da öffentliche Diskussionen der Kammern über Akte, die „die Vergangenheit in gänzliche Vergessenheit“ geraten lassen, nicht „angemessen“ seien, und sprach sich deshalb für die Kompetenz der Regierung aus.

Der italienische Staatsrat scheint hier, in Anlehnung an die „umfassende Vergessenheit der Vergangenheit“, die „französische“ Auffassung der Amnestie zu übernehmen. Eine ähnliche Interpretation geben auch die ausländischen Beobachter, wie beispielsweise auch die deutschen Rechtswissenschaftler, insbesondere zu der Zeit, in der die Einführung der Amnestie in das eigene Regelwerk diskutiert wurde. Man setzte die italienische mit der französischen Rechtswissenschaft gleich und kritisiert das von der Amnestie geschaffene Vergessen:

„Die Französische und Italienische Jurisprudenz allerdings versteht unter Amnestie, der Etymologie des Wortes entsprechend, nur eine Art der Begnadigung, durch welche ein Verbrechen gleichsam als gar nicht geschehen, mit allen seinen rechtlichen Wirkungen als getilgt erklärt wird“.[15]

Die deutsche Forschung diskutierte lebhaft über die Inhalte der Amnestie, ohne jedoch zu einer wirklichen Klärung hinsichtlich der vergessen machenden Tragweite des Instituts zu gelangen. Einzig darin bestand Übereinstimmung, daß es sich um eine allgemeine Maßnahme handele, d.h. daß sie sich auf eine Gesamtheit der Straftäter oder Straftaten beziehe.

---

[14] „(...) gravi considerazioni di ordine pubblico consigliano un eccezione a questa regola, nei casi in cui la natura speciale dei fatti o le circostanze in cui versi il paese, rendano opportuna, nell'interesse dello Stato, la promulgazione di un amnistia la quale ponga in assoluta obblivione il passato, facendo cessare non pure l'applicazione delle pene, ma il corso dei giudizi“. Levi, Amnistia – Indulto (wie Fn. 13), S. 94.

[15] „Amnestie oder allgemeine B.[Begnadigung], *abolitio generalis,* in Bezug auf eine ganze Klasse von Verbrechern oder Verbrechen ergehende B., wobei aber nicht die nothwendige Folge die gänzliche Tilgung der Verbrechen und die Fiktion, daß dieselben gar nicht existirt haben, ist.“, Geyer, B.: Begnadigung. In: Rechtslexikon. Hrsg. von F. von Holzendorff. Leipzig 1880, S. 255.

Im 19. und 20. Jahrhundert wies auch in Deutschland die Bedeutung von „Mildtätigkeit" ambivalente Züge auf. Das Wort ‚Begnadigung' gibt die italienische *grazia* im weitesten Sinne wieder, dieser Begriff umfaßt im engeren Sinne die ‚Gnade' und im weiteren die ‚Abolition'. In der Umgangssprache[16] meint man jedoch mit ‚Begnadigung' die Gnade, d.h. *grazia*, im engeren Sinne.

Die Übergänge zwischen den Instituten blieben unscharf und unsicher. In der Bandbreite der möglichen Lesarten tendierte die Amnestie dazu, sich mit der Begnadigung im engeren Sinne zu decken, die sich an eine Gesamtheit der Verurteilten richtet, bzw. dem italienischen Institut des Straferlasses, dem *indulto,* zu ähnelt, der formell in Deutschland nicht vorgesehen war.[17]

Eine Eigenart der deutschen Debatte besteht in der Frage, ob es angesichts des bereits juristisch eingebürgerten Terminus der Abolition zweckmäßig sei, das Wort „Amnestie" einzuführen. Binding war beispielsweise der Auffassung, daß der Begriff der Amnestie keine wissenschaftliche Basis habe,[18] zudem rief das Wort *abolitio* die *lettres d'abolition*[19] in Erinnerung, die dem System

---

[16] „Wenn man im täglichen Leben von Begnadigung spricht, so bezeichnet man damit meist die Begnadigung i.e.S., nicht die i.w.S." Graebert, Armin: Begnadigung nach altem und neuem Recht unter besonderer Betonung der Staatsrechtlichen Seite. Berlin 1926, S. 8.

[17] Begnadigung „kann erscheinen als Abolition, Niederschlagung, wenn sie Einleitung, Fortführung oder Beendigung eines Strafverfahrens verhindert; als Begnadigung im engeren Sinne, wenn sie die infolge eines Deliktes erkannten Rechtsfolgen ganz oder teilweise wieder aufhebt [...]. Erstreckt sich die Verfügung der Staatsgewalt auf eine ganze Kategorie von Angeschuldigten – im Wege der Abolition – oder von Verurteilen – durch B. i. e. S. – so spricht man von Amnestie." Delaquis, Ernst: Begnadigung. In: Wörterbuch des deutschen Staat und Verwaltungsrechts. Hrsg. von K. von Stengel. Bd. I. Tübingen 1911, S. 374-384.

[18] Begnadigung – im Interesse der Justiz und nicht des Begnadigten gewährt – nimmt die Form von „Abolition" an, und Begnadigung i. e. S. „zerfällt demgemäss in zwei und nur in zwei wesentlich verschiedene Arten; in die Abolition und in die Begnadigung im e. S." Für den Autor hat die Unterscheidung zwischen Straferlaß und Amnestie keinen wissenschaftlichen Wert: „[...] ergiebt aber keine dritte Art der Gnade. Der Begriff der Amnestie ist wissenschaftlich wertlos." Binding, Karl: Handbuch des Strafrechts. Bd. 1. Darmstadt 1991, S. 861 (Nachdruck der Ausgabe Leipzig 1885).

[19] „Sont des Lettres du grand sceau, par lequels Sa Majeité, par la plénitude da sa puissance, abolissant le crime qui auroit été commis par l'impétrant, déclare être bien informé du fait dont il s'agit, sans même qu'il soit énoncé dans les Lettres que le Roi entend que le crime soit entiérement aboli & éteint, & pardonne le cas, de quelque maniere qu'il soit arrivé, sansque l'impétrant en puisse être aucunement poursuivi à l'avenir. Le Roi efface par ces lettres la note que le crime

der Privilegien Nahrung gaben und die Mißstände seitens der Herrschenden und Aristokraten aufrecht erhielten, die die *Encyclopédie* auf das Schärfste kritisierte und die nach der Revolution unterdrückt wurden. So hob Fleischmann hervor, daß in der deutschen Rechtssprache das Wort „Abolition"[20] von einem Ausdruck des altfranzösischen Rechts herrührt, bzw. von der Praxis der *lettres d'abolition.*

Bereits zu Beginn des 18. Jahrhunderts wurde allerdings in Deutschland die Kompetenz, einen Strafvollzug zu unterbrechen als ein Recht der Obrigkeit erachtet und nicht als ein Privileg der Aristokratie.[21] Dementsprechend empfand man nicht die Notwendigkeit, das Wort „Abolition" zu streichen. Und sobald man im 19. Jahrhundert begann, Abolition und Begnadigung zu trennen, bezogen sich die Zweifel vornehmlich auf den Anwendungsbereich[22] und nicht so sehr auf ihre Zulässigkeit an sich.

---

imprime; mais il faut qu'elles soient obtenues avant le Jugement souverain, afin de lier les mains au Juge; & si elles ne sont obtenues qu'après le Jugement, elles ne lavent point l'infamie." Ferrière, Claude-Joseph de: Dictionnaire de droit et de pratique: contenant l'explication des termes de droit, d'ordonnances, de coutumes et de pratique. Bd. II. Paris 1769, S.120. Die „Lettres de grâce „sont celle qui contiennent une pure libéralité du Prince. Elle dépendent uniquement de Sa Majesté ; il les accorde par faveur à qui bon lui semble, & il peut les refuser quand il le juge à propos. Telles sont les Lettres de rémission, les Lettres de grace, les dispenses, les priviléges & autres semblables." Ferrière, ebd., S. 119. Die „Lettres de grâce„ „en matière criminelle, sont des lettres par lesquelles Sa Majesté, préférant la clémence à la rigueur & sévérité des Loix, remet la peine que l'impétrant pourroit avoir encourue. Telles sont les lettres d'abolition, les lettres de pardon, & les lettres de rémission.", Ferrière, ebd., S. 124.

[20] „In unsre Rechtssprache wird das Wort A. [Abolition] über das Französische gelangt sein", Fleischmann, Max: Abolition. In: Wörterbuch. Hrsg. von Stengel (wie Fn. 17), S. 51.

[21] „In Deutschland ergab sich die Möglichkeit, ein Strafverfahren niederzuschlagen, schon früh aus der nicht ohne Eigennutz von den Trägern der Gerichtsgewalt beanspruchten Gnadenübung. Erst mit der Ausbildung des absoluten Staats ist auch dieses Hoheitsrecht ausschließlich in die Hand des Landesherrn gekommen; als frühe Aeußerung die preußische Kriminal O von 1717 Kap. XI: ‚Von Nachlassen der Strafen, vom Begnadigungsrechte und Abolition im Kriminalprozesse'." Fleischmann, Abolition (Fn. 20), S. 51.

[22] „Die Zweifel an der Fortgeltung des A.Rechtes sind zurückgetreten und auch die Zweckmäßigkeit, obgleich vorwiegend für Amnestien, wird sich verteidigen lassen." Fleischmann, Abolition (wie Fn. 20), S. 55. Und Graebert: „Die Existenz von Begnadigung i.e.S. und Amnestie steht im neuen Rechte schon auf Grund der positiven gesetzlichen Bestimmungen außer jedem Zweifel. Anders verhält es sich mit der Abolition. Bereits im alten Rechte herrschte viel Streit darüber, ob die Abolition im Reiche durch die Reichsjustizgesetzgebung von 1879 beseitigt sei oder nicht. In

Andererseits ist auch das Wort ‚Amnestie'[23] nicht frei von Zweideutigkeiten. Die Minderheit der deutschen Rechtswissenschaft, die die Amnestie befürwortete, hatte gerade die Etymologie[24] des Wortes gegen sich. Außerdem witterte man die Gefahr, der Praxis der individuellen Amnestien[25] zu folgen, mit-

der Verfassung war sie nicht erwähnt. Die herrschende Meinung nahm jedoch damals an, daß sie durch die Gesetzgebung nicht berührt sei und weiter existierte. [...] Die Existenz der Abolition muß auch im heutigen Staate bejaht werden. Wollte man ein so wichtiges Institut wie die Abolition es ist, gänzlich ausschließen, so hätte man dies sicher im Gesetze positiv zum Ausdruck gebracht, wie es in manchen Verfassungen geschehen ist. Man hätte sie nicht mit Stillschweigen übergangen." Graebert, Begnadigung (wie Fn. 16), S. 11.

[23] „Pardon que le souverain accorde aux auteurs de certains crimes ou délits [...]" gebraucht man auch als Synonym von Begnadigung, aber „*L'amnistie* diffère de la grâce, en ce qu'elle a un caractère plus étendu et plus générale. La *grâce* est spéciale et individuelle ; elle ne s'accorde qu'aprés la condamnation prononcée : c'est, en d'autres termes, la remise d'une peine ; l'*amnistie*, au contraire, s'applique à toute une classe de délinquants, elle embrasse dans sa généralité les individus condamnés et ceux qui ne sont encore qu'en état de prévention. Malgré ces differences entre la grâce et l'amnistie, toutes deux se trouvent ordinairement réunies dans le même main. En France, le droit de grâce et celui d'amnistie appartiennent au roi." Bescherelle, Dictionnaire national (wie Fn. 2), S. 157.

[24] „Sie lehnt sich stark an die Etymologie des Wortes Amnestie an und findet demnach den Unterschied von der Begnadigung darin, daß die Amnestie über alles den Schleier der Vergessenheit breiten wolle und somit das Verbrechen tilge. [...]. Allerdings kann sie dann folgerichtig sich auf eine einzelne Person ebenfalls beziehen. Dies ist die französische Auffassung, die bei uns jedoch allgemein abgelehnt wird." Graebert, Begnadigung (wie Fn. 16), S. 9.

[25] „La grâce amnistiante, qui apparut pour la première fois, semble-t-il, dans la loi du 3 mars 1879, relative aux insurgés de la Commune, s'était largement développée dans le période contemporaine [...]. La grâce amnistiante ou amnistielle (le législateur a employé les deux expressions) est une combinaison de la grâce et de l'amnistie, à laquelle le législateur recourt pour introduire plus de justice dans l'application de l'amnistie. Le Parlement fixe, dans une loi d'amnistie, les faits délictueux auxquels devra s'étendre la meseure d'indulgence, mais il laisse au président de la République le soin de déterminer ensuite, par voie de grâces individuelles, quels seront, parmi les auteurs des faits prévus, les seuls bénéficiaires de l'amnistie. On évite ainsi le reproche encouru par l'amnistie d'être, du fait de son caractère collectif et anonyme, une mesure aveugle pouvant s'appliquer, notamment lorsqu'elle vise des faits de droit commun, à des individus dangereux." Robert, J.M. : Amnistie. In : Dalloz. Répertoire de droit pénal et de procédure pénale, Bd. I, Paris 1967, N. 99.

hin jenes französischen Instituts, das auch dem einzelnen Begnadigten das Vergessen gewährleistet, das der Amnestie[26] vorbehalten war.

Die Einführung der *Amnestie* in Deutschland schien nur als Synonym möglich oder mittels einer besonderen Art der Anwendung, nämlich der *Abolition*; jedenfalls bevorzugt man weiterhin für lange Zeit den Gebrauch von Wörtern wie ‚Niederschlagung' oder ‚allgemeine Begnadigung'[27].

C. Ein Vermerk für das Gedächtnis: das Strafregister

Genau betrachtet finden sich in Italien dieselben Zweifel hinsichtlich der vergessen machenden Tragweite der Amnestie wieder, wenn man nicht so sehr das Moment der theoretischen Definition der Institute als vielmehr die Gesetzgebung und Praxis im Blick hat. In den italienischen Gesetzestexten[28] sprach man von „abolizione dell'azione penale" (Abolition des Strafvollzugs), möglicherweise jedoch im Sinne der römischen Abolitionsbriefe.[29] Der

---

[26] „Le condamné bénéficiaire de la grâce amnistiante, à la différence de celui qui ne bénéficie que d'une grâce simple, voit sa condamnation entièrement effacée et recouvre ainsi la jouissance de tous ses droits." Robert, Amnistie (wie Fn. 25).

[27] Seit dem 20. Jahrhundert hebt man in einigen Erfahrungen das Wort „Amnestie" hervor, beispielsweise: Thüringen 1921: § 45 Amnestien bedürfen der Zustimmung des Landtags; Hamburg 1921: Art. 47: Der Senat übt das Begnadigungsrecht aus. Amnestien bedürfen eines Gesetzes; Bremen 1920: § 60: Amnestien bedürfen eines Gesetzes; Lübeck 1920: Art. 44 Gegenstand der gemeinschaftlichen Wirksamkeit beider Staatskörper (Senat; Bürgerschaft) sind insbesondere [...] 5. Erlaß einer Amnestie. Herta, Victoria: Die Gnadenhoheit im Deutschen Reich, Darmstadt 1928, S. 26-28.

[28] Das Gesetz zur Tilgung der Straftaten und Strafen des Strafgesetzes aus dem Jahre 1865 sieht im Art. 131 III vor: «Il reato e le pene si estinguono: 1° Colla morte del reo, salvo il disposto dell'art. 15; 2° Coll'espiazione della pena; 3° Cogli indulti, o con ispeciale grazia sovrana; 4° Colla prescrizione nei casi determinati dalla legge.»

[29] „Questa parola significava in diritto romano la soppressione di un procedimento penale, imminente o già cominciato, senza però che fosse cancellato il delitto. Essendo perciò annullato il solo procedimento, una nuova accusa poteva essere iniziata in occasione dello stesso fatto. La parola *abolitio* non si trova impiegata dagli scrittori classici di Roma, del suo significato giuridico di cancellazione dei delitti o dell'azione penale." Nocito, Pietro, Abolizione dell'azione penale – Lettere di abolizione. In: Digesto Italiano, Bd. I, Teil I. Torino 1884, S. 93. Tatsächlich bedeutet der griechische Ursprung des Wortes „Amnestie" „ohne Gedächtnis", „Vergessen", „Vergebung", und wird mit dem lateinischen oblivio übersetzt, das in der römischen Gesellschaft die Metapher der

Rechtsgelehrte Nocito merkte an, daß man sich im Gesetzbuch wie auch in den Dekreten nicht auf einen ‚Tod' sondern auf ein ‚Einschlafen'[30] des Strafverfahrens bezieht.

Das Strafgesetz des Jahres 1865 vermischt Amnestie und Straferlaß, denn der Vollzug der Strafe, die mittels der Amnestie getilgt wurde, konnte gemäß Art. 128,[31] wieder aufleben, sobald der Begnadigte ein neues Verbrechen beging.[32] Für den italienischen Gesetzgeber tilgte mithin die Amnestie nicht das Vergehen, es war nur ‚eingeschlafen'.

Die Einrichtung des *Casellario giudiziale* (Strafregisters) (R.D. 6. Dez. 1865, n. 2644) gibt den Widersprüchen weitere Nahrung: der *Regio Decreto* übertraf die vorherigen Normen, die die Niederschrift aller Verfahrensakten unabhängig von ihrem Ausgang vorsahen, und zielte darauf ab, allein die Entscheidungen aufzubewahren, die dazu dienlich waren, die Vorstrafen der Bürger und eventuelle Rückfälle der Angeklagten zu ermitteln; dennoch wurde die Aufzeich-

---

Schrift, die man tilgt, vorschlägt, (ob-linere, „tilgen"). Siehe Milani, Celestina: Il lessico della vendetta e del perdono nel mondo classico. In: Amnistia perdono e vendetta nel mondo antico. Hrsg. von Sordi Marta. Milano 1997, S. 11-15.

[30] „(...) la parola abolizione dell'azione penale importa cancellare, annullare il procedimento passato, ed impedire il procedimento avvenire. – Oblivione ed abolizione hanno comune l'origine da *aboleo*, *deleo*, ed esprimono insieme dimenticare il passato, onde più non farne parola nell'avvenire. La voce greca [...] dimenticanza, è un segno della loro antica e comune origine [...]. Veramente l'abolizione dell'azione penale può dirsi un sonno od un assopimento della medesima, e non già una sua morte od estinzione." Nocito, Abolizione dell'azione penale (wie Fn. 29), S. 94.

[31] „Coloro, che dopo aver goduto degli indulti od ottenuta una speciale grazia sovrana per reati o per pene inflitte con sentenza commetteranno nuovi reati punibili con pena dello stesso genere o di un genere superiore, si considereranno come se non avessero goduto degli indulti od ottenuta la grazia, e saranno giudicati e puniti come colpevoli di più reati, o come recidivi, a tenore delle disposizioni contenute nelle due Sezioni di questo Capo."

[32] „L'articolo [...] prevede il doppio caso dell'amnistia e della grazia: dell'estinzione del reato o dell'azione penale, e dell'estinzione della pena o della condanna. Quindi dispone, che colui il quale fu amnistiato debba essere giudicato come colpevole di più reati nel caso che commetta un nuovo reato; e colui il quale era stato condannato ad una pena ed ottenne la grazia, debba essere giudicato e punito colla circostanza aggravante della recidiva. Nel primo caso l'azione penale comprende l'antico ed il nuovo reato, e si riprende col nuovo l'antico processo; ed il colpevole è considerato come reo di più reati e sottoposto alle pene dei reiteratori. Nel secondo caso la prima condanna è irrevocabile, come è estinta irrevocabilmente la pena, e solo si tratta la nuova causa, salvo a vedere, in caso di condanna, gli effetti dell'antica pena allo scopo di aggravare la nuova." Nocito, Abolizione dell'azione penale (wie Fn. 29), S. 94-95.

nung der Mildtätigkeits-Dekrete veranlaßt. Die Lehre zeigte sich hinsichtlich der Amnestie schnell ratlos, während sie es als angemessene Wahl begrüßte – anders als Frankreich – die die Strafe auslöschenden Maßnahmen in einer Anmerkung hinzuzufügen.[33] Genau gesehen bestand jedoch auch in Frankreich nicht wirklich die Intention, die Straftaten der Begnadigten aus der Erinnerung zu „tilgen"; in der Tat ergänzte später ein Rundschreiben das Gesetz und sah die Niederschrift im *casier judiciaire*[34] vor.

---

[33] „§ 4 dispone che si conservi notizia nel Casellario dei decreti di grazia sovrana, di indulto e d'amnistia, quando ne sia fatta applicazione a persona determinata. Niuna difficoltà v'è per i decreti di grazia particolare e d'indulto, ed è questa un utile aggiunzione alle disposizioni francesi sul Casellario, ove non è fatto cenno né dei decreti di grazia, né delle sentenze e ordinanze di assoluzione e di non farsi luogo a procedimento; ma gravi osservazioni potrebbero farsi per i decreti di amnistia." De Nava, Giuseppe: Casellario giudiziale. In: Digesto Italiano, Bd. VI, Teil II. Torino 1891, S. 255.

[34] „La condamnation prononcée continue à figurer au casier judiciaire et à être inscrite sur les bulletins [...] La circ. 28 avril 1875 a prescrit la mention des décisions de grâce au casier judiciaire à partir du 1er mai 187" d.h. „Les grâces accordées demeurent sans effet pour l'application des règles sur la récidive". Monteil, Jacques: La Grâce en Droit Français Moderne. Paris 1959, S. 234. Zu Beginn herrscht ein allgemeiner Zugriff auf die Informationen im Vertrauen darauf, damit eine moralisierende Wirkung auszuüben. Mit dem Jahre 1899 erstellt man jedoch drei verschiedene Bulletins, von denen nur das dritte, beziehungsweise ein teilweiser Auszug des Strafregisters veröffentlicht wurde. In Deutschland wird mit Anordnung vom 16. Juni 1882 des Bundesrats (geändert mit Anordnung vom 9. Juli 1896) der Informationsdienst über die Vorstrafen im gesamten Reich vereinigt, wobei es den lokalen Regierungen frei steht, andere Anmerkungen hinzuzufügen. Somit setzt sich das französische gegenüber dem preußischen System durch, das die Registrierung am Wohn- oder Aufenthaltsort der Vorurteilten vorsieht. Die Register über die rechtskräftig gewordenen Urteile der Personen, die in dem Land geboren sind, werden bei den vom jeweiligen Land ernannten Behörden eingerichtet, jedoch die Überwachung und Leitung obliegt der Staatsanwaltschaft bei den Gerichten. Für die Personen, die außerhalb des Reichs geboren sind und von denen man den Geburtsort nicht kennt, werden die Register beim Justizamt des Reichs geführt. Siehe: De Notaristefani, Raffaele: La legge Lucchini sul Casellario giudiziale (30 gennaio 1902, N. 87). Verona 1902, S. XXV. Beispielsweise in Bayern: „Des weiteren ist die zuständige Strafregisterbehörde auch stets in Kenntnis zu setzen, wenn durch eine allerh. Entschließung eine im Strafregister einzutragende Strafe oder Nebenstrafe aus Gnade erlassen, gemindert oder gemildert wurde; zur Mitteilung ist ebenfalls Formular A zu benützen. Im Register selbst ist der Vermerk über die Begnadigung unmittelbar unter den Eintrag der Verurteilung zu setzen; er hat den Inhalt der allerhöchsten Entschließung kurz, aber erschöpfend anzugeben und im Falle des teilweisen Erlasses einer schon in Vollzug gesetzten Freiheitsstrafe ersichtlich zu machen, wann die Vollstreckung begonnen und wann sie geendet hat. (J. MBek vom 23. April 1907)." Müller, Josef von:

Wenn es also Vergessen gab, fällt es tendenziell mit der bloßen Unsichtbarkeit der Mildtätigkeit zusammen und nicht mit dem wirklichen Verzicht auf Erinnerung von seiten des Staates. Man erlaubt das Vergessen im Staat, aber nicht die des Staates.

Das Problem findet in Italien nur mit einem entsprechenden Gesetz (30. Januar 1902) eine Lösung. Der vorschlagende Abgeordnete Lucchini wirkt auf das irrsinnige Paradox ein, dem zufolge die Aufzeichnung in sich eine „ewige Verurteilung“[35] darstellte, was zudem mit dem Institut der Rehabilitation[36] in

---

Vorstrafen und Strafregister, Frankfurt a. M. 1977, S. 36 (Nachdruck der Ausgabe Breslau 1908); und „Insbesondere werden in Preussen im Strafregister andere Nachweisungen, als die durch die BRV vorgesehenen, nicht aufgenommen; nur die sog. Strafaufschubnachrichten werden eine Zeitlang beim Strafregister aufbewahrt (ähnlich wie die in Bayern üblichen Mitteilungen über bedingte Begnadigung).“ (Ebenda, S. 4). Mit Ausnahme von Sachsen tendiert der Geist der Bundesratsverordnung dahin, den Privatpersonen den Zugang zu den Informationen nicht zu erlauben. (ebenda, S. 45). In Spanien: „Sin embargo, se entiende por la doctrina que son efectos automáticos de la amnistía, a no ser que en ella se disponga otra cosa, la cancelación de las hojas de antecedentes penales, en virtud de la Real Orden de 5 de diciembre de 1892 y más recientemente por la Orden de 30 de mayo de 1936 que dispuso que los Tribunales, al aplicar a un penado los beneficios de la amnistía, lo comunicarán con toda urgencia al Registro Central de Penados y Rebeldes. También se entiende que la amnistia, si no se dispone en ella lo contrario, hace cesar con pieno efecto retroactivo las incapacidades para el ejercicio de determinados derechos (como inhabilitaciones, suspensiones, interdicción civil) sin necesidad de un acto especial de rehabilitatción para su disfrute.“ Was den Straferlass betrifft, dessen Auswirkung „consiste en eximir total o parcialmente al indultado del cumplimiento de la condena que se le impuso, por la comisión de un delito, en sentencia-firme dictada por un Tribunal penal, beneficio que no tiene por qué alcanzar a la totalidad de la pena principal, ni a las accesorias“, tilgt nicht die strafrechtliche Verantwortung, die vom zuständigen Gericht kundgetan wurde „salvo en contadas excepciones; la no extinción de los efectos de la imposiciónes de penas, come es el de la inscripción en el Registro Central de Penados y Rebeldes; lo fuertemente condicionado del disfrute del beneficio al buen comportamiento del indultado; y sobre todo que el órgano encargado de conceder el indulto no revise la educación de los echos al derecho no recise la adecuación de los hechos al derecho aplicado en cuanto a la calificación de aquéllos aunquehay excepciones al respecto), sino que su actividad consista en tener cruenta otros ‘datos’ quel el Tribunal no pudo entrar a considerar.“ Linde Paniagua: Amnistia e indulto en España (wie Fn. 3), S. 109.

[35] Lucchini erklärt, dass das Ziel des Gesetzes darin besteht „toglier quanto di aberrante e di veramente incivile caratterizzava le norme vigenti, per cui l'iscrizione nel Casellario riusciva anche più grave e funesta della medesima condanna, che, se temporanea, à termine, e quella durava nei suoi effetti eterna e inflessibile, anche nelle più tenui condanne, anche ove fossero seguìte

Widerstreit stand, zu dem der Amnestierte nur fünf Jahre nach der Gewährung der Mildtätigkeit Zugang hatte. Schließlich bestimmte man, daß die Gerichtsbarkeit die Urteile, die durch Amnestie getilgt worden waren, allein zu dem Zweck erwähne, um zu vermeiden, daß die Strafauswirkungen des getilgten Urteils weiterhin bestünden, daß jedoch die Dokumenten, die von den Bürgern angefragt werden, keinen entsprechenden Vermerk enthalten sollen.

D. Die Gewaltenteilung: eine Frage des Pragmatismus

Das eigentliche Problem bestand also nicht so sehr darin, auch in sprachlicher Hinsicht klare Grenzen zum *ancien régime* zu ziehen, sondern vielmehr darin, ein juristisches Konstrukt der Mildtätigkeit zu finden, das mit den „mo-

---

dall'amnistia o dalla riabilitazione, anche in caso di proscioglimento!" Lucchini, Luigi: Casellario giudiziale. In: Rivista Penale (1906) vol. LXIII, S. 248.

[36] In der Tat zeigt sich im Gesetzestext auch eine andere Inkongruenz zwischen den Vorhersagen der Amnestie und denen des Instituts der Rehabilitation, das lange Zeit ein der „Begnadigung" komplementäres Institut bleibt und in den königlichen Zuständigkeitsbereich fällt. Erst im Jahre 1906 wird die Rehabilitation wieder unter die gerichtlichen Maßnahmen eingeordnet. Bereits in der Sitzung der Kammer vom 24. April 1866 hatte der Abgeordnete Boggio ein Projekt vorgelegt „per essere cancellata la parola *amnistia* dagli art. 834 e 835, cioè che, trattandosi di reato estinto in virtù di decreto per amnistia, non occorra più il bisogno di chiedere la riabilitazione nei diritti politici e civili importando l'amnistia un oblio dei passati trascorsi; di manierachè l'esercizio più o meno dei diritti anzidetti possa essere più opportunamente regolato dal sovrano provvedimento. Epperò sarebbe conveniente cancellarsi la parola amnistia, non solo dall'articolo 834 che rende obbligatoria la riabilitazione, ma soprattutto dal successivo art. 835, che non ammette simile riabilitazione se non cinque anni dopo il decreto di amnistia ch'è in contraddizione con l'obblìo che questa suppone." Saluto, Francesco: Commenti al codice di procedura penale per il Regno d'Italia. Torino 1877, S. 106. Die Artikel 834 und 835 des Kodex der Strafprozessordnung „furono poi modificati con apposita legge del 28 giugno 1866, n. 3008, appunto perché si osservò che l'amnistia avendo per effetto di estinguere la condanna e tutte le sue conseguenze, sarebbe contraddittorio il dire che il condannato amnistiato potesse essere riabilitato." De Nava, Casellario giudiziale (wie Fn. 33), S. 255. Mit Sentenz vom 3. April 1902 (Liperini und Violani) der oberste Strafgerichtshof „giudicò doversi distinguere fra condanna già eseguita e condanna non ancora eseguita, nel senso che, agli effetti della recidiva, dovrebbe tenersi calcolo della prima e non della seconda. Questa distinzione però non regge, e dichiarata estinta per amnistia l'azione penale, tale pronunzia toglie lo stato di recidività per chi ricade nel delitto". Giordani, Francesco: Recidiva. In: Digesto Italiano, Bd. XX, Teil I. Torino 1911-1915, S. 401-402.

dernen" Verfassungsprinzipien und den jeweiligen Zielsetzungen der Strafrechtspolitik in Einklang stand.

Die Verwaltung der Strafjustiz machte in den letzten beiden Jahrhunderten von der Mildtätigkeit großzügig Gebrauch. Aber die Einführung des Prinzips der Gewaltenteilung hatte die Auffassung von ihr grundlegend geändert. Nicht von ungefähr war in Frankreich das Recht auf Gnade am 4. Juni 1791 abgeschafft worden: Die Verfassungsgeber[37] konnten nicht umhin, die Unvereinbarkeit der ‚Begnadigung' mit dem Verfassungsgrundsatz einzugestehen.

Ihr Ziel bestand jedoch nicht darin, auf die Begnadigung als ein das Gesetz ergänzendes Mittel zu verzichten, sondern den Mißbrauch der Begnadigungsbriefe zu bekämpfen: „enlever l'exercice de ce droit au pouvoir exécutif, pour le remettre aux Juré".[38] Die Idee war, die Entscheidungen der Geschworenen aufzuwerten und nicht die Begnadigung abzuschaffen und so überantwortete man das letzte Wort in Sachen Gerechtigkeit der Nation. Die Einrichtung der Geschworenen zeigte jedoch bald seine Anfälligkeit, so daß sich erneut das Problem der Zuständigkeit und der Ausübung von Mildtätigkeit stellte.

Die Verfassungstheorie würde die Zuweisung der Zuständigkeit für die Begnadigung an die Judikative[39] und die der Amnestie an die Legislative nahe legen. Jedenfalls hat die Anwendung des Prinzips der Gewaltenteilung tatsächlich eine Neuerfindung der gerichtlichen Gewalt als „nichtige", neutrale, apoli-

---

[37] Art. 13 (Titre VII – De la Réhabilitation des Condamnés – Code Pénal 1791): „L'usage de tous actes tendant à empêcher ou à suspendre l'exercice de la justice criminelle, l'usage des lettres de grâce, de rémission, d'abolition, de pardon, de commutation de peines, est aboli pour tout délit qui aura été jugé par voie de jury."

[38] Roux-Dessarps, Gabriel: De la grâce. Thèse pour le doctorat. Paris 1898, S. 47.

[39] Die Stellungnahmen der französischen Doktrin für und gegen die Beibehaltung der Begnadigung stimmen, nicht von ungefähr, mit den beiden Auffassungen der gerichtlichen Gewalt überein. Einerseits faßt der Teil der Doktrin, der die Notwendigkeit, das Institut abzuschaffen, unterstützt, die gerichtliche als Staatsgewalt auf, mit der Aufgabe, das Gesetz zu interpretieren: „c'est aux tribunaux et non au droit de grâce qu'il appartient de concilier la loi générale et l'équité particulière". Andererseits fassen diejenigen, die die Notwendigkeit, das Institut in der Verfassung beizubehalten, befürworten, die gerichtliche Gewalt als „Mund des Gesetzes" auf: „Le rôle des tribunaux consiste uniquement à appliquer la loi, en se conformant aux règles de la justice." Gobron, Louis: Le droit de grâce sous la Constitution de 1875. Paris 1893, S. 10-11.

tische, unsichtbare[40] Gewalt bewirkt. Schließlich wurde die Legitimität des Instituts der Begnadigung mit der Dualität[41] ihres Ausübungsaktes begründet. Mit der Gegenzeichnung[42] der königlichen Verfügung durch den Minister

---

[40] Das Prinzip der Gewaltenteilung erfordert eine unsichtbare gerichtliche Gewalt: „Les cours et les tribunaux ne sauraient donc, sans excéder leurs pouvoirs, formuler de voeux, soit dans les jugements de condamnation, soit dans des délibérations postérieures. Mais il est loisible aux membres de ces compagnies de transmettre individuellement au garde des sceaux des observations sur les circostances qui leur ont paru de nature à provoquer une mesure d'indulgence. Ils peuvent également, ainsi que toute autre personne, apostiller une supplique. Toutefois, les magistrats qui ont eu à s'occuper d'une affaire, soit comme juge d'instruction, soit comme officier du ministère public, soit comme membre du tribunal qui a prononcé la peine, doivent s'abstenir avec soin de semblables recomandations." Legoux, Jules: Du droit de grâce en France comparé avec les législations étrangères. Paris 1865, S. 29.

[41] Siehe Stronati, Monica: Torniamo allo Statuto? In: Atti del Seminario preventivo „La grazia contesa. Titolarità ed esercizio del potere di clemenza individuale". Torino 2006, S. 323-328; Stronati, Monica: Il più bel gioiello della Corona. La grazia nella tradizione costituzionale italiana. In: Giornale di Storia Costituzionale (2004) n. 7/I, S. 259-278.

[42] Jedenfalls erkennt man die Schwäche des Mittels, so weist beispielsweise Picot – Presidénte della Société générale des prisons (1899) e secrétaire perpétuel de l'Académie des sciences morales et politiques – auf seine Grenzen hin: „La garantie de la responsabilité ministérielle, essentielle au point de vue politique, est-elle suffisante [...]?" und schließt, dass: „il résulte que l'unique garantie est la conscience du directeur et du chef de bureau des grâces. Eux seuls, d'un trait de plume, peuvent modifier ou supprimer les peines portées par tous les tribunaux de France, confirmées par les Cours d'appel, prononcées par les Cours d'assises, reconnues légales par la Cour de cassation. [...] J'ignore s'il existe, dans le Gouvernement, un pouvoir plus redoutable." Picot, Georges: Rapport sur le droit de justice et sur le droit de grâce. In: Bulletin de la Société générale des prisons (1899) n. 7, S. 904-905. Und Davidsohn bewertet den Verzicht auf das rechtskräftig gewordene Urteil als eine gefährliche Unterbrechung des Ganges der Justizverwaltung: „Als Verzicht auf den durch rechtskräftiges Urteil noch nicht festgestellten Anspruch ist die Abolition aber ungemein bedenklich. [...] darf man nicht die Gefahr einer willkürlichen Handhabung dieser Art des Begnadigungsrechts unterschätzen", unter anderem auch weil die ministerielle Verantwortung dem Autor gemäß nichts als eine Farce darstelle: „[...] der Souverän handelt unkontrollierbar, gleichsam im Dunklen; seine Entscheidungen können und werden willkürlich sein, ohne dass irgend einem das Recht gegeben ist, sie als willkürlich aufzufassen. Eine Ministerverantwortlichkeit hätte bei einer Begnadigung vor erfolgtem Urteil gar keinen Sinn, sie würde zur Farce." Davidsohn, Sally: Das Begnadigungsrecht. Ein Beitrag zur Lehre von der Berechtigung, von dem Wesen und von den Erscheinungsformen der Gnade. Berlin 1903, S. 36-37.

schuf man eine Form von Verantwortung und ermöglichte zugleich die Kontrolle der Ausübung der Begnadigung durch das Parlament.[43]

In Italien wurde die Amnestie, die grundsätzlich mit dem Willen des Gesetzgebers interferiert, nur zu Zeiten der Republik der Legislative zugewiesen. In Deutschland[44] erfolgte dies nach und nach mit den Veränderungen der Regierungsform. In Frankreich hingegen, wo das Prinzip seit 1848[45] Bestandteil der Verfassungswirklichkeit war, schuf man neue Instituten der Mildtätigkeit, die es in der Tat ermöglichten, das Prinzip der Gewaltenteilung zu umgehen und einen flexiblen Gebrauch der Reichweite des Vergessens[46] – beispielsweise mit der *grâce amnistiante* – eröffneten.

---

[43] In Frankreich bürgert sich diese Gewohnheit mit dem etwas entschiedenerem Charakter nur unter der Julimonarchie ein, als Luis Philippe die eigene Rolle in aller Breite ausfüllt und dies Vorrecht ausübt, ohne die Verfassungsgrenzen zu verletzen. Er bedient sich der Redegewandtheit und wendet alle politischen Mittel an, um den gegenzeichnenden Minister von der Angemessenheit des Begnadigungsdekrets zu überzeugen, ohne das Institut in ein persönliches Vorrecht umzuwandeln, was im Kontrast zur verfassungsmäßigen Einrichtung stände: „Louis-Philippe y voyat sa mission propre, sa coopération à l'oeuvre de justice.». Bevor das Recht auf Begnadigung den Thron bestieg «n'avait ni l'autorité d'une application habituelle, ni la puissance de l'initiative. Hors quelques occasions rares et solennelles, le droit de grâce, avant 1830, sommeillait quand il n'était pas invoqué; il attendait toujours la prière du condamné." Picot, Rapport sur le droit de justice (wie Fn. 42), S.921.

[44]Der Übergang ist an die Veränderungen der Regierungsform gebunden: „Mit der Entwicklung des Rechtsstaats zum parlamentarischen Rechtsstaat, in dem das Parlament an der Gesetzgebung erst partizipierte und sie schließlich bei sich monopolisierte, wurde dem Souverän das Recht zur Amnestie entwunden. Während in Preußen nach dem Aufruhr des Jahres 1848 die Amnestie für alle, ‚die wegen politischer oder durch die Presse verübter Vergehen und Verbrechen angeklagt oder verurtheilt worden sind', noch als königliches Dekret Friedrich Wilhelms IV. erging, wurde schon für die preußische Verfassung von 1850 die General-Begnadigung als Prärogative des Parlaments anerkannt." Merten, Detlef: Rechtsstaatlichkeit und Gnade. Berlin 1978, S.13-14.

[45] „Malgré le silence de la Charte de 1830 qui ne donnait au roi que le droit d'accorder des grâces et de commuer des peines, malgré l'opinion de savants jureconsultes et sans pouvoir invoquer d'autre argument que celui d'une regrettable assimilation entre le droit de grâce et le droit d'amnistie, la Chambre des députés avait décidé, en 1834, que le droit d'amnistie était un attribut de la royauté. La constitution républicaine de 1848, réagissant contre cette fausse interprétation, déclara au contraire nettement que les amnisties ne pouvaient être accordées que par une loi." Gouraincourt, P.A. Maxime: Traité du droit de grâce sous la République. Paris 1881, S. 106.

[46] „Mais précisément en raison de son caractère général, l'amnistie ordinaire n'était pas sans inconvénients: opérant automatiquement, sans discrimination des personnes appelées à en bénéfi-

Der Grundsatz, der hingegen im 19. und 20. Jh. die verschiedenen nationalen Erfahrungen zu einen scheint, besteht darin, daß die Mildtätigkeit ein Akt des Staates sein soll, oder ein Verfahren – das verschiedene Formen und Umfänge[47] annehmen kann –, das jedoch einen tendenziell einmütigen Konsens erfordert, sowohl bei der Entscheidung über die Bewilligung als auch in der Befragung der öffentlichen Meinung.[48]

Das Vergessen wird so zum fundierten Gedächtnis des Staates, der nicht vergessen will, sondern vielmehr den abstrakten und flüchtigen Bezug zum Sozialkörper konsolidieren möchte. Einerseits garantierte das Staatsoberhaupt, indem es sich als Organ der öffentlichen Meinung gebärdet, Zusammenhalt und Harmonie unter den Gewalten und andererseits tendierte die Ausübung der verschiedenen Institute der Mildtätigkeit dazu, alle Gewalten bei der Entscheidung einzubeziehen.

---

cier, elle pouvait profiter à des individus qui en étaient absolument indignes." Roux, Pierre-Francis: La grâce amnistiante. Thèse pour le Doctorat en droit. Paris 1940, p. 32.

[47] Das betrifft nicht nur die Begnadigung im engeren Sinne: „Die A. greift in den Gang der Justiz ein, zwar gegen die Regel, aber nicht gegen das Recht; sie ist deshalb weder ein Justizakt, noch ein Spezialgesetz, sondern ein Akt der vollziehenden Gewalt, ebenso wie die „Begnadigung" im engeren Sinne, von der sie sich äußerlich durch das zeitliche Merkmal, innerlich allerdings oft durch das Motiv und vor allem in der Tragweite unterscheidet. Wie die „Begnadigung" kann die A. sowohl für einen einzelnen Fall als für eine Mehrheit von Fällen erfolgen, die bei bestimmtem Anlasse mit Vergessen begnadet werden sollen (Amnestie)." Fleischmann, Abolition (wie Fn. 20), S. 51.

[48] Siehe: Stronati, Monica: L'originalità dell'informazione politica italiana: pubblicità parlamentare e opinione pubblica nel XIX secolo. In: Giornale di Storia Costituzionale (2003) n. 6/II, „Opinione pubblica. Storia, politica, costituzione dal XVII al XX secolo", Macerata, 2003, S. 315-331.

Reconstruction of the *lex Aquilia* as an Example of a Textual Reconstruction of *Ancient leges*

Paulina Święcicka

I am conscious that there are only a few Romanists in the world who have not written about the *lex Aquilia*[1]. This is because the *lex Aquilia* was the most important statutory enactment of Roman private law subsequent to the *lex duodecim tabularum*, and now we can say that it is institutionally fundamental to contemporary delictual civil liability based on the principle of fault. I can also imagine that anyone who dares to offer a new contribution believes, with or without justification, that he has something original to say about it. This is the truth in my case as well. However, the problem which I would like to expose is part of another question, much broader and more general, i.e. the problem with the textual reconstruction of ancient legal sources (e.g. *leges*), which did not remain until our time, using subsequent sources – which is called 'palingenesia'. It is a truism that such a reconstruction is a terribly difficult work. One of the best known examples are the already mentioned Twelve Tables. The text of this *lex* has been reconstructed on the basis of later legal and non-legal sources, such as the works of Gaius (in particular his commentary *ad legem duodecim tabularum*), Livius, Aulus Gellius, Cicero etc; we still do not have the whole text, and a lot of questions remain open[2]. The *Lex Aquilia de damno ini-*

---

[1] In this way, one of the prominent Romanists began his study about one of the aspects of the *lex Aquilia*. See Nörr, Dieter: *'Mortis Causam Praebere'*. In: The Legal Mind. Essays for T. Honoré. Oxford 1986, pp. 203-217, in this case p. 203.

[2] It is difficult to summarize all works about this *lex*. To suggest some of great importance to this problem, see: the old works, e.g. Rotondi, Giovanni: Leges publicae populi Romani. Milano 1912, p. 201f.; Krüger, Paul: Geschichte der Quellen und Literatur des Römischen Rechts[2]. München/Leipzig 1912, p. 8f.; and the new works, e.g. Wenger, Leopold: Die Quellen des römischen Rechts. Wien 1953, p. 357f.; Crifò, Giuliano: La legge delle XII tavole. Osservazioni e problemi. In: ANRW I 2 (1972), p. 123f. ; Diliberto, Oliviero: Materiali per la palingenesi delle XII Tavole. Cagliari 1992, p. 9f.

uria dato seems to be another good example of how difficult the reconstruction and textual criticism can be. But before the examination of the evidence which we possess for this *lex*, I think it would be suitable to say – in a few words – what a textual reconstruction is.

Short Notes on Textual Criticism

Methods of textual reconstruction and textual criticism are used by scholars and editors of ancient texts, especially of Gospels and New Testament texts, but also of classical Greek and Latin texts – non-legal as well as legal[3]. Textual criticism is actually a branch of philology, but, as one can see, it is also very important for scholars who are concerned with ancient sources. The goal of this is to produce a text that is as close to the original as possible.

There are three fundamental approaches to textual criticism[4]: copy text editing[5], eclecticism[6] and stemmatics[7]. Several principles of textual criticism were

---

[3] See in general Schiller, Arthur A.: Roman Law. Mechanisms of Development. The Hague/Paris/New York 1978, pp. 62-83 [Textual Criticism] and lit. cited.

[4] It is worth saying that some techniques from the biological discipline of cladistics are now also being used to determine the relationship between manuscripts. See for this subject – Sober, Elliott: Reconstructing the Past: Parsimony, Evolution, and Inference. Cambridge 1988, passim; and also Peckham, Morse: Reflections on the Foundations of Modern Textual Editing. In: Proof (1971) No. 1, pp. 122-155.

[5] Using copy text editing, one has first to select a base text for a manuscript thought to be reliable. Often, the base text is selected from the oldest manuscript of the text, but not always, because in the beginning of copying and printing, the copy text was simply the version that was at hand, which was not always the first one. After this, one examines the base text and makes corrections, which are called emendations, in places where the base text appears to be wrong. This can be done by looking for places in the base text that do not make sense or by looking at the other texts for a superior version. See more, e.g. Vinaver, Eugène: Principles of Textual Emendation. In: Studies in French Language and Mediaeval Literature presented to Prof. Mildred K. Pope. Manchester 1939, pp. 351-369; Greg, Walter W. (Sir): The Rationale of Copy-Text. In: Studies in Bibliography (1950-1951) No. 3, pp. 19-36, which still is the basis for most current discussions of this issue; and also – The Theory and Practice of Text Editing. ed. Ian Small and Marcus Walsh. Cambridge 1992, *passim*.

[6] Eclecticism is the practice of examining a wide number of versions and of selecting the variant thought to be the best. Evaluation is done by using internal and external evidence. In this

also developed, such as the cannons of Tischendorf[8] or the external and internal criteria of evidence[9].

Not going into too many details and briefly speaking, all methods of textual criticism involve two main phases: i.e. *selectio et recensio* and *emendatio*. *Recensio* is - after an examination of all available material – a selection of the most trustworthy evidence on which a text may be based. *Emendatio* is an elimination of

---

approach none of the versions is theoretically favoured. E.g., one manuscript may have a tendency to omit words, another may have a tendency towards interpolations. After evaluating the opinions, one must decide which variant is the best. There is also another possible situation: Various considerations can be used to decide which reading is the most likely to be original. Of course, sometimes these considerations can be in conflict. See more lit. cit. in footnotes *supra* and *infra.*

[7] Stemmatics is the most rigorous approach to textual reconstruction. It requires the reconstruction of the history of a text by examining the variants for patterns of errors. In particular, critics use the principle that 'a community of error implies a unity of origin', to decide whether a group of manuscripts are derived from a lost intermediate, called an hyperarchetype. Then, relations between the lost intermediates are determined by the same process, so that extant manuscripts can be placed in a family tree, or *stemma codicum,* descending from a single archetype. And after this step, one can do an *examinatio* and a *divintio vel emendatio.* See Studies in Stemmatology. Ed. by Pieter von Reenen; Margot van Mulken. Amsterdam 1996, *passim.*

[8] Some of the most important principles of Lobegott Friedrich Constantin von Tischendorf (1815-1874) are: (1) The text is to be sought from the most ancient evidence, meaning especially the oldest Greek manuscripts; (2) a reading peculiar to a single document is to be considered as suspicious; (3) an obvious scribal error is to be rejected even though it is well supported in the manuscripts; (4) in parallel passages the tendency of copyists would be to make the readings agree, and therefore, in such passages, testimonies are to be preferred which are not in precise accordance; (5) that reading is to be preferred which could have given occasion to the others, or which appears to comprise the elements of the others; and (6) that reading is to be preferred which accords with NT Greek or with the style of the individual writer. After Finegan, Jack: Encountering NT Manuscripts. Grand Rapids 1974, p. 63.

[9] External and internal evidence was summarized by Bruce M. Metzger. The most important aspect in this case is some of the internal evidence dependant upon considerations of paleographical details and the habits of scribes: E.g., (1) in general the more difficult reading is to be preferred – *lectio difficilor potior;* (2) in general the shorter reading is to be preferred – *lectio brevior potior*; (3) the reading, which stands in verbal dissidence with the other is to be preferred. See more Metzger, Bruce M.: The Text of the New Testament. Oxford 1968, pp. 209-210. See also Aland, Kurt; Barbara Aland: The Text of the New Testament. An Introduction to the Critical Editions and to the Theory and Practice of Modern Textual Criticism. Grand Rapids 1987, pp. 275-276 [Twelve Basic Rules].

errors found. It must be stressed that errors could be found even in the best manuscripts, for the reason that, e.g., the copyist has had several manuscripts in front of his eyes and has followed sometimes one and sometimes another; or that a scribe copied a manuscript from one source and corrected it from another; or that copyists were more likely to simplify and smooth a text they did not fully understand[10] etc.

As one of the most famous textual critics said: "Textual criticism is a science, and since it comprises recession and emendation, it is also an art. It is a science of discovery of errors in a text and the art of removing it. That is its definitions, that is what the name denotes"[11].

Lex Aquilia – Problems with its Original Text and Proposal on its Reconstruction

As said, the *lex Aquilia* is one of the best examples of an ancient legal source, the text of which has been an object of controversy for over 60 years[12]

---

[10] One of the techniques mentioned, *nota bene* which was used by several scientists to reconstruct one of the phrases from the text of the *lex Aquilia*, is the *lectio difficilior potior*. This principle is based on considering the more difficult version as the one more likely to be the original. The primary idea is – as mentioned in the main text *supra* – that copyists are more likely to simplify and smooth a text they do not fully understand. See further reflections *infra*.

[11] Hausman, Alfred E.: The Application of Thought to Textual Criticism. In: Proceedings of the Classical Association (1921) No. 18, pp. 68-84, in this case p. 68.

[12] The literature relating to the original terms and the subsequent juristic interpretation of this law is very large. It is very characteristic that all views about the development of this law involve also an hypothesis about the original substance of the *lex Aquilia*. For the old studies, see, e.g., Pernice, Lotar A. A.: Zur Lehre von den Sachbeschädigungen nach römischem Rechte. Weimar 1867, pp. 11-25; Grueber, Erwin: The Roman Law of Damage to Property, being a Commentary on the Title of the Digest ad Legem Aquiliam (IX.2). Oxford 1886, p. 4f., 84f.; Monro, Charles. H.: Digest IX.2. Lex Aquilia. Cambridge 1898; Jolowicz, H. F.: The original scope of the Lex Aquilia and the question of damage. In: LQR (1922) No. 38, p. 220-231 [answered in a Review by Lenel, Otto. In: ZSS (1922) No. 43, pp. 575-577]; Kunkel, Wolfgang: Exegetische Studien zur aquilischen Haftung. In: ZSS (1929) No. 49, pp. 158-187; Daube, David: On the third chapter of the lex Aquilia. In: LQR (1936) No. 52, pp. 253-268; idem: On the use of the term "Damnum". In: Studi in onore di Siro Solazzi nel cinquantesimo anniversario del suo insegnamento universitario 1899-1948. Naples 1948, pp. 93-156; idem: Damages under the lex Aquilia. In: Roman Law: Lin-

and which still creates many problems with its original content and original scope[13]. This is because, as one of the scholars Raymond Westbrook *eleganter*

guistic, Social and Philosophical Aspects. Edinburgh 1966, pp. 66-71; Lawson, Frederick H.: Negligence in the Civil Law. Oxford 1950, p. 4 foll.; de Zulueta, Francis: The Institutes of Gaius. p.II. Oxford 1953, pp. 209-216; Beinart, Ben: Once more on the origin of the lex Aquilia. In: Butterworth's South African Law Review 1956, p. 70-80; Gerke, Theodor J.: Geschichtliche Entwicklung der Bemesung des Ansprüche aus des Lex Aquilia. In: SDHI (1957) No. 23, pp. 61-118 ; Lévy-Bruhl, Henri: Le deuxième chapitre de la loi Aquilia. In: RIDA (1958) No. 5, pp. 507-517; Illife, J. A.: Thirty days hath Lex Aquilia. In: RIDA (1958) No. 5, pp. 493-506; Pringsheim, Fritz: The origin of the Lex Aquilia. In: Mélanges H. Lévy-Bruhl. Paris 1959, pp. 233-244; Kelly, John M.: The Meaning of the lex Aquilia. In: LQR (1964) No. 80, pp. 73-83; idem: Further Reflections on the 'Lex Aquilia'. In: Studi in Onore di Edoardo Volterra. Vol. I. Milan 1971, pp. 235-241; Pugsley, David: Damni Iniuria. In: TR (1968), p. 371-386; idem: The origins of the Lex Aquilia. In: LQR (1969) No. 85, pp. 50-73 ; Schipani, Sandro: Responsabilità ex lege Aquilia. Criteri di imputazione e problema della culpa. Torino 1969, in the case of the text of the *lex* pp. 41-46; MacCormack, Geoffrey: On the third chapter of the lex Aquilia. In: The Irish Jurist (1970) No. 5, pp. 164-178 ; Tomulescu, C. St.: Les trois chapitres de la lex Aquilia. In: IURA (1970) No. 21, pp. 191-196; von Lübtow, Ulrich: Untersuchungen zur lex Aquilia de damno iniuria dato. Berlin 1971, p. 15f.; Honoré, Anthony M.: Linguistic and social context of the lex Aquilia. In: The Irish Jurist (1972) No. 7, pp. 138-150; Witmann, Roland: Die Körperverletzung an Freien im klassischen römischen Recht. München 1972, p. 37 foll.; Cardascia, Guillaume: La portée primitive de la loi Aquilia. In: Daube Noster. Essays in Legal History for David Daube. Edinburg/London 1974, pp. 53-77; Hausmaninger, Herbert: Das Schadenersatzrecht der lex Aquilia[5]. Wien 1996, p. 9 foll.; Völkl, Artur: Quanti ea res erit in diebus triginta proximis. Zum dritten Kapitel der lex Aquilia. In: RIDA (1977) No. 24, pp. 461-486; van Warmelo, Paul: À propos de la loi Aquilia. In: RIDA (1980) No. 27, pp. 333-348; Crook, John A.: Lex Aquilia. In: ATHENAEUM (1984) No. 62, pp. 67-77; Ankum, Hans: Quanti ea res erit in diebus XXX proximis dans la troisième chapitre de la lex Aquilia: un fantasme florentin. In: Religion, société, politique. Mélanges J. Ellul. Paris 1983, pp. 170-183; Nörr, Dieter: Texte zur Lex Aquilia. In: Iuris Professio. Festgabe für Max Kaser. Köln 1986, pp. 211-221.

13 For the recently published studies, see, e.g., Bignardi, Alessandra: Teoph. Par. 4.3.15. Ancora sulla data della lex Aquilia. In: Ann. Univ. Ferrara Sc. Giurid. Nuova Serie (1989) No. 3, pp. 3-38; Cannata, Carlo A.: Sul testo della Lex Aquilia e la sua portata originaria. In: La responsabilità civile da atto illecito nella prospecttiva storico-comparatistica. Atto Illecito. Madrid 1993, p. 25-57 ; idem: Il terzo capo della 'Lex Aquilia'. In: BIDR (1995-96) No. 98-99, pp. 111-146; Westbrook, Raymond: The Coherence of the Lex Aquilia. In: RIDA (1995) No. 42, pp. 437-471; Valditara, Giuseppe: Superamento dell'aestimatio rei nella valutazione del danno aquiliano ed estensione della tutela ai non domini. Milano 1992, p. 1 foll., in this case pp. 2-14; idem: Damnum iniuria datum. Torino 1996, p. 3 foll., in the case of the text of the *lex*, pp. 8-14; Zimmermann, Reinhard: The Law of Obligations. Roman Foundations of the Civilian Tradition. Cape Town/ Juta/

said: "The *lex Aquilia* is a source that goes back to a shadowy period of Roman law for which native historiographical traditions are unreliable."[14]

We have drawn all the information about the origin and content of the *lex Aquilia* from the *Digesta*, *Institutiones Gai* and *Institutiones Iustiniani*, because none of the three parts of the *lex* remained. However, they are preserved, because they were quoted by Gaius, one of the classical jurists, in his commentary on the *edictum provinciale* (I chapter) and by Ulpianus, also a classic, in his commentary on the Edict (III chapter), and since these quotations have been incorporated into the *Corpus Iuris Civilis*. It is obvious that this process must have brought changes to the text of this ancient *lex*[15]. As John A. Crook, one of the scientists who has been occupied with the aforementioned problem, said: "What was quoted as the *lex Aquilia* in the days of Gaius and Ulpianus was a heavily modernized text into which a sprinkling of obvious archaisms had been reintroduced for verisimilitude"[16]. Of course, this statement leads to the question, how far the text of the *lex Aquilia*, handed down by Gaius and Ulpianus, is genuine.

As one may also suppose, it is impossible to reconstruct the original text itself from present sources[17]. The best thing one can hope to attain is the most faithful version, relating to the most direct textual witnesses. Of course, as has been stressed, that fact raises many problems, primarily textual ones, but one can also ask another very important question, i.e. a question about the interpretation of the substance of this *lex*.

As one may know, *lex Aquilia* was composed of three chapters (sections, paragraphs), and each of them refers to various sources.

Deventer/ Boston 1992, p. 953-1049, in the case of the text pp. 959-969; Castresana, Amelia: Nuevas Lecturas de la Responsabilidad Aquiliana. Ediciones Universidad. Salamanca 2001, p. 11 foll., in the case of the text pp. 21-27.

[14] Westbrook (as in 13) p. 470.

[15] As we may know, the juristic works used in the *Digesta* had to some extent been deformed by the time they were used. Also, the compilers of the *Digesta* were not very scrupulous about the exact wording.

[16] Crook (as in 12) p. 76.

[17] Also Westbrook (as in 13) p. 441.

Chapter One

Chapter one refers to three legal sources: *Digesta*[18], *Gai Institutitones* and *Institutiones Iustiniani.* It is worth saying that the fragment of I.4,3*pr.* is almost identical to *Gai* 3,210. This is because, generally speaking, the *Institutiones Iustiniani* are a copy – of course with necessary corrections and modernizations – of the *Institutiones Gai*, and for that reason only the first two sources mentioned will be examined[19], both derived from Gaius, but different.

D.9.2.2*pr*-1[20]: Gaius *libro* 7. *ad edictum provinciale*: *Lege Aquilia capite primo cavetur: "ut qui servum servamve alienum alienamve quadrupedem vel pecudem iniuria occiderit, quanti id in eo anno plurimi fuit, tantum aes dare domino damnas esto"; Et infra deinde cavetur, ut adversus infitiantem in duplum actio esset.*

Gai Institutiones 3,210[21]: *Damni iniuriae actio constituitur*[22] *per legem Aquiliam, cuius primo capite cautum est, si quis hominem alienum eamve quadrupedem, quae pecudum numero sit, iniuria occiderit, quanti ea res in eo anno plurimi fuit, tantum domino dare damnetur.*

---

[18] Some scientists claim that in the *Digesta* we have the actual wording, not only the provisions. I must say that such declaration seems to be going too far, because it is almost evident that Gaius quoted words not from the *lex*, but from the Edict. Also, it can be added that both *Gai* and *I.* seem to be a bit simplistic, and the reason of this was that these two *Institutiones* were made for a specific, i.e for a didactic, purpose. See, e.g., Valditara (as in 13) p. 2 n. 4, idem: Damnum (as in 13) p. 8 n. 46.

[19] Compare with I.4,3*pr. Damni iniuriae actio constituitur per legem Aquiliam. cuius primo capite cautum est ut, si quis hominem alienum alienamve quadrupedem, quae pecudum numero sit, iniuria occiderit, quanti ea res in eo anno plurimi fuit, tantum domino dare damnetur.*

[20] This is a passage from the *Florentine* based on Mommsen's edition, i.e. Digesta Iustiniani Augusti. ed. Th. Mommsen. vol. I-II. Berlin 1870; reed. Berlin 1962-62. This is a critic edition, a basis for an *editio stereotipa.*

[21]This is a fragment from the *Veronensis* based on Krueger-Studemund's edition, i.e. Gai Institutiones. Ad codicis Veronensis apgraphum Studemundianum in usum scholarum edd. P. Krueger et G. Studemund. Inest epistula critica Th. Mommseni. ed. V. Berlin 1905.

[22] It was an obvious and necessary correction of the *Veronensis* manuscript, where it was originally written *constituit.*.

Textual Considerations and Remarks on Chapter One

It must be said that it is very probable that the original beginning of chapter one had the words *si quis*, as we can read in *Gai Institutiones*[23] and also in the VIth century Greek paraphrase of the *Digesta* – Basilica. It is very possible that a copyist had these words in front of his eyes, when he wrote ἐάν τις[24].

The words *quadrupedem vel pecudem* are obviously a later editorial correction. Anyway, it must be stressed that these words in some grammatical arrangements must have stood in the original text. It seems logical that there should be: *servum servamve alienum alienam alienamve quadrupedem pecudem.* In *Gai* and *I.* we also have a phrase: *quae pecudum numero sit.* This phrase seems to be written above all for teaching purposes[25] and did not appear in the original version of the text.

One can also ask about the change of *homo* into *servus*. Was it a necessary replacement, as some scholars suggested[26]? The truth is, that the word *homo* used for a slave is justified by textual references to the literature. In Plautus, we can find the words *servus homo* for a slave but not before Cicero's time was a slave referred to only as *servus*[27]. So I think it safer – but it is not an obvious and necessary change – to replace it, if possible.

The words *quanti id*, which appear in the *Digesta*, can also be found in another passage from this source, however in a different form, i.e. D.9.2.21*pr.* (Ulpianus *libro* 18. *ad edictum*): *ait lex: quanti is homo in eo anno plurimi fuisset.* But *id* is a neuter pronoun and it can be justified here grammatically, because it could appear after the masculine or feminine nouns[28].

---

[23] See I.4,3*pr.*, where in the beginning are words: *Ut si quis…*

[24] Basilicorum Libri LX. ed. G.E. Heimbach. Lipisiae 1850. For this see, e.g., Crook (as in 12) p. 70.

[25] See, e.g., von Lübtow (as in 13) p. 19, Crook (as in 12) p. 70, Valditara, Damnum (as in 13) p. 8 n. 46.

[26] See, e.g., Jolowicz (as in 12) p. 221 by references to other formulas from *edict de servo corrupto* D.11.3.1*pr.*, insisted that in this place should be the word *servus.*

[27] See explanation of Crook (as in 13) p. 71.

[28] For the phrase *quanti is homo velea pecus* in this place see, e.g., Valditara, Damnum (as in 13) p. 8 n. 46. Of course, in this case the question about the word *homo* remains open.

The next difference is the varying order of words in both sources – *dare domino* or *domino dare*. We can suppose that the right sequence is *domino dare*. This can be justified by referring to the other phrases of the *Digesta*, i.e. D.9.2.27.5 (Ulpianus): *domino dare*[29] or much more probable *ero dare*, because *erus* was an old archaic form of *dominus*[30] and Ulpianus, in D.9.2.11.6, writes: *legis autem Aquiliae actio ero competit* .... So one can call *erus* a kind of "legal-archaism"[31].

One could ask now, whether there are any words which are not in doubt? I think, as was suggested before, that the words *servus* or *servus homo* and also *quadrupedem pecudem* in some form must have stood in the original text of the *lex*. Also, the words *iniuria, occiderit* and *plurimi* seem to be original, especially because of the subsequent juristic discussions, which in some way guarantee their presence from the very beginning. The word *iniuria* in chapter one was essential and necessary in order to exclude justifiable killing from liability[32].

It is possible, too, that the rule about double damages *contra infitiantem* stood in this chapter from its beginning, in some form[33].

To end this part, it is to be noted that the word *damnum* does not occur in chapter one[34]. This is a bit odd, because an existence of *damnum*, which means a loss, was and still is regarded as an essential element for the Aquilian liability.

---

[29] See D.9.2.27.5 cit. *infra*.

[30] See also an explanation given by Gaius in case of *consortium ercto non cito*. *Gai* 3,154: *erctum enim dominium est (unde erus dominus dicitur)*. For the literature see, e.g., Capogrossi Colognesi, Luigi: La Struttura della proprietà e la formazione dei iura praediorum nell'età reppublicana. Milano 1969, vol. I, p. 437 and Witmann (as in 12) pp. 44-45.

[31] See further reflections *infra*.

[32] See and compare D.9.2.3 Ulpianus *libro* 18. *ad edictum: Si servus servave iniuria occisus occisave fuerit, lex Aquilia locum habet. iniuria occisum esse merito adicitur: non enim sufficit occisum, sed oportet iniuria id esse factum*. Also D.9.2.4*pr*.-1, D.9.2.5*pr*., D.9.2.7.4, D.9.2.29.7.

[33] See further reflections *infra*.

[34] See Daube, On the use (as in 12) p. 146; Crook (as in 12) p. 72, 74 n. 18.

Chapter Two

The discovery of the Gaius palimpsest in 1816 by B. Niebuhr in the library in Verona brought to light the missing chapter two of the *lex Aquilia*[35]. It is summarized by Gaius and it is obvious that it states only the provisions of words, because in his days this rule was not in use any more.

Gai Institutines 3,215-216: *Capite secundo adversus adstipulatorem, qui pecuniam in fraudem stipulatoris acceptam fecerit, quanti ea res est, tanti actio constituitur.* 216. *Qua et ipsa parte legis damni nomine actionem introduci manifestum est; sed id caveri non fuit necessarium, cum actio mandati ad eam rem sufficeret; nisi quod ea lege adversus infitiantem in duplum agitur.*

It must be mentioned that this passage is the only evidence for the content of chapter two[36] and because it does not purport to quote the exact wording of the *lex,* the point of the textual consideration is out of the scope of this paper. Anyway, one important remark can be made – because of the casuistic tendency in law making in early times, it is reasonable to suppose that chapter two, also casuistic, begins with the words: *si adstipulator* rather than *si quis*[37].

Chapter Three

Considering the last chapter, it must be noted that this is the most problematic part of the examined *lex*. It refers to several legal sources: two fragments from the *Digesta, Gai Institutiones* and *Institutiones Iustiniani.* And as we may suppose, these versions are in conflict.

---

[35] For a review of earlier theories of the content of chapter two – see Cannata, Carlo A.: Considerazione sul testo e la portata originaria del secondo capo della 'Lex Aquilia'. In: INDEX (1994) No. 22, pp. 151-162, in this case specially pp. 151-152; also Birks, Peter: Wrongful loss by Co-Promisses. In: INDEX (1994) No. 22, pp. 181-188; and Tomulescu (as in 12) p. 192-194.
[36] Compare with D.9.2.27.4 Ulpianus *libro* 18. *ad edictum: Huius legis secundum quidem capitulum in desuetudinem abiit*; and I.4.3.12: *Caput secundum legis Aquiliae in usu non est.*
[37] Cannata, Considerazione (as in 35) p. 151; Westbrook (as in 13) p. 447.

Intuitively speaking, D.9.2.27.5 of Ulpianus seems to be the only source that purports to give the exact wording of the statute by saying: *ait lex*. But some scientists hold him not to be quoting the *lex*, but the Edict[38]. On the other hand, *Gai*[39] and *I.*[40] seem to be only the paraphrases.

D.9.2.27.5: Ulpianus *libro* 18. *ad edictum: Tertio autem capite ait eadem lex Aquilia: "ceterarum rerum praeter hominem et pecudem occisos*[41] *si quis alteri*[42] *damnum*

---

[38] See the skeptical notes of Gerke (as in 12) p. 78; von Lübtow (as in 13) p. 21; and van Warmello (as in 12) p. 347.

[39] Gai 3,217-218: *Capite tertio de omni cetero damno cavetur. itaque si quis servum vel eam quadrupedem, quae pecudum numero est, vulneraverit sive eam quadrupedem, quae pecudum numero non est, velut canem, aut feram bestiam, velut ursum, leonem, vulneraverit vel occiderit, hoc capite actio constituitur. in ceteris quoque animalibus, item in omnibus rebus, quae anima carent, damnum iniuria datum hac parte vindicatur. si quid enim ustum aut ruptum aut fractum fuerit, actio hoc capite constituitur, quamquam potuerit sola rupti appellatio in omnes istas causas sufficere; ruptum enim intellegitur, quod quoquo modo corruptum est; unde non solum usta aut rupta aut fracta, sed etiam scissa et collisa et effusa et quoquo modo vitiata aut perempta atque deteriora facta hoc verbo continentur.* 218. *Hoc tamen capite non quanti in eo anno, sed quanti in diebus XXX proximis ea res fuerit, damnatur is, qui damnum dederit. ac ne 'plurimi' quidem verbum adicitur; et ideo quidam putaverunt liberum esse iudici ad id tempus ex diebus XXX aestimationem redigere, quo plurimi res fuit, vel ad id, quo minoris fuit. sed Sabino placuit proinde habendum ac si etiam hac parte 'plurimi' verbum adiectum esset; nam legis latorem contentum fuisse, quod prima parte eo verbo usus esset.*

[40] I.4,3,13-15: (13.) *Capite tertio de omni cetero damno cavetur. Itaque si quis servum, vel eam quadrupedem quae pecudum numero est, vulneraverit, sive eam quadrupedem quae pecudum numero non est, veluti canem aut feram bestiam, vulneraverit aut occiderit, hoc capite actio constituitur. in ceteris quoque omnibus animalibus, item in omnibus rebus quae anima carent, damnum iniuria datum hac parte vindicatur. si quid enim ustum aut ruptum aut fractum fuerit, actio ex hoc capite constituitur: quamquam potuerit sola rupti appellatio in omnes istas causas sufficere: "ruptum" enim intellegitur quoquo modo corruptum. unde non solum usta aut fracta, sed etiam scissa et collisa et effusa et quoquo modo perempta atque deteriora facta hoc verbo continentur: denique responsum est, si quis in alienum vinum aut oleum id immiserit quo naturalis bonitas vini vel olei corrumperetur, ex hac parte legis eum teneri.* (14.) *Illud palam est, sicut ex primo capite ita demum quisque tenetur, si dolo aut culpa eius homo aut quadrupes occisus occisave fuerit, ita ex hoc capite ex dolo aut culpa de cetero damno quemque teneri. hoc tamen capite non quanti in eo anuo, sed quanti in diebus triginta proximus res fuerit, obligatur is qui damnum dederit.* (15.) *Ac ne "plurimi" quidem verbum adicitur; sed Sabino recte placuit, perinde habendam aestimationem ac si etiam hac parte "plurimi" verbum adiectum fuisset: nam plebem Romanam, quae Aquilio tribuno rogante hanc legem tulit, contentam fuisse, quod prima parte eo verbo usa est.*

[41] *Occisos* is an obvious and necessary correction of *occisus* from *Florentine.*

[42] B. Albanese suggested to change *alteri* into *aliter* to justify a rule in chapter three penalizing damages caused in other ways than mentioned in chapter one, i.e. *ociddere.* See Albanese, Bernardo: Una congettura sul significato d'iniuria in XII Tab.8.4. In: IURA (1980) No. 31, pp. 35-36.

faxit, quod usserit[43] *fregerit ruperit iniuria, quanti ea res erit in diebus triginta proximis, tantum aes domino dare damnas esto".*

Another fragment of the *Digesta*, which also seems to be important for this case, is:

D.9.2.29.8: Ulpianus *libro* 18. *ad edictum*: *Haec verba: "quanti in triginta diebus proximis fuit", etsi non habent "plurimi", sic tamen esse accipienda constat.*

Some scientists, e.g. Hans Ankum, think that in this passage, Ulpianus purports to quote the words of the *lex* by writing: *haec verba* and a quotation[44]. They are right of course, although it is only a fragment – an offensive clause in the context of subsequent interpretation.

Textual Considerations and Remarks on Chapter Three

As has been mentioned, chapter three caused a lot of problems from the beginning of the reconstruction of the text of the *lex Aquilia.*

Firstly, it must be said that the opening phrase – *ceterarum rerum praeter hominem et pecudem occisos* – was and still is, as a whole or in part, regarded as an explanatory addition, gloss or interpolation or as an insertion of the compilers. Otto Lenel was one of the first scholars who categorically suggested to omit the whole clause. He regarded it as being suspicious, especially because it is ungrammatical, and he added that it could not refer to both previous chapters, since it was discovered that chapter two was concerned with a debt, not a thing[45].

---

[43] *Usserit* is also an obvious correction of *usuerit* from *Florentine.*

[44] See Ankum (as in 12) p. 178.

[45] Lenel (as in 12) pp. 575-577. Also – before him Pernice (as in 12) p. 14; Jolowicz (as in 12) p. 221; and after him – de Zulueta (as in 12) pp. 210-212; Gerke (as in 12) p. 61, 78; Kelly, The meaning (as in 12) p. 78; von Lübtow (as in 13) p. 21; Witmann (as in 12) p. 40; Crook (as in 12) p. 74, 77; Hausmaninger (as in 12) p. 7 etc. But see Zimmermann (as in 13) p. 960 n. 64.

But not very long ago, one scholar, Tony Honoré, regarded the first two words, i.e. *ceterarum rerum* as genuine[46]. His reasoning about the antiquity of this phrase was based on the text of an aedilian edict *de feris*, where two specific provisions were followed by a general, residuary clause which began with the words: *ceterarum rerum*...[47] Honoré argued that the case of the *lex Aquilia* could be alike. This is possible of course, but I think that the main and primary question in this case should be how a specific clause was used in a particular context[48].

Anyway, going further, Honoré suggested that this clause referred not to things other than slaves or animals, but to matters other than those comprised by the previous chapters[49]. The rest of the disputed phrase, i.e. *praeter hominem et pecudem occisos*, was explained by him as a gloss – an explanatory gloss made by compilers in addition to other passages from Ulpianus, e.g. fr. D.9.2.27.6[50]. Honoré decided that this gloss was necessary in order to give an authentic interpretation of *ceterarum rerum* since without it, this phrase can be either regarded as: 1) things other than slaves and animals mentioned or 2) matters other than killing a slave or an animal mentioned, and, according to Honoré, only the second alternative seems to be covered by chapter three.

As another scholar, Raymond Westbrook pointed out[51], Honoré was not right, because of the fact that there is an obvious absence of a substantive link between chapter one and two; and no provision can be found to deal with 'other matters', because the two chapters of the *lex Aquilia* deal with two en-

---

[46] Honoré (as in 12) p. 144. Also – Zimmermann (as in 13) p. 960, 968 and Cannata (as in 35), Il terzo capo, p. 111.

[47] See D.21.1.42, Ulpianus: *libro* 2 *ad edictum curulium: qua vulgo iter fiet, ita habuisse velit, ut cuiquam nocere damnumve dare possit, si adversus ea factum erit et homo liber ex ea re perierit, solidi ducenti, si nocitum homini libero esse dicetur, quanti bonum aequum iudici videbitur, condemnetur, ceterarum rerum, quanti damnum datum factumve sit, dupli."*

[48] See a critique by Westbrook (as in 13) p. 443 and n.17. See also other examples of *ceterarum rerum a fortiori* – Nörr, Texte (as in 12) pp. 213-216.

[49] Honoré (as in 12) pp. 141-145.

[50] D.9.2.27.6 Ulpianus *libro* 18 *ad edictum: Si quis igitur non occiderit hominem vel pecudem, sed usserit fregerit ruperit, sine dubio ex his verbis legis agendum erit. proinde si facem servo meo obieceris et eum adusseris, teneberis mihi.*

[51] See his very critic examination the propositions of Honoré: Westbrook (as in 13), p. 443 and n. 17.

tirely different matters. Honoré's theory makes sense only under the assumption that chapter two has been omitted, which was of course the situation in Justinian's days[52], or if it is argued that chapter two was disregarded – as Gaius presents[53].

In my opinion, it is possible that the whole phrase was an explanatory gloss. It seems to be very unlikely that in archaic and early-republican times the text was written so extensively.

The next important problem was connected with the word *sum-esse*. As we can see, in D.9.2.27.5 we have *erit* [*fut.pr.*], but in D.9.2.29.8 – *fuit* [*perf.*] and in *Gai* 3,218 – *fuerit* [*fut.ex.*]. This is a very controversial word, in fact the main disputation was and still is concerned with the word *erit-fuit-fuerit*[54].

As can be seen, both Gaius and Ulpianus appear to read the time backwards, but Ulpianus – also forward. How should it be understood then?

One of the most famous philologists of the Middle Ages, Gregor Haloander, in his edition of *Digesta* replaced *erit* in D.9.2.27.5 by *fuit*[55]. And many old and modern authors approve this emendation[56]. The supporters of this approach regarded *erit* as a scribal error and they explained the period in chapter three in the same way as *annus* in chapter one. Also, another modern scholar, Hans Ankum, pointed out that there are other manuscripts and editions of the *Digesta* which are more reliable in this place[57], and he stressed that the word *erit* is not more than a scribal error – *lapsus calami* – in the manuscript

---

[52] See n. 36 *supra*.

[53] See n. 36 *supra*.

[54] For a summary of the discussion on this topic and for the main points of the scholars' views – see specially Cardascia (as in 12) p. 53 and p. 67 n. 1; Ankum (as in 12) pp. 172-180.

[55] Edition of 1529. See Ankum (as in 12) p. 180; Zimmermann (as in 13) p. 963.

[56] E.g. Pernice (as in 12) p. 14; Lenel (as in 12) p. 575; Gerke (as in 12) p. 78; MacCormack (as in 12) p. 169; van Warmelo (as in 12) p. 347; Tomulescu (as in 12) p. 192, 195, 196; von Lübtow (as in 13) p. 21; Ankum (as in 12) p. 171, 179; Cannata, Il terzo capo (as in 35) p. 111; Valditara, Damnum (as in 13) p. 9.

[57] Ankum has examined editions previous to the 1st edition based on *littera Florentina* of de Torelli 1551, such as editions of G. Haloander 1529, edition of Hugo de Porta [Lyon] 1538, edition of Russard 1561. All of them have the verb *fuit* in analyzed phrase. See Ankum (as in 12) p. 180-181 n. 49.

(Florentine) and he gave some etymological and grammatical arguments for a phrase in the past sense[58].

It should be noted that David Daube was one of the creators of the second possibility – that *erit* should be in the original text of the *lex Aquilia.* He even developed the whole, very consequential theory based on this proposition[59]. He argued that in this sense a clause *quanti ea res erit, nota bene* regarded by him as a *lectio difficilior*[60], had the meaning – "the sum this affair will come to"[61]. So the word *ea res* did not refer to the object that had been damaged, but to the affair, and a judge had to assess not the value of that object, but the actual damage suffered by the plaintiff, in particular the mere difference between the full value and the reduced value after interference. And the word *damnum* was here in the sense of a pecuniary loss[62]. 30 days were needed for the plaintiff to see how the injury would develop. Consequently, the *lex Aquilia* in chapter three originally applied only to the wounding of slaves and animals, and the

---

[58] Ankum (as in 12) pp. 171-183, specially in this case p. 177, 179-180, and n. 41 on p. 179.

[59] See the works of David Daube cited in n. 12 *supra.* The theory of Daube must come into consideration because it made a big impact on the subsequent discussion on the text of the *lex Aquilia.* Actually, no discussion on this topic can ignore his propositions and hypotheses, more or less probable. But see the criticism of Daube – e.g. Ankum (as in 12) pp. 175-183.

[60] See the forceful criticism of this argument of Daube by Ankum (as in 12) p. 177, who pointed out that it is *fuit* or even *fuerit* that should be regarded as *lectio difficilior*, because the phrase *quanti ea res erit* is far more common than the others, in *Digesta*, so scribes were therefore likely to write *erit* in error instead of *fuit*, but not in another way. See also Westbrook (as in 13) p. 445, who argued that, of course, a phrase with *erit* is very frequent in *Digesta,* but not universal.

[61] This view goes back to Monro, the first scholar who said that chapter three gave a victim "the amount which the incident would have cost him, if it had occurred at the moment in the month at which it would have cost him the most". Monro (as in 12) p. 36-37.

[62] According to Daube chapter three was not concerned with the value prior to the time of the alleged delict, but a *damnum*, as it might appear in the period up to thirty days subsequent to the alleged delict. So, *damnum* in this context originally meant not a damage, but a pecuniary loss. See Daube, On the Use (as in 12) p. 146; idem Roman Law, p. 66-68. It is also worth stressing that differently from chapter one which is limited, in a primitive style, to a particular kind of injury to a particular kind of property, chapter three shows a general concept of damage – loss. It is *ruperit*, which makes its provision so elastic.

damage to an inanimate object was only included by way of interpretation from *erit* to *fuit*, which took place in the second half of the 1st century BC[63].

This theory was accepted by many scholars[64]. Although it looks consequential and logically correct, there are some difficulties and weaknesses implicit in such an explanation, which make it implausible, especially the subsequent interpretation proposed by Daube, which does not have any supporting information in sources, and the interpretation 'from *erit* to *fuit*' has a regressive character. Such an interpretation in classical times would be an anachronism, not a progress. And the result of changing to *quanti ea res erit* is a thoroughly rational system, so, for that reason, one cannot accept that it existed in the primitive archaic period.

What is the possible solution then? I think that *erit* can be explained as a copyist's error, a slip. This kind of error can happen and thus the explanation is not *per se* implausible[65]. In a way, however, textual emendations always were

---

[63] Daube, On the Third Chapter (as in 12) pp. 262-263. This part of Daube's theory leads to the question about the original scope of chapter three. As has been said, according to Daube this chapter is concerned with nothing else but *servi* and *quadrupedes pecudes*. While chapter one penalized the total destruction of them, chapter three penalized wounding them [*urere, frangere, rumpere* – all of them are originally kinds of wounding].On the other hand, the opponent of Daube, Jolowicz argued that chapter three penalized the destruction of everything else, but not *servi et quadrupedes pecudes*. For this scholar the phrase *ceterarum rerum* was essential. See. Jolowicz (as in 12) p. 220 and just like him also van Warmelo (as in 12) p. 340, 345. However, one can reasonably say that it is almost certain that Roman law was not able to continue for some hundred years with no delict remedies covering damage to inanimate property, as well as *movable*, other than given – in these situations – the actions which are in the *lex Aquilia*. So I think that it was far more likely that *lex Aquilia* included from the very beginning damage to inanimate objects, as well as *res se moventes*, and there is no need to explain any change by an interpretation, which has no references to sources legal and non-legal. See in this way Kelly, Further Reflections (as in 12) p. 238-239; Zimmermann (as in 13) p. 965-966.

[64] E.g. Bernard (as in 12) pp. 450-460; Lawson (as in 12) pp. 8-11; Watson, Alan: The Law of Obligations in the later Roman Republic. Oxford 1965, pp. 234-235; Kaser, Max: In: Review of Daube Roman Law. In: ZSS (1970) No. 87, pp. 535-536 and n. 7 [who *note bene* changed his previous – traditional view form RPR I^1 München 1955, p. 144, 518 because of Daube's theories – see RPR I^2 München 1971, p. 161 n. 60 and 61]; Cardascia (as in 12) p. 53f; Illife (as in 12) pp. 503-505; Crook (as in 12) p. 74, 77, Wittmann(as in fn. 37) pp. 36, 40-43; Hausmaninger, pp. 29-30; Zimmermann (as in 13) p. 967 etc.

[65] See, e.g., Barthélemy, Dominique: Preliminary and Interim Report on the Hebrew Old Testament Text Project. New York 1979, p. IX, who stressed that "when a text was particularly diffi-

regarded as emergency solutions. The theory of interpretation can also be accepted, but in a different way, i.e. from *fuit* to *erit.* Of course, in the time when Ulpianus wrote his commentary, damages under chapter three could be assessed on the basis of loses suffered, but in the beginning we had *fuit* here. After this first primitive period, a new standard was developed by way of interpretation, a standard which was much more suitable for a plaintiff, whose interests could be fulfilled in a better way. The assessment of damages by way of *quanti ea res erit*, that was justified from the classical period[66], gave a possibility to compensate all damages, in other words – the measure of damage was the plaintiff's loss – his *interesse.* To conclude this point, in the beginning we have *fuit,* but in classical law it is very possible that the words: *quanti ea res fuit-erit* have been understood in their current sense, i.e. what the matter comes to.

And the last argument for the word *sum-esse* in the past tense in this phrase is that in Greek Basilica § 60.3.27.5 one can find a word ἦν here[67], so it is very likely that a translator had the word *fuit* in front of his eyes[68].

It is also possible that chapter three did not contain the word *iniuria*, because this word in that chapter would have been superfluous. On the other hand – as one can see – *iniuria* in chapter one was essential and necessary.

The word *plurimi,* which makes references to the highest value, is not in the original text. Such a conclusion can safely be inferred from the subsequent juristic discussion. And as one can know from Ulpianus[69] and Gaius[70], it was Sabinus who definitely resolved this problem on the way of interpretation. Of course, it seems obvious that he cannot have been the first who thought of this as the only possible interpretation.

---

cult, there was a tendency for ancient scribes and translators to simplify the text by employing more fitting lexical, grammatical and stylistic forms (these modifications are often spoken of as 'facilitating')". In the same way also Westbrook (as in 13) p. 447.

[66] See, e.g., D.9.2.33*pr.* Paulus, Gai 3, 212.

[67] The translation of Heimbach is *erat* [*imperf.*]. Analogical situation is in B. § 60.3.29.8 which is an equivalent of D.9.2.29.8.

[68] Ankum (as in 12) pp. 180-181, also n. 44 and 47. See – critically for Ankum – Westbrook (as in 13) pp. 446-447.

[69] D.9.2.29.8 cit. *supra.*

[70] Gai 3,218 cit. *supra.*

And as it was in both previous chapters, the rule about double damages *contra infitiantem* may have been repeated under this chapter in some form.

A question about undoubted words is also present in the subject matter of chapter three. It can be said that three words describing the way on which a damage was caused appeared here in some form. Of course, these were *urere, frangere* and *rumpere.*

Nobody has also – as yet – disputed the presence of the period mentioned in this chapter – *diebus triginta proximis*[71].

Archaic Vocabulary

Finally – I should add a few remarks about the archaic vocabulary mentioned before. It is very important not to be naïve about this, as John A. Crook warns[72], however it is obvious that *lex Aquilia* comes from an age of primitive simplicity – as Cicero said[73] – so the language of the original version must have been archaic. Some linguistic modernizations made in the classical and Justinian periods seem to be almost certain, e.g. a replacement of the term *erus* by *dominus.* But on the other hand, certain archaisms, such as *damnas esto*[74] or *faxit*, were retained. One can of course take them as guarantees of authenticity of the sources – as textual evidences.

Anyway, it is important to say that the linguistic modernizations, which are probable to be made, left the substance of the text unaffected.

---

[71] This was questioned only by J. Illife, who wanted to discover whether it was 30 days after the occurrence of the delict or the discovery of the delict, or better the notification of the delict. He examined for this reason early *leges* from FIRA, which contain a phrase *in diebus proximis.* See Illife (as in 12) p. 503-505. See also Zimmermann (as in 13) p. 968-969.

[72] See Crook (as in 12) p. 76.

[73] Cic. *pro Tullio* 4,8.

[74] For this phrase see specially Liebs, Detlef: Damnum, damnare und damnas zur Bedeutungsgeschichte einiger lateinischer Rechtswörter. In: ZSS (1968) No. 85, pp. 173-252, in this case pp. 242-252.

Two Further Provisions

As it was said, jurists mentioned two further provisions of the *lex Aquilia*: a double penalty against the one who denies the accusation[75] and noxal liability[76].

As was also mentioned, it is difficult to say what form these provisions have taken. It can be supposed that it could be one of three possibilities: 1) a separate clause; 2) a sub-clause within these chapters, or 3) suggestive terms in the three chapters that were interpreted as laying down rules.

Both of these rules are secondary and not specific to the *lex Aquilia* and they are also valid for all three chapters. That is why I think that the first possibility is the most likely[77].

How this *lex* Could Stand

I must admit that this short observation confirms that we cannot pretend to know the exact wording of the *lex Aquilia.*

But, adding information about how ancient *leges rogatae* were composed (*praescriptio* – information about the proponent of a *lex*, date of the meeting of a *comitium* or *concilium plebis, rogatio* – the text of a *lex, sanctio* – rules in case of breach of a *lex*), I can suggest that this text looked as follows:

... Aquilius ... tr(ibuni) pl(ebei) plebem iuore rogarunt, plebesque iuore scivit ... in ... tribus ... principium fuit, pro tribu ... primus scivit[78].

Si quis servum servam alienum alienam alienamve quadrupedem pecudem iniuria occiderit, quanti id in eo anno plurimi fuit, tantum aes ero dare damnas esto.

Si adstipulator pecuniam in fraudem stipulatoris acceptam fecerit, quanti ea res est, tantum aes stipulatori dare damnas esto.

---

[75] D.9.2.2.1 Gaius; Gai 3,216; D.9.2.23.10 Ulpianus; D.9.2.24 Paulus.

[76] Gai 4,76; D.9.4.2.1 Ulpianus.

[77] Also Cannata, Il terzo capo (as in 35) p. 111, different – e.g. Westbrook (as in 13) n. 27 *in fine* on p. 447-448.

[78] See D.9.2.1.1 Ulpianus *libro* 18. *ad edictum: Quae lex Aquilia plebiscitum est, cum eam Aquilius tribunus plebis a plebe rogaverit.*

[Ceterarum rerum] si quis alteri damnum faxit, quod usserit fregerit ruperit iniuria, quanti ea res fuit in diebus triginta proximis, tantum aes ero dare damnas esto.

Adversus infitiantem in duplum actio esto.

Si servus sciente domino faxit, adversus erum in solidum actio esto, si insciente, noxalis esto.

Sanctio

Si quis huiuscelegis ergo adversus leges rogationes plebisve scita fecit fecerit, sive quod eum ex lege rogatione plebisve scito facere oportebit, non fecerit huius legis ergo, id ei ne fraudi esto, neve quit ob eam rem populo dare debeto, neve cui de ea re actio neve iudicatio esto, neve quis de ea re apud se agi sinito.

Final Remarks – How We Should Treat Roman Sources

My essential purpose is to show some problems with textual reconstruction that scholars of ancient laws have had in the past, that they have now, and, I suppose, that they will have in the future. In order to do this, it was necessary to begin with some examples and some details. Of course, I do not pretend to say the last word on this subject, i.e. how to break the code of a particular ancient *lex*, but I think that some general remarks can be made.

1. All in all, I think that in the case of a textual reconstruction, one should firstly look at the text in which its author purports to give the actual wording of the *lex*.
2. Using not only legal sources, but non-legal as well, can have good effects, but in such a procedure a precise distinction should be made between the text that we have received and a historical notice about the law. Of course a text of law is a primary source.
3. Other useful criteria are: the social, economic and historical context of the moment when a *lex* was enacted. E.g., an origin of the *lex* is one of the most important aspects of this approach; e.g., the *lex Aquilia* is re-

garded as a part of legislative reform and certain phrases could be prepared because of it[79].

4. An integral approach is suggested, i.e. regarding the background of the legal sources, also non-Roman ones, which belongs to the common intellectual tradition. E.g., D. Daube based his reasoning several times on examples from the Bible or ancient Near-Eastern law codes (because of a list of cases, remedies, structure, casuistic, grammatical forms: if a man causes X, the legal consequence is Y etc.)[80]. There is no doubt now that in Rome the Twelve Tables belonged to the same scholastic legal tradition as that of the Near Eastern Codes. One can also say that according to evidence, the *lex Aquilia* also belongs to this tradition. Three laws in more or less casuistic form are organized in a pattern which matches exactly the type of structures in which these codes were organized, so a parallel is possible. But of course an Aquilian measure of damage appears to be much more sophisticated than that of the Twelve Tables or any of the Near Eastern Codes[81].
5. It was proven that when a text was particularly difficult, there was a tendency among ancient scribes and translators to simplify it by employing more fitting lexical, grammatical and stylistic forms; these modifications are called facilitating; so by using the criteria: *lectio difficilior potior*, one can find the most probable version.
6. The linguistic and lexical considerations are necessary, because the language has undergone a process of modernization.
7. Of course, the next question must be about interpolations. The juristic language used in the *Digesta* had to some extent undergone deformation by the time they were used. Also, as it was mentioned, the compilers of *Corpus Iuris Civilis* were not so scrupulous about exact wording. So, e.g., one cannot be sure that what one reads is exactly what

[79] See especially, Beinart (as in 12) pp. 70-80; Honoré (as in 12) pp. 145-150; Zimmermann (as in 13) pp. 955-957; Bignardi (as in 12) pp. 31-34. Also von Lübtow (as in 13) pp. 15-16; Birks (as in 35) pp. 181-186.

[80] As did Daube, David: Studies in Biblical Law. Cambridge 1947, pp. 74-85. See also comparative analyze done by Westbrook (as in 13) pp. 438-439, 450-462.

[81] See specially remarks of Westbrook (as in 13) p. 456, 458, 461, 470-471.

Gaius or Ulpianus said in their commentary on Edict, and of course – whether what they said was a real quotation of the *lex*. But of course I do not propose to go back to 'interpolation hunting', in its absurd excess, as it was years ago[82]. Aberrations in every field are dangerous.

8. Circumstantial evidence – some information can be deduced from the later extension of the scope of a source; e.g. in this case – can be deducted from the extension of an action to cover cases of negligent injury to the limbs of a person. Such an extension must clearly be made at the time the *lex* was concerned with. The plaintiff can claim not only the real value of his loss, but also his medical expenses, the loss of wages and the loss of earning capacity.

[82] On this subject see in general, e.g., Schiller, pp. 63-67; also Talamanca, Mario: Esperienza scientifica. Diritto romano. In: Cinquanta anni di esperienza giuridica in Italia, Messina/Taormina, 3-8 Novembre 1981. Milano 1981, pp. 683-753.

Verträge zugunsten Dritter, „Bedürfnisse des Verkehrs“ und Privatrechtsmentalität im Deutschland des frühen 19. Jahrhunderts

Dominik A. Thompson

Mythos „Begriffsjurisprudenz”

Geschichte wird kontinuierlich erlebt, aber in Perioden erinnert – so hörte ich es einmal Aleida Assmann sagen. In Bezug auf die Geschichte des Rechts und dessen Wissenschaft sah das Franz Wieacker wohl anders. Eine Abfolge von „methodischen Neueinsätzen“ gebe die Periodisierung der Rechtsentwicklung sozusagen aus sich selbst heraus vor.[1] Das sich daraus ergebende Bild ist sattsam bekannt. Naturrecht, Historische Rechtsschule, Pandektistik, Begriffsjurisprudenz, Germanistik, Romanistik, Interessensjurisprudenz, Wertungsjurisprudenz, Fortschritt, Rückschritt, das ist das Grundvokabular der heutigen Dogmengeschichte und wohl auch Methodenlehre. Vielleicht aber auch schon jenes der gestrigen. Denn das mit großen Schwüngen von der Hand alter Meister gemalte Schlachtengemälde hat in den letzten zwei, drei Jahrzehnten ein paar Risse abbekommen. Es stellte sich heraus, dass es eine einheitliche „Begriffsjurisprudenz“ nicht gegeben hat. Setzt man die Aussagen von Juristen über ihre Rolle im staatlichen Gefüge in Beziehung zum jeweiligen politisch-ideologischen Kontext, wird offenbar, dass Justiztheorie und Methodenlehre an die jeweilige politische Großwetterlage angepasst wurden, ohne dabei eine inhaltliche Änderung erfahren zu haben.[2]

Die Darstellung der juristischen Tätigkeit als die Ableitung von Lösungen aus einem vorgeblich lückenlosen System hatte demnach vor allem die Funk-

[1] Wieacker, Franz: Privatrechtsgeschichte der Neuzeit. Göttingen 1967, S. 20.

[2] Ogorek, Regina: Richterkönig oder Subsumtionsautomat? Zur Justiztheorie im 19. Jahrhundert. Frankurt/Main 1986, S. 169.

tion, das Rechtssystem nach außen hin abzusichern. Der Ausweis des Privatrechts als etwas, das der Jurist als aus dem Leben gewachsen erkennt, erfüllte so eine doppelte Funktion: zum einen wurde die Bindung des Juristen an das Recht als objektives Verhältnis dargestellt; zum anderen wurde es möglich, der Privatrechtswissenschaft gegenüber den argwöhnischen Landesherren der Restaurationszeit eine gewisse Autonomie zu zuschanzen.[3]

Dieser historische Befund deckt sich mit den Erkenntnissen jenes Teils der heutigen Rechtstheorie, der darum bemüht ist, eine gültige Beschreibung des Rechtssystems von einem allgemeinen, nicht juristischen Standpunkt aus zu erarbeiten. Aus sprachtheoretischer Sicht ist die Vorstellung vom Subsumtionsautomaten eine bedeutungsidealistische und damit unrichtige Verkürzung eines wesentlich komplexeren Vorganges. Und da eine Regel ihre eigene Anwendung nicht determinieren kann, sondern ihre Bedeutung erst dann hergestellt wird, wenn sie gebraucht wird, gilt das ebenso für die Vorstellung eines lückenlosen Begriffssystems, aus dem Lösungen abgeleitet werden sollen. Analytisch betrachtet ist Recht eine soziale Praxis, die sich in ihrer Ausübung selbst steuert.

Beide Erkenntnisse sind freilich bisher im juristischen Mainstream kaum wahrgenommen worden. Umso mehr hat die Vorstellung davon, wie im 19. Jahrhundert juristisch gedacht wurde, eine nicht unbeträchtliche Gegenwartsbedeutung. Die zu strengen Logikern hochstilisierten Juristen vor allem der Jahrhundertmitte dienen als künstlicher Gegenpunkt, um sich immer wieder der Modernität heutigen Zivilrechtsdenkens zu versichern. Das zeigt sich schon an der regelmäßig zu beobachtenden pejorativen Verwendung von »begriffsjuristisch« als ablehnender Bezeichnung für ein formales Argument. Die Existenz dieser Gegenwartsbedeutung ist freilich wenig verwunderlich – aus den eben vorgestellten Gründen ist jeder Zugriff auf Geschichte notwendig instrumentell geprägt.

Eine Untersuchung, die zum Ziel hat, einen Änderungsprozess in einem historischen Rechtssystem besser zu verstehen, könnte folglich die zeitgenössischen Methodenpositionen als unbedeutend zurückstellen. Denn wenn es

---

[3] Dahingehend wohl auch die Analyse bei Haferkamp, Hans-Peter: Georg Friedrich Puchta und die »Begriffsjurisprudenz«. Frankfurt/Main 2004.

stimmt, dass die juristische Nabelschau vor allem der Außenwirkung dient und überdies eine gewisse Theoriefixiertheit eine Eigenschaft ist, die vor allem bei akademischen Juristen anzutreffen ist, bedeutet das, dass die Faktoren, die die Bewegungen im juristischen System verursachen, an anderer Stelle zu suchen wären. Da Dogmengeschichte üblicherweise mit Blickrichtung auf das geltende Recht betrieben wird, kann sie die jeweils gültige Selbstbeschreibung (»Methodenlehre«) kaum kritisch hinterfragen. Weil man an die eigenen Selbstbeschreibungen glaubte – ich erwähne hier nur Karl Larenz und sein österreichisches Pendant Franz Bydlinski –, nahm man auch die Selbstbeschreibungen der historischen Juristen für bare Münze. Ich halte das für den eigentlichen Grund, warum die von Ogorek[4], Falk[5] und Haferkamp[6] eindrücklich belegte Zitatkette Jhering-Wilhelm[7]-Wieacker-Larenz entstanden ist. Sie geht Hand in Hand mit der Einteilung in Schulen und Perioden. Allerdings – und das ist das Problem – beinhaltet der Vorwurf der methodischen Strenge an jene Zeit auch eine entschieden inhaltliche Komponente.

Denn, so liest man immer wieder, das überstarke Festklammern am System habe verhindert, dass die Juristen der historischen Rechtsschule rechtzeitig erkannten, dass man auf die sich ändernden gesellschaftlichen Anforderungen hätte reagieren müssen. Aufgrund der methodischen Einstellung sei man unfähig dazu gewesen, auf „die mobilisierte […] und rationalisierte […] Wirtschaftsgesellschaft der beginnenden Industriellen Revolution"[8] adäquat zu reagieren. Dahingegen scheine es „heute naheliegend, dass Gesetzgebung, Rechtsprechung und Rechtswissenschaft die soziale und wirtschaftliche Realität ihrer Gesellschaft bewusst registrieren und zur eigentlichen Aufgabe ihrer Normen, Entscheidungen und Begriffsbildungen machen."[9]

---

[4] Siehe Fn 2.
[5] Falk, Ulrich: Ein Gelehrter wie Windscheid. Erkundungen auf den Feldern der sogenannten Begriffsjurisprudenz. Frankfurt/Main 1989.
[6] Siehe Fn 3.
[7] Wilhelm, Walter: Zur juristischen Methodenlehre im 19. Jahrhundert. Die Herkunft der Methode Paul Labands aus der Privatrechtswissenschaft. Frankfurt/Main 1958.
[8] Wieacker, Franz: Pandektenwissenschaft und Industrielle Revolution (1966). In: Industriegesellschaft und Privatrechtsordnung. Frankfurt am Main 1974, S. 65.
[9] Derselbe, aaO, S. 56.

Selbstverständlich war den Juristen des frühen 19. Jahrhunderts nicht klar, dass sie fortan in der »beginnenden Industriellen Revolution« leben würden. Dennoch ist damit die grundsätzliche Frage nach dem Zusammenhang von dogmatischem System, juristischem Selbstverständnis und gesellschaftlich induzierter Änderung aufgeworfen. Es handelt sich um ein allgemeines Problem, das sich – auch das darf man zum juristischen Allerweltswissen zählen – immer dann beobachten lässt, wenn beispielsweise technologische Entwicklungen zu Handlungsabläufen führen, die bis dahin gar nicht auftreten konnten. Ein bekanntes historisches Beispiel ist die Entwicklung der Gefährdungshaftung; ein heutiges Beispiel ist der gesamte immaterialgüterrechtliche Komplex, der momentan massiven Irritationen ausgesetzt ist. Heute folgt der Phase der Irritation über das Justizsystem unmittelbar eine Phase der explizit politischen Agitation. Was die deutschen Juristen des 19. Jahrhunderts allerdings die längste Zeit nicht zur Verfügung hatten, war ein aktiver Gesetzgeber. Deshalb war die Änderung von privatrechtlichen Regeln in einen vorgeblich unpolitischen Bereich verwiesen: Das Areal des Volksgeistes, der Gewohnheit, der Sitte, der praktischen Bedürfnisse, der Rechtsüberzeugung und dergleichen mehr, also jener Bereich, der sich etwa auch im Umfeld von Generalklauseln findet.

Ausgehend von diesen Überlegungen wollte ich ein Beispiel von nichtlegislativer Privatrechtsentwicklung unter Beachtung der angesprochenen Aspekte untersuchen. Am besten eignet sich dafür ein möglichst technisches, dogmatisches und insofern auch trockenes Problem, das eben deshalb – zumindest auf den ersten Blick – nicht mit spezifischen Interessen verknüpft werden kann.

Ein solches Problem ist die Entwicklung der echten Verträge zugunsten Dritter im 19. Jahrhundert, die ich im Rahmen meiner Doktorarbeit untersuche. Mein Analysebereich ist fokussiert auf das deutsche gemeine Recht, weil die Lage in Preußen und Österreich, wo es Kodifikationen gab, mit jeweils einem bestimmten Standpunkt der gemeinrechtlichen Diskussion identisch ist. Der Untersuchungszeitraum wurde mit ca. 1790 bis 1870 festgelegt.

Verträge zugunsten Dritter

Zunächst ist das dogmatische Feld abzustecken. Hintergrundfolie ist das unvermeidliche Corpus Iuris, sozusagen der gemeinsame Reibebaum der juristischen Neuzeit. Das zu betonen ist wichtig, es geht nicht um „Römisches Recht", sondern um ein Textformular als Referenzpunkt. Aus heutiger Beurteilung handelte es sich beim älteren gemeinen Recht, das aus der Auseinandersetzung mit dieser Textmasse hervorgegangen war, um ein Privatrecht ohne unmittelbare/direkte Stellvertretung, ohne echte Verträge zugunsten Dritter und ohne materielle Zession; am Vertragsschluss unbeteiligte Dritte konnten nur in wenigen Ausnahmefällen daraus Rechte erlangen.[10] Am Ende stehen die §§ 328 ff. BGB, deren maximale Ausnutzung identisch ist mit einem Gesetzgebungsvorschlag, den erstmals Joseph Unger 1869 an den Schluss einer langen Abhandlung zum Vertrag zugunsten Dritter setzte.[11]

Die Entwicklung dorthin wird gerne als langwieriger Kampf gegen das Dogma alteri stipulari nemo potest dargestellt.[12] Ich meine, dass der rechtshistorische Erkenntnisgewinn eher gering ist, wenn man die momentan gültige Definition eines vorliegenden Rechtsinstituts als Maßstab nimmt, mit dessen Hilfe man sich dann auf die Suche nach dem frühesten Entdecker macht. Denn verfügt man nicht über Kenntnisse des kontinentaleuropäischen Zivilrechts des 20. Jahrhunderts, dann erscheint die Regel alteri stipulari nemo potest nicht als ein Verbot der Rechtsinstitute von Stellvertretung und von Verträgen zugunsten Dritter – die ja unbekannt waren – sondern zu allererst als Grundregel des Vertragsrechts, die in der Form einer negativen Parömie eine Eigenschaft der Stipulation und damit des Vertrages definierte. Daher erscheint es sinnvoller, für die Arbeit am Problem davon auszugehen, dass die Regel in ihrer eleganten Einfachheit nicht nur die Möglichkeit einer Drittbe-

---

[10] Siehe dazu Coing, Helmut: Europäisches Privatrecht Bd. I. München 1985, S. 423 ff; Wesenberg, Gerhard: Verträge zugunsten Dritter. Weimar 1949; Müller, Gerhard: Die Entwicklung der direkten Stellvertretung und des Vertrages zugunsten Dritter. Stuttgart 1969.

[11] Unger, Joseph: Die Verträge zu Gunsten Dritter. In: Jherings Jahrbücher Bd. 10 1869, S. 1-109. Zum 20. Jahrhundert siehe Bayer, Walter: Der Vertrag zugunsten Dritter. Tübingen 1995.

[12] Siehe etwa Zimmermann, Reinhard: The Law of Obligations. Roman Foundations of the Civilian Tradition. Ducksburgh 1990, S. 42 ff.

rechtigung (und -verpflichtung) ausschloss und darin nicht zwischen Stellvertretung und Verträgen zu Gunsten Dritter unterschied, sondern dass sie gerade deshalb das Konzept der Relativität von vertraglichen Forderungen im Corpus Iuris näher bestimmte. Die Regel war im gleichen Ausmaß auch sinnfälliger Ausdruck dafür, dass jemand ohne eigene Handlung und ohne Anwendung anderer, besonderer Rechtsregeln aus einem Vertrag weder Rechte noch Pflichten erfahren konnte. Vinculum iuris und alteri stipulari nemo potest mussten den damaligen Juristen als zwei Seiten derselben Münze erschienen sein.

„Vertrag zugunsten Dritter" bedeutete daher, für sich allein genommen, keineswegs immer das gleiche, da noch gar nicht feststand, was darunter genau zu verstehen sei. Umgekehrt muss eine rechtliche Vereinbarung, die man heute als Vertrag zugunsten Dritter bezeichnen würde, nicht unbedingt so bezeichnet worden sein.

Für die vorliegende Fragestellung erscheint daher eine Orientierung am heutigen Begriff des Vertrages zugunsten Dritter ungeeignet. Der Ausweg besteht in einer funktionalen Bestimmung des Sachproblems, die sowohl von alteri stipulari nemo potest als auch von den Paragraphen des BGB abstrahiert. Sie muss berücksichtigen, dass im Untersuchungszeitraum weder eine einheitliche Rechtsgeschäftslehre, noch eine klar definierte Stellvertretungslehre, eine Lehre von der materiellen Zession, ein Anspruchsbegriff oder die freie Beweiswürdigung im Prozess[13] etabliert waren. Darüber hinaus sind Anknüpfungspunkte im Erb- und Familienrecht zu beachten, ebenso wie der Einfluss von handelsrechtlichen Elementen.

[13] Damit ist weniger das Vorhandensein eines festen Systems aus Beweisarten gemeint, sondern die Frage, wie freizügig Richter mit spärlich formulierten Parteiaussagen umgingen und diese etwa wohlwollend umdeuteten. Siehe dazu die bei Fn. 34 angesprochenen Verträge.

Dogmatischer Analyseraster

Der Sachverhalt:

A vereinbart mit B, an diesen eine Leistung zu erbringen, damit im Austausch B eine Leistung an den unbeteiligten C erbringt. C erfährt später davon und klagt B auf Leistung.

Hier lässt sich in Bezug auf die Verteilung der Leistungen zwischen Stellvertretung und Vertrag zugunsten Dritter kein Unterschied ausmachen. Die dogmatische Einordnung hängt somit vom konkreten Vertragsinhalt ab, dem Ursprung nach also typischerweise vom Verhalten des Versprechensempfängers. Nicht nur müsste deutlich werden, dass der Dritte Gläubiger werden soll, sondern ebenso, ob er dies als Vertretener oder Begünstigter wird. Anders als etwa beim Handkauf wird hier von den Parteien die Bildung eines Willens in Bezug auf eine relativ technische Frage verlangt.

Zunächst ist zu fragen, ob es vorkam, dass die Parteien den Dritten explizit als Klageberechtigten bezeichneten, und falls nicht, ob und wie den Vertragsparteien dieser Wunsch implizit oder explizit unterstellt wurde. Die nahe liegende Annahme, dass die Ergänzung des Parteiwillens unter Rückgriff auf eine Art typischen Parteiwillen erfolgte, ist zu überprüfen. Denn dieser konnte nicht aus den Rechtsregeln selbst, sondern nur aus Anschauungen darüber, zu welchem Zweck solche Geschäfte üblicherweise abgeschlossen wurden, erfolgen.

In einem zweiten Schritt ist nachzuvollziehen, welche dogmatischen Konstruktionen gewählt wurden, um der Absicht der Parteien, dem Dritten eine Klage zu verschaffen, zu einem Erfolg zu verhelfen. In Ermangelung einheitlicher und klarer Regeln zur Drittberechtigung sind ex ante verschiedene Wege denkbar. Es erschien mir hilfreich, der konkreten Analyse eine Art abstrakte Exegese vor dem Hintergrund des gemeinen Rechts voranzustellen, um so das Material besser ordnen zu können.

Eine Möglichkeit zur Herstellung von Unterscheidbarkeit schüfe hier etwa die Einführung eines Offenlegungsprinzips im Sinne der heutigen Stellvertretungslehre. Dies offenbart eine Verbindungslinie zur Rechtsgeschäftslehre: Kombiniert man Offenlegungsprinzip und eine Betonung des Willens im rechtsgeschäftlichen Mechanismus, scheitert das Grundgeschäft in der angesprochenen Konstellation am mangelnden Konsens. Insofern ist die Frage aufgeworfen, inwiefern die sog. Willenstheorie die kreative Suche nach Lösungsmöglichkeiten zur Erhaltung des Grundgeschäfts befördert hat.

Eine andere Möglichkeit bestünde darin, das Konzept von Schuldverhältnis und Stellvertretung dahingehend auszuformen, dass eine Spaltung von Schuldner- und Gläubigerstellung bei Vorhandensein eines Vertretungsverhältnisses nicht möglich ist – mit anderen Worten: dass im vorliegenden Fall nicht der Versprechensempfänger durch eigene Erklärung zugleich Schuldner des Versprechenden und Vertreter des Dritten in Bezug auf dessen Gläubigerstellung sein kann.

Würde hingegen vertreten, dass eine nachfolgende ratihabitio durch den Dritten rechtlich oder faktisch nicht möglich sei, bliebe die Deutungsmöglichkeit als Stellvertretung verschlossen. Dies wäre etwa der Fall, wenn man die Möglichkeit einer ratihabitio bei Klagserhebung ausschlösse oder ein Stellvertretungsverhältnis nur dann zuließe, wenn dem Vertragsabschluss durch den Vertreter ein mandatum des Vertretenen vorausgegangen wäre. Freilich könnte hier ein besonders weites Verständnis der Geschäftsführung ohne Auftrag einen Ausweg darstellen – doch auch das nur dann, wenn man meint, dies könne zu einer Forderung des Dritten gegen den Versprechenden führen.

Das gleiche Ergebnis ließe sich durch die Konstruktion einer gemeinschaftlichen Offerte erzielen: Man versteht das Grundgeschäft als ein Art Vertragsangebot an den Dritten, der dieses durch Erklärung annehmen kann (mit einhergehender Spaltung des Grundvertrages).

Vor dem Hintergrund des römisch-kanonischen Zivilprozesses stünden zusätzlich zwei prozessuale Mittel zur Verfügung. Zum einen die formelle Zession: Der Dritte macht mit Einverständnis des Versprechensempfängers dessen Klage geltend. Zum anderen eine actio utilis oder actio in factum (in der Diktion des gemeinen Rechts mitunter „nützliche Klagen“), aber nur dann, falls diese auch dazu verwendet werden konnten, um eine mangelnde Voraussetzung des Vertragsrechts zu überbrücken.

Allen diesen dogmatischen Deutungsmöglichkeiten ist allerdings gemeinsam, dass der Dritte für den Rechtserwerb eine Handlung setzen muss, was notwendigerweise auch Kenntnis über Existenz und Inhalt des Grundgeschäftes voraussetzt. Demgegenüber steht am Endpunkt dieser Entwicklung die

Möglichkeit eines unmittelbaren Rechtserwerbs des Dritten im Zeitpunkt des Vertragsabschlusses, ohne dass überhaupt seine Kenntnis des Vertrages erforderlich wäre.

Rechtsexterne Faktoren

In der vorhandenen Literatur ist man sich darüber einig, dass als Auslöser für diesen komplexen Prozess Hofübergabsverträge, Wittwenkassen und besonders das Aufkommen der Lebensversicherung „eine Rolle gespielt haben."[14]

- Hofübergabsverträge

Das bisherige Bauernpaar zieht sich von der Führung des Hofes zurück und übergibt den Hof an einen der Söhne. Diesem werden im Rahmen des Übergabsvertrags diverse Verpflichtungen gegenüber Dritten auferlegt; typischerweise Geschwistern, Nachbarn oder diversen Kreditgebern wie etwa der Kirche. Es handelt sich dabei um eine alte Praxis, die auch schon vor der Bauernbefreiung im lehensrechtlichen System nachweisbar ist, dort allerdings offenbar von der Genehmigung des Grundherren abhing.[15]

- Witwen- und Waisenkassen

Eine vorindustrielle Form der Hinterbliebenenvorsorge, die in ihrer Urform allerdings nicht auf versicherungsmathematischer Grundlage beruht. Der Ehemann zahlt einen statutenmäßig bestimmten Kapitalbetrag und/oder regelmäßig Beiträge ein, nach seinem Ableben erhalten Witwe bzw. Kinder ebenfalls typischerweise jährlich für alle Begünstigten in gleicher Höhe festgelegte Zahlungen (kein Umlageverfahren im eigentlichen Sinn, da keine Bindung zwischen ein- und ausgezahltem Kapital bestand). Seit Mitte des 18.

---

[14] Zusammenfassend Coing, Helmut: Europäisches Privatrecht Bd II: 19. Jahrhundert. München 1989, S. 453.

[15] Eine moderne Untersuchung konnte ich nicht finden, zeitgenössischer Text: Puchta, Wolfgang Heinrich: Ueber die rechtliche Natur der bäuerlichen Gutsabtretung überhaupt und mit Althenteilsbestellung besonders. Giessen 1837.

Jahrhunderts überall im Reich gegründet. Typische Form der Vorsorge für Beamte und Offiziere. Ab der zweiten Hälfte des 19. Jahrhunderts allmählich entweder auf versicherungsmathematische Grundlage gestellt oder von der privaten Lebensversicherung verdrängt.[16]

• Lebensversicherung

Vorausgeschickt sei, dass der Zugriff auf die Geschichte der Lebensversicherung dadurch erschwert wird, dass der Großteil der dazu verfügbaren Arbeiten zumindest in enger Verzahnung mit der Versicherungsindustrie erstellt wurde und daher oft die nötige Distanz zum untersuchten Objekt vermissen lässt.[17] Die ersten Lebensversicherungsunternehmen, die das Alter bei der Berechnung berücksichtigten, wurden gegen Ende des 18. Jahrhunderts in England gegründet; von dort wanderte die Lebensversicherung, wie auch andere Versicherungsformen, über den Norddeutschen Raum ein – das Bindeglied war der Seehandel, der schon früh von Versicherungsformen Gebrauch machte. Die ersten Gründungen in Deutschland, die operativ bestehen konnten, erfolgten ab 1829 in Gotha, kurz danach Lübeck; 1831 in Leipzig und Hannover.[18] Im Unterschied zu den Witwenkassen handelt es sich hier um industrielle Unternehmungen, die von Anfang an als Gesellschaften mit entsprechendem Kapitalstock errichtet wurden und auf versicherungsmathematischer Grundlage arbeiteten. Die Entwicklung der modernen Statistik ist eng mit der Entwicklung des Lebensversicherungswesens verknüpft.

Betrachtet man diese Faktoren, die zur Entwicklung des Vertrages zu Gunsten Dritter geführt haben sollen, gemeinsam, so fällt auf, dass sie alle deutlich älter sind als die moderne Konzeption. Hofübergabsverträge hingegen gab es wohl schon seit Alters her; Witwenkassen waren spätestens seit Ende des 18. Jh. weit verbreitet. Selbst wenn man berücksichtigt, dass die Le-

---

[16] Braun, Heinrich: Geschichte der Lebensversicherung und der Lebensversicherungstechnik. 2. Aufl., Berlin 1963, S. 170 ff.

[17] Treffende Worte bei Borscheid, Peter: Die Entstehung der deutschen Lebensversicherungswirtschaft im 19. Jahrhundert. In: Vierteljahresschrift für Sozial- und Wirtschaftsgeschichte Bd. 70 (1983), S. 305-330, 305 f. m.w.N.

[18] Braun (wie Anm. 16), S. 212 ff.

bensversicherungen wohl Zeit gebraucht haben werden, um akzeptiert zu werden – eine aussagekräftige Korrelierung von statistischen Daten über die Anzahl der Polizzen und Versicherungssummen mit Bevölkerungs- und Wirtschaftswachstum hat meines Wissens noch niemand unternommen – liegen immer noch Jahrzehnte zwischen dem Auftreten der Lebensversicherung in Deutschland und der Schaffung des vertraglichen Vehikels, dessen Existenz die Lebensversicherungswirtschaft nach heutigem Verständnis dringend bedarf.

Rechtsexterne Faktoren in der Rechtsprechung

Eine umfassende, systematische Analyse der Rechtsprechung wird durch die vorhin beschriebene Vielgesichtigkeit des dogmatischen Problems bedeutend erschwert. In Bezug auf die Sachverhalte bietet sich ein anderes Bild. Den Großteil nehmen in der Tat Übergabsverträge ein, wenn auch nicht von Bauernhöfen, sondern von Liegenschaften aller Art, u. a. auch Handwerksbetrieben. Dahingegen konnte ich kaum Urteile zu Witwenkassen entdecken.[19] Die Lebensversicherung taucht überhaupt erst ab Mitte der 60er Jahre in der Rechtsprechung auf. So enthält etwa die zeitgenössische Fallsammlung von Busch 62 Urteile verschiedener Oberappellationsgerichte, von denen kein einziges Witwenkassen oder Lebensversicherung behandelt.[20]

Ein Blick auf die verwendeten juristischen Argumente zeigt, dass es tatsächlich nicht auf die Frage der Geltung von alteri stipulari nemo potest ankam. Die Fortgeltung des Prinzips wird fallweise verneint, fallweise bejaht, aber dennoch durch eine Umwegskonstruktion ausgehebelt. Auffallend ist, dass die auf Leistung geklagte Partei sich regelmäßig auf die Geltung von alteri stipulari nemo potest beruft. In den Urteilen finden sich keine Hinweise auf den „Ver-

---

[19] Der Nachweis bei Bayer, Walter: Der Vertrag zugunsten Dritter. Tübingen 1995, S. 70 Fn. 347 geht ins Leere – die Urteile behandeln zwar Witwenkassen, teilen aber bloss mit, dass mit dem Tod des Ehemannes das Verhältnis der Witwe zur Kasse »das ganz einfache Verhältnis von Gläubigern und Schuldnern« werde (Pfeiffer: Die rechtlichen Verhältnisse der Wittwencassen. In: Zeitschrift für deutsches Recht und deutsche Rechtswissenschaft Bd. 9 1845, S. 440-486, 486).

[20] Busch, Ferdinand Benjamin: Doctrin und Praxis über die Gültigkeit von Verträgen zu Gunsten Dritter. Heidelberg 1860.

kehr", sondern – falls überhaupt begründet wird – allenfalls auf eine „deutschrechtliche Praxis" (dazu sogleich). In der Regel wird dem Dritten von den Gerichten das Klagerecht nicht grundsätzlich verweigert. In Bezug auf die notwendige Erwerbshandlung herrschte keine Einigkeit. War sie nicht vor Klagserhebung erfolgt, ließen manche Gerichte die Klagserhebung selbst als solche gelten, andere verweigerten dies. Das Hauptproblem scheint ein anderes gewesen zu sein: es kam vor, dass die Parteien des Grundvertrages diesen nach Tod des Promissars wieder aufhoben. In diesem Fall wurde schlagend, ob der Dritte zuvor eine Erwerbshandlung gesetzt und diese den Rechtserwerb unwiderruflich gemacht hatte. Die Gerichte setzten daher die Tradition des älteren gemeinen Rechts, wie man sie etwa schon bei Glück[21] findet, fort.[22] Trotz aller Unterschiedlichkeit in der Konstruktion erhielt im Ergebnis der Dritte ein Forderungsrecht, sofern er eine entsprechende Handlung gesetzt hatte.

Zurück zur Dogmatik

In der akademischen Literatur des 19. Jh. findet sich hingegen keine »einfache« Konstruktion der Problemlage. Auch hier schlägt eine Zentrierung auf alteri stipulari nemo potest fehl. Was freilich von Wieacker und den ihm folgenden Autoren als „Zurückdrehen des Rades der Rechtsentwicklung"[23] bewertet wurde, weicht inhaltlich von der Position des älteren gemeinen Rechts nicht ab – der Dritte muss, um das Recht erwerben zu können, zumindest eine entsprechende Handlung setzen.

Konkrete Verweise auf Urteile waren in der akademischen Literatur des frühen 19. Jahrhunderts nicht üblich. Aus den Texten geht freilich hervor, dass alle Juristen die Praxis der Gerichte kannten. Konkrete Problemlagen werden allerdings in dogmatischen Monographien nicht berichtet. Hinweise

---

[21] Glück, Christian Friedrich: Ausführliche Erläuterung der Pandecten nach Hellfeld. 2. Aufl., Erlangen 1797, S. 564.

[22] Ähnlich schon Scheuermann, Reimund: Einflüsse der historischen Rechtsschule auf die oberstrichterliche gemeinrechtliche Zivilrechtspraxis bis zum Jahre 1861. Berlin 1972, S. 103 ff, der aber nur auf die Einstellung zu alteri stipulari abstellt.

[23] Bayer, Walter: Der Vertrag zugunsten Dritter. Tübingen 1995, S. 66.

gibt es nur in Aufsätzen von unbekannteren Juristen und Handbüchern für die Praxis.

Seuffert etwa behandelt den Sachverhalt in einer Kombination aus Geschäftsführung ohne Auftrag und Zession im Sinne Mühlenbruchs, was im Ergebnis auf das gleiche hinausläuft.[24] Zentrale Stelle waren aber jene viel zitierten kargen Ausführungen, die Savigny in seinem Obligationenrecht den Verträgen zu Gunsten Dritter widmete, ohne den Begriff selbst zu verwenden. Diese seien nämlich „vom Standpunkt einer richtigen Theorie [...] schlechthin zu verwerfen."[25] Er offeriert eine Lösung über Stellvertretung,[26] was „für den praktischen Erfolg [...] in den meisten wichtigen Anwendungen"[27] ausreichen sollte.

Auch Puchta behandelt die Problematik traditionell als Stellvertretungsfall. So wie Savigny akzeptiert er die gewillkürte, unmittelbare Stellvertretung als den „Exigenzen des Verkehrs"[28] geschuldet. Er geht aber einen Schritt weiter: Der Durchgangserwerb über den Promissar sei dennoch aufgrund der Sicherheit des Verkehrs notwendig. „Dies reicht vollkommen für das Bedürfniß aus. Das Princip, welches dabei festgehalten wird, und das allein eine bestimmte richtige Feststellung des Verhältnisses möglich macht, ist, daß die Obligatio durch den Repräsentanten hindurch geht."[29] Beide ziehen sich also nicht auf das nackte Dogma zurück, sondern argumentieren auch, warum ihre Lösung die beste sei.

---

[24] Seuffert, Johann Adam: Lehrbuch des praktischen Pandektenrechts. Würzburg 1825, S. 204.

[25] Savigny, Friedrich Carl von: Das Obligationenrecht als Theil des heutigen Römischen Rechts. Berlin 1853, S. 84.

[26] Und zwar der »zweiten Art«, siehe dazu Savigny a.a.O., 78. Spätere Juristen wie etwa Busch (wie Fn. 20) und Unger (wie Fn. 11) haben diesen Kniff in der Stellvertretungslehre Savignys – Stellvertretung, ohne dass der Vertreter zu erkennen gibt, dass er für einen anderen kontrahiert – offenbar nicht mehr verstanden.

[27] Wie Fn 25.

[28] Puchta, Georg Friedrich: Pandekten. Hrsg. von Rudorff, 9. Aufl., Leipzig 1863, S. 431. Ein Auflagenvergleich ist von mir noch durchzuführen.

[29] Puchta, Georg Friedrich: Vorlesungen über das heutige römische Recht. 4. Aufl., Leipzig 1854, S. 117.

Die komplexen Konstruktionen der Pandektistik lassen sich somit als Rückübersetzung der Praxis in das dogmatische System deuten.[30] Nicht anders die Lage bei jenen, die üblicherweise als »Germanisten« bezeichnet werden: Sie verneinen durchwegs die Geltung von alteri stipulari nemo potest, verlangen aber für den Rechtserwerb ebenfalls eine Handlung.[31]

Im Ergebnis stellt sich heraus, dass die Frage nach der Gültigkeit von alteri stipulari nemo potest ebenso wie Frage nach der Gültigkeit von VzD in jener Zeit Scheinprobleme waren; tatsächlich bestand inhaltliche Kontinuität bis in die zweite Hälfte des 19. Jh. hinein. Was sich niemand hatte vorstellen können war, dass jemand ohne Wissen und Wollen Gläubiger eines ihm fremden Vertrages werden konnte.

Demgegenüber lässt sich schon 1798 bei Claproth der Hinweis finden, dass die nicht zum Übergabsvertrag hinzugezogenen Kinder diesen schon deshalb nicht anfechten könnten, solange sie nicht in ihrem Pflichtteil verletzt worden wären.[32] Noch 1837 gibt W. H. Puchta das Problem inhaltsgleich wieder;[33] die von ihm angeführten Beispielsverträge lassen erkennen, dass in den Übergabsverträgen nur undifferenziert von „Zahlung an [einen Dritten]“ die Rede war, diese aber nicht explizit als Gläubiger bezeichnet worden waren.[34] Im Revolutionsjahr hält Kirchmann seine berühmte Rede, die in ihrem inhaltlichen Teil auch den konkreten Vorwurf enthält, man habe bei der Erarbeitung des ALR auf den Bauernstand vergessen, weil dessen Erfordernis eines Schuldbeitritts beim Vertrag zugunsten Dritter (§ 75) der Praxis der Hofüber-

---

[30] Ob es sich dabei um das berüchtigte »Kryptonaturrecht« handelt, vermag ich nicht zu beurteilen.

[31] So etwa Beseler, Georg: Die Lehre von den Erbverträgen. Göttingen 1837, S. 76 und S. 80.

[32] Claproth, Justus: Rechtswissenschaft von richtiger und vorsichtiger Eingehung der Verträge und Contracte. 4. Aufl., Göttingen 1798, S. 1101 f. Ihm ging es freilich nicht um die Frage, wie die nicht hinzugezogenen Kinder die versprochene Leistung einfordern können.

[33] Puchta (wie in Fn. 15), S. 96.

[34] Puchta (wie in Fn. 15), S. 80 ff. Windscheid führt die Differenzierung in einen Vertrag mit Leistung an einen Dritten und zu Gunsten eines Dritten erst in der 4. Auflage seines Pandektenrechts ein (1875, §§ 316 f).

gabe widerstreite und daher in Preußen zu den „unerträglichsten Härten" geführt habe.[35]

Anpassungsdruck?

In der Tat scheint es also zwischen der Dogmatik der Pandektisten und dem Leben dort draußen durchaus erhebliche Diskrepanzen gegeben zu haben. Doch bedeutet das notwendigerweise Ignoranz aus prinzipieller Überzeugung, wie das Wieacker interpretiert hat? Ich halte für wahrscheinlicher, dass die angesprochenen Problemlagen einfach aus dem Fokus gefallen sind.

Zum einen gibt es Indizien dafür, dass weder Übergabsverträge, noch Witwenkassen und Lebensversicherung ursprünglich als Probleme des (bürgerlichen) Privatrechts betrachtet wurden.

Wie bereits oben ausgeführt, war die Übergabepraxis unter Bauern schon vor der Bauernbefreiung vorhanden, hatte aber unter Aufsicht des Grundherren stattgefunden. In der ersten Hälfte des 19. Jahrhunderts entstand eine Diskussion über die rechtliche Qualifizierung dieser Verträge, womit unter anderem eine komplexe erbrechtliche Problematik verbunden war. Ob es sich um ein deutsches Rechtsinstitut sui generis, einen Unterfall der Leibrente oder doch um einen Vertrag zugunsten Dritter handelte, war umstritten. Hinzu kam die Frage eines bäuerlichen Sonderrechts.[36]

Ebenso waren die Witwenkassen ursprünglich mit landesherrlichen Interessen verschränkt und nehmen daher ihren Ausgang bei der Guten Policey. Auch hier entstand in der Mitte des 19. Jahrhunderts eine Diskussion über die korrekte rechtliche Einordnung des bereits bestehenden Phänomens, die ein ähnlich inhomogenes Bild zeigt wie die Übergabsproblematik.[37] So hatte etwa das ABGB von 1811 trotz des Verbotes des Vertrages zugunsten Dritter in

---

[35] Kirchmann, Julius Hermann von: Die Werthlosigkeit der Jurisprudenz als Wissenschaft. Berlin 1848, S. 28 f.

[36] Eingehend Puchta (wie in Fn. 15).

[37] Siehe Pfeiffer: Die rechtlichen Verhältnisse der Wittwencassen. In: Zeitschrift für deutsches Recht und deutsche Rechtswissenschaft Bd. 9 (1845), S. 440-486.

§ 881 eine eigene Bestimmung zu Witwenkassen enthalten (§ 1287), ohne beides in Zusammenhang zu bringen.

Die Lebensversicherung wiederum galt ursprünglich als Angelegenheit des (See-)Handelsrechts,[38] was auch ihre enge Verzahnung mit dem Wertpapierrecht erklärt. Die Polizze hatte offenbar konstitutive Wirkung und wurde in der Regel als Inhaberpapier gestaltet.[39] Die Begünstigte musste daher, ebenso wie beim Vertrag zugunsten Dritter nach gemeinem Recht, zuvor eine Erwerbshandlung gesetzt haben, um in den Genuss der Leistung kommen zu können. Noch in den 50er Jahren war unklar, ob die Lebensversicherung zum Handelsrecht oder zum allgemeinen Privatrecht zuzuordnen wäre.[40] Klarheit schuf das ADHGB 1863, es regelte nur noch die Seeversicherung (Artt. 782 ff), nicht aber die Lebensversicherung.

Zusammengefasst scheint es wahrscheinlicher, dass nicht methodische Umbrüche oder ein Schulenstreit den Anpassungsdruck auf die Dogmatik des bürgerlichen Rechts ausgelöst haben, sondern eher die allmähliche Vereinigung der Rechtsschichten in einem dennoch kodifikationslosen Zustand.
Bei all dem ist im Schrifttum eine gewisse Sorge um das Schicksal der Witwe und der Kinder nicht zu übersehen. Unger stützte seine Argumentation für den unmittelbaren Rechtserwerb des Dritten auffallend auf die arme Witwe.[41] Denn Bewegung war in die Sache offenbar erst gekommen, als etwa ab den 60er Jahren die Gläubiger die Lebensversicherungssumme als potentielles Befriedigungsobjekt entdeckt hatten. Nunmehr wurde die Frage des Rechtserwerbs des Dritten mit der Frage verbunden, ob das von der Versorgungsan-

---

[38] Siehe etwa Benecke, Wilhelm: System des Assekuranz- und Bodmereiwesens. Hamburg 1810. Der Autor hatte kurz vor Erscheinen die erste Lebensversicherungsanstalt Deutschlands gegründet, die aber nach wenigen Jahren ihren Betrieb aus finanziellen Gründen wieder einstellen musste. Im ALR fungiert die Versicherung überhaupt im handelsrechtlichen Teil, §§ 1934 ff.

[39] Wolff: Bildet die Lebensversicherungssumme einen Theil des Nachlasses des Versicherten, und sind insbesondere die Gläubiger des Versicherten befugt, ihre Befriedigung aus dieser Versicherungssumme zu fordern? In: Zeitschrift für das gesammte Handelsrecht Bd. 12 (1868), S. 169-190, 174.

[40] Umfassend Staudinger, Julius von: Die Rechtslehre vom Lebensversicherungsvertrag. Erlangen 1858.

[41] Unger (wie in Fn. 11), 75.

stalt ausbezahlte Kapital in den Nachlass falle oder nicht.[42] War es am Ende die bürgerliche Witwe, die man aus Pietätsgründen vor der Armut schützen musste? Zu dieser letzten Hypothese hoffe ich, demnächst Genaueres vorlegen zu können.

[42] Siehe etwa OAG München, Entscheidung vom 11. Februar 1868. In: Blätter für Rechtsanwendung/Ergänzungsband 1 (1869), S. 367 f.

Dealing with the Nazi Past of Legal Scholars in the Classroom*

Viktor Winkler

"In the last analysis, the law is what lawyers are. And the law and the lawyers are what the law schools make them."
Felix Frankfurter[1]

A. The Case of the Serial Killer

As a lawyer let me start with a case: Mister X is a successful law student; he is rather bookish so he strives for an academic career, writes his *Habilitation* thesis and after ten years he secures a chair for legal philosophy. Mister X has written a number of highly successful textbooks and his other publications are widely read. Now we all find out that Mister X is a serial killer; over the last decade he has killed 25 people in the most atrocious way. He is sentenced to life and put to jail. Now the question of the case: Will we still read his books? Will we quote him in scholarly articles? And more importantly: Will we keep using his textbooks to teach young lawyers who want to learn more about, let's say, "The Idea of Justice", one of his bestsellers? You may find the case

---

* The text is presented here as delivered at the Forum. I thank Okko Behrends, Christian Bernd, Michael Brück, Izhak Englard, Ralf Frassek, Thomas Henne, Miriam Saage, Jourden Moger, Travis Ritz, Joachim Rückert, Klaus Schäfer, Folker Schmerbach, Alexander Somek, Andreas Walter and Peer Zumbansen for many discussions on this subject over the years. This article is dedicated to Robin Pierson, who opened my eyes for the place of empathy in legal education.
[1] Letter to Mr. Rosenwald (May 13, 1927), quoted from Edwards, Harry T.: The Growing Disjunction Between Legal Education and the Legal Profession. In: Michigan Law Review (1992) vol. 91, pp. 34ff.

inappropriately bloody, and you might quickly add: Of course we wouldn't. But why wouldn't we? Again, some might say: if his scholarly writing is of indispensable value to jurisprudence we would still deal with it, be it as it may. But how about a variation: What if Mister X were a child molestor, what if he were a serial pedophile rapist? I am rather sure now everybody would stop reading his books in legal academia. But the question remains why?

The jurists I am dealing with today were none of what Mister X is. None had killed anyone, none had physically pushed anyone into the holocaust. But my thesis is that by dealing with their past we inevitably have to answer the same question that we have to answer with Mister X. The standards we use are the same. But what are they?

First I have to clarify what I am dealing with: I am talking here about a number of authors who collaborated with the Nazi regime and whose books have become highly popular and highly influential in legal scholarship after 1945. I would like to point out:

Karl Larenz' "*Methodenlehre*" (4th ed. by Claus-Wilhelm Canaris),[2]
Franz Wieacker's "*Privatrechtsgeschichte der Neuzeit*" (2nd ed. 1967),
Erik Wolf's "*Grosse Rechtsdenker*" (4th ed. 1963),
Ernst Rudolf Huber's "*Deutsche Verfassungsgeschichte*" (7 vol. 1957-84),
but also Ernst Forsthoff's "*Staat der Industriegesellschaft*" (1971),

just to name those that are closest to my *own* scholarly interest. But there are other major influential textbooks, mostly written for use in legal education, such as:

Karl Larenz' "*Allgemeiner Teil*" (9th ed. 2004 pursued by M.Wolf),
Theodor Maunz' "*Staatsrecht*" (31st ed. 2005 pursued by R.Zippelius),
Ernst Forsthoff's "*Verwaltungsrecht*" (1958),
Hans-Jürgen Bruns' "*Strafzumessungsrecht*" (2nd ed. 1974),
Friedrich Schaffstein's "*Jugendstrafrecht*" (14th ed. 2002 by W.Beulke),
Heinrich Lehmann's "*Schuldrecht*" (15th ed. 1958),

---

[2] Expected for October 2006.

Georg Dahm's "*Deutsches Recht*" (2nd ed. 1963),
Edmund Mezger's "*Strafrecht*" (12th ed. 1983 by H.Blei),
Hans Welzel's "*Strafrecht*" (11th ed. 1969).

This list is, of course, by no means exhaustive. And it is important to note that there were also *practitioners* writing or editing influential scholarly works after WW II (such as Eduard Dreher or Franz Schlegelberger). Also, in the classroom the problem of the Nazi past is not limited to the use of textbooks. Instead, students are faced with this problem on a regular basis, with the commentaries they use, the law reviews, the publishing houses that provide them etc.[3] When they are told that these have a certain Nazi past, and I am afraid they are not told too often,[4] students are helpless about what to do with this. Remarkably, consequences for dealing with this background in legal education have scarcely been discussed among legal historians. This, of course, being *pars pro toto* for the general lack of German literature regarding issues of legal education; unlike the USA, we have no substantial scholarly debate about *how we teach* in law school: what *techniques* we use and which are available in the first place, the values we convey, how we ensure student participation[5] – and

---

[3] For the monopolized "Schönfelder"-compilation see Wrobel, Hans: Heinrich Schönfelder – Sammler deutscher Gesetze 1902-1944. München 1997; Redaktion Forum Recht: Warum hat das BGB im "Schönfelder" die Nummer 20? In: Forum Recht Sonderausgabe: Wozu Jura studieren? (2002/2003), p. 28; for the leading "Palandt" commentary see Wrobel, Hans: Otto Palandt zum Gedächtnis 1.5.1877-3.12.1951. In: Kritische Justiz (1982), p. 1ff.; see also Mützel, Philip: Schäffers Grundrisse überdauern die Zeiten. In: Forum Historiae Iuris (2002), www.rewi.hu-berlin.de/FHI/debatte/0202muetzel.htm (accessed on 07/28/06); Becker, Lothar: Schritte auf einer abschüssigen Bahn. Das Archiv des öffentlichen Rechts (AöR) und die deutsche Staatsrechtswissenschaft im Dritten Reich. Tübingen 1999.

[4] To this very day, books appear in which the past of legal scholars is either simply not mentioned or inacceptably blurred. See, e.g., the apologetic volume Blümel, Willi (ed.): Ernst Forsthoff. Kolloqium aus Anlaß des 100. Geburtstages von Prof. Dr. Dr. h.c. Ernst Forsthoff. Berlin 2003. The Nazi past is omitted in Pawloski, Hans-Martin: Nachruf Michaelis. In: NJW (2001), p. 3031; palliating Maiwald, Manfred: Nachruf Schaffstein. In: NJW (2002), p. 1250: the "Third Reich" as a "painful experience" for Schaffstein, who had been a "noble man" with "natural *Liebenswürdigkeit*"; for Erik Wolf see the forgetful reminiscence by Hollerbach, Alexander: Zu Leben und Werk Erik Wolfs. In: Erik Wolf. Ausgewählte Schriften III. Frankfurt am Main 1982, pp. 235ff.

[5] Out of the vast American literature see only Bateman, Paul: Toward Diversity in Teaching Methods in Law Schools: Five Suggestions from the Back Row. In: Quinnipiac Law Review

especially no literature on the very unique situation of the *tutorials* that play a major part in German law school education in the first semesters.[6] And it is in these tutorials where students ask how to deal with the Nazi past of books that we *do recommend* to them. My question is: How are we, as legal historians, to deal with this inquiry made by our students?

B. On How to Deal with Dealing with the Past

Now, the first answer would obviously be that the problem I am discussing here is not a problem to begin with. That we do not *have* to deal with this Nazi background or that we are *unable* to deal with it. The first I call the cynical approach, and the latter I like to call the complexity approach.

(1) The *cynical approach* simply takes note of the fact that these authors are dead,[7] the books have been taken over by others who undisputedly have no fascist notions whatsoever, or, if they have not been taken over, they are no longer read by anyone. But first of all, this is not true for works of legal historians such as Wieacker's "*Privatrechtsgeschichte*" or Huber's "*Verfassungsgeschichte*", both of which have *not* been replaced by any newer works and continue to influence scholarly writings to this day, inside and outside of legal history. Second, the claim that, after new authors have taken over, these books have significantly changed, remains to be thoroughly examined – *e.g.* for Larenz/Canaris' "*Methodenlehre*" it would be rather easy to prove that this is

(1997) vol. 17, pp. 397ff.; Friedland, Steven I.: How We Teach: A Survey of Teaching Techniques in American Law Schools. In: Seattle Univ. Law Review (1996) vol. 20, pp. 1ff.; Rogers, John M.: Class Participation: Random Calling and Anonymous Grading. In: Journal of Legal Education (1997) vol. 47, pp. 73ff.; Kennedy, Duncan: Liberal Values in Legal Education. In: Nova Law Review (1986) vol. 10, pp. 603ff.

[6] Potential inspirations for German discourses may be gathered from, e.g., Wildman, Stephanie M.: The Question of Silence: Techniques to Ensure Full Class Participation. In: Journal of Legal Education (1988) vol. 38, pp. 147ff.; Richmond, Michael L.: Teaching Law to Passive Learners: The Contemporary Dilemma of Legal Education. In: Cumberland Law Review (1995-1996) vol. 26, pp. 943ff.; Reilly, Elizabeth A.: Deposing the "Tyranny of Extroverts": Collaborative Learning in the Traditional Classroom Formal. In: Journal of Legal Education (2000) vol. 50, pp. 593ff.

[7] As far as I can see, Schaffstein and Michaelis were the last among the scholars active in the "Third Reich" to pass away (both 2001).

not the case.[8] Third, even if the books are not read any more, in many cases "new" books are essentially transcriptions of the old ones.[9] Thus, the problem remains to be a problem.

(2) What I call the *complexity approach* is simply the historical assessment that (a) we do not have enough material to make any substantial judgments, and (b) by what we do know of that time, the historical setting here is simply too complex to 'deal' with it in any way. Both arguments are weighty. Indeed, there is a lot that we do not know about these Nazi pasts: Inquiries exist for Karl Larenz, Ernst-Rudolf Huber, Edmund Mezger, Heinrich Lehmann, Heinrich Lange, Ernst Forsthoff, Justus Wilhelm Hedemann,[10] but rather white spots remain to be Hans-Jürgen Bruns, Hans Welzel, Franz Wieacker, Erik Wolf, Theodor Maunz, Friedrich Schaffstein or Georg Dahm.[11]

Moreover, from what we *do* know, the *differences* were enormous: We have post war scholars that, as previous practitioners, were directly involved in

---

[8] A first attempt was made by Rüthers, Bernd: Anleitung zum fortgesetzten methodischen Blindflug? In: NJW (1996), pp. 1249ff.

[9] This is the case for Schlosser, Hans: Grundzüge der Neueren Privatrechtsgeschichte. 10th ed., Heidelberg 2005, who is, as numerous of his colleagues, precisely following Wieacker's "Privatrechtsgeschichte".

[10] For Larenz: Frassek, Ralf: Von der völkischen Lebensordnung zum Recht: die Umsetzung weltanschaulicher Programmatik in den schuldrechtlichen Schriften von Karl Larenz (1903-1993). Baden-Baden 1996. For Huber: Jürgens, Martin: Staat und Reich bei Ernst Rudolf Huber. Sein Leben und Werk bis 1945 aus rechtsgeschichtlicher Sicht. Bern et al. 2005. For Mezger: Thulfaut, Gerit: Kriminalpolitik und Strafrechtslehre bei Edmund Mezger (1883-1962). Baden-Baden 2000. For Lehmann: Depping, André: Das BGB als Durchgangspunkt – Privatrechtsmethode und Privatrechtsleitbilder bei Heinrich Lehmann (1876-1963). Tübingen 2002. For Lange: Wolf, Wilhelm: Vom alten zum neuen Privatrecht. Das Konzept der normgestützten Kollektivierung in den zivilrechtlichen Arbeiten Heinrich Langes (1900-1977). Tübingen 1998. For Forsthoff a brillant and in-depth enquiry is available with Storost, Ulrich: Staat und Verfassung bei Ernst Forsthoff. Frankfurt am Main/Bern/Las Vegas 1979. For Hedemann: Wegerich, Christine: Die Flucht in die Grenzenlosigkeit: Justus Wilhelm Hedemann, 1878-1963. Tübingen 2004.

[11] For Schaffstein see, nevertheless, Hubert, Harry: Jugendrecht im Nationalsozialismus. Frankfurt am Main 2001; for Wieacker see the thoughtful sketch provided by Behrends, Okko: Franz Wieacker, 5.8.1908-17.2.1994. In: SZ RA (1995) vol. 112, pp. XIIIff.; a less sophisticated assessment was given by Kohlhepp, Ralf: Franz Wieacker und die NS-Zeit. In: SZ RA (2005) vol. 122, pp. 203ff.; for Welzel see Hirsch, Hans J.: Zum 100. Geburtstag von Hans Welzel. In: ZgesStrW (2004) vol. 116, pp. 1ff.

atrocities (as were Dreher or Schlegelberger), among the law professors we have openly committed Nazis (such as Koellreuther or Höhn), scholars that had institutional success (such as Carl Schmitt), some who were close to the "*SS*", Himmler and the "*Reichssicherheitshauptamt*" (such as Höhn and Eckhardt), some that had not been, but were members of the then-called "*Stoßtruppfakultäten*" (like Dahm, Larenz, Schaffstein), and some who taught at these law schools without being awarded tenure (such as Wieacker), some that used racist and antisemitic language (as did Schmitt and Forsthoff), and some that never did – some that came into the classroom in their SS-uniform and some, even though very few, that showed certain degrees of resistance facing the expulsion of their Jewish colleagues (as did Werner Flume following the expulsion of his teacher Fritz Schulz in 1933). In general, we do not see a monolithic group of Nazi scholarship. Fitting the overall phenomenon of *polycracy*,[12] we find in legal scholarship conflicting groups between Carl Schmitt and Hans Frank on one side, Himmler and Eckhardt on the other, between a "*rechtspolitische*" and a "*Auslegungs*"-movement, and even just as much conflict *within* these groups, ideologically as well as institutionally.[13]

In addition, the time frame adds to the all but uniform picture: a scholarly article means something completely different in 1933 than in 1943, a seemingly brave and careful criticism of Nazi lawmaking means something far different after the dissolution of Stalingrad than after the establishment of terror in the so-called "*Reichskristallnacht*", NSDAP membership is different if it took place before 1933, in 1933, or after 1937 (when the membership ban from 1933 was disestablished).

---

[12] The best depiction of this phenomenom, I believe, is still available with Broszat, Martin: The Hitler State. London 1991 (first German ed. 1969); for the most recent developments of this topos see Seibel, Wolfgang/Raab, Jörg: Verfolgungsnetzwerke: Zur Messung nationalsozialistischer "Polykratie" und ihrer Auswirkung auf die Verfolgung der Juden im deutschen Herrschaftsbereich während des Zweiten Weltkriegs. In: Kölner Zeitschrift für Soziologie und Sozialpsychologie (2003) vol. 55, pp. 197ff., and Feldman, Gerald D./Seibel, Wolfgang (eds.): Networks of Nazi Persecution: Bureaucracy, Business and the Organization of the Holocaust. London/New York 2005.

[13] See Frassek, Ralf: Steter Tropfen höhlt den Stein – Juristenausbildung im Nationalsozialismus und danach. In: SZ GA (2000) vol. 117, pp. 294ff.

Furthermore, a lot of these scholars, after having participated vigorously, backtracked from the regime before 1945. Though in many cases it is highly questionable whether they did so voluntarily or whether they were simply ousted from power (as I believe most of them were), it is still part of the picture.

But the greatest question must be: What *is* genuine Nazi scholarship? The continuities come to light with almost every element – not even antisemitism in combination with a biologistic language is unique, but has been used in the 19th century.[14] And so was the cynically-called "*Freigabe lebensunwerten Lebens*" when you look at law professor Karl Binding.[15] The entire phenomenon is: The closer we look at the historical contexts, the more Nazi scholarship, in a sense, evaporates – being also a general phenomenon when looking scientifically at the "Third Reich".[16]

But all this should not lead to avoidance: There are things that we *do* know: We have Carl Schmitt's apology for murder from 1934 or Karl Larenz' proposition for section one of the German Civil Code.[17] The unambiguousness of these scholarly contributions we do know. So the question, as far as this knowledge is concerned, remains to be posed.

I would like to discuss three possible standards to do that in the classroom: morals, law and Historization.

---

[14] See, e.g., for Treitschke the evidence compiled by Thomasz Giaro in: RJ (2000), pp. 155ff.; see also Senn, Marcel: Rassistische und antisemitische Elemente im Rechtsdenken von J.C. Bluntschli. In: SZ GA (1993) vol. 110, pp. 372ff.

[15] Binding, Karl/Hoche, Alfred: Die Freigabe der Vernichtung lebensunwerten Lebens. Ihr Maß und ihre Form. Leipzig 1920; see also Riha, Ortrun (ed.): "Die Freigabe der Vernichtung lebensunwerten Lebens" – Beiträge des Symposiums über Karl Binding und Alfred Hoche am 2. Dezember 2004 in Leipzig. Aachen 2005; Klee, Ernst: "Euthanasie" im NS-Staat. Die "Vernichtung lebensunwerten Lebens". Frankfurt am Main 1985.

[16] This is often being ignored by relevant enquiries; see, e.g., Schröder, Imke: Zur Legitimationsfunktion der Rechtsphilosophie im Nationalsozialismus. Frankfurt am Main et. al. 2002, who constructs a "Nazi philosophy of law" and then, rather unsurprisingly, finds very "different" scales of "affinity" to NS en detail (ibid., pp. 185ff., 188).

[17] See Schmitt, Carl: Der Führer schützt das Recht. In: DJZ (1934), Sp. 945ff.; Larenz, Karl: Rechtsperson und subjektives Recht. Zur Wandlung der Rechtsgrundbegriffe. Berlin 1935.

C. The Moral Standard

An approach that, I assume, is quite popular among us, is that moral condemnation is not our task. I agree with that in so far as I believe moral arguments are not generally provable and therefore cannot be verified by the students listening to the professor. I disagree with it when it means that we do not make moral judgments at all. The thing that we forget when we, vaguely based on Max Weber, refuse morals is that it never meant not to do morals but to (1) *separate* moral arguments from those of legal, political etc. nature, (2) to *disclose* that they are unprovable and (3) not to let them take *overweight. This* is what Max Weber meant.[18] Indeed, scholars who made a case for a non-moralist legal scholarship added their own moral convictions in their works, as did Hans Kelsen famously at the end of "What is Justice?" and as did Michael Stolleis in the foreword to his "History of Public Law".[19] We cannot forge a *universal moral judgment* out of our historical knowledge and present it to our students because, as I have indicated, it is not our scholarly business, the differences were considerable and because we do not know enough of the reality to do so.

But my point is: We have to *make a space for morals* for our students, to *enable* students to make their own *individual* moral judgments, even more: their moral indignation, their shame, their mourning. And the classroom has to become a place for that, too. Law students are taught that we have a value-oriented jurisprudence, but when they express their moral judgments in the classroom should we tell them to go home and mourn in private? If Carl Schmitt's participation in the regime has, as Michael Stolleis aptly put it, "darkened his

---

[18] Weber, being disgusted with the blending of rational and irrational arguments, at the same time insistently pointed to the inescapable relevance (and importance!) of the irrational, moral (daemonic) side of all scientific undertakings. He did so most vividly in Weber, Max: Wissenschaft als Beruf. Stuttgart 2002 [1919] (his most significant argument being, perhaps, that mingling the rational and irrational means blurring the tragic disenchantments of modern life – and that only a "coward" would do; ibid., p. 34).

[19] Kelsen, Hans: Was ist Gerechtigkeit? Stuttgart 2003 [1953], p. 52.; Stolleis, Michael: Geschichte des Öffentlichen Rechts III: Staats- und Verwaltungsrechtswissenschaft in Republik und Diktatur 1914-1945. Munich 1999, p. 7.

name forever",[20] where can students ponder these shadows that fall upon them, too? And we should go even further: If a student, because of *moral indignation*, does not want to use Forsthoff, Schmitt, Wieacker or Larenz, should we not allow him to? I believe a student whose family had been a victim of the regime should not be forced (not even indirectly) to read the works of a man who stated that only "arians" had "Rechtspersönlichkeit" in private law.[21]

One might say that this is unscientific because what is in the academic world cannot be neglected – but this is hypocritical: We neglect scholarly literature all the time. We do not read everything. Of course, we always pretend to overlook the literature. We (almost) never do. Some of it is always omitted. Duncan Kennedy has refreshingly vented that: In a footnote providing sources he wrote: "Heidegger is not in here, because I haven't read him."[22] Generally, I believe the guideline we use when selecting scholarly literature is *reliance, trust*. What, our students often ask, could diminish it more than an eminent participation in that regime? Also, we ceased to use a certain terminology because it has a Nazi context such as "*Ausmerzen*", "*Volksgemeinschaft*" and "*Ehre*" even though they have been used long before the "Third Reich". So, quite apparently, we are making distinctions all the time based on moral standards.

To enable students to a moral standpoint, however, would also include a standard of truth and objectivity, including the separation of facts and terms. *Any* writing scholar has this standard, even though not having it is still very fashionable to pretend. I agree with the use of a little irony when talking about *the* truth.[23] I would only like to mention that the elegant postmodern shoulder-shrugging about objectivity, truth and facts reaches its limits when dealing with the holocaust. Thilo Ramm, after a long scholarly life, recently maintained the claim on truth – and he was talking about our topic, remembering

---

[20] Stolleis, Michael: Im Bauch des Leviathan. In: Id.: Recht im Unrecht. Frankfurt am Main 1994, p. 133.
[21] See Larenz (as in fn. 17).
[22] Kennedy, Duncan: A Semiotics Of Critique. In: Cardozo Law Review (2001) vol. 22, p. 1149, fn. 2.
[23] See Günther, Klaus: Von der wahren Souveränität. In: KJ (2005), pp. 434ff.

and forgetting![24] Especially in the field of NS history, scholarly discussions are *overtly* driven by a very strong concept of truth – you can tell by the sometimes harsh and hurtful manner in which these discussions are being led.[25] Thus again, dealing with the Nazi past would be a place to discuss our very basic assumptions. After all, there is no more evidence for that there is no truth than for that there is truth. In that case, we might as well follow a pragmatist view on truth and objectivity,[26] one that enables us to deal with anything in a scholarly manner – not only, but especially the holocaust.

D. The Legal Standard

An approach that is rarely thought of is applying a mere *legal standard* in dealing with scholar's Nazi past in the classroom. That is amazing, considering the fact that most of us and of our teachers are trained lawyers. Scholars in the "Third Reich", however, did not only violate moral standards, but *legal* standards. They disregarded the law of *their* times. They not only misinterpreted it, they clearly broke it. The regime was built on a series of breaches of law, starting with the "*Ermächtigungsgesetz*" which was by no means "legal".[27] Judges heavily broke very determinate legal provisions, not only of Weimarian laws, but quite often even of Nazi legislation, then of course by exceeding it. And so did other lawyers. We do not have to go as far as to Schlegelberger, whose conduct Bernhard Diestelkamp has accurately rated as a committed murder.[28]

---

[24] Ramm, Thilo: Der Jurist und das kollektive Erinnern. In: JZ (2004), pp. 689ff.

[25] See the intervention by Stolleis, Michael: Apologie kraft Interpretation. In: ZNR (1997), pp. 100ff.

[26] For this dilemma see Dworkin, Ronald: Objectivity and Truth: You'd Better Believe It. In: Philosophy & Public Affairs (1996) vol. 25, pp. 87ff.; Rorty, Richard: Objectivity, Relativism, and Truth. Cambridge 1991.

[27] See only recently Dreier, Ralf: Bemerkungen zum ‚Dritten Reich'. In: Festschrift Otte. Munich 2005, pp. 495ff.

[28] Diestelkamp, Bernhard: Die Justiz nach 1945 und ihr Umgang mit der eigenen Vergangenheit. In: Justizalltag im Dritten Reich. Ed. by Id./Michael Stolleis. Frankfurt am Main 1988, p. 133: "That was murder." See also Nathans, Eli: Legal Order as Motive and Mask: Franz Schlegelberger and the Nazi Administration of Justice. In: American Law and History Review (2000) vol. 18, pp. 281ff.

As legal professors these scholars were obliged to teach the law, and this is precisely what they did not do – with only one exception in Anschütz who, out of this very reason, declined his service as a legal professor. Of course, we will not present this fact to our students as long as we ourselves believe that "the political element in law is inescapable",[29] that it is an *unchangeable* task of legal scholarship to "adapt the system to changed political settings", to "reflect the *zeitgeist*", and to "speak about political, economic and social issues".[30]

A second and different legal standard is from today's law. It is almost common sense among legal historians not to apply this standard. The argument is always the same: It is unhistorical to apply today's measures or, simply, we are no judges. I agree with that. Let me only add a very general remark: In a time where morals have lost their universality law is the medium in which societies measure *guilt*. Today's law offers many interesting insights into the guilt of these scholars: Our criminal law punishes bare risk increase and attempt – so even if these scholars were not heard in the regime and did not have any "success" with their writing, it is sufficient that they tried to be heard and thus increased the risk for potential victims to be persecuted on the very arguments they lent to a regime that sought for the legal expulsion of these people. Let me only mention here the changed doctrine of property that was closely knit with "*Arisierung*" and eviction.[31] And did they not profit from a criminal regime – directly and intentionally? Would we not punish that with our criminal law? In any case, this legal standard, of course, *must* extend to events after 1949, such as the case of Theodor Maunz:[32] If we criticize his engagement with the extreme right wing DVU-party after 1945, and I think we should, as teachers of law we also have to make clear that this is a moral or

---

[29] Stolleis, Michael: Lehren aus der Rechtsgeschichte? Zur Auseinandersetzung mit den Thesen von Bernd Rüthers. In: Gegen Barbarei. Essays Robert M.W. Kempner zu Ehren. Ed. by Eisfeld/Müller. Frankfurt am Main 1989, p. 388 (transl. by the author).

[30] Stolleis, Michael: Das Zögern beim Blick in den Spiegel. Die deutsche Rechtswissenschaft nach 1933 und nach 1945. In: Nationalsozialismus in den Kulturwissenschaften I. Ed. by Lehmann /Oexle. Göttingen 2004, pp. 21, 24, 27 (transl. by the author).

[31] Wieacker, Franz: Wandlungen der Eigentumsverfassung. Hamburg 1935; see now Keiser, Thorsten: Eigentumsrecht im Nationalsozialismus und Fascismo. Tübingen 2005.

[32] See Stolleis, Michael: Theodor Maunz – ein Staatsrechtslehrerleben. In: Kritische Justiz (1993), pp. 393ff.

political argument: Legally he was *allowed* to do that. If scholars condemn Maunz' activities *as law professors*, I think they misuse their authority – first and foremost towards their *students* who do not *know* the law yet.

E. Historization?

This brings me to my third and final standard, which I call Historization. The core of this approach is to say that legal history is part of the general discipline of history and is therefore methodologically independent of the normative task of the legal science. The approach first received a great following in the 1920s and 1930s when legal scholars attacked the application of historical knowledge to concrete legal problems, as spotted in 19th century Pandectism.[33] Today, it turns against a neo-pandectist school that applies legal history to find concrete doctrinal solutions for future European legislation.[34] For our problem it would mean that we could only present the historical material to our students, but we could not extract *insight* from it for *today's law*.

Indeed, the exponents of this approach have maintained that legal history could not offer instructions or teachings from the past for contemporary legal science, since this would imply a direct application of historical knowledge, "accusation[s]" of such sort being, as Michael Stolleis said, "scientifically un-

---

[33] See only Wieacker, Franz: Die Stellung der römischen Rechtsgeschichte in der heutigen Rechtsausbildung. In: Zeitschrift der Akademie für deutsches Recht (1939), pp. 403ff.; and already Kantorowicz, Hermann: Der Kampf um die Rechtswissenschaft. Heidelberg 1906, p. 31; pursued by Wieacker, Franz: Privatrechtsgeschichte der Neuzeit unter besonderer Berücksichtigung der deutschen Entwicklung. 2nd ed., Göttingen 1967, pp. 14ff.; Grimm, Dieter: Rechtswissenschaft und Geschichte. In: Id.: Rechtswissenschaft und Nachbarwissenschaften, vol. 2. Munich 1976, pp. 8ff.; Stolleis, Michael: Aufgaben der neueren Rechtsgeschichte oder: Hic sunt leones. In: RJ (1985), pp. 251ff.

[34] For this (temperate) application see only Zimmermann, Reinhard: Europa und das römische Recht. In: AcP (2002) vol. 202, pp. 243ff.; for the USA see Gordley, James: Why Look Backward. In: American Journal of Comparative Law (2002) vol. 50, pp. 657ff.; for the critique see only Giaro, Tomasz: Europäische Privatrechtsgeschichte: Werkzeug der Rechtsvereinheitlichung und Produkt der Kategorienvermengung. In: Ius Commune (1994) vol. XXI, pp. 1ff.

productive".[35] To apply standards and viewpoints of today's law would be "unhistorical".[36]

The *methodological* argument of this approach is convincing because it adheres to the separation of ought and is, as established by Hume and Kant.[37] It therefore may be true for the discipline of historiography. My thesis is, however, that (1) it is incompatible with the place of legal history *at the law school* and *in legal education*, and (2) it itself does not comply with its own declaration to separate ought and is and therefore tends to be a potential danger for legal education.[38]

Let me start with the latter: The historical approach always claims not to draw teachings from history.[39] This is simply untrue. And it is especially untrue for the discipline's past. Respective scholars did not extract consequences from their historical scholarship *for concrete legal doctrine*, but the non-application towards doctrinal details regularly included *a far wider application*: History would now show general, global statements about what law was and is.[40] Their application was thus even more comprehensive. Since they did not have to cling to dogmatic figures, their scholarship became even more essayist, speculative, general. After all, freedom from dogmatic structures has been praised as the great advantage of this approach.[41] Indeed Franz Wieacker, who is one of the fathers of Historization, drew wide, unrestricted conclusions from his alleg-

---

[35] Stolleis (as in fn. 30), p. 24; see also Id.: Vorurteile und Werturteile der rechtshistorischen Forschung zum Nationalsozialismus. In: Id.: Recht im Unrecht. Frankfurt am Main 1994, p. 54.
[36] Stolleis: Vorurteile (as in fn. 35), p. 49.
[37] None other than Hans Kelsen has put this straight for legal history: Kelsen, Hans: Rechtsgeschichte gegen Rechtsphilosophie? Eine Erwiderung. Vienna 1928.
[38] Perhaps surprisingly, these two arguments can also be supported by using Kelsen (see below at fn. 50).
[39] For this premise see only Stolleis (as in fn. 29).
[40] A justly sarcastic critique of this phenomenon was provided by Picker, Eduard: Von Traumen und Träumen der Rechtsgeschicht(l)e(r). Zu Krise, Paralyse und Katharsis einer gebeutelten Wissenschaft. In: Colloquia für Dieter Schwab. Bielefeld 2000, pp. 137ff.
[41] See Stolleis (as in fn. 33), p. 257: "substantially freer", "greater openness and flexibility", p. 259: "dispensed" from restrictions (transl. by the author).

edly non-applicative approach, before and after 1945.[42] So did, after all, general historiography at all times – and does so today.[43]

It is not by chance that the non-applicative approach regularly was found together with a so-called "*sozialwissenschaftliche*" approach.[44] Today's representatives of Historization, instead of clinging to a positivist view, want to show how law was entangled with social and economic "determinants", as they say.[45] Now that is a quite momentous premise: Who says that law *has* these *as determinants*? – and more importantly: Do we, lawyers and historians alike, *really* have the scientific *tools* to examine this complex relation beyond apodictic statements? Such apodictic statements were the basis of very concrete proposals undermining positive law. This is not a danger of the past only. Marcel Senn, an exponent of the "*sozialwissenschaftliche*" approach, wrote 13 years ago: "Legal history does not serve the legitimation of current legal science, but should critically stand opposite to it, as a forum for reflection and critique."[46] I can see you all nodding your heads. But it is a huge difference whether we reflect and criticize current legal science (and practise!) from the standpoint of the law[47] or wether we question the legitimacy of positive law itself. I doubt that Marcel Senn and the vast majority of German legal historians seek for the

---

[42] See only Wieacker's philosophical creed expressed in Wieacker, PRG (as in fn. 33), p. 8.

[43] Most recently in the tremendously silly comparison of Ancient Rome and the US that has become widely popular (Bender, Peter: Weltmacht Amerika – Das Neue Rom. 5th[!] ed., Munich 2004; Münkler, Herfried: Imperien. Die Logik der Weltherrschaft – Vom Alten Rom bis zu den Vereinigten Staaten. Berlin 2005). Conclusions from historical insight have, however, also been presented by more trustworthy scholars such as Rüsen, Jörg: Die Zukunft der Vergangenheit. In: Universitas (1998) vol. 53, pp. 228ff., and Winkler, Heinrich August: Aus der Geschichte lernen? In: DIE ZEIT 30.04.2004, p. 12, the latter refusing "political utility" of history but at the same time seeing himself able to offer some "orientation"(?).

[44] Simon, Dieter, in: Handlexikon zur Rechtswissenschaft. Ed. by Axel Görlitz. Munich 1972, pp. 314ff.

[45] Stolleis: Vorurteile (as in fn. 35), p. 50; see also Id. (as in fn. 33), p. 264.

[46] Senn, Marcel: Stand und Zweck der neueren Grundlagendiskussion in der Rechtsgeschichtswissenschaft. In: ZNR (1993), p. 77 (transl. by the author).

[47] This can (and should) be done radically, see, e.g., for law's indeterminacy Singer, Joseph W.: The Player and the Cards: Nihilism and Legal Theory. In: Yale Law Journal (1984) vol. 94, pp. 1ff.; for reason in legal reasoning Schlag, Pierre: The Enchantment of Reason. Durham 1998; for a balance see now Somek, Alexander: Rechtliches Wissen. Frankfurt am Main 2006.

former. Yet the forum for critique *of positive law* ought to be in politics, not academia.[48] Indeed, from the viewpoint of educating young German lawyers the balance of legal history as a discipline, be it applicative or not, is disastrous. It has provided the Nazi regime with a history of law that told everything but the law. And after 1945, legal history in many ways continued in this very trait. Of course, this is not seen as long as we say that today's law, especially the constitution, could not be the ell by which the history of the 'Third Reich' should be measured, and, as Michael Stolleis put it, legal history should not be "constricted by the juristic optics from after 1945".[49] I believe that the opposite is true: If legal history wants to maintain its place within the law faculty (and it is a historically contingent decision for it to be there), it has to adjust to these very *juristic optics*. This is not a value judgment I take from my moral indignation with the Nazi past. The standard for this comes from the law itself that we have to teach. The paramount German law, the "*Grundgesetz*", does provide a clear standard insofar it is, in its essence, a reaction to the atrocities committed in the 'Third Reich'. Legal history within German legal education being bound to this legal standard means nothing else than that legal history has to say something about one question: Are there any clues to what has caused this anti-constitutional state in the 'Third Reich' and are there any scientifically sustainable ways that might ensure anything like this not to repeat itself?[50] It is important to note that the historical approach, which re-

---

[48] See Unger, Roberto M.: Law in Modern Society. New York 1976, p. 217: "The German case may also serve to point out the enormous dangers to freedom involved in the decline of the legal order and the high risks critical intelligence runs when it attacks the idea of positive law." Of course, one might question whether this "ought" *can* be achieved at all.

[49] Stolleis: Vorurteile (as in fn. 35), p. 49.

[50] This (re)orientation of legal history can be based on Kelsen, too. Kelsen clearly excluded legal history from the "science of law", the former being an explicative and the latter a normative endeavour (Kelsen [as in fn. 37], p. 3; Kelsen, Hans: Hauptprobleme der Staatsrechtslehre, entwickelt aus der Lehre vom Rechtssatze. Tübingen 1911, p. VII). But as Stephan Verosta has shown, Kelsen's "pure" (better: normative) theory of law implies a substantial (though severely restricted!) usage of legal history, namely in pinning the all but clear verges of the Grundnorm – and that calls for a constitutional perspective (Verosta, Stephan: Rechtsgeschichte und Reine Rechtslehre: Zugleich ein Beitrag zum Problem der Beziehung zwischen Faktizität und Normativität. In: Law, State and International Legal Order. Essays in Honor of Hans Kelsen. Ed. by Salo Engel. Knoxville 1964, p. 354). Although Kelsen did not stress this usage, for a normative science

fuses to answer that, also states that the place of legal history within German law schools is a mere hazard.[51] So, behind all this might lie the very essential question whether we are lawyers looking for historical insight or whether we are historians happened to be washed up onto the shore of the law school.

There is indeed certain evidence pointing to the fact that one method is more *susceptible*[52] than the other, that one way of legal reasoning is more prone to abuse than others, or, perhaps, that even one legal history is more susceptible to abuse than the other. This concept is not uncommon: For example, we do fight racism and antisemitism not only because we believe they are morally despicable, but also because we believe they *structurally* lead to horrendous crimes.[53]

For legal history we might "learn" that remoteness from sources, essayist writing, and wide global narrations are particularly susceptible. The best part of legal history scholarship over the last four decades has engaged in nothing but deconstructing these heritages – that has been a true legal history drawing conclusions from *its own* history on the basis of the law. Thus, when dealing with the Nazi past of scholarly writing our task would be to examine not only the biographical backgrounds of the authors but the structure of their jurisprudence, too. This, then, is not so much about atrocious jurists, but about atrocious jurisprudence. The essential question posed in legal education must be: If the constitution is a reaction to National Socialism, how much of the structure of NS law is in today's criminal law, private law, public law, Euro-

---

of law it provides legal history with a role both very limited and enormously crucial – one in particular this article is trying to make a case for.

[51] See Stolleis: Vorurteile (as in fn. 35), p. 48: Legal history as part of legal education "not necessarily justifiable (but useful)" (transl. by the author).

[52] For this concept of "susceptibility" see Vogel, Joachim: Einflüsse des Nationalsozialismus auf das Strafrecht. In: ZStW (2003) vol. 115, p. 643. On the contrary, Bernd Rüther's justly famous enquiries into legal methods in the "Third Reich" have always been suggesting that all methods are alike (see especially Rüthers, Bernd: Entartetes Recht. München 1989). Only recently, Michael Stolleis has renewed his claim that "abstract legal methods" offered no protection against seductability (Stolleis, Michael: Nachwort. In: Id.: Recht im Unrecht. repr. Frankfurt am Main 2006, p. 340).

[53] For a similar concept see Volkov, Shulamit: Antisemistismus als kultureller Code. 2nd ed., München 2000.

pean law etc. – and how much of it is not compatible with the constitution? Especially in criminal law we torture law students with a lot of remnants from the Nazi period and a number of them are unconstitutional.[54] *These* are the darker legacies of the history of law. And what else could be more vital to teaching a legal system that, for the last 60 years, sought to depart from these legacies? What I am suggesting here is very similar to the project of politicizing the classroom established by Duncan Kennedy,[55] because it means disclosing implicit standards of legal education and not pretending to be in a space free from guidelines. We are not free from these guidelines in legal education. Of course, all this is part of asking a lost question: What is the purpose of law school?[56]

F. Standing on the Shoulder of Giants

If it is true that our interest should be led to *patterns*, then it is inevitable that we critically question those who use these patterns without having a Nazi past of their own, but who have done a lot to strengthen democratic values in legal scholarship. As young legal historians, we are standing on the shoulders of giants: Our teachers have deconstructed many of the blurrings made by their predecessors. But today, we have to examine *their* views, the views of *our* teachers, which are, in most part, probably our own. That is, I believe, what Sten Gagnér meant when he said that legal history begins yesterday. If we do not do this, we might as well add to the second guilt a third and a fourth

[54] For an overview see Wolf, Gerhard: Befreiung des Strafrechts vom nationalsozialistischen Denken? In: JuS (1996), pp. 189 ff. I should add that, naturally, tackling these provisions will seem odd as long as German courts maintain the validity of such an utterly and overtly unconstitutional provision as Sec. 185 of the German Penal Code.

[55] Kennedy, Duncan: Politicizing the Classroom. In: University of Southern California Review of Law and Women's Studies (1995) vol. 4, pp. 81ff.

[56] Henderson, Bethany Rubin: Asking the Lost Question: What is the Purpose of Law School? In: Journal of Legal Education (2003) vol. 53, pp. 48ff.

one.[57] Michael Stolleis has said of such inquiries into the history of jurisprudence in the 20th century: "They should be written with civil courage, without fearing colleagues or their disciples."[58] And I agree. Just a few months ago, Michael Stolleis also wrote: "Many of our findings, for sure, will prove wrong from a distance. Gradually falsifying such previous statements is the very aim of the next generation of legal historians."[59]

From this background let me conclude by trying to give an aswer to my initial question: We feel a reluctance to read the writings of Mister X because of two reasons: First, because we feel that his being a serial killer infiltrated his writing, that his writing contains structural patterns that are part of his personal conviction – just as we assume that scholars who once willingly sold the law to power might not be perfectly capable of teaching law to students. This can be wrong, but we have to examine that. The burden of proof lies with the scholars. Most of us have not searched intensely enough.

Second, we feel a reluctance to read the writings of Mister X because we do not want him to profit from us reading him; we do not want to give him this satisfaction. It has something to do with contempt for someone, so it is not the most decent of all intentions. But it is a legitimate answer of the human psyche. And we need a place for that – but we have to show students what to do with it: that we teach not a feeling, but the law. And so their (and our) task is to examine accurately what is consistent with today's law and what isn't. A lot of what is still in our textbooks and standard works is not. Contempt as a motor can thus lead to a valuable insight that, in the end, will be more than mere moral indignation. A feeling of contempt that will not give these men satisfaction will thoroughly examine their works and look for those elements that potentially hinder us from a constitutional condition. Let us not give them the satisfaction that we teach another generation the attitude that law can be written away at any time. Let us not enable them to deprive another

---

[57] Rückert, Joachim: Die erste und die zweite Schuld. In: Nationalsozialismus in den Kulturwissenschaften I. Ed. by Lehmann/Oexle. Göttingen 2004, pp. 657ff.; Giordano, Ralph: Die zweite Schuld oder Von der Last Deutscher zu sein. Hamburg 1987.

[58] Stolleis (as in fn. 30), p. 30 (transl. by the author).

[59] Stolleis (as in fn. 52), p. 340 (transl. by the author).

generation of the law. Law is a weak barrier against power, but it is the only one that we have and the only one that we *can* teach – after all, we are lawyers.

Das Vergessen der sozialistischen Tradition im Privatrecht. Was bedeutet das? Von romanistischen Elementen im sozialistischen Recht und den sog. rein „sozialistischen“ Erfindungen auf dem Gebiete des Privatrechts

Alexander Zezekalo

A. Einführende Bemerkungen

Die historisch nur relativ kurze Epoche der sozialistischen Staaten gab Wissenschaftlern die Möglichkeit, von einer „sozialistischen Rechtstradition“ zu sprechen. Inzwischen ist zu beobachten, daß die postsozialistischen Staaten dieses spezifische Erbe dem Vergessen überlassen haben. Aber was bedeutet das Vergessen der „sozialistischen Rechtstradition“? Um auf diese Frage eine adäquate Antwort zu finden, ist es hilfreich, sich zunächst vor Augen zu halten, um was für eine Tradition es sich dabei gehandelt hat, sofern sie überhaupt jemals existiert hat.

B. Die fragwürdige „Tradition“

Der Begriff der „sozialistischen Rechtstradition“ (*socialist legal tradition*) ist bekannt aus dem Gebiet der Rechtsvergleichung. Die viergliedrige Klassifizierung von David[1], der alle Rechtssysteme in vier große Familien teilt – romanistische (römisch-germanische), sozialistische, *common law* und die Familie der religiösen Rechtsordnungen – hat, wie Sacco bemerkt, einen so „zweifellosen Vorteil“, daß sie es den Komparativisten aus aller Welt erlaubt, einander ohne

[1] David R./G. Grasmann: Einführung in die großen Rechtssysteme der Gegenwart. München, 1966. S. 21 ff.

Mißverständnisse zu verstehen[2]. Dabei wird vorausgesetzt, daß die Rechtstradition – wie Merryman unterstreicht – immer „ein System von tiefen, grundlegenden, geschichtlich bedingten und geprägten Anschauungen auf die Natur des Rechts, seine Rolle in Gesellschaft und Politik, auf die entsprechende Organisation und Leitung des Rechtssystems, sowie auf die Gesetzgebung, die Rechtssprechung, die Rechtserziehung und die Rechtsausbildung" ist[3]. Die Charakterisierung einer Rechtstradition als „sozialistisch" setzt voraus, daß das Recht als ein Instrument einer bestimmten Sozial- und Wirtschaftspolitik betrachtet wird, welche die neue und, von dem Standpunkt der Ideologie aus, sozial und ökonomisch gerechte, sozialistische Ordnung einzuführen anstrebt.

Aber wie kann das sozialistische Recht als eine Rechtstradition bezeichnet werden, nur wenige Jahrzehnte nach seiner Entstehung? Kann sich ein System von „tiefen, grundlegenden, geschichtlich bedingten und geprägten Anschauungen" im Laufe einer so kurzen Frist gebildet haben? Und wenn nicht, woraus erklärt sich der eigenständige Weg, die Absonderung, den es genommen hat? Einerseits kann man den Eindruck gewinnen, daß diese Entwicklung eine logische Folge jener vermeintlichen oder wirklichen Ost-West Trennung war, die schon zu Zeiten der politischen und rechtlichen Spaltung zwischen östlichen und westlichen Teilen des Römischen Reiches ihren Anfang genommen hatte[4]. Aber diese ist viel tiefer verwurzelt als jene und hat mit dem Sozialismus nichts gemein. Andererseits ist bekannt, daß die sogenannte *western legal tradition* als Antipode zum sozialistischen Recht gilt – unter einer Bezeichnung, die während des Kalten Krieges auf dem axiologischen Fundament gemeinsamer Werte wie individuelle Gerechtigkeit und persönliche Freiheit entstanden und populär geworden ist[5]. Diese Rechtstradition umfaßt sowohl das romanistische *civil law* der meisten kontinentaleuropäischen Rechtsordnungen als

[2] Sacco, R.: Il sustrato romanistico del diritto civile dei Paesi socialisti. In: Rivista di diritto civile, Pt. I, 1969, S. 115.
[3] Merryman J. H.: The Civil Law Tradition. Stanford 1975. S. 2.
[4] Giaro T.: Tradizione giuridica dell'Europa orientale – un epitaffio. In: Drevnee pravo – ius antiquum 2 (14), 2004, S. 156.
[5] Giaro (wie in Fn. 4), S. 154 f.

auch das *common law* von Staaten wie Großbritannien und Irland[6]. Es drängt sich der Eindruck auf, daß diese ganze Gegenüberstellung einschließlich der Absonderung der „sozialistischen Rechtstradition" nicht mehr ist als eine Schöpfung der westlichen Sowjetforschung.

Aus dieser Perspektive kann man die Eigenständigkeit des sozialistischen Rechts als Rechtstradition bezweifeln. Zwar ist unbestreitbar, daß sich das Recht der sozialistischen Staaten durch das Vorhandensein gewisser gemeinsamer Merkmale von anderen Rechtsordnungen unterscheidet. Dennoch beobachten wir häufig, daß es sich um nicht mehr handelte, als daß einige Prinzipien der sozialistischen Ideologie einigen bestehenden kontinentalen oder anderen Rechtstraditionen aufgedrängt wurden. Dieser Gedanke ist nicht neu. Insbesondere Sacco zweifelte schon früher mit Recht die These an, daß das Recht der sozialistischen Staaten Modelle hervorgebracht habe, die sich von dem Recht der romanistischen Staaten so mächtig unterschieden, daß eine eigenständige Tradition entstanden sei[7].

Wenn man diesen Gedanke weiter entwickelt, kann man zu dem Schluß kommen, daß das heutige „Vergessen der sozialistischen Rechtstradition" in vielen postsozialistischen Staaten in erster Linie eine Beseitigung vom ideologischen Hauch bedeutet. Jedenfalls hat die Hauptmasse der sozialistischen Neuerungen – unabhängig davon, wie wir ihre materielle Bedeutung beurteilen – ihren Einfluß vorwiegend auf das öffentliche Recht ausgeübt[8]. Aber auch auf dem Gebiet des Privatrechts ist der ideologische Charakter der Ablagerungen höchst offensichtlich. Ein Vergleich des Privatrechts eines sozialistischen Staates mit demjenigen eines westlichen Staates fördert vor allem Gleichartigkeiten zutage, beispielsweise die Identität von allgemeinen Normen und einzelnen Regeln und die strukturelle Ähnlichkeit der Kodifikationen[9]. Hierfür kann man das Recht der ehemaligen Sowjetunion als Beispiel nehmen.

---

[6] Giaro, T.: Westen im Osten. Modernisierung osteuropäischer Rechte bis zum Zweiten Weltkrieg. In: Rechtsgeschichte 2, 2003. S. 123, 138.
[7] Sacco, R. (wie in Fn. 2), S. 115 ff.
[8] Giaro (wie in Fn. 4), S. 163-164.
[9] Ioffe O. Soviet Law and Roman Law, in: Boston University Law Review 62 (1982) S. 701.

C. Die romanistischen Elementen im sozialistischen Recht

Trotz der revolutionären Aufrufe zum entschiedenen Bruch mit der Vergangenheit stellte das erste sozialistische Zivilgesetzbuch (ZGB), das im Jahr 1922 unter der Leitung von Goikhbarg in nur vier Monate geschrieben worden war[10], eine Verschmelzung von deutschen und französischen Modellen dar. Einige Wissenschaftler betonen den Einfluß der vorrevolutionären Entwürfe aus den Jahren 1905 und 1913, die zu ihrer Zeit als schlechte Übersetzungen des deutschen Bürgerlichen Gesetzbuches (BGB) kritisiert worden waren, auf das sowjetrussische Gesetz[11]. Der in dem ZGB von 1922 vorgelegte allgemeine Teil – eine unzweifelhafte Entlehnung aus der Pandektistik[12] – blieb im Laufe der ganzen sozialistischen Periode erhalten.

Es wäre eine nutzlose Beschäftigung, die romanistischen Elemente im bürgerlichen Recht der Sowjetunion aufzuzählen, denn ihr Vorhandensein ist unbestreitbar. Viel interessanter ist es zu untersuchen, in welcher Weise die sozialistische Ideologie diese Elemente in ihren Dienst nahm und wie sie die Anwendung jener oder anderer westlicher Rechtsregeln oder doktrinaler Konstruktionen rechtfertigte und begründete. Überdies hat das sowjetische Recht im Lauf seines Daseins eine Anzahl von sogenannten „Neuerungen" erzeugt, die als Früchte der neuen sozialistischen, als gegensätzlich zu der alten „bürgerlich-kapitalistischen" Rechtsordnung betrachtet wurden. Einige dieser Regeln, Institutionen und Grundsätze, die traditionell als typisch „sozialistisch" angesehen werden, waren tatsächlich nicht viel anders als ihre ideologisch ausgelegten römischen Vorbilder und deren spätere westliche „Doppelgänger". Dabei hinderten die häufig offensichtlichen Parallelen die damaligen Rechtswissenschafter nicht daran zu erklären, daß „die formelle Ähnlichkeit einzelner Kategorien des sowjetischen und bürgerlichen Rechts in keiner Weise ihre qualitative Verschiedenheit beseitigt"[13].

---

[10] Butler W. E.: Russian Law. Oxford 1999, S. 333; Ioffe (wie in Fn. 9), S. 726.
[11] So etwa Butler (wie in Fn. 10), S. 333.
[12] Giaro (wie in Fn. 4), S. 163-164.
[13] Wenediktow, A.: Dogovornaja disziplina v promischlennosti [Die vertragliche Disziplin in der Industrie]. Leningrad 1935, I. § 2.

I. Privat oder persönlich?

Es verwundert nicht, daß die Institution des Eigentums als eine der zentralen Institutionen des bürgerlichen Rechts im Mittelpunkt der großen Konflikte und Widersprüche stand. Die Hauptform des Eigentums in der Sowjetunion war das sozialistische Eigentum. Dieses erschien entweder in der Form des Staatseigentums (das sogenannte „Gemeingut des Volkes"), in der Form des „kollektivwirtschaftlichen Eigentums" oder in der Form des „Eigentums der anderen kooperativen und öffentlichen Organisationen"[14].

Das ZGB der Rußländischen Föderativen Sowjetrepublik (RSFSR) von 1922, dessen Entstehen mit dem Beginn der NÖP[15] zusammenfiel, sah noch das Vorhandensein des Privateigentums vor[16]. Da aber im Jahr 1922 Lenin erklärte, daß „wir nichts ‚Privates' anerkennen, daß für uns alles auf dem Gebiete der Volkswirtschaft öffentlich-rechtlich, aber nicht privat ist"[17], ergab sich ein gewisser Widerspruch, denn die Bestimmungen der geltenden Zivilgesetzgebung liefen den Worten des Führers der Revolution zuwider. Auf die Beseitigung dieses Widerspruchs richteten sich die Anstrengungen der Rechtstheoretiker, und als Ergebnis ihrer Tätigkeit zeichnete sich am Anfang der 1930er Jahre die neue Konzeption ab. Ein Wendepunkt dieses Prozesses war die sowjetische Verfassung von 1936, die das Vorhandensein des sogenannten „persönlichen Eigentums" gesetzlich festhielt. Dieser auf den ersten Blick bloß sprachliche Unterschied trug eine wesentliche ideologische Funktion.

Wie bekannt ist, standen individualistische Positionen dem Sozialismus fern, der sich auf die Idee der Zentralisierung, d. h. die mehr oder weniger vollständige Vergesellschaftung stützte[18]. Es ist zu erwähnen, daß auch das Recht selbst von einigen sowjetischen Theoretikern als „das Opium für das

---

[14] Artt. 5, 6 Verfassung der UdSSR von 1936.

[15] Die Neue Ökonomische Politik.

[16] Artt. 52, 54 ZGB der RSFSR von 1922.

[17] Lenin, W.: Gesammelte Werke, 44. Band, S. 398.

[18] Menger, A.: Das Bürgerliche Recht und die besitzlosen Volksklassen: Eine Kritik des Entwurfs eines Bürgerlichen Gesetzbuches für das Deutsche Reich. Tübingen 1890, S. 4: „In dem sozialistischen Rechtssystem (...) [befinden sich] Die Sachen (...) mit gewissen Ausnahmen im Eigentum des Staates oder staatlichen Verbände".

Volk"[19] oder „konterrevolutionärer Gegenstand"[20] erklärt wurde. Das Eigentum der einzelnen Personen wurde nur als Notlösung zugelassen für die Periode, solange nicht der Kommunismus, das ideale Modell der sozialen Verhältnisse, in dem kein Recht und keine Eigentumsverhältnisse mehr vorhanden sein würden, aufgebaut ist[21]. Demgemäß mußte sich auch das Wesen des genannten „persönlichen Eigentums" von dem bürgerlichen, „Privateigentum" bedeutend unterscheiden.

Die sowjetische Doktrin stützte sich auf folgende Unterscheidung: Privateigentum sei von den Betriebsmitteln unabtrennbar und habe die Ausnutzung der Arbeit zur Folge; „persönliches Eigentum" sei dagegen auf die Konsumtionsmittel beschränkt, die durch die Arbeit der Staatsangehörigen[22] entstünden[23]. Diese ideologisch bedingte Behandlung beschränkte erstens den Kreis der Objekte des persönlichen Eigentums[24] und baute zweitens eine Wechselbeziehung auf, die die Zweckentfremdung des Gegenstandes ausschloß[25].

Der Inhalt des Eigentums im Allgemeinen wurde, dem romanistischen Muster folgend, durch Aufzählung der Machtbefugnisse des Eigentümers definiert. Die romanistische Tradition kannte vier solche Machtbefugnisse (*uti*, *frui*, *abuti*, und *possidere*). Im 16. Jahrhundert reduzierte sich ihre Anzahl auf

---

[19] Goikhbarg, A.: Osnovy chastnogo imuschtschestvennogo prava [Die Grundlagen des privaten Vermögensrechts]. Moskau 1924, S. 8.

[20] Stutchka, P.: Revolutsionnaja roll prava i gosudarstva [Die revolutionäre Rolle des Rechts und des Staats]. Moskau 1921, S. 3.

[21] Wenediktow, A.: Gosudarstvennaja sozialistitscheskaja sobstvennost [Das staatliche sozialistische Eigentum]. Moskau/Leningrad 1948.

[22] In der Sowjetunion die allgemeingültige Bezeichnung für die Personen.

[23] Ioffe (wie in Fn. 9), S. 710.

[24] Gemäß Art. 105 ZGB der RSFSR von 1964 konnten sich im persönlichen Eigentum der Staatsangehörigen nur die Gebrauchsgegenstände, persönliche Konsumtionsmittel, Haushaltsartikel, ein einziges (!) Wohnhaus und Arbeitsersparnisse befinden.

[25] Da die Betriebsmittel, die ihren Wert auf das Fertigerzeugnisse übertrugen, im persönlichen Interesse nicht benutzt werden durften (gemäß dem Abs. 3 Art. 93 ZGB der RSFSR von 1964), konnte solches Vermögen auch kein Gegenstand des persönlichen Eigentums sein. Es war gleichsam re extra commercium für jenes Segment des Verkehrs, auf das sich das Vermögen bezog, das zu den Konsumtionsmitteln gehörte. Das Letzte konnte sich im persönlichen Eigentum der Staatsangehörigen befinden.

drei[26]. Der Artikel 58 des ZGB von 1922 definierte den Inhalt des Eigentums auf folgende Weise: „dem Eigentümer gehören (...) die Rechte des Besitzes, der Nutzung und der Verfügung des Vermögens“[27]. Dabei unterschied das erste Zivilgesetzbuch überhaupt nicht zwischen dem Recht des „persönlichen“ und des sozialistischen Eigentums. Man dürfte erwarten, daß solche Unterschiede mit dem Entstehen der Konzeption des „persönlichen Eigentums“ erscheinen würden.

In dem neuen ZGB der RSFSR von 1964 wurde die Konzeption des „persönlichen Eigentums“ widergespiegelt und weiterentwickelt. Das persönliche Eigentum wurde als diejenige Ableitung aus dem sozialistischen Eigentum erklärt, die der Befriedigung der persönlichen Bedürfnisse der Staatsangehörigen diente. Es wurde vorausgesetzt, daß diese Bedürfnisse, je nach dem Fortschritt hin zum Kommunismus, immer aus gesellschaftlichen Fonds befriedigt würden[28]. Aber mit Blick auf den Inhalt des Eigentums bestimmte Artikel 92 des ZGB von 1964 wie sonst, ohne Unterschied, daß „dem Eigentümer die Rechte des Besitzes, der Nutzung und der Verfügung des Vermögens zugehören (...).“[29]

Vom juristischen Standpunkt aus betrachtet, pflanzte die Konzeption des „persönlichen Eigentums“ der dogmatischen Konstruktion des Eigentumsrechts also nichts Neues ein, sondern beschränkte nur den Kreis seiner Objekte auf die Konsumtionsmittel. Dabei benutzte es ein ökonomisches Kriterium. Die dogmatische Konstruktion des Inhalts des persönlichen Eigentums unterschied sich in der Tat auf keine Weise von derjenigen des so stürmisch kritisierten Privateigentums. Der Gesetzgeber orientierte sich am romanistischen Muster[30].

---

[26] Der Besitz, d. h. possessio; die Nutzung, welche die Befugnisse uti und frui vereinigt; und die Verfügung, d. h. der Akt, dessen Wirkung mit dem lateinischen Verb abuti bezeichnet werden kann.
[27] Art. 58 ZGB der RSFSR von 1922.
[28] Präambel ZGB der RSFSR von 1964.
[29] Art. 92 ZGB der RSFSR von 1964.
[30] Und zwar durch Aufzählung der drei Machtbefugnisse des Eigentümers: Besitz, Nutzung und Verfügung.

II. Ohne rechtliche Grenzen

Im Verhältnis zum dem persönlichen Eigentum hatte das sozialistische Eigentum in der Sowjetunion den Vorrang. Da die Pflicht, „das sozialistische Eigentum zu bewahren und zu bereichern", kraft Artikels 131 der sowjetischen Verfassung jedem sowjetischen Staatsangehörigen auferlegt wurde, mußte man diese Form des Eigentums mit einem stärkeren Schutz zu versehen[31]. Zu diesem Zweck wurde ein echtes romanistisches Prinzip angewendet: *ubi rem meam invenio, ibi eam vindico*[32]. Dieses berücksichtigte keine Unterschiede zwischen *bona fides* und *mala fides*. Diese alte Regel existierte noch in dem römischen Recht, obgleich einige Wissenschaftler[33] bemerken, daß die angeführte Aussage als solche den Quellen unbekannt gewesen sei. Der Inhalt und Sinn dieses Prinzips wurden mit folgendem Fragment von Ulpian (Ulp., 16 ad ed., D. 6, 1, 9) verknüpft: *ubi enim probavi rem meam esse, necesse habebit possessor restituere* – wenn ich bewiesen habe, daß die Sache mir gehört, muß der Besitzer [sie] zurückgeben. Einige Jahrhunderte lang blieb diese Regel im Recht Kontinentaleuropas erhalten und verschwand später allmählich, während die kontinentale Jurisprudenz begann, die Demarkationslinie zwischen Gewissenhaftigkeit und Unzuverlässigkeit zu ziehen[34].

Sowjetische Gesetzgeber haben diesen Grundsatz in Artikel 60 des ZGB von 1922 integriert: „Die staatlichen Behörden und Unternehmen können ihr Vermögen, das rechtswidrig veräußert wurde, von jeglichem Erwerber verlangen"[35]. Später wurde seine Anwendung auf alle Arten des sozialistischen Eigentums ausgeweitet. So lautet Artikel 153 des ZGB von 1964: „Die Heraus-

---

[31] Art. 131 Verfassung der UdSSR von 1936.

[32] Tscherepachin, B.: Vindikatsionnije iski v sowetskom prave [Vindikationsansprüche im sowjetischen Recht]. In: Uchenije zapiski Swerdlowskogo juriditscheskogo instituta [Die wissenschaftliche Blätter des Swerdlowsker juristischen Instituts]. 1. Band (1945), S. 34 ff.

[33] Tusow, D.: Obschtschije utschenija teorii nedejstvitelnych sdelok i problemy ich wospriyatija v rossijskoj doktrine, zakonodatelstve i sudebnoj praktike [Die allgemeine Lehren der Theorie der ungültigen Rechtsgeschäfte und die Probleme deren Aneignung in der russischen Doktrin, Gesetzgebung und Rechtsprechung]. Tomsk 2006, S. 309, der sich auf Meinung Mengonis beruft: Mengoni L. Gli acquisti «a non domino. 3. Auflage. Milano 1975, S. 41, Fn. 12.

[34] Ioffe (wie in Fn. 9), S. 707-708.

[35] Art. 60 ZGB der RSFSR von 1922.

gabe der Sache, die zum Staatseigentum, sowie dem Eigentum der Kollektivwirtschaften oder anderer kooperativen und öffentlichen Organisationen gehört, kann von jeglichem Besitzer verlangt werden"[36].

Gewiß wurde die unbeschränkte Vindikation niemals zu einer Errungenschaft des sozialistischen Rechts erklärt, aber die Tatsache, daß dieses Prinzip mit der Absicht des Schutzes des wichtigsten und vorrangigen sozialistischen Eigentums verwendet wurde, zeigt, daß die wirkliche Herkunft dieser oder jener rechtlichen Konstruktion für den sowjetischen Gesetzgeber keine grundsätzliche Bedeutung hatte, soweit eine bestimmte Konstruktion für die Bedürfnisse des Aufbaus und der Festigung der neuen Rechtsordnung geeignet war. Unter Berücksichtigung des Umstandes, daß dem sowjetischen Recht die Institution der Usukapion (*usucapio*) fehlte[37] und daß die Vindikationsansprüche der staatlichen Unternehmen keiner Verjährung unterlagen[38], bestand immer die unbeschränkte Möglichkeit, staatliches Eigentum von jeglichem Besitzer zurückzuverlangen.

III. Die Ideen „liegen in der Luft"

Auch bei der Behandlung der fundamentalen Prinzipien einiger zivilrechtlicher Institutionen kann man beobachten, daß sowjetische Wissenschaftler erfolgreich westliche Konzepte entlehnten und diese „sozialistischen" Lösungen zugrunde legten. Hier kann man sich beispielsweise an die in der Mitte der 1920er Jahre ausgebrochene Diskussion erinnern, ob man bei der Lösung von Fragen der zivilrechtlichen Haftung dem Verursachungsprinzip oder dem Schuldprinzip den Vorzug geben solle.

---

[36] Art. 153 ZGB der RSFSR von 1964.

[37] Für die Einführung dieser Institution trat zwar voraussichtlich ausschließend dessen Anwendung in Bezug auf das Staatsvermögen Tscherepachin ein, infolgedessen hat er die Kritik an seine Adresse hervorgeruft. Tscherepachin, B.: Priobretenije prava sobstwennosti po davnosti wladenija [Der Erwerb des Eigentums durch die Usukapion]. In: Sowetskoje Gosudarstvo i Pravo 4 (1940), S. 51 ff.

[38] Gemäß dem Art. 90 ZGB der RSFSR von 1964.

Der Anlaß zu dieser Diskussion war eine Rechtsunsicherheit, die darauf beruhte, daß das erste sowjetische Zivilgesetzbuch kein Verschulden des Rechtsbrechers erwähnt hatte[39].

Die Anhänger des Verursachungsprinzips, geleitet vom oben erwähnten Schöpfer des Gesetzbuches Goikhbarg, behaupteten, daß eine solche Haftung „auf der sozialen Grundlage der Verursachung, nicht aber auf der individuellen Grundlage des Verschuldens“ beruhe[40]. Die Haftung sei „als Sanktion wegen des objektiven Zusammenhangs des Schadens mit der Tätigkeit des Verursachers“[41] angelegt. Die Anhänger dieser Auffassung, die auch als die „Theorie der objektiven Haftung“ bekannt ist, rechtfertigten also die Verantwortlichkeit des Verursachers unabhängig von dessen Verschulden.

Auch auf dem Gebiet der wirtschaftlichen Verträge hat diese Auffassung Einfluß entfaltet. Man wies auf die objektive Unvereinbarkeit der Grundlage des Verschuldens mit planwirtschaftlichen Beziehungen hin, weshalb „nur sowjetisches Recht das Schuldprinzip durch die grundsätzliche Unzulässigkeit des Erlasses der Haftung bei Nichterfüllung der vertraglichen Verpflichtung im vergesellschafteten Sektor ersetzen“ könne[42].

In der Literatur jener Zeit wurde unterstrichen, daß das Verursachungsprinzip „dem Geist des sowjetischen Rechts entspricht, daß überall die subjektiven Momente durch die objektiven ersetzt“, und daß das Verschulden den „von den sowjetischen Gesetzbüchern kritiklos entlehnten bürgerlich-kapitalistischen Gedanken“ zugerechnet werden müsse[43].

---

[39] Gemäß Art. 403 ZGB der RSFSR von 1922 war der Erlaß der Haftung möglich, wenn der Verursacher bewiesen hatte, daß er dem Schaden nicht hatte vorbeugen können oder zu dem schädlichen Verhalten berechtigt gewesen war oder der Schaden infolge von Absicht oder großer Fahrlässigkeit des Geschädigten selbst entstanden war.

[40] Goikhbarg, A.: Chozyajstvennoje pravo RSFSR [Das wirtschaftliche Recht der RSFSR], 1. Band. 1924, S. 174.

[41] Ioffe, O.: Razvitije tsivilistitscheskoj mysli v SSSR [Die Entwicklung des zivilistischen Denkens in der UdSSR], II. Teil. Ausgewählte Werke des bürgerlichen Rechts. Moskau 2003. S. 465, mit weiteren Nachweisen.

[42] Wenediktow, A.: Dogovornaja disziplina v promischlennosti [Die vertragliche Disziplin in der Industrie]. Leningrad 1935, IV. § 1.

[43] Ioffe (wie Fn. 41), S. 465 mit weiteren Nachweisen.

Es ist bekannt, daß das Verursachungsprinzip – historisch gesehen – ein Vorgänger des Schuldprinzips war. Das Verursachungsprinzip galt im antiken Recht, als die Haftung mit der bloßen Tatsache der Beschädigung in Verbindung stand. Erst im römischen Recht trat das Schuldprinzip zutage, durch das Bestehen der Regel *casus a nullo praestatur*. Dank der Rezeption des römischen Rechts ist diese Regel in das Recht späterer Völker eingegangen und wurde wohl zu einer der unerschütterlichen Grundlagen beliebiger kultureller Rechtsordnungen[44]. Doch in der zweiten Hälfte des 19. Jahrhunderts setzte eine Gegenbewegung in Richtung des Verursachungsprinzips ein. Den Anstoß dazu gab die sich überschlagende Entwicklung gefährlicher Tätigkeiten. Die Weiterentwicklung dieses Prozesses in der deutschen Rechtswissenschaft kann durch ein Zitat von Gierke illustriert werden: „Mag den Urheber der Rechtsverletzung ein eigentliches Verschulden nicht treffen, so ist doch der Geschädigte noch unschuldiger“[45]. Diese Auffassung fand ihre Begründung in der sogenannten „sozialen Aufgabe des Privatrechts“, die der „romanistisch-individualistischen Verirrung“ entgegengesetzt wurde[46]. Hier können wir uns auch an die Theorie von der sozialen Funktion des Rechts von Duguit[47] erinnern, die nur einige Jahre später entstand. Es liegt also auf der Hand, daß Goikhbarg und seine Anhänger diesen, in der Tat auch „westlichen“ Ansichten folgten und diese nur in geringem Maße zugunsten der bestehenden Ideologie modifizieren. Es sei betont, daß die „sozialistische Erfindung“ des Verursachungsprinzips sich bald als lebensunfähig erwies und in den 1950er Jahren abgelehnt wurde, worauf das „bürgerliche“ Schuldprinzip an seine Stelle trat.

---

[44] Pokrowskij, I.: Osnownyje problemy grazhdanskogo prava [Die Hauptproblemen des bürgerlichen Rechts]. Moskau 1998, S. 286.
[45] Gierke, O. v.: Die sociale Aufgabe des Privatrechts. Frankfurt am Main 1889, S. 25.
[46] Ibid.
[47] Duguit, L.: Le droit social, le droit individuel et la transformation de l'État. Paris 1908.

D. Die sogenannten rein „sozialistischen" Erfindungen

Aber war der Sozialismus auch in der Lage, einige wirklich tiefe und wesentliche Änderungen auf dem Gebiete des bürgerlichen Rechts hervorzurufen? Auch die wiederholten Erklärungen über die eigenartige Rolle und abnehmende Bedeutung des Geldes in der sowjetischen Gesellschaft, das als ein „Instrument der bürgerlichen Wirtschaft, das die Sowjetmacht in die Hand genommen und den Interessen des Sozialismus angepaßt hat"[48] angesehen wurde, führten nicht zum Verschwinden des Geldumlaufs. Wir haben schon gesehen, daß das sozialistische Recht verschiedene romanistische Elemente benutzte und sie dabei entweder mit der „sozialistischen" Deutung untermauerte oder sie ohne jegliche Rechtfertigung und Erklärung übernahm. Gleichwohl gab es einige gesetzliche und dogmatische Lösungen, denen keine romanistischen Entlehnungen zugrunde lagen. Diese können möglicherweise als echt „sozialistisch" angesehen werden. Inwiefern dies stimmt, können vielleicht die folgenden Beispiele zeigen.

I. Die „Kautschukresolution"

Manchmal wurden zu den Überlegenheiten und Eigenarten des sowjetischen Rechts die – vom Standpunkt der Rechtsdogmatik aus – offensichtlichen Mängel der juristischen Technik hinzugerechnet. So verhielt sich es auch mit den Regeln vom Irrtum beim Rechtsgeschäft.

Artikel 57 des ZGB der RSFSR von 1964 beschränkte sich darauf festzustellen, daß das Rechtsgeschäft, das unter dem Einfluß eines Irrtums vereinbart worden war, vom Gericht durch die Klage des irrenden Geschäftspartners für ungültig erklärt werden konnte[49]. Eine solche Formulierung ignorierte alle Errungenschaften der Irrtumslehre, die seit den Zeiten des römischen Rechts nach der Erfassung aller Irrtumsfälle und nach der Ausarbeitung möglichst scharfer und deutlicher allgemeiner Kriterien strebte, die es ermöglichten, einen wesentlichen Irrtum von einem unwesentlichen und unbeachtlichen

---

[48] Wenediktow (wie in Fn. 42), I. § 2.
[49] Art. 57 ZGB der RSFSR von 1964.

abzugrenzen. Auch Artikel 32 des früher geltenden ZGB der RSFSR von 1922 überließ dem Gericht die Entscheidung über Fragen der Wesentlichkeit und der Beachtlichkeit eines Irrtums[50].

In der damaligen Literatur wurde darauf hingewiesen, daß es „prinzipiell richtig ist anzuerkennen, daß in dem sowjetischen Zivilgesetzbuch keine ausführliche Reglementierung der einzelnen Irrtumsfälle vorhanden ist" und daß bei solchen Umständen das Gesetz es dem Gericht überlasse, „das die politische Lage und sozial-ökonomische Momente jedes Falles berücksichtigt, den geeigneten, den Besonderheiten entsprechenden Ausweg zu finden"[51].

Dieser scheinbare Mangel in der juristischen Technik enthielt also einen bestimmten Sinn. Zu den Irrtumsregeln gesellte sich nämlich noch eine weitere Regelung, die wegen ihrer Flexibilität als „Kautschukresolution" bezeichnet wurde. Dies erwies sich in der Praxis als sehr „vorteilhaft" und bildete auch „den Spielraum für ein Manöver"; fast jedes Rechtsgeschäft ließ sich damit auf Grund eines Irrtums vernichten.

II. Widerhall der sozialistischen Rechtstradition?

Einige Lösungen aus der Sowjetzeit, die man auch als eine Errungenschaft bewerten kann, haben bis jetzt ihre Anwendbarkeit nicht verloren. Damit kann man aber auch ihre „sozialistische" Spezifik bezweifeln. So bleibt z. B. eine Konstruktion wie das Recht auf operative Verwaltung trotz ihrer „sozialistischen Herkunft" und trotz der kritischen Bemerkungen über sie im heutigen bürgerlichen Recht Rußlands erhalten. Dieses Rechtsinstitut wurde in der Absicht erfunden, die Befugnisse oder die Rechte der staatlichen Behörden und Unternehmen bezüglich des Staatseigentums zu reglementieren. Um die Natur solcher Rechte zu erläutern, benutzten die sowjetischen Wissenschaftler verschiedene Auffassungen: Die postglossatorische *dominum divisum*-Konzeption, die römische *fiducia*-Konzeption sowie den angloamerikanischen „*trust*". Einen Punkt in diesem Streit bildete das ZGB von 1964, welches das

---

[50] Art. 32 ZGB der RSFSR von 1922: Wer ein Rechtsgeschäft (...) unter dem Einfluß des Irrtums abgeschlossen hat, kann vor Gericht fordern, das Rechtsgeschaft für ungültig zu erklären.
[51] Nowitzkij, I.: Sdelki. Iskowaja dawnost. [Rechtsgeschäfte. Verjährung]. Moskau 1954. S. 103.

Vorhandensein des sogenannten „Rechts auf operative Verwaltung" gesetzlich festgestellt hatte[52]. Später rechtfertigte der bekannte deutscher Jurist Knapp diese neue Kategorie durch die bezeichnende Erläuterung: „Der bestehende juristische Begriffsapparat, der durch das römische Recht geschaffen wurde, war nicht in der Lage, die Natur dieses Rechts zu erklären"[53]. Wie Ioffe mit Recht bemerkt: Wäre dies nicht nur eine gesetzliche Forderung nach der Ausübung dieser Befugnisse des Besitzes, der Nutzung und der Verfügung nicht nur im Rahmen des Gesetzes, sondern auch „gemäß der Bestimmung ihrer Tätigkeit, den Planaufgaben und dem Verwendungszweck des Vermögens", so unterschiede sich diese Konstruktion keineswegs von der romanistischen Konstruktion des Eigentums[54]. Die letzte Bemerkung legt einen besonderen Akzent auf die Abhängigkeit von den staatlich aufgedrängten Zwecken und Aufgaben.

Aber auch nach dem Untergang des Sozialismus blieb das Staatseigentum in Rußland (wie wohl in jedem anderen Staat) erhalten. Man muß dieses Eigentum organisieren und in wirtschaftlicher Tätigkeit nutzen. Folglich bestehen heute wie früher staatliche Unternehmen, die der Staat mit seinem Vermögen versorgt und für die er festlegt, wie sie dieses Vermögen zu verwenden haben. Für die juristische Gestaltung der Rechte solcher Unternehmen ist m. E. die sozialistische Konstruktion des Rechts auf operative Verwaltung geeignet, und ihre Anwendung ist keinesfalls der Widerhall der sozialistischen Rechtstradition.

E. Ergebnisse

Der Begriff der „sozialistischen Rechtstradition" verdankt also seine Entstehung vor allem der Ideologisierung des Rechts der sozialistischen Staaten.

---

[52] Etwa gemäß Art. 93.1 ZGB der RSFSR von 1964 üben die staatlichen, kollektivwirtschaftlichen Unternehmen, denen das Recht der operative Verwaltung auf das Staatseigentum gewährt ist, „im Rahmen des Gesetzes und gemäß der Bestimmung ihrer Tätigkeit, den Planaufgaben und dem Verwendungszweck des Vermögens die Rechte des Besitzes die Nutzung und die Verfügung über das Vermögen aus".

[53] Sacco (wie in Fn. 2), S. 125.

[54] Ioffe, O.: Soviet Law and Roman Law. In: Boston University Law Review 62 (1982), S. 721.

Zweifellos wurde auch das Privatrecht dieser Staaten von der damaligen Ideologie wesentlich geprägt. Aus den oben erörterten Beispiele ergibt sich auch, daß für das Erreichen der ideologischen Ziele alle zugänglichen Mittel eingesetzt wurden. Dazu gehört sowohl die weite Verwendung der romanistischen Elemente und theoretischen Konstruktionen als auch der bewußte Einsatz von juristisch-technischen Lücken. Außerdem ist es der sowjetischen Jurisprudenz gelungen, im Laufe ihres Bestehens eigene Rechtskonstruktionen zu schaffen, die später zu ausschließlichen Errungenschaften der sozialistischen Rechtsordnung erklärt wurden.

Damit erweist sich der Prozeß des Vergessens der sogenannten „sozialistischen Rechtstradition" auf dem Gebiete des Privatrechts, der auf die Beseitigung des ideologischen Hauchs ausgerichtet ist, als ein heterogener Prozeß. Man kann m. E. mindestens drei Richtungen erkennen:

1. Die Entideologisierung und Umdeutung einiger Regeln, Institutionen und Grundsätze gemäß den Forderungen der neuen Stufe der gesellschaftlichen Entwicklung, und zwar dort, wo ein sozialistischer Stempel den romanistischen Modellen oder westlichen Rechtsideen aufgeprägt worden war – auf Grund von verschiedenen Ursachen, die mit den Bedürfnissen der damaligen Ideologie übereingestimmt hatten. Als Ergebnis einer solcher Umdeutung, in Bezug auf die oben erwähnten Fälle wurde das Schuldprinzip als allgemeine Regel auf dem Gebiet der zivilrechtlichen Haftung im Zivilgesetzbuch heutigen Rußlands beibehalten; gleiches gilt für die Orientierung an romanistischen Mustern bei der Feststellung der drei Machtbefugnisse des Eigentümers (Besitz, Nutzung, und Verfügung), vgl. Art. 401, 1064; Art. 209 ZGB der Russischen Föderation. Andererseits wurde die unbeschränkte Vindikation des staatlichen Eigentums abgeschafft. Die Vindikationsansprüche der staatlichen Unternehmen unterliegen heutzutage der Verjährung und bezüglich solcher Ansprüche wird die erneuerte Rechtsinstitution der Usukapion (*usucapio*) verwendet.

2. Wie sich am Beispiel der Irrtumsregeln zeigt, muß in bestimmten Fällen das Vergessen der sozialistischen Tradition in der Rückkehr zu den Errungenschaften älterer Rechtsgedanken und in einer ausführlichen Überarbeitung der jeweiligen Rechtsinstitutionen bestehen. Als Muster dazu kann der heutige Artikel 178 des ZGB der Russischen Föderation genannt werden, der allgemeine

Orientierungspunkte für die Beurteilung der Wesentlichkeit von Irrtümern gewährt.

3. Das Vergessen der sozialistischen Rechtstradition kann auch in der Erhaltung einiger entideologisierter Erfindungen der sowjetischen Jurisprudenz bestehen, die zur Anwendung unter den gegenwärtigen Bedingungen brauchbar sind, wie z. B. die Konstruktion des Rechts auf operative Verwaltung.

Abstracts

Kenneth E. Aldous, New York

The Selective Memorialization of Sir John Fortescue in Early Modern England: A Short Case Study in Legal Antiquarianism

The late fifteenth-century jurist, Sir John Fortescue, occupies a place among those historical figures whom English lawyers during the early modern period re-conceptualized as part of their quest to find new meaning in England's legal history. This article briefly traces the place of Fortescue, and his notion of the English constitution as *dominium politicum et regale*, within an admittedly thin slice of the socio-political disputes that revolutionized Tudor and Stuart society. The general purpose is to examine some of the ways in which exponents, on both sides of those disputes, memorialized Fortescue in aid of their respective legal, jurisdictional and constitutional causes. After previewing Fortescue's life and principal literary achievements, the article briefly discusses how – as part of a process of recollection rooted firmly in an antiquarian consciousness – Fortescue's authority grew as a preeminent source from England's jurisprudential past.

Alfons Aragoneses Aguado, Barcelona

Entre el Dictador i jo: Gedächtnis und Recht der Diktatur im heutigen Spanien

Spain has recently commemorated the 30th anniversary of General Francisco Franco's death. On this occasion, a group of young filmmakers realized a series of short documentaries about the remembrance of the dictatorship in Spain. The author's reflections about this subject start with the description of one of these films which was shown on the Frankfurt *Forum*. He argues that the price of the political transition after the dictatorship had been oblivion of the democratic governments of the 19th and early 20th centuries, and the opposition against Franquism in the social, political and legal systems. This phenomenon can clearly be observed in the field of law. For example, there are still law professionals and academics who do not accept the superiority of the constitution and the "Tribunal Constitucional". Another example is the continuous validity of certain legal provisions from the franquist past.

Laura Beck Varela, Sevilla

Verdammt zum Vergessen – oder zum Erinnern? Kirchliche Zensur und juristische Literatur im Spanien des 18. Jahrhunderts

Among the numerous social practices of forgetting and remembering that operated throughout modern history, few are so clearly linked to the construction of cultural memory as the censorship of books and the ecclesiastical politics of "damnatio memoriae" (damnation of memory), of which the Index of Forbidden Books was the most important instrument. This paper tries to throw light on some aspects of the practice of censorship of law books, presenting the results of a case study on the reception of the Dutch Protestant jurist Arnoldus Vinnius (1588-1657) in Catholic Spain.

Emiliano J. Buis, Paris / Buenos Aires

From Inscriptions to the Dramatic Text: Literary Reminders of Lawmaking in Athenian Old Comedy

The contrast of epigraphic testimonies and comic discourse can shed light on a number of parodic strategies put forward within the dramatic text in order to achieve both artistic and political goals. By reproducing (and distorting) lawmaking schemes on stage, Aristophanes managed to draw the attention of ancient Athenians to the most contemporary discussions on their legal system. Our purpose here is to show how the use of these decrees in Greek comedy consistently reveals a critical approach to the common sophistic interpretation of positive and conventional justice.

Cosmin Dariescu, Iaşi

Physical Pain: An Ancient Legal Remedy against Oblivion

In Moldavia and Walachia (the two states that have been united, since 1862, under the name of Romania), the litigations on the settlement of boundaries were decided by considering boundary marks shown by special witnesses (named "good and old people"). These good and old people remembered the boundaries of a certain land over decades because, in their childhood, they had been beaten at every boundary mark.

Bram Delbecke, Leuven

Le fléau de Van Maanen et le salut constitutionnel. Le souvenir du Royaume-Uni des Pays-Bas et du Congrès national dans les discours sur la liberté de presse en Belgique au XIXe siècle

The constitution of 1831 gave several liberties to the freshly born Belgian state. Most of those liberties were considered as a reaction against the Dutch regime of the past fifteen years. The mistakes of this regime were embodied by its head of the justice department, Cornelis Felix Van Maanen. Freedom of speech, freedom of the press, freedom of religion, freedom of education, and freedom of association had to wipe out the traces of the Dutch regime. Of course, due to the many changes and evolutions in nineteenth-century Belgian society, several aspects of these constitutional liberties were criticized or were said to be in need of a new approach. The changes and evolutions in nineteenth-century Belgian society often led to questioning the position of those liberties. In those discussions, whether on a political, judiciary or academic level, the fifteen years of the Dutch regime were almost always mentioned. The memory of the United Kingdom and Van Maanen did not only function as a warning, but was a main theme of unification in the nationalist discourse, legitimating the existance of the Belgian nation itself.

Fabrice Desnos, Montpellier

Ne pas oublier le crime: le refus d'absolution en Catalogne (XVIe-XVIIIe siècles)

This contribution provides an insight into early modern criminal law in Catalonia. The author studies the deep-seated conviction of the judge in the works of Catalan jurists from the sixteenth to the eighteenth centuries. He observes a refusal to forget a crime when the judge refused to acquit someone whom he believed but could not fully prove to be guilty. The system of legal proof required confession of the defendant or two witnesses with the same deposition. However, the difficulty of obtaining one or the other and the wish that no crime remain unpunished lead practitioners to envision new solutions. The Catalan jurists refused that an established crime be forgotten and a criminal not be convicted despite the existence of many elements of proof, just because they did not conform to the *ius commune*. So these jurists drew up a new system combining elements of Roman law, learned opinions and the current system. By this, no elements of proof were forgotten. Firstly, a crime persisted when the judge refused to acquit the defendant. Then, by the "*élargissement*" and by the "*réserve de preuves*", the basis of the judge's conviction did not disappear. Finally, this school of thought admitted a lesser penalty based on some evidence, simple presumptions or incomplete proof, "beyond a reasonable doubt".

Thilo Engel, Frankfurt am Main

Welche Republik? Der Bezug auf republikanische Traditionen im französischen Verfassungsrecht nach dem Zweiten Weltkrieg

Since 1971, the French constitutional court has declared the constitutional force of several "founding principles" of the republican legal tradition. The court formed these principles using elements of ordinary laws of the time before World War II. Yet, when the French constitutional court declared that these principles had a general validity and constitutional force, it did take into account neither the historical circumstances in which the original laws had been created nor the will of the law-makers to restrain the validity of the principles declared in these laws. The article intends to shows how the reference to a tradition has been used, at different steps in French constitutional history, to legitimate or to disguise the introduction of new norms.

Silvia Falconieri, Frankfurt am Main

La scienza giuridica italiana tra ricordo e oblio della legislazione antiebraica

What was the attitude of the Italian legal community with regard to the anti-Semitic legislation enacted by the Fascist government from September 1938 on? What remains from the categories and the legal institutions introduced by that legislature in the doctrine of the jurists who, after the fall of the regime in 1943, claimed that they would effectively reintegrate the *cittadini italiani di razza ebraica* ("Italian citizens of Jewish race")? At the same time, both remembrance and oblivion characterize those two historical periods. Whereas those Fascist jurists in charge of the study and implementation of the anti-Semitic legislation appear to have constantly attempted to remove the categories of *ebreo* (Jew) and *ariano* (Aryan), the memory of these categories persists in the work of those who were called to eliminate the dichotomy of ebreo/ariano from the Italian legal system.

Birgit Fastenmayer, Frankfurt am Main

„Wohin kommen wir, wenn wir überall Gesetze machen wollen, wo Dummheiten stattfinden…" – Praxis und Gesetz im landwirtschaftlichen Erbgang

The article discusses the relation between practice and law in the rural hereditary course in Germany from the late 19th century up to the Nazi-"Erbhofrecht". The transfer of agricultural real property by intergenerational contracts is brought into focus as an instrument of remembering or forgetting an alleged custom.

Adam S. Hofri-Winogradow, Oxford

Law's Families: Conceptions of the Family in Late Eighteenth Century English Law

The article describes the conception of the family promoted by the late eighteenth century English court of Chancery. The ideal parents of late eighteenth century equity would provide for their children until their majorities, and transfer large sums of money to them soon after their majorities so that they could make their way in the world and enjoy some power over their own children. The ideal children of late eighteenth century equity did not exploit any power advantages they might fortuitiously have enjoyed over their parents; they gave off their own property to pull their parents out of debt, and did not marry without parental consent.

Nir Kedar, Ramat-Gan

Israeli Law as a *Lieu de mémoire (et d'oubli)*: Remembering and Forgetting Jewish Law in Modern Israel

This paper deals with the intricate ways in which Israeli law treats Jewish law. Law has always been an important *lieu de mémoire*, that preserves social conventions, and gives them additional validity, authority and importance. But at the same time, it is also a *lieu d'oubli* that persuades (and sometimes even forces) us to abandon other norms that are now considered "non-law". The establishment of the State of Israel in 1948 and the formation of Israeli law involved many decisions of remembrance and abandonment. One of the most critical decisions was whether to remember or forget Jewish law, whether to turn Jewish law into the law of the land or to relegate it to oblivion. After a brief introduction of Jewish law and some of the problems of its integration into modern law, the paper discusses the complex ways in which Israeli law deals with Jewish law: rejecting it in principle, but embracing it symbolically. The paper concludes by showing that the dynamics of remembering and forgetting Jewish law parallels the difficulty of defining the essence of Jewish law and Judaism, and their relevant roles in Israeli social life.

László Komáromi, Budapest

Institutionen und Ursprung der juristischen Schriftlichkeit in Ungarn im 12.-13. Jahrhundert

The study deals with forms and institutions of the Hungarian State, through which public authorities and society tried to keep alive their legal acts in the Middle Ages. The signs of an increasing demand to lay down legal acts in writing appear in many respects under the reign of King Béla III (1172-1196), who was brought up at the imperial Court in Constantinople as heir to the crown of emperor Manuel I Comnenos. After his return to Hungary, he ordered to put in writing every private lawsuit decided by royal judgment, he stabilized the organization of the royal chancellery, and during his reign began the documentary practice of the so-called "places of authentication" (loca credibilia): ecclesiastical chapters and monastic convents, i.e. corporate bodies who issued deeds on different legal matters and saved a copy of each document. In the literature, both western and eastern institutions appear to have served as possible models or at least as motivating factors to the documentary practice of the chancellery and the activity of the loca credibilia. The paper takes these factors into consideration and tries to show to what extent Hungarian practice was influenced by foreign models and indigenous circumstances.

Henning Meyer, Bordeaux / Augsburg

Die französische Vergangenheitsbewältigung des Zweiten Weltkriegs durch die Rechtsprechung am Beispiel des „Oradourprozesses"

The trials against German and English officials who were responsible for crimes committed during the occupation of France (1940-1944) are important elements of the French memory of that time. The author's contribution focuses on the trials against members of the 2nd SS Panzer Division "Das Reich" who had massacred the inhabitants of the village of Oradour-sur-Glane in June 1944. The proceedings took place in Bordeaux from January 12th until February 13th, 1953. Difficulties arose from the fact that only low-ranking soldiers were accused, and that all but one of the Alsatians – i.e. French nationals – claimed to have been recruited by force. The court imposed rather low penalties. Protests in Alsace pressed the French parliament to pass an amnesty law for all Alsatians only a week after the trial. The few survivors in Oradour reacted with resignation and isolation. It took decades until contacts with the French and German governments were established.

Thomas Mohr, Dublin

Law in a Gaelic Utopia: Perceptions of Brehon Law in Nineteenth and early Twentieth Century Ireland

Knowledge of the legal system that existed in Ireland before the introduction of common law remained limited until comparatively recent times. Scholars in nineteenth and early twentieth century Ireland often presented accounts of early Irish law or 'brehon law' that contained strong utopian elements. This article examines how these utopian visions influenced the development of Irish law in the 1920s and 1930s. It also examines how these utopian visions remain of relevance to the perception of law in contemporary Ireland.

Adam Moniuszko, Warsaw

When to Remember and When to Forget? The Masovian Gentry's Court *petita* in the Vasa Period (1587-1668)

This article focuses on petitions of the Polish gentry from the Masovia region in their court affairs. It indicates many aspects of the petitions: factors in the process of their formation, which institutions they were addressed to, or who were their beneficiaries. The last part of the article contains the gentry's arguments used to support their requests. Their analysis shows legal values which were important to the local gentry in that period.

Christian Müller, Heidelberg

Contested Memories of the Revolution. The Remembrance of Revolutionary Suffrage Laws (1848/49) as Political Arguments in German Discussions on Constitutional Reform, 1860-1875

"We want our right, nothing but our right, but our whole right, complete and undisputed!" This argument was put forward by a deputation from Plauen in Saxony to petition at the Saxon lower chamber of deputies for the re-introduction of the legally instituted suffrage law of 1848. It was illegally abandoned by state government in 1850 and became source of a constant discussion in the Saxon public after 1860. In the light of events like this, the article raises the questions how and for which purposes the memories of the legally instituted suffrage laws were used in the discussions and claims for political reform during the formation of a German nation state, which party formations used the imagined and commemorated legal traditions of 1848, and how these commemorations in political thought and action were forgotten during the 1870s.

Jaime Olaiz González, Col. Paesos de Taxena (Mexico)

Coming to Terms with the Past: The Mexican Juncture between Remembrance and Forgetfulness

Currently, Mexico is experiencing a restoration from more than seventy years of a violent authoritarian regime as well as a political, economic and social transition into a modern democracy. Nevertheless, there is a misunderstanding about the elements that enable such a transition. It is not only by the means of institutional and economic reforms that the country will achieve its democratic consolidation, but, above all, by means of a clear recognition of its recent past in order to fulfill the virtuous circle of Truth, Justice and Forgiveness that Pope John Paul II called the Pedagogy of Peace. The time has come to place Mexico in the juncture between remembering and forgetting its recent past.

Vladimir Petrović, Belgrade

Juridical Memory Making and the Transformation of Historical Expert Witnessing: Contextualizing the Eichmann Case and the Frankfurt Auschwitz Trial

It has been frequently noted that prominent trials make history, not just by rendering important judgments and by influencing the societal development, but also by offering a powerful account which captures the attention of the people and which affects the way societies remember and forget. The impact of such trials on the collective memory has raised a set of legal, moral, political and historical questions which became very urgent in the light of the collapse of communism, the global transition to democracy and the legal reflections on the crimes of past regimes. The aim of this acticle is to address an important, yet frequently overlooked aspect of the present debate: the transformation of the role of historical expert witnessing under the influence of juridical memory making.

Nicolas Rügge, Osnabrück

Steuerung des Erinnerns und Vergessens? Archivische Bewertung von Schriftgut der Justiz

Which processes and legal transactions are permanently remembered, which of them are forgotten after a certain period of time? Contributing to this fundamental decision, the state archives in Germany have developed different strategies of 'appraisal'. Current practice and future perspectives of this complex action, co-forming the basic sources of historical research, should invite to discussion and agreement among archives, justice and (legal) history.

Philipp Scheibelreiter, Wien

„Nicht Erinnern“ und „Übles vergessen“: Zum Amnestiebegriff im klassischen Griechenland

Theodor Mommsen based his theory, that already in classical Greece the "forgetting of past evil“ was officially called *amnestia*, on Cicero´s (Phil. 1,1,1) statement, that for this expression the Romans had to take a *verbum Graecum*. Analyzing the sources of Athenian amnesties in the 5th century B.C., we can see that either their legal consequences or the negative infinitive *ou/me mnesikakein* ("not remembering the evil") were used to denominate *amnestia*, and not the term as such, which, for the first time, appeared in Plutarch´s work (mor. 814b; Cic. 42,3).

Martin P. Schennach, Innsbruck

„Wiewohl von alters her, wie Ihr wißt, ye und ye verboten ist ...": Gesetzgebung als Erinnern an Normen im Ancien Régime

While the conservation, at best the improvement of traditional law was the principal aim of secular legislation in the Middle Ages, the beginning of the 16th century saw the rise of the idea of intentional changeability of the legal system via legislation. The article shows how early modern legislation concernig "good police" ("gute Policey") was nevertheless rooted in traditional law and legal customs. Moreover, it discusses the reasons for constant repetition of laws which characterizes early modern police legislation.

Renate Schulze, Frankfurt am Main

Was tun mit den Dekretalen Papst Gregors IX.? Zum nachreformatorischen Schicksal der Normen des kanonischen Rechts

"What about the decretals of Pope Gregory IX? – Regarding the rules of canon law and their fate after the reformation" sheds light on the work of Justus Henning Böhmer (1674-1749) who provided a scientific basis for the application of canon law within the Protestant Church, published in his famous *Ius Ecclesiasticum Protestantium*. Therein, he analysed each single law of the *decretales* – which constitute the main part of canon law – and decided on their transferability to Protestant ecclesiastical law. Thus the lecture gives examples of continuation and discontinuation of these laws in the Protestant canon law of the beginning of the 18th century.

Monica Stronati, Macerata
Gnade und Vergessen im 19. und 20. Jahrhundert: ein „Einschlafen“ des Prinzips der Gewaltenteilung?

The institution of amnesty is characterized by its ability to wipe out crimes. This ability is recognized as a legal doctrine in times of peace. However, particularly in Italy in the 19th and 20th centuries, the amnesty doctrine assumed the value of temporary sleepiness regarding state penal policies during times of emergency. Amnesty is an instrument of power. It also plays a part in the complex construction of national identity.

Paulina Święcicka, Krakow
Reconstruction of the *lex Aquilia* as an Example of a Textual Reconstruction of Ancient *leges*

The aim of this article is to show that there can be problems with ancient legal sources and with their meaning, and also to give some proposals as to how to deal with them. The first part introduces the methods of textual criticism used by scholars in reconstructing texts. These methods are then demonstrated by a reconstruction of the text of one of the most important Roman statutory enactments, which did not remain *in extenso* until our time, i.e. the *lex Aquilia de damno iniuria dato*. The reconstruction is based on the subsequent texts of Roman jurists, taking into consideration the ideas from modern jurisprudence and Romanist science. The paper concludes by stating some general rules and advice concerning the reconstruction of legal texts.

Dominik Thompson, Wien
Verträge zugunsten Dritter, „Bedürfnisse des Verkehrs“ und Privatrechtsmentalität im Deutschland des frühen 19. Jahrhunderts

The history of the development of contracts in favour of third parties in Germany is usually told as a struggle of the need to embrace Industrialisation vs. the presumably ultra-positivist, retro-minded and utterly hermetic style of jurisprudence said to be dominant in the first half of the 19th century ("Begriffsjurisprudenz"). Starting from the existence of "practical needs" as a common argument in juridical texts of that period, this paper is an attempt of dogmatic history, revisited.

Viktor Winkler, Frankfurt am Main

Dealing with the Nazi Past of Legal Scholars in the Classroom

After decades of research, legal history can provide a remarkably broad and sophisticated (albeit not exhaustive) account of Nazi legal scholarship. This endeavour has provided a vivid picture of the collaboration of those scholars that went on to become the most influential legal writers of German post war legal academia. How are we today to deal with this knowledge when presenting to our students the works of these scholars that are still in use? While exploring possible standards between moral condemnation and a value-free 'facts-of-the-case' presentation, the article criticizes essential deficiencies of post-war legal history and is trying to make a case for a reorientation of the discipline from the point of view of legal education.

Alexander Zezekalo, Tomsk

Das Vergessen der sozialistischen Tradition im Privatrecht. Was bedeutet das? Von romanistischen Elementen im sozialistischen Recht und den sog. rein „sozialistischen" Erfindungen auf dem Gebiete des Privatrechts

Although the socialist countries existed for a relatively short period of time, their existence nonetheless gave legal scientists an opportunity to speak about the so-called "socialist legal tradition". Because today, most former socialist states are forced to get rid of their socialist heritage, this must also imply that they have to abandon the "socialist tradition" in law. But what does it mean, to forget the socialist legal tradition? Has this heritage even existed at all? The following article endeavours to address this issue. A comparative and historical analysis based on examples drawn from the civil law of the former USSR, which served as a model for its socialist counterparts, reveals the three basic processes of "forgetting the socialist legal tradition".